THE LEGEND DIES ON
Gary Green & his "Outlaw Folk"

the poet laureate soul of Folkie Rock & Roll

a roman à clef autobiographical novel **by Gary Green**

THE POET LAUREATE SOUL OF FOLKIE ROCK & ROLL

THE LEGEND DIES ON

Copyright © 2024 by GARY GREEN & PENNY ARCADES PRESS

All rights reserved. No part of this book may be reproduced or transmitted in any form or by any means without written permission from the author.

ISBN: 978-1-7326213-6-7

Library of Congress Control Number: 2024942013

Printed in the USA

THE LEGEND DIES ON — GARY GREEN

About This Book

This book is a *roman à clef novelization*[1] focusing on the *music-related* adventures of the author's very complex life. While both the publisher and the author have used good faith efforts to ensure that the information contained in this work is generally accurate, it is expressly stated that at the time of writing, the author was entering his eighth decade of life and was recalling events from as long as almost 70 years previous. The escapades recounted in this book, therefore, are subject to the recall processes normally associated with the elderly.

Some of these experiences have been, in the roman à clef process, compressed, chronologically reorganized, or completely novelized. Hence, the author disclaims all responsibility for errors or omissions, including without limitation responsibility for damages resulting from the use of or reliance on this *entertainment* work.

In some cases, names and identifying details have been altered to protect the privacy of individuals who played key roles in these event; and in some cases, their contributions have been concealed or excluded entirely, following the author's philosophy of prioritizing family and close-friend protection; a principle instilled by his mother. Despite this, the author acknowledges the vital impact these individuals had on his life, though the roman à clef format allows him to obscure their identities (or not mention them at all) while identifying or novelizing public figures. Nonetheless, the author gratefully acknowledges their vital contributions to his life and notes that without them the events depicted would not have been possible; moreover, the author's life would not have existed as it has without his relying on them for so much ... for *everything*. An historical record (rather than a novelization) would recognize them as the driving force for most of these escapades. The *roman à clef* form of this book allows the author to conceal their identities, roles, or existence while maintaining the identification of public and more well-known figures. Their omission is done out of respect and love and no other reasons.

The author notes that in his life adventures he has subjected them to enough stress, exposure, and insanity: and they don't need whatever is generated because of this book. He adds, *"Make no mistake about it, almost none of these adventures would have been even remotely possible without the unyielding support (and more than that, the influence, the guidance, and the love). I now say THANK YOU and I LOVE YOU."*

Finally, the author reiterates a reluctance to exploit, capitalize, or attach pretentious airs to his routine, day-to-day, activities, relationships, and actions of a life that others might *think* extraordinary when taken out of context. Nonetheless, at the instance of many friends, he offers his story here, in context *(with apologies to those who may feel slighted, misrepresented, or disparaged by the novelization process).*

---

[1] A roman à clef novelization is a novel about real life, overlaid with a façade of fiction. The technique is in the spirit of *Sylvia Plath, John Banville, Truman Capote, Simone de Beauvoir, Ernest Hemingway, George Orwell, Jack Kerouac, Victor Hugo, Blaise Cendrars, Philip K. Dick, Bret Easton Ellis, Jay McInerny, Naguib Mahfouz, Charles Bukowski, Malachi Martin, Saul Bellow, Hunter S. Thompson, James Joyce,* and others writing autobiographical experiences about controversial topics, reporting inside information, or detailing crimes. In this case, it applies to all three.

THE POET LAUREATE SOUL OF FOLKIE ROCK & ROLL

Table of Contents

The **First Movement**..5
- Opus One: *More Than Just A Boogie-Woogie* 7
- Opus Two: *Shaped By My Hillbilly Roots* 15
- Opus Three: *Guitars, "Music City USA" & Johnny Cash's House* 31
- Opus Four: *It's Only Rock and Roll* 54
- Opus Five: *Songs Powerful Enough To Get You Killed?* 76
- Opus Six: *The Captain, Pancakes, Waylon, Pinball, Outlawing* 91
- Opus Seven: *Kristofferson & Iconoclasts Or A Big "F-You" From Nashville*....... 108

The **2nd Movement**..120
- Opus Eight: *Apparently, SOME People DO Like My Music* 121
- Opus Nine: *The University vs. The Founder of Lead Guitar* 131
- Opus Ten: *Vietnam, Wounded Knee, and "Radical" Songs* 145
- Opus Eleven: *Guitar Paint and My Very Own Federal Agent* 161
- Opus Twelve: *New York & The Last Days of Phil Ochs* 173
- Opus Thirteen: *Then I Was An Artist On THE Label*................................ 191
- Opus Fourteen: *Broadside, a Paul Newman Movie, CBGB, Kirk, & Shelley*...... 201
- Opus Fifteen: *Dylan, My $3-billion Rock & Roll Black Eye, & Elvis' Death* 226
- Opus Sixteen: *Nothing Left But To Go Back To Nashville* 252

The **3rd Movement** 260
- Opus Seventeen: *Songs To Die For — Literally*.. 261
- Opus Eighteen: *You Can't Write Songs If You're Dead* 273
- Opus Nineteen: *Don't Mess With An Outlaw Folksinger*........................ 287
- Opus Twenty: *I Kinda Liked The Streets of Baltimore* 301
- Opus Twenty-One: *Túpac Meets Revolutionary Cultural Work & Communists*.......... 323
- Opus Twenty-Two: *I Can Never Play Again, You Racist Bastards*........... 342
- Opus Twenty-Three: *My Dada Life As A Media Event Scoundrel*........... 353
- Opus Twenty-Four: *Arrested At Border Control; Now What?* 365
- Opus Twenty-Six: *God forgives; Outlaws Take Revenge (and own a circus)*.... 380

The **4th Movement** 400
- Opus Twenty-Seven: *My Most Absurd Musical Reinvention*.................. 401
- Opus Twenty-Eight: *The Worst Year Of My Life & My Coda* 412
- Opus Twenty-Nine: *One More Shot, Just For Old Times*........................ 424

Librettist's Cadenza: *These Six Strings Neutralize The Tools of Oppression* **443**

The First Movement
sonata-allegro: *My Developmental Years*

THE POET LAUREATE SOUL OF FOLKIE ROCK & ROLL

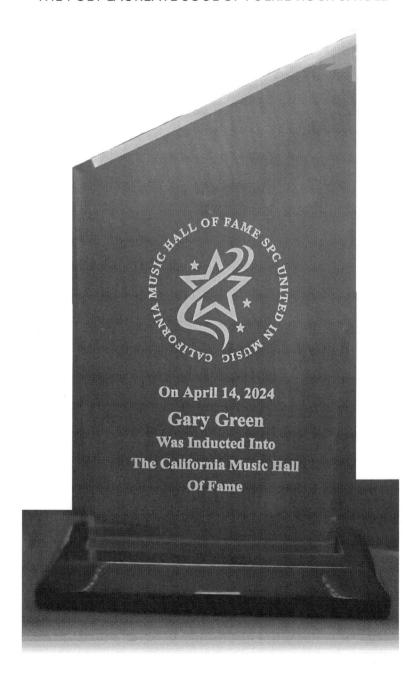

THE LEGEND DIES ON — GARY GREEN

Opus One:
More Than Just A Boogie-Woogie

You know what my momma used to tell me: "If you can't find something to live for, then you best, find something to die for"
—Túpac Amaru Shakur[2]
(about seven years after a year-long daily consorting with the author)

Despite holding a double action standard-issue police .357 magnum revolver, the agent cocked the gun anyway as he pressed the barrel against the back of my head. If he had so-much-as sneezed, the gun would have fired and blown my brains all over the mayor's office.

THAT would have been a hell of a coda to my music. No wonder folk music icon Pete Seeger wrote, *"Hell, there should be a Ballad of Gary Green"*.

The burly cop spittle-screamed as he rammed me against the wall, *"Don't even move, you Communist bastard. Let's see you go to the Grand Ole Opry now!"* His words echoed the September 1973 taunting by Chilean Army officer Pedro Barrientos as he shot folksinger Víctor Jara, "let's hear you sing your songs now, Communist!" So, it wasn't *new* behavior, but damnit, this was America.

The life-threatening assault on me —*with no actual charges*— was just another in a series of post-COINTELPRO attacks triggered by my songs; lyrics apparently deemed *so* dangerous that they warranted a covert government operation to derail "radical" activity that supposedly could pose a threat to the U.S. government. *No, really! This b.s. is documented!* [3]

---

[2] "Something 2 Die 4" by Túpac Amaru Shakur; ©Universal Music Publishing Group, *(with a sample by Curtis Mayfield and input from producer Deon Evans)*, and Warner Chappell Music, Inc

[3] My eventual "escape" from custody —*aided and abetted by a cadre of friendly law enforcement, by members of Congress, a famous civil rights attorney, and a corps of actual celebrities*—led to a harrowing decade of living "underground" as a fugitive, improbable international intrigue, unrestrained violence, eventual capture by United States Border Patrol agents... and eventual exoneration (though psychologically battered, physically crippled, and only a of shell of who I had been before the ordeal). The documentation of much of the program against me is documented in FBI files obtained decades later under the Freedom of Information Act (5 U.S.C. § 552).

THE POET LAUREATE SOUL OF FOLKIE ROCK & ROLL

Had it not been for the badges (and, of course, the gun against my skull), this would have been a comical paranoid exaggeration. I mean, seriously, why ME? I wasn't exactly "famous". There were dozens of much (MUCH) more talented musicians. There certainly were better poets and writers. Hell, there were even more radical folksingers. Few of them were subjected to this kind of nonsense! So why *me*?

I couldn't imagine why anyone would go to all that trouble to get rid of a nobody songwriter. Though, I probably should have been more cognizant after I exposed an undercover Federal agent who'd been assigned to me full-time after my incessant singing raised a shitload of money for a hundred or so Oglala Lakota elders and children inside a church at Wounded Knee South Dakota.

Documents released under the *Freedom of Information Act* indicate that I first garnered attention for being an anomalous white hillbilly folksinger picking guitar at Black Panther Party functions, anti-war demonstrations, and a number of epoch-related rallies[4].

But if the truth is to be told, my musical odyssey really began in the summer of 1957, when I was only three-years-old.

At only 67°, that last Sunday in July, the 28th, was exceptionally mild. I don't remember specifically, but with weather that unseasonably cool my parents probably didn't even have the big grey window fan churning.

I *do* remember that the fan was still grey; Daddy didn't spray-paint it green until sometime in the mid-1960's. That old fan was so big that the constant hum (and occasional squeak) of the belt-driven pulley shook the whole wood-frame rented house. Home air conditioning just wasn't a "thing" in 1957 —at least not at 119 Heather Lane in East Point Georgia.

The fan's hum was perfect for lulling my three-year-old self to sleep, especially since I usually was put to bed long before the summer sun would set sometime after eight o'clock. In my knee-length *Davy Crockett* TV-show seersucker pajamas, the hum usually would sedate me, regardless of my nightly *I-wanna-stay-up* whiney protests. Sometimes the hum sounded like the Davy Crockett theme to match my PJ's. I think that right around the time I learned to talk I was singing that Davy Crockett theme:

| Born on a mountain top in Tennessee; Greenest state in the land of the free; Raised in the woods, so he knew every tree; | Kilt him a bear when he was only three; Davy, Davy Crockett, king of the wild frontier[5] |

---

[4] ibid

[5] Bruns, George and Blackburn, Tom, "*Ballad of Davy Crockett*" ©1954 Wonderland Music Company

THE LEGEND DIES ON — GARY GREEN

On nights when Davy or the fan wouldn't do the trick (or on winter nights when there was no fan) Mother would assure my cooperation by administering a teaspoon of *paregoric* — a camphorated tincture of *opium* that frequently was administered to children in the 18th, 19th, and early 20th centuries. Available without prescription (until 1970, apparently), over-the-counter, the narcotic served as a sedative that my mother ostensibly used to treat "rheumatism", a euphemism for my whining about aching joints from a hard day's play.

That absurd concoction was so addictive, of course, that I often feigned "rheumatiz" just to get my fix. So, around the same time that beat-generation author William S. Burroughs was riding the fame of his landmark novel, *Junkie*, my pre-school self was jonesing for my own opioid. *Is it any wonder that my generation's music festivals were marked by our getting high?*

However, I don't think I was given the paregoric on *that* night. What I also remember from that night was lying in bed in the zombie-world between sleep and awake when my mother rushed into the room to rouse me out of bed as if there was some dire emergency in the house.

I remember it so clearly because the next five minutes would shape the rest of my life. It genuinely was one of those seminal epiphanies that poets, prophets, writers, and musicians attribute to changing everything.

My mother was a public-school piano teacher who also taught students in our home after school and on Saturdays. On Wednesday nights, Sunday mornings, and Sunday nights, she also was the church organist and pianist. Before she married my father, she had starred in her own weekly live local radio program in Forest City North Carolina, playing classical piano pieces and a few big-band hits.

Despite her predilection for the classics and her seemingly endless repertoire of *Southern Baptist* hymns (I think she had memorized all 503 songs in the *Broadman Hymnal*), her signature performance was her own arrangement of *Tommy Dorsey's Boogie Woogie*[6]. It was a rollicking piano boogie spiced liberally with sliding glissandos, breathless triplets, and a metronome-like control of a dominant 7th chord bass blues progression. It never failed to bring the house down and she continued to stun audiences with it well into her 70's when she played it for various retirement community talent shows.

---

[6] Which Dorsey had "appropriated" from African American pianist Clarence "Pinetop" Smith.

THE POET LAUREATE SOUL OF FOLKIE ROCK & ROLL

Classically trained and educated at *Mars Hill College*, (tucked away in North Carolina's Appalachian mountains) she taught hundreds of students across more than six decades with the *John Thompson* piano pedagogy focusing on Western European classical music. As her firstborn, and consequently spoiled, she began teaching me to read music before I could read words; or at least she *thought* she was teaching me to read music.

Looking back on it, I now acknowledge that it is somewhat freakish that I learned to read before kindergarten and learned to spell at about four years old. My parents altered their lives to create an environment for me that was focused exclusively on learning anything and everything. By the time I started *Mrs. Henry's Kindergarten* in College Park Georgia, I was completely baffled that every other toddler couldn't read.

After teaching me to read, my parents quickly realized they could no longer spell out words they didn't want me to understand. So, they both learned *American Sign Language* fingerspelling for their private communications. It took me until I was about five-years-old to learn that skill fluently.

They then switched to speaking *Ceazarnie* —the secret carny language that my father had learned in his youth when he was a traveling carnival roustabout. I never learned that pig-Latin-like language other than a few basic phrases, so they were safe in their communications.

But reading music was an entirely different matter; much easier and something I easily could do at three years old. Reading music was simply learning which of the little dots on the musical staff corresponded to which white key on the piano. It was not really a difficult task since, despite a piano having 88 keys they repeated themselves, starting all over again every few keys.

So, basically, all I had to do was remember which of the 21 little notes of written sheet music matched which 21 white keys in the middle of the piano keyboard. With that, I could "read music" and play piano; memorizing 21 things that never changed.

In the mind of the 41-month-old me, I didn't need to actually understand the music or "read" anything. It was a game of putting the right shaped peg in the correct hole. If I saw a printed note on the musical staff, I identified it as a position on the piano keyboard and touched that key; not as a note name or anything else.

I didn't really "read" music; I just played a game. Seriously, there was nothing *musical* about it. It was the same as the *Fisher-Price* shaped pegs game in nursery schools.

Finally, I learned that if two or more notes were shown on top of each other, then they were all to be touched on the keyboard at the same time. That's it, with that simple memorization, I was "reading music"; or at least that's what it looked like to my mother and anyone else who watched

THE LEGEND DIES ON — GARY GREEN

me. Unfortunately, since I conned my parents into believing that I was reading music, they enthusiastically encouraged my charade, praising the great musical strides I had made.

Even a year before kindergarten, my con-man instincts were fully functional as she praised her music-reading prodigy while in reality I merely played by "ear" and offered exaggerated facial expressions as I "struggled" to follow the sheet music[7]. (Sure, I eventually learned to read music, but as *Chet Atkins* often claimed of himself, "not enough to hurt my playing".)[8]

Nonetheless, it was not unusual for her to push me into listening to live recitals by her students or to watch televised piano concerts, no matter how boring I, as a preschooler, found them. Besides, the pieces that her students were performing in recitals were the same pieces that I was playing over and over *(and over and over and over ...)* and the same pieces that I could hear every one of her students play week after week (after week after week after week after...) as their music lessons in our living room resounded throughout our whole house.

A little better than the incessant repetition of mediocre (to terrible) piano students were the TV shows that featured pianists. I had an overdose

---

[7] Of course, my "technique" meant that I totally ignored time signatures with the obnoxious little stems and flags on notes. It meant that I paid no attention to the notations for rhythm; something that would haunt me for the rest of my life. But, if I heard the song, chances were that I could copy the melody's rhythm fairly closely.

At three-years-old I drilled for hours on *Air from Haydn's Surprise (Symphony Number 94)* and the Stravinsky orchestration of The *Volga Boatmen*.

My mother, of course, thought I was carefully playing the notes printed on the staff; but in reality, I wasn't even looking at the music. Instead, I was "hearing" in my head: *"Papa Haydn's dead and gone; But his memory lingers on' 1-5, 5-1, 1-1-1-5"*. Or, for the Stravinsky adapted folksong, I was imagining, *"Yo-ho, heave ho; Yo-ho, heave ho; Once more, once again, still once more; Yo-ho, heave ho"*.

[8] In hindsight almost three-quarters-of-a-century later, I would not recommend my childhood "system" as a substitute for learning to read music; but at the same time, I think with that kind of silliness, anyone can follow printed sheet music and play the piano at some level. Simple as it was and pretty cool for a three-year-old, it got a little more complicated when the printed music added those pesky ♭ or # symbols that required me to also play on the black keys; but even that was just a matter of rote learning the correlation between the printed notes and the keyboard. The flat (♭) by a note meant playing the black key just before it; and a sharp (#) meant playing the black key just after it. If sharps or flats were at the beginning of the music it meant that every single time that note was shown, it was the black key instead of the white.

I learned much later in life that the celebrated composer Irving Berlin never learned to read music and only played the black keys of the piano. *God Bless America, White Christmas, Alexander's Ragtime Band, Easter Parade, There's No Business Like Show Business,* and about 1,250 more of his songs were all written only on the black keys!

THE POET LAUREATE SOUL OF FOLKIE ROCK & ROLL

of *Liberace, Vladimir Horowitz, Arthur Rubinstein*. and the young Southern prodigy, *Van Cliburn*. Among the more interesting television concerts she pushed on me, I remember actually being fascinated by a tuxedoed Victor Borge playing Rossini's *William Tell Overture* backwards because his music was up-side down. It wasn't until he flipped the sheet music over and played it forward that it was recognizable as *The Lone Ranger Theme*.

It was a gimmick that my mother said she had first seen performed in the late 1940's in high school by a guy named *Wofford Huskey*; her very-talented classmate who had the same piano teacher, an ominously storied "Ms. Wall". (Wofford would reemerge decades later, in my life.)

At such a young age, I was equally amused by the eponymous star of *The Liberace Show*, who, to me, seemed to be as much about his crazy glitter-clothes as he was the piano playing that held my mother's attention. As a fake-player child myself, I viewed his playing as more *show* than the focused concentration of a classical pianist that Mother had shown me. My very-bored impression of him may be why two decades later I was apathetic to Elton John's glitter, while a lot of my friends were captivated by his showmanship. *(Though I do dig a couple of his and Bernie Taupin's songs.)*

On this July 1957 night, my mother (two-months pregnant with her second child) yanked me out of bed and plopped me down in front of the tiny black-and-white screen of our television. I sleepily saw another piano player on TV; but something was different. All my mother could say was, *"look at him Gary, look at him"*. That moment shaped my life, forever.

At 8:00 on Sunday nights the ABC television network, in third place, ran *Maverick* (the Warner Brothers western starting James Garner); CBS ran the much-ballyhooed *Ed Sullivan Show* (which in about seven years would introduce us all to The Beatles); and NBC broadcasted *The Steve Allen Show*. Despite the legacy mythos of the Ed Sullivan program, Steve Allen's show had an average 55.3% audience share vs Ed Sullivan's 39.7% *(leaving poor ABC with only about 5% of the timeslot's audience)*.

Steve Allen not only dominated the time slot, but the night and the entire genre of "variety" shows —TV jargon that described a show that would feature multiple entertainment formats; standup comics, crooners, skits, dancers, acrobats, puppeteers, bands, and anything else that made up that epoch's version of Vaudeville *(including the new genre of Rock and Roll)*.

Despite providing the television debut of many rock & rollers, Allen was not known as a fan of the genre and often tried to ridicule it (rather than promote it like Sullivan did). He had recited Roy Orbison's offbeat

THE LEGEND DIES ON — GARY GREEN

lyrics to *Ooby Dooby* as a satirical poetry reading, complete with pseudo-dramatic pauses at inappropriate points; and he infamously had Elvis Presley sing *Hound Dog* to a live basset hound.

He presented *rock & roll* as a punch line, not a serious musical form; often citing it as an example of what he called *"the cultural decay of society"*.

Nonetheless, he continued to book it on his show. Apparently, he (or the network) had the good sense to see potential dollar signs in reaching the youthful baby boomer market.

So, on July 28th, 1957, his show featured a 21-year-old wild rock and roller from Ferriday Louisiana playing the hell out of the piano (rather than a guitar). Allen himself was an accomplished pianist, and he presented a rock-and-roll piano player as the ultimate mocking of the *alleged* genre.

Jerry Lee Lewis was the rocker's name, and despite Allen's best efforts to make fun of him, the young man riveted the nation to the TV screen. Even when Jerry Lee excitedly and accidentally kicked back his piano stool and it slid across the stage, Allen picked it up and threw it back at him in mock involvement in the excitement as he raked his own greased-back hair down into his face in further mockery.

Apparently oblivious to his host's attempted ridicule, and thinking Allen was rocking with him, Lewis pushed the fevered excitement even further and had the studio audience on their feet. Likewise, viewers across America were equally caught in the frenzy. My parents were among those viewers, *as was I*.

It was more than a backfire of Allen's attempted humiliation; it became a genuine phenomenon of unrestrained musical intensity that forever changed America's perception of rock and roll.

Allen himself seemed to realize that Jerry Lee Lewis was something very real and much more than a punchline begging for a parody. After seeing the ratings and sorting through sack-after-sack of fan mail, he re-booked Jerry Lee for a second appearance; on this one Allen gave a much more serious introduction, asked Lewis to perform the same song, and even got up and danced to the music.

As for his part, Lewis became such a sensation because of that appearance that out of gracious admiration and appreciation, he named his firstborn child *"Steve Allen Lewis"*.

Though clearly that July appearance did not "shatter the foundation of civilization" as one snarky reviewer later wrote, whatever it was that Jerry Lee did on TV that night grabbed America like no one ever had: not even Elvis. I mean, he had my conservative Southern, Sunday-School-Organist mother speechlessly excited.

THE POET LAUREATE SOUL OF FOLKIE ROCK & ROLL

Jerry Lee Lewis had started the song that night with that same left-handed dominant-seventh chord bass blues progression that my mother's boogie woogie featured; but instead of her inverted mixolydian F scale, this kid was hammering a hard-core boogie base line[9] that became more intense as his voice got louder punctuating the lyrics. His right-hand triplets were like hers —but on high-octane jet fuel instead of Sunday School grape juice.[10]

He somehow had merged dance music from Black roadhouses with "holy-rollie" music from white churches to create a feeling far beyond anything that had ever been recorded. He genuinely left the listener (and viewer) breathless and wondering what-the-hell-just-happened.

As he began that lefthand boogie, my mother instantly recognized her own Dorsey-inspired progression… but with something much more intense about the presentation.

That is when she had run into my bedroom, grabbed me, and pointed at the wild man on television. She wanted her music prodigy to see what she saw and to hear what she heard.

I vividly recall standing there, staring at the snowy black-and-white TV screen and actually *feeling* the music. Instantly, for me, my piano playing game … music itself… was something different; something very different. *It was music that caused action!*

For me, as little more than a toddler at that time, it also immediately showed me that even in the face of adversity —when the powerful *(Steve Allen in this case)* make fun of you— you can still come out on top and change everything.

From those few seminal televised moments, when I was three years, five months, and 28 days old, I knew for sure what I wanted … needed… to do in life.

I had to rock and roll!

---

[9] (root-3-5-6 then 7♭-6-5-3)

[10] Watching it in the 21st century, the November 1957 appearance seems more constrained than the first: as if there was a specific cue to JLL to kick the piano stool back and force-repeat the July spontaneity.

THE LEGEND DIES ON — GARY GREEN

Opus Two:
Shaped By My Hillbilly Roots

Now it's a mighty rough road from Lynchburg to Danville,
A layin' on a three-mile grade.
It was on that grade that he lost his airbrakes
And you can see what a jump he made!
—The Wreck of The Old 97[11]

If you asked the best Hollywood fiction-writers to create the archetypical backstory for America's folksinger, all they would need to do is look at my early childhood into my formative years. From *riding the rails* to wandering into black-lung coal mines to elementary school at the birthplace of country music; the universe began singing my song as soon as I was self-aware.

I was born on the first day of February in 1954 in Hamlet North Carolina; a junction of three railroad lines and the regional head-quarters of the Seaboard Air Line[12] Railroad's maintenance shop, roundhouse, shipping yard, and classification yard.

Hamlet was unlike most other North Carolina small towns. Those other towns echoed Merle Travis' lyrics: *I owe my soul to the company store.* Indeed, many North Carolina towns, at that time, were little more than textile mill villages for low-wage workers whose already-meager paychecks were drastically reduced by rent taken out for a company-owned shanty shack and cost of groceries from a company-owned general store. Some mills didn't even pay in U.S. currency; instead, they paid with their own company-issued scrip that was only good for use in company-owned stores and not convertible to real money —*in the f'ing 20th century, for real* North Carolina's mill villages were as close to indentured servitude as existed in early 20th century America.

That was the world in which my mother was raised; both of her parents worked at "the mill" in Caroleen North Carolina and she was raised in a

---

[11] Based on the 1865 Henry Clay Work song *The Ship That Never Returned*; lyrics either by Fred Jackson Lewey & Charles Weston Noell or by David Graves George or "?" (if we believe the US Supreme Court determining authorship).

[12] "Air Line" didn't refer to plans to fly, but rather that the tracks ran "as straight as the crow flies". The Seaboard track from Hamlet to Wilmington NC was the longest straight-line track in America; 79 miles in a straight line. The Hamlet Rail Yard served as a base to dispatch workers along the 4,135 miles of track and branches from Richmond Virginia to Miami Florida.

mill-owned house.[13] Her fond memories of childhood always sounded to me like gothic horror stories; even down to bare-handedly ringing the necks of live chickens and watching their bodies flailing around the yard after they were dead.[14]

Hamlet, though, was a socio-economic anomaly with the railroad providing hundreds of mostly white men with relatively well-paying secure employment including sick leave and even pension plans, negotiated by powerful national unions.

Consequently, Hamlet had a large white middle-class population that often haughtily scoffed at their "white trash" relatives and neighbors that worked at the cotton mills in nearby villages. That was the world into which I was born; albeit in a duplex-house complex of blue-collar specialists. It also was a world that my mother happily embraced as an escape from the carefully whitewashed subjugated life in mill villages from which she'd come.

Although Daddy was from the same mill-dominated county as my mother, his family roots were not from the blue-collar mill hands that her family had been. Instead, he came from a long line of mercantile watchmakers that could trace family roots back to the *Domesday Book* and the landed gentry of 11th century England, hobnobbing with kings and even mentioned in one of Shakespeare's plays. So, he fit well into the *perceived* distinction of the lower middle-class railroad village.

Orphaned at 14, he had run away from his stepmother to become a roustabout and illegal blackjack dealer in a traveling carnival midway. Later trained as an electrician in the railroad union's apprenticeship program and reaching journeyman status in the U.S. Army Corps of Engineers during the second World War, by the time I was born he was working as signal maintainer for Seaboard.

Being dispatched constantly to maintenance yards in Atlanta, Jacksonville, and Winter Haven, his home (at least by number of nights) was

---

[13] Her parents were the only grandparents that I knew; my father's parents had died long before I was born. So, for my entire childhood a visit to the grandparents meant a visit to the mill village and that entirely alternate universe.

[14] The African-American descendants of former slaves, some as few as two generations back, were segregated into even more dilapidated mill houses and even segregated inside the company store and services. As a child, I found it curious that those families often had the same last names as the white families who lived in the less-run-down mill houses. In childish bliss, I was naïve to the realities of history; even when I learned that the Black family who lived behind my mother's childhood home had the same last name as my grandfather.

THE LEGEND DIES ON — GARY GREEN

various cabooses and crew cars along the Seaboard route. Hamlet really was "home" for just me and my mother most of the time.

In 1954, when I was born, America was in the midst of its worst years of the infantile paralysis (polio) epidemic. Leg braces and grotesque abominations called "iron lungs" were very real parts of the lives of afflicted children; and young deaths were rampant. It was a disease that even had killed the most-elected President in U.S. history as well as tens of thousands of children every year; and there was no mass vaccine yet for that highly-contagious illness.

So, six months after I was born, when the Richmond County Quarantine Officer posted a large sign announcing *"INFANTILE PARALYSIS IN QUARANTINE"* on the front door of our neighbor in the duplex we shared, my parents immediately packed our belongings and fled the State to shield me from exposure.

My father's railroad seniority allowed for an easy transfer from Hamlet to the yard in Atlanta. And that is where we were living on the night that Jerry Lee Lewis changed my life.

Gravely shaken and concerned that he should have moved us out of Hamet sooner, my father decided that the best way to avoid such future perils would be for us to travel *with* him. So, while we indeed were based in the Atlanta suburbs, most of every week was spent taking advantage of Seaboard's policy of free family travel.

Repeatedly covering more than 4,000 miles of track, for four years we traveled with him, riding in extra passenger space that hadn't been sold, sometimes in cabooses if there were no empty revenue seats, and on rare occasions in a Pullman berth. I, quite literally, grew up "on the rails" —a great backstory for a Southern folksinger; but one that is absolute reality in my case.[15]

One of daddy's many stories about his rail career was from five years before I was born but was retold so many times that I've been working on a song about it for almost 70 years:

---

[15] Life on railroad trains had a culture of its own, with all the attendant jargon, behaviors, and eccentricities of any substrata of American life. My preschool years were a deep indoctrination into that lifestyle —even down to knowing how to signal a passing train about a smoking "hot box" and other now-archaic behind-the-scenes work not glamorized by those who idealize railroad life, visit round-house museums, and collect model trains.

Even pre-school, I thought it more-than-weird that all the Pullman Porters were named George. Apparently, the Pullman Company, founded during the Civil War and later headed by Robert Todd Lincoln (son of Abraham Lincoln), hired only African-American porters and in the tradition of slaves being named after their masters (like my grandfather's Black neighbors), porters were required to be called "George" after company founder George Pullman. *Seriously, that was a thing.*

THE POET LAUREATE SOUL OF FOLKIE ROCK & ROLL

Daddy was working out of the flat switchyard in Baldwin Florida on January 11, 1949. He and his crew were responsible for the maintenance of the electronic signals between Jacksonville and Miami, including the spur over to Tampa.

In those days one entire wall of every stationhouse was taken up by a large map of the train routes. Along the route-lines, the map had little lights which would be dark until a train crossed one of Daddy's signal junctions. The metal wheels of a train on that section of track would close the circuit and turn on the light at the stationhouse. This system allowed the Station Master to always know the location of his trains by simply seeing where a light was illuminated on the big map wall. A good station master could multitask their normal duties and occasionally glance at the board to note if any train was running late or early.

The flagship of the Seaboard Railroad was the seasonal (and eventually all-electric) "deluxe" passenger train: the highly-celebrated **Orange Blossom Special**[16]. Covering 1,388.7 miles from New York City to Miami Florida, the green and orange painted locomotive was an art-deco sight to behold; though it was not the "streamliner" design as pop culture has remembered it.

On that January day in 1949, Daddy watched the stationmaster stop work and stare intently at the board. The lights indicated that the famous train had cleared both the Wildwood Florida relay light and the Groveland light as it sped south. The next light, at Winter Haven, didn't come on as scheduled. My father prepared to get an electric cart to go repair the failed signal, but the Stationmaster told him to wait.

"I'm not feeling good about this; something's done happened to my Orange Blossom Special," Daddy recalled the Stationmaster worrying aloud.

They both silently watched the board, waiting for either Winter Haven to light up (indicating the train had slowed) or the next signal, at West Lake Wales, to light. The likelihood of two signals failing was remote; so, when the next signal came on that would indicate the first signal was bad. In those days of copper-wire analog signaling, a failed relay was not an uncommon thing; that is why my father, and the other electricians, were assigned to the regional yards.

The West Lake Wales light never came on. They waited and waited and waited and waited... until their silence was interrupted by a ringing phone. My father recalled the voice of the old farmer on the other end of the call: "Is this the

---

[16] In 1938, waiting for another train at the Jacksonville station, musicians Ervin Rouse and Chubby Wise witnessed the brightly colored Orange Blossom Special arrive at the station, long before Daddy worked for the line. They were so taken by the sight of the unusual-looking train that then and there they wrote the fiddle tune that would immortalize the train and later be recorded by Bill Monroe, Johnny Cash, Charlie Daniels, and dozens of others: *The Orange Blossom Special*.

THE LEGEND DIES ON — GARY GREEN

> *Seaboard Railroad? Mister, that pretty Orange Blossom Special of yours is all over my swamp and there are bodies everywhere."*

Daddy retold that story for as long as I can remember; but for me, it is just too daunting to write *anything* about the Orange Blossom Special in the face of the original iconic sawing fiddle song (or the Charlie McCoy harmonica and Boots Randolph saxophone in Cash's version). [17]

Nine years after that incident, my first brother, Ronny, was born in Atlanta (in 1958). That curtailed our train travel to either just weekends or only me and Daddy traveling (with Mother and the baby staying home). Now a genuine family man, my father decided that the best way to spend more time with the family was to leave the railroad life and transition from a blue-collar electrician to a white-collar salesman.

If *life on the rails* was the mythos-perfect beginning for my musical life, Daddy's next move was just as quintessential: to the Holston Valley of upper east Tennessee — the venerated birthplace of country music[18] and only about 15 miles from the home of Americana music royalty, The Carter Family.

My father worked first as a salesman-installer of electronic dictating equipment, then as a traveling appliance salesman for *Sears, Roebuck & Company* (the cataloging giant, before they entered the big-box retail business). Both jobs based him in the rural East Tennessee town of Kingsport[19], and both jobs had him constantly traveling to small towns in East Tennessee, Southwestern Virginia, Eastern Kentucky, and the Southwestern tip of West Virginia.

Neither job, however, gave him the homelife that he wanted. Following the pattern of our railroad days, he decided that we would go with him through Appalachia as much as possible. On the long drives through the mountains, rather than turning on the radio, he and Mother would sing.

---

[17] The reality wasn't nearly as bad as the farmer had reported. A bearing on a traction motor of the locomotive had overheated, causing the motor to seize up and resulting in the derailment of all but two cars. The three Pullman cars were totally on their sides in the farmer's swamp. Seventy-six people were injured, and one died. Two days earlier, another section of cars had derailed as the Orange Blossom had passed Milford Virginia: that one injured 20 people.

[18] The very genre of country music had begun when the new "record business" of RCA's Victor Talking Machine Company sent producer Ralph Peer to the South to find talent. With portable recording equipment, he set up in a small hotel room in Bristol Virginia (on the Tennessee state line and 21 miles from where we lived in Kingsport Tennessee), to hear auditions on August 1, 1927. (More on that later.)

[19] When he started with Sears, we briefly moved back to Atlanta, but soon returned to Kingsport where we remained until the mid-1960's (except for a brief move to Harriman Tennessee, about two hours away).

THE POET LAUREATE SOUL OF FOLKIE ROCK & ROLL

Their driving repertoire included mostly hillbilly train songs: *Wabash Cannonball* and *Fireball Mail* (mimicking Roy Acuff); *I'm Moving On* (Hank Snow); *Casey Jones* (the Burl Ives version from the TV show); *This Train, Hey Porter,* and *Rock Island Line* (aping Johnny Cash); and his (and my) favorite, the Vernon Dalhart version of *The Wreck of the Old 97* (the first million-selling record in the United States).

It wasn't long before I was singing along and we expanded beyond train songs to include: *The Davy Crockett Theme*[20]; *Tennessee Waltz* (Patti Page); *Your Cheating Heart* and *Jambalaya* (Hank Williams); *If You've Got the Money Honey* (Lefty Frizzell); *The Battle of New Orleans* (Johnny Horton); *Walking the Floor Over You* (Ernest Tubb; who Daddy called Ernest "Bucket"); *Thunder Road* (Robert Mitchum's theme from his movie with the same title and not EVEN the Bruce Springsteen rock staple that would be written 20 years later); a few near-traditionals like *Cotton Fields, Going Down The Road Feeling Bad, When The Saints Go Marching In, Swing Low Sweet Chariot,* and *Birmingham Jail*; and a whole set of World War II ballads including: *Coming In On A Wing And A Prayer; Praise The Lord And Pass the Ammunition; White Cliffs of Dover;* the tear-jerker Ernest Tubb song, *Soldier's Last Letter,* that always made my mother cry; and the Red Foley version of the Zeke Clements & Earl Nunn song *Smoke On The Water* (definitely not to be confused with the Deep Purple song of decades later —to this day, I can kick off THAT *"Smoke on The Water"* as surely as Grady Martin did in 1944).

Occasionally they would throw in a hymn or two (which my father would call "a HER" rather than the homophonic HIM/hymn); *Life's Railway To Heaven, Amazing Grace,* and *The Old Rugged Cross.* For the latter, my father would often modify the lyrics to *"On a hill far away, stood an old Chevrolet...".* Such satirical revisions were a frequent part of his repertoire; he usually changed Hank Snow's I'm Moving On chorus to, *"Give me a date and a Ford V8 and I'm Moving On".*

Even that early, I was exposed to parody songs; and that would shape me for decades (re: my *CIA Song* or my *Jesus Christ Was A Republican,* on my first and third Folkways albums).

I memorized all of those songs and like my parents in the 1950's, I have continued to sing them *a cappella* my entire life. The fact that I could pick out the melodies on the piano by the time I was in kindergarten just made the songs more fun to me; and once I learned to add chords with my left hand, I had a concert-ready set.

---

[20] (a la The Wellingtons —who later were known for the Gilligan's Island Theme Song)

THE LEGEND DIES ON — GARY GREEN

In addition to the music education provided on those trips, my young formative-eyes absorbed the depths of abject Appalachian poverty with its cardboard-boxes-for-windows in coal town shanties (that made North Carolina mill villages look "upscale") to no-running-water sharecroppers' shotgun shacks. As we traveled to my father's various destinations, I saw people who only had once-a-day meals of beans-bacon-and-gravy, Sears catalog pages used as toilet paper in outhouses, children's shoes bought once a year and handed down to the next kid, homemade lye soap and butter, patched overalls, and the painfully premature age-lines acidly-carved into the faces and hands of the people there (people in their 40's looked 80).

Family deaths in mine cave-ins, hacking coughs of black-lung disease, route-traveling doctors that made it to town once every few months, elementary schools where teachers were not required to have a college education, and neighborly disputes solved with bullets.

More than just seeing those sights, I wandered through them, alone, as we would stop overnight or even to get gasoline. More than once, I explored a coal mine shaft and returned blowing black coal dust from my nose for days, to my mother's horror. (I couldn't imagine what pneumoconiosis must be like.)

My mother and I were at an in-town restaurant/tavern for lunch one day somewhere when we overheard the two men in the next booth saying, *"I would have just killed him, but they're getting to where they catch 'em for that lately"*. THAT was the lay-of-the-land!

Periodically, our 1949 Ford (with its flathead V8 power-mill and a gravel-induced hole in the rusted muffler that made it louder than normal) would get stopped by "Revenuers" (ATF agents) to see if we had a hidden tank for hauling moonshine; most counties were "dry", and alcohol was illegal.

Barbar shops that sold a 10-cent bath in a hot-water tub for Saturday nights to smelly unbathed people, were not unusual (since no one had hot water at home); as were washboards and coal-oil lamps instead of electricity.

And the local music — *wow!* It didn't sound like anything I'd heard before. Mostly played on front porches or in wood-frame church houses, it seemed to be played super-fast (cut time) and sung by men in high pitched (almost falsetto or contra tenor,) voices. It was bluegrass in its truest form.

Beyond that, the music seemed to be an out-and-out assassination of formal musical rhythm schemes (something that even then *I* could appreciate). With totally unexpected meter changes, the steady structured beat of a song would suddenly break into lightning-speed and just as abruptly

THE POET LAUREATE SOUL OF FOLKIE ROCK & ROLL

return to the slower structure. It violated all the music theory rules but it still was exciting; *no wonder my mother hated it!*

A song might be sung as a waltz (3/4) or in common (4/4) time but at the instrumental break between verses it might suddenly speed to cut time (2/2) or even faster (6/8) before going back to the more restrained verses.

It usually wasn't the controlled crescendo-like change that Bill Monroe famously orchestrated in his iconic *Blue Moon Over Kentucky* as he skillfully manipulated audiences with the sound trick to create a climax. It was more like a rhythmic anarchy that just didn't give a damn about structure; focusing, instead, on what *felt good* to play. It haunted me so badly that later when I would hear music on television or records the instrumental breaks sounded like dull stillness.

I wanted to hear the unrestrained spontaneity regardless of whether it was bluegrass or rockabilly or later acid rock. *That is what the music of western Appalachia did to me!*

Beyond the rhythmic machinations, the real musical mystery, at least to me, was the way the church women in the mountains read music: *shape-note singing.* If you think my reading-music technique of putting square pegs into square holes and round pegs into round holes was a cheat; then shaped note singing is on a whole other plane of confidence games.[21]

The music, the poverty, the squalor, the sights, sounds, tastes, smells, sensations, and interactions that I experienced were exclusively amongst the *White* people, who were the *perceived* "middle class" folk.

Unimaginable as it may seem today, in that time and that location *Black* people were segregated to live in even *more deplorable* deprivation. They made up a whole lower class below even the poverty I was witnessing. It totally confused me, as a preschooler, that people who did the same work, side-by-side, were boxed into such different lifestyle situations. It wasn't something that I fixated on — I was a child carefully ensconced in the

---

[21] Apparently, it actually was a system created by an 11th-Century Italian monk who wanted a quick and easy way to teach music to his uneducated flock. The system had seven shapes of notes; each shape was assigned a name: doe, ray, me, fa, so, la, tee, doe (think of the song from the movie Sound of Music). Each name was assigned a musical pitch; for example, in a C scale, "doe" was a C. "ray" was D, "me" was E... and so on up the scale. The church hymnals were books of sheet music (for pianists to play), with lyrics written under the notes. Each note on the musical staff for the piano was printed as one of the shapes rather than the circles (or ovals) that ordinarily were used for music notations. Using this system, people who could not read a single notation of music could sing pitch-perfect a song that they'd never before heard —simply by singing the correct doe-ray-me pitch indicated by the shape of the printed note. It was a fascinating system that made my childish rote memorization scheme seem like an incredible waste of time.

THE LEGEND DIES ON — GARY GREEN

relative comfort of white middle-class East Tennessee. Nonetheless, I clearly remember a sort of "WTF?" in my observations.

Of course, the managers and mercantilists lived in what would have been middle-class everywhere else but was absolute luxury there. And, evidently, the ownership class lived elsewhere and only occasionally (if ever) visited their fiefs.

All of these experiences, *including the music,* were more than just observations during my preschool-through-sixth-grade years; they were part of the day-to-day life of traveling with my father. These were the foundational images, sounds, and experiences that shaped my life and my music; impressions that I carry even today.

Can you even imagine the impact these things had on a developing child; especially on a child who had the luxury of being able to escape it every week.

My salvation from the wretched imagery was that at the end of every trip I was blessed with the ability to go home to my parents' comfortable house (albeit a rental) back in Kingsport and the stability of *Abraham Lincoln Elementary School* with music lessons, spelling bees, Cub Scout meetings, dance recitals, and French language taught (beginning in the second grade).

From pre-school times, Daddy made sure we had a well-stocked home library; including a 15-volume "Junior Classics" set of reprints from P. F. Collier (my favorite was Volume 10, the poetry book), the complete works of Mark Twain, an encyclopedia and two-volume dictionary, a couple of Charles Dickens books, and a handful of contemporary novels like *The Caine Mutiny.*

Bedtime, 8:30 p.m., on most nights meant that a few minutes after I would crawl into bed, my father would come into the room directly from the living room and a couple of shots of Jack Daniels. It would be time for the nightly bedtime story. There were several regular ones, including a reading of James Whitcome Riley's *"Little Orphant Annie"* poem, or *"The Raggedy Man"* by the same author, or *"The Cremation of Sam McGee"* by Robert W. Service. But the one I requested most was the one that he seemed to enjoy telling the most: *"Br'er Rabbit and the Tar Baby*[22]. Somehow that one story just flowed perfectly with the smell of Daddy's Tennessee sipping whisky and a dissipated cloud of *Roi Tan Perfecto* cigar smoke setting the nightly stage.

---

[22] Despite the 21st century likely-valid view that the tar-baby might be a pejorative racist term, scholars have identified more than 267 versions of the story throughout North American, Latin American, and African folklore.

THE POET LAUREATE SOUL OF FOLKIE ROCK & ROLL

He seemed to take particular pleasure in telling how the victimized rabbit outwitted the oppressive fox. He always made it a point to emphasize that the weaker could overcome the stronger by outthinking him.

The rabbit was, to my father, a brilliant con man. Daddy always liked tales of con men; *The Music Man* was his favorite musical, and *The Flim-Flam Man* became one of his favorite movies. His enthusiasm for the con added to the collage that shaped me.

It was a safe, comfortable, and oblivious childhood. Sometimes, even today, I can close my eyes and almost smell my mother's baking frozen fish sticks or the frying SPAM™ cubes that she would make for supper. Though near the end of her life she stopped cooking anything other than preprepared grocery-store food and canned biscuits[23], I still remember that I have never had hot biscuits that matched the flaky tenderness of hers (and I have eaten a lot of biscuits over the years).

Capitola flour (they had neat little "coins" as a prize in each bag) and later *White Lily* flour, *Duke's* mayonnaise, *Sunbeam* bread (the "Little Miss Sunbeam Girl" mascot was one of Mother's piano students), *Pet Milk* (I used to save bottle-stoppers and trade them for free admission to the Saturday matinees at the State Theater); all visions and smells of home in Kingsport at 713 Biscayne Drive.

It was all part of the comforts of Kingsport homelife, and I easily could have ignored the reality outside of the comparative luxury of Kingsport[24] (as did many of my peers); but to me deep Appalachia was a fundamental part of my life. It was all one package, and I proudly accepted it, flaunted it, and carried it with me ... even today.

In those years from kindergarten through the first few grades, I over-performed academically in school, appeared on local Atlanta television (at five-years-old), had the lead in a folk and square dance group at seven (including, for some strange reason, Romani dance (цыганский танец) taught in an East Tennessee elementary school —probably no stranger than teaching us to speak French in the hillbilly mountains).

When I was in the fourth grade in Kingsport, I consciously wrote my first song (including musical notation) at eight-years-years-old (*The Boys With The Silver Motorcycles,* written with my brother Ronny).

---

[23] An abomination to the Southern concept of a "biscuit".

[24] Kingsport really is in the heart of Appalachia rather than the cultural Midwest of the rest of Tennessee. Geographically, it is closer to the Canadian border than to Memphis, which speaks as much to the vast expanse that is Tennessee as it does to the location of Kingsport. It is, at least, noteworthy that as the Memphis area is arguably the birthplace of Rock & Roll, likewise the Holston Valley is known as the birthplace of Country Music.

THE LEGEND DIES ON — GARY GREEN

Around the same time, I formed an elementary school Beatles cover band called "The Flees" (about the same time The Beatles released *A Hard Day's Night*), and for several years I emceed monthly basement talent shows for the kids in the neighborhood.

We set up a "stage" area against one wall of the basement by stringing a clothesline between two side walls and draping it with a large bedspread to serve as a curtain. After lining up a few quasi-talented neighborhood kids to perform, I stood at the end of our driveway and like a carnival barker called out to neighbors and other kids to "come one, come all". I might have exaggerated a little about the show, announcing that Elvis Presley would be appearing in my basement. Nonetheless, a dozen or so kids would show up every month and Mother would make popcorn for everyone. Adults would come too; Daddy would provide beer or *Jack*. The shows were bad[25], but fun and provided great training in stage-presence and in responding to audience reactions.

Meanwhile, Daddy periodically added part-time or temporary jobs to his activities; sometimes using his electrician skills, sometimes his photography darkroom skills (which he also taught me) like developing blueprints or architectural photographs, sometimes just sales jobs. One such job was business-to-business sales for the *Volunteer Natural Gas Company*.

That company was struggling to find a customer base because the local Kingsport Power Company, a privately held non-TVA company, had painted natural gas as dangerous and likely to explode. The gas company responded with an aggressive sales force (including my father) and advertised that gas was cheaper, more dependable, and safer. As part of the messaging, Daddy convinced the owners to take their campaign to drive-time radio advertising.

For the radio spots, the company listened to any number of ad-agency created jingles; but none of them really got the message across in the way the company envisioned it. Finally, they asked my father to write a jingle that would convey their pitch.

One weekend he and I sat down at Mother's piano and wrote the commercial jingle. Mother then refined the tune to an actual composition and created a score for it. A few weeks later our first radio-airplay song debuted on WKPT radio in Kingsport, sung by an ad-agency choir: *"In East Tennessee For Econ-on-o-my, You Better Heat With Natural Gas. It's Safe And Dependable Too. You Better Heat With Natural Gas."* It was a

---

[25] The shows were sprinkled with our performances of such "classics" as the theme song from the TV show *Fireball XL5* (Barry Gray's first use of an *Ondes Martenot* that spent 12 weeks on the UK music charts in 1963.)

THE POET LAUREATE SOUL OF FOLKIE ROCK & ROLL

three-chord (1-4-1-5-1) common-time song that mother scored with three-part harmony. It sounded exactly like it had been written by an eight-year-old; in other words, perfect for an early 1960's radio jingle. More importantly, I had a "commercially successful" product jingle playing multiple times daily on drive-time radio. Cool cred for a pre-teen!

Every summer, our family would take a one- or two-week vacation to the blue-collar resort town of Myrtle Beach South Carolina. Among the attractions there was the famous Pavilion, filled with pinball machines, shooting galleries, skee-ball, electronic bowling, other coin-operated amusement games, and several 25-cent photo booths where one would get a strip of four "instant" photos shot inside the little booth.

During those elementary school summers, while the family would enjoy the sun, sand, and surf, I usually would avoid the beach, preferring to feed my alienation by wandering the tourist attractions and amusement parks, dressed in long pants, cowboy boots, a US Navy Commodore hat, and a 2,000+ year old shark's tooth on a chain around my neck.

One year, added to the photo-booth area, the Pavilion owners -booth-looking contraption, deposit a quarter, wait for a green light installed a *"Deluxe Voice-O-Graph"*. Using it, a patron would step into a phone to illuminate, and then for the next one minute and ten seconds every sound in the booth was recorded. After a two-minute wait, a 45-rpm record of the recording would be dispensed from the booth. For another five-cents, the machine would also dispense a sleeve for the record.

Daddy wrote a short comedy routine, had us memorize it, and took my brother, Ronny, and me into the booth. We recorded a one-minute record as *"Pea, Wall, and Chess: the Nut Brothers"*. I don't think it was funny, and the record is long lost; but it opened my mind to all sorts of recording possibilities.

The next day, Ronny and I went back into the booth and recorded our song *The Boys With The Silver Motorcycles*. It was a three-chord pop-ballad structure (though sometimes I would make it a four-chord song (1-6m-4-5) that most surely sounded like it was written by an eight-year-old and a four-year-old. Nonetheless, at eight-years-old, I was now, in my mind, a recording artist and I proudly brought my "hit record" back home to East Tennessee.

Meanwhile, things were normal back at school... for a very short time. Though I completely disregarded it, sometime in that elementary school era of my life, school officials and my parents decided to subject me to something called the *Terman and Merrill revision of the Stanford-Binet Intelligence Scale Test*. Allegedly, and *according* to the educators, on the test I scored one of the 22nd highest IQs ever recorded in the world. That meant nothing to me other than the administrators wanted me to undergo

THE LEGEND DIES ON — GARY GREEN

some kind of medical testing, and the school principal wanted me to bypass the rest of elementary school and enter high school years early.[26]

My mother absolutely forbade it, citing that at only four-feet-and-two-inches tall combined with my young age I would be deemed a freak, bullied by older students, and have a generally miserable life. At the time I resented her decision, but in later life I realized not only was she right but that the test itself was culturally biased bullshit that lent itself to being gamed by a con-man kid like me.

The next year, when I was in the fifth grade, Daddy had left the trappings of wage labor to become an entrepreneur of sorts; buying a *Pure Oil* gasoline station in Kingsport (before Pure was absorbed by Union Oil of California the following year). The venture would become the family business known as *Green's Pure Service* in the days when all gas stations were "full service" and pump-it-yourself was an unheard-of imposition on customers.

I worked at the station washing windows, pumping gasoline, and checking oil... as well as removing the coins from the illegal-payout pinball machines in the garage.

I remember, at ten-years-old, wondering why the building came with *three* restrooms instead of two: Men, Women, and "Colored". Two of the restrooms were inside, spotlessly clean, and had good working locks on the doors; the "colored" one was outside, on the back of the building, had no lock on the door, and looked (and smelled) like it had never been cleaned. (Daddy, thankfully, closed the third one and tacitly integrated the business; at a time that such was unheard of in Tennessee).

Around that same time, my parents became regulars at the local VFW club where rockabillies *Eddie and Ron Skelton* played every weekend. Ron was our "Orkin Man" bug exterminator, and his older brother was the star of *The Eddie Skelton Show* on WJHL-TV in nearby Johnson City[27].

---

[26] A 1916 "standardized" test used some sort of scientistic (as opposed to scientific) sketchy math comparing mental age to chronical age (and not without a good deal of white Anglo-Saxon cultural biased). I simply had determined the patterns that were expected of me and then fed back to them what they wanted —just as I had done when I was supposedly "reading music". It, quite literally, was child's play; a stupid game, at that.

[27] Eddie (Etsel) had been a promoter who in the 1950's had brought Chuck Berry and Elvis Presley to perform in East Tennessee. Chuck Berry remained his close friend and often would visit and spend a few nights at the Skelton home. After a brief stint as a hillbilly singer on Don Pierce's Starday Records in Nashville, Eddie returned to East Tennessee to play rockabilly with his brother and a newly-formed band.

THE POET LAUREATE SOUL OF FOLKIE ROCK & ROLL

Once a month Ron would come by to squirt for insects at our house, and often he would bring me a 45-rpm record that he and his brother had made. Their covers of Elvis songs were grittier and, to my young ears, much more exciting than "The King" *(especially after Elvis became a movie star instead of a rockabilly)*.

I must have played the Eddie Skelton version of *Good Luck Charm* a thousand times; the Colonel-Parker-coopted Aaron Schroeder and Wally Gold song that was a number-one hit for Elvis in 1962. I still think the Skelton cover is one of the best post-Sun-Records rockabilly songs ever recorded.

Eddie's own composition, *Yellow Green & Blue*, had what I considered to be every element of a classic country song (even down to a whining pedal steel guitar and the hillbilly harmony). It was never a hit for them, and I doubt if it sold many records at all; but I continued to sing and play it well into the 1980's. I even recorded it myself on my *Live From Bread & Roses* album (though producer Howard Ehrlich edited it from the master tape because it didn't fit with the topical (political) theme he had conceptualized for the performance).

Other than my mother and Jerry Lee Lewis, the Skelton brothers were probably the single biggest musical influence on my elementary school years[28]. I was impressed that the Skelton Brothers actually had day jobs. They were genuine working people who happened to make incredible music —comparable or better than anything on the radio or television. They weren't millionaires, and they weren't aloof; they were "real" people. It showed me, too, that musicians who made great records didn't necessarily make a ton of money, no matter how good they were. That certainly was a lesson to carry forward.

A lesser musical influence on me during that time were twice-a-year charitable "telethons". A few years before the first national *Jerry Lewis Labor Day MDA Telethon,* dozens of TV stations aired week-end-long fundraisers for a Cerebral Palsy telethon or for the *Milton Berle Cancer Telethon,* or for other charities. Inevitably, the shows would end with large groups of exhausted performers all on stage at the same time, performing in unrehearsed jam sessions.

Sometimes there would be random local musicians, sometimes it was Eddie Skelton and his band, and sometimes there would be visiting national celebrities; all singing and playing together. I loved the spontaneity and ad-lib jumping in of various instruments as well as making up lyrics

---

[28] Eddie continued as an East Tennessee promoter, DJ, and regional personality until his death in 2021. Unfortunately, I never saw him again after about 1965.

THE LEGEND DIES ON — GARY GREEN

as they went along. It seemed to say, "hey, just start playing, you don't need structure".

More than a half-century later, I still remember the phone number for one of the telethons because they sung it repeatedly to the tune of *When The Saints Go Marching In*. Something about a message tied to a good song just stuck with me —*a hint of things ahead in my life*.

Amidst all this, along with Daddy's entrepreneurial venture came a dramatic change in fortunes for our family, and not in a good way. I had to withdraw from the tuition-based city school system and enter the county's very-rural school system, where a fifth-grade teacher was required to have only an eighth-grade education to teach.

My 36-year-old teacher resented that I had gone to city schools and could speak French. She vacillated between referring to me as *"Frenchy"* and *"four-eyes"* (after I got my first pair of glasses that year). She also thought that my mother's refusal to allow me to wear jeans to school was some sort of statement that I was some-how "better" than the other students; and she often voiced that in front of the class.

It was less than a pleasant year in school; especially since that teacher had untactfully been told by the school administration that this ten-year-old was qualified for education that surpassed her own eighth-grade level. I prefer to think THAT is why, before I got my first pair of glasses, she announced to the class *"Gary says he can't see the blackboard; he's a such a little pussy. Doesn't anybody want to change seats with the little girl?"* This from a fucking teacher!

It was the same school where my brother, Ronny, entered the first grade and discovered that some of his classmates had never seen porcelain toilets or indoor plumbing and consequently, they wet their pants every day rather than urinate in "such a pretty thing". It's where he was punished for not pronouncing "hiccups" as "hee-cups" and it also was where the school principal got drunk and hung himself after assaulting one of the sixth-grade students.

It was a school where the price of lunch was subsidized by a Federal anti-poverty program so that a carton of milk was 3¢ and the food was a nickel. Eight cents fed a student for the day and, tragically, was often the only meal many of the students got that day. It wasn't the same level of poverty as in the mountains; but it wasn't pleasant either. I drank three-cent *Foremost* milk every day with my nickel lunch.

Fortunately, the gas station project crashed rapidly, and Daddy was forced to return to wage labor; usually not a good thing but in our situation, it was a godsend. Unfortunately, that also meant we packed up and moved from my beloved Kingsport back to Atlanta. This time there were five of us; my parents, Ronny, myself, and my new brother Keith. who had been born in Kingsport four years earlier.

THE POET LAUREATE SOUL OF FOLKIE ROCK & ROLL

We moved to Georgia the same year that the Braves baseball team moved from Milwaukee to Atlanta; and I was instantly a Hank Aaron fanatic. The Dekalb County Georgia public school system at that time was ranked as the top academic jurisdiction in the country; and the sixth-grade curriculum showed it. For the first time in my education, I was actually challenged and had to work; and it was great!

My teacher had a Master of Education degree (a pretty extreme contrast to my 36-year-old eighth-grader who had been in charge of my education the previous year). He was from East Tennessee, a graduate of UT, and the baseball coach for the school, too.

The Principal of the school wanted me to skip at least two grades and jump to the end of Junior High or into High School; but again, my Mother refused to allow it. Instead, my parents took me to *Emory University Medical School* for a series of blood and hormonal tests and x-rays to determine if my abnormal IQ and apparently stunted growth were physiological deformities. *(I still was barely taller than four feet.)* Apparently, they were not, and my parents resolved to let me develop at my own pace; especially since the medical staff also agreed with my mother's decision to keep me with my chronological peers in school.

With my new Georgia-found focus on education, especially biology, there was little time for music; but I did sing (soprano or countertenor) in the church choir and occasionally filled in on the piano when various music teachers were absent.

Inspired by my teacher *(and fellow Tennessean)*, I started playing baseball for the school team; something Daddy seemed happy with as he started taking me and Ronny to Atlanta Braves games on weekends.

I was a busy boy. For a twelve-year-old with two younger brothers, it was a delightfully long way from the Appalachian mountains; both geographically and culturally. But my idyllic Georgia educational experience was short-lived.

By the end of that sixth-grade school year, Daddy was transferred to Bowling Green Kentucky, where we lived in a hotel for about 30 days before he again was reassigned: this time to Nashville Tennessee and it was in Nashville that I first heard the music world singing my name again.

THE LEGEND DIES ON — GARY GREEN

Opus Three:

Guitars, "Music City USA" & Johnny Cash's House

Well, there's thirteen hundred and fifty-two guitar pickers in Nashville
And they can pick more notes than the number of ants on a Tennessee ant hill
Yeah, there's thirteen hundred and fifty two guitar cases in Nashville
And any one that unpacks his guitar could play twice as better than I will!
—John B. Sebastian, *Nashville Cats*, 1966

Only I would be introduced to "The Nashville Sound" through the recordings of an African American bebop jazz saxophone sraw-boss cat; but that's how it happened. *Normal* people, I am told, found more traditional routes into the country music world; but not me.

It was an interesting year: Sergeant Barry Sadler's *Ballad of the Green Beret* was the number one song for five weeks; *Batman* debuted on TV; college military-draft deferments ended for students in the lower academic half of their classes and protesters in dozens of cities demonstrated against the Vietnam War as the *House Un-American Activities Committee* began an investigation of Americans who had participated; Watts was recovering from fires and riots and something called the **Black Panther Party for Self-Defense** was being formed in Oakland by my future friend Bobby Seale; Richard Speck murdered eight nurses in Chicago; the *Dragnet* TV show started reciting something called *Miranda Rights*; Mary Quant coined the term mini skirt; and another future friend, *Nancy Sinatra*, recorded *These Boots Are Made for Walking*.

It was 1966, I was 12 years old, and our family moved to Nashville that fall; just in time for the school year. I'd never heard the term *Music City USA* and had no idea that Nashville was some kind of holy shrine for country music. But… oh boy… I was about to learn. Was I ever!

Shortly after we moved into a three-bedroom rental house in the east-of-town suburb of Donelson, my parents were invited to a night-on-the-town with a group of Daddy's coworkers. They visited the *Carousel Club* in Nashville's then-famous *Printer's Alley* night-club district. There they saw a live show featuring studio saxophone wizard *Boots Randolph* (whose 1963 hit Yakety Sax had become British comedian Benny Hill's theme song). When the nightclub show ended, they bought a 45-rpm record of that hit song and brought it home to me.

Listening to the grind of Randolph's sax for about the 200th time, I developed a feverish obsession for saxophone music. The manager of the local record store (located on the bottom floor of Castner-Knott department store in Donelson) recommended that I listen to *Cannonball Adderley*, the jazz saxophone man in *The Miles Davis Sextet*.

THE POET LAUREATE SOUL OF FOLKIE ROCK & ROLL

Up to that point, my knowledge of jazz was only from one album by *The Dukes of Dixieland* —at that time an incredibly homogenized (and apparently all-white) family band of a father and his two sons along with four friends. The album had come free with the purchase of our first stereo record player, in about 1963 or '64. Released on *Audio Fidelity Records*, it was the first mass-produced American stereophonic long-playing record; and was ideal for demonstrating the sound difference between stereo and regular Hi-Fi. So, Sears-Roebuck and Company included it with the sale of every new stereo console. (What a magnificent time in music history to be a child!)

For a long time, that album, as well as a *Mario Lanza* album, a *HiFi Music To Dine By* album, a Perry Como record, and a *Christmas On The Ponderosa* album (featuring the cast of the TV series Bonanza) made up our entire record collection (other than a handful of Eddie Skelton 45's, one by Marty Robbins (a cover of a *No Signs of Loneliness Here* from New Zealand based *The Keil Isles*), and Bob Montgomery's *Back In Baby's Arms* by Patsy Cline). I listened to the Dukes of Dixieland over and over and over and over; admittedly fascinated with how they seemingly added extra notes at the end of or in the middle of each melody line of their songs.

I had no idea what *that* was all about, but I definitely thought it was cool. The only thing that I had heard using anything like that technique was the Appalachian front-porch Bluegrass music, which by now my mother forbade me to listen to (because of her cultural bias against her own hillbilly roots) and, of course, Jerry Lee Lewis' improvisation-sounding riffs between his melody lines. The Dukes, however, were controlled and tightly rehearsed with their improvisation clearly prearranged. It was... just weird.

Then I heard the Cannonball Adderley record of his *Mercy, Mercy, Mercy!* It was as if someone was playing one my mother's classic piano pieces and just when the piece should come to the coda ... the saxophone would take over and answer the piece, forcing it to start all over again against its will. Each time it would try to swell into a big-band-style ending fanfare, that damned sax would respond and send it back to the beginning.

Rather than the grinding honky-tonk Boots Randolph style saxophone, Cannonball Adderly's sax was more of a not-so-subtle "fuck you" to the band's trying to end the song. It had the elements of the classics, the controlled-improved playing of The Dukes, the rebellious passion of Jerry Lee, and the unexpected changes of those mountain hillbillies. It was as if he had taken the coolest parts of all my favorites and replaced the seemingly rehearsed mechanical-like performances with pure extemporaneous energy.

THE LEGEND DIES ON — GARY GREEN

I could physically *feel* the saxophone-response pounding against my chest; I decided immediately that I needed to learn to play the sax.

𝄞𝄢𝄞𝄢:

Two Rivers High School, a public school in the Nashville suburb of Donelson, was an abomination to progressive educational practices, even in the mid-1960's. Grades 7 through 12 were all lumped together in one school of about 300 students with shared teachers and even some shared classes. That meant ages 11 or 12 through ages 18 or 19 were all lumped together. *What could possibly go wrong in that environment?*

The statistically disproportionate number of pregnant 14-and-15-year-olds (and the associated forced dropouts) was merely a symptom of the unspeakable complexities buried out there on McGavock Pike. Young teens dating high school seniors was neither unusual nor particularly discouraged; it was explained away as "girls mature faster than boys".

The school had one (and only one) Black student. In classes, if he was spoken to at all, almost all of the teachers called him *"Watermelon"*. Another testament to the Tennessee educational system of the era. *No, seriously!* I never heard any teacher (or other student) address him in any other way; and in my twelve-year-old dumbass hillbilly oblivion, it never occurred to me that was not his name but a racial slur. I only "got it" after my father explained it to me. (And, of course, on the day that high school yearbook pictures were shot, he wasn't available to be photographed and be added to the all-white student hardback book. I don't know if he showed up later or what.)

The U.S. Supreme Court *Brown vs. Board of Education* desegregation order was absurdly slow to be implemented across the South. In parts of Tennessee, for example, schools were integrated one year at a time, beginning with the first grade. Stalling the start of the process until 1961, some schools were not fully desegregated until the 1972-1973 school year: twelve years to comply and 19 years after the court ruling!

Remember the *"Scopes Monkey Trial"*? Get this: that 1922 law was not repealed by the Tennessee legislature until the summer that I was between the 7th and 8th grades at Two Rivers. Up until then *(45 years after it was passed)* it was illegal to teach evolution in Tennessee[29]! *Un-fucking-believable!*

---

[29] Tennessee Code Annotated Title 49, Section 1922, signed into law by Tennessee governor Austin Peay, provided for "An act prohibiting the teaching of the Evolution Theory in all the Universities, and all other public schools of Tennessee, which are supported in whole or in part by the public-school funds of the State, and to provide penalties for the violations thereof". It wasn't repealed until May 18, 1967.

THE POET LAUREATE SOUL OF FOLKIE ROCK & ROLL

So, as a middle-class white kid, I was comfortably accustomed to the hidden structures of tyranny. Nonetheless, the "Watermelon" aberration was not so hidden and was a real wakeup call to me that something might be amiss in the simplistic idealism of my world. It certainly was part of the awakening that Two Rivers High School would provide for me; and something that would seriously impact my musical lyrics (as incongruous as that might seem).

Discipline in this grotesque institution was enforced by an abusive wanna-be-tyrant Assistant Principal who on a daily basis, among his many atrocities, required the girls in the school to get on their knees in front of him while he measured the distance from the bottom hemline of their skirts to the floor. Girls were forbidden from wearing pants and required to wear skirts or dresses. The length of a dress was subject to his personal determination of suitability; and hence his daily requirement of having the girls on their knees while he perversely measured and admired their kneeling to his crotch level.

Boys were required to always have their shirts neatly tucked into their pants, and any violation would result in the despot cutting off the tails of the boys' shirts until they did not reach below the beltline. Additionally, boys' hair was not allowed to touch the ears or the eyebrows; any infraction would result in a summary haircut by the Assistant Principal, presumably with the same shears he used to cut the shirttails.

Talking in class when not called on to do so would result in the Assistant Principal slapping the face of the offending pupil repeatedly until he or she "learned to behave". Possession of chewing gum, cigarettes, or snack foods was forbidden, but pocketknives were acceptable; students were subjected to random searches whenever a violation was suspected.

Every-six-weeks' report cards for academic performance included grades for following the rules, willingness to participate in extracurricular activities, and a quarter-page of personality traits measured to the standards of the school's management and staff. Consequently, a student with poor academic performance in any class might improve his or her overall grade by fulfilling the acceptable social requirements of the school or by being a member of the right club or team after school. In fact, one could academically fail a subject and still be an "A" or "B" student just by *fitting in* (and, presumably, not being "Watermelon").

It was *not* my ideal learning atmosphere. In fact, it wasn't my ideal atmosphere for anything. Conversely, the administration of the school was no fan of mine; but they were at a loss for how to deal with my overly-polite passive-aggressive rebellions since I didn't violate their rules — just their propriety.

THE LEGEND DIES ON — GARY GREEN

It was into that culture I transformed from a world of academic overperformance to a new life wrought with missteps that would alienate me from academia permanently and lead me toward an "outlaw" trail into music.

Firstly, I naïvely thought that academic performance would be appreciated in Nashville, like it had been in Atlanta. When I saw a bulletin board notice in the school library calling for extracurricular science papers, I thought it would be an ideal way to use my newfound intense interest in biology to keep me engaged in formal education.

To the detriment of studies for my regular seventh-grade classes, I began spending all of my after-school hours in the Donelson Branch of the Nashville Public Library at 2315 Lebanon Pike; a 15-minute bicycle ride from home. There I focused on researching the two science subjects that cemented my attention.

First, I was fascinated with Albert Einstein's Special Relativity proposition that time and space are an interconnected illusion within a closed circle. I wanted to find a way to travel faster than the speed of light, but from a stationary position; and hence create "time travel". Remember, I was 12-years-old.

Secondly, my Georgia-found obsession with biology had made me really curious about why there was no cure for cancer; especially after I heard a news report that Jonas Salk supposedly had said that any cancer cure would be stalled or blocked by big pharma and the bureaucracy of the patent process.

For my generation, Dr. Salk was widely seen as the man who ended the polio epidemic with his vaccine. When asked who owned his vaccine, he famously had responded, "Well, the people, I would say. There is no patent. Could you patent the sun?" *Tell me THAT wasn't heroic!*

So, at 12, I was fascinated with the conflict between big business and healthcare. Specifically, I was interested in the science that could solve that conflict. It seemed a lot more interesting than music at that point, and certainly more beneficial to society... *so I thought.*

I decided to focus my afterschool research, and the paper I was writing, on the tobacco mosaic virus; a single-strand RNA virus species that in 1966 looked like it could be used to deliver a micro-cellular mutation that would thwart cancerous growth. RNA research, in the mid-1960's, was pretty heavy-duty for serious scientists; for a 12-year-old it was untouchable insanity. I wrote, typed, and then submitted my paper to the address that I had copied from the bulletin board notice; without ever sharing it with any Two Rivers teachers.

About three months later, the school was contacted by *The Ford Foundation* and *The Future Science Teachers of America*, the joint sponsors of the call for papers. I had won first place in the competition and was awarded a four-year scholarship to the university of my choice… until the school's Guidance Office reported to them that I was only (by then) 13-years-old and in the seventh grade. The scholarship was withdrawn and replaced with an "honorable mention" (the certificate for which I still have today).

To make matters worse, I was called into the Principal's office to meet with him and the bullying Assistant Principal to be disciplined for having dared compete with the "upperclassmen" in the school. Ultimately, there was no punishment; but I was warned to stick to my own grade level. (And, of course, there was no winner from Tennessee; so, it wasn't as if I deprived another Two Rivers student of a scholarship.)

Next, I entered the all-grades science fair. Using a cigar box, flashlight, index cards, and hole punch, I made a "data sorter" —a mimic of the UNIVAC 1500 machine that I had seen at my father's office. It was designed to arrange punch cards in specific order by directing them into separate stacks, based on the position of holes punched in each index card.

My 1967 foray into the computer world won first place (I still have that ribbon too); but again, I was admonished by the school administration for overstepping my place. Though, the local newspaper did take my picture along with the other levels of winners.

Still not totally discouraged by the school (yet), I turned my focus to time travel. To shut-down that inquiring-mind adventure, the Assistant Principal ordered me to meet with the physics teacher at the school and explain what I was trying to do. Rather than encourage me academically, that teacher elected to ridicule me in front of the class, comparing my "research" to reading comic books. (Though to this day I argue that there is a lot of educational value in Silver Age comic books.)

Two Rivers High School successfully destroyed my interest in academia for the rest of my life.

Awkwardly, I had already entered the *National Forensic League's* competition for extemporaneous speaking, and it was too late to walk away. With my parents, I attended that competition at a nearby college campus (I previously had won the regional and the state meets). In the national competition, I won first place and that was the last day that I ever paid attention to school.

I vowed to never take another science or math class, even if it was required; and I stuck to that vow until I needed a mathematical foundation for some advanced symbolic logic philosophy classes that I wanted to take at *Johns Hopkins University* about 15 years later. I never even took a book home for the rest of my school days or in college afterwards. Fuck 'em; the school administration completely ignored the accomplishment (and the honor to their school), so I ignored them and all "educators" forever.

THE LEGEND DIES ON — GARY GREEN

Despite being bullied by students empowered by the administration, and despite my decision to coast through school without studying, I transferred my attention to what had interested me up-on arrival in Nashville: the saxophone. Only music mattered to me.

My mother had insisted that, instead of the saxophone, I choose the clarinet, which she argued was more versatile but had the same fingering positions as a saxophone; meaning that I easily could switch between the two. Besides, she had played clarinet in the *Tri-High Marching Band* in her high school in Forest City North Carolina, so I would be carrying on a family tradition.

I wasn't particularly interested in the instrument, even after listening to Benny Goodman and Pete Fountain records. I wanted that Cannonball-Adderly-sound. Still, she pushed, and I reluctantly agreed as I discovered interchangeability of almost all woodwinds.

Daddy bought me a mail-order clarinet and I signed up for the "Junior High School Seventh Grade Band" at Two Rivers. The first few months were simple and fun[30]. Very few of the students could read music, so the classes were all about teaching them to sight-read, learning the finger-positions on the instruments, learning how to use various reed thicknesses and razorblades to trim them, and various marching formations (to be a "marching band").

Daily band practice went well until those aforementioned pesky little flags on notes (♪, ♫, etc.) became part of the rigor. Since my pre-school piano playing, I preferred to read the notes and hear the feeling rather than apply seemingly arbitrary time signatures. Then, after hearing the

---

[30] For me, the hardest part was on-the-fly transposing the B♭ "concert C" scale of most band instruments (including the clarinet and saxophone) to the tunings of a piano or other C instruments. That wasn't even a requirement, but as a piano player, it seemed necessary to me. That mumbo-jumbo meant that if I played a B♭ note on the piano, to play the same tone on the clarinet I had to play the fingering position for a C note; or conversely to play a C on the piano, on the clarinet I had to play a D note on the clarinet. So, to play a duet with my mother (or even with myself on the piano) meant that I had to go through that transposing process on-the-fly (or write out the music).

I learned that there were also other B♭ instruments (and F instruments as well). Why-the-hell they didn't just teach a universal tone for fingering on band instruments was beyond me, because there ARE universal tones available. Developing the ability to transpose on-the-fly was an exercise that would become extremely useful for me in the future, though I could not have possibly predicted so at the time. But then I was just doing it to understand the relationship between the clarinet (saxophone) and the piano.

THE POET LAUREATE SOUL OF FOLKIE ROCK & ROLL

Appalachian mountain front-porch players, I completely discarded any structured rhythm.

(Decades later legendary New York folkie Sis Cunningham politely said that I ignored downbeats and had a "sync-out-sync style"; Túpac's mom, on the other hand, simply said that I was *so white* that I "can't keep rhythm for shit".)

I suspect I frustrated the hell out of the band teacher; he could throw any note sequence at me, and I could *sight-read*-play it, but there was zero sense of rhythm attached to my playing; *none.*

Once I heard a piece, I could "fake" it; but, of course, that kind of anarchy was not acceptable to the tight structure of a band or orchestra. In further lawlessness, I added extra jazz progressions (ii-v-i) to the scores that I thought made the band arrangements sound better; à la Cannonball or The Dukes, I would throw in an extra third or fifth to add either harmony or a nice little run during a musical rest. The band music just wasn't written like that!

Equally, I just wasn't willing to apply the discipline to read time signatures or stick to musical arrangements; and the band teacher (quite justifiably) wasn't willing to put up with my nonsense. Hence, I departed the band; amicably but encouraged to never come back.

I would learn decades later that my rhythm anarchy would frustrate backup bands to no end. The only solace I took in those later years was that my good friend Bee (Dan) Spears, Willie Nelson's longtime bass player, told me that 90% of his job was adding rhythm back to Willie's "all over the place" changes. At least I was in good company with my white-boy lack of rhythm.

I continued to play clarinet for a year or so, following along with 45 rpm records or with my mother's piano playing—where that transposing on-the-fly first came in usefully. *(I had a killer clarinet arrangement of the Hank Mills & Dick Jennings standard, "Little Old Wine Drinker Me".)*

At home, the house still was always filled with music; either my ever-expanding 45-rpm record collection or the three-and-a-half hours every-afternoon sounds of Mother's students banging out their John Thompson pieces for their lessons.

Since the primary industry in Nashville at that time was the music business, many of her students were the children of music industry figures. Probably the most notable were two of the grandchildren of Ernest "Pop" Stoneman.

Apparently concerned that the third generation of the family might not be able to adequately follow in such large footsteps, the kids were enrolled in music lessons. Part of that educational process fell to my mother. My

THE LEGEND DIES ON — GARY GREEN

recollection is that there was no particular outstanding talent shown, but lots of ego and fantasizing about being teen idols.[31]

There was, as I remember, a lot more real talent demonstrated by several children of behind-the-scenes music professionals (announcers, sound engineers, studio executives, etc.). I remember one kid in particular, whose father was an announcer for WLAC-TV and later for the *Hee-Haw* television show, did a spot-on imitation of pianist Floyd Cramer, complete with his well-known rolls between the notes. Talent or not, there was no shortage of musical activity at home.

One Saturday morning Mother and I were at a local music store where she was buying textbooks for her students, and I was buying reeds for my clarinet. At the store I spied a sale on harmonicas and decided to buy one, even though Mother told me that it was a waste of money. She said that she had bought one when she was in high school and was never able to play anything on it or do anything with it other than make harmonic sounds.

Nonetheless, I bought it and, on the way home I began exploring it. It took me about two minutes to realize that the first eight holes on a harmonica when blown represented 1-2-3-5-5-7-2-1 on a scale (for a "C" scale harmonica that would be C, D, E, G, G, B, D, C); and when sucked, it represented 2-5-7-2-4-6-7-4-6 (D, G, B, D, F, A, B, D, F, A on a "C" harp).

That meant that constructing tonic, dominant, and subdominant chords was simply a matter of blowing or sucking on the right section of the harmonica. Moreover, since every note of a major scale is contained in one of those three chords, it meant that I could play the melody along with the chord; at least for simple songs.

Before we got home, I was recognizably playing *Oh Susanna* and two or three other three-chord songs. That, of course, frustrated my mother; but proudly so.

The next weekend, I bought more harmonicas; in the keys of D, E, F, G, B♭, and A along with a metal harmonica holder so that I could play handsfree while I accompanied myself on the piano.

---

[31] Pop, who by then was in his mid-70's, had recorded the classic *Sinking Of The Titanic* in 1926 (which had sold more than a million copies) and had helped Ralph Peer discover Jimmie Rogers and The Carter Family. He spent the next 40 years in relative obscurity until Moe Asch and Folkways Records rediscovered him during the early 1960's folk music revival. By the time my family moved to Nashville, Pop Stoneman hosted a syndicated television show called *Those Stonemans*, featuring his whole family. The following year they were named the *Country Music Association's Vocal Group of The Year*.

THE POET LAUREATE SOUL OF FOLKIE ROCK & ROLL

Around that same time, Daddy bought us a portable "combo" organ (at least portable for *that* era —it weighed about 40 pounds and had long screw-in metal legs). A "combo" was jazz-world jargon for a small, touring jazz, pop, or dance band and these transistorized plastic keyboard units were popular with a lot of rock bands that began popping up in the mid-60's. The combo organs had a unique sound, not like an organ or anything else up to that point; and they were totally keyboard-played with six or eight "stops" to emulate other instruments.

The first time I saw one played was on TV; either Paul Revere and the Raiders on their *It's Happening* daily show (Paul Rever Dick played one) or Steppenwolf (Goldy McJohn very cooly played one that looked like ours) on The Ed Sullivan Show.

I had played goofy portable sort-of organs before; specifically, various Magnus Chord-Organ models. They were three-octave non-polyphonic (single note) devices with six chord buttons. The best I could determine, a simple electric motor forced air through plastic reeds that were exposed to the air when individual notes were played on the keyboard. The chord buttons opened multiple reeds.

The combo organ was a technological wonder compared to those melodica-sounding things. It was polyphonic and used electronic tones rather than reeds. I began hauling the heavy-ass thing around to churches, small parties, and a few events where they wanted free background live music. I dealt with my rhythm challenge by using my left hand to play chords, sometimes inverted, and my right hand to play the melody. It wasn't good; but it wasn't atrocious either.

When I was 14-years-old, I began fanatically absorbing every new 45-rpm top-40 release. I didn't just know *Harper Valley PTA* (Jeannie C. Riley), *Hello I Love You* (The Doors), *Hey Jude* (The Beatles), *Sittin' On The Dock Of The Bay* (Otis Redding) and 95 others; but I knew who wrote them, who published them, the label, the run time, and what key they were in so I could play along either on piano, clarinet, or harmonica.

That obsession landed me a very cool summer job in Corinth Mississippi at the largest record store in the state. Daddy was traveling to Mississippi for his job regularly and I would go with him and work at the record store.

If a customer came into the store and asked, for example, "what's that record that says *We turned cartwheels across the floor?*," I could direct them to Procol Harum's *Whiter Shade of Pale* on Deram Records. If they asked for *that record that says Ride a painted pony*, I could send them to *Spinning Wheel* by Blood, Sweat, & Tears on Columbia Records. I could

THE LEGEND DIES ON — GARY GREEN

tell them all about In the *Year 2525* by Zager and Evans[32], or Desmond Dekker & The Aces doing *Israelites*, or dozens of other 1967-1968 hits. I religiously memorized the Billboard charts every week and I was a walking compendium of pop music trivia. It was a cool summer gig, working two days a week.

Sometime around 1967 or early 1968 I, as a combo organist, was asked to join a *Steppenwolf* cover band with the very-era-sounding name, *Lemon Fuzz*. Compliant with the expectations of the times, I used bottle-after-bottle of hydrogen peroxide on my hair to bleach it snow-white; the idea being that under a blacklight (UVA light) it would give an eerie glow from stage.

Unfortunately, my tenure with the band was absurdly short lived; we did one local Nashville television appearance and then I was out. As the founder of the band later told people, *"Gary was a phenomenal player; he could play anything, no matter how complicated. Better than any of us. But he couldn't keep the rhythm. He couldn't even find the rhythm. If he knew the song, we were fine; but if it was a new song that he didn't know, then he had no idea of how the rhythm worked".* He was 100% right, of course; and I couldn't even follow the band or the drummer.

Not at all discouraged (actually relieved), my musical attentions turned to the all-day Saturdays' television broadcasts of half-hour local country music television shows, some syndicated to stations around the country; *The Ralph Emery Show, The Porter Wagoner Show, The Wilburn Brothers, The Bobby Lord Show, The Bill Anderson Show, Billy Walker's Country Carnival, The Flatt and Scruggs Show, Marty Robbins Spotlight,* and probably a half dozen others that I can't recall.

Before *Hee-Haw*, before *The Johnny Cash Show* on ABC, even before Glen Campbell replaced the Smothers Brothers, those shows exposed me to a who's-who of Nashville country music. That inspired me to visit the *Country Music Hall of Fame* on Music Row and to learn about the *Country Music Association* (I didn't even dream that one day I would be a voting member of that organization).

After learning, at the Hall of Fame museum, about the process of record-making and a little history of Nashville's country music industry, I turned my attention to *The Grand Ole Opry*. I convinced my parents to drop me off at the Ryman Auditorium on Fifth Avenue just off lower Broadway in downtown Nashville every Friday and Saturday evening for a few weeks.

---

[32] Way into the third decade of the 21st century, I bought two of Denny Zager's guitars; after their one-hit, he moved back to the Midwest and became a luthier —and a quite good one at that.

THE POET LAUREATE SOUL OF FOLKIE ROCK & ROLL

I didn't have the money to afford a ticket to the show; but the old church building wasn't air conditioned back then so in the summer months, the windows were raised, and I could lean on the window sill and watch the shows for free.

After a few weeks of being a regular window-peeper, I discovered that the performers took their smoking (and drinking) breaks out the side door in the back alley behind the building. The area was fenced off and there was a security guard to keep pain-in-the-ass fans away; but who-the-hell was going to pay attention to four-foot-nothing 14-year-old dorky kid? Certainly not security.

Who *did* pay attention were some of the performers, who eventually would enlist me to run across the alley, clandestinely (and illegally) for prearranged beer and liquor pickups for them at the back door of a bar on Broadway and bring it back to them in a brown paper bag. Those errands endeared me to some of the performers to a degree that I was considered a (very) young "member of the family" of the Grand Ole Opry.

Additionally, there was a genuine friendly affection demonstrated toward me by *Stoney and Wilma Lee Cooper, Jumping Bill Carlisle, Ernest Tubb, Ernie Ashworth, Charlie Louvin, Tex Ritter* (whose son John from California (later a big TV star) though about 6 years older than me, I had met a couple of times through the National Forensic League where he competed in Drama while I was in Extemporaneous Speaking), *Jimmy Snow* (Hank's son), *Pete Kirby* ("Bashful Brother Oswald from Roy Acuff's Smoky Mountain Boys), guitarist *Joey Edwards, Jack Greene, Dave Akeman* (String Bean), *Jimmy Wakely,* Fiddlers *Mack Magaha* and *Rufus J. Thibodeaux, Little Jimmy Dickens, Ben Smathers, Mrs. Henry Cannon* (professionally known as *Minnie Pearl* and who I would occasionally see as a member of the same Brentwood Country Club as my parents), and especially Opry Announcer/MC *Grant Turner*, as well as probably a dozen others.

As "the kid", an errand runner, at 14-years-old I was "family" enough that usually they would bring me up the stairs and inside the cramped "backstage" of the Opry House. (Though, honestly, it was so hot, smelly, and cramped in there, that I preferred the out-doors.)

Eventually the security guards just waved me in, even if I wasn't accompanied by a member, and I would wander in and out impudently. None of them had any idea that I was a musician of sorts; I was just the kid that hung out and knew all their songs.

On Saturday nights, after the Opry, I would run across Broadway to *The Ernest Tubb Record Shop*, where WSM Radio (which broadcasted the Opry) would broadcast a live show. There, I became friendly with Ernest Tubb's son, Justin, who would occasionally host the show for his Dad; he also had a couple of charting country hits of his own.

THE LEGEND DIES ON — GARY GREEN

One night after The Opry, Justin asked me if I was going to be at the DJ Convention to hear him sing in the RCA Victor hospitality suite. The annual Nashville DJ Convention was held at the storied old Andrew Jackson Hotel on Capitol Hill, downtown. It was a property that I knew well because when we first moved to Nashville, we had lived in that hotel for two months before Mother and Daddy found the house in Donelson.

I had never heard of the Convention and didn't realize what a big deal it was for the industry; but I definitely wanted to come hear my much-older friend play. It turned out to be an industry conference for country disk jockeys from across America; not a fan event at all[33], but a record-pitching event. I, of course, was not registered, but again, who's going to question a kid like me being there? Visting the very intimate performances (15-50 viewers) in the various labels' hospitality suites and attending multiple promotional workshops, I developed an intense interest in songwriting and pitching songs[34].

Besides my Friday and Saturday nights downtown and the Saturday daytime television shows, I was absorbing a lot of music from The *Smothers Brothers Television Show* on CBS. (Though, despite what some have

---

[33] The later-created "Fan Fair" (and even later CMA Week) was put together as a fan alternative to the DJ Convention because fans would show up uninvited and hog celebrities' times that had been set aside to promote records to DJ's.

[34] Meanwhile, on occasional after-hours visits to Daddy's office, I discovered the dictating equipment that he and other executives used day-to-day. He would dictate letters or memos into a hand-held microphone and his voice would be recorded on to a paper-thin seven-inch plastic disk. He would then take the disk and place it in the "in box" on his secretary's desk. The next day, the secretary would slide the disk into her player, listening to it through a head-set, and transcribe what he had spoken.

The disks were not tape-recorded, but instead were lathe-cut into a continuous groove using a sharp needle; the same process that was used to make a vinyl record. Even more interestingly, the little disks were recorded and played back spinning at 33⅓ revolutions per minute: the same speed as a long play vinyl record album. That meant that the little dictation disks could be played on any standard record player; the office playback unit was not necessary to hear the dictation.

When Daddy started bringing home his dictating machine, to work on weekends, he essentially brought home a record-making machine. I of course took full advantage of that and made dozens of records of myself playing organ, piano, clarinet, harmonica, and singing. I became so interested in recording any-and-everything that for Christmas that year my father bought me a reel-to-reel stereo tape recorder.

With that, he created a little monster. I was writing country songs every week. I could record them in stereo on my reel-to-reel. I could dub those tapes into a 33⅓ "demo" record. I was known in country music circles from my Opry visits. So, I was ready to pitch songs on Music Row!

And my interest in pitching songs on Music Row intensified daily. Back then, Music Row was a few square blocks around 16th and 17th Avenues South where many record companies, publishing companies, promoters, and songwriters all kept offices.

speculated, that is not where I first heard Pete Seeger; I first saw him playing along with *Mister Geen Jeans* (Hugh Brannum) on the *Captain Kangaroo* kid's TV show.)

When the network fired the Smothers Brothers and replaced them with Glen Campbell, I became a Glen Campbell and Johnny Hartford fan. In fact, the first paid concert I ever attended was Glen Campbell playing at an auditorium in Nashville.

The following year network television re-"discovered" country music. True, in years gone by, they had flirted with the genre airing the *Jimmy Dean Show, The Tennessee Ernie Ford Hour,* and a few others. But by the end of the 1960's, *The Glen Campbell Goodtime Hour* was just the first of the wave that included *The Johnny Cash Show, Hee-Haw,* and others.

Then in June of 1969 ABC began broadcasting *The Johnny Cash Show* every Saturday night as a replacement for their *Hollywood Palace* show; and everything changed for me. Of course, I used my reel-to-reel to record every minute of every new episode (tapes that I still have —if they have not decayed over the many decades). The show, for me, introduced performers that the rest of the world (and most of my peers) already knew but I had never heard: *Bob Dylan, Linda Ronstadt, Arlo Guthrie, Joni Mitchell, Neil Young, Louis Armstrong, Ray Charles, Stevie Wonder, Carl Perkins, Eric Clapton, Kris Kristofferson, Buffy Sainte-Marie, The Statler Brothers, Kenny Rogers & The First Edition, Ian & Sylvia, Creedence Clearwater Revival, Tony Joe White, The Carpenters,* and dozens that I HAD heard of or seen.

Cash, himself, was amazing to me. He wasn't pretty. He didn't really have much of a singing range (though a really low baritone/bass range). His guitar playing pretty much sucked. The songs he wrote were sort of knock-offs of other songs (and this was before I knew that *Folsom Prison Blues* was totally lifted from *Crescent City Blues*). But his delivery, phrasing, sincerity… was all… just… Johnny Cash!

Besides the TV show, I bought every available 45-rpm record and every available long-play album of Cash. His 1964 *Bitter Tears: Ballads of the American Indian* album, though mainly near-chanted poetry rather than music as I knew it, was the most intensely eye-opening recording I had ever heard. That album, alone, would shape my life, my music, and my work in Indian Country for the next 50+ years.[35]

---

[35] More than a half century later, when my friend and fellow musician (and awesome studio cat) Victor Roche, an enrolled member of the Pechanga Band of Luiseño Indians, named his son CASH… I felt vindicated in my idealization of Johnny Cash's Bitter Tears album.

THE LEGEND DIES ON — GARY GREEN

More than just the *Peter La Farge*[36] songs themselves was Cash's delivery and the passion in his voice. He opened my eyes as well as those of millions of others to the reality of Native America beyond what the television western passion-plays had depicted to my generation. Those La Farge recordings would resurface in my life, time and again.

I was 15 when I bought the *At San Quinton* album, which was released in conjunction with the debut of the TV show. I couldn't stop playing it. One throw-away song on the record, *Starkville City Jail*, particularly intrigued me. The song wasn't really melodic; it was more of a recitation to a sort-of tune. I really liked it because it poetically told a ballad-style story without a sing-songy refrain or moralistic lecture.

But despite my acute ear and uncanny ability to transcribe almost any song, something just wasn't adding up when I tried to follow that recording... on the piano, organ, harmonic, clarinet, or Baroque recorder duct flute (which I had now added to my instruments after Ronny's class at McGavock Pike Elementary School issued them to all 3rd graders). There just seemed to be something impossible to transcribe about that song, despite it being quite easy to emulate the melody in other keys.

Frustrated at my inability to play along I took the problem to my mother, who always had a better ear for these problems than I did. She listened a couple of times and concluded that there was no melody and so there was nothing to transcribe; that I was trying to find musical notation for spoken words that had no pitch other than normal voicing.

I wasn't buying that, though. I heard a tune in there somewhere. Rather than give up on it, I scoured the music stores for sheet music for the *At San Quinton* album. Though I found several books and sheets, none contained that song; it was just invisible. That, of course, only added to my irritation.

I decided to write to the publisher of most Johnny-Cash-written songs, *House of Cash Music* in nearby Hendersonville Tennessee. I didn't identify myself as a 15-year-old, but rather as a pianist who was looking for sheet music for the entire album but had been unable to find that one song. There was no response from them.

After I few weeks, I decided to telephone them and again request it. My voice had not changed yet, so my soprano-sounding self was clearly very young. I talked to a very nice lady on the phone, who obviously concluded that I was a kid. She told me that she would send me a lead sheet for the

---

[36]Peter was another Folkways Records recording artist and for a while deliberately gave the impression that he was Native. He wrote some powerful songs, but he was not Native and apparently was a very troubled individual, dying at 34 years old from either a stroke or an overdose (depending on which source you choose to believe).

THE POET LAUREATE SOUL OF FOLKIE ROCK & ROLL

song. (A lead-sheet was a staff with single-note melody line, lyrics, and associated chords.)

It arrived about a week later. A handwritten one-pager obviously not commercially produced, it even included notations for the *Nashville Charts* numbering system[37]. Nonetheless. following the sheet music, the Nashville Chart, and even the chord symbols above some of the measures, I *still* could not exactly duplicate the sound that Cash and his band produced on that album. My frustration just increased.

After a week or two of messing with it, I decided to call back the nice lady at House of Cash Music. She remembered my name, or perhaps my voice. I explained my problem and I heard her chuckle as I talked.

Before answering me, she asked how old I was. It wasn't the denigrating or patronizing way some adults would ask that after I posed an uncomfortable question. Her asking seemed genuinely curious; and I contentedly told her the truth.

She told me that her name was *Reba Hancock* and that she was Johnny Cash's sister, and in charge of his publishing. She said that I was the first person who had noticed what they all knew to be the issue.

She explained that during the recording of the album, the tape had run out and the engineers had switched to a backup tape recorder while they changed tapes in the first machine. She told me that the motor of the second machine lagged and therefore was out-of-sync with the primary recorder. Nonetheless, she said, Bob (Columbia Records producer Bob Johnston) had decided that the sound was close enough that there would be no problem including the cut on the album. She thought it was hilarious that a 15-year-old was the only person that picked up on it. She assured me that J.R. would be amused too. (At that time, I did not know that "J.R.", was what she called her brother.)

---

[37] I had first seen that system at The Opry where the stage band had to quickly back up songs they may have never heard. Throughout this book, as I have talked about chord progressions, I have used the Nashville Charts system for the non-music reader to understand my meaning. I am guessing the system was designed for musicians that could not read music. It assigns a number (from 1 to 8) to every note of a major scale of the key in which the song is performed. So, if a song is in the key of C and the Nashville Chart indicates the chord progression is 1-4-5-1, then the actual chords are C-F-G-C. Likewise, if the vocal range of the singer requires that the same song be in the key of G rather than the key in which it was written, that exact same Chart applies, but the actual chords played are G-C-D-G. A Nashville sessions player only needs to know the key of the song and the Chart (and presumably the rhythm). This system is the entire music-reading foundation of some of the greatest studio musicians in the world.

THE LEGEND DIES ON — GARY GREEN

We talked for a few more minutes and she ended the call inviting me to call her anytime and that since I was local maybe we will meet someday. She had no idea how wrong it was to offer me that encouragement!

Back at my combo organ, I followed her explanation and realized that the pitch of Cash's voice in that song had started out in one key, was subtly lowered by a half-step musical note, then raised about a quarter-step. Trying to play along note-by-note, I concluded that without a stringed instrument or some very complex electronics for the organ (digital manipulation which at that time had not been invented), it was virtually impossible to *exactly* imitate the song. And, at that point in my life, I had no interest in any stringed instruments.

𝄞𝄢𝄞𝄢𝄞𝄢

I had become completely alienated from the educationally repressive and physically bullying atmosphere of Two Rivers High School. With the benefit of a half to three-quarters of a century of hindsight, I can say that at least part of my inability to adapt to that world was my own failed understanding of where I "fit in" with other students. That is not to say that I should have adopted their racist, sexist, xenophobic, cruelty. Rather, it is looking at the context of everything I experienced and realizing that I was a very troubled boy.

I had come from environments where, since birth, the spotlight was all on *me*... whether from my parents' coddling focus on teaching me to read early to my piano playing to having near-perfect grades in school, to that idiotic IQ test to taking the lead role in school plays, on television, and at any public function. The more I performed and excelled at any of these things, the more I was praised and therefore reinforced to continue and to expand those behaviors. Yes, in my mind it was all about ME; and yes, it is a character flaw.

At Two Rivers High School, not only was the spotlight not on *me* but I was punished for grabbing the spotlight. I was ostracized, harassed, tormented, and belittled by the administration of the school, which in turn filtered to the school tacitly allowing other students to join the bullying.

In the school's defense, there were some genuine *educators* there who grasped the issue and tried to address it. The Public Speaking teacher encouraged me to join the debate team and was the person who sent me to the National Forensic League competitions. She also was the person who made the connection between me and the Steppenwolf cover band. A Social Studies teacher decided to introduce me to her husband who was a political sciences graduate student at Vanderbilt University; she thought that he might be more of an academically intellectual peer for me than the Two Rivers students were. The Chorale Director music teacher at the school tried desperately to integrate my musical interests into his own

THE POET LAUREATE SOUL OF FOLKIE ROCK & ROLL

songwriting and choral productions for the school. None of those noble attempts worked.

Meanwhile, inspired by my Opry visits, the DJ convention, and even my conversation with Reba Hancock, my interest in songwriting intensified and focused almost exclusively on country music.

That same year, America's interest in country music also intensified as Hee-Haw became one of the top 20 Neilson-rated television shows, tying at number 16 with The Glen Campbell Goodtime Hour in 1969. Many of the parents of my classmates at Two Rivers worked behind the scenes on Hee-Haw, though (according to the kids) the entire season was filmed in a week-and-a-half. One of stars, who was also a writer for the show, Archie Campbell, had attended Mars Hill College when my mother was there, though he was a few years older than her.

Despite the show seeming to me like a campy knock-off of *Rowan and Martin's Laugh-In*, it did give exposure to a lot of country music stars which in turn fired up my interest in song writing.[38] I began to think of my songwriting in a much more structured way. I could use complex classical patterns to cover different movements of a melody, and I could identify patterns or templates into which various songs would fit based strictly on their structure.

That latter process included lyrics as well as the music. In 21st century terms, think of it as AI (artificial intelligence) written songs based on past data rather than the gut-feelings of an actual artist. Or, to add a more human touch, think of it as formula writing like those songwriting factories that turn out "beats" and hit-after-hit based on the templates from other

---

[38] It also served to reintroduce me to the work of Buck Owens. I, of course, knew of Owens from his hit *I've Got A Tiger By The Tail*—which he claimed was inspired by Esso (Standard Oil of New Jersey) ads to "put a tiger in your tank" with their gasoline. True to my obsessive behavior of bingeing on musicians, I began to collect not just Buck Owens records but anything country with the Bakersfield Sound, including Merle Haggard.

When that same year Owens released his version of *Johnny B. Goode*, recorded live at the London Palladium, I was completely blown away. Firstly, in my somewhat sterile hillbilly world, I had never heard either Chuck Berry or Elvis do the song; so, it was brand new to me. Secondly, Don Rich's twangy Fender Telecaster guitar was like nothing I'd ever heard, but the reaction of the live London crowd was verification of my excitement as well. Finally, the pedal steel guitar on the recording made an intense sound like some kind of entirely new instrument.

A friend told me that it was a *Cry Baby Wah-Wah Pedal* attached to the pedal steel guitar; but whatever it was, it served to open my ears to expanded genres of music beyond the three-chord triads of Opry bands. If I had been paying attention to the changing landscape of pop and "hard rock" music, I would not have been so ignorant of these sounds. That didn't matter though; I finally heard them!

THE LEGEND DIES ON — GARY GREEN

hits. The only difference was that it was all in the mind of a 15-year-old dysfunctional hillbilly living in the Nashville suburbs.

To test my developing technique, I decided to write a song for Johnny Cash. What I *actually* did was study the music and the lyrics that had worked for him over the years and apply those templates to a sort of a simile with like words and like music.

The resulting "composition" (and I use that word very loosely) was a sophomoric little three-chord song that I called *Jailbird*. It combined Cash-esque themes of prison, railroads, rehabilitation, religion, and hypocrisy into a tight little three-chord song with a melody that was half recitation and half singing but only in the lower register of an A scale. In short, it was a computer-like generation of a song for Johnny Cash.

Having no shame nor, apparently, humility, I decided to submit the song to Reba Hancock. I sat down at my combo organ, recorded a tape of me performing this song, and dropped it into the mail along with a cover letter. When I didn't hear anything from her in a week, I decided to telephone her.

On that call, she clearly remembered me and asked how I had been. She acknowledged receiving the tape, thanked me for sending it, and asked for another couple of weeks to review it. She said that her brother was "on the road" and she would make sure that he heard it as well.

Two weeks to the day, I called her back. Even now I am stunned that she didn't tell this kid to fuck off and never call back. On the contrary, she encouraged me. She told me that she had played the tape for Johnny Cash, and he liked it.

She went on to say that they both felt that there was a lot of potential in my writing but that I needed a little maturity and development to produce some really great songs. Again, she could have / should have blown me off at that point; and they definitely didn't use the song.

Hell, maybe they were that nice to everyone, BUT... instead of just letting me fade away, she asked me if I would like to meet Johnny Cash and sing some songs with him. *Are you kidding me?* This was a dream come true! She invited me to come to something called a "guitar pull" at Johnny Cash and June Carter's home the next weekend. She told me that I would get to hear a lot of songwriters and could learn some techniques.

I didn't have a driver's license yet, so my Mother drove me to Hendersonville and dropped me off with a set pickup time. We rode past the House of Cash publishing company on the left, and less than a half-mile later, turned right into a neighborhood with a tree-lined median strip between the two lanes. We followed that little street down a hill, then to the left up another hill. On the right was the address I had been given, with a little wooden guardhouse in front of the driveway. Mother stopped at the

THE POET LAUREATE SOUL OF FOLKIE ROCK & ROLL

guardhouse long enough to confirm I was "on the list", then she dropped me off. (I don't recall there actually being a guard in the little house.)

To my amazement, I wasn't the only young kid there. Though I didn't know who the others were and still don't, I suspect from the timeframe it might have been Marty Stuart (who is four years my junior and the same age as my brother Ronny) or perhaps one or more of J.R. or June's daughters and their at-the-time boyfriends. The truth is I just don't remember the names or faces of the other kids my age; I was too focused on Cash and a handful of other well-knowns that were all sitting around the room.

What I DO recall is that I was the only person in attendance who could not play guitar. That sort of defeated my purpose for being there, since (as I learned) a "guitar pull" was a sort of roundtable session where people passed guitars around the room and played their latest compositions.

I was intimidated by who the people in the room were. I was intimidated by the fact that I didn't know anything about playing guitar. I was intimidated by being only 15 years old in this group. I was intimidated by the conversations which were way over my head and beyond my understanding. I was intimidated by not knowing anyone in the room. I was intimidated by having a "turn-into-a-pumpkin" departure time.

I was welcomed, more than cordially. People tried to make me feel comfortable; but I was clearly outside of my realm. It was awkward and I retreated to shyness, hardly ever talking.

I sat on the floor beside a huge purple couch kind of unit that took up most of the downstairs room. June Carter Cash was extremely kind to me and encouraged me like Reba Hancock had done; even when I told her that I couldn't play guitar, she told me to listen and learn and grow.

Cash himself seemed uncomfortable in the group too, but clearly everyone's focus, nonetheless. When his sister whispered to him about me, he introduced me to the group and told them that I was a *"fine up and coming songwriter that is going to do great things"*. He also called me his friend (though we'd never met or spoken).

In years since, I have told people that I was invited to a guitar pull at Johnny Cash's house; and that is true. But more specifically, I rarely mention that I was way-too shy and withdrawn to actually participate and I ended up sitting on the floor in a corner beside one of the large sofa units. I never asked to attend again, and I was never invited back. (Though oddly, my friendship with Cash's sister grew and arguably she spurred my recording career.)

In the days afterwards, I was soaring from being there in the first place; but I was genuinely troubled by not being comfortable enough to participate. I decided that if I was going to be "successful", I needed a songwriting partner; preferably one who played guitar.

THE LEGEND DIES ON — GARY GREEN

In my troubled relationship with the school and classmates, I had no actual friends. There were some students who were not mean to me and did not make fun of me, like most did; but there were none that I could actually say was a friend. I needed to correct that.

At first, I over-reached to try to share common interests with the children of some of the people in the music business. My ridiculously encyclopedic knowledge of dozens of subjects made it easy for me to have in-depth discussions about whatever hobby or special interest a targeted student might have. I tried that with a student who wanted to be a radio announcer, another who wanted to be a professional baseball player, another who was a photographer, another who was a huge country music fan, and still another who wanted to travel a lot.

It didn't work, so I modified my technique to not be a "know-it-all" but rather a person interested in their "expertise" in the field. I did this especially humbly with a student who worked on cars. I asked him to explain to me how carbureted internal combustion engines generated mechanical energy vs kinetic energy; okay, probably NOT a typical way of trying to relate to a fellow 15-year-old. Not surprisingly, that too failed.

In biology class students were segmented into teams of two who were assigned as lab partners. Of course, there was no line waiting to be *my* partner, so as the teams were assembled, I was one of a handful of leftovers. Consequently, I was randomly assigned to a shy but intelligent student who also had no friends in the room.

During our time in that class, we begin to talk; mostly making fun of the teacher and the other students. Eventually our conversation turned to music; after all, we were in Music City USA.

His family, like mine, was not in the music business; but he was a guitar player who had written a few songs (and played a way-cool Glen Campbell model Ovation 12-string guitar). Not by planning but by circumstances we became friends and eventually began visiting at each other's homes after school; usually at my house since my "portable" combo organ wasn't really so portable.

It turned out that he was a damned good guitar picker; way too good not to be recognized for his talent. However, he was as shy and wilting as I was over-the-top and spotlight grabbing. (I eventually lost track of him, but I think a couple of decades later he recorded a vanity album or two; but I really still believe that his considerable talent should not have been overlooked. He was a good writer and an excellent picker. Much more technically proficient than me.)

Most of his songs were about the teen angst of unrequited love and had a Beatles-esque flavor to them. He *did* write a pretty decent tongue-in-cheek country song that was along the lines of the George Jones *White Lightening*[39] hit.

We decided to start writing together and our first effort was a very *Peter, Paul, & Mary* like four-chord harmony piece that we called *It's A Hard Road I'm Traveling On*. It wasn't awful and I had abandoned the formulaic template method that had got me in front of Johnny Cash. Content with that composition, we wrote four or five others together: with me at the keyboard and him on the guitar. We also decided to go to the next *DJ Convention* downtown and pitch several of our songs there rather than aimless wander up and down Music Row.

In mid-November, just a couple of weeks before Thanksgiving, Daddy's company notified him that he was going to be transferred to a new regional headquarters they were building in some place called Gastonia North Carolina.

Despite visiting my grandparents several times a year and having spent several full summers in the Tar Hill State, I'd never heard of Gastonia. Mother told me that the town was known as "the meanest place in the state" and was known for having a dangerously high murder rate.

It didn't sound like either a pleasant place to live or a place that I wanted to be. Moreover, I wasn't excited about leaving my "budding career" in country music. In fact, I was near despondent. My friend and I began making fun of the small town, though neither of us had ever been there or heard of it. We facetiously posited that the biggest local music activity probably was listening to frogs croaking at the city fountain.

Clearly, I was not looking forward to the move. Further troubling, it dawned on me that I was about to move out of Music City USA without even knowing how to play guitar. THAT simply was unacceptable. Something had to be done about it; and fast. I asked my friend to teach me to play guitar… quickly.

He was reluctant to do so, but we worked out an arrangement in which I would pay him with a 45-rpm of The Youngbloods' *Get Together* and a *Saturday Evening Post* (Daddy had a subscription) that featured photos and an article about *Blind Faith* (Eric Clapton's newly-formed supergroup replacement of *Cream*).

In exchange for that pay, he would rent to me for one month the guitar that he had learned on: a parlor-size *Harmony* brand *Stella* model six string.

---

[39] *White Lightening*, by the way, while known as a George Jones song, was actually written by J.P. Richardson —professionally known as "The Big Bopper" of *Chantelle Lace* fame and remembered for dying in the plane crash that also killed Ritchie Valens and Buddy Holly.

THE LEGEND DIES ON — GARY GREEN

Additionally, he agreed to teach me three chords: A, D, and E; enough for me to play Cash's hit *Boy Named Sue* (Shel Silverstein song). He also taught me to relative-tune the damned thing, and how to read simple guitar chord charts.

Finally, he taught me a "hammer on" and "lift off" technique, and how to alternate bass strings for those three chords so that I could mimic Johnny Cash's sound (not the chicka-boom, but at least the bass). I was happy; I could now perform *A Boy Name Sue* —a song that didn't require singing; I could recite it.

Our agreement provided that the day before my family moved, I would return the Stella to him, and we would stay in touch by mail, sending reel-to-reel tapes. I was happy with that arrangement, and he seemed to be at least content with it. So, on the day after Halloween in 1969, I became a guitar player... sort of.[40]

In later years I often said that the strings on that guitar were so high above the neck that *"I could pitch a tent underneath them and move in"*. Realistically, that old guitar had horrible action and having never had a callus, my fingers bled daily from struggling to form those simple chords.

Once I discovered that each fret represented a half-step in musical pitch, it became a lot more interesting for me to pick out melodies rather than merely play accompanying chords. Besides not hurting my fingers as badly, that "playing lead guitar" also moved me out of the realm of playing a rhythm instrument (since I was rhythmically challenged).

The week before Christmas I returned the Stella to my friend and prepared to move to North Carolina. My parents decided that we should open Christmas presents before the move and to my surprise they had bought me a "jumbo country-western guitar" manufactured by the storied *Kay Musical Instrument Company* and bearing the store-brand *Truetone*.

The transformation was complete. I was now officially a Nashville guitar picker who was a friend of Johnny Cash; even if I was only 15-years-old and "friend" was a real stretch. Nonetheless, my path seemed clear.

---

[40] My songwriting partner and I had begun to drift apart in our musical taste. I was getting deeper and deeper into traditional country music, especially The Carter Family; and he was becoming a follower of Eric Clapton, Pete Townshend, and a new group called Led Zeppelin. I characterized Eric Clapton as a spoiled punky-boy who was frustrated that he wasn't born Black and from Mississippi and who settled on loud imitation to make up for it. I felt that Pete Townshend's guitar-smashing antics were purely clownish performances to get attention. And I thought Led Zeppelin's Jimmy Page was outstanding at creating psychedelic noise but not much of a musician or songwriter. Contrastingly, my friend thought the Carter Family, Roy Acuff, The Opry, and even Johnny Cash were unsophisticated and out of touch bumpkin hillbillies.

THE POET LAUREATE SOUL OF FOLKIE ROCK & ROLL

Opus Four:
It's Only Rock & Roll

Well, it's only rock & roll keep you jumping all the time
When you really ought to sit this one out
And it's only rock & roll, keep on messin' with your mind
When you don't know what they're talkin' about
All around the world everywhere you go
People got to have it, son, it's only rock and roll
  — *It's Only Rock & Roll,* by Rodney Crowell, Criterion-Lorna Music

The activities director for the *North Carolina Children's Orthopedic Hospital* came backstage to tell us that the beds had all been rolled into the auditorium and she was ready when we were. We already knew that, because even behind the heavy red curtain we could hear the kids chanting, *"Gary – Gary – Gary"*. I told her to raise the curtain just as soon as I stepped up to the microphone. *(Can you imagine what impact THAT had on a 16-year-old?)*

I turned to Stan and asked, "are you ready to rock and roll?" He nodded and said, "let's do this". I turned to Eddie and Jolly; they both nodded.

I took a deep breath, stepped up to the microphone, and a cappella belted out, *"Well it's a-one for the money..."*

As the curtains began to go up the chants from the audience turned into a sustained cheer. I answered the cheer as well as my own voice with a quick and loud "A" chord, sweeping the pick upward across the strings of my hollow-body knock-off of a Gibson ES-335; followed immediately by a sustained E chord with the pick swept downward.

"Two for the show..." I repeated the guitar moves and the rest of the band stayed silent.

"A-three to get ready..." I could see the band fidgeting, eager to play as the couple-hundred kids in their beds and wheelchairs got caught up in the frenzy that I was deliberately creating. With pauses, facial expressions, and body language, I was totally and deliberately manipulating and controlling everyone in that auditorium. And I was only 16-years-old.

"Now go cat go...", I yelled and nodded to the band to start playing.

I was setting up the classic *Carl Perkins* song in the easy guitar key of E; where the chord pattern was E-A-B^7. As I gave that last sweeping E chord, Jolly slid down the D string on his *Vox* bass guitar and began playing a standard boogie-woogie ... in the key of D; where the chord progression was D-G-A^7.

I swallowed hard and prepared to change keys to match him; but with Jolly's bass slide, Eddie took over the rhythm guitar part on his Gibson

THE LEGEND DIES ON — GARY GREEN

SG, with a one-two beat in the key of A; where the chord progression was A-D-E^7.

Hoping that the two guys would see the screw-up, I decided to stay with the original key; and to make certain, I turned toward them so they could see that I was holding an E chord. Then I slid my hands up the neck of my guitar to catch the lead in E.

As I did, Stan stepped up to the microphone to take over the vocal and back up rhythm on his acoustic Martin guitar... in the key of G, where the chord progression was G-C-D ^{7}.

In essence, we were playing four different songs at the same time. I cannot think of a way to write how bad it sounded. The strongest adjectives —hideous, repulsive, atrocious, appalling... shit— can't accurately convey the sound that come from that stage. Even the horrified look on the face of the Activities Director still didn't accurately convey the situation. And the damned band seemed to be tone-deaf oblivious to anything being wrong.

I mouthed to the Activities Director, "close the curtain"; but she didn't understand and mouthed back "what?". I repeated myself and she still didn't understand. Meanwhile the chalkboard-scraping abomination of sound continued to come from my band.

I stepped up to the microphone, as if I was going to harmonize with Stan, and loudly said, "close the damned curtain. NOW".

She did, and as it went down, I said to the band, "Okay, we have a show to do. New Plan".

I asked Jolly and Eddie to leave the stage temporarily. I turned to Stan and commanded, "Folsom". He nodded as I turned back to the Activities woman and told her to raise the curtain again. She complied, but clearly was confused. For some reason the audience thought it was part of the show and showered us with applause.

When the curtain rose again, the room went silent until I stepped forward and played the iconic introductory eight opening notes of *Folsom Prison Blues*. Stan picked up the rhythm, in the right key, and I settled into a very Cash-like boom-chicka-boom accompaniment as he sang the song.

After the first verse, I slid up the guitar's neck and caught the classic Luther Perkins one-string lead as I stepped on my reverb pedal to give the sound an echoing effect. Stan even yelled a good Johnny-Cash-sounding "sooey" as I picked the strings.

When the song finished with unrestrained applause, Stan switched to a couple of slower country standards that we had rehearsed, concluding with the Hank Williams classic, *Your Cheatin' Heart*. His guitar and mine; and it sounded fine.

THE POET LAUREATE SOUL OF FOLKIE ROCK & ROLL

Next, I brought back Eddie and Jolly, with Eddie singing the Henson Cargill song *Skip A Rope*[41], followed by two "Christian rock" songs that he and Jolly had written before I moved to Gastonia. I played a few benign little lead guitar reverse-arpeggio runs behind verses, all-the-while making exaggerated facial and hand expressions as if what I was doing was extremely complex (it was not)[42]. The audience bought into it and seemed to love it.

Having exhausted the entire rehearsed repertoire of the band and unwilling to improvise further after the Blue Suede Shoes disaster, I spent the next 40 minutes alone on stage with my Christmas-present Kay acoustic, playing and singing a mixture of Simon & Garfunkel songs, Peter, Paul & Mary tunes, and Gary Green originals.

And THAT was my debut as a big "Nashville star" who had moved to North Carolina. I had been in Gastonia for a little more than two months. I'd been playing guitar for about four months. I was 16-years-old and had only been driving for a month. But I had been on dozens of stages performing since I was about five-years-old, so this was old-hat to me.

Stan was my 35-ish-year-old neighbor who, with his wife and kids, lived in the house next door to the split level my parents had bought in a just-built neighborhood in Gastonia. He once had dreams of being a rock and roll star but had long-ago set them aside in favor of a job, a wife, and two kids. That is, until I came to town and somehow rekindled his dreams.

Jolly was the son of a prominent local preacher that had named all of his kids "cheerful" names: *Jolly, Joy, Gay, Happy*, and I can't remember the other two. He was a couple of years younger than me, so that made him about 14. He and Eddie had been writing and playing "Christian Rock" songs for a couple of years.

Eddie was the son of a mill-working family and was raised in a mill house with a debt at the company store, not unlike my mother's family. He had an angelic tenor voice and was an adequate rhythm guitar player but was restrained by lack of confidence (probably tied to his excessive

---

[41] If I had known then the history of what Cargill went through to record that song, it might have shaped the next few years of my life and saved me a lot of heartache trying to pitch songs in Nashville. Cargill's seemingly benign lyrics were deemed too-radical for Nashville establishment, and he was rejected by almost every label in town. The song "blamed" social ills and racism on par-ents, teachers, and society in general; and that was much too controversial for Music City. Even Cash, who liked the song, wouldn't record it because Columbia records feared it. Such a benign song scared the hell out of Nashville; THAT should have been a warning to me. But I didn't know.

[42] The idiotically exaggerated facial expressions and faking difficulty was an audience manipulation technique that I had observed watching Roy Clark on *Hee Haw* and earlier watching Liberace on his show.

THE LEGEND DIES ON — GARY GREEN

weight and few opportunities other than the mill). The same age as Jolly, they had met in the church choir, despite living in different parts of town and separated by socially-enforced economic barriers.

Intentionally, there was no drummer because... well, I had that damned aversion to the discipline of structured rhythm.

Together we were *The Gary Green Band*. While we *did* rehearse some of the songs that we performed that night, the *Blue Suede Shoes* debacle was totally my fault.

I had loved that song ever since I first heard Carl Perkins perform it; and I wanted to play it with a band —especially after I learned to pick the lead to it (though I'd been playing it on the piano for years, replacing that lead with a Jerry-Lee-Lewis-style set of glissandos and pounding triplets).

Shortly after moving to Gastonia, I had purchased the *John Lennon Plastic Ono Band Live Peace In Toronto 1969* album. In the first cut on that record, John announced, "you know, we have never played together before, so we are just going to do songs we all know". The band then broke into a seeming improvisation of *Blue Suede Shoes*, presumably never having played together.

In my 16-year-old mind, I thought, "yeah, that works; we don't need to rehearse, we will just do things we know", I asked the three guys if they knew the song and all three said they did. Perfect. I told them when to come in and the structure to follow.

Only what I didn't take into account was that John Lennon's improvised band was made up of Lennon, *Eric Clapton, Klaus Voormann,* and a handful of other seasoned rockers. It just never occurred to me that my guys could not follow along and look at each other's playing to see where they were and what was going on.

When our hospital gig was over, every kid in the auditorium wanted my autograph and a hug; and there were hundreds of them. We were there signing autographs and posing for pictures for almost as long as the concert itself had lasted.

There also were television cameras from nearby Charlotte and photographers from both the Gastonia and the Charlotte newspapers; and the bad start to the show was never mentioned. The hospital had done an incredible job promoting the event and, thereby, promoting me.

No one seemed to notice that we sucked. AND ... *I was hooked.*

𝄞𝄞𝄞𝄞

The dreaded move to North Carolina turned out to be not nearly as bad as I had feared, or that my mother had forecasted. It also turned out to be more of a music-world launch pad for me than Music City USA had been.

First, I was in a school that was actually *just* a high school rather than a catch-all for six grades: grades 10, 11, and 12 only. That within itself was a relief and musical opportunity.

THE POET LAUREATE SOUL OF FOLKIE ROCK & ROLL

Secondly, the system of teaching was an entirely different experience for me. Students in each grade level were required to take some core classes, English and History; but the rest of the curriculum was elective, albeit a requisite number of classes. This meant that rather than the system I knew of the school telling me what subjects, what times, and what teachers that I would have, I was free to choose whatever interested me.

There were, of course, curricula templates; but they were based on the student's plans for post high school life. There were academic and liberal arts electives for students who planned to go to college (photography, journalism, languages, music, art, drama, etc.); further there was an entire core of mathematics and science electives, including pre-nursing and pre-med courses that resulted in an EMT certification; and there were trade-school-like electives for students who planned to immediately enter the workforce (auto mechanics, wood shop, marketing, radio broadcasting (the school even had its own radio station), printing, sewing-weaving-spinning, management, and others).

I signed up for Choral Music, French, Photography, Radio Broadcasting, and driving; yes, the school taught students driving skills beyond the basics to get a license.

On my first day in Choral Music class, I presented my "transferring student" papers to the teacher and told him that I could read music and had some choir experience. He sat down at the piano, played a two-octave extended "E♭" chord and asked me to sing the notes to him as he played each one individually. I did, and he pronounced that my voice was changing so I would be an "alto turning tenor" in his group.

He handed me a six-page tenor score for Paul Simon's *Sounds of Silence* and pointed to an area where I was to sit, presumably with other students in the same vocal range. Wow. A contemporary song that I actually knew! and a far-cry from the self-serving original songs that the choir director in Nashville had forced on his classes.

As the bell rang and class began, everyone took their seats. The teacher again sat at the piano and began sight-reading a piece of music that sounded extremely complex and unrecognizable to me.

After a few bars, he abruptly stopped, shook his head, and flipped his sheet music 180-degrees. He again began playing and this time it was totally recognizable as *Sounds of Silence*.

"Sorry, my music was upside down," he teased as the class broke up with laughter.

Well, most of the class; I just sat there dumbfounded. The girl sitting beside me took pity on me and whispered, "he clowns around like that all the time".

THE LEGEND DIES ON — GARY GREEN

HOLY SHIT! It was the old Victor Borge *William Tell Overture* routine that I had seen back in the 1950's on television. I looked at my class schedule: "Mr. Husky" it identified the teacher.

As soon as class was over, I ran up to the front of the room to talk with the teacher. "Are you from Forest City?" I asked him.

I could see that the question startled him and his hesitating answer of "yes" sounded almost meek. I immediately followed-up, "I think you might know my mother. Before she married my father, her name was Dorothy Mosley".

A huge smile covered his face as he exclaimed, "YOU are Dot Mosley's boy? Well OF COURSE you read music. I suspect you play piano too, don't you?"

"A little," is all that I dared say to someone whose playing I had heard about my whole life.

I couldn't wait to get home and tell Mother that my Chorus teacher was her old friend Wofford Huskey! From that day until I graduated and moved back to Nashville, Wofford and I became friends, despite the 25 years age difference. I spent many Saturday afternoons at his home, listening to him play the piano and talk about music theory. My God! I had a friend who was a teacher!

It was not just the teachers; the entire culture of this school was totally foreign to me. At Two Rivers, daring to step foot off campus during the school day would invoke the most harsh *in loco parentis* sanctions —from corporal punishment to suspension or even expulsion. But at *Frank L. Ashley High School* in Gastonia North Carolina, students came and went whenever they felt like it.

When the lunch bell would ring, rather than all the students silently and orderly reporting to lines in front of the cafeteria to wait their turn to enter in very institutional-like orderly queues, these students would jump into cars and speed off campus to hamburger or pizza joints. Other students would walk to a nearby diner; while others, like me initially, would proceed to the cafeteria where even the menu was different.

For school lunches, I was accustomed to metal prison-style trays with varying size compartments or dividers to keep food organized and portion-control consistent in the fixed-menu, one price, meals with no choices.

At *this* school there were different entrée choices, multiple sides and desserts, multiple drink choices (including soft drinks that were forbidden in my last school), and even vending machines chock-full of junk food choices including Twinkies® and Fritos® (forbidden even in home-packed lunch boxes in Nashville).

In Tennessee, I (and many other students) lived in nightmare terror of raising the wrath of the Assistant Principal. At Ashley, there were two

THE POET LAUREATE SOUL OF FOLKIE ROCK & ROLL

Assistant Principals: one Hispanic man, whose primary duties seemed to be assisting students in preparing for after-graduation life skills as well as overseeing student extracurricular activities including parties; and one (very large) Black man who seemed to serve as both disciplinarian and paradoxically a friend-to-all, especially when it came to pop music.

There was no dress code at this school! Girls wore jeans, sleeve-less shirts, even cutoff shorts... and (God forbid) mini-skirts. Boys wore jeans, tee-shirts (forbidden at my previous school), shirttails out and even hats *indoors*.

The hallways were loud, rather than the required-convent-like-silence that I knew previously. Students talked, sang, yelled... and in languages, slang, and jargon other than "proper" English.

There was an outdoor area for smoking! Students were allowed to bring cigarettes to school and smoke them in designated areas.

Most startling, to this hillbilly product of segregated Tennessee and Georgia schooling, was the ethnic makeup of the student body. More than a third of the students were Black. There were Hispanic students, Asian students, Indian & Pakistani students, Native American students, and the first Jews that I had ever seen.

For me, it was as if I had landed on another planet; and a very pleasant one at that. I could not have even fantasized that there could be a high school like this; it was so far removed from the hell I had suffered for the previous three-and-a-half years (and even the deep hole memories of the fifth-grade nightmare).

Clearly, North Carolina public schools were nothing like Tennessee public schools. And the music possibilities, far from the "business" were even more substantial.

I feared, though, that this amazing new world was set to implode like the planet Krypton, leaving nothing behind[43].

The bad news was that this school, built in 1922, was scheduled to close at the end of that school year. In its place there was to be a new regional feeder school that would combine the student bodies of two of the

---

[43] There were many more complex cultural differences that were just unimaginable in the context of coming from Tennessee schools. No one cared about what job anyone's parents had or what anyone could or could not afford to buy. Having an afterschool job was not frowned upon or discouraged. At Two Rivers there was open racist hostility. The "n" word was more-than frequently used; it was a routine part of conversations, and the slurs are today unrepeatable even in this literary context. Also, at Two Rivers, "fag", "queer", and "homo" were routine insults tossed around between friends, enemies, and strangers. But at this school, not only were those words rarely uttered, the truth is no one cared one way or another. It was a totally different life culture.

THE LEGEND DIES ON — GARY GREEN

county's high schools into one brand-new building. I worried that the utopia might not continue.

The good news seemed to be the location of the under-construction school: it was in my backyard; quite literally and with no fence separating our yard from the schoolgrounds. My parents had chosen the location by design; I was in high school, my brother Ronny would be entering high school in four more years, and my brother Keith would follow him by three years. No school buses, no lines of traffic; we just walked out the back door of our house and we would be at school.

I also developed *friends* at this school; something I'd not experienced since Kingsport or Atlanta. There were no prejudices, no requirements to be in the most popular club or on the "right" team, no special social cliques of the haves and have-nots.

♪♪♪

Shortly after moving to town, Daddy arranged for me to be hired in the record department of a mega-store (think pre-curser to *Walmart*) where, through his job, he had influence with the store's regional and local management.

I had a great school and amazing classes. I had a driver's license and access to a car. I was in the midst of cultural diversity that I had no idea could exist. I was in an atmosphere where individual creativity was encouraged, and artificial constraints and discipline were unheard of. At 16, I had a great job that was ideal for me; and from it I had money of my own to do anything I wanted. Granted, I was only paid $1.60 per hour; but gasoline was 19¢-a-gallon, a new record album was $3.24, a pack of cigarettes was 24¢, and I basically had no expenses.

During summers, several times a week I would drive up to western North Carolina and rent a horse to spend hours riding on known (as well as unexplored) trails through the mountains. I learned to ride and became a fairly good —*for a 16-year-old*— deep-woods scout on horseback. Other days, I would drive to Freedom Park in Charlotte, perch myself on top of the cabin of the steam locomotive on display there, and spend a few hours playing train songs and singing to whoever would listen.

I began buying and absorbing every guitar instruction book that I could find. Then I started buying guitars: a 12-string, a double-neck guitar, a hollow-body electric guitar, a nylon-string guitar, and a dreadnought Martin knockoff. I also bought an assortment of amplifiers, microphones, microphone stands, guitar slides, capos, picks, and string types for different sounds.

When I discovered that a mandolin's standard tuning is chromatically the same as the bottom four strings of a guitar, only in reverse order (upside-down), I bought a "tater-bug" mandolin and began playing. Then, when I discovered that a violin, and related stringed orchestra

THE POET LAUREATE SOUL OF FOLKIE ROCK & ROLL

instruments, used the same (mandolin) tuning, I also bought a violin (fiddle) and began playing it as well (though the bow was not something of which I was fond). Finally, I added a bass guitar to my collection; just for the hell-of-it, since the four strings of a bass just mimic the bottom four guitar strings, only tuned octaves lower.

Reading the various instruction books and following the exercises, I began to experiment with alternative tunings for the guitar. That led to some open tunings and experimenting with slide guitar and then raised-nut slide guitar, and finally a resonator guitar *(Dobro)*. That led me to experiment with some open-tuning instruments themselves; specifically, a tenor banjo (with "C", "G", and "D" tunings) and a five-string banjo (primarily with a G tuning).

I also bought a couple of *portable* reel-to-reel tape recorders (to go with my larger multi-track stereo one), an eight-track cartridge recorder (yes eight-track was a thing back then, especially in cars), and two of the "new" cassette recorders.

In a relatively short time, my small second-floor bedroom was overflowing with musical instruments and recording equipment.

To that growing instrument collection, I began adding multiple lp[44] record albums every week; first buying them at work with my "employee discount" and then buying full collections from garage sales. My 45-rpm collection took a back seat to my new 33⅓ collection.

In Nashville I had bought a 45 of *Donovan Leitch* (who performed simply as *Donovan*) singing "*Atlantis*" with the B-side "*To Susan on the West Coast Waiting*"; but in Gastonia I found his "Greatest Hits" album. That opened an entire world of what I called "sweet-sounding" folk music. That, in turn, took me to *Peter, Paul, and Mary.*

I spent hundreds of hours listening to their incredible harmonies and very tight guitar work. I began thinking about what could be musically accomplished with less instruments rather than more: a sort of minimalist band. Along the way, they provided my first introduction to non-religious "message songs": *Blowing In The Wind, Where Have All The Flowers Gone,* etc.

Between customers in the record department, friends in school, and people I met at church (where Mother had settled in as the organist and piano player, of course), I developed a personal network of other musicians. That is how I met Eddie, who in turn introduced me to Jolly.

---

[44] "lp" is vinyl record era lingo for "long play"; denoting a 33⅓ rpm record as opposed to a one-song 45 rpm recording. (rpm=revolutions per minute)

THE LEGEND DIES ON — GARY GREEN

It also didn't take me long to figure out that being a picker from Nashville relocated to North Carolina made me a much "bigger fish" —even at only 16-years-old— than being one of thousands of "small fish" kids playing music back in Nashville.

The gig at the *North Carolina Children's Orthopedic Hospital* came about just that way. There was no audition, and they certainly weren't soliciting for shows. Instead, I wanted to do something like Johnny Cash's albums at Folsom and San Quinton prisons; but I had the good sense to know that a 16-year-old wasn't going to be able to go into a prison. So, I looked for other institutions.

That State hospital was local in Gastonia, so I called them on the phone and pitched my idea. I told them I was a guitar player and songwriter from Nashville who had just moved to town and started a local band. I told them that I wanted to entertain their patients and that it would cost them nothing. They jumped at the opportunity, set a date, and launched a promotional campaign. (In hindsight, foolishly, I did not tape the show.)

The media publicity and the local word-of-mouth publicity following the show were almost overwhelming. Seemingly overnight, I was a 16-year-old local celebrity. That led to a seemingly unending stream of calls, letters and in-person encounters with local pickers, singers, songwriters, assorted musicians, and partial bands.

If there ever was more than one real-life *Clayton Delaney*, I would nominate *Jim Medford* of Gastonia. He worked in one of the dozens of textile mills in town (Gaston County had the distinction of being the world's largest textile center, with more than 150 cotton mills in the county).

Jim chain-smoked and would tuck the filter-end of a burning cigarette beneath the strings on the upper left side of the head of his guitar. His wife went to our church, *Seventh Avenue Baptist Church*; but Jim rarely attended. She insisted that he and I should meet and play guitar together. It wasn't an unusual request following my newfound celebrity, and I was always eager to meet other pickers; even if most of them only knew three chords and couldn't (as my mother would say) "carry a tune in a bucket".

Wow. To my young eyes and ears, this rail-thin little 30-year-old Jim Medford cat was better than any of the Opry stage band or studio pickers I knew in Nashville. He could play anything and in any key. I would randomly name a country song or just start a song he'd never heard… and he was all over it; and not just the chords but lead and multiple-string harmonies. He was amazing[45].

He kept time by tapping both feet, in opposite beats from each other; the left foot on the downbeat and the right foot on the up-beat. He would also bob his head up-and-down between beats, keeping sort of a counter-rhythm with his neck muscles.

For every song, he would ask if I wanted to hear it "regular style or *Carter Family style* or *Chet Atkins style*". Whichever I chose, he'd make the song sound like it came from the guitar of that artist and sometimes he would switch styles in the middle of musical phrases and make his guitar sound like an entirely different instrument.

Usually, I could follow along and play almost anything he played. But Carter Family style, I couldn't copy because he would play the lead and the rhythm at the same time; that seemed way-too complex. It seemed almost impossible that all of that sound could come out of one acoustic guitar.

He told me that the style was created in the 1920's by a woman named *Maybelle Carter*, who he said was the first commercial artist to use the guitar as a melody instrument rather than just rhythm accompaniment.

I also was fascinated with his playing in what he called the *Chet Atkins style*. He would put a thumb-pick on and alternate between the three lower strings as he rested the palm of his left hand against the bottom of those three strings to slightly mute the sound. With his little finger and ring finger, he would play the melody.

At the same time, with his remaining two fingers, he would brush across the strings to play the associated double-stops (two notes at once) using the 3rd and 6th notes of the scale for the key in which was playing.

All of that made it sound like a chord or counter-melody harmony line being played in conjunction with the lead and the bass parts… all at the same time and on one guitar played by one little North Carolina hillbilly picker.

Yet, for all the world it sounded like three guitars playing together! I couldn't believe the sight and sound coming from Jim and one acoustic guitar.

Jim told me that even though people recognized it as the style of RCA's Nashville President Chet Atkins, it was a style that actually was popularized by *Merle Travis* (who had written the Tennessee Ernie Ford hit, *Sixteen Tons*, among other "standards" including *Dark As A Dungeon, Nine*

---

[45] Songwriter Tom T. Hall often said that his tribute ballad for the best guitar picker ever, *The Year That Clayton Delaney Died*, was based on his childhood neighbor and boyhood hero in Kentucky, Lonnie Easterling who taught Tom to play guitar.

THE LEGEND DIES ON — GARY GREEN

Pound Hammer, and *Steel Guitar Rag*). Atkins, who had begun his professional career as the traveling lead guitar player for The Carter Family, learning from Maybelle Carter had apparently added to the Travis technique by including jazz form chords and runs.[46]

I bought eight or ten Chet Atkins albums, trying to play along with them. Every time Jim and I would get together, I'd ask him to play that style. But I never could do it, mainly because to pull off that complex jazz-style fingering required a tremendous ability to balance multiple tempos simultaneously; and of course, I was rhythmically challenged with even one tempo.

I *did* learn to play Chet's signature *Windy & Warm* (a tune written by prolific North Carolina songsmith *John D. Loudermilk*). A more jazz-form piece, it was doable for me because it didn't require the complex multiple rhythms of Chet's other hits. Eventually I could almost-play his *Country Gentleman* (his best-known recording, written by Atkins and Boudleaux Bryant); but my cover of it was only a shell of what he did to the guitar. That damned rhythm thing, again!

I repeatedly tried to convince Jim to go to Nashville; I even offered to drive him there. I offered to introduce him to friends at the Grand Ole Opry and at WSM Radio. He vehemently refused, insisting that he was not as good as I thought he was. When I argued, he would come up with an unlimited string of inane excuses. He wouldn't even allow me to tape his playing, and he wouldn't do a public gig with me.

He died a very short few years later, while I was a student at the University of Tennessee. After his death, several people told me that he drank a lot (I never saw evidence of that) and that before I knew him he had tried to make a career in country music. Something, of which no one seemed to know the specifics details, had vastly disappointed him and convinced him that the pursuit of a musical career was folly (though he encouraged *me* to pursue a career as a songwriter/performer). After his own disappointment, he would only play at church functions or with me. Making his story even sadder, they told me that after I left town he almost stopped playing altogether, seemingly losing the inspiration.

Around the same time that I was learning from Jim, I also met a really talented local rock guitar picker who was six or seven years older than me. He introduced me to marijuana, cocaine, *The Grateful Dead*, and *Creedence Clearwater Revival*. Of those, I was most enamored with Creedence.

---

[46] Travis apparently had learned the technique from Moses Rager and Ike Everly (father of Phil and Don —The Everly Brothers). Travis and Atkins often credited Rager as the creator of the technique.

THE POET LAUREATE SOUL OF FOLKIE ROCK & ROLL

He said that I was the best guitar player he'd ever heard because I could pretty-precisely mimic John Fogerty's guitar playing on the Creedence songs. We practiced Creedence songs every day for months, and I listened to their albums over and over on "repeat" when I would fall asleep at night. I never had the heart to tell him that my picking was not all that special; that Fogerty had deliberately written the lead guitar parts so that any decent garage band could cover his songs. We never played together in public, but I did learn almost every John Fogerty song or other song that Creedence had covered.

Around the same time, I also became enamored with a song by a country singer-songwriter named Buddy Cagle: *The Guitar Picker*. Cagle had written the song about *James Burton*, the legendary Fender Telecaster picker who had backed up *Ricky Nelson, Elvis,* and dozens of others. Cagle had convinced Burton to play on the cut; on the song about Burton himself. Burton's picking had a unique sound that was instantly recognizable, and I spent hours trying to imitate it; never successfully.

Meanwhile, a friend from high school also introduced me to an album by an obscure Texas hippie cowboy named *Townes Van Zandt*. More than a performer or singer or guitar-picker, he struck me as a brilliant poet who used musical form to tell poetic stories. His verse was like Bob Dylan / Hank Williams mash-up; and it was genuinely unique. Rather than entertaining or something to emulate, he was inspiring —showing that actual poetry could use western/country musical form for its presentation.

I was still playing keyboards in public whenever there was a need; like one Easter Sunday, when Jolly's preacher-father asked me to fill in for their church organist at a "Sunrise Service". Their church was Presbyterian, and mine was Baptist, but that really made no difference, and the songs were the same. The cool thing about Jolly's church was that the sanctuary had a magnificent hundred-year-old *M. P. Möller* pipe organ that could shake the stained-glass windows on certain base notes and could be heard all over downtown Gastonia on certain high celesta-chime notes. For that Sunrise Service, I woke up the town with an as-loud-as-possible rendition of the Robert Lowery hymn, *He Arose* and then followed it with Eddie singing lyrics he and I wrote called *"I Hear The Lord Coming",* sophomorically to the tune of *Folsom Prison Blues.*

In the same months, I started playing with a genuine garage band of guys my age or a little younger; a guitarist/singer, a bass player, and a drummer. We practiced for hours on end and actually prepared formal sets. I know the drummer must have been frustrated with my lack of timing. The mother of the guitar player made it a point to tell us all that she hated my guitar playing because it was "too twangy and sounds like *Duane Eddy*". I wished it had sounded that good!

THE LEGEND DIES ON — GARY GREEN

As tight as we had become with daily practice and formal sets, I decided it was time to get a professional paid gig. I visited the General Manager of the megastore where my record department was housed and convinced him to hire my band for a weekend gig to attract customers.

For the next week, we rehearsed every free minute for the gig set for the next Saturday night. At 7:00 pm on the Friday before the next day's gig, the band members announced that they were firing me because I was too demanding of their time, and I hogged the stage.

They were probably right on both counts. But it was *my* gig. I had booked it, and it had been advertised as *my* band, piggybacking on the publicity from the hospital show. I refused to give them the gig and I refused to cancel.

They offered to let me perform during their breaks, but not be paid for it. I refused and told them they could all be replaced. I packed up the microphones, the stands, the bass, and the guitars (I owned all of equipment except the drum kit).

Stan was out of town. Eddie had to work that Saturday night. My rock friend was not really a candidate (because of his drug use keeping him publicly high) and Jim would not perform in public. That left me and my friend Jolly. I called him, explained the dilemma, and we made plans to get together the next morning at 8:30.

I really needed a rhythm guitar player more than I needed a bass player; but Jolly had never played rhythm guitar (he barely played bass). So, I quickly taught him three guitar chords and I explained how a capo[47] worked so he could change keys for different songs. We worked out body-language signals for me to give him so that he would know when to change chords.

I wasn't going to make the Orthopedic Hospital mistake again. I made a set list of songs that had limited chord changes and that I was sure Jolly knew the lyrics. He would sing and play rhythm guitar with the capo; I would provide harmony and play lead guitar.

That gave me a duo; a two-man band. Unfortunately, the store had bought a lot of television, radio, and newspaper advertising promoting *"Gary Green and his three-piece band: The Reflections of Reality"*. So, we still had to find at least a third person.

---

[47] A capo is a small bar that wraps around the neck of the guitar to apply pressure to all six strings. Doing so changes the pitch of all six strings by one "half-step" musical tone per fret. So, for example, if a player only knew how to play in the key of "E", by placing a capo in the first fret, those "E" chords would sound like the key of "F". Using a capo, guitar players who only know one set of chords can play along in any key with any instruments.

THE POET LAUREATE SOUL OF FOLKIE ROCK & ROLL

We called a friend who wasn't musical but looked good and had a good sense of rhythm. I decided that teaching him to play bass would take too long; but how difficult could drums be? (Clearly, I didn't have a clue.)

Next problem; find drums. We went to the local music store to try to convince the owner to rent us a drum kit for the weekend for which I would prepay. But, despite my (and my mother) being among his most frequent customers, he wasn't having any part of my desperate plan.

The next option was a music store in not-too-far-away Charlotte. That would cost a long-distance phone call to set up the deal; and the store manager there agreed. The rental of a used five-piece drum kit was $26 (plus we had to buy gasoline for the roundtrip to Charlotte and back).

We got back to Gastonia at 4:30; two-and-a-half hours before the advertised time of the show. Even I knew that wasn't a lot of time for rehearsal. We had to stick to three-chord songs; only a few of which were popular. The rest would be traditionals, folksongs. I decided that I would play all electric and perform the folksongs in the style that Creedence Clearwater had done with *Cottonfields* and *Midnight Special*. In case of a lull, I prepared some between-songs patter and jokes.

As late as we could practice and still make it to the show, I drilled the two guys on being a band. My voice was in the midst of embarrassing changes, so we resolved that the two of them would handle all of the vocals.

Before leaving for the gig, Jolly dressed in his American-flag pattern shirt and a cowboy hat. Our "drummer" wore a leather vest and tried to look like a rock star. I dressed in white pants, gold-buckle shoes, a black shirt, and a glittery green choker around my neck —like a used car salesman or a *Christopher Street* hustler.

At the store, the staff had set up a stage in the linen department while the local newspapers and a Charlotte television station had set up to report on the event. There are lots of pictures of that event still floating around today on the internet; maybe because we were so dorky looking.

Just before we started playing, the guys from my original band showed up and announced that they were going to "bust up" the place, kick some ass, and keep us from playing. Their threats lasted almost the entire two minutes it took for the store's security guards, two off-duty city police officers, to "escort" the boys out of the store, out of the parking lot, and threaten to call their parents from the City Jail.

Seemingly miraculously, our little gig started only five minutes late. A crowd had already gathered and was getting restless when they didn't see either equipment or a band. The growing audience relaxed as we quickly set up amplifiers and the drums.

THE LEGEND DIES ON — GARY GREEN

Jolly played my Kay acoustic, with a crude pickup affixed to it. I played my electric hollow-body Gibson knock-off. We had the rented drum kit, and four small cheap amplifiers.

Less miraculous and more predictably, we stunk. I had never seen people leave a concert in the middle of the first song. After the second song, Jolly laid the guitar on the corner of the makeshift stage and announced that he was tired of making an ass of himself.

That left me and the drummer, who decided to stick with me. I played the one song to which the drummer knew the lyrics, Paul Simon's *The Boxer*. For the chorus, I decided to kick (physically) the reverb unit that was attached to my guitar amp; that made a sound like a crack of thunderous lightning after every vocal phrase of the chorus. Back to the verses, I turned off the reverb and went back to a crisp clear guitar accompaniment.

The dispersed crowd returned and surprisingly gave us rousing applause. The problem now was that he didn't know any other songs, and I was certain that with my cracking voice, we would be booed off stage if I sang. I looked into the audience, hoping for a sign of guidance.

As if an appearance by the archangel Gabriel, my 12-year-old brother Ronny ran up to the side of the stage and whispered, "Mother said to play an instrumental of *Wabash Cannonball*". He then faded back into the crowd.

I played the song, and the drummer tried his best to follow me. The crowd got larger as I dragged the song out for about six minutes.

As soon as it ended, my brother returned to whisper, *Wildwood Flower*. I played the Carter Family standard as closely as I could to the Jim Medford style. Again, the crowd grew. I picked up the idea from there; rather than do the songs on the set list or try to sing, I switched to all instrumentals.

The crowd grew even larger, making it impossible to shop in the aisles of the 100,000 square-foot store. They began calling out requests, mostly country standards.

At the end of the night, we were paid in cash, fifty dollars (about $400 in today's money); but the expenses of the drum kit rental and gasoline to and from the other side of Charlotte, the three of us ended up with $6.24 each ($50 in today's money). Nonetheless, it was my first paid gig as a "professional". (I paid Jolly for the show, even though he'd only played on one song.)

After the show, Jolly and several other friends, including Wofford Husky who had come to hear me, told me that it was the best performance they had seen from me. The store's manager wanted me to book once-a-month; and as we were taking apart the equipment, I had four different offers for gigs.

THE POET LAUREATE SOUL OF FOLKIE ROCK & ROLL

One of them was from a much-older and very-rough looking guy who told me that he was a friend of Jim Medford. He asked if I would be willing to audition to be the lead guitar player for his Nashville-based band that backed up a (fairly well-known) country singer named *Red Sovine*. My hunger for Nashville professionalism overpowered my common sense and I agreed to audition. Keeping in mind that I had been playing guitar for only about six months, the audtion was, at least, insane!

On the day of the appointment, I loaded one guitar, amplifier, and a stand-alone reverb unit into the car and drove to the address he had given me. I arrived at a single-wide trailer; it was parked alone in the middle of a pasture. I knocked on the door and inside I could see an entire band of guys in their 30's and 40's assembled and waiting.

They helped me unload my gear and we jumped right into the audition. They started playing Dave Dudley's *Six Days On The Road*; a song I knew well. It was easy to catch the lead to it, and I even threw in some little runs that were not part of the original but were part of Charlie Pride's cover of the song. They recognized it and nodded to each other in approval.

Next, they played *There Goes My Everything*, a Dallas Frazier song made famous by Jack Greene. It was a slower, moaning song and it was obvious that they wanted to see how I handed that kind of tune. When we finished, one of the band members asked if I was Jack Greene's son. They seemed surprised when I said no, knowing that I came from Nashville (and not knowing the spelling).

As we came toward the end of the audition, they asked if there was any particular song that I wanted to play. Without hesitation I said, *Folsom Prison Blues*. I was eager to show off my Luther Perkins picking. They looked at each other and one finally said, "we don't really do Johnny Cash songs; they just cost too much and too much is expected from the audience".

Then the guy who had arranged the audition picked up my guitar and asked, "do you ever do anything like this?" He slid his left hand up the guitar's neck and played a very rigid 12-bar blues progression, two and three strings at a time. It sounded good but contrived; I was impressed and intimidated at the same time. It sounded like a lot of the canned "Nashville Sound" I had heard played by the Opry Stage Band when they didn't know the actual melody lead for a song. It was good, but not exciting. I couldn't, or at least had never, played anything like that; but I answered quickly.

"I've never had the need for that, but I'm sure I can do it," I answered as I took the guitar and played a few measures of Chet Atkin's *Country Gentleman* to show versatility beyond the one-string melody lines that I incorrectly had been calling lead guitar.

THE LEGEND DIES ON — GARY GREEN

I assumed that I had failed the audition, but surprisingly, before I left, I was invited to join the band for their upcoming road tour of seven State Fairs. The leader told me that he had left home and joined a band when he was 15, so my age wouldn't be a problem for them.

I knew there was absolutely no way that my parents would allow me to go on the road like that. Moreover, as exciting as it sounded, the idea of being someone's backup band didn't appeal to me. I wanted to be center-stage doing songs that I wrote. *(What a vastly different life I would have had if I had taken them up on offer!)*

I spent the summer between the 10th and 11th grades playing a few solo gigs, mostly doing either instrumentals or short sets of *Simon & Garfunkel* songs mixed with *Johnny Cash* songs, a few Gary Green songs, and a couple of songs from an album that I had found in the public library: a Folkways album called *Broadside Ballads Volume 1* and featuring *Peter La Farge, Phil Ochs, Gil Turner, Happy Traum, Bob Dylan* (using a pseudonym of *"Blind Boy Grunt"*), *Mark Spoelstra, Matt McGinn,* and *Pete Seeger.*

I continued to write letters, at the very least monthly, to Reba Hancock at House of Cash, to my friend in Donelson who had rented me that Stella guitar, and less frequently to a couple of friends from The Opry.

I also spent more-and-more time with my druggie rocker friend as he introduced me to the music of *Jimi Hendrix, Pacific Gas & Electric, The Who, Sly & The Family Stone,* and *Iron Butterfly.* (I can't imagine what possessed me to spend hours and hours... and hours playing those uninteresting 14 notes of *In-A-Gadda-Da-Vida* over and over on my electric 12-string. [48]) We also revisited my Steppenwolf cover days, focusing on a near-acoustic version of Hoyt Axton's *The Pusher.*

I became especially attached to the *Déjà Vu* album from *Crosby, Stills, and Nash (and Young and Taylor and Reeves).* Their ability to merge rock sounds with country or folk sounds absolutely fascinated me; especially Jerry Garcia's pedal-steel on *Teach Your Children.*

During that summer, I almost completely abandoned my acoustic instruments, opting instead for various electric guitars enhanced with a *Cry Baby* pedal and / or a *Fuzz Box* button. I was drifting from country music to serious rock.

Any public appearances, even those at churches, were all-electric for me and not merely amplified, but distorted and transformed. I wasn't

---

[48] Almost 60 years later, I had a two-minute flashback to those insane days when backstage at an induction ceremony at the California Music Hall of Fame I briefly met inductee Mike Pinera (Ride Captain Ride) who joined Iron Butterfly (of In-A-Gadda-Da-Vida fame) after their 1969 reformation. Interesting cat; definitely flashback material.)

interested in a "pop" sound; but the pre-metal genre of "hard rock". As far as practicing, I spent an inordinate number of hours note-for-note emulating Jimi Hendrix's *Purple Haze* and even more time copying his Woodstock performance of *The Star-Spangled Banner*.

Around that same time, I also destroyed several tube-driven amplifiers and head units, experimenting with feedback, psychedelic sound effects, and overdrive schemes.

Those antics, along with playing *In-A-Gadda-Da-Vida* to-obnoxia, probably in part were driven by my growing use of marijuana and "organic" hallucinogens (mescaline, psilocybin, and peyote buttons) along with an unhealthy dive into lysergic acid diethylamide (LSD) and other not-so-organic chemical psychedelics. All oh-so-healthy for a 16-year-old musician.

Occasionally I would raid Daddy's liquor cabinet, but I found the taste to be less-than-pleasing, and I seriously disliked the burning-sensation when alcohol rolled down my esophagus to my stomach. I could cut the taste a little by mixing orange juice with vodka (a screwdriver); but that was not much better; and the Southern-standard "jack-and-coke" (Jack Daniels Tennessee Sipping Whisky mixed with Coca-Cola) always struck me as an absurd sugar-ball to get the alcohol into my blood system faster. I definitely preferred pharmaceuticals for my highs.

I was physically pretty hyper during that period and slept very little. I tried to treat the near-insomnia with over-the-counter sleeping pills (Sominex, Nytol, etc.). When those proved to be ineffective, I turned to druggie friends to sell me hits of Darvon, Seconal, even Valium; but they were expensive and required me to buy drugs of questionable authenticity from some real goofballs (several of whom, sadly, eventually died from overdoses or drug-related accidents). My childhood opioid, paregoric, was no longer legally available.

Meanwhile, Mother had found us a family physician who was basically a "Doctor Feelgood" type; he would do whatever he was asked, as long as he got paid. It was not at all uncommon for me to call him at the first sign of a minor sore throat and tell him that I needed a prescription of Pentids 200 because I was "developing strep". He would call the local pharmacy, and my mother would pick up the medication for me. Antibiotics for a minor cold were just one of dozens of self-diagnosis prescriptions I successfully ordered by phone from this quack.

I could reveal this goofball's name without fear of reprisal since the truth is the defense of libel; but he defamed himself enough when this "physician" died of lung cancer from his multiple-packs-a-day cigarette habit. *'Nuff said!*

Frustrated with my inability to solve my sleep deprivation and jonesing for my paregoric, I called him and asked for some help sleeping. We

THE LEGEND DIES ON — GARY GREEN

discussed my mother's reliance on paregoric for me to sleep in the 1950's and in response, this lunatic prescribed *phenobarbital*[49] for me; mind you, not the more-moderate secobarbital, amobarbital, or pentobarbital. Granted, it was a small 15 mg dosage ... but fucking phenobarb to a 16-year-old who is whining because he can't sleep?!

Like most drugs prescribed by the Doctor Feelgoods of the world, my tiny little pills worked miracles. I'd pop one each night and I would have no problem sleeping... for the first couple of weeks. Then I started waking up in the middle of the night, unable to fall back asleep. No problem: I would simply pop another pill whenever I woke up unexpectedly.

That too worked for a while; then I began waking more frequently ...and with stomach cramps. I learned that taking another pill would make the cramps go away and allow me to sleep; but it was requiring increasingly more frequent doses.

During a relatively short span, I was taking an entire prescription bottle every week. As my *desire* for them changed to *need* and then out-and-out *addiction*, the good doctor continued to order refills for me.

One morning I realized that I was taking 25 pills A DAY; that was 375 mg every single day... and the doctor kept them legally flowing to me. That was definitely enough to kill me; and I don't know why it didn't.

In hindsight, I can't believe that at least the drug store didn't put a halt to it. Looking back on that collusion between those medical providers makes it easy for me to understand the 21st century news stories about the Sackler family and the Purdue Pharma OxyContin crisis. History has taught us that addiction is a profitable racket at every turn of the supply chain.

Even at 16 years, I knew that taking 25 pills a day was not a good thing; especially since the stomach cramps were getting worse and worse. I was so concerned that I went to the public library to read the *Physician's Desk Reference* indications for the drug. I knew the book was just the legal disclaimers and package inserts for drugs, but it provided a good way to learn about a prescription in the pre-internet years of research. At the library, I learned that a lethal dosage of Phenobarbital was considered 400 mg; and I was only one- and-half pills away from that lethal threshold. As Hoyt Axton had written, I was "walking around with tombstones in my eyes"[50].

---

[49] Phenobarbital, in later years, was/is one of the drugs-of-choice for assisted suicide. It also was the drug used years later by the Gastonia-originated UFO cult *Heaven's Gate* for their tennis-shoed mass suicide in California. That shit kills people!

[50] *The Pusher*, words & music by Hoyt Axton, © Irving Music, Inc.

THE POET LAUREATE SOUL OF FOLKIE ROCK & ROLL

Besides that danger, I was consciously aware that I was becoming mentally impaired; having a difficult time functioning day-to-day. My parents probably just saw it as teenage anti-social behavior; but in reality, it was much more than that and symptomatic of a serious drug-induced psychosis.

I think I began to realize the problem one night at a local concert; or at least that is when it became obvious to other people that something was wrong. A group of guys that I casually knew from school and from the local music store were in the most popular (and by far the best) hard-rock band in the region. Though their music was not like anything that I played, I really enjoyed hearing the music of *Captain John's Fish Market* and their awesome lead singer, *Rick Fitts*.

They were powerful, high energy, and so loud that they could be heard at least a block away from anywhere they were playing. Plus, Fitts had a stage presence that sort of took down the fourth wall as if to share some inside joke with the audience; it was a great stage presence.

I vividly recall attending one of their performances, sitting cross-legged in front of the platform stage, almost touching one of the huge Marshall amplifiers and being totally mesmerized by their lead guitar player's Gibson Les Paul guitar.

It was so loud, and I was so close, that it should have been impossible for me to sit there for more than a couple of minutes; but I sat through all of their sets, apparently without moving or flinching and only occasionally blinking my eyes.

When they finished for the night, I continued to sit there, not moving at all, seemingly just in a fog as they began to pack up their equipment and pass a few joints around. One of the girls from school, who had arrived about the same time as I did, shook me and asked if I was alright. Clearly, I was not; but I was able to drive home. That night I decided to go "cold turkey[51]" and never take another phenobarbital.

That process was easier said than done. For the next week or more I was violently ill and could not get out of bed except to vomit or have diarrhea. (My parents assumed it was food poisoning.) Eventually, I broke the addiction and was sufficiently driven away from any drug other than occasional marijuana or a glass of red wine (which I also would permanently quit about two years later).

Physiologically, I have no idea what, if any, side effects I may have suffered from that brief addiction. Psychologically, however, I was driven

---

[51] *"Cold Turkey"* was druggie-slang for abruptly stopping taking a drug to which one is addicted, usually without a mitigating drug to minimize reactions.

THE LEGEND DIES ON — GARY GREEN

back into the shell of solitude and shyness that high school in Nashville had created for me.

Hearing the magnificent talents of Captain John's Fish Market, the tightness of the touring country band where I had auditioned, the impossible talents of Jim Medford, and even the act of being fired from the band I created for the department store gig... all haunted me with the specter of my worst days at Two Rivers.

Mixing all of that with the normal teen angst one would expect, I also sunk into self-doubt and self-questioning of my own skills, intellect, and accomplishments; all wrapped in persistent internalized fear of being exposed as fraud... despite empirical evidence to the contrary. Still, my entire basis of playing music was borne from a scam of lining up the piano keys to the position of the little dots on the sheet music. Everything else that I had done musically was built on that[52].

Through it all, two of my new friends stood with me as if oblivious to my crises. The first was the one who had introduced me to the music of *Townes Van Zandt* and also suggested that I should listen to *Kris Kristofferson*. The second friend kept telling me that *The Grateful Dead* had country-folk roots and I should pay attention. The encouragement from those two friends kept me engaged with music enough to continue exploring different sounds. At the Public Library I expanded what I had heard on the Folkways Broadside album to discover another Folkways record called *American Industrial Ballads* by Pete Seeger. That album led me to a book called *Hard Hitting Songs for Hard-Hit People,* written by Seeger, Woody Guthrie, and Alan Lomax.

I checked the book out of the library because it contained the sheet-music and lyrics to almost 200 songs; but also, in its pages I discovered narratives and history lessons connected to each song in the collection.

I especially was stunned to learn that some of the most powerful songs, lyrically, in the collection (and on the Seeger record) had been written by a woman who worked in a Gaston County cotton mill and who had been assassinated because of her musical "rabble rousing".

That gave me an entirely new outlook on Gastonia as well as on any genre of music and lyrics powerful enough to make some-one think that murdering the songwriter would seem to make sense. **What kind of songs get you killed?** I needed to know more about that ... *a lot more.*

---

[52] Today, thoughts like that are recognized as the traits of what the National Institutes of Health terms "imposter syndrome"; but 70 years ago, there was no recognition of all that as cohesive symptoms of anything. So as the school year approached, I had not only reverted, but had consciously withdrawn and socially shut-down.

THE POET LAUREATE SOUL OF FOLKIE ROCK & ROLL

Opus Five:
Songs Powerful Enough To Get You Killed?

A hobo must ramble; a cowboy must ride.
Every train has tracks upon which it must glide.
While some will choose the mountain crest,
Some will choose the shore;
But some will jump the track and say,
"I'll run for you no more."
— *The Murder of Ella May Wiggins,* by Gary Green, 1976, as recorded on Folkways Records album FH5351, *These Six Strings Neutralize The Tools Of Oppression*

Apparently, the motive for her murder was that her songs got people too riled up. Not that I wanted to get killed; but I certainly wanted to write songs that could create such powerful reactions. I mean, what was THAT all about?

The more I read about the murdered Gastonia songwriter, the more riveting her story became and the more interesting the *power* of songs became to me. There *had* to be some power beyond just the music or just the lyrics. *Fascinating!*

Moreover, a woman in the very town where I was living had written songs which had so much impact that business owners, the local police, newspapers, and apparently Federal law enforcement all joined together to silence her... AND they determined that the only way to do that was to kill her. That must have been some damned powerful songwriting! I wanted to know how to do that!

Her name was *Ella May*, and she'd been gunned down on September 14, 1929, as she and a group of her friends were driving to a union meeting where she was scheduled to sing her songs; the very songs that were in that Pete Seeger book that I had found in the library.

That millhand woman wrote songs *so* powerful that they got her killed? She wasn't the union's organizer. She wasn't responsible for gathering the most union cards. She wasn't some kind of "outside agitator" that the local newspaper blamed for bringing the union to Gaston County. She was just a mom who wrote and sang songs about her experiences and why she and her coworkers wanted a union.

So, naturally, there was a conspiracy to murder her? How was that even real? Could it be just the songs or was there something else going on? She seemed like the most unlikely target!

I mean, Jerry Lee Lewis shook up the world with his wild antics and then marrying his teenage cousin; but despite generating haters, there was no officially sanctioned plot to assassinate him. Elvis turned the pop music world topsy-turvy and the official sanctions against him had

THE LEGEND DIES ON — GARY GREEN

manifested in drafting him; but that was not an assassination (and actually was a recruiting boost for the Army).

This woman, Ms. May, was no Elvis or Jerry Lee. Lyrically, she wasn't even a Bob Dylan. I didn't get it. There just had to be more to it than her songs.

Besides the "sin" of singing about her hungry children and her shitty wages, this resident of East Tennessee who had relocated to Gaston County (okay, I could identify with THAT) also had committed the social taboo of not "keeping with her own kind". She lived in an African American community rather than in the white mill village.

Though she identified as white, she was half Cherokee; but even in traditional Southern racism that would not have kept her from all-white housing. So, living among the Black workers was her choice, not the mill's edict.

Born in the same East Tennessee town as Dolly Parton, Ella was the daughter of a 16-year-old Cherokee woman and a 30-year-old white man; remarkably the fifth of nine children in the May family when her mother was a mid-teen.

By the time she was in her early teens her family, like many, had moved from small tenant-style farms to logging camps as the paper industry invaded East Tennessee. A center-of-attention popular girl, she spent early evenings around the fireside dinners in the migrant logging camps, strumming a guitar and singing Vernon Dalhart songs and other hillbilly-known favorites.

She began spending most of her time with one particular logger, North Carolina native John Wiggins, who was seven years older. When she was 17, they married and a few months later she gave birth to the first of her own nine children. Her father died that same year, in a logging accident and her mother died a year later.

Amidst all that, husband John Wiggins became permanently disabled in a logging accident shortly after Ella's mother's death. Unable to work, he retreated to long bouts with alcoholism, eventually abandoning the family. That also left Ella with the responsibility of supporting herself and the children.

She moved with her kids to the Cherokee reservation in North Carolina where she had relatives. Unable to find work on the Rez for a single woman heading a family, she soon moved to a plantation in Spartanburg South Carolina where she was hired to pick cotton alongside former slaves and their families. It was hard work and low pay; but she and the kids survived.

In those days the textile companies in Gaston County North Carolina —*a county which had more mills than any other location on the planet*— hired traveling "agents" who served as recruiters. Visiting remote villages and towns, they promised jobs, good wages, and company-furnished housing to people who would move to Gaston County. As an added enticement, the mills would also hire women; a practice that was almost unheard of elsewhere.

A scout for a cotton mill in Bessemer City, about six miles northwest of Gastonia, offered Ella and her co-worker Black field hands money for travel expenses and the promise of good jobs and housing. It was a *streets-paved-with-gold* kind of offer that no poor person could refuse, especially a single mother with a house full of kids and no long-term prospects for her family.

The company operated some of the very few integrated cotton mills in the county; but their small mill-village housing was not integrated. Moreover, unlike some of the larger mills, the company did not operate two sets of housing; so non-white employees were on their own.

Despite identifying as white (rather than Cherokee), Ella and her family were *socially* excluded from the mill housing (probably because of her intimate association with her Black coworkers who also came from the cotton fields). The closest housing for non-whites was about a mile walk from the mill, and it wasn't free (as the recruiter had promised); but her rent could be deducted from her paycheck or paid directly to the landlord.

When four of her children simultaneously contracted whooping cough, Ella stayed home from here "graveyard shift" night work to take care of them, pleading with her employer to put her on a day shift so that she could take care of the children through the difficult nights. Her supervisors would not tolerate her absences nor make accommodation for her to work a different shift; so, she quit.

Around that same time, a fledgling union organizing drive began to spring up at several of the small mills in the county. Frustrated with the heartlessness of her former employer, she began talking with the union organizers who empathized with her situation and hired her as a bookkeeper for the union. She also continued to write poetry and songs and then entertain union members with her singing and guitar playing.

As the union's organizing drive grew from mill to mill, it eventually hit the Loray Mill in Gastonia[53]. Once the workers there started talking union, everything changed in Gastonia and all of Gaston County.

The Gastonia newspaper, business leaders, churches, the local police and the FBI (fresh off the Palmer Red Raids) all joined with Loray owners to oppose the union. Nonetheless, more than 1,000 Loray workers went

---

[53] Named for the merger of the last names of its two founders, John Love and George Gray, Loray was the largest textile mill in the world.

THE LEGEND DIES ON — GARY GREEN

out on strike against the textile giant. As workers from the other mills joined the massive local, the news spread nationwide. The situation became so tense that the United States Congress called for special committee hearings to investigate working conditions in Gaston County's mills and specifically at Loray.

The union took Ella May to Washington to testify before the committee. She returned to Gaston County as a heroine to the millhands and as a serious problem for the mill owners. She led every union meeting singing her songs and building excited rage among the striking workers.

In the eyes of the mill establishment, she was guilty of multiple offenses: not remaining docile about her working conditions; being an outspoken *woman*; and "mixing the races"; along with vocally calling for a union; ... and singing rabble-rousing verses that incited hatred for the owners. Her lyrics pulled no punches and searched for no hard-to-understand allegories.

Look, here's the thing: those were good lyrics; they were sincere lyrics; and they probably were sung with genuine pain and passion. But were they powerful enough to evoke murderous rage? I didn't think so in 1971, forty years after the fact and I don't think so now, almost 100 years after they were written. *I had to be missing something!* Judge for yourself:

> We leave our homes in the morning
> We kiss our children goodbye
> While we slave for the bosses
> Our children scream and cry
> And when we draw our money
> Our grocery bills to pay
> Not a cent to spend for clothing
> Not a cent to lay away
> And on that very evening
> Our little son will say
> I need some shoes mother
> And so does sister May
>
> How it grieves the heart of a mother
> You everyone must know
> But we can't buy for our children
> Our wages are too low
> It is for our little children
> That seem to us so dear
> But for us nor them dear workers
> The bosses do not care
> But understand all workers
> Our union they do fear
> Let's stand together
> And have a union here

— *A Mill Mother's Lament*, **words by Ella May (Wiggins)** *to the tune of the Vernon Dalhart song, The Ballad of Mary Phagan*

Nonetheless, clearly in the minds of the 1929 powers-at-be in Gastonia, something had to be done about that 29-year-old out-of-control trouble making multiple threat woman. Hence, the murder of Ella May Wiggins. *(Note to self: It might NOT be just the songs; it might be the activities of which the songs are only a minor part. Important to note!)*

In the aftermath of the murder, the Gastonia Chief of Police was killed in a gunfight between union activists and anti-union vigilantes; he was with the vigilantes. Ultimately after lots of national publicity, lawsuits,

THE POET LAUREATE SOUL OF FOLKIE ROCK & ROLL

and more violence (though none as deadly as Ella's and the Chief's stories), the union lost, and the mill owners prevailed.[54]

In 1971 when I was first learning about Ella's story, it dramatically changed the way I thought about the power of songs and the role of songs; but there was nothing actionable —only things to ponder. During the next six years, however, the impact of her story on me became more evident as it came to shape my own music.

In 1974, as a young newspaper reporter working for the Gastonia daily newspaper, I got to know the son of one of the police officers that was with the posse that assassinated Ella. His perspective dramatically added to my understanding of the times; especially his hatred of Ella May as he recalled his father's stories about those days, punctuated by his father having been wounded when the Chief was killed.

Also in 1974, my song *"The Murder of Ella May Wiggins"* became my first commercially published song (in Broadside Magazine). There were a number of inaccuracies in my song[55]; nonetheless, as Ella's great-granddaughter, Kristina Horton, wrote about my song in her 2015 book, *Martyr of Loray Mill: Ella May and the 1929 Textile Workers' Strike in Gastonia, North Carolina*:

"However, the chorus accurately and insightfully portrays Ella May's situation. Some accept their fate, others seek better fortunes elsewhere, yet remain firm, demanding better where they stand. This is exactly what Ella May did. Unfortunately for Ella, that day she stood firm in the back of a pickup truck, someone took her life for doing so."[56]

In 1976, the public television station in Charlotte North Carolina produced a half-hour special about the life of Ella May and filmed me performing several of her songs. After that television special aired, I was frequently in demand to speak and play about Ella's life (and death).

At one such speaking engagement, at a church in Cramerton North Carolina, I was approached afterwards by a man who whispered to me, *"Thank you for telling that story. She was my mother, but we never dared tell anybody that and we don't use her name. What you are doing is a true God-send and I know she is smiling on you. Thank you again."*

---

[54] In 2014, the former Loray Mill was gutted inside and developed into luxury condos; complete with a historical marker and a museum where Ella's story was presented.

[55] Ella didn't work at Loray; she worked at American Mill Number Two in nearby Bessemer City, not Gastonia. She did have nine children; but several had died and hence all nine were not alive at the same time. She was shot in the heart, and not in the brain.

[56] *Martyr of Loray Mill: Ella May and the 1929 Textile Workers' Strike in Gastonia, North Carolina*; by Kristina Horton; McFarland; 1st edition (July 11, 2015)

THE LEGEND DIES ON — GARY GREEN

I never had any intention of becoming either a spokesman nor an authority on Ella May ...or on that era of Gastonia history; but I had been fascinated with the impact her songs had on people then. In 1971 when I first learned her story, it was just part of a continuing series of eye-openers about the power of music. For me, it was nothing more than that. My focus, instead, was on the upcoming school year and the new school building that I would be attending. I wondered what musical adventures would be available there.

𝄞♪𝄞♪𝄞♪

The internal finishing work for building the new high school wasn't completed by the time students reported for the first day of classes; so, we shared the hallways with construction workers who were finishing plumbing, noisily installing lockers, and doing some smelly touch-up painting. It was crowded, frustrating, and filled with loud construction noises. It was a series of sounds keeping us all on edge as we attempted to adapt to the new school and whatever the culture of it would be.

To address my reversion to shyness and stage-fright, I registered for a *drama class* among the electives I had chosen. Though I had no interest in acting, I was hoping that taking that class would force me to get in front of people again so that I could overcome the debilitating fear of rejection. I was wrong; it didn't help a bit and only made me more nervous. I was certain that my dreams of performing were over before there even was a real career.

The other creative elective in which I enrolled was the *Student Newspaper*; a journalism class that was tasked with putting out a monthly newspaper for the student body. I thought my photography darkroom skills would be useful in that class.

The first assignment for journalism class was for each student to write a short essay about what we experienced as the first students to be inside the new school building. Like most of the other journalism students, I wrote a blasé little article with the requisite five W's of journalism *(Who, What, When, Where, and Why)* and turned it in with my name and class information. I knew it was boring, but grammatically it was a perfect English mini-term-paper.

I still am not certain why, but I also submitted a second paper, without my name on it and using a different pen, disguising my handwriting, and on different paper. I dropped that one, too, in the box with all the others. That second piece was a biting, sarcastic, cynical attack on the moving-in process and the strain of opening the school before the interior buildout was finished. In my mind it was a *Mad Magazine* style satirical piece.

The next day, the teacher admonished the class that all of the papers turned in were terrible, with one exception: the satirical piece that I had written. She read it to the class, pausing every few sentences as everyone laughed. When she finished, she demanded to know who had written it, since it was unsigned. No one fessed up (because no one knew).

When the class was dismissed, I approached the teacher and confessed. I figured that if she was going to kick me out of class, I might as well take my medicine. Instead of lecturing me about breaking the rules, she told me that it was the best piece she had read from a student in her entire career. There is always a "but..." and in this case, hers was that I could never again submit a "normal" story; that I never again stifle creativity to fit into arbitrary expectations... never ever in life.

She continued her praise with an ominous alert that the kind of writing I had submitted had the ability to "hold readers in the palm of your hand and do whatever you wish to them". On the heels of my Ella May research, this teacher's warning was exactly the encouragement I needed to drive me further into exploring the power of words, of prose, of poetry, of lyrics!

With that acceptance and reinforcement, I immediately came out of my self-imposed shell and refocused on my music and creative writing as a direction in life. I even felt comfortable enough that I began keeping a guitar at school in various classrooms, and whenever even slightly appropriate, I would break into music with other students. I even took a guitar with me on a student trip to Europe during the next summer.

The teacher *did* warn me, "one day editors are going to want to kill you but will put up with your bullshit because your writing is so good", She also added, "but your irreverent attitude toward authority *might get you actually killed some day*".

I didn't question what she meant, and I certainly didn't take it as a harbinger; but it did make me think a lot more about what had happened to Ella May and the power of words & music.

That same teacher also taught the drama class, which was charged with putting on the annual high school play. For this particular year, the students had chosen the Broadway musical *Bye-Bye Birdie*; a tremendous opportunity to highlight the acting *and* musical talents of a wide range of students.

Though like many students I auditioned for a role in the play, I was not an actor, I was not pretty enough for one of the lead roles, and my own ego-driven personality prohibited me from channeling any required persona. So, initially, I remained on the sidelines as stagehand support; my assignment was to operate the lighting control console.

With the licensing of a Broadway musical, even for a high school production, comes an orchestral score; in this case, 158 pages of music. Ordinarily, these were scores that the school band or orchestra could handle with a modicum of rehearsals.

THE LEGEND DIES ON — GARY GREEN

However, Bye-Bye Birdie was different. The play was a musical comedy that revolved around an Elvis-Presley-styled 1950's rock and roller being drafted (as Elvis was in 1957). The plot was about a contest to date the rock & roll king before he left for the Army. While there were traditional orchestra-supported musical numbers (performed on Broadway by *Dick Van Dyke, Chita Rivera, Janet Lee, Paul Lynd, Anne Margaret,* and others) more than half of the score was Scotty Moore style Elvis-esque guitar rockabilly music.

That was far beyond the skillset or instruments of the high school band/orchestra, so the director/teacher called for the best rock and roll guitar players in the school to provide the music. After consulting with the band teacher, the decision was made to assemble a five-piece rock band with the orchestral pieces being played by keyboardist, a couple of horns, with a drummer, and bass guitar player.

The entire Broadway score was written in the key of B♭ major and the closely related keys of E♭, A♭, and F. Unfortunately, those are not common keys for guitar players, especially pop music guitar players from garage bands. Further contributing to the music debacle, the score was written for an orchestra dominated by B♭ instruments and not a piano; and there were no guitar chord charts above the lyrics.

After paying the licensing fee for the play, and several weeks into dialog and blocking rehearsals, the organizers came to the realization that the music wasn't working. Two weeks before the scheduled opening, the problem still had not been resolved, despite great efforts by student musicians.

The horns, piano, and guitars just weren't playing the same songs no matter how they tried to adapt. It was like my Orthopedic Hospital fiasco, only a lot more complicated because these were actual music students aware of the problem and trying to make it work. But no matter what they tried, it didn't sound like rockabilly or Broadway; and the excellent guitar players they had drafted were all "hard-rock" players more attuned to Jimi Hendrix than Carl Perkins.

That weekend, I took the score home and transposed all 158 pages to the guitar-friendly keys of E, A, and C. I then rewrote the piano parts for easier accompaniment of the guitars. Next, I rewrote the B♭ instrument parts also to the key of natural-E. Finally, I added the Nashville numbering system and decided to teach it to the band at the next Saturday afternoon play practice.

I loaned my best acoustic guitar to the play's star so he could accompany himself on stage for his solo ballad (once I transposed it for guitar). On Monday, I borrowed a friend's Fender Stratocaster guitar (pre-CBS, by the way, for those wondering) and sat in with the band to play all of

THE POET LAUREATE SOUL OF FOLKIE ROCK & ROLL

the lead parts myself. That crazy transposing exercise that I did when I learned to play clarinet finally had come in useful!

For the rest of my time in high school my focus was almost exclusively writing songs. I had been playing that Kris Kristofferson album over-and-over; specifically, a song called *The Law Is For Protection Of The People*. It struck me as a contemporary follow-up to what Ella May Wiggins wrote 40 years earlier; it was a "message song".

I still needed to know more about songs that could cause reactions like her murder. That was much more interesting to me than the seemingly never-ending drone of unrequited love songs.

Around that same time, the number one rated television show in the country was *The Smothers Brothers Comedy Hour*. Tom and Dick Smothers hosted a more-hip-than-normal variety show that included writers like *Steve Martin, Rob Reiner, Don Novello, Mason Williams, Lorenzo Music*, and others who in the next decades would help shape American entertainment culture.

From the onset, the brothers were in conflict with the official CBS TV censors over content. The censors removed a segment featuring Harry Belafonte singing *Lord, Don't Stop the Carnival* while a video of the police riot at the 1968 Democratic National Convention played behind him. They censored a skit by comedian David Steinberg making fun of Judeo-Christianity as he played Moses. They totally prohibited an entire episode of the show in which folksinger Joan Baez sang a song dedicated to her then-husband, David Harris, who was entering prison for resisting the draft.

Pete Seeger appeared in one show singing his song, *Waist Deep In The Big Muddy*, an allegory about US involvement in Vietnam that drew comparisons from the line "the big fool said to push on" to Lyndon Johnson's escalation of the war. President Johnson complained to CBS CEO William S. Paley, who immediately cancelled the show. The brothers filed a lawsuit which they eventually won; but the damage had been done and the show was gone[57].

---

[57] About 35 years later, I met Dick Smothers on an elevator at the Delta Airlines Crown Room lounge in Atlanta. In what I am certain must have been an uncomfortable fan-boy like conversation from me, I showered him with my own praises of the show. Modestly he lamented that they had been just a couple of regular guys trying to get along in life.

Unwilling to let it go at that, I lit in on him with a long recitation of how he and his brother had changed the world for an entire generation by bringing into our homes ideas,

THE LEGEND DIES ON — GARY GREEN

From all of that, clearly there were official-esque sanctions for singing songs that confronted the power establishment. It wasn't assassination; but it definitely was a reaction to the "message" of certain songs[58].

After their show was cancelled, I became even more interested in Seeger and his cohorts. That *American Industrial Ballads* album had led me to *Woody Guthrie*, whose records weren't available at any local record stores but were in the Public Library. Guthrie was praised at every turn by Seeger, who proclaimed him to be the biggest influence on his own music.

I was more-than fascinated with the way Guthrie had taken familiar songs and added not just new contemporary lyrics, but powerful thought-evoking calls to action. It's what Ella May had done with her Mill Mother's Lament; but it was a generation later (and better written).

In a ballad about the outlaw *Pretty Boy Floyd*, Woody Guthrie paraphrased O'Henry and wrote, *"some people will rob you with a six gun, and some with a fountain pen"*; but not leaving it there, he also sang a barb toward home foreclosures: *"...as through this world I roam, I've never seen an outlaw drive a family from their home"*.

In a song to the tune of Jesse James, he wrote a ballad called *Jesus Christ Was A Man*, in which he sang *"He said to the rich, "Give your goods to the poor, So they laid Jesus Christ in his grave"* and also, *"It was the landlord and the soldiers that he hired, That nailed Jesus Christ in the sky"*, and *"if Jesus was to preach today like he preached in Galilee, They would lay Jesus Christ in his grave"*.

For a boy raised Southern Baptist hillbilly, those lyrics were either blasphemous or revolutionary or both; either way, it wasn't something one would expect to be sung and especially not by a guy with a Southern accent, like Woody.

---

music, views, humor, emotions, and writing that otherwise we would have never known. I "accused" him of being one of the most significant driving forces of the late 1960's and early 1970's hippie culture.

If he even remembered that airport encounter with me, he probably concluded that I was insane and added me to a permanently banished list somewhere. He should have.

Nonetheless, I stick by my thesis about the brothers and their role in shaping our culture. And for myself, their ordeal really did show me that there were contemporary sanctions taken against the writers and performers of certain songs

At least ten years after my encounter with Dick Smothers, I met his brother Tom in Sonoma County California. We talked for hours about those days and the influence he had on me and millions of others. We stayed in contact occasionally up until his death in December of 2023.

[58] Not unlike the 2003 blacklisting of the country group *The Dixie Chicks* after they were ashamed to be from Texas, the same state as President George W. Bush who had ordered the invasion of Iraq.

THE POET LAUREATE SOUL OF FOLKIE ROCK & ROLL

Using the tune of the folksong "John Hardy", he paraphrased Steinbeck, concluding one song with "...wherever little children are hungry and cry; wherever people ain't free; wherever men are fighting for their rights; that's where you're going to find me".[59]

Using lyrics in such a way had never occurred to me and I'd never heard anything like it. Then I heard Woody Guthrie's original version of *This Land Is Your Land* and that just totally blew me away!

It was a song that almost every kid in America learned in elementary school, but it had been written by Guthrie because he was tired of hearing Kate Smith singing Irving Berlin's *God Bless America*. Two verses of Guthrie's original song were not taught in schools, and when I heard those two verses it changed the whole song for me. In fact, it changed everything I knew about lyrics for songs. It was a lot more impactful, for me, than Ella's songs.

Everyone knew the schoolhouse chorus and the four verses of This Land that were often on television, in plays, and recorded by dozens of artists. But Guthrie's original version of his song also had more:

"One bright Sunday morning
In the shadow of a steeple.
By the Relief Office
I saw my people.

As they stood there hungry.
I stood there wondering if...
This Land Was Made For You and Me"

In that one verse, he attacked poverty, the inefficiency of government programs, and the aloof self-righteousness of churches. But he wasn't finished; there was another untaught verse:

"There was a big high wall there
That tried to stop me
And a big sign painted that said
'Private Property'

But on the back side
It didn't say nothing except
This Land Was Made For You And Me." [60]

Not only did those lyrics serve as a powerful provocateur but the very fact that I (and most people) had never heard them —*though the song was taught in almost every public school* — was itself eye-opening. It made me wonder what *else* had been hidden from us; but more germane to developing my own writing, it made me further understand how lyrics could be threatening to the status quo.

---

[59] Upon hearing it, Nobel-prize winner John Steinbeck quipped, *"If I had known Tom Joad's story could have been told so concisely and so passionately in a song, I would have never written Grapes of Wrath".*

[60] © Copyright 1956 (renewed), 1958 (renewed), 1970 and 1972 by Woody Guthrie Publications, Inc. & TRO-Ludlow Music, Inc. (BMI); used here exclusively in journalistic context for the purpose of explanation (like all lyrics herein).

THE LEGEND DIES ON — GARY GREEN

It occurred to me that if someone could write such powerfully inciting lyrics but attach them to more popularly mainstream musical forms... then those would be amazing songs.

Guthrie's recordings, voice, and musicianship were not exactly the quality that would be played on commercial radio stations (at least not by the late 1960's and early 1970's) and his brilliant writing, consequentially, was lost to millions of people.

What I wanted to do was write songs with that kind of power in content but with a form that would reach a broader audience.

I needed to present the painful passions of Ella May, the powerful lyrics of Woody Guthrie, the musical intensity of Creedence Clearwater Revival, and the working-class audience appeal of Johnny Cash.

I wanted to write a song that could change the world. I wanted to write a song that could make white people think twice before attaching the name "Watermelon" to a Black guy in school. I wanted to write a song that could stop the violence, the wars, the hatred, and the other tumultuous ills that haunted the end of the 1960's (and every other decade). *That seemed like a simple-enough task, right?*

That impossible dream came crashing down for me in a revelation through the most unlikely source: a song performed on *The Lawrence Welk Show* on television[61]. As far from Welk's genre as imaginable, during that same era there was a one-hit-wonder group called *Brewer &*

---

[61] Welk was an accordion player (no, really), bandleader, and television personality known as *the champaign music maker*. He was known for his signature phrase "and-a-one-and-a-two" with which he started every song that his mini-orchestra would play.

Born in 1903, Lawrence Welk hosted a nationally syndicated television series from 1951 to 1982 and was considered by much of my hippie generation (as well as the Beats before us) to be the ultimate personification of a "square".

He assembled a television cast of some ... interesting ... performers; a cast that was homogenized, never controversial, never ethnically accented, and all white except for one Black tap dancer who stereotypically was regulated to grinning minstrel-like performances.

For most in my parents' generation, his show wasn't at all hokey; for them it was a broad-based variety show. But among my coming-of-age *Woodstock Nation* generation, the show was at best a comical parody of America and at worst a denial of the turmoil of the Civil Rights era, the Vietnam War, and the American turbulence of the late 1960's.

Lawrence Welk, himself, pitched his show as television's one remaining bastion of old-fashioned conservative family values amid the wasteland that had delivered such irreverent programs as the sexually suggestive *Rowan and Martin's Laugh-in* or the blatantly antiwar *Smothers Brothers Comedy Hour*.

Apparently, his show had a large enough following that it attracted advertisers and constantly aired on between 80 and up to 217 television stations around the country on any given week for three decades.

My parents, of course, loved the show and it was often on our TV during its early Saturday night timeslot.

THE POET LAUREATE SOUL OF FOLKIE ROCK & ROLL

Shipley. They were a sort of *Byrds/Gram Parsons* style folk-rock band with a popular song about being high from smoking marijuana; *One Toke Over The Line*[62]. That connection to Welk should have been a Monty Python routine; but it was very real or at least surreal.

Each week in preparing for his show, Lawrence Welk and his producers would look at the list of the top Billboard hit songs, listen to any new ones, and determine if any of them lent themselves to the show's format. That process, apparently, was the Lawrence Welk Show's way of staying contemporary from week to week, at least in their minds.

One Toke Over The Line, at the top of the chart for a few weeks[63], contained a chorus with lines including "I'm one toke over the line, sweet Jesus" and "Waiting for the train that goes home, sweet Mary".

Having no idea what a "toke" was, but hearing "sweet Jesus" and "Mary", the out-of-touch Welk concluded that the song was a Christian religious song. Because it was obviously popular (as reflected by the Billboard charts), he decided that it would be ideal for the weekly gospel song segment that his show always featured.

On that week's broadcast, two well-dressed (and as-far-from-hippie-as-imaginable) singers performed an orchestra-driven sing-songy version of the Brewer and Shipley drug song. *Gail Ferrell* and *Dick Dale* were Lawrence Welk's go-to middle-America white "clean-cut" conservative-looking and always-smiling cast members.

Their harmony was church-choir perfect as they stood in front of a stained-glass window with halo-ish stage lighting around them. When the song ended, a smiling Welk announced to his conservative television audience, *"here you've heard a modern spiritual by Gail and Dale"*.

---

[62] A "toke" was hippie-drug jargon for drawing a puff of marijuana smoke. (Clearly, this was before the days that the FCC forbade radio stations from playing pro-drug songs.)

[63] Unfortunately, they never had another song to chart the way One Toke Over The Line had, though they did have two minor-hits a year or so later. For the most part the duo faded into obscurity, though as of the 2020's Michael Brewer and Tom Shipley were still touring and still singing that hit song. They remain a really good folk-rock duo. The song, even with its brilliantly harmonized melody, might have benignly remained obscure if two things had not happened.

Firstly, the conservative (and later convicted felon) Vice President of the United States, Spiro T. Agnew, named Brewer and Shipley as the architects of *the subversion of American youth*. Mainstream America almost completely ignored Agnew's rant as just the latest in his seemingly never-end anti-hippie attacks. But for my generation, it made Brewer and Shipley, who we'd pretty-much never heard of, big stars and drove their drug song to the Billboard Top 40.

Secondly, the thing that was completely over-the-top was the relationship between that drug song and The Lawrence Welk Show.

THE LEGEND DIES ON — GARY GREEN

Between that comical misunderstanding and the Vice-Presidential assault, *Brewer & Shipley* and their song briefly became countercultural heroes for a while; so much so that the first chapter of Hunter S. Thompson's novel *Fear and Loathing in Las Vegas* featured Dr. Gonzo singing the line "One toke over the line, sweet Jesus, one toke over the line" while driving with Duke from Barstow to Vegas.

But for me, the entire Lawerence Welk incident was extremely troubling and paradigm-shattering. To me, it showed that if a melody was too sweet or too complex or too loud or too… melodic … the lyrics could get lost and even be completely ignored. Or if the lyrics were uncertain to the general population, they equally were lost.

Clearly, some degree of grit was necessary to keep the audience from getting lost in the music. That was an important lesson for my understanding of the difference between sing-songy lyrics and call-to-action lyrics: escapist music versus lyrical poetry.

At the same time, it indicated to me that the music needed to be pleasing enough to hold their attention[64].

I began frantically writing song after song, experimenting with both lyrical and musical impact on listeners. I wrote several songs that successfully made the mothers of some of my classmates' cry from my carefully-chosen emotion-evoking buzzwords and phrasing. The music, though, was still a puzzler. It was a deliberate exercise in manipulating feelings and it worked. I learned "trigger words" to elicit varying reactions, regardless of context; and I learned stage expressions, movements, body language, and specific sound combinations to engineer other reactions.

---

[64] THAT was a lot more complex than I had initially considered. Lawrence Welk had shown that to me, as had the near-incomprehensible lyrics on several big-selling rock bands. It, incidentally, was a feeling that was validated about seven years later when CBS Television aired a show called *WKRP in Cincinnati* in which the closing lyrics were pure gibberish. As songwriter Jim Ellis explained, "There were no lyrics, and I was just sort of scatting gibber-ish. Well, Hugh (Wilson of MTM Enterprises) and Tom (Wells who wrote and produced original music for the show) thought that was funny and that it made a joke about the general unintelligibility of rock lyrics".

Validation or vindication, years before that series debuted, I was aware that really addictive music could obscure lyrics or at least make lyrics unimportant. What else was the aforementioned "*In-A-Gadda-Da-Vida*" by Iron Butterfly? To make lyrics that could change the world, I needed to find a way to have attractive music that would not obscure the message. Further, I wanted to find a way to mesh the words and music into poetic form. Not an easy challenge!

THE POET LAUREATE SOUL OF FOLKIE ROCK & ROLL

I was also extremely interested in Johnny Cash's *talking* part of a song and singing part of it. His Carl-Perkins-penned *Daddy Sang Bass* was a perfect example (not to mention Shel Silverstein's *A Boy Named Sue*).

I kept writing. Prolifically building a notebook of multiple styles and genres, I concluded that I should focus on my writing rather than on performing. Part of that decision was driven by my fixation on the power of a well-written song, part by the encouragement of the teacher who praised my writing, and part by my damned war with rhythm. Okay, and a major part of it was my insecurity with my voice and musical skills[65].

For the rest of my high school days, I carried out the expected senior-class ritual of applying for college admission. At the urging of the school's guidance counselors, I applied to multiple schools, since they told me most students get rejected except at their own state university.

I sent applications, transcripts, and test results to *The University of Tennessee, University of Georgia,* and for journalism, *Columbia University*; I had no interest in North Carolina schools though I should have.

By spring, when the acceptance letters began arriving, I had *less-than-zero* interest in attending any college. (I was accepted at all three.)

I had heard Kristofferson's refrain to *Me & Bobby McGee*: "Freedom's Just Another Word For Nothing Left To Lose..." and, well, I absolutely had to find the person who wrote such words.

I had to write songs like that. And...harking back to Ella May, I had to understand how a song could be so moving that it would make powerful institutions conspire to murder a songwriter. I wanted to change the world with music; and for me I thought all of that had to start back in Nashville... "down on Music Row".

---

[65] During this period, my focus was on subliminal cues that could be worked into words, sounds, and visualizations. I discovered that there was an entire science of subliminal manipulation, often used in advertising but occasionally (at that time) used in entertainment. Though I would circle back to that in later years, I decided it was not the direction I wanted to take my writing at that point.

THE LEGEND DIES ON — GARY GREEN

Opus Six:
The Captain, Pancakes, Waylon, Pinball, Outlawing

> Trail-dust that once covered his boots
> Is now dust from another terrain.
> But the bar is still open.
> And the ladies keep coming...
> And trouble still rides with his name.
>
> — *The Cowboy*, by Gary Green, 1976, as recorded on Folkways Records album FH5351, *Allegory, Gary Green Volume Two*

With my guitar slung over my shoulder and a seven-inch reel tape in my hand, I probably looked a lot like a thousand other kids who over the years had walked along 16th and 17th Avenues South — Nashville's storied Music Row. Two hours after my high school graduation ceremony, I had left for Nashville with a dream of stardom and a loose-leaf Blue Horse binder filled with the 85 or so songs that I had written.

I even had the requisite cowboy hat (which for the next ten years I almost never took off, and only then when I replaced it with a Greek fisherman's cap). Hip-hugger bellbottom jeans with a wide leather belt and oversized buckle, a pearl-snap (rather than but-tons) dress shirt, leather vest, and high-shaft cowboy boots finished my daily wardrobe —or costume, as the uninitiated might have de-scribed my attire.

The only accessories to my daily garb were a pocket watch with its braided leather fob and the bullwhip tied to the right side of my belt. Yup, a *bullwhip*.

When I was about 10 years old, my family visited the tourist attraction *Oconaluftee Indian Village* owned by the *Eastern Band of Cherokee Indians* in the mountains of western North Carolina. A sort-of reconstructed 18th-century Native community, the village featured demonstrations of basket making, shooting bows & arrows, blowguns, and tricks with bullwhips.

I was especially fascinated with the amazing skill of the Native bullwhip performer as he snapped out the flames of candles, snatched cigarettes from assistants' mouths, and disarmed "cowboys" holding "loaded guns". He could use the whip as a near-lethal weapon or he could use it gently to caress the neck or wrist of his target, once using it to bring his pretty assistant to his side.

I was so impressed with his super-Zorro or Lash-LaRue magic that at the village's giftshop I convinced my parents to buy me a "Genuine Cherokee Indian Bullwhip", made in Japan. For the next eight years I practiced with that whip almost as much as I practiced music. I carved a series of

THE POET LAUREATE SOUL OF FOLKIE ROCK & ROLL

X-like notches covering the entire wooden handle to rough-up the slick finish so that the whip could not easily slip out of my hand.

Since that time, tying that bullwhip to my right side had been part of my daily wardrobe as essential as I imagined strapping on a six-gun had been for the heroes of the TV westerns. I wore it everywhere, except to school of course. I didn't hang up my whip for another nine or ten years; after the first *Indiana Jones* film came out — and then only because I got sick of people assuming that the character in the film was why I carried it. My whip-snapping predated George Lucas' imaginative Harrison Ford by at least a decade-and-a-half.

When I hit the streets in Nashville, my guitar, recording tape, and cowboy hat were pretty much *comme d'habitude* on Music Row; but the rest of my comportment might have been a little eyebrow-raising; even in a town where men costumed in rhinestone sprinkled polyester and women wore crinoline petticoats.

I had driven the 458-miles from Gastonia to Nashville in my eight-year-old hand-me-down 1964 Plymouth Valiant loaded with assorted clothing, a sleeping bag, one tape recorder, a "portable" record player with the best of my record collection, a few musical instruments, and a bag of groceries.

With my father's soon-to-expire gasoline credit card and twenty-four dollars in my pocket, I was ready for Nashville! Alas, Nashville was not quite as ready for me.

Somehow, I had expected Music Row to throw open the doors welcoming the return of the prodigal son. I mean, I'd only been gone three or four years, and I had kept in touch through monthly letters and tapes. Why wouldn't they be thrilled and get busy spreading the word that I was coming home?

In the early 1970's Music Row was a vibrant center of creativity and energy, with an openness unlike anything that ever existed in the formal business world of music[66]. Never actually a "row" of anything, it was a six-blocks-long ladder-shaped neighborhood just southwest of downtown Nashville. The two arms of the ladder were provided by parallel 16th and 17th Avenues South; the rungs were six cross-streets between them.

Along the ladder were dozens, probably hundreds, of recording studios, publishing companies, agencies, and support services. Except for four, maybe five, actual office buildings, the companies and studios were all

---

[66] Other than a few very corporate buildings, most of those businesses are long-gone. Those streets have been renamed and are part of an historical-register district called Music Square.

THE LEGEND DIES ON — GARY GREEN

located in converted single family homes that at one time probably made up an upper middle-class neighborhood[67].

In the two months that I'd been back, I had settled into a routine of visiting several companies each day; but it seemed like the people at every stop were telling me the same thing, *"Kid, get a job. Get a place to live. Then come door-knocking with your songs"*. It was either that or *"Kid, get out of Nashville; we don't want you back here. You're a hippie-freak"*.

Never one for authoritatively sage advice and always looking for shortcuts, for me, getting a job (other than as songwriter or country music superstar) was the farthest thing from my 18-year-old mind (except maybe for attending college, which was equally uninteresting). Nonetheless, getting an actual place to live didn't sound too bad; I had been sleeping in my car for more than 30 days. All I needed to do was find a $20 apartment[68]. *Riiiight!*

During my first month back in Nashville, I lived in the *Holiday Inn* on West End Avenue, just off of Music Row; courtesy of Gulf Oil, or more accurately, courtesy of my father via his Gulf credit card.[69] But after that first month, I'd been living in the woods, sleeping in my car, and only eating every other day... or less.

When I left North Carolina in the middle of the night, I brought along the Gulf Oil credit card that Daddy had given me to buy gas locally around Gastonia. That card was how I had been able to afford gasoline for the long drive and then to tool around Nashville once I arrived. It also was how I paid my Holiday Inn bill... until the card expired 26 days into my staycation.

Since the expiration, I had been living outside of Nashville at campsites that had been built and then abandoned by the U.S. Army Corps of Engineers when they constructed various projects for the Tennessee Valley Authority. My usual campground of choice was about 30 miles east of Nashville. I would drive along a dirt road as far into the country as it went; from there on it was a Jeep-trail that led to a few obscure Army campsites which at first had been reserved for a Boy Scout camp, but now had been abandoned to nature... and to me.

---

[67] Today the term *Music Row* had become a less-than-flattering metonymic for the country music business (much like the once vibrant *Tin Pan Alley* had become in New York).

[68] The equivalent of about $149.44 as of this writing.

[69] A *Gulf Oil* gasoline credit card could also be used for *Trailways* bus tickets (which I didn't need), rooms at *Holiday Inn* motels (which I definitely needed), and in a number of restaurants across the country (which I also utilized).

THE POET LAUREATE SOUL OF FOLKIE ROCK & ROLL

In those days most Gulf stations also gave patrons *S&H Green Stamps* with all purchases[70]. With my gasoline purchases before the expiration, I had collected enough stamps to fill collection books sufficient to redeem them for a "Girl Scout Camping Cook Set", which included a quart pot with a lid, a frying pan, a metal plate, a fork-spoon combination utensil, and a collapsible drinking cup. That gave me the kitchen supplies that I need for my home-in-the-woods.

For food, I would occasionally shoplift one or two potatoes from a random grocery store. Sometimes I would splurge and buy a 25-cent loaf of bread or a 13-cent day-old loaf. I also would go into McDonalds restaurants and get free packets of ketchup and mustard, or earlier in the day, free packets of jelly and peanut butter.

About every-other-day I would have "a good meal" of a fried potato with ketchup and mustard used as the oil to fry it. There were no other "meals" after I left the Holiday Inn. It didn't take long for my ribs to jut from my skin, my clothing to slip off a bit, and for my waist to shrink to 26-inches. (I knew that from the notches on my belt).

Early every morning I would wander through a Nashville neighborhood and steal a morning newspaper from a driveway before anyone awoke. That allowed me to keep abreast of the news as well as to scan the daily want-ads. The latter was essential to find a $20 apartment, as well as to see if any taverns were hiring brilliant young songwriter guitar pickers. *(They were not)*.

Finding an apartment was making more and more sense to me. Besides, I was seriously tired of not having running water, a shower, or a way to wash my now filthy (and smelly) clothes. I equally was tired of the long drive to my campsite and back from Nashville and the incessant nightly swarms of mosquitoes that lived at the campsite.

Every few nights, to save gasoline and the long drive, I would park in the lot of the apartment complex behind the house where my family had lived in Donelson. It was safe and had a great view from a cliff high above Elm Hill Pike. I didn't make that parking spot a "permanent" home because periodically it was patrolled by Metro Police, and I didn't want to run the danger of being arrested for sleeping in my car. Little did I know how valuable a skill it would become to look innocent as if I belonged when police patrols showed up.

I used restrooms at gas-stations and fast-food joints to brush my teeth and for a toilet; but a bath required a little more creativity. Usually, I

---

[70] Those stamps were a multiple merchant loyalty rewards program and could be traded for merchandise at redemption centers.

THE LEGEND DIES ON — GARY GREEN

would drive to the rear parking lot of a random large family-friendly motel. In my car, I would remove my boots and change from my clothes to my bathing suit. Then I would walk barefoot along the motel's corridors until I found a housekeeping cart where the staff was inside a room working. From the cart, I would cop a towel, a tiny bar of soap, and a bottle of shampoo.

Draping the bath towel over my shoulders and around my neck (and concealing the soap and shampoo), I would deliberately walk into the lobby of the motel and say something to the desk clerk like, "did you see my mother walk through here? Red-headed lady, with a blue bathing suit?"

The desk clerks, without fail, would see the skinny young boy, and attempt to be helpful to an obvious son of a guest at the motel. When they would tell me they had not seen her, I would cheerfully announce, "oh okay. Well, I'm going to go to your restroom then go back out to the pool to find her. Is that okay?" It never failed to work, and I would use motels' swimming pool to take a bath a couple of times a week at different motels; all right-under-the-nose of management.

Creative as that might have been, this was not an ideal existence. So, after a month or so scanning the classifieds in driveway-stolen newspapers, I found an ad for a three-room furnished apartment for only $15 weekly[71]. From a pay phone, I quickly called the number and then reported to the address given to me by the landlord.

I had been camping in those woods outside of Nashville for too many nights, and on the drive to the address my mind filled with sugar-plum-fairy visions of a real apartment with a real bed, walls, electricity, and maybe even wooden floors.

I pulled the Valiant up to a 19th-century two-story house and I walked toward the giant double doors, being careful to dodge the swarms of honeybees buzzing around dozens of colorful flowers and shrubs in the front yard. A small Asian man came to the door, didn't speak a word, but led me to a bench beneath one the yard's leafiest trees. There I filled in the lines of a printed rental application that he had put into my hands, still without speaking a word. It looked like a form-application that he could have bought in bulk at any office-supply store.

When I finished, he still didn't speak to me but walked to the door and loudly called out, *"Mamma. Mamma... M-aaaaa-mmmmmmm-a, come an' see whaz is wanning tos get the apart-to-mint"*, at least, that is sort-of what it sounded like to me.

---

[71] A little more than $450 a month at the time of this writing.

THE POET LAUREATE SOUL OF FOLKIE ROCK & ROLL

Around the corner and from a side door came a plump Asian woman about 65 years old. She looked at me and authoritatively said, "How are you son? My husband doesn't read in English. Let me read this."

She looked over the application and when she saw that I had left blank the line for "occupation", she sternly stared at me before speaking again. "What do you do for a living, son? How shall you pay me every week?"

With all the pride and confidence that I could muster, I answered, "I'm a musician; a songwriter".

Surprisingly, I saw big tears swell from her eyes, genuine tears. I could tell that she had heard my tale before and in a saddened tone that revealed a pain in her heart she began to tell me what was on her mind.

"Why do young people never listen?" she scolded me. "You are not a musician. Music is no good. It is like art. An artist is no good until he is dead. After he dies, then people pay $500 for his work. While he is alive, he is no good. It is the same with music."

She sat down in a wicker chair, by the bench, as she continued. "Listen to us. We are Chinese. We are old. We know what you can't know yet. Years ago, our daughter said she wanted to be a big musician. We sent her to the finest music school in New York. She taught in college. She conducted orchestras. Still, she is not a musician. They will not listen. She is not a musician until she dies".

Totally disarmed, I said nothing as she continued, "Listen to me. Don't tell people that you are a musician; they will not listen to you. Tell them you are an electrician or doctor or student. These are people of respect. There is no respect for music. Tell people anything but musician; they will believe you and show respect".

The tears continued as did her lecture, "You listen. Someday you will remember what the Chinese lady has said to you. Then you will know. Music is bad. I know", Her voice was almost pleading with me.

It didn't look like she was willing to rent to me, so thinking fast, I assured her that I was already a *successful* musician, and that Johnny Cash was going to record one of my songs. That didn't work; she didn't buy my lie for even a second. She immediately countered, "then why isn't Mister Johnny Cash getting you an apartment? You are not a musician until you are dead."

Now fully in defense mode, I lied further and assured her that my "rich" father in North Carolina was sending me money regularly. It was a double-lie; he wasn't rich, and he sure-as-hell wasn't going to send money.

Still clearly not believing me, she demanded to know if his money was how I was currently living and where I was staying now. I told her that I had been staying at the Holiday Inn on West End Avenue; and as "proof", I showed her a room key (that I had forgotten to turn in when I checked

THE LEGEND DIES ON — GARY GREEN

out the month before and where it had been tucked into this cleanest pair of dirty jeans that I had switched to before coming to see her).

That seemed to do the trick; and based on seeing the hotel key, she agreed to show me the apartment. I guess she thought that if he was paying costly hotel bills then he would probably pay her meager rent too.

She and her husband got into their car, and I followed them toward the section of Nashville where the apartment was located. After a couple of miles, as they continued driving straight, I abruptly and without a signal turned right and sped away toward Music Row; the opposite direction from where she was leading me.

For some reason that I didn't understand, I was afraid of her and her words. I didn't want to disappoint her, and I didn't want to keep lying to her. I decided to go back to camping rather than have to see any more of her tears. Living in the woods seemed an easier choice than facing her disappointment and by extension, the surrogated disappointment of my parents back in North Carolina.

Months earlier, when I had told Daddy that I wanted to go back to Nashville, he had asked "why won't you listen to me? Music is bad for you. How will you pay the rent and buy groceries? You are not Perry Como. Nobody wants to hear you sing. You can't even carry a tune".

Trying to defend myself, I had argued, "Neither can Johnny Cash or Bob Dylan and..."

He cut me off, "Johnny Cash is a bum. You aren't a bum. But you will turn into one if you try to be like Johnny Cash", He shook his head and repeated loudly and angrier, *"Johnny Cash is a bum!"*

I'm sure he thought his words fell on deaf or at least defiant ears, but in reality, I loved his line about Cash. I coopted it into the chorus of a song that I wrote shortly after that: *"Love is a bummer; Life is a bummer; and Johnny Cash is a bum..."*

We had fought constantly about my choice to follow music and in part that is why I had decided to leave home in the middle of the night and with no "goodbye". I had, though, stayed in touch by collect-calls home every week and eventually daily. I was certain that I would "make it big" in Nashville and buy them a big white mansion, just like Elvis had bought for his mother with *Graceland* in Memphis.

Hearing the Asian landlady's scolding words just hit too close to home and her tears were more than I wanted to deal with. Nonetheless, after another month or longer sleeping in my car in the woods, I was ready to reconsider the apartment hunting issue... but there was no way I could again face the kindly old Asian couple.

Plus, there was a new problem: my twenty dollars had dwindled to eleven dollars since I had no credit card for gasoline, and I also had been buying bread.

THE POET LAUREATE SOUL OF FOLKIE ROCK & ROLL

Between the hunger (unquenched by my every-other-day camp-fire meals), the lack of a bathroom, and the discomfort of sleeping in the car, I decided to take a few musical instruments to a pawn shop and get cash for an apartment. The pawnbroker offered me only $66, and I desperately accepted it for a Gibson LG-0 concert-size guitar and a silver-coated Selmer flute... neither of which would I ever get out of hock and consequently never see again.

In the newspaper ads, I found an apartment for $25-a-week plus a $15-deposit. This landlord didn't care what I did for a living as long as I could pay the rent every week. The rent also included electricity, water, a refrigerator, and a couch. Electricity! I could plug in my tape machine and record new songs for demo tapes! Making it even better, it was located at 2120 Belmont Boulevard —less than a mile walk to the heart of Music Row!

Thrilled, I moved into the third-floor Apartment A-8, and that very morning, as soon as I was alone, I took a long-long overdue shower. No soap. No shampoo. No washcloth. No towel. BUT it was a shower! Soaking wet, I laid down on top of my sleeping bag on the floor; at last, in my own real apartment![72]

I was jostled back to reality a little before ten o'clock that night by a roach crawling across my face. I flung it to the floor and walked into the back room to get dressed. It was mid-summer, and even late at night it must have been ninety-eight unairconditioned-degrees. With clothes on, it would feel even hotter.

I fumbled through the cardboard box where I stored my clothes to find one of my least-smelly shirts (since none had been washed in months). I put on my boots, my hat, and strapped my bullwhip to my side.

Several more cockroaches scurried from under my box, and I snapped them to their deaths with sharp cracks of my whip. I didn't care; it was a real apartment; it was indoors. I considered myself lucky; I was healthy (albeit starving), I had a roof over my head, and I had a plan. Pollyannaishly, I figured *that* made me much more fortunate than many homeless, aimless, songwriter-hopefuls wandering the streets in Nashville.

Dressed, I walked to the window, pulled back the newspapers which the last tenant had used for curtains, and looked out onto the dark street. As I turned back toward the room, another roach crawled across the toe of my boot. I supposed it was the seventy-fifth or sixth that I had seen since moving into the apartment a few hours earlier.

---

[72] As of this writing, the "historic" Albemarle Apartments building is still there; but apparently has different ownership and has been totally gutted and remodeled. Judging from on-line photos, the apartments look really nice.

THE LEGEND DIES ON — GARY GREEN

Still, it was an indoor apartment and that was better than outdoor living with who-knows-what wild animals and the ability of any stranger to wander up to my campsite.

In the bathroom, I flushed the toilet and watched the water overflow to flood the room, into the living room and roll down the sloped floor toward the kitchen where it seeped down the plywood wall and poured to the outside of the building.

Shaking my head, I kicked a spool of recording tape toward the kitchen just for the amusement of watching it roll downhill into the slime of the next room. I suspected that once-upon-a-time there had been support beams underneath the floor; but they had long-ago collapsed and allowed the plywood/linoleum floor to slant sharply at about a 15-degree incline.

The previous tenant had left a few things in the refrigerator, including a can of Budweiser and a bag of hard pretzels. The landlord had already told me that it would be best to keep all food in the refrigerator rather than in the pantry, so the roaches and rats couldn't get to it. That sage advice, apparently, wasn't foolproof because somehow the little bugs had found an entrance to the refrigerator and had infested the pretzels (though I saw no indication that the rats, too, had found a way into it). It didn't really matter, though, I had no food to store.

As I walked into the kitchen, I spotted the long grey tail of one of those rats slip around the corner and through a hole in the wall. Back in the living/sleeping room, I saw another scurry of tails fly through the holes in walls there, apparently startled by the sound of my boots on the floor.

I plopped down on to the filthy couch that had come "furnished" with the apartment; careful to avoid jabbing myself on one of the exposed protruding springs. That sent another rush of roaches running from the cushions.

I decided I was going to need some household furnishings and insecticides, but it was too late at night to go shopping. Those moneyless adventures would have to wait until tomorrow.

Meanwhile, I was starving and had a little bit of money left; so, I decided to splurge on some "silver-dollar pancakes" late at night in a clean restaurant (or at least more sanitary than my new digs).

During my first month in Nashville, I had eaten a lot of meals at Gulf-credit-card supported restaurants. One of those restaurants was an all-night pancake joint located on West End Avenue, just off of Music Row and adjacent to the Holiday Inn. They made a great 24-hour-a-day breakfast platter that included six tiny pancakes about the size of the new Eisenhower silver dollars, one egg any style, two pieces of bacon or one piece of sausage, and grits (it was the South, so yes, grits). They called that dish their "Silver Dollar Special". I wasn't a vegetarian yet, so it was one of my favorites.

THE POET LAUREATE SOUL OF FOLKIE ROCK & ROLL

Since living in the woods, I had not been able to afford to go back there. In fact, other than my campfire specials, I had not had a hot meal since the Gulf card expired. So, on this night, I decided to splurge with the little bit of the cash I had left. Plus, as an added inducement, the all-night restaurant was a very short walk from my new apartment.

It was about a quarter-until-eleven when I got to the restaurant. Though it was open, the little diner was almost empty. I sat down in an open booth across from the only other patrons at that hour; two rough-looking guys who eyed me suspiciously as I walked in. I had never eaten there late at night, so as far as I knew those two derelicts could have been regulars.

In those days, there were two types of guys that hung out as part of the Nashville music scene. There were throwbacks to "old Nashville" who looked like they should have been rock and rollers in the 1950's; nicely dressed, shiny greased-back hair, and a slightly dangerous look in their eyes. If they wore jeans (most wore dress pants instead) the jeans were creased from having been ironed along with their starched shirts. As likely as not, they would say a blessing over their food before eating. Their drink of choice was almost any alcohol (but they avoided illegal drugs).

The other type was a cadre of near-hippies with long hair often in need of shampoo, faded wrinkled jeans, tee-shirts, or western-snap shirts, and with a stench of smoked marijuana streaming from their clothes, hair, and pores; and they generally were badly in need of a bath.

The two guys in the adjacent booth were of the latter ilk, as, I suppose I came closest to fitting, at least visually. They were engrossed in some deep conversation about nothing and didn't really acknowledge my presence except to look at me as I sat down; presumably acknowledging one of their brethren.

They definitely were high; I could smell that cannabis remnants. I guessed they were probably 20 to 25 years older than me; though age is hard to pinpoint when people have lived hard (or at least druggie) lives.

I ordered a Silver Dollar Special and when the waitress asked me what I wanted to drink, I ordered a large cold glass of milk.

That drew a rude guffaw from one of the two guys. Rather than just laugh, he decided it was necessary to punch his buddy in the arm and loudly ask me, "did you just order a glass of MILK?"

I took a deep breath and answered him, "Yeah, I did. You gotta problem with that?" I knew it was a confrontational answer, but I was tired and hungry and didn't really care. And, what-the-hell, I am Southern.

As he stood up to further provoke me, his boothmate touched his arm and said, "Come on Capt' leave the kid alone".

"Capt" answered, "I'm just going to show him my sticker". As he spoke, he drew a Bowie knife with about a seven- or eight-inch blade. It

THE LEGEND DIES ON — GARY GREEN

was scary; and would have been scarier if he had been sober and not weaving a little when he stood.

I was young, generally aggressive, and had the infamous too-quick-to-react Southern temper. Rather than brush it off, I just had to answer his challenge. *"I sure hope that thing isn't too sharp; I wouldn't want you to get cut when somebody shoves it up your ass"*.

His partner laughed out loud and then pleaded with him, "Capt, sit down". But rather than heed, he walked toward my booth, almost laughing rather than threatening. He stood in front of me, and said, or slurred, *"I'll tell you what: Let's me and you go outside and if you can take me, I'll buy your milk and one for myself. But if you can't, I won't cut you too bad, and you'll buy supper for us"*.

His partner now addressed me, "don't do it; he's the world knife-throwing champion". I didn't heed the advice.

We walked out to the sidewalk, and he began performing juggler's tricks, tossing the big knife from hand to hand. It was comical and clear to me that there was no real threat, but some bullshit macho positioning. It was equally clear that both he and his companion definitely were high as kites.

I watched the super-skinny, goofy-looking wanna-be cowboy juggling for a couple of minutes, then untied my bullwhip, cracked it behind me to get his attention, then slung it to wrap tightly around the big blade. As I jerked the whip back toward me, it pulled the knife from his hand and sent it spiraling into the grass near my side of the walkway.

His stunned silence and my fear were only broken when his friend spoke, "come on, Capt, you've been needing a glass of milk lately". We walked back insider just as the waitress brought my meal to the booth.

Inside the restaurant, everything changed between the three of us. It was as if we were all old friends. Capt was laughing hard, as was his friend, and eventually I joined in.

We talked, we laughed, we complained about the attitudes of publishers and record executives on Music Row and the failure of radio stations to play quality music not on corporate-approved playlists. We made fun of the greasers and discussed the role of marijuana in the creative process.

About 15 minutes before midnight the waitress interrupted us, saying, "Captain, you've got to go", He looked at his watched, moaned, "oh shit" and jumped up to leave. He looked back at the waitress and said, "put his milk and his whole damn meal on my tab", Then he was gone.

I turned to his left-behind comrade and asked, "does he turn back into a pumpkin at midnight?" His friend answered, "Damn hoss; he's Captain Midnight. He's got to be on from midnight till seven".

Whoa! Every kid in Middle Tennessee knew the legendary *Captain Midnight*: the most famous DJ in the state!

THE POET LAUREATE SOUL OF FOLKIE ROCK & ROLL

When I was in school at Two Rivers, there were three dominant AM radio stations in Nashville (and many other less dominant ones). WSM was the 50,000-watt clear channel station that owned The Grand Ole Opry and served as the mother church of country music as well as the go-to source for news and sports. For the younger set, there were two competing rock stations: WMAK and WKDA.

The disc jockeys at the ratings-dominant WKDA were collectively known as "the good guys" and were local celebrities themselves. One of the good guys, Roger Schutt, was known statewide as sort of the regional equivalent of *Wolfman Jack, Johnny Holliday, Murray the K,* and the like. Schutt was the coolest-of-the-cool and called himself *Captain Midnight*.

He had been a childhood radio hero of mine; he also was the stoned knife-fighter at the Pancake House who bought my milk and Silver Dollar Special that night and on many other nights to come. His companion, I learned later, was Tompall Glaser of the Glaser Brothers; a moderately successful country-folk group in the 1960's.

That night, they were just a couple of stoned fellow Nashville iconoclasts struggling, like me, against the music business establishment.

I had no clue —nor would I until years later— that they were in the midst of working with another Music Row rebel named Waylon Jennings *(who would eventually become part of our regular pancake group)* producing the seminal record of what would become the "Outlaw Music" genre of country rock[73].

I walked back to my genuine-indoor-real apartment, to spend the rest of my night with the roaches and rats. Early the next morning, I would go "shopping" as it were. By mid-morning I was awake and ready to furnish my apartment.

Motels, and especially hotels, were great for all sorts of survival techniques other than my using their pools as a bathtub when I lived in the woods. The housekeeping carts, which provided my towel for my little charades there, were an excellent source of "free" mini-bottles of shampoo, bars of soap, toilet paper, and Kleenexes, as well as towels and wash clothes (sheets too, if I needed them).

Fine hotels, rather than motels, were even better. Those housekeeping carts often had glasses, toothpaste, mouthwash, razor blades (disposal

---

[73] I love the Wikipedia entry describing the genre: "The music has its roots in earlier sub-genres like Western, honky-tonk, rockabilly, and progressive country, and is characterized by a blend of rock and folk rhythms, country instrumentation and introspective lyrics. The movement began as a reaction to the slick production and limiting structures of the Nashville sound developed by record producers like Chet Atkins".

THE LEGEND DIES ON — GARY GREEN

razors were not widely available yet), replacement light bulbs, and an entire bevy of other household necessities, including cleaning products.

When my family first moved to Nashville in 1966, we had stayed in the historic *Andrew Jackson Hotel* for a few weeks, and I had come to know well the behind-the-scenes life inside that grand old-style classic inn. In addition to the cache of household products, such nicer hotels would routinely host meetings or small conventions which would be catered with buffet-style meals or at least coffee breaks and happy hours. Those buffets usually were set up in a separate room from the actual meetings, and during breaks the attendees would move to the lounge-style food set up. (The Andrew Jackson had been the location of those DJ conventions that I crashed as a kid.)

More often than not, after setting up the small buffets the staff would lock the doors to that room rather than wait there until the break. They would return a few minutes before the break to unlock and prepare the line.

When I was in the early days of my science-fair years, I had signed-up for a mail order locksmithing course. Besides teaching students to make keys (for which a key-cutting machine and blanks were included), the course also taught students how to open locks if keys had been lost (basically, *Lockpicking-101*). By the time I was 13 or 14 years old, I was a certified locksmith and quite skilled at opening most tumbler-based locks, including deadbolts.

The uncovered latches of the buffet-room doors were child's play (literally). Hence, a-keep-from-starving buffet before attendees arrived was always a possibility, providing that I could dress in such a manner not to raise the eyebrows of hotel detectives (fortunately, there were no security cameras in those days).

Though it would not stock my (and my roach-roommates') refrigerator, hotels also could be a source for a quick snack while I was out "shopping". Soda vending machines in those days often had a long glass door behind which the customer would see the drink bottles and grasp-and-pull the bottle after depositing the requisite coins in the machine. However, for a broke hippie-songwriter, it was possible to open the glass door, survey the choice of beverages, and without inserting coins, simply use a bottle-opener to pop the top of the bottle and insert a straw to slurp out the contents. Hungry people often will go to great extremes.

The hunger and the associated poverty, enhanced by either my stubborn refusal to get a job or by my passionate idealism about "making it" overnight in the country music world, justified for me all sorts of absurd petty-crime nonsense.

My new apartment did not include free trash pickup. Tenants were required to pay a fee to a pick-up service to haul away garbage and trash. I had no money for that; but I did have a solution to keep the refuge from piling up in the apartment and at the same time amuse me.

At the public library I would read the latest issues of a number of magazines; they often were littered with BRE[74]-prepaid-postcards (or envelopes) to order subscriptions or any number of products and services. My favorite was the prepaid mailer to the U.S. Army to order information about enlisting.

Every few days, I would collect all of my garbage into a cardboard box (which I would get free from the dumpsters behind grocery stores). I would then seal the box, tape a prepaid postcard or envelope to it and drop it off at the post office. Yes, it would have been just as easy to toss the trash into the dumpsters where I nabbed the empty boxes; but it would not have been as much anti-establishment fun.

The agreement that businesses had with the Post Office to allow the prepaid mailers required the businesses to pay the postage for anything that was mailed using the reply card; and no return address was required. So, it gave me a special smile to weekly mail 15 pounds or so of garbage to the U.S. Army recruiters or to any number of large corporations that solicited business with prepaid mailers.

The most serious (and complex) of my petty crimes during my self-alienated poverty was what was then called "phone phreaking". Before the popular availability of digital telecommunications, long distance phone calls were per-minute expensive and made on analog phone lines by "dialing" a phone number. The dialing was actually a standardized series of electronic pulses that would interrupt the otherwise-constant "dial-tone" of a line. After a number was dialed, the telephone company's analog switches would then be triggered by additional electronic pulses and interrupts that would indicate the billing route of the call: operator-assisted, direct-dial billing, or third-party billing.

The handheld part of a pay telephone had a mouthpiece that could be unscrewed exposing the carbon microphone so repair technicians could easily replace it. When the microphone was re-moved, it exposed two direct-current electric poles.

Using a short strand of shielded copper wire, a skilled thief could touch both polls briefly and simultaneously in sequences and durations that would tell the analog switch how to bill the call. Once the instructions had been received the call would be placed and the microphone could be re-inserted into its cradle.

---

[74] Business Reply Envelopes

THE LEGEND DIES ON — GARY GREEN

I had learned the different pulse patterns when I was about 10 or 11 years old and since that time, I had the ability to make free calls from a pay phone to anywhere in the country without being charged. It was a fun science experiment that I rarely used; but in my new life of self-imposed poverty, it was a useful (if not necessary) skill.

My "outlaw" escapades during this time were merely my way of continuing a near-middle-class lifestyle without working for a living. I justified it as a general antiestablishment zeitgeist and my rebellious part of it. In reality, though, it was neither organized nor particularly profitable; it was merely a survival technique. Clearly, it was not a lifestyle that could sustain me nor that I could sustain.

I was occasionally able to pick up a little bar gig here and there; but the pay for those was essentially non-existent. Some "let me play" for "the exposure in Nashville", others paid a percentage of the amount of beer sold during the gig. I never did get a gig that actually paid out-and-out for a performance; but in fairness, the competition were some fine seasoned Nashville musicians, and I was just a hillbilly hippie with a rhythm issue.

Whenever I had a little extra cash, I would go back to eat at the Pancake House late at night. After selling more instruments and equipment, I was able to eat there a couple of times a week until I left Nashville.

Some nights, the Captain, Tompall, Waylon, and a handful of their other cohorts would be there; sometimes not. When they were, I sat with them, talked with them, laughed with them, and mostly listened to them, since they were all at least a couple of decades older than me and had been in Nashville a lot longer than I had. They also would pay for my meals.

I was much more thrilled at actually meeting and hanging out with Captain Midnight than I was at knowing Waylon Jennings at that time. I knew of Jennings as one of those lard-in-the-hair country singers who a few years earlier had a hit called *The Only Daddy That Will Walk The Line*. I always thought it was a cheap copycat way to exploit Cash's *I Walk The Line*. I didn't know that he and Johnny Cash had been roommates in a cheap apartment in Madison Tennessee.

In fact, long before I met him, Waylon was the example I often used to make fun of the worst things about commercial country music; he had the perfect name and perfect hair to be made fun of by a hippie rocker, despite his having an incredible voice. Moreover, his music was so countrypolitan-establishment that it practically made fun of itself. He had a recording of *House of the Rising Sun* that I thought was one of the worst records I'd ever heard.

By the time I was semi-regularly eating pancakes with him and the others, he had abandoned the greased-back hair in favor of longer (albeit a little nasty-looking) locks and he had gained about 50 pounds to strain the shirt buttons across his stomach. Unbeknownst to me, he had also declared war on Music Row and that God-awful canned sound.

Like the rest of the late-night pancakes troupe, Waylon came with a stench of tobacco and marijuana, seemed like he was always high, and usually needing to have his clothes washed as well as needing a good bath. But he, apparently, was Captain Midnight's best friend, so that made him okay in my book.

As I would drink my milk, we all often talked about music, writing, phrasing, what moved people and what was lame. Waylon loved lyrics; especially ones that had multiple meanings. Late one night we all pondered Jimmy Webb's lyrics of *MacArthur Park*, recorded by Irish actor Richard Harris. We concluded that it most likely was the impressions from an acid trip; either that or something that was just too deep for mere mortals like us to understand.

I vividly remember Waylon noting, "Don't you love it when a song does that? You have no fucking idea what it is about, but you know there is something there. You go home thinking about it and can't get it out of your head."

After that ponderance, he looked at me and said, "write a song like that, hoss". First, Waylon called everybody "hoss" no matter how casually he knew them. Secondly, I hadn't mentioned yet —at least to him— that I was a songwriter, so Waylon's advice was most-likely just generic rambling rather than actual guidance to a developing young writer.

In other conversations, they all talked about who on Music Row "had their head up their ass" and who knew a good song when they heard it. I listened, took mental notes, and learned. Listening, sponging, observing, studying, talking, and having many silver dollar pancake nights with some of the original "Outlaws", I have always —even then, before it had a name— thought it was an attitude, not a sound.

At the time, I may have been too young and naïve; but I didn't even think about what was going on as a commercial endeavor. In my mind it was about *frame-of-mind* and willingness to break rules[75].

---

[75] It has never been clear to me who actually coined the term "Outlaw" for the genre of country music that these guys were creating in those days.
Some said that it was a P.R. term created by Tompall's office manager-publicist-manager, Hazel Smith. She seemed to be a nice-enough lady, but I only met her once or maybe twice; so, I didn't really know her (nor the incredible influence she ultimately had on the genre). Some claimed it was a country disc jockey named Ron Roach at WCSE radio in Asheboro North Carolina, working with Ms. Smith after he played nothing but the genre
continued at bottom of next page

THE LEGEND DIES ON — GARY GREEN

Commercial value was the last thing I would have considered. By that time, they all knew that I was a songwriter, but it never occurred to me to pitch to them, and they never asked. I think they appreciated that from me; I wasn't selling anything, just hanging out and drinking milk. It was attitude. Come to think of it, I never asked what they were working on either; we just hung out and talked shit —occasionally about music.

In the decades since, I've often wondered what might have come from those friendships if I had not decided to leave Nashville (again) that summer. Most likely my songs wouldn't be part of the Smithsonian's collection. I probably wouldn't have moved deeply into the folk world. I definitely would've never traded political poetry with Túpac.

At the same time, if I had stayed, it is unlikely that would have been necessarily a positive thing. It's unlikely my music would have developed alongside theirs; I was vastly younger and had entirely different motivations and interests. Though, I would have held onto some great friendships.

On the other hand, it was those very friendships that helped shape me into the character that "Nashville" would chase out of town… so there was *that*.

---

for a week and decided to label it. I should have tracked him down and asked him about it a few years later when I was an editor of the newspaper in Asheboro that was owned by the WCSE owner, but I never did.

Still others supposed that it came from a music magazine writer who turned out an article about the creative conflicts between formulaic orchestra-enhanced music versus a grittier garage-band sound.

I've heard some people say the term came from songwriter Lee Clayton's tune Ladies Love Outlaws, which actually mentions Waylon in its lyrics.

There was another school claiming that RCA Records producer Jerry Bradley created the term to promote a compilation album he created of Waylon, Tompall, Willie Nelson, and Jesse Coulter (Waylon's wife). I am pretty sure that the term was being tossed around before the 1976 release of that record.

If the etymology of the term was convoluted, a definition was even more complicated. The record labels posited it as a performance style punctuated by a five-piece band. A number of artists defined it as a type of song; certain kinds of lyrics interwoven with a type of music.

In the 21st century, it has been rolled into a genre called Americana; the Americana Music Association defines that genre as "contemporary music that incorporates elements of various American roots music styles, including country, roots-rock, folk, bluegrass, R&B and blues, resulting in a distinctive roots-oriented sound that lives in a world apart from the pure forms of the genres upon which it may draw".

Waylon told me, years later, that the "outlaw" term "was all a load of bullshit. People trying to sell."

Opus Seven:
Kristofferson & Iconoclasts Or A Big "F-You" From Nashville

> *For the ones who you couldn't trick*
> *You laid a special plan:*
> *You called them outcasts and criminals.*
> *And banished them from your land.*
> — *Hymn*, by Gary Green, as recorded on Folkways Records album FH5353, *Allegory*

Singers, songwriters, and wanna-bees like me were welcomed, *and encouraged,* to walk in the front door and pitch songs at any of the dozens of companies along Music Row. There were no security guards, and only rarely receptionists. As likely as not, we could walk in and talk to a well-known artist or publisher or producer without any gate-keepers blocking access.

Rather than merely drop off a tape, chances were that someone would take the tape and ask questions or make comments with me sitting in the office or studio with them while they listened. Sometimes the decision-maker preferred live performances over tape and they more-than welcomed opening a guitar case and singing my latest song. It was a down-home folksy charm that made Music Row something really different from any other music center in the country.

Even a "quick" pitch visit sometimes could take a couple of hours, depending on how engaged the listener might be and whether the visit was tape-playing or a live impromptu concert. Weirdly (at least to me), there wasn't necessarily a correlation between the length of a pitch meeting and the likelihood of financial success; the amount of time was more related to how much fun or how interesting it was for the listening executive.

Almost anybody was welcome to drop in anytime, day or night, as long as a light was on or as long as a recording session wasn't underway (and in some, even sessions were sort-of open). In many studios, no one was there until after seven or eight o'clock at night, anyway. That didn't mean people didn't take the work seriously; it simply meant that it was an informal atmosphere —even if they hated your songs, they might dig the picking and singing in their offices[76].

It was no wonder that we were called the *Country Music Family*. But like all families, we were plagued with the nutty uncle, the forgetful

---

[76] This wasn't the case with the handful of large corporate offices along Music Row; they were caught-up in formalities, gatekeepers, security guards and other haughty trappings of self-importance in an otherwise irrelevant atmosphere.

THE LEGEND DIES ON — GARY GREEN

grandfather, the philandering brother-in-law, the alcoholic cousin, the golden child, the bumbling screw-up, the goofy dad, the flirty sister, the martyred long-suffering mom, the angst-suffering rebel, the hopelessly goth, the zealot, and Thanksgiving Dinner fights.

No shit, every one of those roles was assignable to specific stalwarts of Nashville music at that time; some good, some bad, some just ... weird. Come to think of it, I could probably write an interesting book (or at least an article) assigning specific names to those roles and then citing the specific behaviors that earned those roles[77].

When I would visit a company on Music Row, I never knew if I was going to be amongst hippies or greasers; and consequently, I didn't know which songs to pitch until I was inside. *(That may have been part of my later problems with Nashville; my songs weren't necessarily universal, and I had to focus on "the market" rather than the material.)*

The differences were a lot more than hair style, clothing, and hygiene. The disagreements weren't political; we had right wingers, left wingers, anarchists, and the decisively apolitical in our "country music family". It wasn't even a generational thing either; both camps had young and old adherents. While the family differences definitely were distinct, they weren't a new byproduct of the rebellious 1960's either. Nor were the differences something that would end with the birth of the Outlaw movement.

As far back as 1940, Pee Wee King (who wrote *The Tennessee Waltz*, the official Tennessee State Song) was told that his band's electric guitar and drums would not be allowed to play at *The Grand Ole Opry*. Loretta Lynn was barred from singing one of her biggest hits because it encouraged birth control. Buck Owens, star of the network TV series Hee-Haw, was banned from The Opry for what they termed as "creative differences" over the definition country music. Even Elvis had been rejected; after his one Opry appearance, managers there told him to forget about music and go back to driving a truck.

Despite the clear African-American roots of much of the music (even the iconic banjo was born of African antecedents), there was no Black performer invited to join The Opry until the 1990's and it was 2012 before a second African American member was invited to join.

---

[77] Old-time Nashvillians from those days already know exactly who fit into which of those roles; and here I have not even scratched the surface of the eccentric behaviors and dramas within our country music family. And I am not even talking about ridiculous-looking male wigs, over-the-top promiscuity, or turf-protecting maneuvering. Come to think of it, we had some real assholes in the mix. If you're a writer wanting to go down that road, reach out to me for some background color; or better yet to my dear friend Tim Ghianni, author and former entertainment editor at The Nashville Tennessean.

THE POET LAUREATE SOUL OF FOLKIE ROCK & ROLL

So yeah, the "family" differences had a very real impact on the business and on the music itself; what made it to records or to stages was a function of which controlling wind was blowing on any given day.[78]

In the summer of 1972 when my boots were getting dusty from walking the sidewalks of those two celebrated streets of music companies, the greasers and hippies were the primary opposing forces on Music Row; and it was not a friendly competition. In fact, somedays it was out-and-out nasty at worst and at best just spirit-breaking discouraging. It also made it damned difficult for a young man who didn't want to choose sides; it was like a kid having to choose which parent to live with after a divorce.

One day on my door-knocking rounds, I walked into a publishing company where the only person there was a 45-year-old slicked-back songwriter named *Cecil A. Null*. He had written the country classic, *I Forgot More Than You'll Ever Know About Her* that over the years was recorded by *Sonny James, Jeanne Pruett, Johnny Cash, Jerry Lee Lewis, Patti Page, Kitty Wells, Jimmie Rodgers, Roy Drusky, Del Reeves, The Statler Brothers, Slim Whitman, Wanda Jackson, Patty Loveless, Dolly Parton, Loretta Lynn, Tammy Wynette Elvis Costello, Tom Petty,* and even *Bob Dylan*. So, he definitely had some actual credibility.

---

[78] Even the most divisive conflicts had followers on both sides; as illustrated in the inglorious split up of the legendary bluegrass group, *Flatt & Scruggs*. That epochal tale, at least as told by bluegrass great *Sonny Osborne*, was that Earl Scruggs' sons had become respected musicians independently of the family name, establishing themselves in progressive country rock genre. It was the world of *The Byrds, the Eagles, The Nitty Gritty Dirt Band, Buffalo Springfield, The Flying Burrito Brothers, The New Riders of the Purple Sage, The Stone Canyon Band,* and even *The Grateful Dead*. It was also the genre that was going to give the world the transformed versions of Waylon Jennings, Willie Nelson, and the genre of Outlaw Music. Earl Scruggs, arguably the greatest banjo player that ever lived, wanted to play with his sons... and to crowds of eight-to-ten-thousand people. His wife, *Louise Scruggs*, was a groundbreaking legend as one of the first women to manage a big-name artist. She also was known to be a ruthless negotiator. She positioned her sons and especially her husband into superstar and then the icon status that he became. She moved Earl Scruggs from the state fair and school auditorium circuit to filling stadiums. Lester Flatt, according to Osborne, was content playing for smaller crowds of a couple of hundred people who just wanted to hear unaltered mountain bluegrass. That vision wasn't copacetic with Earl's playing to a football stadium filled with hippies. I had heard at The Opry that Flatt had refused to play on stage with any male who had long hair over his ears or collar. I suspected that was not true, judging by the length of 14-year-old Marty Stuart's hair when he was in Lester's band during that era. Moreover, Lester and his new band played with *Kool and The Gang*, as well as with the *Eagles*. So, whether that version of the rift was true or not, Osborne's story was illustrative of typical philosophical differences that surfaced in our "family".

THE LEGEND DIES ON — GARY GREEN

He invited me into the studio with him, put on my tape, and started listening. After the first verse of the first song, he said, "That sounds like Kris Kristofferson and some of those California hippies. It's not a Nashville song and we have too-much hippie stuff here already. Do you have other songs on here?"

Answering himself, he sped the tape fast-forward to my next song. He only listened to about half of one verse before stopping it and saying, "That sounds like Bob Dylan and that New York bunch; that won't work in Nashville either". He listened to a third song and stopped it early too, less than 30 seconds into it. He looked at me for a minute —longer than he had listened to any of my songs— as if he was sizing me up for something profound. After a couple of very awkward moments of silence, he finally spoke again.

"You have some good writing here and you're a pretty good guitar man; it's just not in the right direction. You need a Nashville hook to your songs. I have a new one called *Don't Blow Smoke In A Kangaroo's Face To Get Your Kicks.* You need to write like that",

While I was trying to figure out if he was serious or joking, he kept talking, "I think you can do that. I like your turn-of-a-phrase. I can tell that you are from good-Southern stock. You can do this. Let me ask you this, how do you plan to fulfill your military obligation?"

I was dumbfounded. Between that idiotically comical song title and his asking me about military service during the height of the Vietnam War, I didn't know what to say. It was hilarious and infuriating at the same time. (Besides, the apparently-unwelcomed Kristofferson had taught at West Point; so, Cecil didn't really care about military service to condemn som.)

I wanted to say, *"what the hell does that have to do with the price of cotton?"* [79]; but I didn't. Instead, I meekly answered, "well my draft lottery number was really high, so I didn't get the call".

He still wouldn't let it pass. *"You don't need to be drafted to serve. I suggest you enlist in the army. Let them make a man of you. Then come back here to Nashville. We can work together then. I think you could make it."*

Rather than argue, I decided just to thank him and leave (as if there were any conditions under which I would have wanted to work with him). I didn't know if he was encouraging me or trying to discourage me. Looking back on it, he probably was offering me a rare opportunity and trying to be nice. Absurd or surreal as the whole situation sounded, it was not at

---

[79] That was a Southern colloquialism about irrelevant conversations, that probably came from the French, *"Quel est le rapport avec la choucroute?",* which translates to "What does it have to do with the sauerkraut?"

THE POET LAUREATE SOUL OF FOLKIE ROCK & ROLL

all outrageous in the context of Music Row. Nashville had crazies on all sides; and every song-pitch encounter was its own little adventure.

On another day, I walked into an old house that was the head-quarters for *Jerry Reed* and his publisher; and both were there. Reed, often remembered for his co-starring role with Burt Reynolds in the *Smokey and the Bandit* movies, was a well-established songwriter (he had written Elvis' *Guitar Man*), was a fine performer himself with hit records, and was a true virtuoso guitarist.

After hearing the first song on my tape, they wanted to know if I had something up-tempo. On the tape I did not, so, picking up my twelve-string Fender acoustic I did my song *Morgo The Mighty Meteor*, a semi-nonsensical piece that I sort-of stole from a Monty Python skit. It was the song that contained the lyrics expanded from my father's lecture, *"Love is a bummer, life is a bummer, and Johnny Cash is a bum"*.

They couldn't stop laughing; Jerry said I was on the road to becoming the funniest writer to hit Nashville since Roger Miller or Ray Stevens.[80] I took that as a high compliment, though I had not intended to write a comedy or novelty song. I asked if they would be interested in publishing it or recording it.

The manager answered, "I would love for Jerry to record that, but there is just no-way-in-hell that we could do that. Johnny Cash just agreed to record Jerry's song and if we came out with that it would kill the deal and kill Jerry here in Nashville" [81]. (That was a red-flag to me about the damned family-fight nature of Music Row.)

Apparently seeing the disappointment on my face, Jerry Reed tried to offset the blow and spoke up, "There's nothing wrong with the way you just did it for us, and you got in some good licks on that 12-axe. You ought to take it out to California and play it for some of the clubs out there. You've got something, son, but this town ain't ready for it".

Once again, I didn't know whether to be disappointed or flattered; but at-the-end-of-the-day, nobody was publishing me or writing me a check.

---

[80] Harold Ray Ragsdale (known professionally as Ray Stevens) wrote and performed *Gitarzan, Harry The Harry Ape, Ahab the A-rab, The Streak,* and a handful of other novelty songs in the 1960's and 70's. And Roger Miller, of course, was... Roger Miller.

[81] Reed wrote A Thing Called Love that was a hit record for Cash, Jimmy Dean, Elvis, Glen Campbell, Dave Dudley, and others. At that time, I was not aware of Cash's insider-well-known highly-competitive insecurities

I had heard, years later, that while on "The Highway Men" tour he often measured the number of steps from wall-to-wall in his, Willie Nelson's, Waylon' and Kristofferson's dressing rooms to make certain no one had a larger room than his.

THE LEGEND DIES ON — GARY GREEN

That is how all of my door-knocking went. I got responses at every extreme of interest and no-interest, but without offers of contracts or money.

Based on the Jerry Reed meeting, I took that song to the aforementioned Ray Stevens. He listened to the entirety of the first song on my tape and then asked, "Is *that* on purpose?"

Not understanding his question, I asked him what he meant. Unfortunately, he answered me, "That's not music. There is no tempo. It starts, stops, changes. If you were trying to be funny, it doesn't work".

Imagine my misery hearing that... given my rhythm issues anyway. I had no response other than devastated disappointment.

The highest plateau, contrasting to Steven's stinging, was at *Combine Music*. I had heard that Bob Beckham at Combine Music mentored promising songwriters; he was the publishing partner of Fred Foster's Monument Records. Combine and Monument had their own new bright-green office building and studio at the top of Music Row. It smelled like success and was complete with security guards, receptionists, secretaries, and all sorts of gatekeepers to keep the likes of me out. It definitely was more New York or Hollywood than Nashville.

Rather than deal with that structure, I walked in and brazenly ordered the receptionist, "Tell Bob that I am here", She looked confused, so I pushed further, "Bob Beckham is expecting me: Gary Green", (a pretty ballsy con for an 18-year-old, huh?)

She fell for it and answered, "Oh, sorry. He's at the house". As if I knew where that was, she directed me out of the building and pointed down the street to one of the older wood-frame houses.

I responded, "Sorry. My fault. He told me that. Bye." I walked up to the windowed front door of the designated house expecting that she had called ahead, and I would be met by security; but no one was there. I walked through the house, calling out "Hello? Mr. Beckman?" No answer: so, I kept looking.

One of the back rooms had been converted to a studio and there were two people there; but neither was Bob Beckman. However, one was ... *Kris fucking Kristofferson*! It was THE guy I had come back to Nashville to find. Yikes!

He asked, "Can I help you?"

I quickly answered, expecting to be thrown out on my ass, "I sure hope so. I'm pitching songs".

Kristofferson looked at me for a second as if half-amused and half-trying to decide how to deal with me, and then said, "Well, show us what you've got".

I played the guitar rather than handing him a tape, and to my shock he didn't stop me as I ran through all of the verses of three songs. I'll probably never forget the next few minutes.

THE POET LAUREATE SOUL OF FOLKIE ROCK & ROLL

After the first song, he nodded his head and only said one word, *Righteous*. THAT alone was as good as a record contract to me. Kris Kristofferson was digging my songs!

When I finished the third song and as I was putting away my guitar, he told me, "These are songs that I enjoy hearing, sitting around with friends. This is the stuff legends are made of. You need to go to Greenwich Village or to Santa Monica and record these yourself. You are too political for Nashville; you'll scare the hell out of 'em here." He chuckled after that last statement as if he had someone in mind that needed a good scare.

I started toward the door. He walked with me as I protested that I couldn't record them because I can't sing. He said, "Have you heard Dylan? Have you heard *ME*? I said the same thing. Do it yourself and don't worry, you'll find your *Bobby McGee*; you've got it in you. You are a poet."

When I left the house, I was even more confused. No contract. And it seemed that once again, I was being told to get-the-hell-out of Nashville, this time by a writing hero of mine. About 20 years older than me, Kristofferson seemed more like a peer or at least a well-traveled older brother; and HE was telling me to leave Nashville. *Well damn.*

Poet? What was THAT all about? I was a hillbilly singer, not some high falutin' librettist bard. And political? I had no clue what he was talking about. I didn't have the remotest idea that I had written anything political. Granted, I wasn't writing standard cry-in-your-beer country love songs, and I wasn't writing strictly to fit the three-minute-and-fifteen-second AM-radio format.

I was writing what I felt was right; but I wouldn't call what I wrote "political". I was writing observations of things I saw or learned; but there certainly was no political agenda. I didn't care if the listener was a democrat of republican or communist or whatever.

In fact, usually when asked about politics I would often tell people that Democrats and Republicans were just *"Tweedledum and Tweedledee"*: two identical sides of the same dirty old coin and I really didn't give a damn. So, I just couldn't see "political" in anything I wrote.

Of course, upon reflection more than a half-century later, it is clear that what I was writing in my mindset of counter-culture hippiedom indeed might have been considered political at the time. Indeed, it may have been seen as political hippie-stuff rather than a "Nashville Sound" country song ready for a Nudie Cohn suit and The Opry Stage Band; even if the form of the music that went with it was straight-out-of-Appalachia.

In my hind-sighted defense, it was the restless era of Woodstock Nation, anti-establishment youth rebellion, and COINTELPRO. I wasn't so far out there for the pulse of hippie baby boomers —just for the greased

THE LEGEND DIES ON — GARY GREEN

establishment types that wanted me to *Blow Smoke In A Kangaroo's Face.*

Despite my outrageous (and not very good) lyrical content, the musical form really was Appalachian Mountain hillbilly. The Nashville Establishment just did not want to hear traditional Carter-Family-style music desecrated and blasphemed with outrageous hippie lyrics... or *poetry* as Kristofferson had put it.

Hence the admonitions I was receiving from friend and foe alike to get-the-hell-out-of-Nashville. In that regard, old Cecil Null might not have been real-far off the mark.

After the Kristofferson praise and rejection, I decided to retreat to the company of fellow freaks, misfits, and outcasts in Nashville.

The first stop, of course, was the Pancake House, earlier in the evening than I normally showed up. Captain Midnight was there with two or three friends, but not the full cadre of musical outlaws that I had hoped to see. He introduced me as *"The Milk Man"* and they either knew what he was talking about or just nodded at a typical Captain handle for people; he had nicknames for everybody the same way Waylon called everybody "Hoss".

I ruminated aloud my woes on Music Row, and in classic Captain style, he advised, *"Joke them if they can't take a fuck"*, I just closed my eyes and shook my head, actually appreciating his Dada-like "advice" to my crisis.

In the midst of that wisdom, Tompall and Waylon had wandered in and Tompall chimed in, "I second that motion," though he had no idea what we were talking about.

I thought perhaps I could get actual advice from Waylon Jennings; after all, he had been part of that conservative greaser world before warping into whatever he was becoming. He didn't seem to be particularly interested in listening to my despondency over Music Row. Staring off into space and occasionally blowing cigarette smoke toward me, it was clear that he'd heard it all before and probably experienced a lot of it.

When I finished babbling, he showed the first indication that he'd even heard anything I said. Seemingly speaking more to Captain Midnight than directly to me, he opined, "Country, Hillbilly, Rock and Roll, Folk, Gospel. It's all the same thing". That was it. No elaboration, no explanation, no encouraging words; that little bit of opinion was all he offered.

I finished my silver dollar pancakes and I stood to leave. Roger was still buying my meals there and I was grateful. Waylon then spoke directly to me, asking if I wanted to go play pinball. That wasn't code for anything; he and The Captain were pinball junkies and played for hours and hours ... and hours and hours. Inviting me to play was as close to empathy

THE POET LAUREATE SOUL OF FOLKIE ROCK & ROLL

or comradery as I could hope for from him. It's just the way that Waylon was… at least around me.

I thanked him but said no and started walking back to my apartment. The Captain called after me, "Don't let the bastards kick you".

Back at my vermin-infested apartment, I decided to get my car and drive downtown to The Opry. I knew that the backdoor reprobates there were outcasts too and would probably have more actionable advice than Captain Midnight or Waylon or Tompall.

My dejection must have been written all over my face, because the first thing "Little" Jimmy Dickens said to me when he saw me was, "Are you alright my friend?". I politely told him I was, and he continued up the steps to the stage entrance as I stayed outside. He was always nice and "on" to everyone.

About a half-hour later a security guard appeared and asked me to leave. I don't think anyone asked him to do that; he just took it on himself. If any of my friends had been around, I am certain they would have brought me inside; but this rent-a-cop was on his own when he told me to beat it. I'd never seen him before; in fact, there were several "new" security guys. That was a first! And my comic-book loving self probably thought "It's an omen".

From the backdoor, I wandered down the hill on Fourth Avenue to lower Broadway and across the street for a half-block to the *Ernest Tubb Record Shop*. Maybe someone there would offer me the revelation that I was seeking. It was an after-opry hangout for a handful of pickers and singers. The shop also hosted a live-performance show on WSM radio at midnight on Saturdays.

My friend, *Rhinestone*, was out in front as he usually was on weekend nights. Rhinestone, whose real name was *David Allan Coe* —though at that time I rarely remembered his actual name— was one strange cat; but always friendly and fun to talk to. He lived in a bright red 1956 Cadillac Superior hearse with a big chrome siren on top. Almost every Friday and Saturday night he illegally parked in front of the record shop and played original songs to harass tourists on his Buck Owens style red-white-and-blue acoustic guitar.

When I say he "lived in" the hearse, I mean it quite literally. He was doing what I had done months earlier in my Valiant. The difference was that the casket space of the hearse made a much more comfortable bed than the seats of my small Plymouth. Also, he had all sorts of graffiti written on the vehicle calling for the support of Country Music.

Rhinestone was part counter-culture hippie, with long hair, bell-bottom jeans, and an anarchist kind of attitude about most things. Contronymically, he was also part greaser, complete with that damned bacon-grease-

THE LEGEND DIES ON — GARY GREEN

like lard in his long hair and deep respect for old-style country music (of which he had encyclopedic knowledge that rivaled even mine).

He leaned against his home…ah, hearse… played guitar and sang some weird-ass songs that made my *Average Minded American* seem very mainstream. Despite his admiration for the country standard bearers, his music was a lot more Rolling Stones than Ernest Tubb.

Like my father's satirical rewrites of the lyrics of country standards, Rhinestone had a habit of doing the same thing. Only Rhinestone's rewrites were totally off-the-wall nonsensical sometimes. He took a fine Townes Van Zandt song, *If I Needed You*, and changed the lyrics to something about laying in "a field of stone". It was a song that he'd eventually get covered by lots of artists; but at the time it was just weird. And, of course, he never shared credit with Townes Van Zandt, whose melody he clearly lifted and whose lyrics he twisted.

Rhinestone did all sorts of weird shit like that. Also weirdly, he said he had spent a lot of time in prison, not mythologically like Cash or misdemeanorly like Merle Haggard, but genuine felony prison time. In the "joint" was apparently where he picked up a lot of body ink, a somewhat unhealthy disregard of any authority, and a genuinely offensive seemingly dislike of anyone whose skin wasn't lily white.

He was worse than your run-of-the-mill Nashville outcast; he was a genuine goofball outcast (who within the next six or eight years would sell millions of albums and write massive hits for himself and other artists). I figured that if anyone could put my troubles into perspective it would be Rhinestone.

He and I always seemed to click on some level and despite being a decade older than me (and the whole prison thing and his racism) he somehow saw me as a kindred soul. I think it was because he really viewed himself as a poet; and since my Kristofferson encounter, I openly self-proclaimed that I was a *rock-and-roll poet* (as opposed to a country singer).

Hardly a weekend went by that we did not have some pseudo-philosophical conversation, no matter how brief or merely observational... or superficial. Actually, less than conversation it was more like him lecturing or rambling or pontificating and me throwing in a few "ah's" or "hmmm's".

So, on that night, I unloaded my Music Row lament on him in hopes of getting some sage advice. He listened. After a couple of songs, he offered his advice, "If I was you, I'd saddle up and get the hell outta Dodge". Once again, I was hearing the same-old message: *leave Nashville*.

For the next few days, I continued my routine door-knocking. During one afternoon door-knocking spree, I met painter, sculpturer, songwriter, singer, and all-around renaissance man *Gil Veda* (Luis Gilbert

THE POET LAUREATE SOUL OF FOLKIE ROCK & ROLL

Sepulveda). Gil had been the first Hispanic person to play on the stage of the Grand Ole Opry. He had written songs that were recorded by dozens of country stars. I had heard that as a painter, he had been commissioned by the White House to paint an official presidential portrait.

He also held a very healthy iconoclastic opinion of Music Row; even though much of his career had been spent there (including recording in RCA's historic "Studio B" where Chet Atkins had created the "Nashville Sound" genre in one of those "family fights" between "honky-tonk" and "sophisticated country" music).

He listened to my tape —the entire tape. Afterwards, he asked me, "What do you want to do with it?"

I told him that I wanted to get my songs published, and he answered immediately, *"Why? What will that do? Anybody can publish you. You need to record those songs. Published is nothing. You want them published? Hire a pretty girl to wear a short skirt and take your tape around; you'll be published immediately. It means nothing",* He opened a filing cabinet and pulled out a contract form and then continued talking.

"Here," he said as he pushed the paper toward me. *"I will sign a publishing contract right now. I will publish your songs; they're good songs and I will be happy to take the publishing rights to them away from you. But that doesn't give you money. That doesn't mean anybody will ever hear your songs. It doesn't mean anything".*

"If you want these songs heard, then you need to record them. Then a publishing contract is worth something. Then somebody will cover them. But nothing until you make that record. And it needs to be you",

"Who else can put your feelings into those songs like you do? Nobody at first. You need a record company, not a publisher," he finished his first lecture, adding, "Then people will cover them".

We talked for about four hours. He was totally serious about offering me a publishing contract; he even filled in the blank spots and signed it but cautioned me not to do the same. I didn't. (I still have that contract somewhere among my boxes of old files.)

It probably was the most helpful conversation that I had with anyone in Nashville except Reba Hancock; and it was more intense than any of my many discussions with her.

I told him about what I had run into all along Music Row. He wasn't surprised and told me that what I was trying to do overnight takes people years to do; and he cited several examples of famous country stars who were "overnight sensations" after 15 years of poverty.

"Take my contract with you, and if you think that is really what you want to do, then come back tomorrow and sign it and turn over all your publishing rights to me. But what I suggest is that you give some serious thought to what we've talked about and then make some plans to record

THE LEGEND DIES ON — GARY GREEN

your songs. Let me know what you really want," he said as he walked me toward my car.

I needed to seriously think about what I wanted to do; Gil was right. One thing was certain: the lifestyle I was currently in was neither healthy nor sustainable. I was debating with myself whether to stay in Nashville or go to New York or, more likely, take my songs to Los Angeles or San Francisco.

Miami was also a possibility, at least for a detour. Tens of thousands of music-loving young people were planning to converge on South Florida for the biggest anti-war protests since the infamous 1968 Democratic Convention in Chicago. Richard Nixon was President and the Watergate crimes had not yet surfaced, but the "secret" bombing of Cambodia had become public knowledge. The Republican National Convention was scheduled in Miami Beach for late August, which was only about a week away.

Chances were that if my audience was going to be my peers, they would be there, and I could find out once and for all.

THE POET LAUREATE SOUL OF FOLKIE ROCK & ROLL

The 2nd Movement
andante: *Why I Chose the "Outlaw" Trail*

THE LEGEND DIES ON — GARY GREEN

Opus Eight:
Apparently, SOME People DO Like My Music

What sphinx of cement and aluminum bashed open their skulls and ate up their brains and imagination? — Howl, by Allen Ginsberg [82]

*I*n Miami Beach's Flamingo Park, late one afternoon just as I was stepping off the stage and the Yippie leadership was playing Frisbee in front of the park, three rented yellow school buses pulled onto the grass at the edge of the park. The doors opened and from each bus about 25 members of *The American Nazi Party* stepped out.

They were dressed in their brown shirts and carrying baseball bats, axe handles, and bicycle chains. They unfurled a large swastika-flag beside an American flag. Their leader announced that they were here to "rid the park of the jews, commies, queers, and nasty hippies, in defense of White man's America".

I saw Alan Ginsberg run away from the group, dart behind the stage, and disappear beyond the parking lot. I looked at the sound engineer on stage and she said to me, "well, he is all four". The situation was way-too tense for me to laugh.

The Nazis stood in formation and began singing *God Bless America*. (I was starting to develop Woody Guthrie's distaste for the song.) In the midst of their song, the leader gave some order, and they began marching toward us, holding their weapons ready.

Before we had the chance to flee them, Ginsberg reappeared... with about 50 really muscular, short-haired guys who were even more scary-looking than the Nazis. They lined-up between us and the Nazis, crouched in a football-line formation as if they were ready to charge.

One of the guys stepped forward and screamed at the Nazis, *"I am a United States Marine"!*

He paused for a movie-script-worthy dramatic effect before continuing, "Let that sink in. We are *Winter Soldier*. If you want to get to these people, then you have to come through us. Better men have tried, and they died".

Before the Nazis could respond, the entire Winter Soldier line, in unison, yelled, *"Oo-rah!"*

Without another word, the Nazis turned around, got into their buses, and drove away. We never saw them again.

---

[82] Renewed copyright ©1984 by Allen Ginsberg

THE POET LAUREATE SOUL OF FOLKIE ROCK & ROLL

As I approached Ginsberg, he said to me, "Meet VVAW. Get somebody to buy them some cold beer".

Well, this was one hell of a welcome to Miami Beach; and it was about the least of the drama about to befall me.

Music had been a key part of the culture of the protests at the 1968 convention, with performances by *MC5, Bob Dylan, Joan Baez, Graham Nash* (of Crosby, Stills, and Nash), *Country Joe McDonald* (of Woodstock fame), *Peter Paul & Mary, Phil Ochs* (I knew of him from that *Ballads of Broadside* Folkways record), and lots of others.

Somehow, I got it into my head that if I went to the Miami Convention that I could play and I could take my mixture of hillbilly roots and contemporary rock-poetry lyrics to my own generation. Perhaps Nashville wisdom had been correct; that I should be in New York or L.A.; and if that was the case then Miami Beach on August 21st, 1972, would give me access to both audiences to see how it would go. Perhaps, if the reaction there was positive, it would give me a direction for what to do.

What-the-hell. I had decided to skip out of my apartment (the rent was due anyway) and drive the 1,002 miles down to Miami. Along the way, I picked up a menagerie of hitchhiking fellow-travelers who were also en route to the demonstrations, though none were musicians.

Cruising south in my unairconditioned fire-engine-red 1964 Plymouth Valiant, we shared songs, marijuana, and campfires. We were stopped and threatened by police in south Georgia and again in Florida. A Georgia State Trooper told one of my passengers that he was going to handcuff him and cut his hair. (He didn't follow through; though driving through Atlanta we did see a billboard that said, "Keep America Beautiful, Get A Haircut".) In north Florida a cop said that if he saw me in Miami Beach with the bullwhip that was tied to my side, he would "shoot first and ask questions later".

The constant police harassment just because we had long hair and looked like "hippies" made me genuinely wonder what life must be like for Black people who drove through white towns or even white neighborhoods. The huge difference was, I could cut my hair, put on a suit, and be acceptable to the cops and establishment; my African American friends did not share that privileged luxury —changing skin color was not an option (nor desirable).

It really was terrifying; we never knew if we would be arrested, beaten, or even shot. That alone, was unnerving; but beyond that, it caused us to develop a fear, animosity, distrust, of *all* police officers. We could not even imagine what it would be like to live in that abyss our entire lives.

Our group was from The University of California at Berkley, from Brooklyn, from Boston, from Chicago, from Denver, and ... me. And we were packed like hot sardines into my car. When we finally arrived in

THE LEGEND DIES ON — GARY GREEN

Miami, everyone had a place to crash except me. I was the only one who showed up with no plans and no arrangements.

After dropping everyone off at their respective locations, I headed to *Flamingo Park*, which had been designated as the gathering area for all of the counter-convention events. It was also where the stage was set up for music, speeches, and assorted rabble-rousing. I parked my car, pulled out my 12-string and strapped it across my back as I walked toward the stage. My motivation for the trip was primarily musical; my dislike for the war was, at that point, secondary —not well-researched, but firmly opposed to seeing dead friends shipped home with a flag draped over them without any clear reason why.

Abbie Hoffman was speaking from the stage, and he was getting the crowd wound-up. I was psyched just to see him in person. That might make the whole trip worthwhile!

As I got closer to the stage, a very-organized looking woman spotted me and came down the stage-steps toward me. "Do you know *Alice's Restaurant*?" she asked without even asking who I was. (Alice's Restaurant was Arlo Guthrie's very long semi-talking comical anti-war song.) I answered, "All 18 minutes and 17 seconds of it", With her obviously New York accent, she shot back, "Good. As soon as Abbie finishes, you are on. Just walk up beside him and start".

And THAT is how I became the troubadour of the three-day "Be-In" in Miami Beach. As soon as I finished the song, Yippie leader Stew Albert took over the microphone and I stepped off the stage where I was greeted with bear-hugs from poet Ed Sanders (of the rock band The Fugs and author of a book about Charlie Manson, *The Family*) and by the legendary Allen Ginsberg the revered poet laureate of the Beat movement.

The musical "stars" that were part of the event were treated like celebrities; and that was fine. They came in, made their appearances, sang a few songs, and then were escorted away by drivers taking them to their nice, air-conditioned hotels. But despite all of that, for three days I remained the "go-to" non-celebrity musical interlude that the organizers came to between speeches or to gather a crowd or to calm or to incite.

At the end of that first night, I still had no place to sleep. About nine o'clock a woman backstage was asking if anyone spoke Spanish; apparently no one did. Next, she asked if anyone knew ASL (American Sign Language). I told her that I was a very fast ASL finger-speller, but not a signer. She asked if I could communicate with a deaf person that was offering to rent a house to a group of organizers.

Apparently, the deaf landlord could only read Spanish but could understand ASL, as well as ASL finger-spelling in English. Of course, I agreed to translate. When the negotiations were finished, the organizers were so grateful to me that they asked if I wanted to stay in the house with them while I was in Miami. I had a place to crash!

By the end of the second day, my musical interludes from the main stage had garnered me a following. People were actually asking me what label I was on or what was the name of my album. Wow! Fans!

Also, by the end of that day, it occurred to me that I had not eaten in almost two days. Apparently, my skin-and-bones look sent the signal that I was starving. A heavy-set woman, who identified herself as Julie, asked me when the last time was that I had a hot meal. I truthfully told her that it had been several days (a campfire special on the drive down). She announced to me that was not acceptable and marched me to a nearby deli where she instructed me to order anything on the menu.

After paying for my huge meal, she walked with me back to Flamingo Park and told me that if I get hungry again to find her. I thanked her profusely and then she disappeared into the crowd as I mounted the stage to sing Dylan's *Blowing In The Wind* and a couple of rallying songs.

About lunch time on the third day, I finished another short set with my song *The CIA*. The stage schedule called for an announcement that box lunches provided by a local synagogue were available at the back of the park. The stage was to go dark (silent) for about an hour.

That typed-out schedule was abruptly changed when Allen Ginsberg bolted to the stage as I finished my song. He took the microphone and motioned for me to remain on stage. Then he announced to the crowd that he thought he had written the best (if not *only*) CIA song ever when he wrote his *CIA Dope Calypso* song earlier in the year. He continued, "That is until I heard Gary Green's song today".

He continued, "I am inspired by the music of this young poet and his balls to expose the drug-trafficking menace that is the Central Intelligence Agency of the United States". (My song doesn't mention drug-trafficking, but, what-the-hell anyway.)

Allen-fucking-Ginsberg praising MY writing made up for every Ray Stevens, Cecil Null, and pissed-off Gastonia band that I'd ever met. AND, he said he was inspired by my music. AND Allen Ginsberg called ME a poet! Let me repeat that: *ALLEN GINSBERG CALLED ME A POET!*

Allen Ginsberg was digging my song. The audience liked my performance. There was —almost— nothing that could rain on this perfect parade of life for me. *Almost.*

Then about midway through that next afternoon, Julie approached me again. "How well do you know the people at that house where you are crashing?" she asked me.

I didn't recall telling her where I was staying, but I answered her anyway. "I don't know them at all. I don't even know their names," I laughed

THE LEGEND DIES ON — GARY GREEN

a little embarrassed. I explained to her how I ended up being in the house thanks to my ASL finger spelling skill.

Her voice suddenly took a very serious tone that I'd not heard from her before. She warned me, "You need to get out of that house. Now. Don't go back at all. Something really bad is going to happen there", Then once again, she faded into the crowd.

Ordinarily, I would have laughed off such an ominous warning, but there was some resolve in her voice that seemed like I should heed her words. The event was almost over anyway, so that night instead of returning to the house, I drove down to Key Largo and found a place to camp out in my car, Tennessee-style.

On the island, there were so many mosquitoes that almost every exposed part of my skin was bitten. It was too hot to roll up the windows, so I suffered the welts. The next morning, I started driving toward Nashville, still high on the Ginsberg experience.

It wasn't until almost ten years later that I learned that Julie, known in the movement as "Fat Julie", was an undercover FBI operative and all of the people in that house had been arrested the night I left. The FBI and ATF had raided the house and charged the occupants with manufacturing incendiary devices and conspiracy to bomb the convention. Julie had saved me; but I didn't know it at the time. I also didn't know they were making bombs there!

When I arrived in Atlanta, about 10 hours later, I weighed the distance back to Nashville (265 miles) versus the distance over to Gastonia to visit my parents (223 miles) before going back to Music Row. I decided to detour east to Gastonia; I was hungry.

♪♪♪

Still riding the high from being praised by the esteemed poet of *Howl*, I didn't even think about how I looked (or smelled) when I pulled into my parents' driveway. The months of near-starvation had gnawed my weight to a little less than 85 pounds. My sweaty body was covered with welted mosquito bites. My hair was stringy, and my clothes (which no longer fit me at all) were more than filthy; they reeked (as did I). Years later, my mother told me that I looked like a walking skeleton at death's door.

My family always lived by a credo that "right or wrong, we are always family; and family comes first", True to that mantra, I was welcomed home as if I'd only been away on holiday.

While I was in the shower, Mother sorted through my dirty clothes to wash them and, quite literally, burned the worst. She then set about preparing a very large meal, again as if I'd only been on an extended vacation. My two brothers, Ron (14) and Keith (11), were equally welcoming but uncharacteristically quiet about the whole thing.

THE POET LAUREATE SOUL OF FOLKIE ROCK & ROLL

There were lots of family complications, but the biggest was, "what now?" My father wanted to know if I was ready to "calm down and get a job". My mother wanted me to go to one of the universities where I had been accepted. And I, of course, planned to go back to Nashville.

The next few days of daily clean clothes, roach-free nights, regular showers, and fattening up on hot meals —home cooked— all were making me evaluate the self-alienating roller coaster of door-knocking in southwest Nashville. The more-than-acceptance (and actually asking for my "album") in Miami Beach only added to my rethinking the plan; or rather the lack-of-a-plan lifestyle.

For every one Gil Veda or Kris Kristofferson, I had suffered a half-dozen Ray Stevens' and Cecil Null's pejoratively asking me, What's your Plan B? How long are you giving yourself? and Do you have anything else lined up in case it doesn't work out for you?

Because our family had always been so close-knit, I am certain my parents also were struggling with the what-next debacle that I had rained onto our otherwise always-sunshine world. On my third-or-fourth-day home they presented me with a way-too-generous plan of their own. On hindsight, it really was an over-and-above expression of love and support.

They proposed that they would go back to Nashville with me, rent me a nice apartment (ostensibly vermin free), and stock it with groceries. BUT... at the end of two months, if I had not found financial success in music, then I would accept my enrollment at the University of Tennessee in Knoxville (which was on the quarter-system rather the semester system of most colleges). They would pay the out-of-state tuition costs.

Some serious decisions needed to be made. But, at 18 years old, I still was a hard-core product of the Margaret-Mitchell-esque *Oh fiddle-dee. I'll think about it tomorrow; after all, tomorrow is another day.*[83] Consequently, my parents' offer, which would force incredible pressure on me, was the ideal motivator. Moreover, without spending most Nashville days worrying about shelter and my next meal, my focus could be exclusively on getting my songs heard... or now my *poetry* heard — thanks to Ginsberg, Sanders, and the whole Miami Beach experience.

In Nashville, later that week, they found an apartment for me at the *Madison Square Apartments*, in a northeast Nashville suburb. To add icing to the cake of this apartment, the legendary *Mother Maybelle Carter*

---

[83] One of the (many) negative byproducts of the absurd IQ and charmed life I had lived for 18 years was that I tended to put things off until the very last possible minutes; serial procrastination followed by frantic pressure to complete. That bad behavior was reinforced and perpetuated by my charmed life allowing things to always work out (either that Pollyannaism or my aforementioned Scarlett-O'Hara-attitude.

THE LEGEND DIES ON — GARY GREEN

lived about four minutes away at 1020 Gibson Drive in Madison. It was a great location for me!

To my further delight, a neighboring apartment in the same complex was home to one of the three guitar pickers from The Grand Ole Opry Stage Band. After I got to know him (and reminded him that I was the kid that used to hangout backstage five or six years earlier), he made the complex even better by telling me that Johnny Cash and Waylon Jennings shared one of these apartments before Cash married June Carter!

When I talked to him about the troubles that I had pitching songs on Music Row, he shook his head almost moanfully, and told me, "*It's going to get worse. The Opry just bought the buffalo pasture at Rudy's Farm in Donelson. They are going to build a country music Disneyland and move The Opry out to the middle of it. There's not going to be room for anybody that doesn't fit into the Disneyland mold. So, unless you've got some mouse-ears in that guitar case, you might want to just go to California instead.*"

Even that gloomy visual didn't deter me; but it did give me further resolve to be myself rather than conform to a product mold —just the opposite of most of the advice I had been getting. I immediately set into a new Music Row routine. This time, instead of trying to adapt to the occupants of whatever house/company I came to, I decided to present myself with a "what you see is what you get" unapologetic approach. Born from the confidence of the Miami Beach adventure, my new attitude would certainly expedite things; if they hated me, I would know immediately and could move on, rather than anguish wondering.

"Hippiebilly", "Alt-Country", "Progressive Country" and "Americana" were not yet recognized genres; nor, for that matter, they weren't even real words. *Gram Parsons*' flirtation with country music forms was more likely to be labeled "folk rock". And my middle-of-the-night pancake buddies had not yet been labeled "outlaws"; in fact, it was still almost a year before Waylon's *Honky Tonk Heroes* album would springboard that handle.

Moreover, while many of us were unabashedly rebellious against Nashville's establishment (and clearly were out-of-place in the mainstream), we had little else in common universally. At least after my Miami Beach adventure I understood what Kristofferson had meant by "political".

While the new Nashville iconoclasts were unified in our disdain for the corporate "Countrypolitan" autocrats, beyond that we were no more of a cohesive group than any other random collection of creators. We each had our own specialty, niché, and interests; whether we were good, bad, or average at it.

I wasn't the best writer and certainly not the best musician or singer, but I probably was the most "beat" of the outsiders trying to get inside.

THE POET LAUREATE SOUL OF FOLKIE ROCK & ROLL

At least, that's how I decided to approach my pitches. Thanks again to Ginsberg.

Beginning from the comfort of my new Madison digs, I decided to drop in, unannounced, on Reba Hancock. Her office at House of Cash in Hendersonville was a much shorter drive for me than it would have been from my old Nashville apartment; 12 miles versus 24 miles.

As always, she was more-than gracious and nurturing, welcoming me as if I was an old friend, rather than the uninitiated child that I actually was. I told her that I wasn't there to pitch songs but to get her advice. It was true, and she seemed to appreciate that enough to take time out of her busy day to mentor me for a few minutes.

I told her about my encounters along Music Row. She laughed at the Cecil Null story, especially at the *Don't Blow Smoke In A Kangaroo's Face* advice. She seemed to be genuinely outraged at my Ray Stevens story. And I had the good sense not to tell her about the Jerry Reed meeting. She seemed completely neutral to my Pancake House adventures (which I shared sans bullwhip story); except she *did* ask me if Waylon was sober (she apparently knew him).

When I told her about the Miami Beach adventure, she shifted to a very pensive expression, seeming to hang on to everything I shared. *(I left out the FBI raid, Julie, the Nazis, and near-starvation.)* At some point she interrupted me to say, "That is exactly the kind of show JR loves".

After I finished, she looked at me for a minute and then told me, "You know, Kris isn't totally wrong", I am sure I looked confused as I waited for her to explain.

She said, "You should record your songs yourself to start. Have you thought about sending a tape to the people in New York at that…" She paused, not like she was trying to remember but as if she was distracted, thinking about something else that might have been going on that day.

"Folkways Records?" she concluded. I told her that I knew of the label but had never thought about sending them a tape to pitch songs. She told me, "You aren't pitching songs; you are pitching YOU".

BING-BING-BING; alarm bells went off in my head. Her advice was genuinely inspirational; it reinforced what at least *some* others had been telling me and certainly what I wanted.

Driving back to Madison, I was even further empowered to jump right back into taking on Music Row; perhaps a little too enthusiastically.

When I got home (yup, "home"), I grabbed one tape and my 12-string; I was no longer in the frame-of-mind that I needed to have different tapes for different types of publishers. I also had resolved to not just call on publishers; I now was going to visit *record companies*. I wasn't just pitching songs; I was pitching me.

THE LEGEND DIES ON — GARY GREEN

During the next two weeks, I not only was rejected by every record company on Music Row; but I was actually thrown out by a security guard at one of them, refused admission or drop-off of a tape at two others, and showered with insults by low-level A and R flunkies at the rest.

Still, I didn't have enough sense to stop. My friend *"Jumping" Bill Carlisle,* a longtime member of The Grand Ole Opry, had suggested that I go see a guy he knew at a booking agency that also negotiated record contracts and provided personal management for a handful of Opry members. I did.

After hearing my tape, that guy unleased a tirade at me, *"I agreed to hear you because our mutual friend called ahead and asked me to. But I am sure that he, and you, would want me to be 100% honest with you and not blow smoke up your butt."* (I mentally noted that was materially different than blowing smoke in a kangaroo's face.)

"You are a hippie, and Nashville is just not ready for hippies. I've got nothing against you and even think some of your songs are pretty good. But there is no place for you in Country Music. I'm telling you like it is. We don't want you here. This is a business, not a rock festival. The best advice I can give you is either get a haircut and lose the hippie lyrics or move to California. Even the guys here that are open to that kind of thing, a Bobby Bare or Kris Kristofferson or Mae Axton's boy, wouldn't touch you with a ten-foot pole. Politics and music don't go together; you can't piss off half your audience".

He read the disappointment and pain on my face and attempted to soften the scolding he had given me, *"Look, I don't mean any offense; I am trying to do you a favor and be the first person in this God-forsaken town to tell you the truth and not try to pick your pocket. I've been here a long time, and I have seen everything. Believe me, Nashville will never welcome this kind of stuff. These guys are too conservative."*

He spoke about the Nashville establishment as if he was not part of it, though clearly, he was. His lecturing monologue, which he called "a heart-to-heart talk", sliced through everything, and cut right to the heart of all that I had heard and experienced in the previous six months. I actually appreciated his honesty.

Driving back to my apartment I weighed all he had said against everything I had experienced in Florida. I was missing something; there was something I was just not processing.

I made a brief detour to stop by Gil Veda's gallery and tell him that I was taking his advice and planning to pitch myself rather than songs. We talked for a few minutes, and I thanked him again for his support.

Heading home, on Gallatin Road about a mile from home, I was stopped at a traffic light when my poor little car was rear-ended by a guy that didn't even hit his brakes. Hitting me at about 45-miles-per-hour, he totaled my fire-engine-red Valiant.

If my comic-book mind thought it had been an omen when the Opry security guard had blocked my entrance to the backstage door, then totaling my car was my ultimate moment of the proverbial "a bat! That's it! It's an omen. I shall become a bat-man!"

After the police report, I phreaked a phone call to my father to report what had happened. He asked if I was ready to go to The University of Tennessee and I reluctantly said yes. (I could have called collect, but it was more fun to fuck with AT&T by stealing a call.) I knew exactly where I stood with Nashville and where Nashville stood with me.

THE LEGEND DIES ON — GARY GREEN

Opus Nine:
The University vs. The Founder of Lead Guitar

Romantic life of a rambler ain't all it's cracked to be.
And living the life of a Gypsy ain't always living free.
— *The Last Minstrel,* by Gary Green, 1982, as recorded on
Folkways Records album FH5356, *Still At Large*

When I tried to accept that it was supposed to take four years to get through college, I could not imagine putting my music on hold for that long. *No way!* I had to come up with an alternative to that nonsense. It turned out that wasn't nearly as difficult as it sounded. It also turned out that there were many more options surrounding the university than being molded into a socially productive automaton.

The University of Tennessee had a rule that students could take no more than 16 credit-hours per session. At that rate, it was no damned wonder it took four years to get out of prison ... I mean college. Seemed logical to me that if I could take 32 hours each session, I could cut the sentence in half; but even that two-year stretch wasn't terribly appealing.

Not so simple! The University would only approve that heavy class load if I could show *academic aptitude and performance* to justify it. In short, they wanted to see good grades for a regular term before they'd let me double up. That would mean that for my two-years-and-out goal I probably would need to take 36 hours per session to make up for the "loss" during the first session. Bureaucratic bastards!

During the orientation, the school's volunteer docents told the incoming class about a student coffeehouse that had open microphone nights every Friday and Saturday. Needless to say, that was the first stop of my collegiate experience; in the audience, and not with a guitar. I wanted to hear what people were listening to and digging.

The most popular performer that first night was a way-too-pretty-for-his-own-good boy who did a short set of covers from the band *America* (never one of my favorite groups for lots of reasons, though I do appreciate Dewey Bunnell's writing). The student performance was lively, engaging, and self-deprecating enough to make the audience feel like they were part of some kind of inside joke. With his closing song, *Horse With No Name*, he had most of the audience singing along with him.

Without exception, the rest of the performers provided me with an almost-painful flashback to my mother's student piano recitals —the music was technically accurate but without passion or engagement. There was nothing really exciting the whole night; at least not to me, and apparently not to most of the audience.

THE POET LAUREATE SOUL OF FOLKIE ROCK & ROLL

The next night I showed up with my guitar and signed up for the open microphone. It turned out that I was the only freshman to do so; the rest of the performers were "seasoned" and apparently regulars on the little stage; they all seemed to know each other. That made me nervous; and even more so when the organizers relegated my time slot to near the end of the night. That meant, to me, that I would be "judged" against all the people who came before me, and the only people left in the audience would be the stragglers and the bored.

I had already decided to do only one song rather than subject the audience to a mini-set; so, the time slot wasn't really a big deal to me. I had been debating with myself whether or not to hit them with one of the get-'em-on-their-feet anthems that had garnered enthusiasm in Miami Beach; maybe even do the 18-minute Arlo Guthrie *Alice's Restaurant* that launched my Miami popularity.

I was leaning, though, toward introducing a new down-tempo teen-angst whiner that I had been working on about my brother Ronny. There was plenty to cause angst for my generation; angst far beyond Jim Stark's coming of age traumas[84]; so, I opted for that new song. It was untested, but to my delight it won applause and calls of "more, more". I declined, promising that I would be back next week.

As soon as I stepped off the stage I was approached by a tall, skinny guy with long dark hair whose first words were, "We have a band that I want you to hear".

I know I must have looked at him like he was crazy, and whatever the expression on my face conveyed, he realized I was caught completely off guard. He quickly started over with, "You don't remember me, do you?" I didn't; *I had no frigging clue.*

---

[84] Jim Stark was James Dean's character in the classic teen angst film *Rebel Without A Cause.*
- Historically, it was an epoch when anyone under 21 was legally a minor —a child subject to arbitrary in loco parentis from university officials.
- The voting age had just-that-year been lowered to 18, and the drinking age had recently been raised to 21 on campuses but not elsewhere, though the military draft age had always been 18.
- Abortions were criminal activities.
- On the average one student out of every two high school graduating classes would die in Vietnam. Four students recently had been murdered on campus by the National Guard in Ohio, two on a campus in Mississippi, and police routinely sicced dogs on Black students seeking equal rights.
- Possession of even one-joint of marijuana could land you prison for up to 10 years. The State of Oklahoma, for example had the most severe marijuana laws; prison for one year for possessing any amount of marijuana on a first offense and 2-10 years for a second offense. Fines for selling any amount of marijuana started at $20,000.

THE LEGEND DIES ON — GARY GREEN

It turned out that he was one of the kids I had known in elementary school back in Kingsport. It shouldn't have surprised me that lots of those classmates would be at U.T.; after all, it was THE state university, and therefore the cheapest college education in the state.

Truthfully, I had not thought of any of those classmates since the day my family left East Tennessee. I had gone to Kindergarten in Atlanta, started elementary school in Kingsport, in the 5th grade moved to a Sullivan County school, then for half of the 6th grade to a different Kingsport *city* school with the second half of the 6th grade in Atlanta, then 7th through the 10th grades in Nashville, the rest of the 10th grade through high school graduation in Gastonia. Hell, I could barely remember the names of the schools and certainly not all the teachers. There was no way I could remember the names of classmates in every grade at every school[85].

This guy's name was Jimmy and he and three other guys from Kingsport had a band that played covers from a new California rock band called *Eagles*. It wasn't exactly country, but not hard rock either. I had never heard of Eagles, but I agreed to meet Jimmy and his friends in a music practice room at the Student Center the next day.

All four guys in the band were my former elementary school classmates and, allegedly, they all had fond memories of me (even if I had no recollection whatsoever about any of them). Their band was actually pretty good. I wasn't too impressed with the songs; but the keyboard, bass, drummer, and guitar were all good musicians. They played with that soulful Appalachian passion that took me back to the Skelton Brothers, but their song choices were more contemporary folk-rock-ish.

As they played, I watched their chord changes and tossed in a few little one-string lead riffs. Having never heard the songs, I had no idea what they were supposed to sound like. I must have done something right, because after they ran through their set for me, they asked me to join them for gigging and the quest for a record contract.

I thanked them profusely but told them I didn't want to be a lead guitar picker. As I was trying to politely turn them down, Jimmy interrupted me, "No, no, no. We don't want you to play Eagles songs. We want to play *your* songs. Like the one you did last night. We want to be your band." The other guys nodded in agreement.

I was totally surprised. I didn't know what to say; so, I decided to run through four or five of my songs with them. Even with my weird rhythm thingy, they followed along; stopping only to discuss different things they

---

[85] Looking back on that, in my "elderly" years, I see that as a *good* thing; it indicates that my current inability to remember names and faces is likely not some early onset dementia but rather a lifelong debility.

THE POET LAUREATE SOUL OF FOLKIE ROCK & ROLL

could do and where I should pause for them to do stuff. After that, they still wanted to be my backup band; maybe even more so.

Baffling to me, the drummer especially wanted to play with me. Clearly that guy had some masochistic issues to subject himself to drumming with my rhythm problems; either that or he wanted to save me from myself. *(I should have let him!)*

We rehearsed together a couple of times a week for about a month or so. Then, in probably the biggest musical mistake I ever made, I decided that I didn't want a band. Instead, I wanted to be a solo acoustic Woody Guthrie kind of character, only a solo rock-and-roll version. Besides, playing with a band full-time required way more discipline than I had; at least I knew that about myself.

More pointedly, with just me and my guitar I felt like I could create my own emphasis on my words, my own speed, my own stopping and going as the mood called for from one day to the next. Even the inconsistent rhythm that Ray Stevens had hated so much could be used to emphasize the emotions I was trying to convey. In fact, my changing tempos from one phrase to the next really was driven by the feeling I wanted the listener to get from the lyrics. It wasn't written to dance to; I wrote poetry *to be heard.*

I never heard from them again, but I am convinced that the more I tell this story, one day someone is going to tell me, "oh yeah, those guys formed such-and-such band and sold triple-platinum albums before they were inducted into the Rock & Roll Hall of Fame". I just know that will happen; but not in the fall of 1972.

Jimmy's band, which I truly believed had great commercial potential, provided for me a real *ah-ha* epiphany. Playing with them I realized that I didn't fit any of the new music molds that were developing. *(Hey guys, if you are still alive as I write this and aren't in a band, zap me an email and let's get it right this time.)*

But, before totally swearing off playing with other musicians, I continued to experiment with small groups, jams, and just get-togethers to see what might come about. I just wasn't sure.

The burgeoning progressive country music movement in Nashville that was being spearheaded by my old silver dollar pancake buddies (and would eventually be called "Outlaw"), was really about control of the presentation of the music. It was a reaction to the corporately canned "Countrypolitan" bullshit. It was a move to replace the old presentation with a new one that was different only in form but not necessarily content. That wasn't me; I was dialectical... *content AND form.*

Out in California the *Eagles* (that had been introduced to me by these guys from Kingsport), and *The Byrds, The Flying Burrito Brothers...* were all more about the art. Their making music was genuinely an art

THE LEGEND DIES ON — GARY GREEN

form, and they truly were artists. What was California-transplant Gram Parson's Nudie suits all about other than a *performance art* transformation of country music? I was sure that I was about as far from being an actor as one could possibly be. So, *performance art* was out.

Even all of the excellent writing and music that was starting to come out of the newly-opened *Exit Inn* venue in Nashville —from people who on the surface might have appeared to be my peers— was not what I was doing. True, for the most part they were living and performing outside of mainstream convention and expectations. They were styling differently in both form and in content; but they were a far cry from genuine Bohemianism. Rather, I saw them as the foundation of what I thought would be the next iteration of Nashville mainstream. *(I was right, by the way; that eventually became the new establishment in Country Music.)*

All of these movements were made up of incredibly talented people producing music that (for the most part) I truly loved to hear and even play for myself at times. But what I grasped from playing with the Kingsport band was that I didn't fit into any of those groups. While I had some degree of affinity with all of them... plus adding the traditional mountain hillbillies... I wasn't part of any of them. I was even alienated from the alienated outcasts.

That alienation was what, a few years later, would be part of the liner notes of my first Folkways album, "I'm just a little writer who sometimes uses a typewriter and sometimes a guitar" (a recurring theme, that I continue to preach).

That alienation is the thing I learned during my first days of college. So far, then, higher education was worth it.

♭♪·♭♪·♭♪·

I was set to major in journalism, so one of the first classes on my schedule was, not unexpectedly, Journalism 101. Unfortunately, for me, I got off on the wrong foot from the very first day in class.

As soon as the students had settled into our seats, the "Professor" announced, "Grading in this class will be based on three exams. Now I have heard from some other teachers that certain female students approached them and offered to trade sex for better grades. I want you to know that in this class if any of you have such an idea, my office hours are Tuesday and Thursdays from 11 until 3 and I do keep condoms in my desk".

If it had been an attempt at humor, no one laughed. The room was silent, until I broke the tension. I stood, looked at him, and quietly addressed him, "Get the fuck out of here you asshole".

I stormed out of the classroom, to the College of Communications office, and changed "sections" to take the course from a different professor. The other section was taught by the Chairman of the department; so, I assumed it would be better. I couldn't think of a way that it could be worse. *As usual in academia, I was wrong.*

Our first written assignment was for the entire class to attend a visiting lecture on campus given by Pierre Salinger, former press secretary for John F. Kennedy and later for Lyndon B. Johnson. We were to attend his lecture, take notes, ask questions, and write a "newspaper story". The stories were to be turned in during the next morning's class, with no late papers accepted because "newspapers have deadlines".

I already thought the assignment was boring, and I couldn't imagine 65 (the number of students in the class) articles all saying the exact same thing written in the exact same *who-what-when-where-why* form. I couldn't bring myself to turn in the *same-ole-same-ole* dribble that everyone in the class would be writing.

Not duplicating the comedy script style that I had turned in on the first day of high school journalism class, I still did not feel compelled to turn in a perfectly straight newspaper story. Instead, I wrote a piece that provided the requisite setting in the first paragraph, but after that I transitioned to satirical piece stereotyping my classmates and speculating what they were actually thinking versus what they were writing in their class papers. Admittedly, it was a little mean-spirited in my dismissal of their work based solely on their clothes or hair styles or makeup; but I still thought it was funny.

The professor, however, unlike my high school journalism teacher, was not the least bit amused; a fact that he made very clear by affixing a bright-red "F" (for failing) to my paper. Apparently, that alone was not enough, because he decided to publicly scold me in front of the class, as if my paper had somehow been an affront to his authority or to the grave significance of the assignment.

"Mister Green, I have already been warned that you are a troublemaker," he began. Apparently, the previous asshole had put the word out about my storming out of the first-day-of-class.

He continued, "I can tell from reading this, no matter how erudite you think your writing is, it is not. You should consider changing majors immediately, because it is obvious that you will never get a job at a newspaper. You lack discipline, respect for authority, and the ability to follow instructions. Your writing will never be in print, anywhere."

I had suffered authoritative scolding-humiliation before: from that teacher in the 5th grade in Sullivan County schools and later from the administration at Two Rivers High School. *BASTA!*

I didn't care that this cat was the author of the required introductory textbook there and at other schools; I was not going to accept his abuse no matter how important he was supposed to be. I followed his advice and

THE LEGEND DIES ON — GARY GREEN

immediately marched to the registrar's office to withdraw from *Communications* and switch to the *College of Liberal Arts*.[86]

That move allowed me to further focus on my initial educational goal: to get-the-hell-out-of-there in less than four years. With an undeclared major, I had the freedom to explore multiple fields across all of the colleges in the university system. What that meant was that I could cherry-pick courses for that first session; courses that would allow me to over-perform so that I could double up and triple up in coming sessions.

To further prove my "performance excellence" (so that I could take the heavy course load), I showed my "academic maturity" by declaring a major despite not being required to do so. I chose the then-new field of *American Studies*. It was an unstructured liberal arts discipline that had been created to appease liberal faculty members without offending conservative stalwarts. Because it was new and only a placation, the few students in the major were free to do whatever they wanted as long as we cloaked it academic mumbo-jumbo.

I signed up for *Guitar Playing 101* and also *Music Theory* in the College of Music. I signed up for *Introduction to French* (though I had been taking French classes since the 2nd grade). I topped those academic non-challenges off with *Creative Writing, Introduction To The History of Western Civilization,* and *Black Religion in America.*

At the end of the term, I was certain that when the report of my grades were mailed to my parents, my father would be less-than-amused at my class choices for his out-of-state-tuition investment; but I was equally certain that my mother would be impressed with my stellar grade point average (which, indeed, was high enough to qualify me for the increased load of classes moving forward). I was right on both counts.

To prove to myself that the journalism professor was wrong, I applied for a position as a reporter at the student-run newspaper. That paper came out daily and, because of the large student population at U.T., it was actually the fourth-largest daily paper in the state; an almost-guaranteed steppingstone to a post-graduation job at any daily newspaper in Tennessee.

---

[86] Less than ten years later, when I received an official confirmation letter of my first *Pulitzer Prize* nomination at a daily newspaper, I sent him a photocopy of the letter along with a container of *Vaseline Petroleum Jelly* and a note from me that read, *"You probably don't remember me being your student for two days, but I wanted to share this with you because you were such an influence on me; and I included this lube so that when you stick this up your pompous ass it won't hurt as much"*. It was a departure notice technique that I would use frequently over the years with various employers. For him, I also sent him a copy of my university documents showing that a year after his class, I switched back to majoring in Journalism and my early-out credits.

THE POET LAUREATE SOUL OF FOLKIE ROCK & ROLL

As a writing sample, I submitted a first-person essay about my encounter with the Asian landlord couple in Nashville. The editor of the paper told me that they reserved their reporter slots for senior journalism majors positioning themselves for a job after graduation. Instead, she offered me a three-days-a-week *columnist* role because she liked my writing. With the column, she gave me the freedom to write about any subject and with any voice. We named the column for my angst song that I had played at the coffeehouse: *America's Child.*

♩♪♩♪♩♪

About a month or so into that first academic quarter, I glanced up the northern sky to see huge bat-signal-like beams of carbon-arc spotlights rotating above Knoxville. Searchlights, as they were called, usually indicated a theater premier, a store grand opening, a fair, or carnival. It was a common advertising gimmick to promote events to attract the public.

My late-great fire-engine red Valient had been replaced with a Ford Maverick (once again courtesy of my supportive, if not vocally so, father). Bored and curious (and always a sucker for carnivals), I jumped into the green-and-black Ford and headed toward the lights.

It turned out that the searchlights were coming from the local Chevrolet dealership, which probably meant nothing more than a sales pitch to announce that year's new car lineup. But, curiously, in the center of the parking lot was a flatbed trailer with a couple of amplifiers and microphones positioned in the center of it. That makeshift stage probably indicated that there was going to be live music to mark the introduction of the new car lineup.

I wasn't particularly excited about seeing a used-car salesman's kids in a garage band; but what-the-hell, I'd driven across town and had nothing better to do. So, I decided to stick around and see what kind of characters would be playing.

I surveyed the milling-around crowd, who apparently had seen some other advertising for the event and already knew who would be on stage. From the comportment of that crowd (if one could call that small handful of people a "crowd"), I surmised that it would be a country act. The potential audience was about as working-class lily-white hillbilly as I could imagine; most would have called them "redneck", but to me they were just East Tennessee home-folks.

After a few minutes a long, black Cadillac Brougham pulled up beside the stage, and out poured four women and two men. As they were walking toward the makeshift stage, I realized that the woman in the rear was *Mother Maybelle Carter* —the creator of the *Carter Family Churchlick* style of guitar playing that I had learned from Jim Medford. I was about to see living history!

THE LEGEND DIES ON — GARY GREEN

I cannot over-emphasize the significance of seeing her; not just for myself, but in the context of the history of both Country Music and of *any* popular music that uses guitars. The very genre of country music had begun when the new "record business" of RCA's Victor Talking Machine Company sent producer Ralph Peer to the South to find talent. With portable recording equipment, he set up in a small hotel room in Bristol Virginia (on the Tennessee state line and 21 miles from Kingsport), to hear auditions on August 1, 1927.[87] On that August afternoon Peer recorded a local family trio called *The Carter Family* and in doing so he created the entire genre that would become Country Music; but much more importantly, it also set the foundation for pop music…and rock and roll.

The group was made up of patriarch 36-year-old A.P. Carter and his wife Sara along with his brother's wife, 18-year-old Maybelle (who was Sara's first cousin). A.P. wrote original songs (or adapted folk songs) and sang. Sara sang and accompanied the group on autoharp or guitar. Sister-in-law Maybelle played a second guitar and provided a second female voice, usually for harmony. A.P.'s brother, Maybelle's husband, served as the business manager and booking agent for the family band.

It was that second guitar —*Maybelle's*— that would change everything about music in America, influencing of course country, bluegrass, and folk, but also creating the *form* for pop and even rock music. Quite simply, Maybelle Carter invented playing *lead guitar*.

Until Maybelle Carter, the guitar was strictly a rhythm accompaniment instrument. She introduced the addition of a melody line played on the

---

[87] One appointment was with a band led by a Mississippi-born gandy dancer for the Mobile and Ohio Railroad who had been a panhandling busker to supplement his meager wages. Later promoted to a brakeman, young *Jimmie Rogers* had quit the railroad when he was as diagnosed with tuberculosis at the age of 27 and formed a band performing hillbilly versions of Broadway and Vaudeville songs. *(A "gandy dancer" was a railroad term for a section hand (general laborer); and a brakeman was the person in charge of coupling and uncoupling cars at train stations)*

Literally minutes before their appointment with Peer, the band fired Rogers over his being the "front man" of the group. *(Apparently my Gastonia band adventures were rooted in a long history of such shenanigans.)* Both the band and Rogers reported to the audition for Peer, competing for the producer's favor. To everyone's surprise, Peer dismissed the band, but asked Rogers to stay and record with just a guitar and no band. Years later, Peer said that he liked Rogers' voice and passion in singing, but the song selection wasn't what The Victor Company had sent Peer to find. His mission was to scout for new original material; not rehashes of copyrighted Vaudeville standards. He invited Rogers to come back in a couple of months with fresh material. Rogers pivoted to singing White-yodeling versions of African American blues songs that he had learned from his mostly-Black coworker railroad section hands. Those recordings and the Rogers' subsequent studio records became major successes for the label. Sadly, the tuberculosis spurred pleurisy, and the singer died in 1933.

THE POET LAUREATE SOUL OF FOLKIE ROCK & ROLL

guitar. Other than a few classical and jazz musicians (like Andrés Segovia, who weren't *commercial*), no one had ever done that.[88]

Beyond that innovation, she also created a style of playing that produced multiple sounds simultaneously from one guitar. Though she modestly claimed that she learned the technique from other Appalachian mountain pickers, it is indisputable that her usage of it was the first commercial introduction of guitar melody lines or first-position in bridges between verses.

Since that day in 1927, her guitar style has been imitated (or, rather, attempted) by any guitar stylist worth their salt, regardless of their style of music. It is generically known as *The Carter Lick* or *The Carter Scratch* or sometimes *The Church Lick*. When you hear it, there is no mistaking what it is.[89]

---

[88] That innovation involved her playing the guitar chords like any picker would do, but she used only the treble strings of the guitar to play the chord triad. Simultaneously, she used her thumb to alternate the bass strings on the guitar —creating the sound illusion that there were two instruments: a bass guitar and a rhythm guitar. But earth-shatteringly beyond that already revolutionary innovation in guitar play-ing, she would also play the melody of a song —at the same time that she was playing rhythm and bass. Combing a complex series of hammer-on and pull-off string techniques with bass-note runs, she was a one-woman-band of accompaniment; at the time, no one had ever done those things.

[89] After the original family group disbanded (and Sara and A.P. divorced) Maybelle continued to tour with her three young daughters. Helen age 16, June age 14, and Anita age 10. By the age of 40 she was being booked as Mother Maybelle and the Carter Sisters. Touring with the girls, She hired a young Chet Atkins as the guitarist to backup for them F . But by the late 1950's their popularity had waned, and they became a secondary or tertiary act relegated to small-audience events.

As the early 1960's folk music revival hit the northeast, urban folkies rediscovered the guitar-legend of Mother Maybelle and she enjoyed a fame resurgence playing folk festivals and New York clubs (without her daughters). In 1963, she and her daughters began touring with and backing up Johnny Cash. Five years later, her middle daughter, June, famously married Cash.

In the late 1960's ABC television's The Johnny Cash Show was a ratings behemoth and Mother Maybelle, and her daughters once again were nationally famous. Cash would often tell the Ralph Peer story to the nationwide television audiences before introducing her and singing along.

But by the early 1970's, Cash was on the downside of one of his less-in-demand periods, so Mother Maybelle and the daughters (sans Mrs. Cash) were once again on the tertiary tour circuit. Hence, the flatbed trailer stage at a car dealership in east Tennessee where they played to a crowd of less-than 50 people. She had another brief resurgence of fame a few months after the Knoxville appearance when California country-rock band *The Nitty Gritty Dirt Band* released their seventh album, *Will The Circle Be Unbroken*, featuring Mother Maybelle and a who's-who of traditional hillbilly musicians. The album's title-cut was, of course, one of The Carter Family's best-known songs.

THE LEGEND DIES ON — GARY GREEN

The next few hours were truly seminal in my development and the rest of my life; and it was far-more impactful than merely attending a concert. On that night, at a Chevrolet dealership in Knoxville Tennessee, I was pressed against the edge of a flatbed trailer to see the founder of Country Music and the originator of lead guitar playing. I was less than two-feet from her; so close that when Mother Maybelle tapped her foot, the dust from the truck bed went up my nose.

Near the end of their performance, Mother Maybelle asked the small assembly if there were any requests for songs. I began calling out some old ones from pretty-obscure Carter Family records; songs that featured the guitar style that Jim Medford had introduced me to in Gastonia. She didn't simply pick one and play it; *she played all of them!*

We've already established that I didn't look like your run-of-the-mill hillbilly or like a Nashville establishment cat. In fact, I didn't look like your average college-student hippie either; though my fringed jacket and jeans might have passed, my cowboy hat, boots, snap-button shirt, and vest sent a clear visual that there was something up with me.

And there I stood in all my glory, pushing against the stage, knowing every Carter Family song and singing along with them.

By the time the show was over, 63-year-old Mother Maybelle apparently was about as anxious to find out "who-the-heck is the young kid" as I was to meet and talk to the legend. She was 45 years older than me; so yeah, I was definitely a *young kid* at 18.

As she came off the stage and saw me approaching, she made a beeline straight toward me rather than avoiding an obvious fan (like many stars would have done). When she was directly in front of me, she asked if I wanted to go inside and talk away from the crowd.

Gee, let me think: Mother Maybelle Carter wants to know if I'd like to talk privately with her!

We went into the showroom where the dealership had prepared a temporary private green room in one of the sales offices. Once we got inside, she formally introduced herself. It was almost comical when she put out her hand to shake mine and said, "I am Maybelle Carter"; as if I didn't know!

I introduced myself and at the same time answered the question that I was sure she was going to ask: how/why did I know all of her songs. I told her about my fascination with her family and her guitar style. I told her about my history, about Jim Medford and my struggle to play *The Carter Lick*, at least as well as he had played it.

Something about what I said must have interested her, because she smiled and asked me if I would like for her to show me how she does it. Speechless, I nodded a "yes" and managed to squeak out a "please". I mean what else could I even think of to say?

THE POET LAUREATE SOUL OF FOLKIE ROCK & ROLL

I could not believe this was happening. This was more amazing than Allen Ginsberg calling me a "poet"! *I was getting a guitar lesson from Mother Maybelle Carter!*

As she reopened her guitar case and once again took out that famous arch-top Gibson guitar, it occurred to me that the word "legend" is thrown around too cavalierly; and "icon" falls short of the influence she had on American music.

Beyond that, the guitar itself is (as I write this) a museum piece. That 1928 *Gibson L-5* guitar is today behind glass at the Country Music Hall of Fame in Nashville. But I can honestly say that not only have I played that very guitar, but I received a guitar lesson on it from Maybelle herself! *No, really!*

She asked what I'd like to learn, and somehow, I was able to get the words out, "Could you teach me to play the *Wildwood Flower?*" (Probably the most iconic Carter Family song[90].)

Without hesitation, she slid a *Hamilton* capo up to the fourth fret of her Gibson guitar[91]. Then came the heart-stopping moment. She handed me *that* guitar; the very guitar that had started it all… *the very guitar where lead guitar playing was invented.* She put THAT guitar into my hands.

It was as if Thor had handed me his hammer; as if Leonardo had put his paintbrush in my hand; as if Babe Ruth had said, here's my bat, let me show you how to hit! I would not have been surprised if there had been a thunderclap and a bolt of lightning as I touched it![92]

---

[90] Calling any Carter Family song THE icon is pretty difficult. Their originals, other than Wildwood Flower, include: *Wabash Cannonball, Can the Circle Be Unbroken, Worried Man Blues, Keep On The Sunny Side, There'll Be Joy, Joy, Joy, See That My Grave Is Kept Green, My Clinch Mountain Home, Lulu Walls, Lonesome Valley, Little Darlin' Pal of Mine, John Hardy Was a Desperate Little Man, Jimmie Brown, the Newsboy, Gospel Ship, Foggy Mountain Top, East Virginia Blues, Bury Me Under the Weeping Willow, Black Jack Davy,* and dozens more.

[91] As noted earlier, a capo (pronounced with a long-A rather than a short one like a Mafia boss), is a clamp placed on the neck of a guitar to transpose and shorten the playable length of the strings—hence raising the pitch. It allows a picker to play in a difficult key by playing more-simple chords and just raising the pitch.

[92] Up close and with no one it the room but us, the first thing I noticed was the tuning; it wasn't standard. It seemed to be tuned at least a whole step lower and maybe even two steps lower than standard. Rather than E-A-D-G-B-E, it seemed to be tuned D-G-C-F-A-D. I had used a drop-D tuning on my bass E string, but I'd never tuned-down a whole musical step. When I asked her about it she told me that it made the strings last long and she needed it for her alto voice.

THE LEGEND DIES ON — GARY GREEN

It only got more surreal and better. She told me to pick-it-out. As I tried, she came to the front of the guitar to watch me then she walked back behind me to look over my shoulder, as I struggled.

For the next 45 minutes to an hour, she held my right thumb and guided it, lifted my left fingers on and off of strings, pushed my right fingers brushing across strings; joking with me the whole time about how nervous I obviously was.

When she finally felt like I "got it", she sang as I picked. Mother Maybelle Carter sang Wildwood Flower while I picked her guitar!

Incidentally, the alternating bass strings and the tapping of her patent leather shoe seemed to instantly cure my rhythm issue... at least for that evening and that song.

The lesson might have lasted longer, but we were interrupted by her daughter, Helen, who walked in to say, "come on Momma, we're ready to go", then she apologized for her mother hogging MY time.

What-the-hell, Maybelle Carter taking up *MY* time? On what planet in what alternative universe had I landed?

As she packed up to leave, Mother Maybelle gave me an address in Nashville to write to her if I had any questions. I recognized the 16th Avenue South address as a business office; and I knew that she lived out in Madison (near my former apartment). Nonetheless, for the next three or four years I semi-regularly corresponded with her; I'd write to her and a couple of weeks later she would respond, always encouraging and a few times discussing the finer points of the Carter Lick.

I also bought an autoharp and learned to play it because of my meeting her. *(The autoharp was her other instrument.)*

Postscript About Mother Maybelle

Sometime just before Halloween of 1978, I received word that Mother Maybelle, at 69 years old, had unexpectedly died of pneumonia the week before. (She told me that she had developed Parkinson's Disease and almost stopped any public appearances; but her death still was a total shock to me.)

I was too far away to make it to a funeral. Anyway, I was certain it would be a commercial circus with every Nashville social-climber jockeying for a position in the funeral service. I did send a telegram to Reba Hancock and asked her to pass my sincere condolences to J.R. and June and tell them that Mother Maybelle had taught me to properly play guitar.

I also sat down and wrote a song about her, which I taped and sent to June Carter Cash at the Hendersonville lake house where she and J.R. lived.

By then I had already recorded my first two Folkways albums. On my third album, I was obliged to include that tribute song. Moe Asch

THE POET LAUREATE SOUL OF FOLKIE ROCK & ROLL

allowed me to give a three-or-four-minute monologue before the song, talking about that night in Knoxville. That little talk is immortalized on the Smithsonian recording. The song follows:

Travlin' on the road since she was 17 years old.
Her mother never knew it'd turn out this way.
From a Scott County church to a Bristol hotel room...
Every town is different; but every town is the same.

There'll be no more flatbed trailer stages.
No more electric fans in high school gyms.
No more one-night- stands.
Or nights without her man.
The last Minstrel is coming home.
Romantic life of a rambler ain't all it's cracked to be.
And living like a gypsy ain't always living free.
Tryin' to raise three kids in a backseat and floorboard:
Singing is her trouble, but happiness is her reward.

No more electric fans in high school gyms.
No more one-night- stands.
Or nights without her man.
There'll be no more flatbed trailer stages.
The last Minstrel is coming home.

From the greasepaint on her face that makes the minstrel seen
To the rhythm in her fingers that helps the minstrel sing
How many generations have grown up with her name?
How many still sing the songs that she sang?

There'll be no more flatbed trailer stages.
No more electric fans in high school gyms.
No more one-night- stands.
Or nights without her man.
The last Minstrel is coming home.

— *The Last Minstrel*, by Gary Green, 1982. as recorded on Folkways Records album FH5356, *Still At Large*

THE LEGEND DIES ON — GARY GREEN

Opus Ten:
Vietnam, Wounded Knee, and "Radical" Songs

Don't you ever cut your hair.
Don't accept the white man's shame.
Don't forget the truth you bear.
Or forsake your grandfathers' name.
— *Sovereign Nation*, by Gary Green

Make no mistake about it: I never intended to become any kind of radical or a "political" anything. I was —and still am— just a wide-eyed hillbilly "git-tar-picker" *(and not a particularly good one, at that)*. But I was raised to try to understand things and if something was wrong, to try to do the honorable thing and fix it. That's why my uncle went to Europe to fight the Nazis and why Daddy went to the Pacific to fight Imperialism. The late sixties and early seventies were confusing times for a young man bred into the bowels of such honorable intentions *(no matter how convoluted they may have become)*.

One thing that became crystal-clear to me from my college days was that some people, in positions of power, thought that guitars were more dangerous than six-guns[93].

Though for me to understand why songs got Ella May Wiggins killed it would take a clandestine Federal agent's report that my music was dangerously "subversive" and that I used it as a cover to run guns through a U.S. Army blockade. *No, really, that's what he said.* And I just wanted to sing hillbilly songs!

I suppose my understanding of not only Ella May but the potential power of songs, began from my being bored one Sunday night and deciding to go to a Methodist church campus ministry service. Innocent enough, no?

Though I was raised *Southern Baptist*, by college I adhered to what Woody Guthrie famously said when the administrators at Bellevue demanded that he list a religion on his admission form, "All or none; it's

---

[93] Queen Mary I had degreed that there could be no *"books, ballads, rhymes, and interludes without royal authorization"*; Plato had warned that *"Any musical innovation is full of danger to the whole state, and ought be prohibited (it) imperceptivity penetrates into manners and customs; whence issuing with greater force, it invades contracts between man and man and goes on to laws and constitutions, in utter recklessness, ending at last by overthrow of all rights, private as well as public."* And, of course Woody Guthrie had said, *"one good song is worth 10,000 of your best speeches and a couple of armies."*

THE POET LAUREATE SOUL OF FOLKIE ROCK & ROLL

your choice". Like Woody, I saw myself as a religious or atheist egalitarian; pick your own flavor.

I had played organ in a *Presbyterian* church in Gastonia. I had played guitar in an *African Methodist Episcopal Zion* church in Knoxville. In Charlotte I sang campfire songs at a *Synagogue*.

Guitar-less, I had meditated and listened to chanting at a *Buddhist Temple* in Atlanta. And I had *tried* to rhythmically chant Qur'an verse at a *Sh'ia Mosque*.

Also *(and most significantly)*, since my matriculation at the University of Tennessee, I had started going to the *Epworth Ecumenical Church* for their regular series of folk music events. So, visiting the Methodists wasn't really a radical departure for me.

It wasn't like I was joining one of the campus churches or anything like that. Besides, I had already been way-too intimidated by the amazing musicians at Epworth to spend too much time in any church community. Those Epworth gatherings were hosted by some phenomenal musicians whose talent and skills were just so over-the-top that I wouldn't even take a guitar with me or tell them that I was a musician[94].

Nonetheless, they provided immeasurable inspiration... and education... for my hungers, curiosity, and continuing search for direction.

---

[94] At the top of that Epworth list was an incredibly versatile talent named *John McCutcheon*. Only a couple of years older than me, but far more skilled than I could ever be, he played 12-string, autoharp, banjo, fiddle, mountain dulcimer, acoustic six-string guitar, and most notably a 29-string trapezoid called a hammered dulcimer (named for the four little hammers used to play the strings). That circle-of-fifths contraption itself was enough to intimidate me; but John's overall talent and his very Pete-Seeger-like folksy charm just totally shut me down. When John played, it was like attending the most interesting educational session ever. I never failed to learn something when he played and talked before and after songs. He was like a performing ethnomusicologist... only interesting. Despite leading very-compelling sing-alongs, he always left me thinking, "I could never do anything like that, but I wish I could". Equally intimidating was a Knoxville-local African American musician-songwriter-storyteller named *Sparky Rucker* (okay, his name was James; but he was called *Sparky*). Eight-years older than me and six years older than John, Sparky had created a way to merge folk and gospel sounds with bottleneck blues and theme it all with poignant civil rights and labor lyrics. When Sparky would play, it was impossible to not become totally absorbed in the force and intensity that he exuded. It was as if the fate of the world depended on adherence to his passion. And he added to those powerful songs, riveting storytelling that just wouldn't let go of me. If I had been looking for a living Ella May Wiggins character, whose music could change the world (without getting assassinated), then its name would have been Sparky Rucker. He was that powerful. Between those two Epworth cats, there was just no way my little 18-year-old wannabe songwriter self was going to let on that I might pick a little bit of guitar and sing some original songs.

THE LEGEND DIES ON — GARY GREEN

To further the intimidation, and my fascination, sometimes those shows were put on in conjunction with the historic *Highlander Research and Education Center* in nearby New Market Tennessee. I had read about Highlander in follow-up research from that book that had introduced me to Ella May.

Just meeting people from Highlander would have been a significant educational experience; but attending one (or multiple) of their events was an incredibly special experience. It was my first, but certainly not last, encounter with Highlander[95].

On those Highlander nights at the church, the performers would include a living Who's-Who from that Seeger-Guthrie-Lomax book I had found in high school, *Hard Hitting Songs for Hard-Hit People*. That group included coal-country singer/songwriter *Sarah Ogan Gunning* (sibling of *Aunt Molly Jackson* and of *Jim Garland*), *Nimrod Workman, George Tucker, Hazel Dickens* (who a decade later I would share a bill with), *Alice Gerrard, Guy Carawan* (co-writer of *"We Shall Overcome"*), and several other fabled Appalachian activist musicians.

The Epworth-Highlander nights were often hosted by another folksinger named *Anne Romaine*[96]. Though I didn't know it at the time, Romaine was from Gastonia; but, as noted, I was much too intimidated by all of them to get into discussions about roots and backgrounds.

In fact, I rarely spoke to any of the key people there, with the exception of Sparky *(who was just super-friendly to me)*. For the most part, despite its folk music bent and educational opportunities, I treated Epworth as if it were just any *church social*[97].

---

[95] Founded in 1932, Highlander was one of a handful of labor schools that trained activists and union organizers across generations. Among its alumnae were *Rosa Parks* before her famous bus-boycott-triggering Montgomery action, *Dr. Martin Luther King, Ralph Abernathy, John Lewis* and many SNCC members. By the 1960's and 70's Highlander was focused on worker health and safety in the coalfields of Appalachia. The school was often a target of violence from the KKK as well as law enforcement groups accusing them of being a "communist training camp", with attacks continuing well into the 21st century (including a 2019 arson that left behind white supremist graffiti).

[96] Besides bringing Nimrod Workman and other roots writers to young audiences, she was the founder of *The Southern Folk Cultural Revival Project*, was a close friend of Mother Maybelle. and co-founded Atlanta-based *The Great Speckled Bird* —the south's most-read "underground" newspaper.

[97] Being from Southern culture, I viewed churches not always as exclusively religious institutions but also as community, social, economic, educational, and music gathering places. Accurate or not, that was my (and the general Southern) opinion. Hence, in the big picture, my attendance at the Epworth events was just the latest in attending not-necessarily-religious events at various church denominations over the years.

THE POET LAUREATE SOUL OF FOLKIE ROCK & ROLL

So, I had absolutely no reservations about adding another flavor by going to the Campus Methodist Center on that fateful night in the fall of 1972. That afternoon I had seen a flyer on campus announcing an evening showing of a film providing "a Christian perspective on the Vietnam War".

I already was nominally against that War, and my entire Miami adventure, essentially, had been a three-day-long anti-war demonstration. Less of a traditional hippie "peacenik" or any kind of anti-war activist, I was just a guy troubled by having seen so many of my high school classmates sent home from Vietnam in body bags. It didn't make sense to me because it didn't seem like a clear attack on us as World War II had been.

And of course, like most Americans I was pretty freaked out by the revelations of the mass murder of more than 500 civilians by U.S. troops at Mỹ Lai. But also, like most Americans I hoped (and believed) that was an isolated incident and certainly *could not* be American foreign policy.

So, on that Sunday evening, I thought it would be interesting to see what a conventional church had to say about the war. What I expected to be just another church social, turned out to be... not even what I had expected.

The preacher began the meeting by introducing a short documentary movie showing grim footage of children who had been maimed by razor-sharp springs shot from bombs insidiously disguised as stuffed animals and other toys. *Seriously, WTF?*

It showed other non-lethal (but maiming) bombs that had been disguised as pineapples and guava fruit spewing almost-impossible-to-remove steel pellets to rip flesh or shooting out spiderweb-type strings to trigger more explosions. There were still other anti-civilian bombs that were disguised as animal dung and triggered by complex urine-sniffing and audio-tracking detonators.

Even more alarming, the film identified the manufacturers of some of the most insidious of these devices as *Honeywell* (the maker of thermostats and heating regulators found in millions of American homes), and *ITT* (who at that time also manufactured *Hostess Twinkies* and who, during the second world war, had made payments to finance Heinrich Himmler).

The film equally indicted *General Electric, Dupont* (makers of the antifreeze in my car), *Lockheed Martin, Raytheon,* and *Thiokol* (makers of the *Morton Salt* on most American dinner tables); all as makers of weapons designed specifically to maim civilians and their children or destroy their crops... not military targets.

When the film was over, the preacher introduced a decorated Vietnam veteran to verify and comment on the claims made in the film. He was a representative from a group called *Winter Soldier: Vietnam Veterans*

THE LEGEND DIES ON — GARY GREEN

Against The War—a group that I knew extremely well from my recent adventure in Miami Beach.

The vet confirmed the atrocities that were shown in the documentary and then explained that the mission was not *to kill enemy soldiers*, but rather to *mutilate children and the elderly too infirmed to fight*. It was a carefully orchestrated tactic created to demoralize the people of the country so they would pressure their government into surrendering, he detailed, adding that his orders specifically were to "clean-up" after the demoralization process.

He said that since he'd been back home, he had heard defenders of the policy say, "well there are atrocities on both sides". He shook his head as if to answer those people, "I can assure you, that simply is not true. No one is planting bombs in toys distributed to American children." He added that more than 4,700 of those devices had been dropped during the previous May alone.

Propaganda or not, the film was like my generation's version of what my parents must have felt when they saw the first pictures of the liberation of Nazi concentration camps: the stark horrors of *pure evil*, but in this case inflicted on children. AND, in the case... WE were the perpetrators.

It is safe to say that most of us attending that church service left with the distinct feeling that buying a *Hostess Twinkie* or using a *Honeywell thermostat* was a tacit endorsement of the maiming of children on the other side of the world. It was no wonder that many returning veterans were met with, "how many babies have you killed?" rather than some kind of heroic welcoming party. *(To this day, I have a hard time with that "thank-you-for-your-service" bullshit.)*

As for myself, I certainly came out of the church thinking that by being silently complacent in our day-to-day lives, we were all accomplices, accessories in those crimes against humanity.

Among the many songs that I had grown up singing was The Marine's Hymn and especially the last verse: *"if the Army and the Navy every look on heaven's scene; they will find the streets are guarded by United States Marines"*. I would never be able to sing that again —at least not with the same awe and reverence.

More complexly and troubling, I also lost all respect for any Vietnam veteran who had not become a vocal opponent of that war after seeing it firsthand. I decided that they were either oblivious, stupid, or in collusion. Either way, I had no use for them and considered them war criminals as surely as the Nuremberg criminals who claimed, "I was just following orders". War resisters (like VVAW), draft resisters, and people marching in the streets of America all seemed much more heroic to me.

Following the first-hand advice from Reba Hancock, of Kris Kristofferson, Jerry Reed, and the published advice from Woody Guthrie and

THE POET LAUREATE SOUL OF FOLKIE ROCK & ROLL

Pete Seeger, I decided to write about what I saw in the world. On that day, what I saw was this horrific exposé on film. So, as soon as I got home, I sat down and wrote my first anti-war song. But it wasn't an *olive branches & doves beating-the-swords-to-plowshares* song. Rather, it was an angry indictment of all of us, myself included.

The next weekend, at the campus open-mic room, I began with my popular "angst" song and then followed it with my new song, *You're Just As Guilty*. Not only was it not as well-received, but the operators of the venue asked me not to come back... ever. "This is a safe-place for people to drink, dance, sing along, and have a good time. They don't come here to be preached at," the organizers lectured me as they fired me. Wow! I got fired for being too passionate! Talk about confusing!

A few days later, someone from that Methodist church contacted me and asked if I would play at an anti-war meeting that they were having on Saturday. My song got a much more rousing reception there than it had at the campus open mic.

In fact, it was so well-received that during the next few weeks I was invited to play for an entire alphabet-soup of antiwar and peace organizations: *PCPJ, NPAC, SANE, AMFP, WRL, SDS, WSP, FTA, PFOC, Yippies, NMCEWV*, and a handful of others including my friends at VVAW[98]. It seemed that I was becoming the darling of the antiwar protester circuit, not by plan but by default.

Shortly after the Christmas break, that church and several of those alphabet-soup groups asked me to come with them on a Christian bus trip to Washington DC they were planning for late January to sing peace songs at Nixon's second inauguration. They estimated it would be a 12-hour bus trip. I agreed to play but opted out of the bus ride and decided to drive, knowing I could make it in half that time.

They had arranged housing at George Washington University in DC. That whole trip was an adventure within itself *(the conservative University of Tennessee had no coed dormitories, so housing at the GW campus was a whole new world)*.

Far beyond that, though, were the pivotal events of the next day that changed everything for me. The event was set for the National Mall. On the mile-or-so walk from campus to the Mall the next morning, I took a

---

[98] PCPJ = Peoples Coalition For Peace & Justice; NPAC = National Peace Action Coalition; SANE = National Committee for a Sane Nuclear Policy; AMFP = Another Mother For Peace; WRL = War Resisters League; SDS = Students for a Democratic Society; WSP = Women Strike for Peace; FTA = Fuck The Army; PFOC = Prairie Fire Organizing Committee; Yippies = Youth International Party; NMCEWV = National Mobilization Committee to End the War in Vietnam.

THE LEGEND DIES ON — GARY GREEN

shortcut and inadvertently walked into the staging area for the Army National Guard that President Nixon had activated for the occasion.

The guardsmen were, more-or-less, my age and easily could have been my high school class peers. I am sure I made quite a sight for them as I cut through their ranks wearing my leather jacket with 24-inch fringe from the sleeves, cowboy hat, jeans, and boots, my hair down to my shoulders, and a guitar slung over my back. They were just as weird-looking to me, with their GI-cropped hair, olive-drab uniforms, and combat boots.

As I cut through, I watched them affix bayonets to the end of their rifles; and I watched them receive their issue of live ammunition for their belts.

It occurred to me that those long knives and the bullets were for me and my friends. These American soldiers were preparing to stab me or shoot me because I had the audacity to sing songs opposed to hiding razor blade bombs inside teddy bears and disguising explosives to look like fruit to give to starving people (starving because we had burned their rice fields with Napalm and Agent Orange).

There was something seriously wrong. This was not the America that I knew. The demonstration was not anti-American; in fact, the speakers were members of *The United States Congress,* leaders of labor unions, movie and television celebrities, and student leaders. Yet, our own military was prepared to kill us. *I just didn't understand.*

It was January 20, 1973. The National Mall was covered with ice and about five-inches of snow. I had expected the demonstration to be large; maybe as many as 500 to 750 people. I did not even expect the more-than 100,000 people that were the official DC Police estimate of crowd size. *My God! That was more people than most towns that I had lived in.*

The National Guard took up positions circumnavigating the entire mall; in effect creating a human fence around 100-thousand shivering-cold people and only 75 port-a-potties.

Just as the speeches began, the soldiers stepped aside to allow a large open-back truck to pass through and toward the stage. The bed of the truck was filled with a rough looking mixture of hooded KKK members and other assorted thugs who were later said to be from something called "The National Caucus of Labor Committees" (though *that* was never confirmed as far as I know). As demonstrators jumped out of the way, the truck plowed through the crowd with no regard for not hitting people.

As it approached the stage, Reverend Ralph Abernathy and U.S. Congresswoman Bella Abzug stood at the microphone and spoke to the crowd, *"That truck must not be allowed to reach this stage. Stop them no matter what".*

I watched 100,000 people stand and turn toward the truck. In mass we walked toward it, ready to turn it over or whatever else we needed to do. Talk about "Power To The People"; *holy-crap!*

THE POET LAUREATE SOUL OF FOLKIE ROCK & ROLL

Realizing the danger, the driver of the truck switched to reverse gear and slowly backed down the path he'd come. As he did so, the crowd narrowed in tighter. Speakers on stage instructed the crowd to let the truck leave and when the driver reached the perimeter, the National Guard again opened their ranks to let the truck pass before reclosing their ranks.

I still was not even 19 years old, and I just could not grasp that what I saw was in the America where I had grown up. This was the first of the life-changing events that hit me that day.

As I stood trying to understand what had just happened, Pete Seeger mounted the steep stairway to the stage and with only his banjo began singing *We Shall Overcome*. In seconds, tens of thousands of people were singing along with him and holding hands on the Mall.

Pete was able to completely take away the tension that the near-attack had caused. It was the magical power of music; of a good song and a good man. I watched him, stood beside him singing, and I read the words painted around the head of his banjo: **This machine surrounds hate and forces it to surrender.** Indeed, it did; he did.

The calming power of the music consumed me so much that I didn't even digest the super-cool fact that I was sharing a stage with *Pete Seeger* —the cat that I had "discovered" in the Gastonia library, who had pissed off CBS during his Smothers Brothers appearance, who I'd seen singing with *Mister Green Jeans* on *Captain Kangaroo*, who had co-written the book where I discovered Ella May, who had written the banjo lesson book that I'd used to learn to play, the guy who… well… who was Pete Seeger. That was awesome that I was standing there with him. I mean, how many kids hang out with a cat that they read about in the library?

Then, as I stood backstage surveying the crowd and trying to understand, my eyes turned toward the Washington Monument. There were 50 U.S. flags around the monument, one representing each state. Someone began lowering those flags and re-raising them upside down. *(Any upside-down national flag was an international nautical signal of a ship in dire distress.)*

I felt tears rolling from my eyes as I watched and realized that indeed, my country was a ship in distress; dire, deep-seeded distress.

During the decades since that day, I have often looked back on seeing those flags and realized that it was in that moment that I was radicalized. That was THE decisive event.

I looked at the flags and I looked at our own military ready to shoot at 100,000 of us because we didn't want children killed with exploding toys. It really was that simplistic and that stark… at least in *my* mind.

♩♪♩♪♩♪

Back on campus the next week, I began getting requests to play at all sorts of activist events; some were paid gigs and some not. Many of the

THE LEGEND DIES ON — GARY GREEN

leaders of those alphabet-soup antiwar organizations were also members of other social-justice organizations. They had heard me perform and hoped that some of my songs would be a good fit for their other groups.

One of the first to contact me was an organizer for the *United Mine Workers Union*. The union had contracted with a Methodist-church-owned hospital to provide health care for their members in Pike County Kentucky. That hospital group had been refusing to treat new cases of pneumoconiosis —*black lung disease* that plagued coal miners. Negotiations over the issue had broken down and the union had decided to picket the headquarters of the hospital company; and that headquarters was located in Knoxville Tennessee, about five miles from campus. The organizer wanted me to come to the picket line, sing, and pep-up the spirits of the people on the line.

I loved the idea. First, I knew the area well. Pike County in northeastern Kentucky was one of the places I used to travel with my father in my preschool days, singing as we drove. Added to that, it would give me a chance to sing a bunch of very cool coal miner songs that I had learned from that *Hard Hitting Songs* book, from Epworth Church, and in Nashville from Merle Travis.

The attending miners and their families loved that a long-haired hippie was authentically singing the hillbilly songs they grew up on. They liked it even more when I spiced those traditional songs with the *Carter Family Lick* that Mother Maybelle had taught me; when I added a flat pick to my playing it *almost* sounded like *Bluegrass* music. We bonded over my stories of traveling through their towns when I was a child.

At one point, some company goons decided the hippie was the easiest of the group to attack. The miners immediately surrounded them and the wife of one of the miners reached into her bra and pulled out a .38-caliber revolver pointing it at the hecklers as she chased them away *(don't even ask me how she had it stuffed in there; she was a big woman, though).*

Unbeknownst to me, the building where the hospital company rented offices also rented space to the Knoxville field office of the FBI. I learned, years later, that Federal Agents took some outstanding action pictures of me; in fact, they shared some of them with the news wire services.

One of those pictures of me, in my cowboy hat, long hair, fringed jacket, and carrying a picket sign instead of a guitar, appeared in newspapers all over the country. At that time, I had no idea that the FBI had shot it; the credit line simply read: "The Associated Press".

The publicity from that pro-union picture led to an invitation from the *United Food and Commercial Workers Union* for me to come to Atlanta for an organizing drive at the 150-year-old Riches Department Store. Apparently, the store systematically paid Black workers significantly less than White workers doing the exact same jobs.

THE POET LAUREATE SOUL OF FOLKIE ROCK & ROLL

The union had teamed up with SCLC *(Martin Luther King's organization)* and the ongoing strike against the stores had become a cause célèbre. The two organizations were planning a high-profile action in which SCLC leaders *Ralph Abernathy* and *Hosea Williams* would both be arrested in front of TV cameras.

The organizers of that action wanted the White hippie folksinger to lead the crowd singing at a midnight vigil outside of the Fulton County Jail, calling for the release of the leaders and for Riches' acquiescence to the demands for equal pay.

I'd never met Hosea Williams, but Doctor Abernathy remembered me from the demonstration stage in DC. He was all-in with the plan, though I was a little creeped out about showing up at midnight at a Georgia jail. But what-the-hell, as I often paraphrased, *"it's only rock & roll"*.

My reception in Atlanta, and specifically working with SCLC, mushroomed into requests from many civil rights groups wanting me to play, sing, and occasionally write a song about their struggle. By this time, my portfolio of original songs included (as one cynical friend critically told me) *"all the usual suspects: civil rights, unions, anti-war, women's rights, housing discrimination, prisoners' rights & anti-death penalty, mine disasters, and police brutality"*.

As I continued to neglect my classes and focus on my music (and rabble rousing), I shifted my academic focus to courses more in tune (no pun intended) with my avocation. One of those courses was a graduate-level seminar on the history of Black religion in America following up the undergrad course I had taken earlier. To no one's surprise, I was the only white student in the class; but my impetus had been singing for SCLC.

From those seminars, the TA (teaching assistant) put together a public forum comparing and contrasting the political action philosophies of Martin Luther King to Malcolm X; Christian-Baptist & Islam. I was asked to attend and sing two songs: *We Shall Over Come* and Jimmy Collier's *Nothing But His Blood*.

The latter is a much more radical song, with lyrics that brilliantly can be taken either as a deeply religious call for salvation or an angry radical call for the White man's blood. I thought the two songs were appropriate illustrations of the two philosophies.

After the forum ended, a tall skinny guy (who identified himself only as "Brother Sherman") approached me. As he came toward me the first thing that I saw was the button pinned to the lapel of his black leather jacket; it was the face of Huey P. Newton with no words on the pin. That pin, his black beret, blue shirt and black pants, the jacket, and the unflinching expression on his face were all parts of a "uniform" that I had seen in Miami Beach.

THE LEGEND DIES ON — GARY GREEN

"Surprised a White guy singing that song," he said in a low, almost-whispered voice as he tried to stare me down without blinking.

I returned the stare and answered, "I'm surprised a member of *The Black Panther Party* is at a religion forum".

He finally smiled, "I guess we're both motherfuckers. You want to get a drink?"

We walked off campus and toward one of the taverns on Cumberland Avenue. I ordered a fairly-cheap bottle of Blue Nun Riesling. When the server opened the bottle, Sherman looked at me, shook his head, and laughed loudly. "Your wine has a CORK! You are a crazy mother!"

"Hell, yeah it has a cork. That god-damned Ripple and Boone's Farm twist-off shit tastes like old shoe-polish," I laughed.

"Shit, you ain't never been poor; You drink what you can when you have to", he shot back.

"Fuck you, I answered. "I was homeless for most of last year, lived in the woods, shoplifted potatoes, and only ate every couple of days".

He looked at me for a few seconds, trying to decide if I was serious, and I cut back in, "oh, and I lost 50 fucking pounds".

When he finally realized that I was serious, he shook his head laughing and said, "yeah, you definitely are a crazy fuck".

He stared at me some more and then shifted deliberately so that I could see the Colt .45 automatic tucked into his waistband. *"Why aren't you afraid of me?"* he asked with a serious tone in his voice.

"Afraid? Man," I sighed, stretching out the "man" to "maaaaaaan". "My people have done a hell of a lot more to your people than your people ever did to mine. Why aren't you afraid of *ME*?" I almost-flippantly answered.

Suddenly very serious, he responded, "because we are the self-defense vanguard party for our people. We are militant, not hostile". Equally seriously, I answered, "Yeah, I read *Soul On Ice*"[99] Then I added, "but you're not in Oakland; you're in East-fucking-Tennessee. What's up with that?"

"We police The Police. Who else can our people call?" he answered.

"Well, first-off, I'm not the police. And next, I am totally with you on that; I'd call The Panthers any day before I'd call "Johnny Law".

He poured more wine and answered with big smile, "I already told you. Cause you are a crazy motherfucker. Damn White man reading that shit".

We laughed and talked for about two hours; mostly about why anti-war activists seemed to be ignoring what he was calling "the war at home".

---

[99] A collection of prison essays by Black Panther Party Minister of Information Eldridge Cleaver.

THE POET LAUREATE SOUL OF FOLKIE ROCK & ROLL

War at home was a good phrase. I thought I knew exactly what he was talking about; but I didn't and *couldn't*. It would take a few more weeks before I even had a clue. But for the time being, it was a great potential hook for a song.

With the Methodist Church documentary and my experience in DC still heavy on my mind, I completely agreed with him, though most likely we were talking about two entirely different fronts.

When the bottle was empty, we decided to part, but promised to stay in touch; though we didn't trade phone numbers (and there was no email back then). I guessed that I'd probably never hear from him again.

About a week later, I received a call from an organizer of a Knoxville group fighting with the City over maintenance neglect at one of the city's housing projects. He didn't say how he had found me, and I didn't ask, but from the tone of the conversation, I assumed it was an SCLC or other civil rights connection.

The group had planned an early morning free-breakfast distribution and organizing drive for the residents of *Lonsdale Homes Public Housing*. They asked me to come to help serve the food and then sing songs.

I had been in the *Projects* no more than five minutes when the woman in charge of the food line stormed up to me and loudly demanded, "who invited your white ass? This isn't for you people". Apparently, whoever asked me to come did not spread the word that I'd be there; and in fact, I was the only white face present.

Two other organizers rushed to her aid and began yelling that I was a cop sent in to spy on them because there was no other reason a white guy would be there. They started demanding to know who had sent me, which law enforcement agency.

Before it turned any uglier, from behind me I heard a familiar voice speak firmly to them, *"Minister Eldridge said if Malcolm could change and if Eldridge Cleaver could change and if certain whites can change, then there is a movement. Gary Green is with us. I know him. He is movement-people. He stays".*

Their attitudes immediately changed, almost to submission, as the most aggressive woman answered (now softly), "Yes, Brother Sherman; Nobody told us".

Of course, there was no apology nor acknowledgement of me; but that was okay because I was certain my songs would validate me.

During the next few weeks, I was invited to more Black Panther Party functions, meetings, and food distributions than I was to anti-war events. On campus, people started thinking of me more as a civil rights troubadour than an anti-war activist; especially since I repeatedly had made it clear that I was not a pacifist.

THE LEGEND DIES ON — GARY GREEN

Around this same time, *Opryland USA* came to the University of Tennessee campus to hold auditions. Mistakenly thinking that the talent call was for Opry-style performers, I showed up with my guitar and picked Carter Family Churchlick style. To my amazement, I was called back for a second audition to be held in Nashville (180 miles away).

At that national audition, they provided a pair of overalls and a straw hat that reminded me of the famous Almanac Singer's audition at Rockefeller Center's Rainbow Room. My reaction was much more hostile than Woody Guthrie's playful reaction had been: I screamed, cussed, and kicked over their stool and stand when I stormed out.[100]

♭♪♭♪♭♪

Near the end of February, I received a desperate-sounding call from a Jewish organization called *The Anti-Defamation League of B'nai B'rith*. They asked if I would sing at a campus fundraiser in support of the Indian occupation at *Wounded Knee*.

I had been interested to Native American issues through Johnny Cash's *Bitter Tears* album and from listening to Folkways records featuring Peter La Farge (just as Cash himself had done). Moreover, as a songwriter, I wondered if there was another Ira Hayes or Lake Perfidy story that needed to be told. *(Little did I know at that time; there were thousands of them.)*

I certainly agreed to play; but at that point, all I knew about the situation was what most white Americans knew from watching the evening news or reading daily papers:

> Tribal members and activists from the *American Indian Movement* had occupied a church on a reservation in South Dakota as Federal soldiers surrounded them and cut off water, electricity, medical supplies, food supplies, and eventually banned media coverage of the siege. Most of the people in the church were Tribal elders, and children. Shots had been exchanged and at least two Indians had been killed.

That was all the information available; but of course, there *had to be* a lot more to the story. I wanted to know the background of what led up to the siege. More pointedly, I wanted the story, the characters, and the elements that would make a song.

---

[100] *Opryland* was an ill-conceived amusement park, Opry-themed with a sprinkling of homogenized musical shows. The park opened in 1972 and struggled for 25 years through multiple owners, always failing to draw the "Disneyland" size audiences that the developers had promised. Nonetheless profitable from the first year, the property was plagued by floods, intense competition, and unengaged operators. Located in a former buffalo pasture purchased from Frank & Dan Rudy (the owners of Rudy's Farm Sausage company), beginning in 1974 it stood adjacent to the new home of the Grand Ole Opry and in 1977 a huge hotel was added. Finally in 1997 the latest ownership group demolished the park and built a 178-store shopping mall.

THE POET LAUREATE SOUL OF FOLKIE ROCK & ROLL

Even though I instantly agreed to play, I also wanted the caller to provide all of those details as well as the proposed format for the event. Their format was to be a report of what led up to the occupation, a same-day dispatched update from South Dakota, and a couple of songs (one to open the event and one at the end). Their hope was to raise a couple of hundred dollars to send for food and supplies that could be smuggled into the church through holes in the barricade. The caller also provided me with the detailed information that I wanted to hear.[101]

Once I understood the background, I felt that the scope of the event they were proposing was much too small. The whole affair seemed more important than just another academic panel and a couple of *"Kumbaya"* songs to make people feel good about donating a few dollars.

Instead, I proposed a highly publicized event in a full-size auditorium with Native speakers, musicians, and if possible, a first-person report from Wounded Knee. I believed the issues were extremely important and could get broad-based support if properly presented to a large diverse

---

[101] Ten days into the ordeal, the Traditional Chiefs declared the territory of Wounded Knee to be the independent Oglala Nation and granted citizenship to those who wanted it, including non-Indians. They also smuggled their senior elder through the blockade so that he could address the United Nations to petition for recognition as sovereign nation and then demand negotiations with the US Secretary of State. B'nai B'rith's director explained that on the Pine Ridge Reservation in South Dakota The Council of Traditional Chiefs and the Matriarchs of the Clans for the Oglala Lakota were trying to impeach a corrupt Tribal President. They had accused him of facilitating 64 unsolved murders of political opponents and acquiescing to Federal land-grab and decertification programs. Fearing more violence aimed at them, the elders asked for help from AIM; and the Tribal President responded by calling for their arrests. He created a personal militia that he called Guardians Of the Oglala Nation *(with the surprisingly appropriate acronym, GOON)* and ordered them to arrest the leaders. About 200 people (more than half of them elders, women, and children) moved into a church at the site of the infamous 1890 massacre at Wounded Knee. Despite the GOONs opening fire on the church and killing some of the occupants, the leaders refused to surrender, and expanded their demands to include the US Government reopening treaty negotiations with the Traditional Chiefs. The Tribal President responded by setting up a 15-mile-parameter barricade around the church. To support it, he asked for help from the Federal Government. For the first time since the Civil War, US Troops were dispatched for a domestic operation. The 82nd Airborne, still deployed in Vietnam, and the Sixth Army were dispatched to join US Marshals, National Guard from five states, and FBI agents. **A full battalion of snipers, supported by daily flyovers by Air Force F-4 Phantom fighter jets, made a stand against the 200 elders, women, and children inside the wood-frame church. To hold back this "Indian uprising," the military brought in 17 armored personal carriers, a dozen .50-caliber machine guns, 41,000 rounds of M-40 high explosives for M-79 grenade launches, helicopters, 130,000 rounds of M-16 ammunition, and a procession of helicopters. Seven hours away at Fort Carson, Colorado, an armed assault unit was billeted to 24-hour full alert.**

THE LEGEND DIES ON — GARY GREEN

audience. I wanted to see the event taken mainstream and potentially the rally could do just that; especially with local clergy involved.

After much discussion and my trying to convince them that the potential size of the audience could raise more money, they agreed to put together a coordinating committee to consider organizing an event more along the lines that I was proposing.[102] I wasn't a fan of committees; but in this case the plan was that the members of the committee would also be the speakers at the event. So, I was good with it; especially since this was a pretty broad-based committee.

A few days before the date of the reconfigured program, the St. Paul AIM leadership told us that they had become wrapped up with the logistics at Wounded Knee and could not send a representative. Reports from South Dakota indicated that the situation had become grave; so, they couldn't send anyone.

In their stead, they recommended an Indian singer-songwriter who could also speak about the struggle. They sent *Floyd "Red Crow" Westerman*, a Sisseton Wahpeton Oyate Indian singer-songwriter; eighteen years my senior but decades wiser. His real name was *Kanghi Duta*; but "Red Crow" was the anglicized name that he used.

As we got to know each other, Kanghi Duta told me that before he was ten years old, he had been taken from his family and forced to attend an Indian Boarding School, 70-miles from home and in another state. Forbidden to see his parents, his traditionally long hair was forcibly buzz cut American military style. If he was caught speaking his native language, school officials would washout his mouth with burning lye soap. If he dared practice his people's traditional religion, he would be locked in a guardhouse with only bread and water for several days.

His painfully tearful recollections combined with the vivid La Farge/Cash poetry gave me vignettes of American Indian history that I prayed were isolated incidents. Unfortunately, they were not, and that reality fueled my outrage. Fortunately, it also fueled my songwriting.

I wrote a song called *Sovereign Nation*; based on Kanghi Duta's story. It was a powerful song; but I knew it was empty. No matter how much emotion I poured out, it was impossible for me to convey what I didn't know. As a White male from the working-class South, my childhood was highly privileged compared to the gruesome terrors that he had endured

---

[102] The committee meeting attracted religious leaders from all over Knoxville, university anthropologists with deep interest in Native Americans, a local television producer, a representative from the nearby Eastern Band of Cherokee Indians expressing solidarity, the Chief of the (Federally decertified) *Skuarureaka Tuscarora People* from Eastern North Carolina, celebrated civil rights activists Carl and Anne Brade, and by speaker-phone a representative of the American Indian Movement in St. Paul Minnesota.

as a child. Regardless of how creative my writing might be, it was impossible for me to produce a credible representation of that shear horror.

I sang the song privately for Kanghi Duta and I saw his eyes tear up. He insisted that I do the song at the rally; and after I raised my concerns, he offered to join me on the chorus... which he did; and it was one of my most poignant moments ever on a stage. *(Nonetheless, I chose to never record Sovereign Nation or sing it again; it just seemed, to me, wrong for a white guy to be singing a first-person Native song.)*[103]

With free admission, we structured the event like an old southern rival meeting. We cloaked subtle lectures about sovereignty around the Wounded Knee issue. The event drew the largest *issue-based* crowd that U.T. had seen; a little more than 25,000 people —more than 10% of the population of the entire county.

Adding to the drama that we presented, the Cherokee speaker had just been at Wounded Knee with two other Cherokee Tribe members; one of whom was killed by an FBI sniper a week before our rally. This was a war, and our audience knew that. Moreover, it was the quintessential example of what my friend Sherman had called the "war at home".

Passing my cowboy hat (and two dozen Kentucky Fried Chicken buckets) for donations, to everyone's surprise, we raised little more than $10,000 on the first pass and another $40,000 on the second pass. *(As of this writing, that 1973 $50,000 would be equivalent to raising $353,095 at the rally; a significant amount of money!)*

The Wounded Knee occupation began on February 27, 1973, and lasted 71 days. As of 2024, one of the Natives involved —*Leonard Peltier*— is still in Federal prison as of this writing.

---

[103] In his later years, Kanghi Duta performed *with Jackson Browne, Willie Nelson, Bonnie Raitt, Harry Belafonte, Joni Mitchell, Kris Kristofferson, Buffy Sainte-Marie, Sting,* and lots of other music world well-knowns. He also eventually had an acting career and appeared in dozens of featured roles in TV shows like *MacGyver* and *Walker Texas Ranger*, and movies including *The Doors*, and *Dancing With Wolves*.

THE LEGEND DIES ON — GARY GREEN

Opus Eleven:
Guitar Paint and My Very Own Federal Agent

Dear Mister Kelley at the FBI:
Listen to my song and the words I cry.
I heard the man say it on my TV.
You've been takin' notes on Americans like me.
— *Dear Mister Kelley At The FBI*, by Gary Green, 1976, as recorded on Folkways Records album FH5351, *These Six Strings Neutralize The Tools Of Oppression*

Wounded Knee — which was only the beginning of my dive into Indian Country. My adventure in Washington DC with American soldiers affixing bayonets and flags for the ship in distress. The revelations of razorblades in toys. Everything that had happened since I arrived at the University of Tennessee. All had dramatically changed my songwriting. I was transformed from a hillbilly guitar picking songwriter to a radicalized topical singer seeking to change the world with a song. *Yikes!*

That musical transformation was fueled by how effective those words stenciled around the head of Pete's banjo had been: *This machine surrounds hate and forces it to surrender.*

I had seen that in action; Pete lived it and made it happen. It was simply amazing. And especially for me, it was an entirely different way of looking at songs. It began to redefine everything and bring together the whole Ella May inquiry.

With Pete, it wasn't just a song hook; it was his philosophy of music and his philosophy of life. And he wrote songs that took that philosophy from theory to practice; peace songs that... well, forced hate to surrender.

Pete often said that he got the idea for the writing on his banjo from a little sign that Woody Guthrie had taped to his guitar: *This Machine Kills Fascists*. Woody's songs were hard-hitting and pulled no punches.

Besides those hidden verses of *This Land*, there was no mistaking Woody for a pacifist after hearing his other songs... like *Ludlow Massacre*. When he sang first-person as one of the miners that gunned down State Troopers, you totally believed him. Many of Woody's songs had that kind of *warrior* undertone.

Pete could never have written warrior songs; he was a total personification of the word pacifist; and that was a wonderful thing! During the Second World War, he even registered as a conscientious objector. By contrast, Woody had enlisted in the Merchant Marine (and his ship was torpedoed by a German U-boat).

THE POET LAUREATE SOUL OF FOLKIE ROCK & ROLL

It's arguable that Pete was a warrior in his own way; and that is valid. But the signs on the two instruments clearly showed the different approaches of the two men to the same issues.

As for myself, I idealized Pete but knew that I was a lot more like Woody and certainly not a pacifist. There is no doubt that what I had seen was moving me from being an iconoclastic anti-establishment hippie-freak hillbilly guitar player toward being a genuine activist who wanted to wield my guitar like some sort of weapon —deliberately and with malice.

As I began to come to grips with what I was becoming, I thought more about the words on Woody's guitar and on Pete's banjo. I decided that it would be appropriate for me to make my own statement. So, around the body of my acoustic guitar, in big blue letters, I painted:

These Six Strings Neutralize The Tools Of Oppression

That seemed much more in line with a philosophy that best defined ME. It wasn't too "Woody", and it wasn't too "Pete"; but it was very "Gary". A couple of years later, in the liner notes for my first *Folkways* album, I explained:

> The idea for the paint-job grew from a little sign that Woody Guthrie taped to his guitar: This Machine Kills Fascist. I figured that there were probably more oppressed people out there than fascists running around, so I decided to neutralize a few tools. Only problem is that I've found so much oppression floating around that I'm seriously considering taking up the 12-string guitar just to get six more tool-neutralizers."

I spent the next year crisscrossing almost every flavor of "The Movement" (as Sherman had called it), singing my songs, a few of Woody's every now and then, and just for good measure throwing in a little Carter Family here-and-there.

I constantly played for the Panthers, for SCLC, for the peace movement, for the ERA, for pro-choice, for unions, for political prisoners, for voting rights, for environmentalists, for… damned-near anybody that would give me an audience and some appreciation.

During all of that, my primary focus was aligned with the *American Indian Movement* and multiple struggles for sovereignty, so I spent a lot of time living on the Rez[104] with various Tribes. But for the other gigs, I spent nights in public housing ghettos, dorm rooms, supporters' spare bedrooms, tents, band houses, and highway rest areas (a *lot* of those).

Around that same time, I began to notice a series of non-descript cars with government license plates clumsily following me. I periodically verified my paranoia by going through a comical series of inappropriate U-

---

[104] Rez = Reservation

THE LEGEND DIES ON — GARY GREEN

turns and driving the wrong way on one-way streets; and my pursuers would follow. Invariably, the cars would follow me on the same awkward (and often illegal) maneuvers.

At first it was funny, but eventually it became annoying, and finally it moved to genuinely creepy. Never mind that some agency was spending their time and money following around a guy whose biggest crimes were writing bad poetry and using acrylic paint on the finish of an otherwise perfectly good guitar.

At one organizing meeting for some esoteric protest march, one attendee was trying so hard to instigate violence that even the stereotype *agent provocateur* label was too comical for him. While he was on one of his rants, I excused myself to find a restroom; in reality I slipped outside to his car, used a coat-hanger to unlock it, and then rifled his glove compartment. There I found his Federal ID and gun. At least my suspicion was verified.

Still, it was all a big joke to me, and I started talking about it from stage and performing Arlo Guthrie's *The Pause of Mr. Claus* — a comedy song about his own experiences being followed to gigs by FBI agents. When I would finish that song, I had canned patter that I would add:

"People ask me how I deal with being followed around like that. Well, I am here to tell you how I deal with it and to teach you to do so too. In the tradition of the great folksingers, I have a sing-along that will help us all deal with that and with any number of other traumas that may be visited up on us. You all know the tune: it's the same as *Frère Jacques*. So, I am going to teach you the new lyrics and ask you all to join in with me; and let's sing it as a "round" with this half of the room coming in after the first line of the song. Ready? THIS is how to deal with being followed by The Man: *"Mari-juana, Mari-juana; LSD, LSD; Her-o-in and cocaine. Her-o-in and cocaine. THC. THC... Now, everyone sing along!"*

The whole *cops follow the folksinger* thing remained comedy relief for me to melodramatically use on stage... that is, until I got assigned my very own full-time Federal agent.

Of all the hazards and tribulations of a traveling musician —and I had heard a lot of them from backstage friends at The Opry and at the Pancake House— this was one that was just too bizarre. I had never heard of it happening to any Nashville cats; or to anyone other than Arlo Guthrie.

If it were not for testimony before a Congressional committee a few years later and the passage of the *Freedom of Information Act*, I probably still would not know the extent of the agent's assignment. Even after that, I never learned the specific details of his work.

Bear with me for a minute here: At 19-years-old I was writing and singing songs that someone in authority somewhere thought were so dangerous that your (and my) tax dollars were spent to hire a fulltime employee to do nothing but follow me around and pretend to be my friend. I was a hillbilly folksinger who wrote songs about things I saw; and that earned me a dossier. *Wow! WFT??!!*

THE POET LAUREATE SOUL OF FOLKIE ROCK & ROLL

That Wounded Knee event was the largest crowd that I'd ever done a *solo* performance in front of (for the 100,000 people in DC, I was just a "sing-along" on stage with Pete Seeger). The publicity generated from it had brought lots of requests for me to play and sing and had created a national, albeit esoteric, reputation for me and my songs.

Unfortunately, it also attracted the attention of the remnants of the FBI's COINTELPRO domestic surveillance program[105]. Federal agents visited my professors, friends, and people I had only casually met. They even blocked my father from being appointed as a Bankruptcy Trustee for a Federal Judge because, as the judge told Daddy, "your son is a known communist". *(More on that later.)*

Years later, heavily-redacted documents released under the *Freedom of Information Act*, revealed that the FBI had speculated that my traveling around the country singing was actually a front to cover my "clandestine activities" of running guns through the Wounded Knee blockade.

There was speculation that the guns that I somehow magically transported in guitar cases, or something, were used in an armed defensive activity at Wounded Knee that resulted in the death of two FBI agents. *(For the record, that was nonsense.)*

The documents also conjected that my songs were actually sophisticated propaganda, subversively written for mind-control to incite people against government authority. While I snidely was flattered that anyone thought so highly of my writing, the absurdity of it was matched only by the overriding issue of creating Secret-Police-type dossiers on Americans.

As I repeatedly said, I just wanted to sing hillbilly songs! Nonetheless, in fairness, consider these facts that might have made agents at least raise an eyebrow:

- At the crash-house in Miami Beach, almost everyone there had been arrested for manufacturing incendiary devices. Gary Green was there; allegedly as a folksinger, *but was that all?*
- Members of The Black Panther Party in Knoxville (including Sherman) had recently been arrested on firearms and other charges. Gary Green was a "known associate"; allegedly as a folksinger, *but was that all?*
- A number of supposed anti-war peace organizations had been heavily influenced by *The Communist Party USA* and the *Socialist Workers Party* (not that either was illegal). Gary Green was there; allegedly as a folksinger, *but was that all?*

---

[105] COINTELPRO (FBI *Counter-Intelligence-Program*) tactics that have since come to light in recent years have included smearing reputations with forged documents, false arrests and wrongful imprisonment, planting false media stories, illegal violence, and even assassination. *This is in AMERICA!*

THE LEGEND DIES ON — GARY GREEN

- Members of *Southern Christian Leadership Conference* in Atlanta had been arrested for a sit-in at Richs department store. Gary Green was there — across state lines— allegedly as a folksinger, *but was that all?*
- A picket line in front of the FBI's field office in Knoxville was allegedly organized by union members; but... Gary Green was there; allegedly as a folksinger, *but was that all?*
- The Wounded Knee "armed uprising of renegade Indians" was so severe that it had required action by the United States Army. Somehow food, blankets, *and guns* were smuggled through the barricades; probably purchased by the tens-of-thousands of dollars raised in Knoxville. Gary Green was there —across state lines again— allegedly as a folksinger, *but was that all?*

Congressional testimony, a decade later, revealed that the FBI had employed a former MIA (Military Intelligence Agency) white man to infiltrate the American Indian Movement. For the undercover role, he grew his hair long, dyed it black, shaved three times a day, and slept under a sun lamp to change the color of his pale skin. For good measure, he courted and eventually moved in with a Navajo single mother and her kids; further "establishing" his Indian credibility. Then, after he was successfully ensconced into the leadership of the American Indian Movement, he secured board positions on several leftist organizations by providing perceived diversity as a token Indian (including Angela Davis's *National Alliance Against Racist and Political Repression*).

Following the success of the Knoxville fundraiser, he used his AIM role to contact B'nai B'rith to ask about how all that money was raised. They gave much of the credit to me; and as a result, his focus turned to my activities. After consulting with his superiors, or whatever pinheads planned domestic surveillance of guitar pickers, he was instructed to move his family to Knoxville and become a folk music fan.

He raised my suspicions, about three months later, when at a planning meeting for a second event he suggested taking the donations to Atlanta to buy several thousand-dollars' worth of marijuana and reselling it for a large profit, possibly doubling the value of the donation[106]. He was adamant about his recommendation; and I was just as obstinate telling everyone that I would not be singing at an event to raise money to buy dope. I told them all that it was hairbrained and reckless to even consider.

The other thing that really bothered me about him was his supposed interest in my music. My songs had become lyric-heavy and required that they be *listened to* in order to appreciate them. I would watch this spy-cat while I was performing; he almost never paid attention to what I was

---

[106] As noted earlier, possession of more than an ounce of marijuana was a felony; possession with the intent to resell was punishable by life-in-prison in some jurisdictions.

saying. That was fine, of course, but it was not the behavior of a supposed "fan". At least that part of his story stunk from the get-go.

A more troublesome indication that something was amiss came when he insisted that I travel with him to rural Eastern North Carolina to meet with a Native leader there. I agreed and after being warmly welcomed into a local home, my "spy" tried to convince the local Tribal officials (and me) to bomb the nearby Federal Courthouse as a sign of our refusal to recognize the legitimacy of the U.S. Government.

Talk about classic "agent provocateur" shit! At that point I knew that this cat was not everything that he claimed to be. I did not know, at that point, that he was a white Federal agent. And he continued to play the role, despite my refusal to be part of either the bombing or the drug selling plan.

Despite claiming to acquiesce to my refusal to participate in a felony, after the next campus event he took the new money that was raised and left town with it, ostensibly to buy drugs and return with a small fortune. Before leaving, he apparently got into a fight with his girlfriend and severely beat her.

I accompanied the event's organizer to visit her at the hospital, she told us that the beating had come after she discovered an envelope containing identification papers. She said the papers showed that he had another name; and she suspected that he was most likely white rather than Native.

All of that was far beyond the scope of picking-and-singing, even within the realm of the topical music that I was writing. I decided to take the whole problem to the people at the Highlander Center; they were a lot more attuned to these kinds of things than I was. They had been dealing with spies, duplicities, and associated violence, since the 1930's. By comparison, I was a virgin at being a "known-subversive".

They were far more alarmed than I'd been. They listened to my tales of being followed, then his showing up, the plot to sell marijuana, and his suggestion to bomb a courthouse. They concluded that I had been targeted and was likely in severe danger of being arrested on trumped-up charges *(like marijuana possession)* or even killed during an arrest *(like had happened to Chicago Black Panther leader Fred Hampton).*

They also warned me that it could take several years, but with that much attention it was beyond dispute that I eventually would be targeted for either arrest or assassination. I didn't totally laugh-off the warning; but I didn't take it as life-threateningly serious either. (Part of that may have been my youthful feeling of being (figuratively) bulletproof.)

Very clandestinely, they gave me a powerful .303 British Army rifle for defense of the Native family. I promptly gave it to the spy's (by then "ex") girlfriend to protect herself and her children.

THE LEGEND DIES ON — GARY GREEN

They also suggested that I be extremely careful with my public appearances and that I should avoid doing anything even remotely illegal. For the first time, I realized that the whole spy-on-the-folksinger thing was actually very serious and not *even* a game. Consequently, I took a number of extreme steps to protect myself. I drastically cutback my public performances, to less than one-a-month. Even then, I was extremely selective about where I played or what "cause" might be associated with my name. I changed my major back to Journalism and focused myself on my early-out plan from academia rather than songwriting and touring. I wanted out of Tennessee. I stopped using marijuana or any illegal drug and let it be known that I had stopped. I also became vocally opposed to any illegal drugs. That way, I reasoned, I could not be framed for a drug offense[107].

Unable, or at least unwilling, to stop music altogether, I began attending (as a spectator) a number of concerts of musicians that played various venues in Knoxville: Chuck Berry, George Jones, Leon Russell, The Allman Brothers, and most importantly to me... at long last I saw Jerry Lee Lewis in person. *(I couldn't wait to call my mother after that one and tell her that I had seen him!)*

I refocused my own music back to my Appalachian roots. Setting aside, for a while, my guitar with its big blue letters and replacing it with a 150-year-old fretless hillbilly banjo, along with a mandolin, and an autoharp.

I also started practicing a few times a week on a grand piano in one of the rooms at the student union on campus.

I developed an absurdly-large repertoire of traditional mountain ballads, Roy Acuff songs, and especially train songs (throwing back to my childhood roots riding the rails with my parents). I was singing and playing those oldies almost exclusively. (To this day, I know and play a lot of train songs.)

For the very few gigs I did, I was known as a traditional musician (today we would call it "roots music"). In short, the whole affair (culminating in being given that military rifle) either scared the shit out of me or it taught me to be extremely wary, guarded, and security conscious. (The latter paranoia has remained with me ever since.)

I also reached out to union activist (and writer-producer) Ed Spielman, who had created the *Kung Fu* television series. Almost exactly ten years my senior, he had been studying Chinese martial arts since the early 1960's. Without detailing my drama, I asked for his advice on how to

---

[107] I also stopped consuming any form alcohol, because I did not want to have less than 100% awareness and control of myself. *(I have not used either alcohol or drugs since that day in early 1973. In fact, even as of this writing more than a half-century later, I won't even take painkillers.)*

THE POET LAUREATE SOUL OF FOLKIE ROCK & ROLL

pursue some weaponless martial art. I didn't want to risk a weapons charge, and I wasn't sure that I'd always have my bullwhip available.

He put me in touch with Sophia Delza, a woman born in 1903 and who was one of the first popularizers of Chinese martial arts in the United States. She and I began a long series of back-and-forth correspondences with her outlining a training regimen for me.

It was also during this period that I became a vegetarian (and have not eaten meat since). My life was filled with changes... so I thought.

In March of 1974, *Ms. Magazine*[108] ran a profile story on *Agnes "Sis" Cunningham*; the woman often credited with introducing the world to Bob Dylan, Phil Ochs, Tom Paxton, Janis Ian, The Freedom Singers, Buffy Sainte Marie, Len Chandler, Malvina Reynolds, and scores of other "message song" singer-songwriters.

A friend and former bandmate of Woody Guthrie, in 1962 she and her husband, Gordon Friesen, had founded *Broadside Magazine*; a publication hugely influential in the folk-revival. The *Broadside Records* album that I had listened to in high school was produced by Sis and Gordon through their magazine and in conjunction with Folkways Records.

The biographical article began with her early life in Oklahoma and teaching music at the Commonwealth Labor College (an Oklahoma version of the Highlander Center). It told of her marriage to Gordon and their fleeing Oklahoma because of the harassment for their membership in the *Communist Party*.

It followed her joining the *Almanac Singers* behind Woody Guthrie, Pete Seeger, and others in New York and her songwriting for the *New Lost City Ramblers* and for *Ry Cooder*.

Finally, the article described the founding of Broadside Magazine and the profound impact it had on not just the folk music "revival" of the early 1960's, but on rock, country, and pop music as well as American youth culture. Dylan, Ochs, and many others recorded some of their first songs in Sis and Gordon's living room. Sis transcribed the music, and Gordon wrote articles and political commentary. *Rolling Stone Magazine* called Broadside "the single most important publication in musical America".

Until the Ms. Magazine article, I was not aware that Broadside was still being published. Like most who knew about it, I assumed it ended sometime in the sixties when the folk revival ended. Amazed that the magazine

---

[108] *Ms. Magazine* was/is a feminist monthly slick magazine co-founded in 1971 by journalist and social/political activist Gloria Steinem and touted as viewed as a voice for women by women.

THE LEGEND DIES ON — GARY GREEN

still existed, I wrote Sis and Gordon a fan-boy letter and briefly told them about my musical history. I also told them that I wrote topical songs and sang them at rallies.

To my surprise, I received a really long return letter from Gordon Friesen; lamenting that there were no "young people" coming along to continue the legacy of Broadside.[109] Thus began an intense two-years of weekly very long letters (sometimes more than weekly) between me and Sis & Gordon.

In one of our letter exchanges, after I had told them about one of my musical escapades, Sis casually asked me if I had mentioned that *(whatever it was)* to Pete Seeger. In the 21st century, it is very difficult for me to express how ludicrous-sounding that question was to me in the early 1970's. She had tossed out the question as if it were the most natural thing in the world to routinely talk with the legendary folk music icon (which, of course, it definitely was not); though in her world it may have been.

The casual in-passing, "have you mentioned it to Pete" question was, at least to me, tantamount to "have you discussed this with the President of the United States" or "have you asked the Pope what he thinks". But Sis Cunningham was beyond iconic; she was the driving force for much of the activist music that had cemented my attention, so I had to take her question seriously.

At that time, Seeger was already a genuine American icon; widely-recognized as a sort of grandfather of American Folk Music. He was a

---

[109] In late 1961, Sis and Gordon had been talking about founding a magazine exclusively for "protest songs". The "steering committee" that met regularly in their living room included their old friend *Pete Seeger* (from Sis's years as accordion player and singer with the Almanac Singers), *Gil Turner* (singer, actor, and Master of Ceremonies at *Gerde's Folk City*), west coast music journalist *Ralph Gleason* (who later co-founded *Rolling Stone Magazine*), *Moe Asch* (founder & owner of Folkways Records), and a small circle of other friends. At the second meeting, to determine content for the first issue, Turner brought by his latest discovery —a 20-year-old unsigned Jewish songwriter from Hibbing, Minnesota named Robert Allen Zimmerman. (Just before arriving in New York and connecting with Turner, Zimmerman had taken to calling himself Bob Dylan. The (then-recently-defunct) American Labor Party donated a discarded mimeograph machine for producing the magazine. Turner would bring by a seemingly never-ending parade of topical songsters who had showed up at Folk City. Asch agreed to issue compilation albums. I was in the second grade in February of 1962 when their first issue printed songs by Sis, Bob Dylan, Gil Turner, Malvina Reynolds, and Ernest Marrs. The masthead read: Publication: Sis Cunningham (Editor), Gil Turner, Advisory: Pete Seeger (SIC: that typo was theirs). The next few issues included contributions from *Eric Andersen, Len Chandler, Jr., Bob Dylan, Larry Estridge, Richard Fariña, Tuli Kupferberg, Jonathan Kwitney, Peter La Farge, Julius Lester, Ewan MacColl, Ernie Marrs, Matt McGinn, Bernice Reagon, Patrick Sky, Mark Spoelstra, Gil Turner, Vanessa Redgrave,* and a newly discovered Ohio journalism-school dropout named *Phil Ochs.*

THE POET LAUREATE SOUL OF FOLKIE ROCK & ROLL

Columbia Records recording artist, had written some of the most important (and frequently recorded) songs of the century (*We Shall Overcome, If I Had A Hammer, Turn-Turn-Turn,* and more), had pretty-much launched the early 60's folk revival (through his group *The Weavers* and their covers of songs that they moved into the lexicon of American standards (*Goodnight Irene, On Top of Old Smokey, Wimoweh, Kisses Sweeter Than Wine, Kumbaya, Aunt Rhodie,* and many others).

As noted, he also was the impetus for the paint job around the body of my own guitar. "Legend" was too casual a word to define Pete.

Even though I had been on stage with Seeger at the Nixon counter-inauguration demonstration, I didn't *know* him, and he certainly did not know me. The only reason I made it to the stage with him was that Pete was a notorious egalitarian and anyone with a guitar and progressive frame of mind was welcome at his table —or in this case, on his stage. I had been booked as a minor performer in DC and he waived me up to the main stage to join with him.

Sis and Gordon seemed genuinely surprised that I didn't know Seeger; apparently *everybody* knew Pete. They responded by nonchalantly sending me his home address and phone number. Looking back on that, it seems outrageously absurd that they would do so. It was even more bizarre that when I contacted Pete, he welcomed me like a long-lost friend.

In addition to the weekly letters to and from Sis & Gordon, Pete Seeger and I began writing back and forth almost as frequently. While my "conversations" with Sis and Gordon were almost exclusively about Broadside, the letters from and to Pete were a lot more general. We discussed everything from the tribulations of my academic life to Kanghi Duta and AIM to why I thought *Ralph Nader's Public Interest Research Group* was inane to Pete's thoughts on the Palestinian and Israeli conflicts.

We occasionally discussed Broadside, but Pete's general attitude about the magazine was that it was perfectly suited for the early 1960's but the early 1970's the world needed something entirely new. At that point, we didn't spend much time elaborating or exploring what that would mean.

The Pete Seeger and Broadside letters were almost my only real musical activity for several months[110]. I did no appearances, and only rarely wrote anything.

Around this same time, the University of Tennessee started a "Free University"; a tuition-free group of classes in a wide range of subjects taught by anyone who was an expert in the particular field (without regard to

---

[110] It's funny what one finds in one's memories, looking back a half century or more later; I still have many of those letters.

THE LEGEND DIES ON — GARY GREEN

academic qualifications). The teachers were paid a small stipend that was based on the number of students that enrolled in the class. Each session was six weeks long.

I decided to offer a class on how to play the Carter Family Churchlick on the guitar. To my surprise, and clearly the surprise of the administrators, 36 students signed up for my class —apparently a really large number for Free-U classes. I had them bring their guitars to class and I believe that by the end of the six weeks, I had taught most of them to play at least Wildwood Flower.

The Free University's administration asked me if I could teach any other subjects that might equally draw a "large" turnout like that. I thought about it for a while, and drawing on my own knowledge and experience, I offered a course called *Folk Music and The American Left*.

The syllabus outlined classes that would navigate the often-in-the-news alphabet soup of lefty organizations that I knew so well, I would talk about the relationship between various songs and musicians and with various demonstrations and rallies.

I prepared a custom taped musical playlist to illustrate my lectures. I began with the Ella May murder and concluded with the Vietnam War and Broadside. It helped that I could talk first-hand about a lot of what I was teaching. *More than 250 students filled a lecture hall for those classes!* I set a record for the Free University.

During the Woody Guthrie segment, one of my students commented, "Yeah, yeah; that was really interesting back then. But today, we have to realize that just could not happen. Unions aren't important anymore and besides, nobody could just wander around from town to town singing songs and expect to make a living".

Her comment enraged me so much that today —more than a half century later— I am still pissed off at her. At the time, my visceral side wanted to give her a big "fuck you" and storm out of the class to a union hall and start singing. Instead, discretion prevailed, and I diplomatically told her that lots of us in "The Movement" did just that. I then challenged her (and the class), "if you don't believe me, watch the next few years; then come back and say it can't happen today".

Other than that one *almost*-confrontation, the class went even better than the Carter-Family class. Because of that, the Free University asked me to teach another session of it for the next quarter. I was just on the cusp of being 20-years-old and was a paid "college professor" with no degree yet. *What a strange world!*

Meanwhile, my two-year spree of doubling-up-on-classes was just about at its end, so I began investigating the job market for young journalists. My first target was the *Knoxville News Sentinel*; but my musical and Wounded Knee notoriety preceded me, They had no interest.

THE POET LAUREATE SOUL OF FOLKIE ROCK & ROLL

My next target was near my parents at *The Gastonia Gazette*, a 35,000-circulation afternoon daily newspaper. The editor remembered me from my high-school journalism days and hired me on-the-spot. Thus began my new career as a newspaper reporter.

I'd been working there for about six months when the FBI and the Chief of the local police visited the paper's publisher to inform him that he had hired a *"dangerous subversive communist folksinger who was in regular contact with Fidel Castro and trying to take his seditious music to your newspaper articles"*. No, really, that's what they said.[111].

What they didn't count on was that the newspaper publisher was some sort of political *libertarian* who was adamantly against government intervention in citizens' lives. Fortunately for me, that position also included opposition to government spying on American dissidents and college students; *especially* on the "working press".[112]

He kicked the cops out of his office, and in the next Sunday's paper ran a frontpage story with the headline, *Comrade Green: He Marched For Peace*. It included a three-column print of the photo that the FBI had shot of me in front of their office in Knoxville.

As for my music, finally out of college, it was more of a hobby than a profession. I wasn't sending tapes or pitching songs. I wasn't even writing any new songs at that time. I had finally picked back up my blue-words-painted guitar; but I was only playing hard-core country songs. I didn't even go to concerts. The closest I came to having any contact with music was weekly letters with Sis and Gordon and with Pete Seeger.

I now was officially on a career track as a journalist. It was the era of *Woodward and Bernstein* and hero-reporters. It was the age of *Walter Cronkite* and trusted newsmen. It was decades after *yellow journalism* and decades before *fake news*. It was a highly respected —and often feared— fourth estate. And I was planting my flag firmly in it.

---

[111] On that *Broadside Ballads* album, Phil Ochs had a song called *The Ballad of William Worthy*, about a journalist who had his passport revoked after flying to Cuba to interview Castro (in violation of a travel ban). Since hearing that song, I had signed up for a free subscription to the English-language weekly newspaper published by the Central Committee of the Communist Party of Cuba. Each week it came to my post office box; but, of course, I was NOT in contact with Fidel. Likewise, I had a free subscription to the Soviet-subsidized daily newspaper published by the Communist Party USA (*The Daily World*). I also subscribed to a dozen other political publications. So clearly, the Federal agents had some information; just not totally accurate.

[112] The lunatic publisher was also opposed to public funding of highways, schools, police and fire departments, and any other "creeping socialism" as he called it.

THE LEGEND DIES ON — GARY GREEN

Opus Twelve:
New York & The Last Days of Phil Ochs

New York City Ain't No Place To Be
Searching for the gods you'll never see,
Looking for a dream in a devil's hideaway
And never knowing There's Ain't No Easy Way
— **There Ain't No Easy Way,** by Gary Green, 1976, as recorded on Folkways album FH5351, *These Six Strings Neutralize The Tools Of Oppression*

Sis & Gordon and I continued our very-intense and very long weekly letters, even well into my newspaper career; as did Pete Seeger and I. Eventually, Sis asked me to send them a tape of some of my songs, which I was reluctant to do for dozens of not-very-good reasons.

Eventually, after her continued coaxing, I relented and mailed them a reel-to-reel tape with two songs: the song I had written based on my friend Kanghi Duta's childhood; and my song about the murder of Ella May Wiggins.

They wrote me back and told me they hated the Indian song for the same reason that they had rejected Jerry Jeff Walker when he had sent them *Mr. Bojangles* in the late 1960's. They felt that his song was racist; that a white guy writing that song was more patronizing than tributing[113]. *(Much the reasons I never performed it.)*

I totally got it, though: Sis and Gordon felt that my writing and singing, first-person, about Tribal life was a racist hypocrisy in the same way Jerry Jeff's song had been. But they had not rejected my music, my style, or even my performance: only the content of that one particular song. At least that was *something*.

Before I could be too devastated by that rejection, they vehemently praised my *The Murder of Ella May Wiggins*. In fact, they wanted to publish it in the next issue of their magazine.

I was ecstatic! The first official publishing of my music was going to be in the same magazine that first published Bob Dylan! Thinking back to when I first heard the *Broadside Ballads* album in the summer after the 10th grade, this was the ultimate in fulling-an-adolescent-dream. Or at least it would be if there was going to be a "next issue" of Broadside.

---

[113] Clearly Sammy Davis Jr. disagreed with that characterization when he made it his theme song (as did *Nina Simone, Neil Diamond, the Nitty Gritty Dirt Band, Bob Dylan,* and others who recorded it). On the other hand, Sammy Davis Jr. also performed for Richard Nixon; so, he wasn't exactly without controversy.

THE POET LAUREATE SOUL OF FOLKIE ROCK & ROLL

In her letters, Sis often mentioned how draining it was to publish the magazine. They had dropped from monthly to quarterly because of the amount of labor involved and the lack of funds (they refused to accept advertising and survived only by donations).

To relieve her of some of that labor, at least for my song, I transcribed the song myself and sent it to her "camera-ready" for printing in the magazine. Apparently not many of their contributors had the skills (or at least the propensity) to do that.

I guess my doing that shocked her and Gordon. The next series of back-and-forth letters revolved around their curiosity about my skills beyond songwriting. They didn't know that I could read, write (and transcribe) music. They also didn't know that I understood the printing and production processes; and they were really interested that I had been doing the actual printing of flyers, posters, and newsletters since my junior-high-school days.

They seemed to be fascinated that I had hands-on photo darkroom experience dating back to my childhood in the 1950's. They also wanted to know more about my new journalism career. Gordon had started *his* career as a journalist, first with *The Detroit Times* and later with *CBS News* in New York *(where he remained until he was blacklisted in the 1950's for being a member of the Communist Party)*. As he put it, he had "printer's ink in my blood".

He and I bonded over our mutual journalism backgrounds; and cemented that bond when I told him about the FBI visiting my publisher. He saw that as the equivalent of his being targeted in the 1950's blacklisting.

Gordon said that he thought that I could never outrun the *outlaw* label that the government agencies were attaching to me. It was a word that I took to heart and filed away! Hmmm; "OUTLAW".

Our next few letters focused on preserving *Broadside Magazine*; Mostly Gordon's ideas for making certain publication could continue. Those letters were filled with dozens of schemes, some harebrained, some outrageously expensive, and some just pipe-dreams; but none actually feasible... at least not in my limited experience.

Gordon, especially, was pushing hard for me to consider taking over for them: becoming the next generation of Broadside. The letters I received during that period were almost patronizingly laudatory for my skillset being the ideal match for his hopes and dreams for the legacy of Broadside.

Sis, however, seemed more reluctant to turn her life's work over to me... actually to *anyone*. The tone of her writing was much more tied to the finances (or lack thereof) and the too-obvious lack of support from the folk music community in general. She blamed commercialism, record

THE LEGEND DIES ON — GARY GREEN

labels, personal managers, and the seduction of wealth for artists along with an ever-changing political landscape that seemed more conservative than in Broadside's heyday.

Almost buying into Gordon's vision, I tried to assure Sis that none of those pressures applied to me, so there was less-than-zero danger of me being pulled away. I stopped short of formally offering to step in to take over their work.

She responded that even so, I didn't have access to the funds it would take to continue the magazine. Still defending Gordon's position, I told her that new energy and the prospect of a "new birth" for Broadside could be used as a fundraising launchpad; part of the rebirth would be a concise fundraising plan.

She was a lot more cynically skeptical than her husband. During the past decade, they had seen too many of their hopes burned by unfulfilled promises from musicians who would stick around only long enough to use them and then move on, never to talk to them again.

Almost conspiracy-theory sounding, Sis' letters seemed to carry a tone of resolve that people who got close to Broadside (or to them) somehow always seemed to be pulled away.

The magazine's future had two main hurdles: Sis & Gordon's ages and energy levels; *and* the money to pay for publishing and postage.

Both born in 1909, so when we began talking, they were already 65 years old; but tired beyond their years from decades of poverty and struggle. They needed youthful energy to carry on *with* them (not *for* them).

The finances were an entirely different matter. On principle they had always refused advertising and instead depended on donations from wealthy friends and supporters. But most of those people had died, moved on, or lost interest in Broadside… or lost interest in Sis & Gordon themselves[114].

---

[114] Sis' perceived lack of support may have been self-inflicted, at least to some degree. I didn't see it at the time; but there were widespread feelings in the folkie community that Gordon, and especially Sis, were difficult to work with. Some critics wrote them off as embittered old Stalinists who never recovered from the 1950's blacklisting ordeals and remained dogmatic in their lives and politics.

Late one night a few years later in a backstage dressing room, Arlo Guthrie told me that Sis and Gordon were bitter and spent too much time being angry at people. He said it gave off a bad vibe that nobody wanted to be around. He blew them off as insignificant and didn't even want to talk about them.

After I moved to New York, I *did* notice that many of the people who originally rallied around Broadside were conspicuously absent from helping them, a mere 10 years later.

THE POET LAUREATE SOUL OF FOLKIE ROCK & ROLL

It was clear to me that the Friesen's were trying to convince me to become part of Broadside on some level other than as just another songwriter. Clearly, that would have been a possible solution to the time and energy deficits. I, on the other hand, was not ready for (nor particularly enamored by) that prospect.

I had only been to New York a couple of times, and I didn't really have any idea of what regular trips up there would be like for me. I needed to have a good handle on *that* before I could seriously consider anything that Gordon Friesen was hinting.

I was a long-time mail subscriber to the weekly *Village Voice* newspaper[115]. In the back pages there were always one-column ads for that week's musical line-up at the coffeehouses in Greenwich Village. One of those clubs often featured musicians that I had heard from their Folkways albums or had read about in various folkie journals. That club also featured an open-mic night, once a week. I'd had a great experience at the University of Tennessee's open mic coffeehouse —well, until I pissed them off with a topical song. I decided that a short set of train songs with my hillbilly accent might hit-the-spot with the New York City folkie set. So, I fired off a letter and a tape, asking for a spot; and they responded with an invitation to play.

It was for an open-mic night, so there would be no publicity by name. I decided to just slip into New York and not tell anyone that I was there. The only issue would be the cost of getting there and back; my $60-a-week reporter's salary didn't exactly lend itself to a jaunt to one of the most expensive cities in the world.

I had two weeks of vacation coming, so I decided to take one of the weeks. It was a relatively direct route of major highways to New York from Gastonia (unlike from Knoxville); Interstate 85 then on Interstate 95 in Petersburg Virginia and that was it; straight into New York. There

---

They, apparently, had fallen out with their cofounders Gil Turner before his death in 1974 and with Ralph Gleason. Of the original corps of topical folksingers, only Pete Seeger and Phil Ochs were still regularly in the Broadside circle; and that within itself was curious. On the other hand, Pete was known for supporting a number of folk projects from *SingOut! Magazine* to various topical collectives and gatherings; and Phil, by then, was deep in the throes of personal demons that eventually took his life.

Eventually, I too, saw the bitterness (especially from Sis); but I knew more about their backgrounds, the blacklisting that led to poverty, and their being ostracized for unbending political beliefs. So, I was more sympathetic and forgiving than most. Pete Seeger also discussed their bitterness with me; and he, too, was more tolerant than most —either for the same reasons I was, or perhaps because that was just Pete's nature.

[115] At that time still an alternative cultural paper for avant-garde arts, literature, and music.

THE LEGEND DIES ON — GARY GREEN

would be lots of traffic and lots of trucks; so, I decided to hitchhike; that would save money, for sure.

I rolled my clothes into an over-sized backpack (at a time in our culture when backpacks were rare sights and usually only seen with hikers or other naturists). I had a guitar case with a shoulder strap; so, my acoustic axe would be safe.

I reasoned that the only issue would be making certain that I got one ride from at least the North Carolina line all the way to DC, because hitchhiking was illegal in Virginia at that time. Optimism had me expecting one ride from Charlotte (just east of Gastonia) nonstop to New York; but I might as well have believed in Santa Claus and the Easter Bunny — *it just didn't happen.*

For the trip, I imagined climbing up into a truck, taking my harmonica out of a pocket, keeping time with the windshield wipers, and singing up every song that driver knew... or some other such Kristofferson-ish Kerouac trip. Unfortunately, on the road I learned that wasn't going to happen either.

Just to make the 220 miles across North Carolina to the state line took seven rides and 19 hours on the road. Southerners weren't eager to pick up a hippie-looking character on the side of the road holding a little cardboard sign that read "New York".

. The longest ride through the state was about 45 minutes with a burley truck driver who looked like he killed hippies for sport. I was expecting a Cecil Null incident with him asking me about military service and Vietnam. As soon as I climbed into his cab, he asked "what do you do?" I told him I was a hillbilly singer, and I asked him what he did. "I am into prophylactics," he answered.

"Huh?" I responded. "Rubbers," he answered.

I nodded, "yeah I know what they are…"

"You know those 25¢ condom machines in bathrooms at gas stations and truck stops?" he asked me and then continued before I could acknowledge. "Well, I supply them. This whole trailer is full of thousands-and-thousands of rubbers," he proudly concluded as I was trying to decide if he was serious. He was.

He was going about halfway to Petersburg, but I opted to be dropped at the state line rather than having to risk looking for a ride in Virginia. Besides the no-hitchhikers-allowed law, rural Virginia was known to be very *Easy-Rider*-like toward long hairs[116].

---

[116] *Easy Rider* was the 1969 Peter Fonda, Dennis Hopper, and Terry Southern, film that ends with the shotgunning of two hippies because they … were hippies.

THE POET LAUREATE SOUL OF FOLKIE ROCK & ROLL

Mister "condom driver" dropped me at an exit ramp near the state line and I wandered up the hill to a roadside *Stuckey's Shoppe*[117]. Using many of the survival skills that had kept me alive during my living-in-the-woods days outside of Nashville, I crashed that night in a field behind the store, brushed my teeth and washed the next morning in their men's room, and hit the road early with my "New York" sign.

I needed a ride that would take me all the way through Virginia, but no one was stopping for me. I turned down several rides that told me they were only going part way through the state. Though I had started early, by sundown I still had not found a through-ride and I was starting to worry.

Finally, around eight p.m. I accepted a ride that was going only to Richmond. That at least would get me to Interstate 95; but it also would keep me stranded in Virginia for the night. Even though Richmond was less than a two-hour drive from Stuckey's, it would be after ten o'clock when I arrived in the capital city.

Once again calling on my Nashville-homeless-days skills, I found the 19th century *Jefferson Hotel* on Franklin Street and put in place all of my tricks from the Andrew Jackson Hotel in Tennessee. I slept pretty comfortably that night by picking the lock on the door of one of the hotel's meeting-rooms and crashing in a corner. Using supplies from a housekeeping cart, I copped toiletries and linens to take full advantage of the oversized restrooms down the hall.

Early on day three of this journey I set out again for New York. Rather than risk arrest for hitchhiking, I walked to a truck stop near an entrance ramp and decided to accost truckers in the parking lot. I figured that whatever hostility I might run into there would be immeasurably better than a roadside run-in with *Johnny Law*.

The first trucker I approached welcomed me to ride as far as he was going. It was only to Washington DC; but that at least was out of Virginia. That meant that I could accept shorter rides without fear of arrest. Also, from my protest-singer days, I knew people in DC and especially at

---

[117] Stuckey's was a roadside chain then owned by the Pet Milk Corporation, but in its early years was known as a safe haven for all travelers and was even included in the famous Green Book travel guide as a safe haven for Black travelers during the Jim Crow years. In the 1950's and early 60's when I traveled with my family, stops at Stuckey's were mandatory and their pecan pralines were a required treat. Despite corporate ownership, most of the franchised stores were still pretty safe, even for long-haired hippie freaks with guitars. *(And today, the founder's granddaughter has repurchased the family business and begun revitalizing the great brand.)*

THE LEGEND DIES ON — GARY GREEN

George Washington University; so, worst-case, I could crash and eat safely and for free.

It turned out that rides out of the District of Columbia were not as easy to get as I had hoped. After a few hours, I wandered to the student union on the GW campus and looked for bulletin board postings ride shares. I found one that was going to New York City early the next morning; so, I called the number that was dangling on the cutaway tag on the flyer.

The guy who posted it was driving into The City early the next morning. He was looking for companionship and someone to share the driving on the five-hour trip. I told him that I was a folksinger headed to The Village for a gig and if he supplied the car and gasoline, I would drive all the way. *Done deal.*

I just needed a place to crash for the night. Since the Nixon inauguration, the campus had tightened up access to the dorms; so being smuggled in for a free room now required a complex, but doable, charade. A friend, who was a grad student at GW, met me off campus and brought with him a bottle of some cheap liquor. We waited until about 10 pm and then he poured it all over me so that I would smell like I was drunk. We went back to the student union and into one of the cafeteria-style restaurants there. He then led me behind the food line and into the kitchen where the workers just ignored us as if we belonged there.

A hallway from the kitchen led directly into the dormitories of Crawford, West End, and Schenley residence halls. We left my backpack and guitar in the hallway, for him to retrieve later using his student ID so there would be no questions asked.

Stairs from the hallway came up in a lobby area that was inside the security perimeter. Coming in that way rather than through the front door, could have been interpreted as we were already inside the complex and would not need to show student ID cards to the security guard who was at the desk at the front door. Just for good measure, he had me slump as if I was fall-down drunk and with his arm around me he was leading me back to my dorm room; hence me smelling like cheap gin. *(Drinking age then was 18.)*

It worked like a charm and soon I was safely ensconced for the night in a comfortable quad with four female students who were happy to welcome the hippie folksinger and his guitar, which arrived about ten minutes after I did. Very early the next morning, one of the girls accompanied me to the communal shower on the floor and guarded the door while I showered and dressed in non-alcohol-soaked clothes.

An hour or so later, I met my ride and was driving up Interstate 95 toward the New Jersey Turnpike and then through the Holland Tunnel. He dropped me off in Washington Square Park about four hours before my open mic gig. That gave me time to go into the NYU (New York

THE POET LAUREATE SOUL OF FOLKIE ROCK & ROLL

University) student union and post a notice on several bulletin boards there; some to the effect of:

> **H-E-L-P** Topical songwriting folksinger from the South needs a warm corner to roll out a blanket at night and take a shower in morning. In return can offer only token payment and original stereo tape of songs and photocopies of original manuscripts of 2 books. Will also throw in a vast repertoire of southern folk songs &train songs. I am no trouble and will be out most of the time. Please help. I will be under the arch playing guitar.
> Thank you.

It was a different era (and of course no cell phones). I opened my guitar case under the arch and started playing Southern traditionals. A few passersby tossed coins into my open case and after about a half hour a guy came by and asked if I was the person who had posted in the student union.

He told me that he was a professional musician and lived in a commune in Brooklyn where I was welcome to stay. He gave me the address on Flatbush Avenue and told me if he wasn't there just to tell folks that Ben sent me. *(I told you it was a different era.)*

I still had a couple of hours to kill before my gig, so I decided to continue playing and collecting donations so that I could afford food later. An essay-worthy interesting cast of characters stopped by to talk with me between songs. They were all New York architypes of one kind or another and thus to me were comical parodies[118]. When I finished playing, I packed my gear and headed toward the coffeehouse.

---

[118] Probably the most memorable was an undercover cop who unsuccessfully tried to entrap me into any number of crimes. My brief career as a newspaper reporter had embedded me for stories with undercover vice cops so often that I could almost smell the tactics. If it had been five years later, I could say that he was costumed like a reject from *The Village People*; but they had not been formed yet. So, for the time, it was just a silly, exaggerated "undercover" get-up.

First, he approached to ask me, in a whisper, if I had any marijuana to sell him. I laughed him off. After another song, he came to me again; this time asking if I had any "coke" (cocaine). Again, I laughed and told him no. He still didn't leave. His third approach was to ask me if I wanted to "make some money hustling".

This time I stopped playing and strongly said, "look, I am just here to play guitar and sing a few songs; nothing else".

Clearly taken aback, he responded, "No way. I mean, come on. What's with the cowboy hat, the boots, even that fake accent? You are playing *Midnight Cowboy*; don't bullshit a bullshitter".

I started packing up my guitar, took a deep breath, and decided to confront the situation. *"Look officer, I can smell you guys a mile off. Trust me on this, I know more about vice-*

THE LEGEND DIES ON — GARY GREEN

The first thing I learned was that "coffeehouse" was a euphemism; there was a hell-of-a-lot more beer sold there than coffee. The gig, it turned out, wasn't simply an open-mic welcoming all comers. Rather, it was an audition for a paid gig at the bar; it was just cloaked as an open mic night. That was fine, but I did take mental note of the duplicity of scamming musicians into playing for free while the owners sold beer.

Allowed two songs, I opened with a fairly innocuous rendition of *Wabash Cannonball*. I received minor applause, but no one really looked up from the beer other than to see if my Southern accent was authentic. Sticking with my train-song theme, I decided to wake them up with my arrangement of *The Wreck of the Old 97*.

Rather than the traditional version, I started slowly, like the typical ballad; but into the second verse I sped up (with that weird-o rhythm thing of mine) to the Johnny Cash version which was in cut time (about twice as fast as the ballad version). That unexpected speed-up raised a few eyebrows, but I still didn't "have them". When it came to the break between the next verses, I played it with the Carter Family Churchlick that Mother Maybelle had taught me; only very fast, to demonstrate my picking chops. That got the crowd's attention and even elicited a gratuitous "*Yee-Haw*",

At the end of the night, the owners invited me back for a paid gig. I took their information and told them that I would get back to them. I thanked them and headed out for the commune.

The biggest problem at that point was that I had not spent a lot of time in New York; I did not know about the Burroughs. I had no idea what Brooklyn was. *No, really.*

---

control than you will ever know, even if you already have a gold shield. You are wasting your time with me, hoss." I blurted frustratedly.

He just wouldn't let it go, *"So you are saying that if you didn't think I am cop, we'd do something?"*

That was the last straw for me. I opened the side pocket of my backpack, where my wallet was, and pulled out my press pass. As I shoved it in his face, I growled. *"Look you goddamned yankee asshole, I am Working Press. I am not a fucking hustler or drug dealer, and my accent is as real as a heart-attack. Now do you want to get the fuck out of my face, or do you want me to out your undercover ass as loud as I can in this park right now?"*

He took a step backwards before he spoke again, *"Wow. Sorry man. I didn't know. You are good. I won't mess with you. Just one thing, how'd you know?"*

I was calmer by then, *"I am a police reporter and I've spent most of my adult life dealing with undercover. You were trying too hard and you mixed vices. Sex and drugs are not the same guys usually, unless they're junkies; and it's obvious I ain't no hype"*. (I didn't bother to tell him that my "dealing with undercover" was from the bastards following me around at gigs.)

He left without further incident; he even thanked me and wished me good luck.

THE POET LAUREATE SOUL OF FOLKIE ROCK & ROLL

I walked to the West 4th Street subway station, went down the stairs, and walked up to the only official-looking person there. "Which one of these trains here goes to Clinton Street in Brooklyn?" I asked just as nicely as I knew how.

The man, who had been keeping a close guard on the fading yellow subway gate to make sure no one carried it off, turned to look at me. He said nothing. I could see his eyes walking from the top of my dusty hat down my hair to my jacket, then to my jeans and on down to the toe of I my boots. I waited for his eyes to climb back up to mine before I spoke again.

"Look, I just wanna know which one of these ramps takes me to the "A" train so I can get the "double-C" train," I told him.

Careful not to violate the strict New York City rule which forbade strangers from having a decent conversation with each other, the little man answered me:

"Godowntothebarbarshopandgetonthe"A"ramp—thatleadstotheBroadwaylocalnumberoneandgotothe—portauthoritythere'snofreetransfertheresoyoumight--wanngotofifty-ninthstreetand-columbuscircleand—changethereforthe "A"orthe"AA"trainandtakeitto--"Hoyt-Schmieterhorn"theregetonthe"GG"trainand—thesecond stopisClinton."

I didn't understand a damned word that he said, but rather than make a total ass of myself by having him go through all that again, I sort of mumbled "Thank-ya" and walked in the direction he had pointed. I must have done the right thing because I didn't hear him yell at me or anything.

I somehow got to the right platform, after having to cross a mezzanine to get to the other side of the tracks. I was beginning to think that all of New York was *the other side of the tracks*[119].

Since being in New York City just a few hours, I had been: harassed by two of "New York's finest" who didn't like the words printed across the face of my guitar (which was always slung across my back as I wandered around); followed on two subway trains by a guy about 45-years-old and dressed in (are you ready for this?) a black leather jacket, no shirt, too-tight black leather pants, no socks, black leather shoes, black leather gloves, a black leather "cab-driver" cap, and rolls of silver-chrome chains hanging from all of his leather; stopped by a drunk who wanted me to give him my guitar so he could go trade it for (you won't believe this either) an egg sandwich; chased out of Washington Square Park by a police car that drove across the grass to park within 15 inches of where I

---

[119] "Other side of the tracks"...hmm... strange expression; down home it would mean the side of town that nice little middle- and upper-class family boys (to say nothing of girls) should never wander through... especially at night.

THE LEGEND DIES ON — GARY GREEN

was sitting and playing my guitar; followed for three blocks by an aged-before-her-time young woman who seemed unable to say anything other than "Come on Mister Cowboy you want a date don't you?"; and followed by a Latin guy who wanted God-only-knows-what.

At any rate, I had concluded that New York City was no place for this cowboy to be![120]

Still unsure of the exact directions, I decided to approach a Transit Cop that was watching the trains. In my best Southern twang and exaggerating my accent, I said, "Ah, 'scuse me Oss-i-fer, could ya'll tell me what a Brooklyn is?" *No, I really* did *say that.*

He too looked at me from head-to-toe and surmised that I might not be putting him on. He decided to take pity on me and tell me how to get to Brooklyn. Then he asked where in Brooklyn and I gave him the address. He even told me which stop on the train to get off and the direction to walk when I did. NYPD; got to love 'em… at times. I thanked him with my best *Andy Griffith* like, "I 'preciate it". With that, somehow, I made it to Clinton Avenue, found the house (a run-down brownstone house just off of Flatbush Avenue), and walked in.

Ben wasn't there, but he had called ahead, and the other residents were expecting me. There was a light, but not unpleasant, scent of marijuana permeating the rooms. A very Janis-Joplin-lookalike woman assigned herself to being my hostess and led me to an empty room. There was no bed or other furniture, but I was able to layout my bedroll beside a steam radiator on the broad-board hardwood floor.

I was tired...I'd been awake for about 26 hours. I dropped my backpack in the corner and propped my guitar against it. I unfolded my blanket against the radiator and looked for a match to light a candle. I found it and in the flickering light I pulled off my boots and my socks. I hung my hat

---

[120] I wasn't sure that the one guy was following me until I walked around the block twice, ducked into a subway station, rode a train for two stops and then turned around and came back where I started. He was still with me at every turn. So, I decided to end the whole thing; after all, it was getting a little bothersome). I walked down a subway ramp to some vacant tracks that looked like they weren't used except during rush hours. This was not a rush hour. Sure as shit falls, this guy followed me. I lured him to the end of the tracks where I knew he could be certain that no one could hear me cry out if he attacked me. I stopped, lifted my guitar off of my back, laid it on the concrete, threw open the flaps of my jacket and began walking toward him like I was going to tear life out of him and leave it for the rush-hour commuters on the track below. I straightened one hand and fisted the other as I got closer. When we were no more than 15 feet apart...just about "white-of-their-eyes" drawing distance, he turned and literally RAN, bounding stairs and fading into the crowd on the level above heading toward the streets. I never saw him again.

THE POET LAUREATE SOUL OF FOLKIE ROCK & ROLL

over the tuning pegs of my guitar. I threw my coat over the pack and tossed my shirt and tee-shirt over it.

With the top half of my red long johns showing as a shirt and my jeans covering the rest of me, barefooted I walked out of the room in search of the communal bathroom. There I filled my coffee mug with hot water and returned to the room to pour in a packet of instant grits —the first food I'd had all day. When I finished, I washed out the bowl-cup slipped out of my jeans and rolled up against the radiator. I went to sleep feeling like even when I was inside, I was somehow outside.

Though my city gig was over, I didn't have to be back at work for almost a week. So, I decided to stay in New York and absorb all that I could in those few days. From about 8:00 every morning until around midnight I wandered around Greenwich Village or took in the typical tourist sites *(Statue of Liberty, Staton Island Ferry, Empire State Building, World Trade Center, NY Public Library, Macys, the Chrysler Building, Grand Central Station, Madison Square Garden, Times Square, the Port Authority, the various sites in Central Park, and on and on)*.

Around lunchtime every day I would open my guitar case and play for tossed coins either along Central Park West across from the Essex House, or up at Columbus Circle, or on Fifth Avenue near the stores. Lunch goers and tourists alike would walk by and toss me coins or subway tokens. At the dinner hour every evening I would go back down to The Village and sing Paul Simon, Hank Williams, and Johnny Cash songs for tossed coins.

Late nights I would return to the commune house to sleep. Every now and then, I would get a roommate who needed a place to sleep for a night. Hey, it was rent-free, so... whatever. Also, periodically in the middle of the night my Janis-esque hostess would wander in, clothed or not, and wake me up to talk about pretty much of nothing.

On the night before I was set to leave, Ben told me that since I was sleeping with a guitar and a handful of original songs, he saw "a real comradeship between us". He asked to hear some of my songs, and of course I agreed.

After I played for them, Ben said, "You better stay away from that stuff. Politics will kill you in this business quicker than anything. Don't touch politics", I thanked him, politely.

Despite that warning, incredibly surprising to me I made more money street-singing than I made per week as a daily newspaper reporter. That put the whole Gordon Friesen plea into a new perspective. Perhaps, I thought, I actually could make it work... if I decided to step back into my life's calling into music.

The finances to support Broadside, however, were a whole different matter. Way out of my proverbial wheelhouse, I decided to learn more

THE LEGEND DIES ON — GARY GREEN

about that situation by asking Pete his thoughts. I decided to write to him as soon as I got home.

The trip home was a lot faster than the trip north. I had made enough money on the streets to afford a train ticket from Pennsylvania Station to Charlotte North Carolina. A long-haul passenger train trip was like a flashback to my preschool years; I felt at home the instant I boarded.

At home, before I went back to work, I fired off a letter to Seeger. He responded in less than a week and surprisingly, at least to me, Pete thought that Broadside should gracefully fade away. In its place, he proposed, a new "project" that would be far more than a monthly (or quarterly) publication and reaching far beyond just topical or political music.

He envisioned a combination of a magazine, record label, concerts, booking agency, library-educational resource, a historical repository, and a creativity hub. He wanted to call the massive new project, *I Hear America Singing*, borrowed from the Walt Whitman poem of the same name and first published in *Leaves of Grass*.

He proposed that the initial Board of Directors for the project be himself, the *Reverend Frederick Douglass Kirkpatrick* (an associate of Martin Luther King Jr. and widely known as the official troubadour of Dr. King's historic 1968 Poor Peoples' March on Washington), and *Phil Ochs* (probably America's most famous perennial protest singer). He proposed that Sis Cunningham and Gordon Friesen serve on a separate "Board of Advisors" along with *Moe Asch*, and a handful of other luminaries in Pete's general circle.

He said that I should be the "Executive Director" of *I Hear America Singing*, and he asked me to put together a working plan for the project. While I was doing that, he would talk with Kirk (which is what friends called Reverend Kirkpatrick) and with Phil. He left it to me to tell Sis and Gordon about the plan.

I was still working, pretty intensely, as a daily newspaper reporter; and I was racking up a string of press awards for my spot-news reporting. Nonetheless, I started writing what was, essentially, a business plan for the new project. Via our weekly letters, I gave progress reports to Pete. He suggested that when I finished it, I should come to New York to meet with him to lay out the next steps for the proposed Board.

Working full-time as a spot news / police reporter, it was difficult for me to arrange two or three consecutive days off; and I didn't want to use the remainder of my vacation unless I had to. Also, if I went back to New York for Pete's meeting, it would be a 12-hour drive, since I had sworn off hitchhiking for a while.

Nonetheless, my music was starting once again to come first in my life, and I convinced the editor to let me take the time off (though I certainly didn't tell him why).

THE POET LAUREATE SOUL OF FOLKIE ROCK & ROLL

I set a target date for my trip and wrote to Pete. He said that my choice of dates was ideal, because he was going to be in "The City" (New York jargon for Manhattan) then. He was scheduled to begin a cruise up the Hudson River on *The Clearwater* and he would send me details of where to meet him. A few days later, he sent me a postcard asking if I could meet him at an address in lower Manhattan and the promise to "answer all my questions then".

I sensed from the tone of the letter that came before the postcard that he didn't actually believe that I would drive the 663 miles from historic Gastonia up to New York. That explained his startled reaction when I showed up at the dock, walked up to him, and in my very-best Johnny Cash, announced, "Hello, I'm Gary Green".

Clearly shocked, he looked at me for a minute, taking in my cowboy hat, western-cut dress-jacket, and wide-bell jeans. After a long silence, he put out his hand and said, "Well, I'll be God-damned. You came".

For *I Hear America Singing*, I had typeset (in the newspaper composing room; there were no personal computers in those days), printed, and bound the business plan. We sat on the dock while I summarized the contents and he read it, sitting on a wooden dock piling.

When he finished reading and I finished talking, he looked upward as if he were staring off in space. Then he spoke. "This is good. This is real God-damned good. This is what we need," he pontificated.

Just as I was feeling really good that I had so-pleased the legendary Pete Seeger, he dropped a bomb on me. "You've got to move to New York immediately, so we can get this going".

Move to New York? Yikes! That thought had never occurred to me; even in my intense discussions with Gordon about revitalizing Broadside, I had never considered that it would require moving to New York. Even after my week at the commune, my thoughts were only about visiting New York frequently; not living there[121].

Before I could think of words to respond to Pete, someone from the Clearwater crew called to him that they were ready to shove-off. As I turned to leave, he asked, "where are you going?" And, before I could answer that, he said "you are coming with us. Get on board". [122]

---

[121] There was no "remote" work in those days; and no electronic networks to enable such things.

[122] *The Clearwater* was (and I think still IS) a sailing sloop (a one-masted sailboat with a fore-and-aft mainsail and a jib) that Pete and his wife, Toshi, had built to bring attention to his campaign to clean up the heavily-polluted Hudson River. It became the springboard for an environmental non-profit organization they founded as well as an annual environmental-themed folk festival.

THE LEGEND DIES ON — GARY GREEN

There were no free spectator rides on The Clearwater. I learned that we were going to jump the halyard (apparently the act of the full crew of unskilled workers all hoisting the main sail) under the supervision of the rigging monkey in the bosun's chair!??

The lead slave-driver of this conscripted amateur work force had an incredible voice that took on a natural amplification as he led us all singing *Sailin' Up, Sailin' Down* and other appropriate sea shanties, working, and environmental songs. During the next four hours cursing that toxic river, I learned that he wasn't the lead slave-driver at all; in fact, he wasn't even a regular part of the crew. Instead, he was a 29-year-old folksinger named *Don McLean* who spent a lot of time on The Clearwater with Pete and the crew; he also had just had a mega-hit song on United Artist Records called *American Pie* (so titled after the name of the plane in which Buddy Holly et. al had died).

Pete introduced us during one of the (very few) rest breaks on the trip. Pete told him that I was "working on a big project" and we should stay in touch. I don't think he was very impressed and likewise, I wasn't a fan of American Pie.[123]

By the time the sloop returned to the dock in lower Manhattan, I was exhausted and had callouses on the palms of my hands that were matched only by the aches in muscles that I didn't even know I had. I also had a tiny-insight into the work of 19th century sailors; and at that moment I knew that I was really glad that I was not a pirate. *Jean Lafitte can have that shit!*

Back on dry land, Pete told me to let him know when I moved to New York. More-than-reluctant, I told him that I had to figure out what I was going to do about my newspaper job, but I'd let him know. As I left, I assumed the project was dead.

As was always the case in my relationship with Seeger, I underestimated him. His weekly letters were filled with more thoughts on my business plan and his ideas about how to bring it to fruition.

He convinced the *War Resisters League* to donate us office space on Lafayette Street in lower Manhattan; and he set the date for the first meeting of the Board of Directors for himself, Kirk, Phil, and me: Saturday, April 10th.

I still had one more week of vacation coming, so I took off from work on Friday the 9th with a plan to return to work on Monday the 19th.

---

[123] Cruelly, I thought that rather than his magnum opus, it was more of a pop one-hit-wonder. So, there was no follow-up from either of us. Probably a mistake on my part, because among other things, Don McLean is an incredibly talented singer and songwriter with much more depth than that one song. I wish I had developed the friendship.

THE POET LAUREATE SOUL OF FOLKIE ROCK & ROLL

On Friday morning, April 9th, I set out on the long trip to The City. That same day, Phil Ochs, who had been living at his sister Sonny's house in Far Rockaway Queens, went into the bathroom and hung himself. His body was discovered by his fourteen-year-old nephew.

Needless to say, the Board meeting was cancelled; Pete didn't even come into The City. He told me about it on the phone, and I didn't tell him that I was already in New York when I called. I had intended to, but as soon as he heard my voice, he told me the news.

I had not known Phil for long and we never met in person, though I knew his music really well. Still, I took his death really hard; and not because it fundamentally changed the plans for *I Hear America Singing* (though, of course it did that too).

We never met face-to-face, but we had multiple really-long phone conversations that Pete had arranged. In the months between my first trip up and down the Hudson on The Clearwater and April of 1976, I had concluded from those many calls that the once-brilliant Phil Ochs was quite insane.

I did *not* suspect that he was suicidal. Perhaps I was not worldly-experienced enough to see it. But I definitely could see that he was nuts. On the phone Phil would ramble for hours; often slurring like an old drunk (he was only 35); then he would also have moments of startling lucidity… in the same conversations.

Sometimes he would call and claim to be "*John Train* the murderer of Phil Ochs". Other times he would tell me that he found out that Bob Dylan was dead, and his soul had been transplanted into a Norcross Georgia folksinger named *Sammy Walker* who Phil… or John… was producing for Moe Asch and also for *Warner Brothers Records*. He would tell me that, and then two days later call and tell me the exact same thing, as if it was the first time that he had said it. *(Sammy was a real person and Phil actually did produce records for him on both labels.)*

One time Phil called me, whispering during the entire call, to tell me that the FBI was following him to murder him because the CIA had created an android to replace him and discredit everything he'd ever done. He told me to not trust anyone who calls me claiming to be Phil Ochs unless he gave me the code word "Butler" —which he told me was the secret middle name of John Train.

Many of the calls from him were about slain Chilian singer *Victor Jara*, whose hands were cut off before he was murdered by the CIA-backed junta that had overthrown the democratically elected Chilian government. (I later referenced that situation, as told to me by Phil, in a song I called *Ain't No Two Ways About It*).

Gordon Friesen told me that many times in February of that year when there was snow on the ground in New York, Phil would show up at the

THE LEGEND DIES ON — GARY GREEN

Broadside apartment barefoot, shirtless, and having pissed in his pants. Gordon said that he and Sis would bathe him, dress him, nurse him well, and then he would disappear again.

Some of the calls from Phil were seemingly perfectly normal. We would talk about journalism, topical music, and phonograph records being *modern journalism*. Not long before he died, Phil told me that he had quit drinking, was *"getting some help"*, and *"when you get to New York, we're going to do this right"*.

Presumably, he was talking about *I Hear America Singing*. I never heard from him again after that call.

After Pete told me the news, I didn't really have a plan. He didn't know I was in New York. I was too bummed-out to call Sis and Gordon and tell them I was there. I had no clue what to do.

On some level, I took Phil's death as a sign to me. As we know, my omens always fizzled to have no significance whatsoever; but my sense of melodrama didn't want to accept that. Besides, at times during that last year of his life I was as close to Phil... or John... or Butler... as (I suppose) anyone. Though, I truly regret that I never knew the *REAL* Phil Ochs; the pre-mental-illness Phil: *the creative genius*.

I took Phil's death as a sign that my music days finally were over; not just our *I Hear America Singing*, but the whole New York direction. I needed to enjoy my vacation, then get back to my career as a newspaper reporter. This definitely was the end of my musical road.

If I had any regret about my crashed-before-it-started music "career" it was that I never had the guts to submit a tape to Folkways Records. I had always been afraid to do so because a rejection from Folkways would have felt like the end of the musical world for me.

It was the label of Woody Guthrie, of Pete, of Broadside, of Phil, of dozens of historical figures who not only changed the world but who were inseparable from American culture itself.

A rejection from Folkways wouldn't be like the corporate rejections on Music Row. It wouldn't be a rejection by hack commercialism; it would be a rejection of my writing, my literature, my value in the big picture of the world.

So, I had never submitted to Folkways because I just couldn't handle the inevitable rejection. BUT... since I had resolved that Phil's death was the end of my career, I now had nothing to lose.

I thought about just turning around and driving back to North Carolina; but I'd never been much north of New York City, so I decided, instead, I would drive up to the Berkshires in western Massachusetts. I'd always wanted to see Stockbridge; the village that was the location of Arlo Guthrie's *Alice's Restaurant Massacre*. It would make a nice vacation.

THE POET LAUREATE SOUL OF FOLKIE ROCK & ROLL

In those days, I never traveled anywhere without a guitar and at least one demo tape; on this trip I actually had three tapes with me. So, I decided, *what-the-hell*, I might as well do a final slamming of the door on my music. On my way out of town I decided to stop by the Folkways Records office on West 61st Street behind Lincoln Center and drop off one last tape. No point sticking around, they could mail it back to me with the rejection letter; my address and phone number were on the tape box.

I chose a demo tape that was a combination of my originals and my covers. I reasoned that it was probably the best representation of the "whole package" of me rather than just one dimension.

The tape began with one of my favorite train songs, *The Wreck of the Old 97* —my crazy superfast arrangement that had been a hit in Greenwich Village. The next track on the reel was my *The CIA Song* that Allen Ginsberg had praised.

The CIA opened with a mock-ragtime intro on a kazoo. Rather than a standard three-chord triad folk or country song, it had a seven-foundational-chord jazz progression but sung hillbilly style and played so simplistically that an untrained ear would never hear the jazz underpinnings.

It was a sneaky little subliminal music trick that I liked to use to seduce an audience into a false sense of the mundane before punching them in the face with something completely unexpected. Words aside, the presentation itself was a parody. Add the words and the song was pure irreverent sarcasm aimed at our otherwise sacred spy agency.

The final song on that demo tape was one that I had just written from my hitchhiking trip to New York City. *There Ain't No Easy Way* was a sung-poem that summed up everything I felt on that trip: from my thumb out on the road to arriving in The City… to wandering the streets and watching the people… to ultimately making decisions about my music.

I took the elevator up to the Folkways office and marveled at the mixture of African Art and seemingly unorganized stacks of papers and files and boxes of who-knows-what. A very nice woman named *Marilyn Averett Conklin* seemed to be in charge of everything.

She very graciously took my tape, wrote down my contact information, and thanked me profusely. She was probably the single nicest and most accommodating person I'd ever met in the music industry; it amazed me that she was in New York — I definitely had a stereotyped image of New York behavior, and it was *not* her totally unexpected welcoming kindness.

I gave her the tape, and thus ended my music career, as far as I was concerned. It died with Phil Ochs in Far Rockaway. Before coming to New York, all I knew about the city was what I had seen on TV during the Macy's Thanksgiving Day Parade (and a few movies). Finally coming to The City, it came to represent the end of my musical dreams.

♪♪♪

THE LEGEND DIES ON — GARY GREEN

Opus Thirteen:
Then I Was An Artist On **THE** Label

"To give you a sense of the breadth of this collection, here are just a few of the familiar names found on the label: Lead Belly, Woody Guthrie, Pete Seeger, Phil Ochs, Jean Ritchie, Mary Lou Williams, Ella Jenkins, The Carter Family, Lucinda Williams, Janis Ian, Martin Luther King, Bertold Brecht, Margaret Mead, Langston Hughes, W. E. B. DuBois, and Bob Dylan (under the pseudonym Blind Boy Grunt)".

— anthropologist Dr. Michael Asch, discussing his father's record label in a paper for Canadian Society for Traditional Music/Société Canadienne four les traditions musicales

The Berkshires were pretty, I suppose; but not fundamentally different, visually, from the Blue Ridge Mountains of Appalachia that were my childhood home. As for the storied town of Stockbridge, despite my affection for the Arlo Guthrie song, I was underwhelmed. Rather than leave immediately and just to get the full New England experience, I also drove up to Vermont then New Hampshire, just to say I had been there.

Not bummed out but not enthusiastic either, I headed back south. I could have stayed on Interstate 95 and bypassed New York City, but I wanted to eat at *Le Figaro Café* on Bleeker Street —my favorite New York eatery. After pastries, fruit, and hot tea, I decided to call Folkways Records before leaving town; perhaps I could pick up my tape and save the trouble of their having to mail it back to me. I wasn't very excited about calling the record company, because I already knew they didn't want me; but from a pay phone in front of *Café Reggio* on MacDougal near West 3rd, I dialed the number.

Even in my certainty, I still was nervous about calling the mother church. When Marilyn answered the phone, I just started babbling; I didn't even identify myself. "Hi. I dropped off a tape at your office a while back and I am in New York for a couple of hours today. I was wondering if I could come by and pick it up," I asked.

"Of course," she began, again in that unyieldingly pleasant put-you-at-ease voice that had impressed me before. She continued, "what is your name?"

A little embarrassed that I had not begun the call by identifying myself, I answered, "oh, sorry. This is Gary Green".

There was a short pause before she responded, then the pleasant professionalism in her voice changed to something different; good, but different. It was as if I could hear a smile come across her face as she again began speaking.

THE POET LAUREATE SOUL OF FOLKIE ROCK & ROLL

"Gary Green! We have been trying to get in touch with you. We called everywhere. Mr. Asch wants to talk to you. Can you come to the office?"

Okay, that was weird. MOE ASCH wanted to talk to me! I still could not imagine why. I simply answered, "when?" She asked if I could come "right now". I told her that I was in The Village but had a car and could be there in a half hour. Always accommodating, she asked if I remembered where they were located. *My God, it was Folkways Records; how could I not remember?*

The office of 71-year-old Moses Asch was not at all what I would have expected for the man who gave the world *This Land Is Your Land, Goodnight Irene,* and hundreds of treasures of my childhood and of American culture. Or... maybe it was.

There were very neatly arranged shelves with hand-carved pieces of African Art; pieces that obviously even to an untrained eye were authentic and not mere decorations bought at *Pier One Imports* or *World Bazaar*. At the same, the office was packed with cardboard boxes, file folders, papers, tape boxes, record albums, and a lot if unidentifiable electronic gadgets —not really equipment, just component gadgets. The actual identifiable equipment included a record player and a monaural reel-to-reel tape player/recorder.

He did not introduce himself at all; it would make sense that I knew exactly who he was. He pointed to a chair in front of his desk, motioning me to sit down. Sorting through a stack of tapes and letters on his deck, he found my tape box and put the tape on to the machine. I was intimidated from the get-go.

Listening to my rendition of *The Wreck of the Old 97* (a song I am sure he had heard hundreds of times), he abruptly stopped the tape in the middle of my *churchlick*. It was a move I'd seen repeatedly on Music Row when I was about to be thrown out.

With the tape stopped, he leaned forward in his chair and peered at me over top of the frame of his glasses (which had slipped down on his nose). Then he spoke: "No, No, No! Young man do not ever do that again. This is a sad song about a train wreck that was so tragic that people are still singing about it today, 73 years later. You have turned it into a square dance! It is not a celebration; it is mournful. Don't ever play that song that fast again".

I didn't have time to collect my thoughts enough to be impressed that he knew exactly how long ago that train wreck had happened. I was too busy suffering my reprimand. All I could muster was a soft, "Yes, Sir".

He turned the tape back on and fast-forwarded to the next song. As *The CIA Song* began, he again abruptly stopped the tape and sternly stared at me over the top of those glasses. I felt another scolding coming as he spoke, "Young man; is that a kazoo you are playing there?"

THE LEGEND DIES ON — GARY GREEN

Of course, I fessed up and managed another, "Yes, Sir", He nodded his head as if to congratulate himself for recognizing it; and then he spoke again, "Very good".

I didn't know what that meant; but he listened to the song until the end. Then he listened to *There Ain't No Easy Way,* my New York City song. When the tape ended, he sat silently for what felt to me like a very awkward long time but probably was just a couple of seconds.

Then he spoke again, "Do you prefer a check or cash?"

I had no clue what the question meant, and the expression on my face must have revealed that, so he clarified, without my asking. "You look as if you need some cash; do you prefer cash or a check?"

"For what?" I cautiously peeped.

He looked at me as if I was crazy and answered me as if it were the most natural and expected response, "your first record for me; the advance". And, yes, he emphasized "first" and "advance".

I desperately needed cash; but I also had a full-time newspaper job waiting for me back in North Carolina. I also had the historical awareness to know the value of having a check from Folkways-fucking-Records! Still stunned, I answered, "a check?", almost as a question if that was acceptable to him.

He called out to Marilyn to bring him a contract and a few seconds later she appeared with two thermal-paper photocopies of a contract. He took it and asked her, "where is my checkbook?" When she asked him which one, he responded, "Chase". As she left the room, she glanced at me and raised her eyebrows as if acknowledging the special occasion.

I did not know until months later, talking to other Folkways artists, that Moe Asch almost never gave advances to new artists. And I didn't know until more than 47 years later, talking with Marilyn's son *Charles* (who was practically raised by Moe) that the amount of my advance was huge in the context of Folkways Records. It was equivalent to amounts that were reserved for Pete Seeger and Ella Jenkins and almost never for the few unknowns that received any advance at all.

I watched with indescribable excitement as he opened the big looseleaf check book and made out and signed check number FC7836 drawn on The Chase Manhattan Bank branch at 1441 Broadway. In the notation area on the check, he scribbled at an angle one word, "Agreement". He tore it along the perforation and slid it across the desk to me.

Next, he turned his attention to the contract. It was a typed single sheet of paper with spaces (not lines) left blank as if the missing terms were to be typed in later: Name and address of the artist; what was to be recorded; consideration (royalty amount); and signature lines. He used a felt-tipped pen and filled in those spaces, copying my address from the outside of the

THE POET LAUREATE SOUL OF FOLKIE ROCK & ROLL

tape box. He then copied what he had written to the second copy of the contract and passed them both to me for my signature.

He gave me my copy and then addressed the logistics. "When can you go to the studio?" he asked.

Thinking about what this would mean for my newspaper job, I answered, "I have to go back to North Carolina tonight. I have a home studio; I could do it there". He looked skeptical but then said, "Okay. Send me a tape. Your own songs only".

He walked me to the elevator and as we waited for it he said, "this is an open contract. It is not one record. Whenever you have new songs, bring them to me. I will make a record".

The significance of that did not fully sink in until a few years later when *Marjorie Guthrie* (Woody's widow and Arlo's mother) told me that as far as she knew, Woody, Pete, Ella Jenkins, and me were the only people that Moe had ever given that. *(I do not believe that is accurate; but it was pretty cool that Marjorie Guthrie felt that it was.)*

As I took the elevator back to the ground floor, I was thinking, "I wish I could call The Captain, Tompall, and Waylon. Not only do I have an open recording contract with a major label; but I had the producer's creative control that they had been fighting with RCA to get for themselves". *(In retrospect, I wish I had not been given the latter; I didn't have the studio chops those cats had. In fact, I had none!)*

𝄞:𝄞:𝄞:𝄞:

This changed everything. In my newspaper career I had begun winning a string of journalism awards. NOW I had just signed a recording contract with ... not just *a record label*, but with THE record label of my dreams.

I needed to decide if I wanted to be a journalist or a musician (it didn't occur to me that I could do both). In light of being a "recording artist", I needed to decide what I wanted to do about *I Hear America Singing*. I needed to address the Sis & Gordon's discussions about the future of Broadside Magazine.

Besides the philosophical issues, I had logistics to plan as well. I had written almost 200 songs; I needed to determine which 12 or so I wanted on my album. I needed a name for the album. Oh, and all Folkways Records had an eight-to-twelve-page booklet of lyrics and notes inserted into the album cover; so, I needed to write and design that. And photos... oh yeah, photos.

And I needed to decide if it would be just me and a guitar or if other musicians were appropriate. And did I want the album to be a random collection across the spectrum of my songs or should it be political songs or should it be themed (like Pete's *Industrial Ballads*, or Woody's *Dust Bowl Ballads* or Willie Nelson's *Red Headed Stranger* that had come out

THE LEGEND DIES ON — GARY GREEN

the year before or the *Desperado* album from the Eagles). And… lots of other decisions to make.

The career choice was indirectly made for me by the Publisher of the newspaper where I worked. I had just won my 27th consecutive national press award and I was called into his office; I assumed it was to be a congratulatory talk for bringing more acclaim to the paper. *It was not.*

Instead, he asked me to sit down, and he began lecturing me, "I see that you are getting more of these awards and a lot of attention from our readers. You may start thinking that you are some kind of crusading journalist or a great writer. Before this goes any further, I need to help you put this into perspective".

Well, that was unexpected, and I wasn't sure where he was going with it. He continued his lecture, "As a reporter, you are a whore, a prostitute. You write what I tell you to write. You write the length I tell you to write, in the style I tell you to write, with the slant I tell you to write. I use the product you create at my discretion to sell advertising. You are just a whore, my whore right now. If you don't like that, then you are free to go sell yourself to someone else. It really is that simple. That is how America works, and it is how journalism works".

When he finished that sentence, I stood up, thanked him and said, "well, I was looking for a job when I found this one". It was a line that later that night I would make a song title, but at that moment it was just the right thing to say. I might not have been so bold if I had not just signed a recording contract with the largest record label in the world, but then again, I might have been.

I think it was not the reaction he was expecting, and as I walked out the door of his office, he started to say something more… rambling about how producing a daily newspaper was like working in a factory. Before he could finish, I added to my goodbye, "oh, and you can go fuck yourself". That was a parting line which I would use often when quitting jobs under less-than-ideal conditions. It was, alas, more blunt than the *"Take This Job And Shove It"* song that my Nashville friend "Rhinestone" had written, but it was much more… me.

When I got home, I fired off a very long letter to Sis and Gordon. I told them about my Folkways contract, and I sent them a tape of *There Ain't No Easy Way.* I also wrote to Pete.

During the next few days, as I waited for replies from the letters, I was contacted by the educational TV station (public television) in nearby Charlotte. They were producing a half-hour documentary on the infamous Gastonia labor strike and the murder of Ella May. Someone had told them that I was a Gastonia-based folksinger who knew many of Ella May's songs and could perform them.

THE POET LAUREATE SOUL OF FOLKIE ROCK & ROLL

I drove to the studio, and they taped me talking and singing, including my own *The Murder of Ella May Wiggins* song. The only parameter they gave me was, "Please don't mention Mister Nixon; there's enough bad publicity about him and Watergate". *What-EVER!*

It wasn't my first television appearance. The Public Broadcasting station in Knoxville had done two half-hour shows about me and my music; but my first TV appearance had actually been in 1959 when I was a guest on an Atlanta kids' program. I was completely comfortable under the lights, finding my mark, the makeup chair, and taking directions.

After the Ella May show aired, about a week later, I got a call from the *Cultural Arts Committee of Mecklenburg County*. The County had just purchased an old church in downtown Charlotte, and they were converting it into an arts complex with theaters, galleries, classrooms, and meeting spaces. They were planning a huge grand opening gala for the newly named *Spirit Square* and wanted a folksinger to perform at the event, which, of course, I did. So, I was back on stage.

In Pete's response to my letter, he wanted to meet face-to-face to discuss the next steps since Phil had died. He recommended getting together on July 4th for the bicentennial celebration in New York, where he would be taking *The Clearwater* up the Hudson River as part of the celebration flotilla.

I started making plans for that, then the next week he sent another letter telling me that he had been asked to perform at a bicentennial event on the National Mall in Washington but had to turn it down because of the flotilla commitment. He wanted to know if I would be interested in doing the DC event in his place and postponing our meeting until later.

It took me no time at all to answer: Pete Seeger was asking me to fill in for HIM at a gig! Even if I was not interested, there was no way that I would have said "no" to him. In this case, it really helped because I wanted to do the gig anyway.

Meanwhile, letter conversations were on going with Sis & Gordon. We continued to explore various options for saving Broadside and assuring that it would continue. It was becoming more and more evident that we were moving toward me relocating to New York. First, though, I had an album to create.

As I tired to keep all of these things juggled around creating my first album, it occurred to me one afternoon that I had *already* named the album; those big blue letters written around the body of my guitar gave me the perfect name for the record:

These Six Strings Neutralize The Tools Of Oppression

I decided to open the album, side one band one, with *There Ain't No Easy Way* and follow it with *The Murder of Ella May Wiggins*.

THE LEGEND DIES ON — GARY GREEN

I wanted to make the rest of the first side all topical songs; about current events. While not overtly political, I tried to put a commentary "zinger" into those songs.

I transitioned into more topical songs with an allegory about my departure from the newspaper. It was sung first-person from the perspective of a disgruntled factory worker leaving North Carolina and wage labor forever. The song, metaphorically about a textile worker, was about my decision to leave the "job" and step into music full-time.

The next two songs were pure gazetteer topical: one about a Kentucky coal cave-in that year in which 26 people were killed after the mine had been cited 735 times for violations of Federal safety standards; and a second song about a random racist murder committed by a white woman who later was acquitted by an all-white jury.

I ended that side of the record with *The CIA Song*. Then I had to decide what to do with the "B" side of the album.

I wanted to put some of my "country" songs on the album. I had written another New York City song that was a modern cowboy song transposing standard old-west imagery to 20th century urban reflections. I opened side two with that song.

I decided to drop a couple of overtly political songs on the album as well. I recorded *You're Just As Guilty* (my antiwar song that I wrote after seeing the anti-personnel bombs film) and I recorded a new song that I had written called *Dear Mister Kelley At The FBI*. That one was about the ordeal that I went through getting the release of the files that the FBI's fake-Indian undercover agent had created about me.

Between those two songs I inserted a pure-country song about a cowboy's revenge, *I Wore His Gun*; a tribute to Sis & Gordon called *The Ballad of Broadside*; and my teen angst song that had been popular at the college open mics, *America's Child*.

There were six songs on side one and six songs on side two; but timewise, side two was about three minutes too-short for my tastes in value for a record album purchase. I needed another song. I didn't want overtly political; that was covered more-than-enough on the lp. I didn't want to be too sarcastic; my CIA song covered that. I didn't want another cowboy or overtly hillbilly song because I wanted the record to appeal to urban audiences; and people could get those kinds of songs in Nashville recordings if that's what they wanted.

What I really wanted was something that would have a broad appeal without being preachy or whiney. There was nothing in my blue notebook of my almost-200 songs that I thought would fit the bill and was a good length for the remaining time on the vinyl album.

I had been screwing around with a minor-key variation for several old spiritual standards, but the variations had modified the melodies so drastically that the standards were no longer recognizable. Still, I liked the progression I had created from the guitar's natural E minor pentatonic scale (rather than the eight-not piano or orchestral scale).

I also was using that progression to help me with my meter (one-two; one-two). Sitting at the kitchen table with my guitar, trying to decide what to use for the last cut on side two, I absent-mindedly began picking that progression.

I had been reading Phil Foner's four-volume *History of the Labor Movement in the United States*[124] *(it contained one of the only academic accounts of the murder of Ella May)*. One of the volumes was on the kitchen table and I was using it to serve as a sort of bookstand to slightly elevate my song notebook as I flipped through page-after-page of songs.

Just as I was oblivious to the sound coming from my guitar, I was equally unmindful of the words that I was attaching to that one-two staccato. Thus, was born my two-minute-and-eight-second anthem to labor unions, *The Hammer*. And that became the final track on the album.

The imagery for the song was more than merely inspired by the Foner books. During the first four years of my life, when my father was a railroad laborer and electrician, he also was a shop steward and national delegate for his union. I had lots of memories of him and his coworkers. Then, in college, the Highlander Center sessions had provided vivid details of coal miner union struggles; perfect for me to glean material.

Besides finishing up the album, that song became my most requested for the next decade, at least among certain audiences. I received the most enthusiastic and raucous applause I ever had when I sang it five years later for a crowd of more than 450,000 union supporters on Saturday September 19, 1981, at the *Solidarity Day March on Washington*. (You can't imagine what standing in front of almost a half-million people is like until you've done it! I wasn't selling number-one-Billboard-hit country songs; but I was being heard by a hell-of-a-lot of working people!)

I packaged the master tape along with a camera-ready eight-page liner note and lyrics brochure and sent it overnight to the Folkways office. I even included a mock-up of a front cover and back cover; both in the minimalist Folkways Records style that was radically different from typical album cover style. I was determined to make this as easy-as-possible for them. Years later, I regretted doing that because it deprived me of the design work of Ronald Clyne who had created the iconic Folkways look.

---

[124] Before his death, Dr. Foner's labor history series expanded to 10 volumes; but in 1976 there were only four. Doctor Philip Sheldon Foner (December 14, 1910 – December 13, 1994) had been fired from City College of New York and blacklisted during the mid-century "red scares". By his death, he was a professor of history at Rutgers University.

THE LEGEND DIES ON — GARY GREEN

Then I waited. And waited. And waited. If I had not required a return-receipt from the post office, I would not *even* have known for sure that they received my package. Thanksgiving came and went, then Christmas and New Year's Day. I didn't dare call the label's office; I was too nervous and didn't want to rock the boat.

Meanwhile, Broadside Magazine issue 134 announced: "In preparation: "*The Songs Of Gary Green*" and "*God Guts And Guns*" by Jeff Ampolsk." The same issue printed, on page 13, my *There's Ain't No Easy Way* with an announcement on that my soon-to-be-released record would be *Broadside Album #12*. (It was NOT; Moe Asch made the decision not to have me as part of the Broadside series. At the time I was disappointed, but I came to truly appreciate his decision after Marilyn told me that Moe wanted me to be part of Folkways for a series of my own.[125])

Near the end of January 1977, I received an envelope from Marilyn Averett Conklin. No letter, but it contained a half-dozen copies of the Folkways Spring 1977 Catalog. On the first page was a box around "New Releases", and a photo of my album covers with a brief description of two records: FC 7666, *Ella Jenkins — We Are America's Children* (which actually had been released a few months earlier, but not announced) and **FH5351, Gary Green — These Six Strings Neutralize The Tools Of Oppression.**

A few days later, I received a box with 12 copies of a genuine Folkways album with my face on the cover! I immediately opened one and put it on the record player and listened to both sides; just to make sure that it sounded like a Folkways record. Next, I took a copy to my parents' house (I think they were happy for me but less-than-impressed with the record.) I then packaged a copy to send to ASCAP in New York.

Before the album was shipped, a distributor-industry newspaper called *Midwest Record Review* published a pre-release review that, among other accolades wrote: *"there is no doubt that the genre of protest music is still viable, alive, and well in the person of Gary Green"*.

I was ecstatic. I felt that I had just inherited the mantle of Woody Guthrie, Phil Ochs, and (early) Bob Dylan... even if only in my fantasies.

About two months after the release, I received a huge (for the time) royalty check from ASCAP. Something on the album was getting massive radio play; and I could not imagine which song it could be. None of them were what I *(or almost anyone else)* would consider commercial

---

[125] It turned out that even though Gordon had asked Moe to make my album part of the *Broadside* series, Moe had decided that it was going to be the first of a series of his series of me; and he wanted to keep that series on the Folkways label, not the Broadside sub-label. So, the album instead of a Broadside number 12, was Gary Green *Volume One*.

THE POET LAUREATE SOUL OF FOLKIE ROCK & ROLL

broadcast quality. Before I deposited such a large check, I decided to call ASCAP[126] in New York to tell them they had made an accounting error. They promised to research the issue and get back to me. Three days later, they called me back to report that there was no error and that in fact I had the number-one radio-played hit song in *Sweden*. The check represented thousands of air-plays of one of the songs on the album.

Even more perplexing, the song was a throw-away on the album; a track that even I didn't consider to be good... or even a decent song. *Dear Mister Kelley At The FBI* was a sing-songy thumb-to-my-nose that I wrote to prompt the FBI into releasing their files on me[127].

Meanwhile, my letters to and from Sis & Gordon were becoming more and more intense. Finally, they asked me to move to New York to help out with the next couple of issues and plan what to do next. They said that I could move into their apartment rent free. Between that offer, the folk clubs in The Village, and the success of my album... moving to New York seemed to make sense.

---

[126] There were, at that time, three major performing rights organizations: *ASCAP* (The American Society of Composers, Authors & Publishers); *BMI* (Broadcast Music Inc.); and *SESAC* (Society of European Stage Authors and Composers). All three collected and paid royal-ties for live performances and broadcasts of songs. SESAC was known as primarily European and BMI was what most Nashville songwriters were using at that time. I opted for ASCAP just as further rebellion against the Nashville establishment that had essentially chased me out of town. *(ASCAP was also the oldest and at that time most "mainstream" of the three. It had been founded in the very early part of the 20th century by Victor Herbert, Irving Berlin, and a handful of Tin Pan Alley songwriters.)*

[127] My *Freedom of Information Act* request for the files was turned down; first with the claim that the FBI had a huge backlog, and they were too busy to get to it. I appealed that decision directly to Kelley *(the FBI director who succeeded the recently deceased J. Edgar Hoover)*. The FBI then claimed that releasing those specific files would "compromise national security".

That assertion was so ludicrous that it just begged for a smart-ass parody. So, I wrote the song and as soon as the album was released, I sent a copy with the lyrics to Director Kelley. I mean, the FBI already was making files on me; so, what did I have to lose?

There were two, most unexpected results: firstly, the FBI released my files (albeit heavily redacted); and secondly, the damned song became a hit record in Sweden of all places. *I still don't understand that! Moe didn't understand it either; but he knew that whatever the reason, it made my album do something most Folkways albums never did: **it made money.***

THE LEGEND DIES ON — GARY GREEN

Opus Fourteen:
Broadside, a Paul Newman Movie, CBGB, Kirk & Shelley

Oh, they never gave an inch.
No, they never gave an inch.
And it's time their story, it was told!
No they never budged an inch
They said they would not flinch.
And all they have to show for it is their soul!

— *The Ballad of Broadside*, by Gary Green, 1976, as recorded on Folkways Records album FH5351

*E*arly that spring, I took a train to New York's Penn Station and moved to 215 W. 98th Street, Apartment 4-D. It was a huge pre-war apartment, under New York's rent control law, with lots of bedrooms. The apartment served as the office and production facility for Broadside Magazine as well as the residence of Sis and Gordon... and their daughter Jane ...and her daughter Ellie... and Gordon's brother Ollie and... whoever else might need to crash for a night or two. With all of that, there was still a spare bedroom for me to move into (though I think Ollie moved out of that room in order for me to move in).

There were two items on my New York agenda: producing Broadside and funding it. The latter also meant, of course, finding a way to supplement the meager Social Security payments that provided Sis' and Gordon's only income for paying the rent and living expenses.

By this time Sis had heard a lot of my taped music and had taken it on herself to work on my rhythm issues. I warned her that it was a losing battle because I'd had the issue since childhood; but she was a stubborn woman and refused to give up on it.

She told me that ten years earlier, when Bob Dylan first started visiting them, the only rhythm he could play was waltz (¾) time. Sis said that Dylan seemed to have a mental block prohibiting him from keeping common (4/4) time. Before his first album, she spent hours-on-end sitting on the couch beside him with her hands moving his right hand on the guitar strings and counting out "1-2-3-4" to teach him the rhythm. She said that on his first Columbia album she can hear his struggling.

She concluded that my (allegedly similar) issue was related to my failure to understand a downbeat (the first beat of a musical measure). Instead, she surmised that I almost always would start singing (or playing lead) on the upbeat (the last beat in the previous bar).

We spent hours every single day with her counting the beats for me, showing me where to come in, and literally moving my right hand. I was ridiculously frustrated, and I could tell that she was too. To make it worse, I was doggedly arrogant, insisting that "I wrote the damned song, I know how it goes".

Despite having been a music teacher for more than 50 years, she seemed unable to crack my seemingly-deliberate obstinance in learning to stay within the confines of a constant count. Metronomes, foot tapping, pointing at me like a conductor; none of it seemed to work on me. Nonetheless, she kept trying.

She had requested that we include my song *There Ain't No Easy Way* in the next Broadside. It was Gordon's favorite of my songs, and he had rejected several other images-of-New-York type songs that I thought were from far better songwriters than me. Gordon actually told one of the writers, "Gary Green has already written that song better than anyone else can."

Flattering as it was, I did not agree. In fact, I pointed to several songs that had been submitted to Broadside that I thought had far better imagery of The City. I especially liked Steve Forbert's *Grand Central Station*. Between Steve visiting the apartment and my championing his song, Sis decided to override Gordon and include it.[128]

Meanwhile, Sis raised the issue of my rhythm *challenge*[129]. When we published *There Ain't No Easy Way*, I could see that she was not happy with the transcription I had done. She explained that it wasn't just my rhythm problem when I performed, but it was in my music notation too.

---

[128] Apparently, I was not the only fan; the next year CBS signed a contract with Forbert and included the song on his *Alive on Arrival* album for *Brian Epstein's Nemperor Records*. In fact, Steve's first four albums all charted on the Billboard Top 200. He also appeared as Cyndi Lauper's boyfriend on her *Girls Just Want To Have Fun* video.

Mississippi-born almost-punk-rocker *Steve Forbert* was my same age and he seemed to be wondering about my role and at one point after some of my random (and probably arrogant) lecturing from me, he asked, "are you some kind of musicologist or something?"

Steve never knew that Gordon had argued with Sis and me that he wasn't impressed with Steve and didn't want to include him in Broadside. Sis, however, really liked one of his songs (*The Oil Song* about the disastrous oil tanker the Argo Merchant); and as noted, I especially liked his *Grand Central Station*. We outvoted Gordon; and Steve became a featured songwriter in several issues.

Since the 1970's, I have not seen him or any of two-or-three dozen other songwriters from those days. I am certain that he had no idea that I'd been his advocate on multiple occasions (if he even remembered meeting). I didn't tell him or any of the visitors that I championed at the time; and there was no reason to do so.

[129] If I have any regrets about those years, they revolve around not appreciating Sis Cunningham more and not showing my gratitude to her. Though in later years I did send them a lot of cash, anonymously, it didn't even provide the gratitude that I should have given her.

THE LEGEND DIES ON — GARY GREEN

To explain the problem, she transcribed the song to reflect my rhythmic weirdness. She noted (in writing), *"This isn't exactly exact, but it illustrates what I'm trying to say in my explanation. The song might be better written in 2/4 time to eliminate more signature changes."*

At the time, I was really irritated by Sis' notation and the tone in her voice as she lectured me. It wasn't until years later that I realized how lovingly she was trying to help me, guide me, and resolve my lifelong rhythm issue.

By the time I arrived in New York Gordon had practically become a shut-in. He would lie in bed almost all-day every day, fully clothed (usually in a white shirt, grey pants, and black shoes).

Every few days, he would walk into the living room-office to run the mimeograph machine or look for a particular tape. Once a week he would venture onto the street to buy fresh vegetables from a neighborhood bodega (the apartment was in a neighborhood that at the time was known as *Spanish Harlem*).

Other than that, he stayed in bed. The reel-to-reel tape machine was by the bed, as was an IBM-Selectric® typewriter that he and Sis used to "typeset" the magazine. He read the mail in bed, took his meals in bed, and made phone calls from bed.

He even took visitors from bed. It was a rare event when he would venture into the living room to sit on the couch for a visitor. I think I only saw him do that once or twice. While I lived there, dozens of songwriters paraded into the bedroom where Gordon would rise from his normally supine position and sit, hunched-over, on the edge of the bed to meet them.

Eventually, I had a permanent chair at his bedside so that we could spend our days talking and planning… and working. Whenever any of that never-ending stream of young folksingers came by, he would have them come into the bedroom with their guitars or tapes or just to talk to both of us.

I'm sure some of those visitors were wondering what-the-hell I was doing there; I was their age or younger but self-importantly holding court alongside the great Gordon Friesen. That stream of visitors gave me a great understanding of what the previous 20 years had been like for Sis and Gordon.

By the time I was living with Sis & Gordon, Broadside was not the substantial cultural force that it had been in the *Bob-Dylan-folk-revival era*; so, appearance in our little magazine really had no significant impact on most careers.

Nonetheless, if people looking back on it decades later see it as significant, then so be it. For me it was … only rock and roll (only life).

THE POET LAUREATE SOUL OF FOLKIE ROCK & ROLL

In my mind, the "value" of being part of Broadside was the provenance of Sis and Gordon. It was the thrill of being in their orbit and the vibe of the folk music world. It definitely was not a quest for musical fame and fortune that drove *me* to Broadside (and if it was, then it certainly wasn't a well-planned quest, given the status of Broadside at that time).

I spent a lot more time with Gordon than with Sis (probably in part because my "office" was at his bedside). He became my mentor for folk music, the music "business", politics, and urbanization: sharing stories, advice, and sending me on various musical errands around New York.

Gordon and Sis both had incredibly interesting and never-ending stories of their lives in post-Bohemian pre-Folk-Revival, Beat-era New York. Opening their home up to partnering folksingers and writers like me was not a new behavior for them; they had been doing it for decades beginning with their first long-term New York roomie, *Woody Guthrie*.

All from Oklahoma, and all in the lefty folk music scene in The City, it was natural that the three of them would team up. Woody sang and Sis played accordion in *The Almanac Singers*; a Popular Front singing group very loosely affiliated with the *Communist Party USA*.[130]

There are conflicting stories attributing the founding of the Almanacs, but Sis insisted that she and Gordon[131] were among the first organizers — at least of one version of the group. What is clearer is that at various times the group had as many as 16 members with a core of *Millard Lampell, Lee Hays, Pete Seeger, and Woody Guthrie*.

---

[130] *Popular Front* was a term created by the *Communist International* (Comin-tern), for their wartime program to put aside differences with capitalist governments in favor of fighting Nazi fascism. In the USA, that objective was expanded to promoting racial and religious inclusiveness as well as workers' rights.

The role of the Communist Party in the American folk music scene has been much debated; spiced with nutso accusations from the right and ludicrous denials from the left. Many of the musicians who were accused of being "communist" were no more communist than your kindergarten teacher. But, while most "folk revival" musicians were oblivious to the actual role of The Party, for many of the older folkies, Party "club" membership or association was a very real thing (as was the occasional financial backing, either tacitly or overtly).

Still, the hordes of young folksingers, songwriters, and enthusiasts had no reason to know about it (there certainly was no recruiting drive). As for myself, I definitely would have never met Túpac, gone to Eastern Europe, or eventually provided venues for so many mainstream artists had it not been for those associations with the Communist Party USA.

[131] Several songs on my second Folkways album were inspired by Gordon (*I Guess He's Rather Be In Oklahoma, Ashes Of A Fire, No Great Loss*); I wrote others on that record at Gordon's suggestion —or insistence— and research help (*Fort Apache The Bronx*, and *The Semi-Local Branch of the Loyal Order of The Tour-ing Cockroach Club*).

THE LEGEND DIES ON — GARY GREEN

The Almanac Singers group was created with goals focusing on popularizing anti-war, anti-racism and pro-union songs. Twenty years later, that agitation through topical music would become the model for Broadside, which in turn would be massively influential in the commercially popular folk music revival. In discovering, nurturing, and promoting some of the most important musicians of the era, it is not a stretch to see Broadside's straight line from the Almanacs.

In those days before the blacklist and when the Soviet Union was a U.S. ally, Gordon worked as a newswriter for *CBS Radio*; so, he had a salary, unlike most of the other members of the group. He was able to take over rent payments at the Almanac House on West 10th Street, the semi-official home and occasional crash pad for traveling Almanacs. A non-musician, Gordon also managed the group while the other members wrote songs, played, and sang. (And of course, they recorded on Moe Asch's label.)

Woody Guthrie eventually moved in with them, just as I had; so, if nothing else, I felt that I was in the company of folk music royalty with my living arrangements. I loved hearing Sis and Gordon talk about those days, especially the anecdotal adventures around the lifestyle. Most of their more-outrageous Woody Guthrie tales came from those days. Among the MANY stories:

> One night, Sis and Gordon heard strange noises coming from Woody's bedroom. They knocked on the door to see if everything was alright. When there was no answer, they became concerned, and Gordon decided to enter the room. He told me that when he opened the door, he saw Woody dressed in a bright pink bunny-rabbit suit, jumping up and down on the bed as if it were a trampoline. On both sides of the bed were two *less-than-fully-clothed* young women who were making what they perceived to be rabbit chirping sounds as Woody hopped around.
>
> *On another day:*
>
> Sis awoke early and went into the third-floor kitchen to make coffee. In the middle of the kitchen, she found a tin lithographed advertising sign for Coca Cola in the shape of a policeman holding a school zone warning sign. It was five-feet tall, 36-inches wide and sat on a 22-inch-diameter cast iron base which was encased in a 200-pound concrete block. It was too heavy for her or Gordon to move out of the center of the room. (Woody was smaller than either of them.)
>
> Later in the day when she and Gordon asked Guthrie how he got the absurdly-heavy piece up three flights of stairs, Woody simply said, "He just showed up here last night. I didn't ask him how he got in".

THE POET LAUREATE SOUL OF FOLKIE ROCK & ROLL

The colorful stories made me feel even more a part of a very special history of folk music and an equally special culture. There were so many of those vignettes:

> One time Mill Lampell, who later in life would become a respected (but blacklisted) movie and television writer, arranged to book the Almanacs at the highly-prestigious (and very high-paying) *Rainbow Room* on the 65th floor of 30 Rockefeller Center. Excited about the big paycheck, the group put together a set list and headed to midtown for the gig.
>
> When they arrived, the venue's manager handed out straw hats to them, overalls for the men, and checkered square-dance dresses for the two women in the group. He also told Woody that he looked the most authentic and therefore he should chew on a long piece of straw that the manager provided.
>
> According to Gordon, Woody looked at the manager without answering. He surveyed the room and saw the large cocktail party buffet and open bar that had been arranged for whatever group would have been the audience.
>
> Without saying a word, Woody walked over to the two-story curtains at the window overlooking midtown and with all of his weight ripped them from their rods. He wrapped one of the curtains around himself like a toga. He then marched across the room to the bar, grabbed two unopened bottles of vintage *Dom Pérignon*, put one under each arm and stormed out of the room. The group was summarily fired, with no cancellation fee and certainly no big paycheck.
>
> When Sis and Gordon got back to the walkup, they found Woody pacing back and forth. Excitedly he approached Gordon and said, "give me twenty dollars". As Gordon reached into his wallet, he asked Guthrie, "what do you need it for?"
>
> Woody answered, "'Cause I know a guy uptown that will sell me a pistol for twenty dollars, and I am going to buy it to kill that goddamned Mill Lampell".
>
> When Gordon told him he would not give him the money, Woody became furious and eventually stormed out of the house yelling, "Well I will get it somewhere else; he's as good as dead", Of course, he didn't kill Millard Lampell and after a few days Woody seemed to have forgotten the entire incident (according to Gordon).

Hearing those and scores of other intimate-*life-of-Woody-Guthrie* stories was not only fascinating from a history-student standpoint; but for a young fanboy it was an unimaginable dream. I felt like I had been invited into an intimate circle, as if Woody were still alive and sitting there.

Beyond the emersion into the depths of that era of the folk music scene, Gordon and I bonded on lots of other levels, beginning with journalism. We both were aficionados of purple prose: what the Roman poet Horace

THE LEGEND DIES ON — GARY GREEN

described as *"weighty openings and grand declarations often (that) have one or two purple patches tacked on"*. Gordon had a great purple-prose story from his earliest days as a newspaper reporter:

> He had just started as a young general assignment reporter for the *Detroit Free Press*. A major thunder-storm was coming ashore from Lake Erie, and Gordon was sent out to cover the damage. The paper was on deadline, but the City Desk wanted coverage; so, his job was to survey the damage and call in his story, dictating it to his boss.
>
> Arriving at the scene and impressed by the awesome destructive power of the storm, Gordon called the desk and began dictating:
> *"The heavens open up from Lake Erie this morning and the hand of God threw his wrath at the city..."*
> Before he could continue, his editor cut him off with, "Stop right there Friesen. Forget the damned storm. Get me an interview with God!"

The young reporter got the *Purple Prose* message, and despite that penchant for colorful words went on to a great career as a journalist, eventually landing a job as a national reporter-writer for CBS radio.

And, then there was the blacklist and despite the later lauded heroics of CBS' Edward R. Murrow, Gordon and others were fired for their political associations.

Years later, a *New York Times* journalist. who had known Gordon in those reporting days, confidentially told me, "you know, his wife was a communist and it just looked bad on him." I couldn't even respond to the multiple levels of absurdity in that statement.

Sis, Gordon, and their two daughters were left with no income and were more-or-less forced to move into the New York City housing projects; ghetto-living with two small children. Connections within the Communist Party arranged for a clerical job for Sis at the Czechoslovakian Embassy; but it was at a minimal salary. Essentially, the family lived in poverty with the other poor people in the projects.

But those hard times didn't quell their zeal for topical music, their leftist politics, nor their *you-can-always-sleep-at-our-place* policy for visiting musicians, songwriters, and assorted "fellow travelers".

It was in those living circumstances that Broadside was born and was printed on that discarded mimeograph machine.

Running a "business" (even a rinky-dink not-for-profit one) was forbidden under the housing projects rental agreement from the *New York City Housing Authority*, so Sis would bundle the magazines and hide them in the folds of blankets inside the stroller when she'd take her youngest daughter, Jane, to Central Park. Once out of the complex, she'd go to the post office and to various distribution points.

Fifteen years later, when I arrived in New York, they were long out of *The Projects* and had "inherited" the rent-controlled apartment where I was crashing with them on the Upper West Side.

THE POET LAUREATE SOUL OF FOLKIE ROCK & ROLL

Our work putting out the magazine was not nearly as simple as I had imagined that it would be. Rather than just writing a little editorial copy, transcribing a few songs, printing, binding, and mailing; there was *real* work involved — especially the mechanical preparation for production.

Despite its enormous influence on popular culture and the music world, since its beginning Broadside was only a little mimeographed[132] newsletter. But by the time I was living with Sis and Gordon, mimeograph technology had significantly advanced since they had begun 15 years earlier. It allowed for a much better-looking magazine; but it also meant a tremendous amount of production work was involved in getting an issue out.

Making the process more complex, the tasks weren't chronological. We might print one page the same day that we are transcribing for another page or before we had even determined all the content for that issue. Sometimes it took an entire day using transfer letters just to get headlines right for one single page.

Remember, this was decades before there were personal computers in every home or office… or anywhere, for that matter. Terms like "font" or

---

[132] *Mimeograph*, at that time, was a stencil-based printing process that began with a "master" inserted into a typewriter. That "master" was a normal-looking sheet of white paper but with the entire back treated with a carbon-paper-like coating. The resulting typed sheet made holes in the "master" in the shape of each letter typed. In addition to typing, a metal (or wooden) stylus could be used on the master for hand-drawn headlines or drawings.

That typed and/or drawn process created a "stencil", which then was wrapped around an ink-filled rotary drum. The drum was rotated with a hand crank. As it rotated, the drum pulled single sheets of paper from a loading bin and then squeezed ink through the holes in the stencil as it pressed the stencil against the paper and thus the printed page was created. Mimeograph ink was a spirit-based ink with a noxious smell that required heavy ventilation to avoid user asphyxiation. So, in the Broadside apartment, we had to have the windows open on printing days; regardless of how cold it might be outside *(in the summer, windows were already open, because there was no air conditioning)*. By the mid-1970's, the hand-crank had been motorized, and a then-high-tech process called "thermofax" could be used to make the stencil. That new process allowed the user to create a mock-up of what the printed page should look like, including photographs and typeset headlines. The thermofax would then use an infrared process to "burn" the stencil. The burner was an expensive machine, so many print shops would burn a thermofax stencil for around $1.25 per page; thus, creating another expense for Broadside. This new process allowed the previous type-only newsletter to mimic a professional magazine, complete with photographs or even reprints from newspapers and magazines.

Two other technological advances further enhanced the visual outcome. First, the use of the IBM Selectric® typewriter allowed the typist to change fonts by changing a small globe inside the typewriter, allowing more professional-looking fonts than just a typewriter. It was limited, however, to either 10-point or 12-point size type because of the size of the typewriter. Headlines were an entirely different matter.

THE LEGEND DIES ON — GARY GREEN

"point size" were at best highly esoteric and at worst technical jargon for experienced typographers. Even creating headlines was a highly-technical labor-intensive process[133].

One more reason that Sis and Gordon had invited me to be part of Broadside was that I understood and had a good deal of experience in those production and printing processes. Beyond being a journalist and a musician with a similar social/political bent, I had been using mimeograph, transfer letters, and thermofax stencils for several years creating flyers and handouts to bring people to my gigs or to rallies.

On final production days, it was an entire household event; everyone in the apartment pitched in to get the magazine ready to print, then the actual printing, collating pages, stapling, sorting, bundling, and mailing. Their daughter Jane and even their granddaughter Ellie were essential workers, with experience and skills far beyond most print-shop employees.

For mailings, even for the proper counts, labeling, zip-code sub-sorting, postal group stickers, and grouping, were all specialized labor-intensive tasks. Probably the single most tedious task (even more so than lining up transfer letters) was the three-digit sorting process and affixing colorful code-stickers to mail bundles; required in order to be accepted at the lower bulk-mail postage rate. [134]

Besides the exhausting production tasks, we had to make content decisions; a difficult process given the number of submissions Broadside

---

[133] The other important enhancement was the creation of "Dry Transfer Letters" —which would come to play an important role in my personal musical future; especially the multi-million-dollar lawsuit surrounding the Bob Dylan album I produced for Gordon.

Transfer Letters were decals of individual letters of the alphabet. Multiple decals of each letter were affixed to a plastic backing sheet. The sheets were sold individually, packaged by font and point size (i.e., "36 point Helvetica).

To create a headline, or other text, users would line up each individual letter to the position on the page mock-up. Using a stylus or a popsicle stick, the user would burnish the backing plastic and *that* action would apply the decal to the paper. It was a long and tedious process to align and transfer the letters for each individua word.

Like followers of *Wheel of Fortune*, manufacturers of dry transfer letters knew that certain letters are more commonly used than others (more "s" and "e" than "z" and "u", for example). Each sheet had more of some letters and fewer of others. While generally this was accommodating, for users with limited budgets it was problematic; often we would not have enough letters of a certain font or size to construct the words for a specific headline. Hence a good deal of planning and creativity was required just to have resources available to write even the simplest headlines.

[134] It had only been about six years since the United States Postal Service had been created to replace the US Post Office Department. Besides converting the constitutionally budgeted cabinet department to an independent agency, the creation of USPS also gave the world a new universe of bureaucratic work requirements for mailers; tasks before performed by the Post Office Department.

THE POET LAUREATE SOUL OF FOLKIE ROCK & ROLL

received every month... even then. There were lots of typical A&R decisions, political decisions, originality decisions, and more.

Most importantly, at least from my perspective, I knew that the simple act of determining whether a song or artist was or was not a good match for Broadside could be monumental. Such a decision had the potential to be incredibly inspiring to an artist or it could be devastating. Not every submitter would be impacted to such extremes; but for some of us, it could be life changing.

So, I was hyper-sensitive to that and tried to make every decision from the standpoint of the artist as well as the intrinsic music or political factors and the potential broad audience appeal.

At the same time, we each had our own tastes of what we liked and disliked of the tapes and visitors to the apartment. My personal favorite from that time was a New Orleans hippie-cowboy named *Jeff Ampolsk*[135]. He had written a nice little talking blues called *God Guts & Guns*; but rather than playing the standard Guthrie/Dylan chord progression, he spiced it up with some Cajun guitar licks for the chords themselves. It sounded very Churchlick-like but Cajun-style and with a flat pick. It was a lot like listening to Jerry Reed play chords on the guitar —rather than a static chord, there was always movement on the notes with hammer-ons and lift-offs.

We featured him in a couple of issues of the magazine and apparently, Moe Asch heard the same thing in Jeff's songs that I had heard. Moe recorded him. It turned out that I wasn't the only person pitching him to Folkways Records.

We did a few gigs together in Greenwich Village; but Jeff was content with some clubs' policy of paying entertainers in beer rather than money. I was not; so, after a few such gigs, I stopped going downtown with him.

Shortly after that, Jeff excitedly told me that he had been booked to play in a then-very-famous venue in The Village. Excited for him, I indiscreetly asked what they were paying him at such a well-known club.

He told me that they were *not* paying him but were giving him "exposure". When I began ranting incredulously against that arrangement, he further confessed that in order to get the booking, he had to agree to stay after the club closed that night and mop the floors and take out the trash.

Genuinely confused, I asked, "How in the hell does that work and why would anybody be fool-enough to fall for it?" Looking back on it, I guess

---

[135] Sadly, I lost track of Jeff when I left New York and recently I learned that he had died in Nashville in early January of 1989. He was 38.

THE LEGEND DIES ON — GARY GREEN

it was a little rude, since Jeff was so excited about it; but actually, it was not an uncommon situation imposed by bar owners.

Jeff told me that it was like a *hoot*[136] but *without passing the hat*. In the 1960's when this particular bar had been run by previous owners, the saloonkeepers would allow the folksingers to play and pass a hat on weekends. The practice provided entertainment to keep customers coming into the bar to drink and eat; at the same time, the musicians made a little money too. During the weekdays when there were no hoots, the saloon paid musicians who were often hired based on who had excited a "hoot-day" crowd and hence had potential to draw customers.

I wasn't a fan of even that audition process; but the new owners' system was even worse. The new paradigm still had free entertainment but instead of passing a hat or a tray around, the saloon keeper charged people to walk through the front door: a cover charge of which 100% went to the saloonkeeper. The musicians got NOTHING... except "exposure" and a "chance" to get paid "if they are good". So, the owners got money for food and drink, money from the cover charge, a required minimum number of drinks sold, AND free entertainment.

If all that wasn't enough, the young guitar slingers, like Jeff, had to audition before a live crowd just to be allowed to play on a hoot night; and still no passing the hat or getting paid.

That bar owner, whose memory is often lionized today as a patriarch of the folk revival, knew that there were enough drifting guitar players starving in the street that there'd be no shortage of free entertainment. Those musicians often simply were blinded by the stars painted in their eyes by the saloonkeepers like him who exploited the names of famous people who'd played in their clubs decades earlier. Some surviving musicians even credit that bar own with giving them their first "real break" in music. *Barf!*

Making it worse, Jeff's guitar was stolen from inside the bar one night while he was mopping the floor.

Still, after Jeff told me all of these things, I restrained myself; I didn't cut loose on these exploitive bastards. It wasn't my fight, and I didn't want

---

[136] Most people I know credit the term "hootenanny" to Woody Guthrie who supposedly made it up. Whatever the origin, the word has now worked its way into Webster's Dictionary: *hoo-te-nan-ny (hoot), a gathering at which folksinger sing and 'pass a collection plate or hat.* Apparently, the original idea was to feed the starving folksingers and to heat their houses. (It gets as cold as a Montana well digger in New York.) A bunch of singers would get together, do their things together or individually or both and then pass a hat to the people who dropped by to see the show. Then, after the show was over, they would divide up the hat and eat or warm or whatever.

THE POET LAUREATE SOUL OF FOLKIE ROCK & ROLL

or need the trouble that would be sure to follow if I opened my controversial Southern bad-ass mouth to the Greenwich Village club establishment.

It was about ten o'clock one night when Jeff talked me into going into that saloon with him. He said he was sure that we wouldn't have to pay the cover charge since he was the floor cleaner. He was wrong.

After a little talking (which sounded like pleading to me), the man at the door agreed that I could sit at the bar ...but nowhere else... IF I would pay one dollar. I couldn't believe it. I wanted to rock the whole bar to silence and punch out the son-of-a-bitch, but Jeff restrained me by saying that the dollar would cover the cost of my first drink and then "when nobody was looking, we can sneak back to the regular seats". SNEAK? After paying the bastard a buck to walk through his door? After the floor-mopper showed up? Like hell!

So, in addition to not paying for his singers and charging a cover charge, there was a requirement that everybody had to buy at least two drinks! I don't even drink (and didn't then either). I loudly asked Jeff, "has there ever been bullshit any deeper where you could still walk through it?" I was about to explode over the whole thing. I was ready to slug the guy at the door and then roll the bar over on top of the asshole behind it. I glanced through the candlelit darkness toward Jeff, who had already walked toward the bar. He looked back at me like I was crazy.

I would like to say that Jeff understood what I was thinking and that he was pleading with me not to do what I was thinking about doing; but the thought didn't even bubble in the back of his head that I was seriously considering delivering a sermon of song and anger followed by an adrenaline kick through the table at the door that would have sent the money flying, the crowd crawling, the owner cussing and the law running.

The words to a song were already dancing around the ropes of grey brain matter under my hat when Jeff spoke, "Come on in. It's worth it. We can go on back."

I called him back to me, "Look, it's really not worth it. I don't need to be inside there that much. You go ahead —I'll catch you later. I'm not going in there. This guy's full of shit."

Jeff said something to me and then disappeared into the crowd of bodies mingled inside the dark bar. The man sitting behind the table at the door looked at me and snarled, "If you ain't going to come in then get out of the door so paying customers can."

I slammed my palm down on his money table so hard that I thought I had torn through the cardboard top. The man looked up at me like he thought I was going to rob him. I pressed tightly against the table and put my face to his. The music was so electric and loud and most of the customers were so drunk that very few people saw what was happening. (Loud electric music in a supposed "folk" venue just put the proverbial

THE LEGEND DIES ON — GARY GREEN

icing on the cake for me.) I was already talking before the man behind the desk had time to say "what the hell..." I spoke loud and angry, "My name is Gary Green. The day is gonna come that you're gonna remember that I came into this joint. The day will come that the *Musicians' Union* will force you to sign a contract that guarantees that you'll give the singers all of the door money and you'll settle for your food and drink take."

He interrupted, standing up a head taller than me, "Look here..." I got louder and he stopped to listen, "Mark my words...that day is gonna come when you'll be happy if people just walk through your door. You remember this when that day comes you motherfucker."

I turned and started to walk away but he grasped at my arm and started babbling something. I grabbed my wrist with my other hand and twisted it backward toward his pulling arm until the pressure turned on his arm as if it would break. As gracefully as David Carradine would have done before TV cameras in *Kung Fu*, I snapped my arm back to my side and darted out the door into the street.

There I stood for a second trying to decide whether or not to go back inside or to come back the next night or forget about the whole thing. I heard him yelling something at me through the door, but he didn't come out, so I walked away.

As one might expect, striking a blow for musicians' rights, earned for me... the high honor of being banned from almost every club in Greenwich Village and the reputation among my peers of being an asshole.

I especially earned the ire of Village folksingers who were not part of the "topical music" world of Broadside. I repeatedly was warned that I'd never work again; during the next few weeks that seemed to be accurate.

To make money for food I began street singing, opening my guitar case for donations as I usually stood across from the mid-town hoity-toity hotels —*Essex House* or *The Plaza*— and occasionally somewhere in The Village. I sang my songs, Woody Guthrie songs, train songs, and threw in a few old gospel songs for their power to be heard over noisy traffic.

Late one afternoon after a very intense day of transfer letter headline creation, I didn't feel like going the forty blocks down to midtown. So, I set up my little street corner serenade stand in front of a (really great) taco stand on West 89th Street at Broadway. The passersby tossed a few coins, but nothing equal to the day's wages I usually made at those high-end tourist locations.

Hoping to increase the donations and be heard over passing traffic, I decided to switch to the gospel songs, which were more boisterously loud than my typical songs. I started with a long, sustained G-chord and near-acapella I loudly sang out, "I looked over Jordon and what did see?" (the opening of *Swing Low Sweet Chariot*).

THE POET LAUREATE SOUL OF FOLKIE ROCK & ROLL

I gave the chord for the second line of the song, but before I could sing it, from behind my left shoulder I heard a powerful baritone voice sing out in perfect pitch and with a soulful passion that I could only dream of, *"Coming for to carry me home"*.

Partly surprised, but more impressed, I turned to see what street derelict had chimed in with such precision. If I had been susceptible to a heart attack from shock, then I would have had it when I turned around. There stood a genuine living legend: *Reverend Frederick Douglass Kirkpatrick*; the celebrated civil rights troubadour (and more recently, renowned Sesame Street semi-regular).

Before Phil's death, Pete Seeger had planned for Brother Kirkpatrick (as he was known) to be on our board of *I Hear America Singing*. Once the creation of that project went dormant, I never had the opportunity to meet him. Then, here he was standing beside me and singing on the street.

I was stunned; and silent. "Don't stop; keep it going," the big man said as he opened his own guitar case and joined in with me. Holy crap! Not only did I get to meet Kirk, but I was standing on a New York City street corner, singing with him. *Just wow.*

After we finished the song, he stayed. And he stayed. And stayed. He stood there singing with me for about two hours. When we finally tired, I split the money in my guitar case with him. He looked at it and said, "Son, that is more money than I made last week playing at a club in Harlem. I going to stick with you".

I loved the sentiment, of course, but knew it was "just talk" ... at least so I thought. I was wrong. At least three times a week, Brother Kirk and I played somewhere; pretty-much rehearsing on stage. We played mostly traditional civil rights songs, occasionally threw in one of his or one of mine, and a few of Woody's.

Between gigs we talked for hours about anything and everything. He also invited me to play with him at several of his gigs at churches and coffeehouses in Harlem and The Bronx, and at campus functions at Columbia, NYU, The New School For Social Research, Barnard College, and CCNY.

When I told him about my misadventures at the bars and clubs in The Village, he wasn't surprised. He told me that he had not been allowed to play down there in years; ever since he called out that same famous owner of one of the same club as a "racist, elitist pig", We both got a good laugh out of that, but then pondered other venues.

Kirk had recently applied for a permit for a folk music venue inside Central Park; but that was in the bureaucratic processes of the city and the NYPD, so there was no-telling how long that would take.

He suggested that I try to play at a club way-downtown on the Bowery; a club called *Country, Bluegrass, Blues, and Other Music For Uplifting*

THE LEGEND DIES ON — GARY GREEN

Gormandizers. [137] He said that place only allowed original songs and was becoming famous since *Patti Smith & Lenny Kaye* had gigged there as well as *The Ramones, The Talking Heads,* and *Blondie* had played there.

The absurdly-long-named club was known by its initials *CBGB & OMFUG*; and it was referred to by the acronym CBGB's. Steve Forbert, on a visit to the Broadside apartment, had said that he was booked to play there; but it didn't register to me what it was other than something way downtown.

I took Kirk's advice and dropped my album off, leaving Sis & Gordon's phone number as my contact number. A couple of days later a guy in his mid-forties named *Hilly Kristal* asked me to come see him at the club. When I met him, he began by telling me that "Hilly's" was not just punk rock or new wave and that he was a big fan of what he called "Hilly-Billy" music.

Despite his personal tastes, the mid-1970's New York City punk audience was one weird scene; especially to a Nashville guy who learned his music in rural Tennessee and North Carolina. Extemporaneously and on-the-fly, I modified my set list to include less overtly political and a lot more of my counter-culture songs (*Average Minded American, Morgo The Mighty Meteor* (the "Johnny Cash is a bum" song), *America's Child* (my teen-angst song), and others). Realistically, I didn't become a CBGB favorite by any means; but I was very well-received.

The appearance also led to a call the following day from *WBAI 99.5 Radio*, the progressive *Pacifica* network's New York City affiliate. They did almost an entire half-hour of interviewing me and me playing my songs in their studio. I really couldn't tell if the guy that interviewed me was genuinely interested in my music or if he had been given an unpleasant assignment of having to do it or if he was actually tongue-in-cheek mocking me. It was just an awkwardly weird interview, and he seemed as genuinely amused as I was uncomfortable.

During the interview, I even got in a very-light slap at those Village club owners. When the host of the show complimented me for appearing for New York audiences and noted my good reception at CBGB, I answered, "Well thank you, that's very kind of you. I'm not sure everybody agrees; some of the clubs in Greenwich Village chased me out." He responded, laughing, "That's because they are afraid of how blunt your songs are about some touchy subjects. Too close to home?" He then asked me to play *You're Just As Guilty.*

---

[137] CBGB's "gormandizer" is defined by Webster's as "one who eats gluttonously or ravenously".

THE POET LAUREATE SOUL OF FOLKIE ROCK & ROLL

That did nothing to help my relationships in The Village, but it did wonders for me Midtown and Uptown. I received several invitations to play for the more hoity-toity, which I shared with Brother Kirk.

Throughout all of this, I was deep into production of the next few issues of Broadside; I was only gigging late at night. Gordon had just finished writing liner notes for an album for Moe Asch and he asked me to drop them off to Marilyn at the Folkways office.

When I arrived at 43 West 61st Street, Marilyn welcomed me like a long-lost relative. Mr. Asch was in his office and when he looked out and saw me, he motioned for me to come in.

Without any salutation, he began speaking immediately, "Go buy a New York Times and write some songs about what's happening now. Like a newspaper, let's make a record".

I was stunned. My album had been out less than six months, and Moe Asch himself had just asked me to make another record for him!

"I have a lot more songs," I said; but he dismissed that, answering, "I know. But I want to hear some songs about what is happening now. Today's newspaper stories".

I told him I understood and would start that day. He answered again, "Good. Bring me a tape next week".

Holy crap, again! No pressure or anything. Wow. I rushed out of the office, bought a paper, walked to the Columbus Circle train station, and took the Broadway Local up to the stop near the Broadside apartment. Inside, I couldn't wait to announce that Moe wanted another Gary album.

I think Gordon was probably as excited as I was. He immediately pulled out an over-stuffed file folder full of clippings from newspapers that he had been saving. Quickly going through them, every few clips he would pull one out and hand it to me, giving me a synopsis of the story with his own political commentary.

I still had to write the songs, but in essence he was co-producing the album with me. He was suggesting songs; albeit, not quite written yet songs, but songs, nonetheless.

Under Gordon's tutelage, my writing was becoming overtly political and nothing short of that. My lyrics were becoming noticeably angry. It wasn't anything that I had planned or intended; but there was no doubt that because of it I was known as a "topical" singer. I *wanted* to be a country singer, but instead I was seen as a "political activist".

Forty years later, a curator at The Smithsonian wrote a catalog description of my second album:

"Folksinger - songwriter and political activist Gary Green's second album for Folkways Records offers more original material on the themes of poverty, social injustice, corruption, and political issues of the mid-to-late 1970's ("The Siege of Fort Apache," "Rev. Ben

THE LEGEND DIES ON — GARY GREEN

Chavis"). Influenced by Woody Guthrie, Green sings a posthumous letter to the singer ("Dear Woody Guthrie"), telling him what has become of his legacy. Green dedicates this album to Guthrie, Pete Seeger, and Moses Asch. An introduction written by the artist and lyrics for all tracks are included in the liner notes."

That damned "*political activist*" label just wouldn't go away. But, in 1977 living in Sis and Gordon's apartment on the Upper West Side, without a doubt, I definitely *was* writing political music.

And, as I said, very angry political music! One song on that second album contained the charming chorus. *"Burn. Burn. Burn. And I'll watch you die!"* While that certainly summed up the depth of the angry-young-man radicalism that I had become, it also pigeon-holed me into that radical-activist box and completely obscured by country music flavor and my Ginsberg-inspired poetry roots.

I tried to discuss the labeling-me issue with Moe Asch *(it was not something that would not have been appropriate to raise with Gordon or with Sis)*. Moe seemed indifferent to my concern. His only advice was a shrug and "you want to be a poet? Put a poem in the brochure."

In hopes of reaching beyond the confines of the pop culture label of "Protest Singer", I decided to try to reach the literary world. I knew that I could get my album in front of my friend Allen Ginsberg; so, I reasoned that if I offered it as a literary creation of poetry that happened to carry a political edge that would be cool.

I had been reading a lot of lyrical long-form epic poetry; especially *Percy Bysshe Shelley*. Known as a political radical during his short lifetime (he died at 29), after his death he became recognized as a founder of a movement of English romantic poets who redefined literature against the more staid neoclassical poetry.

My God! 155-years before me, here was a "political activist" whose poetry eventually defined an entire style of classical literature. THAT is what I wanted to do. I wanted to be a *classical poet* ... who also happened to be —in the mold of Percy Bysshe Shelley— a "political activist" ... and a hillbilly. No complexity there at all... right?

That synthesis of literature and topical music was what I wanted to accomplish with the second album. To facilitate that desire, Moe Asch expanded the print format of the booklet insert to accommodate my epic poem (though he reduced the size of the type to barely-readable).

I decided to take up the entire front page with my poem, *The Poet, The Prophet, The Writer, and The Musician*, which I dubbed an "allegorical epic" and in keeping with my goal, Moe let me name the album *Allegory*.

The actual recordings on the album were a lot more direct than allegorical, despite the name of the album. While any single cut might agitate or

THE POET LAUREATE SOUL OF FOLKIE ROCK & ROLL

incite on its own, the most controversial song on the album turned out to be what I had thought to be the most innocuous.

The South Bronx had been plagued by an epidemic of fires —some that burned down entire neighborhoods. There were so many fires that photos of the area around *Hunts Point* and *Longwood* looked like World War II photos of bombed-out Dresden. From *Westchester Avenue* to *East 163rd Street*, there was virtually nothing but burned-out ruins.

Throughout New York it was widely accepted that greedy landlords had paid arsonists to destroy the buildings because the insurance covering the buildings was more profitable than renting apartments to the impoverished population of the South Bronx.

There were almost-nightly demonstrations at the local police station from residents that had been left homeless by the arsons. Demonstrators were demanding that the police go after the landlords and the arsonists; and many of the demonstrations were marked with rock throwing, Molotov cocktail throwing, and other violence.

The cops working out of the precinct felt that they were getting inadequate support from *One Police Plaza* (the then-new headquarters of the New York City Police Department). Officers began calling the 41st Precinct "Fort Apache" because, they said, they felt like an abandoned outpost in the midst of "no man's land".

Ignoring the clearly racist overtones of that nickname, police management often blamed "rampant violence" on the culture of poor Black and Hispanic people who live there (and, of course, not on the arsonist and landlords). As the stories and moniker circulated around New York, Gordon sent me up to The South Bronx to survey it for myself and write a song about my impressions. That fit right in with what Moe Asch had asked me to write; so, I was all over it.

Around the same time, The New York Times, New York Magazine, and several other media outlets sent reporters up there to do essentially the same thing that I was doing: observe and write.

I wrote a very radical song called *The Siege of Fort Apache* and unleashed lots of anger at the situation. Even before the album was released, I began singing the song all over New York; at every gig everywhere. The issue was *that* hot and it was widely accepted every time I'd sing it.

By the time the album came out, the *Fort Apache* term was widely known, and all the major papers and magazines had used the term. Whether or not they got the imagery from my song or from talking to the cops, is just not clear and should not matter to me; but it turned out to matter in a really big way.

Academy-Award winning film producer *Martin Richards*, working with *Time-Life Film Division*, began working on a movie about it all,

THE LEGEND DIES ON — GARY GREEN

starring *Paul Newman* and *Ed Asner*. It took them four years to film and release it; but they announced work on it right after my album was released.

At Gordon's urging, we obtained Richards' phone number and called him to ask if they wanted to use my song in the film. He responded that we should send the album to him so he could hear it *again* and let us know. Operative word: *again!*

We sent him the record, and a few weeks later called him for a follow-up. Gordon made the call, but I was listening. The producer said, "it's a powerful song, but it is too ethnic for us to use. So, no."

WTF? "Ethnic"? I had never thought of my hillbilly accent as "ethnic". Was Johnny Cash "ethnic"? What-the-hell?

Gordon wasn't letting him get away with that simple "no". He pressed the producer, demanding to know what sort of payments the production company would be making to me and to Folkways Records for using our imagery, theme, and title. When he informed Gordon that there would be no payment for our creativity, Gordon accused him of plagiarism and told him that he would be hearing from our attorneys.

Thus began a multi-year legal entanglement for Moe Asch, for me, for *Time-Life*, and for *20th Century Fox* (who distributed the film). Eventually... sometime in the 80's... they "settled" by sending me and Moe checks and giving me credit in future releases of the film. As of this writing anyway, IMDB has my name, along with the score's composer, listed under "Music By" for the movie. We could not have imagined that this silly legal nonsense truly was a harbinger of the drama I would bring down on Moe and Folkways Records.

Meanwhile, I continued to work on the magazine, play the places (other than in The Village) that would accept me, and meet other people in the New York folk and music universe.

Moe Asch wanted me to get a personal manager/agent. He sent my two albums to *Manny Greenhill* on the west coast, and he asked me to drop in on *Harold Leventhal* in Manhattan. Harold, over the years, had represented *Frank Sinatra* for a *Benny Goodman* event and managed The *Weavers, Woody Guthrie, Pete Seeger, Alan Arkin, Judy Collins, Theodore Bikel, Arlo Guthrie, Joan Baez, Mary Travers, Tom Paxton, Don McLean* and lots of other Folkies. Manny was Joan Baez's manager and handled a number of political singer-songwriters.

When I showed up, unannounced, at Leventhal's office he was not there. However, there was a flurry of activity. Woody Guthrie's widow, *Marjorie*, had founded the *Committee to Combat Huntington's Disease* (now called Huntington's Disease Society of America) —the disease that had killed Woody at 55 years old. The Committee operated out of Leventhal's mid-town Manhattan office.

THE POET LAUREATE SOUL OF FOLKIE ROCK & ROLL

Only one person was working on Harold's side of the business, but Marjorie and her team were hard at work. I as thrilled to meet Woody Guthrie's widow than anyone I had met in New York. She was warm and welcoming; and told me that she was absolutely thrilled that there was a new generation of Woody Guthrie devotees showing up in New York with their guitars. She also immediately put me to work stuffing envelopes for a mailing the Committee was preparing.

The entire time she continued talking to me about Woody, about the disease, about the folk scene in general. She was not a fan of Sis or Gordon but had a really warm spot for Pete and of course for Moe.

When she learned that Moe had recorded me, she asked if I had a contract and when I told her about the contract terms and Moe asking me to do the second record, that is when she told me that the only other people that she knew of that Moe had offered an "open" contract to were Woody, Pete, and Ella Jenkins. She asked me to bring her my albums, which of course I did.

Marjorie and I remained friends for years and wrote back and forth regularly. A few years later when I performed on The National Mall at the *Smithsonian Folklife Festival*, I appeared as *her* guest in her segment there. She gave me an amazing introduction from the stage, actually comparing me to Woody. *What higher praise could I have imagined!* It was an incredibly special moment that I wish had been recorded.

Back at the Broadside apartment, Sis was less-than-thrilled that I had spent time helping stuff envelopes for Marjorie. I sensed there was some animosity there that I probably didn't want to know about; but I could have been wrong.

Gordon, meanwhile, had conceived a fundraising idea that he wanted to experiment with and try out on me. Without telling me what it was, he said that it involved Moe Asch, and I should go see Moe the next day to discuss it. I hadn't seen him in a few weeks except one street encounter.

A few days earlier, Moe walked by a street corner in Greenwich Village where I was playing and singing with my guitar case open. He and the guy he was walking with stopped in front of me, and Moe introduced me as one of *his* artists. He introduced his companion simply as "Bill". I later learned it was *William Kunstler*, the celebrated civil rights and activist attorney... who also would play a major role in my life eventually.

Moe asked me how much I needed to collect that night. I told him that a box of *Golden Grain Macaroni and Cheese* was 33¢, a stick of butter was a quarter, a quart of milk was 85¢, and a subway token back uptown as 50¢. He chuckled at my precise answer (I rarely saw him chuckle) and carefully placed a twenty-dollar bill into my open guitar case. Kunstler did the same. *Jackpot!*

THE LEGEND DIES ON — GARY GREEN

When I dropped by his office at Gordon's request, Moe told me that he had two projects for me. He said that over the years he had sent several producers into "the field" to record New York City street musicians. He told me that he had made records of those tapes, but he wasn't satisfied. He said that he thought since I was a sometimes-street-singer that I might have a unique perspective on what is happening with street music. He asked me to take recording equipment around the city and tape what I thought accurately reflected "what is out there right now".

I had written a song for my second album called *Annie and Her Violin* about one of those street performers and the scenes on the streets of midtown Manhattan. Moe wanted me to find her again and record her as well.

The second project was a new Phil Ochs album that was to be released on Moe's *Broadside* label. He wanted me to "look into it" and tell him what I thought of the project. I felt greatly honored that he wanted *my opinion* on a project that had nothing to do with me.

Sis and Gordon already had released two posthumous Phil Ochs albums; one a poor-quality tape of a coffeehouse concert he had done, and the other a series of conversations between Gordon and Phil in the 1960's that was promoted as *Interviews With Phil Ochs*.

Gordon was proposing a second interview album; but this one was likely to be much more controversial than merely Phil's radical politics. He wanted to "expose" what be believed to be the CIA's role in Phil's death.[138]

After Phil's death, Gordon picked up that conspiracy-theory mantle and insisted that the U.S. Government had assassinated Phil. In an article published in Broadside just before I moved in, Gordon made his argument. Citing the government campaigns and murders of *Joe Hill, Fannie Sellins,* and *Ella May Wiggins,* as examples, he continued citing actual documented examples of Federal and State government campaigns against *Seeger, Molly Jackson, Woody Guthrie, Martin Luther King, Fidel Castro, The Black Panther Party,* and the entire COINTELPRO project… as well as even Sis and himself.

I wrote it off, in my mind, as totally nutso stuff; but my own experiences in the next few years had me revisit that first impression.

---

[138] Before Phil's death, and especially during his "John Train" mental illness, Phil had repeatedly ranted that the CIA was going to assassinate him. He had cited the murder of Victor Jara but also his own near-murder in Tanzania during which bandits attacked Phil near *Dar es Salaam*; but the would-be thieves did not steal anything —instead they crushed his vocal cords. Phil was convinced that the attack was from the CIA attempting to silence him. When Gordon told me this story, I wrote it off as insanity; but in the coming years… it came to seem at lease *plausible*.

THE POET LAUREATE SOUL OF FOLKIE ROCK & ROLL

Gordon pointed to Phil's being deported from Ireland after the CIA communicated with the Irish government. *That one* is officially documented and not even debatable; so, there was *some* reality to the CIA harassing a folk singer in that case. Gordon concluded citing the attack in Africa and then Phil's plans to set up a project to make records, print a magazine, and make films; noting that Phil had already picked out a building to buy in SoHo[139].

Gordon wanted to issue a new Broadside album with tapes of Phil talking about government surveillance of him. It was to be spiced by commentary from Gordon. Moe was mildly concerned about the content that Gordon was proposing, though he had not heard a tape yet. He wanted me to look into it for him and report back whatever I found.

If I had not been so wide-eyed naïve, I might have felt weird about being placed in the middle of whatever was going on between Moe's concerns and Gordon's certainty. Instead, though, I blindly plowed on, feeling loyalty to both "sides" in getting or not getting the album out.

I kicked into newspaper-reporter mode and decided to track down as much of the "story" as possible. I set about it in the most structured way I could imagine; as if I had been handed the assignment by the City Editor rather than by the most important record company owner in America.

I began, sitting at Gordon's bedside and asking him to go over "the facts" with me, which he happily did. Radical politics aside, Gordon Friesen presented a very reasonably compelling argument that the United States Government had a verifiable history of following, harassing, attempting to discredit, and even orchestrating the murders of American leftist political activist. Those activities were well documented and through the decades had been reported almost to obnoxium in respected mainstream newspapers and magazines.

The Washington Post and other media outlets revealed memos from FBI Director J. Edgar Hoover's program with the stated purpose to *"enhance the paranoia"* of antiwar activists. That led to the revelation of the FBI's Counterintelligence Program (*COINTELPRO*) which was revealed to be a series of covert, and often illegal, surveillance, infiltration, discreditation, and the disruption of domestic political organizations and individuals — including actions that led to murder.

The targets of the program were not always the highest-profile activists; and with the benefit of 21st century hindsight those targets look pretty insignificant as being any kind of *real* threat. But Hoover's obsessed

---

[139] Phil had code-named the project *Barricade House*; but in fact, it was our *I Hear America Singing* project... which Phil may have conceived, taken to Seeger, and then Seeger co-opted it.

THE LEGEND DIES ON — GARY GREEN

machinations were epic, and his influence was so great that it permeated the entire culture and mission of the FBI.

I knew-well the reach of his paranoia; it was the remnants of those programs that had the taxpayers of this country funding the fulltime operative that had been assigned to me at U.T. and had created the reluctance of the FBI to release even the highly-redacted version of their files on my music appearances. So, lesser-targets and targets who in reality were of *zero threat* to anything were still pursued by the programs.

Hence Phil, who arguably had a huge following and had even been an unindicted co-conspirator (and defense witness) at the *Chicago Seven* trial, would have been a likely target for *at least* surveillance. Depending on the level of official paranoia about his sway, it was totally *plausible* that some official badge-carrying mandarin could have targeted Phil for assassination.

Years later, I interviewed a former Federal Agent who told me that one of *his* assignments had been to be on standby in the event of a leftist takeover to assassinate novelist *Norman Mailer*; so, in hindsight and in that context (if the agent was truthful), Gordon's ascertain wasn't as insane as it sounded.

Even more concerning, it is well documented that Hoover's dossier-creating, career-destroying obsessions leeched into the entire structure of the Federal Government. President Lyndon Johnson was asked, after Hoover's death, why he did not fire the Director. LBJ famously responded, "I'd rather have him on the inside pissing out than on the outside pissing in."

Then, Gordon's presentation was, at the very least, plausible. He did not share with me enough tangible evidence to justify the dogma of his assertion; but, then again, if such a murderous conspiracy existed, there would likely be no hard evidence available.

I, however, was in full reporter mode and therefore one source was not sufficient for me to file my story. I decided to take the A-train out to Far Rockaway to meet face-to-face with Phil's sister, where Phil was living when he died. Sonny Ochs (who became and remains a dear friend).[140]

Sonny, and her brother Michael (a noted rock and roll photo-journalist) were adamantly opposed to the claims that somehow mysterious operatives slipped into Sonny's home and hung Phil. They were certain, rather, that Phil's mental illness had taken his life. *(Despite Gordon's adamance,*

---

[140] Since the 1980's, she has hosted her a weekly political-folk radio show on WIOX FM, in the Catskill's. She has featured me and my music on the show on multiple occasions in the half-century since Phil's death.

THE POET LAUREATE SOUL OF FOLKIE ROCK & ROLL

I had to agree with the family's analysis regardless of how "too close" to the situation they were.)

Having talked of suicide for years, Phil had been receiving psychiatric treatment and had been prescribed drugs to help control his psychoses. While he had assured Sonny that he had been taking his medication, later investigation revealed that he had *not* been doing so.

Sonny readily acknowledged that it was unequivocal that the FBI, the CIA, and other governmental authorities had massive surveillance dossiers on Phil. (And in subsequent years, many of those files have been released under the *Freedom of Information Act*). Further, she agreed that it was at least likely that Federal agents had participated in some disruptions and infiltrations of events where Phil had played.

So, while there probably had been some legitimate basis for his paranoia, the mental illness had taken a toll on him; not the least of the signs being the whole *John Butler Train* thing. His failure to take his medication provided further evidence that his death most likely was at his own hand.

Phil's family was unalterably opposed to Gordon's propagation of the murder conspiracy theory. Without saying it directly, it appeared that Sonny was also telling me that she considered the entire conspiracy theory to be an exploitation of Phil's mental illness and a grossly unfair representation of the tragic reality.

I also got the impression that should the album be produced... the family would vigorously fight for its withdrawal. *And I wasn't sure that I would disagree with them.*

I reported my findings to Moe and then to Gordon. Moe had no response other than a nod and a slight grunt. Gordon was more talkative. He said that Sonny did not understand the extent of the government's hatred of Phil and that she and the family were blinded by their grief.

Apparently, the decision was made by both Gordon and Moe to move forward with the record. The tape and the booklet-insert had already been finished before I even began my inquiry, though I didn't know that at the time.

Gordon offered to list me as co-producer because of my legwork and support, and he even went as far as to paste a one-line credit for me on one version of the back cover art sent to Moe. I, however, declined the honor; partially out of my journalist's sensibility that the reporter should not become the story, and partly because I just didn't want to be involved in the drama that I was certain would ensue.

For Moe's other project, the New York City "field recordings" project, I took a tape recorder to the streets and began taping. I recorded an awesome harmonica player from Brooklyn who I ended up playing along with and taping us both on the street and again back in the Broadside office.

THE LEGEND DIES ON — GARY GREEN

Sis and Gordon were less-than-impressed with him because there was no topical angle; it was pure blues harp performance.

I recorded the aforementioned violinist, Annie, who by then was playing with a string quintet on Fifth Avenue near Tiffinay's. I taped a steel-drum player from some Caribbean island who was playing near the arch in Washington Square Park. The tape also included three folksingers recorded at various street-corner locations uptown and midtown. I concluded it with a recording of Kirk and me on the corner where we had met, and I arranged the mix so that the street sounds were as loud as our performance.

I prepared the booklet, the cover, and tape itself; then took the entire package down to the Folkways office.

While I was there, Moe asked me to record a "third volume of Gary Green songs about the news". I began working on that tape as soon as Sis, Gordon, and I finished the next issue of Broadside.

I cranked out that third volume in less than a week, which Moe really liked because of its "news-magazine" like turnaround time. It was made of 13 more songs; 7 of which were explicitly political commentary on current events, with the remaining six being overtly Country Music with no political overtones except an occasional "zinger" last couple of lines.

Both that album and the *Street Sounds* album, however, were put on "hold" and eventually never issued. In the way of their release was Gordon's next project: our fund-raising scheme for the revitalization of Broadside.

THE POET LAUREATE SOUL OF FOLKIE ROCK & ROLL

Opus Fifteen:
Dylan, My $3-billion Rock & Roll Black Eye, & Elvis' Death

Hey man who writes better songs than I do? Name me somebody! Creedence Clearwater? (something unintelligible) I don't think he was as good as all that; just a bunch of faggot bullshit all wrapped up in about two or three lines.
— Bob Dylan, speaking on the album, *Bob Dylan vs A.J. Weberman*, produced by Gary Green, 1977, for Folkways-Broadside Records album FB5322

Rock and Roll history is full of strange and unlikely adventures; and ranking near the top of the bizarre was the release and then court-ordered recall of the album that spurred an FBI raid and a lawsuit demanding what in today's money was the equivalent of $3.22-billion.

I mean, can you *even* imagine how irritated someone must have been to instruct corporate attorneys to wage that kind of war against a goofball 23-year-old hillbilly poet? Then, imagine the law firm's dismay when Federal authorities told them to modify the lawsuit *in the interest of national security!*

The shitstorm was over the infamous record called *Bob Dylan vs A.J. Weberman – The Historic Confrontation.* It also was the first record to have printed on the album cover: *Produced By Gary Green*; AND it almost destroyed Folkways Records, Broadside Magazine, and me.

That 1977 vinyl record remains so notorious that as of this writing, bootlegs still sell for around $100; and a few of the originals that popup on eBay and collector-sites go from a few hundred to a few thousand dollars. At this writing, there is even one listed on *Amazon.com* for $1,495.

I want to be very clear about this: Bob Dylan was as much (or more) of a victim of the ensuing madness as I was. I certainly meant no harm, malice, or anything negative toward Bob Dylan; he was set to be the savior of Broadside Magazine and a genuine roll model for many of us. I thought. Further, I didn't know Dylan then, I don't know him now, and either may or may not have talked to him on the phone twice; at this point, it is just not clear. What IS clear is that it was a bizarre adventure with unintended consequences all around.

The strangeness began, as such things do, with an innocent string of absurdities and no thought or intention of releasing a record album. Even more ridiculous, the real target of most of the eighteen counts of the lawsuit wasn't even aware of the album or the activities that led up to the album. Nonetheless, CBS Inc. representing Bob Dylan came after us like a category five hurricane hitting a wood frame shanty shack.

With no thought of producing an album, Gordon Friesen, Sis Cunningham, and I finally got around to addressing the elephant in the Broadside

THE LEGEND DIES ON — GARY GREEN

Magazine room: *raising enough money to keep the magazine afloat.* We had been toying with ideas for months before Gordon finally came up with a plan that seemed to be the most likely to succeed.

We decided that one of the magazine's greatest assets was the roster of "stars" that had begun their careers in that living room. Gordon conceived a huge *Madison Square Garden* benefit show featuring some of those big-names from the magazine; almost ten years before the first giant multi-artist fundraising concerts (*Live Aid, Farm Aid,* etc.).

He outlined three steps of the process: (1) get commitments from the artists, (2) secure the venue, and (3) promote the concert.

Gordon reasoned that promotion would come free because of the publicity such a collaboration of stars was sure to generate; so that one was off the checklist, as far as he was concerned. That left the line-up and the venue as the immediate tasks; and so, we began lining up performers.

Sis asked me, totally seriously, "have you called Bob yet?" She meant Dylan and she was asking as if picking up the phone and calling Bob-f'ing-Dylan was as routine as ordering a pizza. When she learned that I had failed to carry out even that very basic task, she *humphed* and made the call herself.

As she opened her little notebook, I could only imagine what a treasure chest of legendary talent must be in those pages where she kept the personal phone numbers and home addresses of the musicians who had brought songs to Broadside over the years. Not only did she dial one of the secret numbers from her book, but apparently Bob Dylan, himself, answered the phone.

Even more amazing to me, she said that he agreed to headline the show; instructing her who to call to work out the date he could be available and the details of making it work.

Sis next called a woman named *Naomi Saltzman*, who was identified as Dylan's personal business manager and assistant. After a brief conversation, they selected several target dates that he would be available.

Gordon, Sis, and I began making a list from the Broadside archives of potential stars to share the stage. Gordon felt that a personal plea from me would be more persuasive than from either of them. He said that it would send the message that a young person had come along to revitalize the magazine and would indicate that the concert would be a new beginning. *(It may also have been that people they had alienated would be open to a new person).*

Once the list was completed, I began writing personal letters to each artist, explaining what we had in mind and that the benefit show would be at Madison Square Garden headlined by Bob Dylan. During the next two weeks, I received more than two-dozen positive responses and no

THE POET LAUREATE SOUL OF FOLKIE ROCK & ROLL

negative ones. It was beginning to look like the show was actually going to happen.

The very first response I received was from Janis Ian, who was first published in Broadside when she was 12-years-old and still using her family name of *Fink*; *Janis Fink*. She not only agreed to appear, but she also showered me with the kindest accolades and fond memories of Sis Cunningham. She was so nice and supportive that it was almost surreal; my little hillbilly self didn't know New Yorkers could be so nice.[141]

With a list of commitments from Broadside alumnae *(and, of course, my plan to perform on stage with that platinum lineup)*, the next step was to secure the venue. Gordon instructed me to make an appointment with management at "The Garden"; and I made the phone call.

With all the New York arrogance toward a Southern accent that I had come to expect, the person on the other end of the call was haughtily dismissive... until I began reciting the list of performers who would be appearing in the show. Then, suddenly, his tone changed, and we were like long-lost friends reuniting. He set a time for an appointment (get this: at *MY* convenience!).

I am sure that my arrival in his office raised a few eyebrows among the all-white and all-male business-suited executives gathered to meet me. I was costumed in my should-be-trademarked cowboy hat, long-fringed suede jacket, wide-bellbottom jeans, over-sized belt buckle, and pointed-toe cowboy boots.

Looking at the "WTF" expressions on the faces of the buttoned-down people gathered in the meeting room, I decided to exaggerate and thicken my already-heavy Southern accent. I opened the conversation with a Cash-esque "Hello, I'm Gary Green" Then just for good measure I added, "who might *ya'll* be?" As they each introduced themselves and put out their hands, I responded with an equally-over-the-top accented "How ya'll doin'?", in my best *Beverly Hillbillies* imitation.

They, of course, had no idea that I was fucking with them; but that was okay because I knew it would disarm them and allow me to gather more

---

[141] Though I have not talked with Janis Ian in a half-century, Janis Ian and I shared a number of correspondences for several years. She was one of, if not THE, nicest person I ever met from that Broadside universe. As of this writing, she continues to be an incredibly talented writer, musician, and spokeswoman for change. She appeared on the 1967 Folkways-Broadside album *Broadside Ballads, Volume 4: The Time Will Come and Other Songs from Broadside Magazine*. For that record she used the name *Blind Girl Grunt*, taking the pseudonym from Bob Dylan's appearance on the first Broadside album as *Blind Boy Grunt*.

228

THE LEGEND DIES ON — GARY GREEN

information. They clearly weren't sure if they were dealing with a rock-and-roll hippy or a genuine nut.

They asked me to repeat the description of the show and lineup of committed performers. When I finished, they immediately began talking about something called *four-walling*[142] Madison Square Garden; I had no idea what-the-hell that meant, but like a good little newspaper reporter I took copious notes and shorthanded exact quotes of what they said.

By the end of his presentation, it was clear to me that putting on the show would cost us tens-of-thousands of dollars and we would have to hire everyone from security guards to lighting technicians to ushers and everything else. We'd have to set up a ticket booth and validate the tickets (there was no *LiveNation* and *Ticketmaster* was a little Arizona start-up that no one had heard of).

All of that was before the cost of renting the venue itself. It was clear to me that the total price tag for this show easily could top a hundred-thousand-dollars; and most of that would be payable *in advance*.

FUCK! If we had $100-thousand available, we would have used it to put out the magazine and we wouldn't need the damned fundraiser. Dejected, I returned to the West 98th Street apartment to break the news to Sis and Gordon.

Rather than throw-in-the-towel and forget the whole thing (which I probably would have done), they began plotting ways to raise a hundred-thousand-dollars to produce the concert. I was thinking, "well damn; if they can come up with a way to raise that much money, why exactly do we need a concert?" I was not, though, bold enough to ask that obvious question. Instead, I listened to the various schemes they were coming up with and rejecting just as fast, for seemingly (to me) inane reasons.

Finally, Sis took a deep sigh and said to Gordon, "We could use the *Weberman* tape." I had no idea what she was talking about, but Gordon nodded favorably and said that he could call Moe and get it released on Folkways as a *Broadside Record Number 12*. They seemed to agree that they had found the 100-grand solution to the problem.

When they realized that I had no idea what they were talking about, Sis began sorting through their stash of reel-to-reel tapes that had been submitted to Broadside during the past 15 years. Like packrats, they never threw any submissions away, even the rejected ones. When she found

---

[142] "Four Wall" is promoter's jargon for renting a venue with the owners providing nothing other than the "four walls" of the empty building. The show producer provides all staffing, insurance, and other expenses while in turn keeping 100% of ticket sales revenue.

THE POET LAUREATE SOUL OF FOLKIE ROCK & ROLL

what she was looking for, she took the tape into the bedroom and threaded it into the machine.

For more than an hour, I listened to a series of recorded telephone calls between Bob Dylan and a person named *Alan Weberman*. When the tape had ended and Gordon asked me what I thought, I told him that I had two reactions: Firstly, it gave me a lot of insight into Bob Dylan the person rather than the superstar; and secondly, that this guy, Weberman, was a total goofball. That amused Gordon.

Apparently, I had met Weberman in Miami in 1972 when he had been one of the Yippie organizers of the demonstrations at the Republican National Convention in Miami, (where I had been Ginsberg's favorite stage performer). I did not remember him at all. It turned out that he had no recollection of me, either. *Thank goodness.*

Even as of this writing, I have never met Alan Weberman in person and have only had one or two phone conversations with him *(neither of which were pleasant)*; so, everything that I know about him came from Gordon and Sis (or later from the affidavits in the massive lawsuit).

Gordon explained that Weberman was a self-proclaimed *garbologist*. Garbology, believe it or not, is actually in the *Oxford English Dictionary* and defined as Anthropologist William Rathje's term for "the scientific study of the refuse of a modern society; the investigation of material discarded by a society considered as an aspect of social science". *(You can't make this shit up!)*

Gordan said that in addition to sorting through various celebrities' garbage, Weberman had become obsessed with Bob Dylan and had narrowed his activities to, specifically, Dylan's trash. Weberman coined a term for that focus: *Dylanology*. (A few years later, *Rolling Stone Magazine* called him, "the king of all Dylan nuts".[143])

At best, Weberman was a 60's counter-culture *character*. More than a footnote of obsessive fandom or the lunatic fringe, he was a genuine anti-authoritarian activist who not only questioned but upset the status quo with uncomfortable questions and conclusions. Among his supporters were *John Lennon, Yoko Ono, Jerry Rubin*, and other well-known anti-establishment luminaries of that epoch.

With that kind of backing, Weberman focused on many 60's rock figures that he said had "sold out", targeting them for demonstrations, posters, and underground newspaper articles. His many articles, speeches, and media appearances were filled with the jargon of the era.

---

[143] *Man no fan of Dylan family*, Rolling Stone, July 4, 1997; and again *The wildest people from David Kinney's new 'The Dylanologists: Adventures in the Land of Bob'* By James Sullivan, May 16, 2014

THE LEGEND DIES ON — GARY GREEN

His seeming fixation on Dylan had Weberman, at various times, claiming Dylan was a heroin addict, a spokesman for "the capitalist pig establishment", and turning his back on his fans. In fact, Alan built an entire persona, if not career, around his Bob Dylan obsession. Reportedly:

- He organized demonstrations in front of Dylan's home.
- He sorted through Dylan's garbage looking for information about the star's personal life.
- He wrote underground press articles with stories like "Bob Dylan's Sex Life".
- He taught a "Dylanology" course at a Free University.
- He allegedly attempted to climb through the windows at Dylan's home.
- He called Dylan's business manager at midnight.
- He staged an unauthorized party for Dylan's 30th birthday, where more than 500 people showed up in front of Dylan's home where Weberman served a birthday cake decorated with hypodermic needles (illustrating Weberman's contention that Bob Dylan was a drug addict).
- The invitation to that "party" used a modified Peanuts comic strip and triggered attorneys for Charles Schulz (the comic's creator) suing Dylan for copyright infringement (assuming he had authorized the party invitation).

That list of madness that Gordon described to me went on-and-on including dozens of either authorized or unauthorized tape recordings of phone calls between Dylan and Weberman. At one point, according to Gordon. after Weberman had promised to stop Dylanology activities, Alan again was caught going through Dylan's garbage. That supposedly resulted in a physical fight between Dylan and Weberman.

Somewhere along the timeline of this lunacy, Weberman was served with either a "C&D" (cease and desist) or some other court order to leave Dylan alone. [144] Yet, through it all, *again according to Gordon,* Dylan continued to take Weberman's calls and even invited him to his studio and his home at various times.

Apparently, the songwriter was *trying* to make peace. Objectively (at least based on the seven-year-old taped conversations that Sis and Gordon played for me) it appeared that when the interactions between them began, Bob accepted Alan as a sort of "super fan"; but it is clear, from a series of civil court cases, that Dylan had tired of Weberman and his antics.

According to one related affidavit, Dylan had come to consider Weberman to be a physical threat to him and his family. At the time, New York had no "celebrity stalker" laws to deal with this bullshit. So, get the picture of A.J. Weberman? (Or at least the picture that was painted me).

---

[144] Weberman's attentions did not seem to wane when Dylan's popularity subsided. Forty years later, after Dylan was awarded the *Nobel Prize in Literature,* Weberman claimed, in a *YouTube* video that he was responsible for Dylan's being awarded the honor; an absurdist claim that was bolstered by *Salon* magazine characterizing it as having "a scrap of truth in it".

THE POET LAUREATE SOUL OF FOLKIE ROCK & ROLL

As I said to Gordon, it was my opinion that Weberman was a goofball[145]. *But the weirdness was just beginning.*

To this picture, Gordon added that one of Weberman's closest friends and collaborators was a proto-punk rock-and-roller named *David Rosario*, who used the stage name *David Peel*. Gordon explained that the "Peel" name was adopted from the pop-culture story that smoking banana peels could induce hallucinations (it cannot, by the way).

Rosario and Weberman had co-founded the "Rock Liberation Front" to taunt financially successful "sell-out" musicians. Rolling Stone Magazine's *Jon Wiener* described the group's mission as "exposing hip capitalist counterculture rip-offs and politicizing rock music."

Rosario with his band (*David Peel and the Bunch* and occasionally called *Joe Bananas and the Bunch*) had submitted a song to Broadside called *The Ballad of A. J. Weberman*, a song about Alan's obsession with Bob Dylan. Shortly after submitting the song (which Broadside never used), Peel's third album was released — produced and paid for by former Beatle *John Lennon*.[146]

Gordon wanted to use Peel's Weberman song as the introduction and closing for the album. I listened to that tape as well. The song was... different... not something I might have picked; but Gordon felt it was appropriate.

Gordon had one other musical piece that he wanted to add to the album. In one taped conversation about other songwriters, Dylan asked Weberman, "Does Grace Slick even write songs?" Grace Slick was the singer-songwriter-confounder of the legendary rock band *Jefferson Airplane*. Several years earlier, she had submitted one of her songs to Broadside for consideration. Gordon dug out that tape as well and suggested that it be added to the album; inserted at the point where Dylan questions her songwriting.

That conversation was part of Weberman and Dylan debating the quality of Dylan's then-recent songwriting. Dylan demanded that Weberman name anyone who wrote better songs. Weberman named a string of

---

[145] Though he continued his Dylan focus for decades, Alan Weberman also co-wrote a book claiming that the "two bums on the grassy knoll" at the JFK assassination in Dallas were actually Watergate burglars E. Howard Hunt and Frank Sturgis and that CIA had orchestrated the Kennedy Assassination. That book, based on his work with Texas Democratic Congressman Henry Gonzalez and Republican Senator Richard Schweiker, was cited as evidence by the United States Congress when they convened a special inquiry into the assassination, scrutinizing and questioning the Warren Report.

[146] Beginning his recording career with Elektra Records David Peel went on (before Lennon produced him) to be a leading early punk rocker in the New York scene.

THE LEGEND DIES ON — GARY GREEN

writers and bands, which is where the Grace Slick question arose. In that same conversation, Weberman named Creedence Clearwater Revival (John Fogerty) and several unintelligible things after that. To that, Dylan responded, "I don't think he was as good as all that; just a bunch of faggot bullshit all wrapped up in about two or three lines."

There were other equally offensive comments on the tape and the phone conversations themselves were at best contentious; though it was clear that Dylan and Weberman were not always adversaries. At several points on the tape, Dylan invited Weberman to visit him "again" at home — which was consistent with what Gordon had said about the relationship between the two.

Nonetheless, the conversations were something that an image-conscious celebrity probably would not want the public to hear. For example, during several of the taped conversations, Dylan pitched childlike tantrums; at one point telling Weberman, "Man, I'm going to write a song about you and tell everybody that you're a pig."

Weberman-weirdness aside, the conversations with Dylan provided more insight about the Dylan-the-man than any of the biographies that I had read, including what was then considered the ultimate bio by newspaper journalist Anthony Scaduto. The tape humanized Bob Dylan (in a good way) and gave the listener a really good understanding of the normalcy of Dylan's life; so normal that at one point he talks about building shelves in his garage. In those days, glimpses into the ordinary lives of celebrities were rare; so, it was unusual as well as potentially fascinating.

Gordon called Moe Asch and convinced him to press it as the next Broadside album. He then set about writing the booklet insert. He assigned me to take the three tapes to the Folkways Records office on West 61st Street for Moe hear.

I sat with Moe as he listened to the tape of the phone calls. I could see that he was amused at what he heard, but at the same time concerned. When the tape ended, he asked me, "this was all on the telephone?" I answered, "yes, Sir; I think so".

At that time, New York State had a law that prohibited the taping of any telephone call unless both parties were aware that it was being taped. The law, a backlash to the Watergate-revealed Nixon phone taps, required notification to the party being recorded as well as an audio reminder every 15 to 30 seconds during the call.

Several times on the tape, Dylan and Weberman discussed that the calls were being recorded; but the tape did not have the requisite "beep" reminders. At the time the conversations were recorded, apparently in 1970, that law did not exist; but Moe was still uncomfortable.

He made an appointment with the studio and asked me to take the tape there for editing. He instructed me to overdub a loop of a "beep" sound every thirty-seconds so that the listener would believe there was constant notification that the calls were being taped. Okay, pure deception, but no actual representation being made.

He also asked me to dub, between the different calls, the sound that a caller would hear when a phone was ringing, to give the illusion that it was a complete call on the tape. Finally, he asked that I supervise the splicing of the David Peel song and the Grace Slick song into the master tape at the appropriate spots.

In the studio, I also had the engineer insert short silent spots between portions of the taped conversations; that was to create tracks on the record, making the vinyl album easy to navigate on a record player.

After several hours in the studio booth with a technician, I had the "final cut" of the album. I took the new 12-inch master tape to Folkways' office and the original five-inch and seven-inch tapes back to the Broadside apartment uptown.

The next day, we began designing the album cover. We had zero budget: *not one penny*. So, we had to use materials that were already available in the office-apartment. We didn't even have a photo of Dylan; and certainly not one of Weberman.

Gordon found a really bad photocopy of an abstract-art photo-montage of Dylan that had accompanied an article in an earlier issue of Broadside. He chose that as the picture for the cover.

As he finished the eight-page insert, I wrote the very-short liner notes for the back cover. For that one-paragraph back cover, I wrote (sic):

PRODUCER'S NOTE

Several people have asked "Why would you want to release an album like this?" The important thing to realize is that beyond the "star" syndrome that has been cast around Bob Dylan, is the fact that Dylan is one of the major poets of our historical time period. This is a record which will give a rare insight into the workings of Dylan the man, rather than Dylan the "star".

This is a historical album. —Gary Green

Then typesetting! Remember those pesky "transfer letters" that we used for headlines in the magazine —the ones that I said would come to haunt me eventually? Well, they did haunt me!

We sorted through the office-supplies closet for sheets of transfer letters (and the requisite popsicle stick to apply them). To our disappointment, the only sheets in the closet with enough letters to spell both "Bob Dylan" and "A.J. Weberman" was an absurdly-large 150-point Helvetica (plain sans-serif) font. It was all we had, so it was our only choice. It didn't have enough letters for "Alan"; so, we opted for "A.J." (which fit with the Peel song anyway). To give you, the reader, an idea of the type size, below is a 150-point example of the transfer letters we had in the closet:

There were not enough letters for the "vs" or for "The Historical Confrontation"; but we found smaller letters on a combination of other transfer-sheets that would work.

The rest of the typesetting was done on the IBM Selectric® typewriter by Gordon's bed; and the album back cover looked unprofessionally exactly like it was set on a typewriter rather than a typesetting machine.

The next day, we packaged the front and back covers along with the camera-ready copy for the inserted liner notes. I took them to the Folkways office and delivered them to Moe. Then we waited.

Converting a tape to a record master, pressing the records, affixing the labels, printing the covers, assembling them, inserting the records into sleeves and the sleeves into the covers, shrink wrapping, and preparing for shipping... these were not overnight nor high-tech processes. They took weeks that usually turned into months.

If I'd had any idea of the commotion, havoc, and ultimately banishment, that would rain down with the release of that record, I probably would not have been so impatient. On the other hand, if I'd had even the most isolated clue of the notoriety, fabled renown, and enduring mythos that would come with it... I probably would have been even more impatient. And, if I could have imagined the comically melodramatic wrath it would bring from some corporate comitatus; my impatience would have been even more nerve wracking.

THE POET LAUREATE SOUL OF FOLKIE ROCK & ROLL

But, meanwhile, we continued to struggle to put out the next quarterly or semi-annual issue of the magazine. Money was becoming tighter; stencil prices had increased, there was a postal rate increase, and Sis and Gordon's already large household expenses had further grown with me living there.

I was pretty-much unaware of the severity of our poverty; not totally oblivious to it, but not really grasping the intensity either. New York City urban poverty in "Spanish Harlem" was markedly different from my time living in the woods outside of Nashville and going days without eating. Part of my ignorance of the situation probably came from the stereotypes of New York poverty that so many of us not from The City had imagined.

We were overrun with cockroaches, but no rats or other expected vermin. We were impoverished but we were not living in disrepair or in a slum. We were poor, but we were clean.

Squalor and poverty, however, are entirely different things. And rather than a stigma of "being poor", the reality of the situation gestates a frame of mind around survival and an *us-versus-them* between the *haves* and *have-nots*. Sis and Gordon had lived in that world for so many decades that it was, in fact, their lifestyle. It was, however, new to me.

I was still unable to grasp the depths of that life, especially in the context that these two people had contributed so much to popular culture and in turn to corporate and individual wealth. The disparity just seemed non-sequitur.

What I did understand was why Sis felt so bitter toward so many former Broadside protégés who had turned their backs on Sis & Gordon after using Broadside as a springboard. I also understood their disdain for almost anyone who had even moderate wealth.

Our poverty was very real. It impacted their ability to received medical care and prescription drugs. It impacted clothing purchases. It impacted what food they could eat; even with the Federal Food Stamp Act of 1964, there were strict limits on what could be purchased. Poverty was a lifestyle; and not one by choice but one they had been forced into because of the blacklist. It was an economic sanction against their social and political activities.

In their lives, neither Sis nor Gordon had held traditional jobs long enough to qualify for the maximum Social Security and Medicare benefit payments. Ollie had; so, there was that meager income for their household of five; five not counting my arrival. For years, their survival really depended on donations from supporters; and those donations had trickled to near-nothing. My presence was an additional drain on them, though I never ate their food.

On the positive side, when we focused on putting together the album and the fundraiser, Gordon seemed reenergized, at least to some degree.

THE LEGEND DIES ON — GARY GREEN

He was out of bed almost every day, and he had a seemingly endless stream of new ideas and dreams, not just for Broadside but for multiple political music projects.

I was supposed to be writing songs for a "what's happening now" third album for Moe, but the day-to-day financial concerns kept me preoccupied trying to get gigs in The City. The clubs in The Village still considered me a *persona-no-grata*; so, most of my income came from standing on streetcorners with my open guitar case, singing my heart out, and selling one-dollar copies of a 62-page mimeographed booklet of my songs and prose. (It had never occurred to me that a "successful recording artist and producer" had to worry about how to buy food for the day.)

Gordon seemed oblivious to it all, but Sis' stress level was clearly rising every day. It was becoming clear to me that I needed to move out of their apartment in order to take some of the financial pressure off.

I raised my concern with both of them. Sis said nothing; and her silence spoke volumes. They both agreed to help me find a temporary job as a writer; the trade for which I had a track-record.

As I went to multiple job interviews, played a few gigs, and we waited for the release of the album, I raised another concern that added to the tensions in the apartment. It had occurred to me that no one had obtained releases or even permission to use the tapes for the album. No one had contacted Dylan, Weberman, Peel, or Slick; and they all appeared on the record.

I raised that issue to Sis and Gordon, more as a question than a criticism. Nonetheless, Sis seemed genuinely irritated that I questioned the process. She asked me why I had not contacted those people if I was so concerned about it. Her tone made me feel like she was thinking, "who does this hippie kid think he is to question our judgement".

Gordon, on the other hand, brushed my concern off completely, noting that the tapes had been submitted to Broadside with the understanding that Broadside would use them as they saw fit with no compensation to the submitters.

In this case, "as Broadside saw fit" was putting out a record album with the recordings on it. Gordon maintained that no payments were necessary: only attribution.

That thinking seemed to be consistent with one section of the tape where Dylan asked Weberman if he was making money from his "Dylanology", and Alan assured him that he submitted everything for free with no payment whatsoever.

I also asked why we didn't note on the album cover or liner notes that the album was being produced as a fundraiser for Broadside Magazine. That question brought an even sharper response from Sis, who rather than address the issue, became further agitated about my hindsight. She was

THE POET LAUREATE SOUL OF FOLKIE ROCK & ROLL

taking it as personal criticism and not as the innocent question that I had intended. *Stress*.

Clearly it did not help things months later when both of my questions proved pivotal in the legal entanglements the album would create for all of us.[147] I was just too naïve and inexperienced to know how to handle the situation.

Our discussions, though heated, never became divisive; but they were not comfortable either. It was the first disagreement we had ever had; and I felt that the issue potentially could be monumental. Without a doubt, tensions were developing between us, and I didn't want to see our relationship deteriorate.

I discussed the situation with Brother Kirk, who agreed with my assessment that I should move out. He was quick to add that I certainly should continue to work with Broadside, just not as a live-in editor.

He suggested the name of a woman who might be able to provide me temporary living quarters while we waited for the album's release; *and* she was a longtime financial supporter of Broadside. Kirk agreed to reach out to her.

Sis seemed overjoyed with the idea and immediately called the supporter to secure the arrangement. I moved out the next day. It actually was on good terms, because Sis felt that some of the pressure (financial and emotional) was being lifted. I continued to come to the apartment every day to work on Broadside; I just didn't live there anymore.

Meanwhile we waited and waited and waited some more for Moe to release the record. My new living arrangement was just to be temporary; only until the album was released and funding was available. So, we waited. Whenever I made a little money from a gig, I would donate at least half of it to Broadside, even though I had moved out.

The new apartment was on West End Avenue at 95th Street; one block west and three blocks south of the Broadside apartment. I moved in on Tuesday afternoon, July 12, 1977; in the midst of the notorious summer of the "Son of Sam" murders and a massive heat wave in The City. The next day was the infamous New York City blackout that paralyzed The City and set the stage for massive looting sprees.

It was too hot to remain indoors, so I, of course, was on the streets in the midst of all of it; though not as a participant. The closest looting to my new upper-middle-class digs was over on Amsterdam Avenue, two blocks away; and the targets were… interesting. I wandered among the

---

[147] Usually, in those days a half-century ago, people were not as litigious as they would become in the 21st century; a lawsuit was not even a concern, though it definitely *should* have been a concern.

THE LEGEND DIES ON — GARY GREEN

looters, talked with some, but didn't give in to participating (despite the temptation).[148]

By the end of the second day, the electricity was back on, and some semblance of normalcy began to return to the streets. Gordon and I had several long conversations about the looting, and he asked me to write a song about it. Instead, I began writing an article for the next issue.

Our waiting for the release of the Dylan-Weberman record again turned to weeks then to months. My "temporary" housing was starting to feel way too permanent... and imposing, since it was rent-free.

Despite now having two albums, I was not getting a lot of offers to play; at least not in New York City. Concerned about income, I decided to visit the Folkways office for a progress report, but Moe was not there. Marilyn told me that the album had been delayed because Moe wanted a legal opinion about its content before he sent it to be pressed. (The production had not even begun!)

Since my living situation was only supposed to be interim, I thought it might make sense for me to return to The South until the release of the album. At least in North Carolina or Tennessee I could get a job at a newspaper and have regular income; that would allow me to save some money, support myself, and send money regularly to Sis and Gordon.

Before taking such a drastic step, I needed to discuss it with Kirk, Pete, Moe, and of course, Sis and Gordon. So, I started taking steps to make that happen.

Kirk was teaching a history-of-political-folk-music class at New York University, so I took a train down to The Village to see him. Unannounced, I walked into the back of his classroom after it had already begun for the day. I had planned to silently listen and then talk with him after class[149].

---

[148] For a long time, there had been verifiable indications that some grocery stores, consumer goods stores, and even small bodegas increased their prices in poorer neighborhoods. Even anecdotally, the 33-cent boxes of mac and cheese that I bought downtown were 50-cents in Harlem and 55-cents in the South Bronx. There are endless sociological, business, law enforcement, and ethics discussions of those occurrences; but none of the academic or business analyses mattered to the poor people who, like us, couldn't afford a subway token to go downtown to buy.

When the looting began, the targets that suffering the most damage were the stores that had inflicted the most exploitation on the areas' poor. That is not say other businesses were not vandalized and looted; but there was clear popular support amongst the poor for looting the biggest offending merchants.

As part of that culture of poverty, we were in solidarity with the majority of the looters, though not necessarily the vandals. *It was a thin line of distinction.*

[149] In those days, no one saw a need for high-security; so, I was able to just stroll into the building and the classroom.

THE POET LAUREATE SOUL OF FOLKIE ROCK & ROLL

When I stepped through the door, he abruptly stopped lecturing. With a big smile on his face, he addressed his class after a short silence. "I want you all to turn around and look at what just walked through our door. THAT is exactly what everyone of you is trying to learn about and some of you are trying to be. Forget Woody Guthrie, he's been dead for ten years. Forget Pete Seeger, he's an old man. What just walked into our classroom is the living, breathing, real thing. That is a folksinger. He lives it while you are reading about it."

I remember it so well because it was probably the nicest public acknowledgement I had ever had up to that point; it captured the essence of what I was trying to be. Also, Kirk and I discussed it many times for years afterwards.

After the class, I told him of my plan, and he agreed with my decision. He also agreed to fly down south to wherever I ended up and gig down there with me.

The next day, I took a train up to Beacon (the town where Pete and Toshi Seeger lived) and met Pete at the station. He, too, agreed with my decision. Surprisingly, he also expressed skepticism that the album would ever be released. He thought the Friesen's were too dogmatic, Moe was too cautious and would never pay us the actual royalties, and (even though he had agreed to appear at Madison Square Garden) the show to save Broadside was *not* a good idea.

Pete still insisted that Broadside should be allowed to die a graceful death and we should revisit some version of *I Hear America Singing*. He strongly supported *Sing Out! Magazine*, but told me that its mission was not topical and was more of a commercial enterprise than a tool for social change.

He said that he thought that my returning to newspapering in the interim would be a good idea because it would give me money to work on the project. *(He had no idea how poorly-paid newspaper reporters and editors were.)*

Finally, I met with Sis and Gordon to talk about it. Though he took it stoically, Gordon's facial expression showed much more than disappointment... almost devastation. Sis, however, did not seem surprised at all, not in the least bit. Less than either disappointed or relieved, her expression seemed more resolved, as if it was what she had expected from the onset. She had said repeatedly that every time she had put her hopes into "new people" (as she termed me) coming along, she had been disappointed.

She had often lamented that people would come around every day for a while, then trail to weekly, then to almost never. So, she accepted my departure as nothing different from the dozens of young people who had come to her and Gordon during the past decade and a half. And she dismissed my vow to return and support them as the empty promises that she and Gordon were accustomed to hearing.

Just about a month after the blackout, I returned to North Carolina, at first under the auspices of my parents. The plan was that I would stay with them until I could find a job back in the newspaper world.

At the time that I arrived, my father was in the midst of the process to be appointed as a Trustee for U.S. Bankruptcy Court; a paid post taking advantage of his business acumen to oversee business reorganizations and dissolutions on behalf of a Federal judge. The Federal Trustee Program is a component of the U.S. Department of Justice.

Once I moved back into my parents' home, the FBI met with the judge and informed *His Honor* that my father was "harboring" a dangerous threat to national security. The Justice Department, naturally, could not employ a family member of a known-communist (or cohort of known communists). Consequently, my father lost that job. (His contact inside the Judge's office told him the backstory of the rejection.)

It was clear that government surveilling, discrediting, disrupting, and infiltrating had not ended with the death of J. Edgar Hoover, the change of political party in power, the passage of the Freedom of Information Act, and the "official" end of the COINTELPRO program. Unknown to me, at that time, the continued Federal interest in radical folksingers would also shape the upcoming lawsuit over the Weberman-Dylan album.

My immediate focus was to get out from under my parents' roof so that my demons would stop disrupting their lives and the lives of my two brothers. As an award-winning journalist with an impressive set of clips (by-lined stories from newspapers), I assumed I would not have a hard time finding a newspaper job; as usual, I was wrong.

Before I could start floating resumes, *Tuesday August 16, 1977* happened. That was the day Elvis died. To me, Elvis dying at 42 years old sitting on the toilet … just was not possible.

Despite coming of age during the violent 1960's with the assassinations of John Kennedy, Martin Luther King, Robert Kennedy, Fred Hampton, Malcolm X, and others, I had no real concept of the emptiness of a loss from death. With exception of a great grandmother (who I barely knew and had died 20 days after I turned three-years-old) no one in my family had ever died. Even with Phil's death, I had no real personal perspective on death.

Perhaps that is why I took the Vietnam War so hard —because classmates died; people I actually knew. Perhaps it was why I was so passionate about the civil rights movement —there was so much death that I could actually see.

THE POET LAUREATE SOUL OF FOLKIE ROCK & ROLL

Even having covered more than 30 murders, in some cases discovering the bodies myself, as a newspaper police reporter; I did not *know* death. It was still an abstract concept that did not touch me directly.

But *Elvis* died. That changed everything for me. For the first time in my charmed life, I had to come to grips with mortality. If Elvis could die... then ANYONE could die. Even the *concept* of Elvis dying seemed unreal to me. How could it possibly be true?

Unlike the induced tears of heartbroken fans, I was completely debilitated by the possibility that Elvis *could* die; and I was devastated that he in fact *did* die. I could not get out of bed for almost two weeks. I could not eat. I vomited constantly. I shook; I trembled. *Elvis died!*

No matter what uncertainty there was in my life, Elvis had always been there consistently; Elvis was there my entire life. Presidents came and went; by then I had lived through six presidencies. But Elvis Presley was always there. Friends were temporary; with all the schools in all the places I had lived, I knew that friendship was momentary. But Elvis was consistent, no matter where I lived. Whether it was the skinny rebel Elvis or the too-much-makeup-on-the-eyes Elvis or the movie-star Elvis or the *Comeback Special* Elvis or the fat Las Vegas jumpsuit Elvis that kissed Nixon's ass: *Elvis was always there.*

The funny thing was, I wasn't even a big Elvis fan. As far as I was concerned, the "King of Rock and Roll" had abdicated long ago to Jerry Lee "The Killer" Lewis. The movie-star Elvis was as predictable as a bad television show, and certainly not interesting (though some of his co-stars were quite interesting).

The white jumpsuit and sweaty scarf Elvis was a joke topped only by his meeting with President Nixon to be an anti-drug spokesperson for "American youth"; what the hell did he know about youth culture anymore? He was irrelevant and a parody of himself. But... he was always there, and he was ELVIS!

You might have told me that God was dead, or there would never again be a springtime, or the moon had disappeared. Elvis was part of the fabric of existence. For him to suddenly cease to exist shook the foundation of everything for me.

When I heard the news, I immediately ran into the bathroom where I lost all control of my bowels and in a diarrhea-frenzy emptied my guts into the toilet bowl. When the irony of that hit me, I began to tremble; my legs shaking out-of-control. I couldn't stop them and therefore I could not stand up. My arms were shaking, my hands would not stay still.

When my insides were completely emptied except for some clear slimes and blood, I was able to make it to bed. But the shaking would not stop until I passed out and slept. As soon as I awoke, the shaking would start again, with severe stomach cramps. If I tried to eat, I would vomit immediately.

There were no tears. There was no sadness. There was no mourning. There were none of the conventional accoutrements that accompany hearing of a tragic death. It was something else for me.

Beyond the physical debilitation, was the mental exasperation. Nothing mattered any more. Music didn't matter. Civil rights didn't matter. Writing didn't matter. Peace didn't matter. Poverty didn't matter. Family didn't matter, because eventually they would die too. My own life didn't matter. Elvis died; *everything* was over.

A half-century later, the obsessiveness of my behavior truly seems mad; but at the time, it gripped my life and shocked me from the safety of the childhood that had protected me into my mid-20's. It wasn't an epiphany, but it was a great awakening.

And whatever it was that woke up, was not a welcome or pleasant thing. The world of Oz suddenly turned black-and-white. There were no rainbows anymore; only dark clouds looming and waiting to open up on my world. Why would I want to get out of bed to face that?

From my Southern Baptist childhood, I vividly could feel *the stars of heaven falling to the earth*[150]; no, really! Lying in bed aching and trembling I imaged the power to *kill with sword, and with hunger, and with death, and with the beasts of the earth*[151]. The much-cliched and melodramatically-used pale horse was real to me as was *the name that sat on him was Death, and hell followed with him.*[152]

Morality itself; good, bad, evil, pure... who cared? It would all eventually die anyway. The evil that men do lives after them; *the good is oft interred with their bones*[153]. So, who-the-fuck cared?

The realization of mortality that Elvis' death forced on me triggered a psychotic breakdown and loss of will. Hallucinations would have been a welcome relief from the physical and psychological suffering that was jerking me into reality.

The pain. For the first time, I realized that my entire life had been a child's game. Sheltered. Safe. Even adversity was just a game and could be changed as easily as changing the channel on the television. Captain Kangaroo or Dragnet; it was all only entertainment. *It was Only Rock and Roll.* But now... Elvis had died.

---

[150] Revelation, Chapter Six, Verse Thirteen; King James Bible

[151] ibid, Verse Eight

[152] ibid

[153] William Shakespeare, Julius Caesar, Act 3, Scene 2, lines 74-86

THE POET LAUREATE SOUL OF FOLKIE ROCK & ROLL

The bastard, reality, kicked in my door and grabbed my throat. The demon reached down my choking throat and wrecked my body from the inside to the out. Leaving me weak and unable to respond, he then fried my brain.

At some point during those weeks, I reached beside the bed and grabbed the notebook where I wrote lyrics and I scribbled, "*I lost it all; whatever it was that I had found.*" Other than that, I had nothing.

A fetal position would have been a relief from the torment of existence. For the next few days, I slipped further and further away from motivation and deeper and deeper into questioning what exactly could be wrong with me. I was lucid enough to know I needed medical attention; but I could not imagine for what.

I focused on trying to convince myself that there would be some good reason to seek that medical attention; but I just couldn't see it. Elvis was dead; anything else was only momentary. Why, exactly, should I give a fuck? I just did not have the will... to do anything.

Every day was a struggle to find the energy... and motivation... to go to a doctor. Eventually I forced myself to roll out of bed and go to a doctor's office to see if anything was actually wrong with me. After a thorough examination, the doctor concluded that there was nothing physically wrong but that I was nuts (his words, not mine). He patronizingly prescribed some kind of in-vogue-at-the-moment psychotropic drugs to "calm my nerves".

I had already met the demons of drug-altered behavior and despite the prescription I refused to take them; not even one. I just refused to go back to bed and in a very *Scarlet O'Hara oh fiddle-dee dee; I'll think about it tomorrow* moment, I cranked up my hunt for a newspaper job.

I plastered every daily and weekly newspaper in the state with a carefully packaged booklet of my clips, resume, and letters of recommendation. It was more like a marketing campaign than a job hunt.

Unfortunately, the FBI's visit and my abrupt resignation from my last newspaper job haunted me in the industry, at least in North Carolina. At some papers I would actually get as far as an interview; but then in the final approval process my past would somehow pop up.

The Executive Editor of *The Charlotte Observer*, the largest paper in the state, called me back for three in-person interviews and it was looking good. Then, in a monumental lapse of judgement I submitted a Sunday Op-Ed piece to his editorial committee without telling him that I was doing so.

To make matters absolutely horrible, the piece was a defense of the New York City blackout looters, condemning the practice of price-gouging poor neighborhoods. Just for good measure, I predicted —and *might*

THE LEGEND DIES ON — GARY GREEN

have called for— similar looting in North Carolina unless certain reforms were made in the state.

What I was actually trying to do ("trying" being the operative word) was paint for the working middle class a vivid picture of the culture of long-term poverty. I wanted them to feel what it was like and therefore understand why the looting took place. That, of course, killed any possibility of me ever working at *The Charlotte Observer*.

Added to that bad judgement, my job prospects were not enhanced when it was reported that the "folksinger, recording artist, and former newspaper reporter" visited in prison a high-profile civil rights clergyman who had been designated by the United Nations and Amnesty International as a "political prisoner" in North Carolina.[154]

In hindsight, it might not have been a wise job-hunting move; and the job offers were not filling my mailbox. However, I was inundated with requests for me to play at campus coffeehouses, rallies, demonstrations, arts councils, churches, and public television.

Kirk flew down to North Carolina, as he had promised, and we did a short educational tour across the state. He adapted key selections from his *Ballads of Black America* Folkways album to gospel ("spirituals") duets with me, and a handful of my own civil rights songs. We constructed a chronological narrative from slave ships through the 1960's Civil Rights Movement to the Panthers and into the then-contemporary mid-1970's. (We had a killer-version of *Amazing Grace* with me doing the narrative of the white slave-ship captain who freed his captives before writing that song).

As the tour ended, a small daily newspaper in central North Carolina offered me a job as their wire-services editor and I eagerly took the job. To my delight, the editor also named me "Entertainment Editor" and allowed to me to produce a weekly entertainment tabloid supplement to the paper. That gave me a free hand and press-access to television, theater, film, and music. Truthfully, it was a great job, and it allowed me to send money back to New York to Broadside.

I began each day around 5 a.m. pulling stories from the three wire-service teletype machines that fed us national news. I would determine which

---

[154] North Carolina, at that time, had more prisons than any other state. It had more people on death row than any other state; and per capita a greater percentage of the population was in prison than in any other state. The State had the lowest average wages and fewest unions of any state. It had the only fugitive law in the country that allowed any person declared a fugitive to be "shot on sight" by any citizen without repercussion. It had an all-white State Legislature. And it had at least ten people in prison that *Amnesty International* had proclaimed "political prisoners".

THE POET LAUREATE SOUL OF FOLKIE ROCK & ROLL

national stories would go into the paper as major news, which would be filler space, and which would be feature stories.

Early one morning, after I had pulled the news stories, I began to sort through entertainment stories for my weekly tabloid. As I tore the stories from the long roll of teletype paper, one in particular made me freeze into a blank stare:

```
ROCK AND ROLL STAR BOB DYLAN FILES
MULTI-MILLION LAWSUIT AGAINST SMALL
RECORD LABEL, MUSIC MAGAZINE, INTER-
     VIEWER, AND RECORD PRODUCER
```

Folkways had finally released *Broadside Album Number 12, Bob Dylan vs A.J. Weberman – The Historic Confrontation,* Produced by Gary Green. With the initial pressing, Moe was suddenly flooded with phone calls for interviews and orders for enough copies of the album that it would be Folkways first "gold record" if he produced and shipped the number that had been ordered.

The raw, uncensored Bob Dylan (from a seven-year-old tape) may have been the proverbial last straw for Dylan in his history with Alan Weberman. I certainly don't blame him if it was. He had taken Weberman to court in the past and clearly it had not stopped the madness.

Of course, Dylan wasn't aware that Weberman didn't even know the album existed. Most likely Bob Dylan saw the album as just the latest in the seemingly never-ending series of obsessions of Alan Weberman.

From that perspective, without the context of the album, and with the benefit of a half-century of retrospection, I might have had the same reaction. On the other hand, after having agreed to appear at the Madison Square Garden fundraiser, when seeing that the album was under the auspices of Broadside, if I was Dylan I would have called Sis Cunningham and asked, "WTF" or at least, why Broadsided had embraced Alan Weberman.

None of that temperance, however, took place. Instead, Dylan's management turned the issue over to CBS Inc., the record label where Bob Dylan recorded.

Just two years earlier, in 1975, a New York court agreed to a settlement of a lawsuit filed by CBS against Weberman; in that settlement, Weberman had signed an agreement to stop Dylan-related public activities and specifically not issue recordings. Dylan's people and CBS viewed our album as an overt violation of the court-ordered agreement.

Again, they did not know that Weberman was not aware that we released the album; nonetheless, his supposed "violation" of that ordered agreement was the crux of their lawsuit over our record.

Merits of their case aside, the first serious complication for them arose when they contacted the United States Attorney and the FBI for

THE LEGEND DIES ON — GARY GREEN

investigation of what their lawyers argued was a criminal activity. Specifically, the alleged Federal crime was a supposed violation of Bob Dylan's civil rights by publicly defaming him —vis-à-vis publishing a record album that was sold across state lines.

There is both written and physical indication that the FBI did, in fact, open an investigation into the complaint coming from attorneys for the huge media corporation. The criminal cause of action was to parallel a civil lawsuit with named conspirators being Weberman (of course): Folkways Records, Moe Asch personally, Sis Cunningham, Gordon Friesen, Gary Green, Broadside Magazine, and 100 "John Doe's" who were unnamed coconspirators who distributed or sold the album.

Obtaining a warrant at the onset of their investigation, the FBI met with Moe Asch with an order to seize all copies of the album that had not been shipped. Moe escorted the Federal Agents from his office to his warehouse, a block away.

My friend *Charles Averett*, Marilyn's son, was working in the warehouse when Moe and the agents arrived. Almost a half-century later, as I prepared this book, he recalled the incident for me.

Charles said that it was very calm and uneventful. He said that the agents were wearing suits and did not want to get dirty handling boxes in the warehouse. Moe instructed Charles and the warehouse manager to box all copies of the record and carry them to the waiting government vehicles outside. They did.

Meanwhile, the Justice Department's investigation immediately revealed that the FBI already had files on the political activities of Weberman, Moe Asch, Sis Cunningham, Gordon Friesen, and me. As The Bureau drilled into those files, field agent memos indicate that of the group, only I was subject of an *open* investigation, and I was still identified as a member of the *working press*. The other defendants were "known radicals", but their files were inactive.

Both the open investigation and, especially, the "working press" designation created a number of bureaucratic complications for the Department of Justice, the FBI, and any on-going action.

I suspected that the lawsuit might potentially shine a light on all sorts of illegal *black bag* activities that the government cloaked as "national security"; specifically, the remnants of COINTELPRO, which supposedly magically ended the day Nixon resigned (but clearly didn't)/

Once Dylan's team was notified of the complication, CBS attorneys decided to focus the lawsuit on Weberman and refer to me as an "unnamed agent, employee, or one acting on behalf of the defendants".

With that change, CBS also decided to engage an outside law firm with significant expertise in intellectual property (IP) law

Apparently, those lawyers were never given "the rest of the story" [155]. Having said that, even the best IP experts can only operate on the information they have. Dylan's people seemed emotional about it (as evidenced in the text of Naomi Saltzman's affidavit), and CBS Inc. appeared to be in a combative mode over their perception that Weberman had dared defy their corporate power and the earlier court order. Neither position was particularly conducive to providing objective data for the attorneys to evaluate and build a case.

Apparently, no one ever told the legal team that Weberman didn't even know about the album. I suspect Dylan himself, who likely was justifiably outraged by the whole affair, was as much in the dark as his representatives. Clearly a victim, he had no way of knowing (or probably even caring about) the backstory; the whole affair was in the hands of lawyers and Bob Dyland could, ostensibly get on with his creativity and life without such nuisance side-tracking.

Consequently, the complaint that was filed (and that I learned about from the wire service news report) was full of both inaccuracies and absurdities. Some of the counts in the lawsuit document were overtly offensive to the defendants. Gordon Friesen's outrage is clear, in a letter he sent me discussing reaction to the suit:

> "We are especially offended at being declared to be "barbarians", outside the pale of "civilized society", by a man, Bob Dylan, whose wife is suing him for divorce, charging he beat her mercilessly when she objected to his bring other females into their house for sexual purposes".[156]

The suit charged that *Weberman* had issued the album "out of vengeance" in a "conscious-shocking and malicious campaign of harassment" against Dylan. *But in reality, Weberman didn't even know about it.*

Among the many absurdities charged was the allegation that the typesize and font on the album cover were carefully chosen in a subliminal design trick so that consumers would believe that the record was a music performance by Dylan. *(As you recall, the font actually was chosen because it was the only transfer-letters sheet we had in the closet).*

Another count claimed that "the producer" (me) was attempting to "practice medicine without being a licensed physician". That charge grew from my album cover notes in which I described "Dylan the man, rather

---

[155] One of the "of counsel" attorneys engaged by the firm went on to become one of Columbia Law School's leading lecturers on copyright litigation and as of this writing remains a highly-respected authority on the subject.

[156] This is directly quoted from a letter from Gordon Friesen, dated February 8, 1978. It is presented here in in journalistic context, reporting the thinking of the defendants at that time.

THE LEGEND DIES ON — GARY GREEN

than Dylan the star"; supposedly that characterization was my diagnosing Bob Dylan as having "dissociative identity disorder"; specifically, multiple personalities: Dylan the "star" and Dylan the "man". *No really, that was an allegation!*

The suit also alleged that there was no indication that the record was not a Bob Dylan *musical performance* and that the two musical performances on the album were cloaked to appear Dylan was performing on the record. Apparently, they ignored the announcements printed on the record label itself *(underlined emphasis added for this book)*:

- *"BOB DYLAN vs AJ WEBERMAN <u>a Telephone Interview</u>"*
- *"This <u>Interview</u> Was Produced By Gary Green"*
- *"Song "A.J. Weberman" by David Peel and Group"*
- *"Song "Father Bruce" by Grace Slick © 1965 Grace Slick"*

Or the front cover:

- *"THE HISTORIC CONFRONTATION"*

Or the back cover:

- *"Sound Effects Courtesy of Alexander Graham Bell"*

The suit even suggested that the Dylan voice on the album might be a Bob Dylan impersonator that we had hired to sound like the star. *(Thank God AI didn't exist then, or they might have claimed THAT too.)*

The filing also claimed that Gordon's liner note booklet was filled with "bizarre and libelous statements". *(Not sure I could argue with the "bizarre" portion of that.)*

Though not one single claim of the lawsuit was 100% accurate, the firestorm that it released was devastating. It also made for one of the more bizarre adventures in the history of rock and roll.

Combined, each count against each defendant constituted CBS (and thus tacitly Bob Dylan) demanding $636-million in damages against us all —*an astonishing $3.22-BILLION[157] adjusted for the time of this writing!*

CBS also took the extraordinary step of obtaining an emergency court order enjoining Folkways Records from distributing any more copies of the album until the lawsuit was settled. Effectively, they got the record off the market before there was even a hearing on the suit.

After I pulled the wire story, my first call was to the Folkways office. Marilyn told me that I needed to let things settle down a little before I talked with Moe. He was meeting with lawyers and working to resolve the situation. She suggested I call back in about a week.

---

[157] Using the U.S. Department of Labor's CPI inflation calculator, the $636-million lawsuit filed by CBS Inc. and Bob Dylan against Folkways Records, Broadside, and me would be, at the time of this writing, the equivalent of a $3.22-billion lawsuit against us.

THE POET LAUREATE SOUL OF FOLKIE ROCK & ROLL

Instead of letting it settle, I fired off a *Western Union Mailgram* (same-day delivery letter) to him and another to Sis and Gordon. In it, I wrote:

> "I can understand why Bob Dylan is upset with the album. After all, it does present him in a light that he has tried to keep undercover for all of these years.
>
> But it seems to me that any fool would know that we can check the voice print in court if he is denying that it is his voice. And as far as "bizarre and libelous statements", that is purely subjective. Besides, as you well know, malice must be proved in such cases. And we certainly had no malice in mind or heart when we produced that album.
>
> I have given much consideration to the whole thing. The album is in fact a Broadside and Folkways project. Nevertheless, my name is on it a PRODUCER of the album. And you have said several times that if it were not for me, the album would have never come out. Therefore, I consider it MY problem just as much as it is either of yours (even though Moe is the only one of us that stands to lose anything; after all, what can you take from someone who has nothing?).
>
> Therefore, whereas Bob Dylan is such a prominent and forceful person in the commercial music world, and whereas his saying these things about the album which I produced casts an aura of fraud around the album and in fact around the producer (me), and whereas I feel that Dylan's suit is a smite on my reputation and will affect any future records that I may want to produce by having this aura of fraud cast around me, I therefore think I should file a countersuit charging defamation of my character and real damage to potential income from future albums produced by me."

There was no response from Moe, but Gordon responded immediately:

> "Just got your mailgram. Enclosed find all the information we have. We feel that a countersuit should be instituted and would have tried to undertake it ourselves if we weren't so old and sick and housebound. I am supposed to report back to the hospital right away.
>
> If you decided to go ahead, you should sue for at least $5-million, since you are a young man with your future ahead of you and are being irreparably damaged and especially since the false allegations by Bob Dylan and CBS are being widely disseminated to the nation's media. I think you have a good case because the charges are a mish-mash of misrepresentations as you see when you read through them.
>
> You might put in there that Folkways and Broadside are highly respected nationally and internationally for their work in keeping a history of important musical developments.
>
> I think a strong case can be made that in no way is this record a "PERFORMANCE", but an interview/dialogue protected by the freedom of the press provision in the first amendment of the U.S. Constitution."

THE LEGEND DIES ON — GARY GREEN

Based on Gordon's letter and subsequent phone calls, I decided to discuss the situation with a local lawyer. That poor fellow seemed genuinely overwhelmed with even the suggestion of filing a suit against CBS and Bob Dylan. He said that in his opinion no attorney would handle the case on contingency because he believed that it would be impossible to defeat CBS' attorneys, and it would take many hours of research and time.

He told me that not only was he not interested, but that if I was "adamant about tilting at windmills", I would need to consult a large law firm in either Charlotte or Raleigh and be prepared to pay a sizable retainer to find that firm.

I was not amused; and I decided that if I was going to move forward, I would need an attorney that specialized in entertainment law and underdogs. I needed a *Sancho Panza* that would enable my charging at the windmill; and I wasn't likely to find that lawyer in a small town.

I did, however, resolve that I might need to sock away money for a retainer if I was serious about this. I also realized that I was not going to be able to create that nest egg on my meager editor's salary.[158]

---

[158] Using the U.S. Department of Labor's CPI inflation calculator, the $636-million lawsuit filed by CBS Inc. and Bob Dylan against Folkways Records, Broadside, and me would be, at the time of this writing, the equivalent of a **$3.22-billion** lawsuit against us.

THE POET LAUREATE SOUL OF FOLKIE ROCK & ROLL

Opus Sixteen:
Nothing Left But To Go Back To Nashville

I'm Gonna Head For Tennessee One More Time.
I'm Gonna Leave A Cloud Of Dust At That North Carolina Line
— *Down The Road & Over The Hill,* **1976**, as recorded on Folkways Records album FH5351, *These Six Strings Neutralize The Tools Of Oppression*

I was ready to leave that job anyway; I felt underpaid for my value and unappreciated for my contribution. Likely neither was accurate, but in light of my awakening following Elvis' death, I also reasoned, "what have I got to lose?"

Even though I maintained a connection to the music world through my weekly tabloid and all the freedom it afforded me, I still was not *creating* music. I was feeling too far removed from that 1957 night when Mother woke me up to see Jerry Lee.

On top of that, my ranting and raving about the Dylan suit wasn't all hyperbole. In reality, I felt estranged from my record label since Moe wasn't talking to me amidst all the drama. Sis and Gordon, while clearly supportive of my reaction to the suit, were not as open-arms welcoming as when I had arrived in New York; *Sis had more-or-less kicked me out.* I'd alienated myself from the Greenwich Village bars. I was isolated from *mainstream* music because, as the movie producer had said, I was "too ethnic" (read "too hillbilly") And, perhaps most disappointingly, my hillbilly-self had in essence been kicked out of Nashville for being *"too political".*

The combination of all that was sending me signals that maybe my music and writing weren't all that good in the first place. Maybe whatever Moe had heard was a mistake, an anomaly. Maybe everything I had been about since pre-kindergarten was all bullshit. At 24-years-old, maybe it was time for me to decide what I wanted to be when I grew up.

My lefty-notoriety had waned, and I had continued to win press awards garnering a lot of attention in the journalism world; so, I knew that finding another job in newspapering would not be difficult. Perhaps I could find something that would let me create *and* would pay me enough to afford a legal retainer for a counter-lawsuit.

I floated resumes and clips all over the country and in less than two weeks I was hired, with no in-person interview, as the Executive Editor of a small newspaper on the Upper Peninsula of Michigan. So, in the midst of a winter snow and ice storm, I packed everything into a rental truck, hitched my car to the back of it (after removing the drive shaft from the car), and began the estimated 21-hour drive.

THE LEGEND DIES ON — GARY GREEN

By the time I reached Nashville on Interstate 40, only eight-hours into the long drive, snow on the roadway was six-inches deep. I had read that the town where I was heading averaged 208-inches of snow annually. The little six-inches of snow was insignificant by comparison but incapacitating to me. And ... I was back in Nashville. It was *home*. It was music. AND... there would be entertainment lawyers.

I called the editors at *The Nashville Tennessean* (the morning daily paper) and *The Nashville Banner* (the afternoon daily). Neither had an immediate opening but asked to see my resume and clips. I then started calling daily papers in several towns nearby.

When I reached the paper in *Clarksville Tennessee*, about 50 miles away (up on the Kentucky border), I talked with one of the coolest cats I'd ever run across, a guy named *Tim Ghianni*. I think he was an assistant managing editor or maybe a sports editor or something. The guy was so encouraging that I really wanted to work there; and he told me they had a copy-editor job open. He handed me off to his boss, a true classic newspaperman, named *Max Moss* who made me stop and think, *"these guys are for real"*.

Getting hired, however, required the blessing of the Executive Editor. I had called on a Saturday night, so it would be Monday morning before the editor could meet with me. On the phone, he told me that he was actually looking for a "design editor"[159] and invited me to meet him for an interview. *Yes!*

I brought a portfolio of clips for the editor to review. He tossed them aside, telling me that he had already called my past employers and knew everything he needed to know about me. I assumed that was the end of the interview; but instead, he offered me the job. (Apparently Max or Tim or both had rah-rah-ed me; and I genuinely bonded with the two of them.)

To my delight, he told me that the paper also produced a string of weekly newspapers from across middle-Tennessee as well as the *Music City News* (a well-known music tabloid that was part trade journal and part fan magazine founded by country music star *Faron Young*). They also produced country music star *Conway Twitty's* monthly fan tabloid. AND part of my job would be design duties for those music publications. It sounded like the perfect newspaper gig: near Nashville and plugged into country music.

---

[159] Many newspapers in that era were in the process of converting their printing process from lead type letterpress to offset printing. That opened an entire new world of the layout and design of the pages of the paper: the look and readability. It was an actual science of typography and layout; and I was a track-recorded master of both.

THE POET LAUREATE SOUL OF FOLKIE ROCK & ROLL

Making it even better, the newsroom of the paper was organized by Max Moss who was, as I had sensed, a very cool managing editor. He also was plugged into the *Grand Ole Opry* community, differently than I had been a few years earlier. He was mentoring, nurturing, knowledgeable and so laid-back that he made it a joy to work there. When he found out about my music background, he called the Opry manager and made press arrangements for me; regularly assigning me music stories and interviews in addition to my editor duties.

In relatively short order I settled into the comfortable little job, bought a used Porsche, and had enough money to approach a lawyer about the lawsuit. I wanted to find a lawyer who was more than just an encyclopedia of entertainment law; I wanted a suspender-popping, seersucker suited, *Atticus-Finch*-passionate, *Perry-Mason*-wily, evil-bastard lawyer. I wanted some Nashville hillbilly cunning to run circles around the New York City white-shoe law firm.

When I found him, in a little white house on Music Row, he was so intrigued by my story that he took the case on contingency: no retainer even. He loved my idea of a countersuit, but not as "limited" as Gordon and I had conceived. He wanted CBS to suffer the same pain that I had felt; and he wanted them to pay dearly for inflicting their clearly-misdirected wrath on me, on Folkways, Broadside, Sis Cunningham, and Gordon Friesen.

He wasn't even concerned that I was no longer named in the suit; because it was implied by my being clearly identified as the Producer. They had sued for $636-million; exclusively punitive damages since there was no actual financial loss alleged.

We didn't countersue. Instead, we filed an entirely new lawsuit: for $36-million in projected real damage to my budding career as a record producer for an influential label and as a singer-songwriter-recording-artist. *(That would be $187-million as of this writing.)*

The legal strategy he devised was so brilliantly complex that it was simple. Rather than defend against that suit, since I was not a formal defendant anymore, he decided that I should go on the offensive. After talking with Moe, Sis, and Gordon, and reviewing the facts of the case, he decided to focus exclusively on Bob Dylan, personally. *(I didn't feel too good about THAT; but what-the-hell, lawyers know stuff.)*

Our contentions were based on the accusations and the ensuing publicity in the original suit. We argued that I had suffered *irreparable damage* within the industry and publicly from misrepresentations, sloppy research, and complete lack of facts about the album. We argued that Dylan had manipulated an unaware *CBS* to be his weapon and therefore had

THE LEGEND DIES ON — GARY GREEN

acted with negligent malice and disregard for who, *other than Weberman*, would be destroyed by his blind rage.

Though we weren't answering the original suit, he countered each of its claims by matching new counts, turning their entire strategy inside-out and focusing on Bob Dylan. He painted a picture of a multi-millionaire ego-maniac blindly raging against anyone associated with his target *(Weberman)*; a rage without regard for the carnage created along the way.

He showed evidence and affidavits to support the facts compared to the speculation and falsifications in the original suit. Their litany of absurdities —like the supposed-conspiracy of the cover design— were put into the context of irrational mania by the empirical facts (of the transfer-letters and no budget, in that example).

Because I was a resident of The State of Tennessee and significant elements of the recording industry were in the state, we filed the suit in Tennessee Court. It was our specific intent to make the venue inconvenient for Dylan and requiring him to obtain local counsel. Further, my evil-bastard lawyer filed in a county where the judge likely to be assigned the case would be exceptionally friendly.

He topped off this carefully-constructed attack by painting a stark contrast between me and Dylan. I was a *"good ole Baptist boy"* from the hills of upper east Tennessee, just trying to get by with my hillbilly music. Bob Dylan *née Robert Zimmerman* was a millionaire New York rock & roller entangled in all the evils of that lifestyle, *even down to having a fake name.*

He argued that the malicious New Yorker was guilty of *transferable intent* in his out-of-control temper tantrum in the latest of his prolonged quarrel with another New Yorker. He argued that Dylan was civilly (if not criminally) negligent when his misrepresentation brought my budding career to a halt and destroyed my future.

Perhaps a bit melodramatic; but they were arguments that would play well in Tennessee courts, especially in its obscene stereotyping[160].

When it came time to serve him, personally, the hired process servers were told by CBS that Dylan was homeless, and it would be impossible to find him. They were told that as a result of the damage caused by our record album, his wife had expelled him from their home and since that

---

[160] Disgustingly, and over my objections, it also played to the prejudices, racism, and biases that were prominent in Tennessee at the time (and still are in some places). I strongly suspect that my attorney's constantly referring to Dylan as *"Zimmerman"* was deliberate to raise unspoken antisemitism; especially since he mentioned in the pleading that I was raised in the *Baptist Church*. His continuous references to *"New York City"* was an intentional north-versus-south allusion; just as was the "good ole boy" contrast to "rock and roll star".

THE POET LAUREATE SOUL OF FOLKIE ROCK & ROLL

time he had no home. There is no evidence that I have seen that any of that characterization was true; but it was part of the report of the catchpole's failure to serve Bob Dylan.

Not to be deterred by their failure, my attorney cooked up a definitely-Tennessee scheme to both serve Dylan and send the message that we were damned serious about our lawsuit.

Bob Dylan's 1975-76 *Rolling Thunder Revue* tour had been a massive success and launched him to true "superstar" status. That tour was followed by a 1978 *Bob Dylan World Tour* which was scheduled to hit Memphis on December 1st and Nashville on December 2nd.

When the private jet landed in Memphis, the entire legal strategy from my team came to a head. My lawyer told me that *Shelby County Deputy Sheriffs, U.S. Marshalls*, and two process-servers, bordered the plane with a court order to seize the plane, its contents including musical instruments and equipment, and hold them for the court until Bob Dylan accepted service of our subpoena and lawsuit. He said that without the release, the equipment would not be available for the shows and transportation would not be available. Without much legal consultation, I was told, Dylan accepted service. He then had been officially notified that I was suing the shit out of him, and he had been ordered to appear.

Looking back on this to verify it a half-century later, I could find no evidence of the suit being filed and certainly of no such dramatic service of the folk rock superstar. Nonetheless, it is what was reported to me.

Two days later in my apartment up in Clarksville I received what I thought was a prank call from one of my friends *(and I STILL contend that it may have been.)* I answered the phone and heard the worst Bob-Dylan-parody accent I had ever heard, "Gary, this is Bob". The accent was so obviously phony that it immediately reminded me of the character "Alias" played by Dylan in the 1973 Sam Peckinpah film *Pat Garrett and Billy the Kid*. In the film, Alias inventories a general store and has about a minute of dialogue saying nothing but, "*Beans. Beans. Beans. And Beans.*" THAT was the accent on the phone call. It was the worst "Dylan" ever.

"Yeah right. Who-the-hell is this? Cut the shit," I answered, wondering if it might be my brother Ronny who I knew did a spot-on imitation of "beans" from the film.

I was wrong. The person convinced me that it really was Dylan. I wish I had recorded the conversation so I could know for sure today; but then again, this whole debacle began with recorded phone calls with Dylan. As a journalist, I always had a cassette recorder and suction-cup earpiece by the phone; but I exercised the prudence to not engage it, once I believed that I was talking to *THE* Bob Dylan.

THE LEGEND DIES ON — GARY GREEN

It was a weird conversation, with the alleged Dylan doing most of the talking. He began by actually apologizing for letting everything get "out of hand". He confirmed that the entire drama was initiated because (as he explained it) Weberman had been harassing him for years and had refused to stop. He acknowledged that Folkways and Broadside were not the real targets, only Weberman. (THAT made me wonder if the call was from someone put up to it by Weberman and doing a spot-on Dylan; but I dared not raise that nor try to contact A.J. Weberman since my last call with him had been him yelling obscenities at me for getting him sued.)

This "Dylan" expressed surprise that I was involved, because he was aware that I was not a target of his suit. (He, apparently, was not aware of why my name had been pulled; or at least he never mentioned the FBI.) His dismay seemed genuine, and he was very convincing arguing that things had spiraled beyond his intent.

It was obvious that he had read our complaint because he said that he was surprised that I had never talked to Weberman. (At the time we filed, I had not.) Almost pleading, he said that he did not know me and noted that I do not know him, and we had no "beef" with each other. *(I noted the usage of the very non-midwestern term "beef", since he was from Minnesota.)*

Seeming to relax a little he almost scolded me, saying that Sis or I should have called him before we "got involved with that guy."

He said that even before he was served, he had intended to call me to see if I could talk to Weberman and get him to "stop his shit." I suspected that was a lie, since Dylan wasn't aware that the producer of the album was even involved in the legal action until all of the latest developments.

His tone then softened once more, and he repeated that this was all a big mistake caused by "that fucked-up guy". Again, almost pleading, he said that he didn't mean for things to end up like this. (I felt a con-job coming.)

He asked me if we could just forget about everything; he would drop his suit and I would drop mine and "everything will be cool". He said that "the lawyers" can deal with "that other guy".

I thought about it for almost ten-whole-seconds before I agreed. I asked for his assurance that Moe, Sis, and Gordon would be completely released from any action. He responded with a "yeah, yeah, yeah". I told him that I agreed.

The conversation ended with an upbeat tone in his voice and an invitation to be his guest that night at the *Nashville Municipal Auditorium*. I graciously declined but thanked him, nonetheless.

I returned my focus to my newspaper job and being backstage at *The Opry* every Friday and Saturday night. After I wrote a feature about my old friend *"Jumping" Bill Carlisle*, who then was 70-years-old, he and I

THE POET LAUREATE SOUL OF FOLKIE ROCK & ROLL

became closer friends than we had been years earlier as just acquaintance-friends. I had his home number and he and I talked on the phone a couple of times a week every week.

At the paper itself, as *"design editor"* most of my time was spent outside the newsroom and instead, upstairs in the composing room where the papers were physically prepared for printing. The more time I spent there, the more aware I became of the tyrannical work rules and management procedures.

Four years before my arrival, the long-time family-owned paper chain had been purchased by a South Carolina based chain of small papers and television and radio stations. Their corporate employee relations were archaically out of the mill-village era and the more the headquarters put budget performance pressure on local management, the more oppressive life became for the blue-collar employees.

That corporate pressure eventually leeched into the newsroom and increased the workload on the editorial staff. The otherwise congenial Executive Editor was forced into what must have been a very uncomfortable adversarial relationship with his own newsroom. In hindsight, I feel terrible for him; but at the time, I was at war.

I contacted the *Newspaper Guild* and asked them to organize our paper. They arrogantly informed me that there is no place in the State of Tennessee that would "qualify" for membership in The Guild because Tennessee was a "remote location", had a small population, lacked a sophisticated staff, and our pay was too-low to interest them. *Union solidarity, Wow.*

Only partially discouraged, I reached out to the *International Typographical Union*, the largest and strongest of the 19th century AFL labor unions. They jumped at the chance and sent an organizer to meet with me. He prepared documentation for a complex bargaining unit made up of the newsroom, compositors, typographers, and pressmen.

The South Carolina company that owned the paper hired an anti-union law firm that began a campaign that eventually landed them in court over a string of unfair labor practice charges. As for me, they first gave me a $260-a-week pay raise —apparently an attempt to buy me off. When that didn't quell the union, they changed my duties from "design editor" to "copy editor" and put me under a "supervisor" who (among other things) wrote such headlines as *"Shawl Of Iran Removed"* (for Shah).

The organizing drive stretched out for months with the company's anti-union tactics becoming more and more intense. Most of my organizers were fired on trumped-up charges, despite doing so being overtly an *"unfair labor practice"*. The handwriting was on the wall; I began job-hunting.

THE LEGEND DIES ON — GARY GREEN

In relatively no time, I was offered a job by a retired *U.S. Congressman* to be editor of a small newspaper that he owned about 65 miles east of Nashville. In not-one-of-my-more-eloquent moments, I wrote a resignation letter to the anti-union editor; its entire text read: "I quit. Fuck you. Love Gary."

A week later I was installed as editor of the new paper and the Congressman was suggesting investigative stories to (as he put it) "get you and this paper on the map". It never entered my mind that my previous singing at political rallies would create a whole new drama.

Meanwhile, about a week after my phone conversation with the I'm-not-so-sure-it-was-Bob-Dylan guy, Moe Asch's attorneys received a "Settlement Agreement" from CBS Inc. That document proffered that CBS would agree to forgo all "damages" in exchange for Moe agreeing to a permanent cease-and-desist from selling that or any Bob Dylan recording, withdrawing the recording from the current and all future catalogs, a reaffirmation from Weberman of his previous cease-and-desist, and the destruction-burning-incineration of all outstanding records, and the "Master Tape and all copies" in the presence of CBS representatives.

Mister Asch eagerly accepted the terms and set the appointment at an incinerator for the ceremonial destruction of the Master. The CBS representatives tossed it in and watched it crackle and burn. The albums from the warehouse had already been seized by the FBI, so Moe had none to be destroyed. Broadside Album Number 12 disappeared forever[161].

All during the drama, from the first filing, Moe had no communication with me and would not return my calls. I was certain that I was on his shit list, and I was ruined forever (despite having more-or-less settled the lawsuit for him by my intended countersuit).

Nonetheless, about a week after the incineration, I received a *Federal Express* package from *Folkways Records & Service Corporation*. No letter, no note, no explanation; only a 12-inch studio tape reel in a box.

I threaded it into my tape console and hit "PLAY". It was the original studio master tape of the controversial album. I have no idea what Moe burned at the incinerator; but it was not the master tape; THAT is in my possession today, damned-near a half-century later.

A couple of years afterwards, Moe told me, "hold on to it for a few years; someday it will be worth a lot, and you can tell this story." At the time of this writing, I still am holding on to it and THIS is the first time I have told the *whole* story.

---

[161]To this day, it remains one of a very few (if not the only) Folkways album(s) not available through the Smithsonian.

THE POET LAUREATE SOUL OF FOLKIE ROCK & ROLL

The 3rd Movement
minuet: *"Don't Ya'll Think This Outlaw Bit's Done Got Out of Hand"*[162]

---

[162] (from the song of the same title) ©1978 Waylon Jennings Music, 3817 17th Avenue South, Nashville

THE LEGEND DIES ON — GARY GREEN

Opus Seventeen:
Songs To Die For — Literally

You know what my momma used to tell me:
"If ya can't find something to live for
Then you best, find something ta die for"
—Túpac Amaru Shakur[163]

Despite it being a double action standard-issue Police .357 Magnum revolver, the *Tennessee Bureau of Investigation* agent cocked his gun and pressed the barrel against the back of my head. If he had so-much-as sneezed, the gun would have fired and blown my brains all over the mayor's office.

The cop yelled at me as he shoved me against the wall, *"Don't even move, you Communist bastard. Let's see you go to the Grand Ole Opry now!"* His words resounded the September 1973 taunting by Chilean Army officer *Pedro Barrientos* as he shot folksinger *Víctor Jara*, "let's hear you sing your songs now, Communist!"

With the benefit of almost a half-century of hindsight, I can confidently say that those agents probably were not consciously part of any conspiracy or plot to silence a folksinger. They simply were following orders to arrest a "dangerous communist agent" who was "attempting to extort" a former State Trooper. Nonetheless, it clearly had something to do with my music or they wouldn't have mentioned *The Opry*.

Truly living in a naïve oblivion, I genuinely saw myself as nothing more than a hillbilly guitar picker with a penchant for rock & roll and a country-church-infused belief in "truth, justice, and the American way".

Driven straight out of the moral passion plays of black-and-white primetime television, I really had no grasp that my typewriter and guitar could have been actual weapons that would cause trembling rage in the corridors of power.

The cold blue steel barrel of that gun against my skull was more than an epiphanical revelation. It showed me the dreadful reality of life contained in all of the colorful ballads and adventures that had enthralled me since childhood. It showed me that merely singing a song or putting words on paper actually could get a person killed. *It changed everything for me.*

Equally disturbing, it showed me that overlord suzerains could convince or pay (or both) never-ending legions of simple folks to carry out

---

[163] "Something 2 Die 4" by Curtis Mayfield, Deon Evans, and Túpac Amaru Shakur; ©Universal Music Publishing Group, Warner Chappell Music, Inc

their disdainful vengeance. Foot-soldiers with the most noble intentions could be convinced to carry out malevolent acts under the guise of righteous duty. A decade later, I might have called it *an old Jedi mind trick.*

Perhaps ... just perhaps... that explained why so many otherwise good people willingly participated in the atrocities against the Vietnamese people in the name of "American patriotism" and "protecting freedom". It defined what Brother Kirk had once said to me, "There is no creature on God's green earth more confused than a Black man who becomes a policeman."

Perhaps manipulative subterfuge was *that* powerful. Maybe such false-duty was driving the badged and official gunmen threatening my life on that night.

Whatever their motivation, wielding that gun at my head gave me visions of the assassination of Ella May Wiggins; and this was not exactly what I had in mind when I wanted my songs to have the kind of impact that hers did. Nonetheless, I felt death knocking at my door and I opted for cooperative silence rather than confrontation; probably a prudent decision, and one that allowed me to be here today to tell this story, my dear reader.

Ostensibly, it had begun innocently enough with a series of dramas related to my new job and the search for a new audience for my songs. At the time, it just didn't enter my mind that it actually was the culmination of years of investigations into my music, my lyrics, and my choice of venues. I should have picked up on that underlying reality when the would-be assassin mentioned *The Opry* and called me a *Communist.*

None of that was clear to me until famed radical lawyer *William Kunstler* took my case. (The New York Times had called him "the country's most controversial and, perhaps, its best-known lawyer".) He built a strong argument that the arrest had little to do with newspapering drama and more to do with my music and political activism.

The funny thing was (if funny is even an appropriate description) I still did not consider myself to be a "political activist" I really saw myself as that hillbilly folksinger who sang about injustices. But I certainly wasn't going to debate the point with America's best-known lawyer.

At that time, in my mind, the ordeal started in January of 1980 when I took the job (at a $4,000 cut in pay) as editor and general manager of the Congressman's newspaper. I had thought I was escaping the drama of the union-organizing drive's management harassment.

Boy was I wrong! All I did was make it easier to silence me. The whole concept that I had an audience large enough that I would be considered a threat... was just absurd to me. It was even sillier than Phil Och and Gordon Friesen thinking the CIA had crushed Phil's vocal chords; and Phil had an actual following.

THE LEGEND DIES ON — GARY GREEN

I could name a hundred singer-songwriters with real followings and who were a lot more "dangerous" than me with their talents and lyrics. Granted, they might not also be award-winning members of "the working press" and legitimate candidates for U.S. Congress mentored by a 15-term Congressman; but, damn, they were a lot more talented, had "fans", and large audiences.

Yes, I had just been appointed to the Board of Directors of the *American Indigenous Music Ensemble*, sharing Board status with *B. B. King, Leonard Bernstein, Chet Atkins,* and other *actually* notable people. But that didn't make me on the level with such luminaries; I felt like I was appointed just to have a token hillbilly hippie.

With the benefit of a half-century since that gun was put against my head, I mention all of these after-the-fact reflections to share my frame-of-mind as it was happening. I mean, yeah, I was "well-known" in limited circles; but come on! I was not a real "threat" to anyone — and especially not to government powers.

The whole thing was just too fantastical to be real. Though, I *should* have been tipped off a few years earlier when FBI Director Clarence Kelley had *personally* responded to my questions about the redacted sections of my FBI files by saying release of the information would pose "a threat to national security".

This terrifying guns-drawn arrest had grown from the events around my second day at work at the Congressman's newspaper. On that day, I discovered that the company books had been altered and the newspaper was $26,000 in debt with another $13,000 in bad checks floating around the county. *(In 2020's money that would be about $93,000 and $46,500 respectively.)* More alarmingly, there was not enough money in the bank nor from Accounts Payable to meet the upcoming payroll for the staff.

The best I could tell, the Congressman had no idea that the money had been stolen or that the books had been doctored to hide it from him and other members of his Board of Directors. Convinced of their innocence in the scam, I agreed to work with the Board to arrange a financial bailout by selling their failing paper to a small regional chain. I negotiated a deal for them in which they would retrain minority ownership, with the chain as the majority owner and sole decision maker.

During the lull between discovering the financial discrepancies and closing on the bailout sale, I had no income and eventually filed bankruptcy. Shortly after I filed, one of the board members stepped up to help me by offering to bankroll a printing and publishing business for me. I eagerly agreed, withdrew the bankruptcy before it was processed, and accepted 49 percent ownership (and profits).

THE POET LAUREATE SOUL OF FOLKIE ROCK & ROLL

I also contacted the *International Typographical Union*, where I was still paying dues, and signed a union contract for the shop. That gave us a "union label" for our printing and an easy-in for political print jobs.

In addition to printing contracts, we began publishing a weekly entertainment magazine, which allowed me to continue press-access to the Nashville country music world as well as national television, film, and theater access. It also gave me the ability to write and publish a book-length analysis of changes in the Country Music industry. (I worked with my old friend Justin Tubb for that piece.)

All of that spurred the retired Congressman to also come to my aid; at least in his mind that is what he was doing. Again, in hindsight, what he actually did was inadvertently set me up for a near-assassination, a legal nightmare, and the pivotal climax of the FBI's focusing on me from their Wounded Knee infiltration and anti-war surveillance. I should have listened to the folks at Highlander Folk Center when they gave us the rifle.

The Congressman, however, was not part of any of that; and, apparently, the FBI didn't even bother to notify him that he was dealing with such a "dangerous" character. His plan was that he wanted me to run for his old Congressional seat. *Seriously.* That seat was again going to be open because the holder of it, 30-year-old Al Gore Jr., was planning to run for the U.S. Senate. The plan appealed to both my ego and my desire for progressive change in government policies.

And... it wasn't unprecedented. Ricky Nelson's piano player, singer-songwriter *Jimmie Davis*, had been elected Governor of Louisiana. He wrote *You Are My Sunshine* and Hank William's *I Heard That Lonesome Whistle*; and even had a number one country hit song while he was Governor. Also, Roy Acuff had run for (and lost) Governor of Tennessee. I thought it would be cool to have a folk-singing rock-and-roll poet as a member of the United States Congress from Tennessee.

Retired from Congress for three years, Joe L. Evins had served 15 terms in Washington and had been a close confidant of President Lyndon Johnson, heading the Democratic Party's patronage committee. Even in retirement, Congressman Evins was still a powerful political "mover and shaker" in Tennessee as well as in D.C.

Despite being a conservative Democrat voting against the Civil Rights Act of 1964, he was a key vote for Johnson on the 1965 Voting Rights Act. He had the same kind of voting record on the Vietnam war; at first supporting every escalation, eventually seeing the reality of it and strongly opposing escalation. His political track record was complex, and at times questionable; but he knew my background and even listened to me play guitar and sing my songs. He said that he believed the time was right for me to be a member of the United States Congress. *No, really!*

THE LEGEND DIES ON — GARY GREEN

He recruited a former aide to the Governor of Tennessee as well as a number of other statewide political leaders and began training me to run for office in the mostly-rural district. At least rural Tennessee folks were "my people", from my childhood.

His plan was two-fold: firstly, he wanted me to become known to the voters; and secondly, he believed that I needed to be recognized not as just a hillbilly hippie singer but as a successful businessman and a crusading journalist fighting for the rights of the voters in the district.

For the first goal, he began driving me around the district in his blue Chrysler New Yorker; he asked me not to drive my Porsche, because it was "too high-falutin" (as he put it) for "a man of the people" (even though I paid less for it than he paid for that big Chrysler). Visiting constituents, door-to-door, was a daily grind, but incredibly educational about the methodology of local (or at least Congressional-district-level) rural campaigning.

Our campaigning also introduced me to the tremendous amount of data on voter registration tapes *(computers in those days were huge mainframes with data stored on magnetic tape media)*. Understanding what information was available allowed me to see all sorts of potential for matching individuals' backgrounds with specific issues. That part of playing politics was genuinely interesting.

His second goal was more complex. Congressman Evins arranged to have my 49% ownership in the printshop converted to 16% ownership of the just-sold newspaper. (I have no idea what metric for valuation allowed him to come up with that percentage.) He then began conspiring with me to transform the newspaper into an organizing tool for my campaign, despite our not having decision-making authority at the paper. I *did* remain on as editor, at least nominally.

The stories that he suggested to serve the purpose were to be an exposé series reporting on vote-buying schemes across the state; something the Congressman knew well because he had benefited from it. We ran the first of the series, citing anonymous sources (who in reality were Congressman Evins and my campaign manager who had *purchased* votes on behalf of the sitting Governor). After the first story in the series, dozens of people contacted me to become sources for the series of stories; and *that* confirmed that the scope of the voter fraud reached across the state and all the way to the Governor's office as I had been told initially.

That series also brought a number of violent reactions. Hot tar was poured on the door of the newspaper office, jamming the locks to enter the building. Then our receptionist was attacked with hot tar and feathers poured on her car and forearm.

THE POET LAUREATE SOUL OF FOLKIE ROCK & ROLL

Rather than deter us, the attacks made us even more resolved to crusade; and suddenly I was in demand as a speaker at civic associations and social clubs. It perfectly followed Congressman Evins' plan.

What did *not* follow his plan was my outraged reaction to the tar-and-feathering. Until then, I didn't even know *that* was a real thing; I thought it was some bad-movie bullshit for colorful dialogue. Turned out, nope, it definitely was real. I was furious.

At each speaking engagement I angrily challenged the perpetrators, "if you have a problem, then come after ME and not after my people. Don't be cowards; come face ME!"

The Congressman scolded me for those outbursts. He also warned me that I might be opening myself up to direct attacks, which could hurt me "politically".

The next installment of my series of stories included a photograph I had taken with a hidden camera; the picture showed a local businessman making a cash payoff to a precinct captain for a block of votes. It also contained a confession from a mayoral candidate, telling me exactly how many votes would be cast in his upcoming election and the number by which he would win the election.

On the day of the city elections (exactly a year before my Congressional election-day), I walked out of the vote count and across the lawn at the county courthouse. The businessman who I had photographed paying for votes, appeared from one side of the building. Six of his employees surrounded me as he walked forward. Weighing in at around 300 pounds (compared to my then-only 150 pounds), he began beating me while his compatriots held my arms and legs.

The brutal assault on a well-known editor (and Congressional candidate) brought wire service along with national newspaper and television attention. New investigations were launched by several major newspapers and TV stations; and they too found the vote frauds that the Congressman and I had exposed.

One of those investigations revealed that a state election fraud criminal investigation, eight years earlier, had been quashed by a regional district attorney —who, himself, was an elected official (and, according to the Congressman, benefited from bought votes). That investigation also revealed that the district attorney was the business partner of the man who had assaulted me. This did not bode well for a happy ending for me —*especially after I wrote a banner headline exposing that connection.*

Eventually there was so much press pressure (as well as political pressure and public outcry) that a Grand Jury was convened to investigate the claims. To avoid being called before that Grand Jury, Congressman Evins decided to take his annual extended vacation to Florida, essentially

THE LEGEND DIES ON — GARY GREEN

leaving me on my own with only a phone number to call in Florida if there was "an emergency".

At that time, Tennessee law allowed automatic immunity from incrimination for any Grand Jury witness who offered evidence that would aid in prosecution of others. Armed with that knowledge and having talked to my news sources, I testified before the Grand Jury *and revealed the names of those sources* that had agreed to testify under that immunity law.

I did not, however, reveal the Congressman or other sources who did not agree in advance. My hope was that with the immunity law, my sources would sing like birds as they had indicated to me that they would.

Several of my sources were called before the Grand Jury, one-by-one; but all were gathered into a waiting room together. This allowed them to see each other (and thus be revealed to each other). The district attorney forced each witness (under threat of not being allowed to testify for immunity) to sign a waiver of that immunity. He also refused to subpoena a number of witnesses who were probably immune to his threats —including local clergy that had firsthand knowledge of the voter fraud.

I continued my stories for the paper and in the investigation, I learned that several members of the Grand Jury were family members or employees of the man who had assaulted me. I demanded that those jurors be recused, and when the district attorney refused, I appealed to the district judge.

Small town politics: The judge, of course, turned out to be a childhood friend of the district attorney; so, he also refused to act. Finally, a call from my campaign manager to the Governor's office spurred the State to intervene and remove the questionable jurors. The judge then replaced them with other employees of the district attorney's partner; effectively nullifying the removal.

In the midst of all of this absurd small-town drama, the President of the local NAACP, who knew of my reputation in the Civil Rights Movement, contacted me. He said that the son of one of his Board members had been offered $5,000 to murder me. *(I thought I should have been worth much more than that.)* He added that the offer had been refused, but cautioned me that since it was made, then there likely would be other offers until someone agreed to kill me.

A Tennessee State Senator, loyal to Congressman Evins, also came to see me, reporting that he had been told that a "contract" had been put out to assassinate me. He said that the order had come from "somebody high up the political ladder" *(whatever that meant)*. He would elaborate no further.

Then the town's former Chief-of-Police visited me at home late at night to tell me that his "informants" had told him that someone in official law enforcement circles already had been hired to kill me.

THE POET LAUREATE SOUL OF FOLKIE ROCK & ROLL

The chairman of the election commission, who had provided much of the information for my stories, advised me to "get out of town before they get you".

And, then the High Sheriff of the County advised me to get a gun and make plans to get out of town. He said he had heard that I was going to be killed.

The Sheriff and the sitting Town Police Chief also told me that the Grand Jury investigation would "not go anywhere" and that several of the witnesses had been threatened by Grand Jury members.

A couple of days later, the Sheriff told me that he had heard rumors that the owner of the chain of newspapers was going to be visited at home late at night and threatened as well. Shortly after that warning, the owner called me to tell me that there would be no more investigative reporting and going forward I would only report "good news".

A few days later, the Grand Jury recalled me; this time questioning me about my motive for writing the stories and demanding to know who had "put me up to it". They asked if I knew the stories were lies or if I was just repeating what someone had ordered me to write.

I could see that the process was a waste of time. It was equally clear that I could no longer work for the newspaper chain and the congressional plans would be lost once the Grand Jury blasted the paper's credibility. Even if that were not the case, all of that drama did not interest me at all. And, for the first time, I was starting to be concerned about the death threats.

I decided to call Brother Kirk in New York. His advice did not surprise me; he told me to get out of there and head back to The City. He chastised me for "getting involved in local politics". In hindsight, I should have listened to him too.

During the same week, the newly-elected mayor, a retired State Tropper, approached the advertising manager of the paper and asked him to offer me one-thousand-dollars for each percentage of ownership that I had in the paper. He said that he wanted to buy me out and run me out of town but needed someone else to approach me. The advertising manager did so.

Finally, I decided to call the Congressman's emergency number in Florida. I told him everything that had happened, including the rumors about my impending murder. His advice was short, sweet, and to-the-point: he said that I should accept the mayor's offer for my stock and leave Tennessee for Washington DC. He cautioned me to get a cashier's check for the sale and prepare a stock transfer document. He added that he would "make arrangements" for me when I reached Washington. He also cautioned me not to mention his name to anyone. I agreed.

THE LEGEND DIES ON — GARY GREEN

Following his guidance, I called the mayor and accepted the offer to sell my interest. I requested the certified check, and he agreed. He asked me to come to his office later that evening.

At 7:30 p.m. the mayor tossed me a cloth bag full of hundred-dollar bills: no check, all cash. As he presented the bag, he loudly announced to me, "here is your money, if this is the only way to stop you from writing the lies, I will pay you off."

Stunned that his tone that was nothing like what he had said before, I asked what he was talking about. I told him that I could understand why he was upset with all the political turmoil, but I didn't know what he meant about lies since he was one of my sources.

Before I could say another word, the door to his office opened and the agents charged in, guns drawn. That is when the first agent pulled back the hammer on his gun and put the barrel to the back of my head.

For the next two hours the agents and two investigators from the District Attorney's office questioned me about additional sources for the vote-buying stories. They asked about my campaign manager. They asked about "communist agitators in the State". They asked "what else" I was planning to report. They asked me if I had any new records coming out with any country music stars singing with me. They never asked about the newspaper sale, the money, nor my conversations with the mayor; and when I raised those issues, they changed the subject.

At the end of their questioning, I asked if I was being arrested. The lead agent answered, "not by us. It's up to the Sheriff". They handcuffed me behind my back and took me across the courthouse square to the Sheriff's office at the County Jail. They kept the cash and my stock certificates.

The Sheriff, himself, met us just inside the door. He led me to a "holding cell" where no other prisoners were being held. Then he disappeared to confer with the agents that had delivered me to him.

After about 45 minutes, he returned and led me to his office. No one else was around. Inside his private office, he removed my handcuffs and asked me if I was "okay". Oddly enough, I was, and I told him so.

He told me that my "enemies" (who he did not name) had paid an inmate in the county jail to kill me that night. He reminded me that he was loyal to Joe L. Evins, and he was going to release me. As he let me go, he told me that if I was smart, I would leave the county immediately.

After packing my car, I pulled out of my driveway and was immediately arrested by town police for running a stop sign. There, of course, was no stop sign at my driveway. The officer demanded to see my driver's license.

When I handed him the license, he put it in his pocket and arrested me for "driving without a license". He handcuffed me and took me back to the jail; but stopped first at the county magistrate's office.

THE POET LAUREATE SOUL OF FOLKIE ROCK & ROLL

The judge there placed me under a $500 bail, which of course I did not have money to pay. Fortunately, the bail bondsman working at the courthouse was the brother-in-law of my campaign manager and he immediately posted the bond for me, advising me to get out of the county immediately.

Taking back roads, which I knew were rarely patrolled, I made it across the county line. However, a few seconds after entering the next county to the east, a Silverado pickup truck pulled in behind me. After coming within a couple of feet from my rear bumper, the driver leaned out the window and began firing a rifle at me.

The shot was missed, and I downshifted my little Porsche 914 to accelerate away from him. The ordeal turned into a high-speed chase, filled with sharp curves on roads that I was unfamiliar with, but that my pursuer seemed to know well. He continued shooting and thankfully continued missing.

When we reached an intersection with a main highway, I could see two State Police cars parked in a median strip. I pulled up to them, bounded from my car, and ran up to them. Breathlessly, I reported that I was being chased by a guy shooting at me from a pickup truck. Both officers perked up.

A few seconds later, the truck pulled up and the driver stepped out, holding a badge in his hand. He identified himself as the Assistant City Police Chief back in the town where I had escaped. He told the Troopers that I was a fleeing extortion suspect, and he was taking me back for questioning at the County Jail.

I told them that he was lying, but they chose not to believe the hippie in the sports car; especially after he added that I was an "outside agitator" sent into the county to "cause trouble" for their former co-worker who was now mayor. The Troopers agreed to escort me to the County Jail and turn me over to the Sheriff. *(I was certain that if they had not escorted me, the Assistant Chief would have murdered me.)*

Once again, the Sheriff took custody; and once again he released me as soon as my escorts left. He suggested I drive west rather than east this time. I, of course, complied. I was getting very nervous about the whole situation.

This time, rather than a backroad, I took the Interstate Highway. Nonetheless, as soon as I crossed the county line, I was pulled over by a deputy sheriff in *that* county. He demanded to see my license, and when I told him I didn't have it with me, he arrested me and took me to his county jail, where I was met by *his* sheriff.

That sheriff was even more friendly than the one in my county. He told me that my car and description had been radioed to every county in Middle Tennessee with instructions that I am armed and dangerous. He said

THE LEGEND DIES ON — GARY GREEN

that he was certain that the purpose was to get me shot "by some hothead deputy".

He explained that he had been loyal to Congressman Evins for decades and he knew what was "going on with these guys". He volunteered to give me a police escort through the rural counties all the way to Nashville where he said, "you'll be safe". I accepted his offer and spent the next few nights in the relative safety of Nashville. At least there I knew the "lay of the land" in case I had to escape.

Meanwhile, an attorney for the mayor told a trustee for the Federal bankruptcy judge that my earlier filing and withdrawal of the bankruptcy had been part of a scheme to avoid paying taxes on unreported stocks and thousands of dollars in cash that the mayor had paid me.

The next morning, the Grand Jury reconvened and issued three sealed indictments against *ME*: apparently charging extortion, fraud, and conspiracy. One of the members of the Grand Jury tipped off the bail bondsman who in turn called Congressman Evins. The Congressman immediately issued a public statement that said, among other things:

"It is my personal opinion that Gary Green was attempting to render a public service. However, I think he made his biggest mistake by including the District Attorney General as somehow being involved when some of the candidates were charged with vote buying."

I made several strategic phone calls from pay phones in Nashville, using phone-phreaking techniques that I had learned as a child. I called the Congressman. I called William Kunstler. I called Pete Seeger. And I called Moe Asch.

After Bill Kunstler agreed to take my case, Congressman Evins sent a large retainer check to him in New York. They also talked on the phone after Kunstler gave me specific instructions for avoiding arrest and what to do if I failed.

"Why, anyone can see that they've set you up for this," the Congressman told me on the phone, adding, "the Grand Jury will never go for it."

Moe Asch suggested that I record a new album for Folkways Records and the advance plus royalties would be used for my legal defense fund, which he suggested that I get someone to set up for me immediately.

He also gave me a phone number for *Ewan MacColl*, a well-known folksinger in England. Two years earlier Ewan (whose real name was James Miller) had married *Peggy Seeger* (Pete's half-sister). Moe sent a letter to Ewan and Peggy, telling them about my plight and suggesting that we make plans to get me to the UK for at least safety, if not asylum.

Ewan and Peggy sent Kunstler money for my defense and sent a letter to my parents' address inviting me to come to England and connect with them. Pete and Toshi Seeger also sent money to Kunstler for my defense. Pete also said that he would talk with Moe Asch about ideas for my defense fund album.

THE POET LAUREATE SOUL OF FOLKIE ROCK & ROLL

Meanwhile, the local police lost track of me and called the FBI to report a new felony: *Interstate Flight To Avoid Prosecution*. Of that one, I actually was guilty, though the pending prosecution was bogus.

My campaign manager's relative who had posted my bail, panicked when he was questioned by the FBI. To show that he was not a "co-conspirator" he agreed to list me as a *fugitive* who had jumped bail. He then sent my file to a national bounty-hunter agency that he used.

Added to that, the guy who had assaulted me in front of the courthouse offered a $1,000 cash reward to any bounty hunter who would "capture or kill" me. *Great*.

I learned, a few months later, that the Tennessee authorities had listed me as "armed and dangerous" on NCIC (the FBI's *National Crime Information Center* computer network connected to most police departments in the country). That designation meant that I should be approached with guns drawn and the intention to shoot me.

Thus begin a new life for me: folksinger *and wanted fugitive.*

The most famous lawyer in the country was warning me that he was concerned that someone wanted to murder me not just because of the voter-fraud exposé, but because of a decade of writing and singing songs that challenged powerful people. *Serious stuff!*

While on the surface I was caught up in the fantasy-drama of it all, more seriously I was trying to deal with the stark terror of it all and the fear of actual execution. Amid those roller-coaster emotions, I could also felt a deeper anger growing inside me. It reminded me of Arlo Guthrie's lyrics in *Alice's Restaurant*:

"I mean I'm sittin' here on the Group W bench, 'cause you want to know if I'm moral enough join the army, burn women, kids, houses and villages after bein' a litterbug." He looked at me and said, "Kid, we don't like your kind, and we're gonna send your fingerprints off to Washington."[164]

Only, my situation was a lot worse; instead of *sending my fingerprints off to Washington*, they were going to murder me... *just like they did Ella May Wiggins*. For the horrendous crime of exposing voter fraud — *actually, for openly singing opposition to the power structure*— I was ordered dead. I had been beaten in the town square, run out of town, and now slated for death. *And I wasn't even famous!*

Well, at least I reached my goal: *like Ella May, I had written songs that could get me killed.*

---

[164] Alice's Restaurant Massacree lyrics © Primary Wave Songs, Appleseed Agt, Appleseed Music Inc. Words & Music by Arlo Davy Guthrie

THE LEGEND DIES ON — GARY GREEN

Opus Eighteen:
You Can't Write Songs If You're Dead

And I can still hear Rudy's Farm praise Tennessee.
Lord I can almost taste that sassafras tea.
I don't know where I'm going, but I know where I've been.
And I know I can never go back home again.
— *I Can Never Go Home Again*, as recorded on Folkways Records album FH5356, *Gary Green Still At Large*

*I*n my most "radical" days back at the University of Tennessee, I had been part of a new "underground railroad" network that arranged housing, food, and transportation for political fugitives and radicals living "underground". Today we'd probably call it "living off the grid"; but in those days it was the leftist underground part of something called "The Movement".

I was a facilitator with an apartment, a car, food, an encyclopedic knowledge of rural backroads throughout the South, and a good understanding of clandestine operations. The existence of the network was an in-plain-sight secret known not only to law enforcement but to general pop culture. One of the "big five" publishers even issued a trade paperback *Guide To Underground America* that listed contact addresses and phone numbers —including my apartment in Knoxville.

Despite that in-your-face publicity, there also was a hidden side to that world which genuinely facilitated harboring fugitives. The public side of it just meant that the actual clandestine activities required extraordinary security since we all knew we were being watched.

Though I had grown into that "secret" role through my work with pacifist church groups, the FBI was totally justified in their surveillance of me; and I certainly wasn't a pacifist. Among the many wanted fugitives that spent nights harbored at my on-campus apartment were members of *The Weather Underground, The Irish Republican Army, The Symbionese Liberation Front, The Black Panther Party, The War Resisters League, The May 19 Communist Organization, The Black September Organization, Baader–Meinhof Group, American Indian Movement, Organization of Iranian People's Fedaian, The Black Liberation Army*, as well as dozens of "infamous" names of 1960's and 1970's leftwing political fugitives, and a handful "draft dodgers" en route to Canada. Hell, I even had a connection to the Patty-Hearst-related *Symbionese Liberation Army*.

It's funny that looking back on those days, a half-century later, what I remember most is who needed a bath and who were the nicest people. The rest of it is pretty much a blur, because at no time was it ever a major activity. Being part of the underground railroad was just an availability that I had when called upon.

Made up of members or supporters of *Clergy and Laity Concerned* and other devout religious zealots, the semi-informal network was driven, in part, by romantic fantasies of historical underground movements. We even tossed around code terms like *Cross of Lorraine, Follow the Drinking Gourd*, or *John Has A Long Mustache*; all from once-outlawed resistance movements for freedom.

This role-playing drama reinforced that *The Movement* was an historically righteous resistance to illegal government oppression rather than a conspiracy to harbor actual criminals. It seemed like a noble service that could be performed by the folk-singing rock-and-roll poet amidst everything else that I was doing.

As part of all that, I became intimately familiar with the *Soundex* algorithms for encoding real and fake drivers' licenses, the *Modulus 10* algorithm for verifying social security numbers, with which states' vital records were easiest accessible and easiest alterable, which state drivers' licenses did not have photographs on them, and with an entire library of the tools and tricks of hiding out "underground".

As a facilitator for some of those high-profile political fugitive cases, I also had spent many hours training in defensive driving techniques, identifying "tails", and leaving fake trails for law enforcement to follow. As part of that network, I knew how to create cues to send investigators in the wrong direction and to tie them up for days (if not weeks) of following false leads. I even had an actual toolbox of electronic "bug" detection devices and equipment along with a series of telephone scripts to mislead people on the other end of such surveillance.

I had installed "kill switches" in cars so that the brake lights would not come on when the brakes were applied. I even experimented with a very James-Bond-ish triangular wedge to mechanically rotate three different license plates for cars; though I never put that into use. I did, however, several times install kaolinite dumps into carburetors and gas tanks to create massive Bond-like smoke screens to obscure a car from pursuers.

I also had the names, addresses, phone numbers, and code-words for an entire network of similar sympathizers, genuine (not pop culture) underground resistance members, and facilitators all across the US and Europe.

Added to those college-years shenanigans was an intimate knowledge of law enforcement methodologies and procedures that I later learned as a daily newspaper police reporter. My time riding with the undercover operatives of the Vice Squad provided a great understanding of official surveillance techniques.

If ever there had been a person "ready" for the life "underground", it was me. And who, other than Movement people or people who knew the

THE LEGEND DIES ON — GARY GREEN

history of Ella May Wiggins, Victor Jara, and others, would believe that I was slated for death because I wrote songs. I was so obscure that it was unreal, even to me; but then again, so was Ella May. Nonetheless, with my life credibly in danger and the FBI actively looking for me, I pulled out all stops for self-preservation. *So, the adventure began.*

The first step was a trip to the Davidson County (Nashville) Public Library branch where I had researched my award-winning *Tobacco Mosaic Virus* paper. Libraries kept telephone directories and city directories (which contained property records, among other things) for every major city (and many small towns). I pulled the Los Angeles directories and looked for people with the last name Green. I found a longtime resident named Benjamin Green.

I wrote a long rambling letter about my situation, beginning it with the salutation, "Dear Uncle Ben". I ended the letter with a paragraph telling him that I was driving to Los Angeles to "hide out with you, until this blows over". I threw in a few personal things about my brothers and my parents and then signed it, "your favorite nephew, Gary". I, of course, had no Uncle Ben and no California relatives.

I gave that letter to my (former) campaign manager to mail from the post office across the street from the newspaper office. I also gave him a second letter to mail from Nashville exactly one week later.

The second letter was addressed to a friend who worked at a large newspaper in Georgia. In it I also outlined my troubles, but I ended it explaining that I had fled to California to see my Uncle Ben but the police had been watching him so I might be coming to Georgia now, but for the time being I was back in Nashville.

Years later I learned from that friend that the FBI had shown up at his office with warrants to search for any correspondence from me. Clearly, someone was monitoring any mail that came from me (as my paranoia had allowed me to suspect). The agents began questioning him about my whereabouts until his paper's attorneys halted the questioning on First Amendment grounds.

Based on that raid, I cannot imagine what havoc I caused for whoever Benjamin Green was; but I have *no* aunts or uncles anywhere and had picked his name totally at random. *If you are still alive, Sir, I apologize.*

Remember, this was an era just post COINTELPRO when FBI (and other agencies) surveillance without warrants was commonplace. Political dissidents were especially targeted; apparently even obscure ones.

Meanwhile, as the FBI was on those wild-goose-chases, I covered my car with a light coat of mud, making certain to slightly obscure my license plate —but not enough for it to be criminally obscured. I then waited until the heaviest traffic times (afternoon and early evening) and began driving Interstate-only toward the northeast, careful to obey the speed limits.

THE POET LAUREATE SOUL OF FOLKIE ROCK & ROLL

My goal was ultimately to get to New York City to meet with Kunstler, but my immediate target was the city of Baltimore Maryland. My parents had moved there two years earlier, and I knew I could "hideout" there even if authorities came looking for me.

I arrived in Maryland without incident, pulled my car into the backyard behind my parents' house, and told my parents the whole story. They, of course, were more-than supportive.

We unloaded my car and covered it with a weather-tarpaulin. Then they bought me a roundtrip Amtrak (train) ticket to New York so I could meet with my lawyer.[165]

While I was in New York, my Father converted a windowless basement storage room to what I came to call my "Ann Frank Room". Walking through the basement, the entrance to the room was disguised as part of the stairway and a back wall. Unless you knew where to look, you would not know there was a bedroom back there.

Ever since I was a small child, my Mother had instilled in all three of her boys, "Family First". No matter what, the Family comes above all else; right or wrong. Unfortunately, I inadvertently was putting that mantra to the test for her; but she didn't flinch.

In New York, I called William Kunstler from a pay phone down in Greenwich Village, speaking only a prearranged code phrase when he answered. He gave me the name of a deli on Christopher Street where he would meet me. From there he walked me back to his apartment, taking a series of alleyways and streets where we walked against traffic and in the opposite direction of his home. The walk took about twenty minutes, but I learned that his home was only about a half-block from where we had started. The long walk was anti-surveillance subterfuge.

For the next few hours sitting in William Kunstler's home-office at 13 Gay Steet (rather than at his *Center for Constitutional Law*), we discussed strategies to keep me free and to defeat the charges against me. Every few minutes he would get up to check on his wife who was in a leg cast after having been hit by a drunk driver while she was walking across the street near their row house.

We decided to take advantage of the offer from Ewan MacColl, at least visibly. Kunstler arranged a mail drop forwarding service for me in Liverpool at 41 Mill Hill Road in Irby, Heswall: Merseyside England. We would put the word out that I had fled to Ewan and Peggy. For anyone wanting to reach me, that would be my new address; and for anyone wanting to arrest me, it seemingly would require an extradition hearing.

---

[165] In those days, you could travel anonymously by train; no identification was required.

THE LEGEND DIES ON — GARY GREEN

We then planned how to set a false trail to lead investigators there. With my father, my lawyer helped plant the "clues" that we would leave. Meanwhile, he would contact the prosecutor in Tennessee.

When I returned to Baltimore, I drove my car to Dulles International Airport in Virginia, 82 miles from my parents' house. My father followed in his car, to drive me back to Baltimore.

I parked my Porsche in the long-term parking lot, expecting that after some period of time Airport officials would check to see if the car was abandoned. The plan was they would call the police, who would check the tag and determine that it was the car of a Federal fugitive. The hope was that some bright investigator would conclude that I had parked the car there and fled, with the intent of returning. After all, who would abandon a Porsche?

To help them with the myth, I grabbed a Pan American Airlines timetable book from inside the airport and dog-eared a page that listed flights from Dulles to London Heathrow. I then "hid" that timetable book in the car's glove compartment; hoping that a "good" investigator would "find" it there and draw his (or her) own conclusions.

I then went into the international terminal and from a pay telephone called Kunstler, speaking a pre-arranged script. We assumed that his phone was routinely tapped, and this was a call from a fugitive client reporting to him that I was leaving the country for the United Kingdom. I repeated the same call with Congressman Evins, my mother, and two different newspaper colleagues. We assumed that at least one, if not all, would have tapped phones and the false trail would be set even further.

My father then drove me back to Baltimore to continue the plan. The owner of the address in Liverpool was set to forward letters from me back to the USA, with British postmarks. I sent him a mail-packet of five letters addressed to people we assumed would have their mail intercepted. He mailed them on my behalf.

As the reality of this melodrama began to weigh on me, I became aware that a real anger was starting to build in me; and that was even more scary. I didn't know what kind of *David-Banner-Incredible-Hulk* monster might emerge from my already borderline psychotic personality. Frankly, I didn't want to know. I preferred the escapism into my adventure. Unfortunately, that fear-to-anger was bubbling toward something really bad.

A few days later, an FBI agent showed up at my parents' front door. We saw the nondescript Ford with government license plates and realized what it was before he rang the bell. Terrified, I stood behind the door as my mother opened it.

I cannot emphasize enough how horrible the situation was to me, even at the time. Remember, I had been told by reputable authorities that elected officials and law enforcement officers had ordered that I be

THE POET LAUREATE SOUL OF FOLKIE ROCK & ROLL

assassinated. There was strong evidence (and I believed it) indicating an officially sanctioned plot to murder me. A respected United States Congressman, a sitting Sheriff, and the most famous lawyer in America had all told me to flee because I was going to be killed otherwise.

The last time I had contact with a plainclothes agent, he had held a cocked gun against the back of my head.

So, there I was in my parents' home and a potential hitman was ringing the doorbell and my parents were in equal danger with me. This wasn't an adventure anymore; this was life-and-death.

Genuinely terrified, I held a snub-nose police revolver in my hand; and truthfully, I was so scared that if he had forced his way into the house, I would have killed a Federal agent.

Looking back at it, I can't believe that I was that scared and that it had come to that; but I had authoritatively been assured that law enforcement wanted to murder me.

How could this even be happening? I really-really-really wasn't a well-known or particularly successful singer-songwriter. Yet the original arrest had mentioned my music life. On the other hand, if it was only about the newspaper stories, it seemed like a pretty trivial thing to cause a murder. There was just nothing about this that made sense. *Nothing.*

Holding the door, without allowing him inside the house, my mother told the agent that I was living in England, and she had no idea when or even IF I would return. The only follow-up question he asked was, "is he playing in a band there or did he go alone?".

She told him that she had no idea who I was playing with because I had not contacted her other than to say goodbye.

He seemed to accept her sincerity and after handing her his business card (which I still have today), he left. We never saw a Federal-plated car in the neighborhood again. More importantly, I was spared the hell that would have unleashed if I had pulled that trigger; it was bad enough that I even *considered* such a thing.

A few days later, another agent showed up in Gastonia to question one of my brothers who was working at an auto-repair shop there. When I heard about that encounter, I actually felt sorry for the agent.

The repair shop had been having problems with unruly customers walking into the garage or behind the counter, rather than staying in the waiting room. To halt that behavior, the manager had posted more than a dozen signs throughout the waiting room announcing, *"Authorized Personnel Only Behind The Counter"*. Apparently not fully understanding Southern culture nor Gastonia exceptionalism, the agent arrogantly walked through the waiting room, pushed his way behind the counter, and in his heavy New-York-accent announced that he wanted to see my brother. The manager looked at him, pointed to one of the signs, and responded, "can you

THE LEGEND DIES ON — GARY GREEN

read?" The agent, flashed his badge and scolded, "I am with the FBI!" The manager picked up an iron tire tool and walked toward the agent, snarling at him, "I don't give a god-damn who the hell you are with. Get the fuck out from behind this counter, you damned-ignorant-yankee." The agent actually retreated and then politely asked to see my brother. *Welcome to The South; and welcome to Gastonia!*

He asked my brother if he knew where I was. "Nope. My parents said he moved to Europe or somewhere. He was living in Tennessee. But I haven't seen him in years," seemed to satisfy the agent, and he left without follow-up.

So, it appeared, at least for the time being, that I had successfully painted the picture that my interstate flight had become *international* flight. If they checked, they would have found that I did have an active passport (which in those days would not have been recorded on departure.) Basically, they were shit-out-of-luck if they were expecting an easy apprehension.

𝄢𝄢𝄢

Baltimore was the long-time home of a syndicated leftist radio program called *The Great Atlantic Radio Conspiracy*. Broadcasted on more than 200 public radio stations, including the Pacifica network, and many college stations, the weekly show was the product of an intellectual anarchist collective. It was the brainchild of *Doctor Howard J. Ehrlich*, a renowned sociologist and frequently published scholar who also was a Movement contact for the underground railroad.

Shortly after I arrived in Baltimore, the city held its annual City Fair— a celebration of Baltimore's quirky neighborhoods— with live music, food vendors, craft beer, community service tables, and arts & crafts booths. The list of vendors, printed in the local newspapers, included The Great Atlantic Radio Conspiracy (GARC).

After seeing that ad, I visited the street fair and immediately went to the GARC booth. There I introduced myself as *"Charles M. Levy"*. That was the code to identify that I was a fugitive "on the road"[166]. I extended a hand to Howard.

At first, he reacted as if I was any one of hundreds of locals who stopped by the GARC booth. Then he visibly did a double-take and repeated back to me, "Charles Levy". He nodded his head as acknowledgement and understanding. Reminiscent of the film Casablanca's *Berger* flashing his

---

[166] The code name was some fanciful leftist silliness. Karl Marx had shortened his last name from the original *Marx-Levy*, to allow some anonymity to his family which was made up of some leading German rabbis. And, of course, the Anglicization of Karl is not Carl, but rather, Charles. So, "Charles M. Levy" was "Karl Marx". *Like I said: lefty silliness.*

THE POET LAUREATE SOUL OF FOLKIE ROCK & ROLL

ring to *Victor Lazlo*, Howard Ehrlich said, "I am at your service; what do you need?"

I told him that I had a place to stay, food, and transportation but I would be staying in Baltimore for a while and likely would need a support network. He scribbled his home address onto a little note card and told me to come by anytime, 24-hours-a-day.

I took him up on his offer and began spending long days at 2743 Maryland Avenue, two blocks from the campus of Johns Hopkins University (where Howard had taught until his politics got him fired). To his delight and my amusement, once he learned my actual identity, he revealed that The Great Atlantic Radio Conspiracy had often played my *CIA Song* during multiple programs they produced.

He seemed to be very pleased that he was helping hide a "famous" topical folksinger. He asked me to accompany him to *The Bread and Roses Coffeehouse*; a music space reminiscent of 1960's Greenwich Village folk clubs but located in inner-city Baltimore. He assured me that the "collective" that operated the space was made up of all *Movement People* who would protect me at all costs. I agreed to go with him that night.

There I learned that while the Coffeehouse was, in fact, run by a collective of leftist hippies, it had been founded by The Black Panther Party. Though by the time I arrived in Maryland the local Panther chapter was near the end of its organizational strength (with its primary organizers in prison on trumped-up charges).

At one time The Black Panther Party had a phenomenal presence in Baltimore City. In the inner-city Greenmount Avenue/Waverly neighborhood they had organized a food co-op, a free health clinic, breakfast distribution, bookstores, a meeting hall, this music coffeehouse, and even a Federal Credit Union to provide banking for poor people disenfranchised from traditional banks.

After I met with two of the original local Panther organizers, I felt even more comfortable in Baltimore. I knew The Panthers were all about self-defense; and it turned out that both of them had worked with my friend Sherman from Knoxville. So, after checking my bona fides, they determined that I was "cool". They suggested I go to see a supporter who taught at Baltimore's historically Black *Morgan State University* and I agreed to do so.

That worked out really well because Howard had been teaching a class at Morgan called "Ethnoviolence In America". He offered to make the introduction for me. The contact there, who was friendly but not active, suggested that I visit a professor at another Baltimore university who was a "long time political activist". He gave me the name of Doctor *Walt Fuchs* at Towson State University.

THE LEGEND DIES ON — GARY GREEN

Howard was not thrilled with that recommendation because Fuchs identified himself as a Marxist. There was a long history of antagonism between Anarchists and Marxists; and America's New Left had not let go of those 100-year-old animosities. I decided to make that trip later.

Meanwhile, Howard also connected me to his own network of anarchist and anti-war activists in the city. Most of those activities revolved around various collectives that Howard had been part of; GARC, a Free University, an anti-violence group, and other disenfranchised hippies. To several of the collective's members I was a celebrity of sorts; though to other members I was an untrustworthy authoritarian outsider who might even own a gun.

Then, without Howard, I also set up a meeting with the director of the largest labor union council in the city. Anarchist academics rarely had a high level of solidarity with hard-core trade unionists; so, I didn't want to cause waves. Going through an activist Jesuit Priest for the introduction, I was taken to *Ernest B. Crofoot,* head of Council 67 of *The American Federation of State County and Municipal Employees, AFL-CIO.* Though Crofoot was not part of The Movement, *Father Tom* was.

As a bonus, like Howard Ehrlich, Ernie Crofoot knew of my music because he had heard my *The Hammer* song a few years earlier at an AFL-CIO sponsored rally in Washington DC. Though I never told Crofoot that I was a fugitive, Father Tom assured me that the union leader was totally trustworthy and a great contact if I ever needed *political* protection.

Next, I finally traveled to the Baltimore suburb of Towson, where the former State Director of SDS[167] taught philosophy. Wolfgang "Walt" Fuchs (recommended to me from the Panther supporter at Morgan State) was a brilliant, tenured, scholar at Towson State University. He also was part of The Movement underground railroad network. When I arrived in Towson, he was teaching a graduate-level seminar on American Marxism.

I walked into the back of the classroom just as someone auditing the class might do. That day's lecture was a rather detailed discussion of the sub-division of "The New Left" during the last years of the Vietnam War —mostly a discussion of which group split from which other group over which non-issue.

His lecture turned to the role of folk music in The Movement and specifically Woody Guthrie and Pete Seeger. When he read to the class those

---

[167] SDS, Students For A Democratic Society, was the largest student anti-war group during the Vietnam War. At one point it was reported (by the FBI) to have had more than 30,000 members.

THE POET LAUREATE SOUL OF FOLKIE ROCK & ROLL

two "lost verses" of *This Land Is Your Land*, I knew I had found another comrade!

The class was a seminar, conducted in *Socratic* format. Near the end of the 90-minute session, the discussion turned to the students wondering why there were not "modern" versions of Guthrie and Seeger. Walt acknowledged that there probably were, but like Guthrie in his own time were probably obscure. It reminded me of my Free University class that I taught at the University of Tennessee.

That opening seemed perfect for me to chime in and talk about the current crop of Folkways and Broadside artist and to laud *Reverend Frederick Douglas Kirkpatrick* as well as *Phil Ochs* and lesser-known brilliant writers like *Mike Glick, Mike Millius*, and others. My legal status tempered me from mentioning myself.

When the class ended, Walt approached me in the hallway outside and asked, "Who exactly are you and why are you in my class?"

I looked at him and said, "my name is Charles M. Levy". Without a moment's hesitation he responded, "Doctor Marx, I didn't recognize you." A big smile came across his face, and he asked me if I felt safe enough to get a pizza with him. Besides the fact that I was starving, I really wanted to talk with him; so, we walked off campus to a nearby pizzeria.

Walt was a genuine intellectual, completely wrapped in academia and with a mind as sharp as any I had ever come across. Talking with him was both a joy and a cerebral challenge. We talked for several hours, until well after dark. When we finally departed, We both promised to stay in close contact.

With a local protection network in place and the cover of a large city population, I felt confident that I could hide with some relative safety while William Kunstler and Congressman Evins worked to get the charges dropped. Nonetheless, I still wanted to have in place an actual escape plan, should worse-turn-to-worst.

I had read somewhere that the *Constitution of the Soviet Union* provided asylum for politically persecuted people. I certainly met that requirement, though I was not eager to move to cold-ass Russia. However, I was not eager to be in a shoot-out with trigger-happy police assassins either. So, I decided to open up that option as well.

I couldn't very well waltz into the Soviet Embassy on Wisconsin Avenue in DC; it obviously was under constant surveillance. So, I decided to look for less public ways to pursue that option.

One possibility was tucked away on the Eastern Shore of Maryland. The Soviet Union had an official retreat compound there that was protected under international law and flew the Soviet flag. It technically was Soviet soil, just as their embassy in Washington was. If I could get there

THE LEGEND DIES ON — GARY GREEN

and if I could get inside and if I could convince them of my viability ... that was a lot if "ifs" with no plan to fulfill them. But I was desperate.

Within The Movement there were connections to anarchists, communists, revolutionaries, religious fanatics, academics, clergy members, elected officials (Republicans and Democrats) and all types. What united them was an acknowledgement that the United States had political prisoners, regardless of what was projected to the world (and domestically). I was relatively certain that within that network, I could find access to that Eastern Shore complex.

With that process underway and a local Baltimore network watching out for me, I decided to get to work on the new album that Moe Asch had suggested. My legal defense fund was going to need cash, and I needed to decide what to put on it, how much of my situation to make public, what to call the album, and how to best situate it as a fund-raising tool.

I tried to look at the complexities of my situation as objectively as I possibly could from the inside looking out. I reasoned that, realistically, there was a genuine possibility that I would be killed but almost no likelihood of imprisonment. *Prison was never the goal of my pursuers; they wanted me silenced.*

That meant, again trying to look at it realistically, this could be my last album. I wanted to record something that would "close the book" on the Gary Green musical story. In conjunction, it needed to be something powerful enough to raise the money I would need to end the legal nightmare.

For the "book closing" part of the need, that seemed clear enough for me. Moe had tagged the subtitle *Volume Two* on to the *Gary Green: Allegory* album (tacitly implying that that *These Six Strings...* was Volume One). Hence, I decided that whatever I ultimately titled this record, it should have *Gary Green Volume Three* attached to it.

At first, especially after the release of *Allegory*, attaching a volume number to my albums disappointed me. Moe didn't tell me that *Allegory* would be *volume 2*; I didn't discover that until the record was released. I felt that putting volume numbers on my writing was too temporal, too fixed, too finite. It was as if there was a clear beginning and ending; it was as if they had to be listened to in chronological order and there was some reason for that.

It bothered me for a long time that Moe had boxed me into a structured beginning and ending. I decided not to mention my disappointment to anyone, and to be content that I was on Folkways Records at all. It wasn't until several years later that I casually mentioned it to Marilyn Averett while I was visiting the Folkways office in New York and Moe was not there. She was surprised that I was upset at all. She told me that it was a great honor that Moe decided that there would be multiple volumes of *Gary Green* and that I was not another Broadside one-album discovery.

THE POET LAUREATE SOUL OF FOLKIE ROCK & ROLL

She pointed out that Moe had done the same thing with Woody Guthrie: attached volume numbers. She said that Moe was so pleased with his discovery me that it had inspired him to revive the volume-labeling practice not just for me, but for a number of other new artists as well.

When I related that conversation to Walt Fuchs, in Baltimore, he brushed off my concern with an almost-flippant, "Oh, like Led Zeppelin II, Led Zeppelin III, Led Zeppelin IV; yeah, nobody does that."

Point taken, from both Marilyn and Walt. The new album would definitely be *Gary Green volume 3*; but I wanted a tag line like I had done with *Allegory*.

Howard's radio shows began and ended each of their more than one-thousand episodes with the tag line *"This is The Great Atlantic Radio Conspiracy: We Are Still At Large"*. I loved that *We Are Still At Large* line and decided to co-opt it, with Howard's blessings.

Thus, I had the title for the new album: *"Gary Green volume 3 Still At Large..."* The ellipses were an essential part of the title; I wanted the reader to be able to take the title literally relating to my legal status as a fugitive as well as taking it as a continuation from my previous albums.

The next step was to decide on content. To help me determine what to include, I reached out for advice from a handful of trusted people.

Moe Asch told me that I should continue what we had begun with *Allegory*, "Write songs about what is happening now." He had wanted that "gazette" album structure for decades and had tried it over and over. A lot had been going on in the world since my Allegory album. Politically, the country had taken a decisive turn to the right; to the *far* right compared to the late 1960's and early 1970's. There were plenty of subjects begging for a good topical song.

Bill Kunstler said that whatever I recorded I should make certain that the liner notes clearly showed that I was a political fugitive. He thought emphasizing that would be critical to my defense in "telling your story". He also said that I should include the British address for my defense fund.

My family suggested that I should record whatever I felt like playing, not necessarily what anybody was expecting to hear from me. Especially if I felt that it would be my final album, it should contain my musical legacy. *THAT* was the most challenging of any of the suggestions.

Walt and Howard, despite their political differences, both thought that I should record hard-hitting political songs. They both said that I should clearly draw a line in the sand, calling out the people who had come after me —not merely the toes I'd stepped on in Tennessee but the bigger picture going back to domestic spying and harassment from the time I first spoke out (or sang out) against the war and for civil rights.

It was all a lot to think about. I began planning the album, both visually and in content. I was reluctant to put my picture on the cover, because I

THE LEGEND DIES ON — GARY GREEN

was in the process of changing my appearance and I didn't want to show law enforcement or bounty hunters what I looked like. So, the cover was also something to think about.

The easiest to address was my lawyer's concern; so, I got to work immediately on the eight-page insert booklet that went into all Folkways albums. I wrote a somewhat rambling four-and-a-half-page tirade about what had happened. I punctuated it with buzzwords, rhetorical hyperbole, and rabid-ranting against the entire "establishment" and system that had framed me. In the midst of my rambling sermon, was the core of truth of what had happened. There was absolutely no ambiguity about whether or not this was a political frame up. As Kunstler had insisted, I included a full page explaining how to donate to my legal defense fund, including the drop-box address in England.

With my mind on my mortality and the potentially fatal ending of my escapade, I concluded the eight-page booklet in the frame of mind that it might be my last testament to the world. I decided to include a long list of "thank you" messages and acknowledgements, not just for the one album but for everything leading up to it.

I, of course, thanked my family profusely, but I also wrote:

> One must above all thank Moe Asch and his Folkways Records for production of not only my three albums but for the thousands of historically important recordings that he has made available over the years...
>
> ...Thanks also ... to Richmond journalist Kenny Powers ... to Georgia photojournalist Larry Grayam ...
>
> Then things get complicated: Since the work on this album did not spring spontaneously from me but was the result of millions of interactions and processes of my life, acknowledgements must be made for the influences on me from a number of friends. So then, thanks are due to:
>
> Rev. Fred Kirkpatrick; (singer-songwriter) Mike Glick; Bernie Deimer (close college friend); Dr. Walt Fuchs; Pete Seeger; former U.S. Congressman Joe L. Evins; Jerry Stroble and the promotions department at the Grand Ole Opry in Nashville; the Clarksville (Tennessee) Leaf-Chronicle newspaper's back-shop and pressmen who make up the Clarksville Chapel of Nashville Local Number 20 of the International Typographical Union; ITU Representative Billy Mitchell; Bee Spears (bass player for Willie Nelson); Willie Nelson; Waylon Jennings; Captain Midnight; Bill Lee (journalist); Wayne Trotter (editor); Tim Wheeler (staff writer for The Daily World; Communist Party newspaper); Gordon Friesen; Sis Cunningham; William Kunstler; Mike Clark and the Highlander School; Rev. Ben Chavis (civil rights activists and political prisoner of the Wilmington 10); Dr. Helen Olthow (Rev, Chavis' mother); Reba Hancock at Johnny Cash's House of Cash Music in Hendersonville, Tennessee; and dozens of others who will understand why I did not list their names here.
>
> Finally, there is thanks to you, the listener and the reader -the workers of the world whose brains and muscles turn the gears that keep the world moving. Workers of all countries unite!

For the content of the record, I decided to treat the album truly as my last musical will and testament. Side one would be that Gazette-esque that Moe wanted; songs about *what is happening now*.

THE POET LAUREATE SOUL OF FOLKIE ROCK & ROLL

I also decided to pull out all stops and write the new songs with all the anger, fear, and bitterness that the ordeal of being a fugitive had created in me. Without restraint of perspective, I allowed myself to fume and then explode with my anger. The result was a series of very angry but pretty good songs.

Regardless of the "politics" of my first two Folkways albums, the political songs on *this* album were beyond "protest songs" and were truly preachy "message songs". Any semblance of mainstream music was gone. The first side of the record was a radical railing against social and political injustice, presented in bitter cynicism and out-and-out hatred.

For the "B" side of the album, I decided to treat it as an entirely different album; disjointed from the anger and radicalism of the first side. The second side of the record was to be my musical farewell; it was to be what my music might have been if I had not been perverted by the long string of events that began when I attended that Methodist Church anti-war film at the University of Tennessee. It was lighthearted, apolitical, unashamedly country, and concluded with a six-and-a-half minute tribute to Mother Maybelle Carter.

For the cover of the album, since I had decided not to use my "new look" photo, I opted for just a picture of my guitar. In keeping with the semi-comic-relief design of the booklet, I chose a typeface (font) that looked like it had bullet-holes shot in it.

Moe released it early in 1982 and graciously used the full extent of his distribution network to get it into circulation. Donations to my defense fund rolled in almost immediately.

Meanwhile, Kunstler finally had a long conversation with the prosecutor in Tennessee. From a pay phone in New York, he called my mother and told her that he needed to meet with "our friend". Once again, I boarded a train for New York.

THE LEGEND DIES ON — GARY GREEN

Opus Nineteen:
Don't Mess With An Outlaw Folksinger

Don't you think this outlaw bit has done out of hand?
What started out to be a joke, the law don't understand
— Waylon Jennings[168]

Mindset of a genuine outlaw is hard to explain. On the most basic level: Federal, State, and Local agents, acting in their official roles, decided to assassinate me because they didn't like the lyrics to my songs. *No, really!* And as hard-to-grasp (and paranoidly insane) as *that* seems, my reaction to it all was even more bizarre.

I was at the intersection of fear, survival, and rage; none of which were conducive to good behavior. It's hard to explain the feeling —*physical as well as psychological*— that came with ever little ripple that could challenge my freedom. It was nothing like the despair and resolve that came a half-century later when doctors told me that I might have the same prostatic cancer that killed my father. Instead of depressed anguish and melancholy regrets, I was filled with a hateful anger.

Every near confrontation, even the seemingly most benign, triggered an explosion of terror and an associated backlash of defensive posturing. I am sure it appeared as aggression to my victims who had no idea of what triggered it; but it really was just the opposite —defensive cowering. Admittedly, it created many new enemies; people who should have been friends and allies. But there was so much more.

Forget the burning acids constantly climbing my esophagus. Ignore the daily uncontrollable diarrhea each time I would fret over an incident. Ignore having to sleep so light that a city-rat running across dry leaves outside would awaken me ready for defense. There was so much more to it.

What must have been seen as anger, an out-of-control-temper, or generally bad attitude; all were only self-preservation reactions. Remember, I had been told by *government officials* and *law enforcement* that I was going to be assassinated; murdered. I had fled to survive. I had been ready to blow the brains of a Federal agent all over my mother's dress. I was more than cornered. I was terrified.

So, when there was a confrontation, a disagreement, even the most minor slight, it was absolutely necessary for me to interpret it as a life-or-death situation. This is why a half-century later I was still telling people:

---

[168] ©1978 Waylon Jennings Music, 3817 17th Avenue South, Nashville

THE POET LAUREATE SOUL OF FOLKIE ROCK & ROLL

"PLEASE think before you confront someone; you never know what their mental state is and what they are willing to do."

Many times, I felt that since I was going to be killed anyway, I had nothing to lose. So, something as minor as a cross word toward me, or pushing to the front of a line, or (God forbid) bullying of any kind against anyone... could have very easily ended in tragedy.

I was quick to draw my guns. Quick to physically assault. I fought. I pistol-whipped. I screamed. I kicked. I destroyed. And, it didn't even have to be an attack on me; it could be anyone in my orbit. It could even be a perceived attack on a group of people. *(Thank God I was not in that state of mind when the Nazis attacked in Miami Beach; we wouldn't have needed VVAW because I would have either taken them out or died trying.)*

On *many* occasions, I stopped traffic, at gunpoint forced drivers from their cars, and pistol-whipped them in the street; often in front of crowds of witnesses.

I had no control whatsoever; only a desperate clinging to survive. It was a fucked-up behavior; but it was desperate. As I wrote in the lyrics to a song at the time:
>Carrying your life in your hand; For so long you can't recall,
>Makes you a hard and desperate man so
>Ride fast and ride hard; If you're that desperate of a man.

A bullying, racist, sexist, or even slightly aggressive rudeness was as likely as not to trigger unrestrained violence from me. And should anyone dare be fool-enough or confrontational enough, my mindset was that *I had nothing to lose;* so, killing them meant nothing to me. *Raise a hand at me or mine, and die:* it was that simple.

It was ugly. It was scary. It was wrong. It was psychotic. But it was survival. And I couldn't tell anyone about it. They just had to deal with my shit or avoid me. *(To those people who knew me then and who are still around (and reading this), I DO apologize; you couldn't have known, and I couldn't tell you. Even if you knew that I was some kind of fugitive, you could not have known the stress of that lifestyle.)*

It was exhausting. Constantly on high alert. Unable to safely sleep soundly. Having to be suspicious of every new person, but also of even familiar faces around me. Paranoia that was a reality; even when I routinely cleaned one of my guns, I would keep another fully loaded with safety off and within reach. I couldn't afford to be vulnerable; they had announced that they were going to kill me, and they had sent law enforcement to carry it out!

Many times, I wondered how the great mythological outlaws —*Jesse James, Bonnie & Clyde, Doc Holliday, Pretty Boy Floyd*, even *Robin Hood*— could stand it. I mean the movies and books and articles never talked about what they felt and how they held themselves together. Did

THE LEGEND DIES ON — GARY GREEN

Jesse James puke up blood? When John Dillinger pulled off that bank-robbery-disguised-as-a-movie-crew, did he stay awake all night with overpowering dysentery? Did Billy the Kid tremble? THOSE questions were never answered or addressed in even the most academic books. What was the blueprint for being an outlaw?

It wasn't a matter that I somehow didn't "have the stomach" for the violence. My time as a police reporter had taken me to the front lines of violence; often arriving before the cops did at bloody murders and in one case actually performing a radio-instructions assisted tracheotomy. I certainly wasn't squeamish.

What was I missing about being "an outlaw"? Because, clearly, I was not dealing well with it. For me, the mechanism I chose to handle the stress was to ignore it. I threw myself into the role of being an outlaw; but more than a mere role, it became a lifestyle. Fuck with me and die. Only, I wasn't sloganeering; I meant it. Not good; not good... NOT good.

The Tennessee District Attorney General probably wasn't citing Aristotle when he dropped the old *Out Of Sight —Out Of Mind* epigram on William Kunstler. He probably wasn't even citing playwright John Heywood[169] who turned the cliché into a well-known proverb. Nonetheless, it was exactly what he told my lawyer.

William Kunstler told me that the verbal agreement reached was that if I would agree to stay out of Tennessee, the State would agree not to prosecute me. Further, the D.A. agreed that when the term of the Grand Jury expired, the sealed indictments against me would also expire if they had not been served.

The bad part of that "deal" was that I would remain "wanted" and a "fugitive" until that term expired.

Not clearly understanding what that meant for me, I asked Kunstler, "Am I still an outlaw? Am I still a fugitive?" He explained that I was not, *as long as I didn't get arrested*. He added that my in-limbo status would be "only" for two years, then it would all go away.

Kunstler said that he felt that the offer was the easiest resolve to the whole thing. He advised me that I needed to just not get arrested, not get a speeding ticket, and not give law enforcement any reason to run "wants and warrants" on me for the next two years; then everything would be fine and eventually just fade away.

"So, what exactly am I supposed to do for a living for the next two years?" I incredulously whined. He told me to do whatever I normally would do: "Go to work at a newspaper, tour with your music, go back to

---

[169] Actuality Aristotle had written, "memory is the residue of thought"; but it was essentially the same concept that Heywood memorialized.

THE POET LAUREATE SOUL OF FOLKIE ROCK & ROLL

college for an advanced degree, work for your union. Do whatever you would normally do; just do not get arrested for anything."

I didn't tell him that newspapers would never hire me because I had been blacklisted in the industry as a union organizer by the *Multimedia Newspapers* chain. So, a return to that "career" was out. I had a portfolio of award-winning clips, had brought two Pulitzer nominations to my papers, but I was barred from the industry.

Still dazed, I asked, "What name do I use? My real name or a code name or a stage name, or what?" He told me that I was perfectly free to use my real name, though he again cautioned me not to get arrested. He added that if there was any trouble I should give him a call, but other than that, it seemed to be over.

I asked what I should do with the legal-fund donations that would continue to come in from my *Still At Large* album. He reminded me that fortunately, what the cover of the album actually said was "a *portion* of the royalties from sale of this album will go to the fight to free political prisoners". It did not specifically identify a fund for me. So, he said, that I did not need to worry about any kind of misrepresentation when I no longer needed a legal defense fund and the records continued (hopefully) to sell.

All of this out-of-sight-out-of-mind turn of events did not give me the sense of relief that I would have hoped to feel. If anything, it kept me even more on edge and made me even more angry at the system itself.

To further complicate these turns in my life, the company that employed my father had decided to close their Baltimore office. My parents were moving back to Gastonia to the office there. That meant that I would have no place to live unless I returned to Gastonia with them.

When I told Kunstler that I might move to North Carolina, he was adamant that I should not even consider it.[170] He warned me that I was more likely to be murdered there than returning to Tennessee. In Tennessee it would be only law enforcement officers gunning for me; in North Carolina, any citizen could legally kill me.

---

[170] At that time, in the late 1970's and early 1980's North Carolina had more *Amnesty International* designated political prisoners than any other state. Despite not being in the top-ten states population wise, North Carolina had more State Prisons and prisoners than any other state (not per capita, but actual numbers). It also had the highest number of prisoners on death of state. It had the largest number of women and of juvenile prisoners. The State Legislature had no minority members; it was 100% white even though 26% of the population was non-white. It was the main battleground for the ongoing vicious race-baiting anti-union campaign of the *J.P. Stevens* textile company; and it was the home state of the world-known *Wilmington Ten* civil rights political prisoners (who I had sung about on my 2nd album).

THE LEGEND DIES ON — GARY GREEN

North Carolina, at that time, had the only remaining shoot-on-sight fugitive law in the United States. That law allowed that without fear of reprisal, any citizen could kill any officially-declared fugitive. North Carolina had invoked that legal-murder law as recently as three years earlier against political prisoner *Joan Little* (who Kunstler also represented).

The option of returning to Gastonia with my parents was not a sound possibility. I was not eager to return to the South anyway.

Besides, I had created a new support net in Baltimore —one of the 25 largest cities in the country (and number four in crime rates in America). It was only about two hours from New York and a half-hour from DC. I had no idea how I could afford to live there or what I would do; but perhaps my advisors in my support network would have some suggestions.

Howard, the most anti-establishment of my new friends, was totally skeptical of the D.A.'s deal, especially since there was nothing in writing. He felt that I should be extremely wary of everyone and everything; but he totally supported my thoughts about staying in Baltimore.

He also said that I could make a living by *"Do what you are infamous for: be the best-known topical folksinger in the country."* He also offered to book me to teach several courses at his Free University, *The Baltimore School* (which was a paid gig). Then he made a couple of phone calls and arranged for me to be hired as an indexer for *The Alternative Press Index*[171]. After setting me up with that gig, Howard took me to a community organizing rally at the Bread & Roses Coffeehouse. He asked me to bring a guitar and he would put me on stage to sing.

It was a small gathering with less than 150 people. He gave me a pretty powerful introduction, telling the audience that regular listeners to *The Great Atlantic Radio Conspiracy* already knew my music. Then he said, "Please welcome Folkways recording artist and political activist, Gary Green." I was surprised at the rousing applause that brought.

I decided to open with my *Ain't No Two Ways About It* from the new album. It was an angry song and I performed it with the bitterness, pain, and hatred that my ordeal had gestated. The enthusiastic support of the

---

[171] *The Alternative Press Index* was — a library resource that was sort of a *Readers' Guide to Periodical Literature* for leftist journals, newspapers, and magazines. My job was to take a stack of periodicals home, read every article, and index it. Then I would take my indexed notes to the "computer lab" at Johns Hopkins University where I would type the notes for each issue onto an IBM 12-row/80-column punch card. The cards were then sorted —using an electronic version of the device that I had made from a cigar box to win the 1967 Science Fair in Nashville, so I knew what I was doing. Finally, the printed results were bound into a library reference book. Though I indexed many different publications, my primary assignment was *The Black Panther*, the official organ of *The Black Panther Intercommunal News Service*. I indexed every issue.

crowd at each phrase made me deliver an even more powerful performance. When I finished the song, the applause turned into a standing ovation and people actually rushed the stage to slap me on the back and thank me for coming. A woman from the remnants of the local Panthers asked me to stay in Baltimore and help with "the struggle". I was hooked. I was back in music!

Meanwhile, Walt Fuchs' first reaction was, "I suspected this would go out with a 'thud' rather than with a lot of drama." He then echoed one of Kunstler's suggestions (without knowing the lawyer had said it too): go back to college. When I laughed at the suggestion and cliché-quipped "easier said than done", he took a draw from one of his constantly-present cigarettes and matter-of-factly said "bullshit".

Over pizza and beer (and in my case diet-Coke®), he outlined a way to pay for tuition, books, and other university related expenses, including a portion of my housing costs. It was an off-the-wall guerilla tactic that I would have more-likely expected to come from anarchist Howard than from Marxist Walt. It also required co-conspirators back at Morgan State University, from where I'd first been referred to Walt.

In a clear conspiracy against the university's acquiescence to a recent reactionary Supreme Court ruling[172], I was admitted to the historically Black school as a "minority" student. Under that program, I was awarded a number of grants that had been set aside for actual minorities but were to be cancelled unless the school should show they were not race based.[173]

Stupid as that was, our contact at the University viewed me as that solution; the programs could be salvaged by demonstrating that not all of the recipients were traditional minorities. I, of course, was only a minority *in that context*; but it meant that I could receive the grants and the University could preserve the grant program by meeting the court guidelines.

---

[172] It was absurd, at best. About a year earlier, the U.S. Supreme Court had ruled (in a case called *Regents of the University of California v. Bakke*) that a university's admissions criteria which used race as an admission decision violated the *Equal Protection* clause of the *Fourteenth Amendment* and of *Title VI of the Civil Rights Act of 1964*. The troublesome thing about that ruling was that Bakke was a white man who claimed he'd been denied admission because he was white.

Not only did the reactionary ruling set back *Affirmative Action*, but it legitimized a new anti-civil-rights fervor in the country. Under the new banner of "reverse discrimination", the ugly heads of racists rose to attack the last two decades of civil right progress.

Tragically, a number of traditionally minority institutions sheepishly complied without a fight and consequently began searching for ways to show they were not guilty of "reverse discrimination".

[173] In that regard, then, my being awarded the grants did not deny any minority student the grants; they were to be dormant if not taken by a non-minority. *(Absurd as that is.)*

THE LEGEND DIES ON — GARY GREEN

As our contact described it, "win-win"; but I saw it more as bowing to the racism of the court ruling.

My tuition and books were covered, as well as part of my housing costs. To add icing to the proverbial cake, there was a co-op arrangement between *Morgan State* and *Towson* (where Walt taught) as well as with *Chopin State College* and the highly-prestigious *Johns Hopkins University*. That meant that I could (and did) take classes, free, at any of the four schools. I later learned that it also meant that I could officially transfer, under the same grant program, to any of the schools.

At Towson, Walt arranged several seminars and classes for my personalized curriculum and he lined-up similar situations for me at the other universities. I spent the next two years in part-time academia, attempting to pioneer theoretical work that would consolidate behavioral science with dialectical and historical materialism[174].

More interestingly, he asked me to attend a meeting of a leftist student organization that he sponsored, *Section Twelve*[175]. Though we chose to withhold my legal status from the group, Walt did announce that I had more political experience than even he did and that I was a "famous" topical singer from the antiwar and civil rights movements. Needless to say, I was welcomed with open arms.

Meanwhile, Howard pushed me to begin teaching at his *The Baltimore School*. I taught my course in how to play the Maybelle Carter Churchlick, my multimedia course on *Folk Music & The American Left*, a class teaching how to get coverage in newspapers (that I titled *The Nine Postulates of Propaganda*), and a Political Organizing 101 class that was a rehash of the campaigning techniques I'd learned from Congressman Evins.

Between those teaching gigs and the grant money, I was able to afford an apartment in an inner-city Baltimore neighborhood.

In the early days of all of that academia, I saw an advertisement announcing that *Willie Nelson* would be performing at a huge outdoor arena between Baltimore and Washington. The afternoon before the concert I deduced at which hotel his entourage would be staying, and I telephoned

---

[174] Toward that end, I began an intense series of correspondences with Harvard's B.F. Skinner (often cited as the father of "behaviorism") and with several leading Soviet psychologists. Skinner became my de facto advisor on that part of my studies.

[175] The name of the group was another one of those leftist insider jokes. The original "Section 12" was part of Karl Marx's First International organization. The section had been expelled from the International because (depending on which version of the story one chooses) either because of the section head's advocacy for intersectional feminism or because that founder owned a Wall Street brokerage firm. *(Both, incidentally, were true and whichever was the impetus for expulsion, the group clearly was feminist during an historical epoch when it was considered unreasonable radicalism.)*

THE POET LAUREATE SOUL OF FOLKIE ROCK & ROLL

my old friend *Bee Spears* — Willie's longtime bass player. As I expected, he invited me backstage for the gig that night; it was something I had done many times at Willie Nelson concerts.

Bee often told me that he got a kick out of my rhythm, or rather, lack thereof. Whenever I would apologize for it or whine about it, he would assure me that Willie Nelson suffered from the same malady. I never believed him, but years later after his death I read that he was quoted in Rolling Stone Magazine saying:

> *"Willie is all over the place with his vocal phrasing. He'll take you up a creek and dump you in a minute. My main role in the band is to make sure he knows where the 'one' is, so he can come back to it."*[176]

(Sounded to me like Sis Cunningham trying to focus me on downbeats!)

Willie rarely acknowledged me other than a smiling "hello" every now and then; and Willie's best friend (and drummer), Paul English, disliked me either because of my open aversion to alcohol and drugs or because there was a Washington DC Secret Service agent named Gary Green who was a good friend of Paul.

Standing in the wings of the stage watching the show, I was in great company; a collection of visiting music celebrities (including Kris Kristofferson, who surprisingly seemed to remember me). The stage monitors were so loud that in the wings we couldn't really talk to each other, except to occasionally open a cooler for beer or water and yell "want one?".

As I stood there, someone tapped me on the shoulder. Rather than turn around, I leaned back to hear what the tapper had to say. All I heard was, "where do you take a leak around here?" Rather than turn around, I leaned further backwards and yelled, "follow me, I need to go too". I didn't turn to see who had asked the question until we both stepped up to urinals.

It was the President of the United States! Totally stunned, I asked, "Mister President, what are YOU doing here?" He flashed that famous Jimmy-Carter-smile and quipped, "the same thing you are, what people usually do in the bathroom".

A few minutes later, for the last song in the show, I watched the sitting President of the United States and his 14-year-old daughter join Willie on stage and sing *Whiskey River* with him. Even without the urinal adventure, it was just *too* surreal.

Okay, think about that encounter. I was a Federal fugitive. Wanted by the FBI. Armed and dangerous, supposedly. There I was in the rest room, with the President of the United States, alone and with no Secret Service in there with us. *WTF?*

---

[176] Rolling Stone Magazine, December 9, 2011

THE LEGEND DIES ON — GARY GREEN

After the concert, I wrote an anonymous op-ed piece and submitted it to the widely-circulated alternative *Baltimore City Paper*. I identified myself only as "a political prisoner living underground in Baltimore". Apparently, the editors were as amused as I was and ran a promo for the story on the front page of their tabloid weekly paper.

Besides that bizarrely close encounter with the most powerful man in the world, the other thing that I got from that Willie Nelson concert was the much-needed inspiration to return to music full time. Live concerts often had that effect on me; but every time I saw Willie, or Waylon, or Cash it was more intense.

Perhaps because of the intensity of my situation, or maybe because I was in limbo about what to do; but whatever the reason, this particular backstage visit convinced me more than anything else... that it was time for me to come back to music in a big way.

Academia aside, my first focus was to go back to the *Bread & Roses Coffeehouse*. Howard had wanted me to join "the collective" that owned and operated the venue. Now I was ready, so I dropped by Howard's house and told him what I wanted to do. He called two members of the collective and arranged for me to attend their next meeting; Howard agreed to go with me.

Without mocking or making fun of the collective, it is difficult to describe what that meeting was like. There was no structure, no real organization, and no bank account for the coffeehouse. All transactions were cash and there were no books or accounting kept. There were no permits or an actual company.

Membership in the collective was determined by showing up at the meeting; consequently, the number of members and their identities changed from day-to-day. Decisions were made by consensus.

Howard later explained to me that the coffeehouse had initially been organized by a coalition of Panthers and white social democrats, community activists, LGBT activists, and assorted white radicals. It had been part of an entire alternative community that also included *(Uncle) Sam's Belly Food Co-op*, the *People's Free Medical Clinic*, and other free or low-cost enterprises. In the years since that founding, many of the original group had moved on to other things or died, gone to prison, left Baltimore, or just lost interest. Slowly the governing body had deteriorated to the unorganized collective that I witnessed.

Nonetheless, it seemed to work; so, who was I to question the structure? I was welcomed at that meeting as a full member of the collective and was expected to participate in discussions and join the consensus decisions.

As a member of the collective, I was also expected to show up at concerts at the venue and provide free labor. Some of that labor meant making

THE POET LAUREATE SOUL OF FOLKIE ROCK & ROLL

homemade sandwiches or cookies to sell at concerts. I wasn't really into beansprout and avocado whole-wheat sandwiches, so I opted to work during the show itself.

I volunteered for the next concert, which was the upcoming Saturday night. The collective had booked a local *punk* band with the charming name, *Mouse In A Blender*.

As a hillbilly guitar picker, despite my political bent, I was not a fan of Punk Rock in general; but from my *CBGB* days I did have a healthy respect for *Patti Smith* and especially her version of the Hendrix classic *Hey Joe* to which she added references to Patty Hearst and the Symbionese Liberation Army. And, admittedly, I was amused in a pleasant way by *Lou Reed, Sid Vicious, the Ramones, Lemmy Kilmister's Motörhead*, and a handful of the genre's pioneers. Pleasant amusement in the sense of *Dada art*; not fandom. Though I did actually like *Jello Biafra* and the *Dead Kennedys*; so, the genre was not totally lost on me.

Nonetheless, I showed up on that Saturday night to work the door, the bar, and whatever else needed to be done. To my disgust... no, to my horror... *Mouse In A Blender* lived up to their name when on their final song they plugged-in a *Waring Blender*, dropped a live mouse into it, and ground the poor creature to death as they sang and *sort-of* played their instruments. *Seriously!*

The next day when I reported to Howard what I had witnessed, he was not surprised but was amused. I, however, was not amused and was definitely surprised. Mostly, I was horrified that such a great community venue —located in an historic art deco era former U.S. Post Office— was being so wasted.

Howard's advice to me was, "then convince the collective to change things." That was all the encouragement I needed. I knew what I actually needed to do, and it wasn't going to be nice; but then again, neither was the bloody mouse killing.

Political organizations in general, but especially the Left, have a long and ignoble history of in-fighting, splinter-group slits, and deviously undermining of other. Marx had been part of the ouster of the anarchist faction as well as the aforementioned Section 12 from his *International Working Men's Association*. Lenin had written an entire book calling his internal leftist opponents "either blockheads or charlatans". Leftist infighting had a long and stupid history.

One of the fun things about teaching my *Folk Music and the American Left* class was charting the dozens of splits in the Civil Rights and Antiwar movements in the U.S. since the mid-1960's. As a veteran of performing for many of the alphabet soup of organizations before my newspaper days, I was uniquely positioned to have seen the innermost workings of dozens of the splinters. First-hand, I had seen an encyclopedic collection

THE LEGEND DIES ON — GARY GREEN

of duplicities, conniving, conspiring, and power-grabs. Navigating through it was either an art or a science, depending on one's perspective. But even the most elementary manipulations would be child's play on the Bread & Roses collective member goofballs.

First, I need to use their structure of an "open collective" against them. I needed to stack it. Then I would need to get the non-stacked members so angry that they would storm out of the meeting, leaving decision making to the remaining members: my stacked group.

I devised a two-step process for accomplishing that first goal. I went back to Towson State and met with Walt's Section 12. I needed to get them to adopt *Democratic Centralism*[177] as a decision-making model and then I needed to convince them to attend a *Bread & Roses Collective* meeting with me.

I'd expected changing the organizational structure to democratic centralism would be difficult, but the majority acquiesced, if not based on my arguments, then at least based on my experience within leftist organizations and in community organizing. Actually, it turned out to be relatively simple to convince the group of wanna-be lefties to blindly adopt the model as being somehow noble and true to their beliefs. Then getting 30 or so college students to attend a music organizing event at a lefty coffeehouse was even easier task. I positioned it as a party and a field trip escape from the humdrum campus life.

To provide more vocal backup for the Towson interlopers that I was bringing in, I reached out to a group in Silver Spring Maryland, about thirty-miles south of the coffeehouse. There had recently been a highly-publicized demonstration in Silver Spring against an outfit called the *Institute of Behavioral Research*; a company conducting cruel, and deadly, testing on monkeys. A new organization had been launched to protest not just the animal torture in Silver Spring but worldwide. The new group called itself *People for the Ethical Treatment of Animals: PETA*. It was not a difficult argument to convince them to show up for a hostile takeover of a group that allowed the tossing of a live animal into a blender.

My forces were lined up to attend the next collective meeting, set for the middle of the following week. All I needed to do was make sure the discussion at the collective meeting was offensive enough that the regulars would storm out and leave my group in control.

---

[177] Democratic Centralism is a leftist organizational structure created by the Lenin. With it, decisions are debated internally within the group and then voted on. Simple majority rules and is binding on all members. Then, when the decision is taken public, the organization speaks with one voice. No public disagreement is allowed; publicly, the organization and members are always consistent. It was simple to convince the group of wanna-be lefties to blindly adopt the model as being somehow noble and true to their beliefs.

THE POET LAUREATE SOUL OF FOLKIE ROCK & ROLL

It turned out that I didn't have to take that second step at all; I managed to piss them off four days before the meeting. In fact, some were so angry at me that they refused to attend a collective meeting where I would be present. They didn't want to be in the same room as me. In my mind, though, it came about quite innocently; I did no preplanning at all.

There was one more concert at the coffeehouse before the next collective meeting, and I had signed up to work as a volunteer, just as I had done at the *Mouse In A Blender* gig. The group playing at that show was not offensive at all, at least they didn't kill anything on stage *(well, except maybe the cover of a Neil Young song, which they clearly murdered)*.

The concert was uneventful until about a half-hour into it a really suspicious-looking guy wandered into the coffeehouse. He just looked too straight[178] to be attending an event at Bread & Roses. I, and a number of the volunteers, eyed him warily but did nothing unwelcome.

The volunteer behind the bar that night was the girlfriend of the lead singer of the band that was performing. On the counter at the bar were three loaves of homemade bread that had been donated by other volunteers and a serrated knife to slice the bread.

I watched the straight guy as he seemed to take in the layout of the room. He clearly had no interest in the music and seemed irritated by it. I couldn't blame him for that, but something just didn't seem right with him. Straight-looking as he was, he didn't carry himself with the same arrogant comportment that I had seen from undercover cops trying to blend in. He was just... out of place. The expression on his face as he looked around the room indicated that he was even more disgusted with the clientele than with the music.

When the band took their break, he made a beeline for the back of the bar. From the countertop he grabbed the knife that had been put there to cut the fresh bread. He grabbed one arm of the singer's girlfriend and twisted it behind her back as he held the knife to her throat. She screamed.

The room went silent, and all eyes were on them. He was screaming racist, homophobic, sexist, rants at the *"communist bastards"* in the room. He demanded the money from the till and threatened to slit her throat unless we complied. Then he demanded everyone present empty their pockets and give him that too; all as he continued to rant hatred.

As the terrified patrons and volunteers complied, something snapped in my head. It may have been his hurtful raving at the crowd. It may have been the "communist bastards" phrase. It may have been that the stress of

---

[178] In those days, the term "straight" didn't refer to sexual orientation but rather to being an "establishment" type rather than a counter-culture type.

THE LEGEND DIES ON — GARY GREEN

being a fugitive was catching up to me. It may have been the anger that I was carrying, but whatever the cause, something snapped.

I looked at the knife that he held to the terrified woman's throat. It was that serrated blade bread knife; so dull that it barely cut through the bread. He would have had a really difficult time slitting her throat; as a newspaper reporter, I had seen enough cuttings and stabbings to know that it would have taken tremendous strength to seriously harm her with that knife. Stout as he appeared, he didn't look like he had that much strength, or at least didn't realize how much it would take. I decided that she was in no real danger, at least not life-threatening danger.

His eyes looked crazed and his offensive raging at the crowd continued. I could tell that there was no happy ending to the situation possible. Only a few seconds had passed. I felt my spine get tense as I took a deep breath. Indigestive acid rose from my stomach and burned my esophagus. All of the anger I had been suffering seemed to come to the surface at once.

His distraught robbery forced me to come to grips with my own reality. I was an outlaw. I was a fugitive. I was somehow a threat to social probity. My lifetime belief that rules did not apply to me had come to a head as I was officially outcasted. And now... amongst my supposed peers... I was again being subjected to bullying and oppressive actions from an idiot.

Basta! Enough! I felt myself snap. In the silent panic of the people in the room, I calmly walked toward the back of the bar. From the small of my back, underneath my jacket, I pulled out one of the three guns that I had been carrying daily since the near-encounter with the FBI at my parents' house. I aimed the gun at him.

"I'll kill her, drop the gun" he screamed with his own panic obviously taking the forefront. Without hesitation I responded, "Kill the bitch. She's nothing to me. But you are one dead motherfucker either way."

There were audible gasps from the crowd as I continued. "There's one way out for you. Lay down the knife and I'll let you walk out the front door. You have five seconds." I began counting, "One... Two... look, I have nothing to lose. I am already a dead man. If you want to go to hell with me, then don't drop the knife. Let's rock and roll! ... Three."

He dropped the knife, let her go, and slowly walked toward the door. As he stepped beside me, I slapped him across the face with the side of my pistol. Blood erupted from his cheeks, and he mumbled, "You lied."

"Fuck you," I answered as I shoved him out the front door, down the metal steps, and to the sidewalk. Back inside, no one thanked me. No one spoke to me. No one made eye contact with me. So, I decided to leave. I calmly walked out the door and disappeared into the city streets.

Word of what had happened spread quickly in the tightly-knit leftist community. It was not, however, the word that I would have expected. The story told was that a needy man had come into the coffeehouse and desperately tried to get money to support himself. His need was met by an armed *authoritarian* who mercilessly beat him and chased him away.

By the next afternoon when I saw Howard, he too had heard the story. When I recanted my version, he just smiled and said, *"Well I wouldn't worry about it too much; none of that group would dare call the police. So, you are safe."* That was it. That's all he had to say on the subject.

At the collective meeting a few days later, most members left immediately when they saw me there. The few who stayed thought that they could get consensus to ban me; though I am not sure how they could reach unanimity since I was a member of the collective.

Before the issue was raised, the PETA representative asked for a resolution to ban animal cruelty and specifically banning *Mouse In A Blender*. Several of the remaining original members objected to "more authoritarianism"; they felt that banning a group because of "differing opinions" would not be appropriate. One member said that it was *"a typical Stalinist tactic to ban those you disagree with"*. When I pointed out that was exactly what they were trying to do to me, most of those remaining members gathered their belongings and stormed out of the meeting. The few that remained voted to support the resolution to protect animals.

Next, the spokeswoman for Section 12 made a (prearranged) motion to convert the organizational structure from a collective to a not-for-profit limited liability company. She presented the argument that we had constructed in Towson and then asked for consensus. Everyone present agreed. That ended the collective and *decision-by-committee*. With no need for consensus, I knew that the PETA folks and most of the Section 12 students would not be back; even if they did return, they certainly had no interest in operating a venue.

The next day I set up the company, applied for an IRS tax identification number for the business, and changed the locks on the doors. I set up the new company not as Bread & Roses, but as *Bread & Roses Two*.[179]

Suddenly, I was the operator of a Baltimore Maryland music venue. I couldn't have known it at the time but my visceral reaction to *Mouse In A Blender* was the beginning of an adventure that would shape the rest of my musical life and the musical lives of —quite literally— hundreds of other musicians, comics, actors, and performers.

---

[179] The original name for the coffeehouse came from reference to a 1912 union song written to support a textile mill strike in Lawrence Massachusetts. The lyrics included, "we are fighting for bread, but we fight for roses too". My choice for the new name if the coffeehouse was a play on "roses too" with the double entendre of it being the second Bread & Roses at that location.

THE LEGEND DIES ON — GARY GREEN

Opus Twenty:
I Kinda Liked The Streets of Baltimore

As we come marching, marching, a hundred million dead
Go crying through our singing their ancient cry for bread.
Small art and love and beauty their drudging spirits knew.
Yes, it is bread we fight for, but we fight for roses, too.

— *Bread & Roses*, from the *IWW Songs to Fan the Flames of Discontent*; by James Oppenheim and Caroline Kohlsaat; written for Lawrence, MA textile strike of 1912

Biting off more than I could chew would have been one of the least cliché things I could have said about gaining control of the coffeehouse. Years of no record-keeping, no one in charge, no official structure, and haphazardly booking acts like the live animal sacrifices had taken a toll on the poor venue and on what little following remained.

The coffeehouse had become less than irrelevant; it was obscure, fringe, poorly attended and not break-even profitable. In a city with a population that fluctuated between the seventh and tenth largest in America, *Bread & Roses* concert nights struggled to attract even 20 people.

Making matters worse, it also still clung onto the shell of the Panthers' original vision; at least physically though not philosophically. The interior was littered with calendars, a "free library" of books, children's toys, propaganda brochures for the alphabet soup of lefty organizations, religious tracts from a handful of eastern religious sects, and several very healthy colonies of cockroaches.

There was no formal stage, just a back area of the room where people played. There was no lighting system and no sound system. There was no air conditioning nor heat; small fire-hazard electric heaters that often blew fuses provided the only warmth in the cold-ass Baltimore winter months.

The "tables" were salvaged spools from telephone wire that had been discarded at one of the city dumps. The chairs were a disjointed collection of classroom chairs that had been trashed by the city. Ambient lighting ... no, the *only* lighting ... was from small anti-mosquito candles burning on each spool-tabletop. There were no licenses for food service or alcohol, and in fact, beer had been routinely served illegally and to *any age* customer. And there certainly had been no health department inspections for anything that was served to customers.

It seemed to me that there was no wonder why no one came to the coffeehouse: not only did the venue suck, but it was almost completely unknown. On the bright side, since the venue had never been advertised they operated "under the radar" so that government agencies most likely were not even aware they existed. That, of course, made repositioning them a double-edged sword; especially once a fugitive "owned" the business.

THE POET LAUREATE SOUL OF FOLKIE ROCK & ROLL

William Kunstler had told me that I could use my own name, and I could go back to music; the only caveat was that I should not get arrested. Feeling emboldened by my angry confrontation with the would-be robber, my seizing the coffeehouse, and being awarded the academic grants, I decided to push Kunstler's advice to the limit.

First, I plastered all four campuses (Hopkins, Towson, Chopin, and Morgan) with crudely made flyers announcing a *hootenanny* at the Bread & Roses on May 1st. I didn't announce the new name or any other changes. I wanted to see what size crowd I could draw with just the flyers.

I couldn't have been happier! Fifteen performers showed up and, including their friends and families, an audience of about 135 people. Even better, a whole new cadre of people wanted to get involved with bringing an alternative venue to Baltimore; especially one that highlighted labor, civil rights, and "movement" music.

One of the performers approached me afterwards and asked me to serve on the board of an AFL-CIO sponsored labor heritage festival that he was organizing. He wanted me to be in charge of the workshops for the festival. Other performers and audience members wanted to know when the next "hoot" would be and asked what they would have to do to be booked for a solo gig at the coffeehouse.

I decided that the venue needed an internal facelift; and I needed money to do that. I called Harold Leventhal; he was Pete Seeger's manager, and it was in his office that Marjorie Guthrie had set up the *Committee to Combat Huntington's Disease*. He also was the agent that Moe Asch had sent me to see years earlier. I told him that I wanted to put together a large folk concert as a fundraiser for my coffeehouse, but I was willing to pay the performers. He told me that he could book legendary folksingers *Tom Paxton* and *Dave Van Ronk* (affectionately known as the Mayor of Greenwich Village). He asked if I would be willing to play, myself, and if I would be willing also to book *Hazel Dickens*. Hazel was one of the incredible performers I knew from Highlander and Epworth in Knoxville.

I agreed, knowing that by putting myself on the bill I would be part of whatever publicity blitz was created. That could mean drawing law enforcement attention to me.

After I accepted, I called Kunstler and asked what he thought about generating publicity with my name on the billing. He told me that he could see no reason that law enforcement would check warrants and wants on headlining musicians. He said he thought it actually would be a good thing, because it would indicate that I wasn't hiding anything or in fear of anything. Then, of course, he cautioned me *again* not to get.

Clearly the coffeehouse wasn't large enough to handle the size crowd that I anticipated with that line-up, so I needed to find another venue. My experience with Madison Square Garden had given me a good understanding of what it took to four-wall an event, so, I set about searching for a suitable location with terms that I could meet.

Working through Father Tom, the movement priest who had introduced me to Ernie Crowfoot and the union, I arranged a meeting with Kathleen Feeley who ran *Notre Dame College of Maryland*. Based on his endorsement, she offered *LeClerc Hall* auditorium with terms that I would have been a fool to turn down. The school would require no upfront money; on the night of the show, they would collect the rental fee as well as money for insurance, security, and staffing (all of which they would provide).

Before advertising the event, I wanted to see what free publicity I good generate. Calling on my newspaper experience, I put together a press release package for *The Baltimore Sun* and targeted the managing editor personally (rather than the entertainment editor or the features desk).

It worked. Oh boy, did it work! He sent a reporter with a photographer and gave me three-quarters of the front page of the paper's "Nightlife" entertainment section, including a four-column photo. Under a 36-point headline, *Just Plain Folk Making A Comeback In Baltimore*, he placed me on the page above an article about famed violinist *Itzhak Perlman* appearing in the city.

In the newspaper interview I didn't announce the location of the fundraiser concert nor the line-up other than *Tom Paxton*. Even though the concert date was only nine days away, I had not signed the Notre Dame contract and Harold had not confirmed Dave and Hazel (Hazel was looking for a local pickup bluegrass band before she confirmed). In an interesting break from newspaper policy, the paper graciously included our phone number in the body of the story[180].

Not having a venue signed until eight days before the event was an absurd timeframe in which to sell tickets. But it was the only date that Harold could confirm Tom and the lineup; and he didn't do that until Thursday, May 20, 1982 — the day the story actually came out. I quickly signed the contract for the 28th and began a guerilla blitz for selling tickets with only a week before the show.

Another problem that arose was the lack of union-label print shops in Baltimore that could print poster-size. The few that existed could not do the one-day turnaround that I desperately needed. As a card-carrying Typographical Union member, I refused to print in a non-union shop *(an*

---

[180] Incidentally, a phone number for Bread & Roses was a new thing; the previous collective members had determined by consensus that installing a telephone was too conforming with authorative convention. I suspected that nonsensical aloofness actually meant that they didn't want to pay a monthly telephone bill. I continued to defy tradition by installing a business telephone line at the coffeehouse ... and buying an advertisement in the yellow pages.

affliction I still hold today, even though the ITU disappeared years). I finally found a shop by calling Ernie Crofoot for some union support.

When the newspaper story hit, the phone began ringing; 15 hours a day without a break. After a couple of days, I found a used answering machine at the *Goodwill Industries* store and recorded a message giving ticket-purchase information.

With no advertising budget and the short window until the concert, ticket sales depended on the newspaper story, our plastering the one-thousand-plus posters all over Baltimore City and County, and word of mouth. Of course, it was not a sell-out; but it sold a respectable number of tickets.

After the college collected their fees and we paid Harold Leventhal, there was almost no money left for the coffeehouse. However, the publicity generated by the show was invaluable; we were covered by all three daily newspapers[181], the weekly City Paper, and all four TV stations.

Moreover, the demographics of the attendees were beyond anything the old Bread & Roses had ever drawn. Both of Maryland's sitting United States Senators were there, a cross-section of Maryland academia, a huge student turnout, dozens of old folkies, and most significantly (to me, at least) a large African-American turnout.

Bread and Roses *Two* was officially on the map! I, also, was officially on the map; as both a noted Folkways recording artist and as the "owner" of a major new folk music venue. Now I had to keep that momentum going… oh yeah, and not get arrested.

Besides bringing the coffeehouse to the attention of a much broader audience, the concert also put it on the radar of touring musicians and singer-songwriters. Almost immediately our mail delivery was filled with tapes, records, and letters from people wanting to be booked. Some of those people were really well known; others, *not-so-much*.

Thinking about how to deal with the newfound fame, I enlisted volunteers to help me clean out and remodel the big room. We held a massive sidewalk sale to get rid of the books, toys, and other left-behind items from the collective. With the money from that, we bought a used lighting system, a really nice used Sony tube-driven sound system and tower speakers, and (most exciting to me) a used upright church piano.

Other improvements included an internal paint job, a thorough extermination and cleaning, and having the steam radiators repaired so the building could have heat in the winter. Volunteer carpenters built an actual stage and volunteer electricians rewired the electrical system. We

---

[181] The Baltimore Sun, The Baltimore Evening Sun, and The Baltimore News-American.

THE LEGEND DIES ON — GARY GREEN

painted the spool-tables and covered them with checkered table clothes, upgraded the chairs to more consistent seating (though still second-hand).

The coffeehouse was located in north-central Baltimore on 31st Street, bridging two neighborhoods: the student hipster ghetto called *Charles Village* and the African American edge-of-the-ghetto community called *Waverly*. Walking distance to both *Memorial Stadium* and *Johns Hopkins University*, the coffeehouse was situated between the two and could have claimed either neighborhood (in a city where neighborhood identification was actually a "thing"). Based on the location, I decided to position the branding image of the coffeehouse to take advantage of the publicity proclaiming us to be a new folk venue: *Greenwich Village 1962; Charles Village 1982. Folk Music Is Back!*

I had decided to only book live music on Friday and Saturday nights at first, because I didn't think we could draw enough people for weeknights; especially since so much of the clientele was made up of academics and working people. I went on a booking spree, combining fairly well-known performers with up-and-comers. We were so busy booking and promoting that I had to have two employees that did nothing but arrange bookings.

Everything revolved around my monthly (and later twice-monthly) hootenannies. I made arrangements with a local radio station to broadcast tapes of our hoots and that just made us more popular —and a more desirable venue for musicians. In addition to booking national touring acts, we also booked local musicians based on their performances at the hoots.

Hoot nights became so popular that the crowds were truly unmanageable; hundreds of people spilling out onto the sidewalk and eventually blocking the street. We would run the hoots for about eight hours (6 p.m. until 2 a.m.) and some nights there would be as many as 100 performers with each one bringing one to five supporters/fans. So, on those nights we would have as many as 500 people attending a venue that was set up to hold about one-tenth that many.

With the concert nights (non-hoot) door collections going exclusively to pay the musicians, raising the on-going operating costs of the coffeehouse was problematic. The old collective had sold alcohol to sustain the business; but they had done so without the benefit of a license.

Hearing William Kunstler's constant reminders, "do not get arrested", I decided that selling alcohol illegally wasn't really a road I wanted to travel. Hence, the Bread & Roses Two menu included a selection of teas, some coffees, and fresh pastries (delivered by a local French).

Even if I had wanted to legitimately sell alcohol, the legal licensing process in Baltimore City was (to my thinking) a criminal enterprise itself. It was no wonder at all that the collective had refused to participate. The scam operated like the New York City taxicab medallion system: the City issued a limited number of licenses, no more than that arbitrary number.

THE POET LAUREATE SOUL OF FOLKIE ROCK & ROLL

In order for a new business to obtain a license, that business had to buy a license from an existing license-holder — at whatever price "the market would bear." Some of those license-holders actually owned several licenses, holding them dormant and on the market for sale. So, if the City had originally sold licenses for $500, a license holder could resell a license for any price... say $20,000, a tidy little 4,400% profit and THAT was common. Even after such a private sale, the purchaser would still be subjected to an investigation by the City and a large fee to "cover the costs of the investigation". Just another reason for me to distrust governments.

One of our regular audience members, especially on hoot nights, was a local Precinct Captain for the Democratic Party. He held an obviously-patronage job as an inspector for the *Baltimore City Board of Liquor License Commissioners*. He was a strong proponent of almost everything we were doing with the coffeehouse; and he was a Gary Green fan.

One evening he asked me why I had not applied for an alcohol license. I, of course, wasn't going to tell him that it was because I was a fugitive wanted by the FBI and didn't want to be subjected to the background check. And, knowing that he worked for the board, I didn't want to tell him that I thought the system was a scam. Instead, I told him that the process was too costly, and as a not-for-profit[182] we couldn't afford it.

He told me that there was a little-used section of the City's licensing code that allowed non-profit organizations to receive a "special event" alcohol permit for one weekend at a time. With such a special permit, no permanent license was required.

The next night, he brought the form by and offered to submit it for the coffeehouse... weekly. I noticed that the form required neither proof of non-profit status nor the name of an owner (since non-profits do not have owners). From then on, we were legally licensed to sell beer and wine during our "special events".

In late July, Moe Asch asked me to record a live album at Bread & Roses Two. Howard Ehrlich arranged the engineering and equipment though The Great Atlantic Radio Conspiracy and we flooded Baltimore with invitations to be in the audience for the recording of a live album. About 100 people crowded into the room along with three television news crews and reporters from three newspapers.

The publicity surrounding that recording was almost overwhelming. *The Baltimore Evening Sun* printed a half-page review of the show on the front of their entertainment section. Among their comments:

---

[182] I had organized the new Bread and Roses Two under an obscure Maryland tax category called "Not-For-Profit Company". Not a Federal IRS-approved Section 501 tax-exempt non-profit organization, but still proclaimed non-profit in structure in the State.

THE LEGEND DIES ON — GARY GREEN

> "By the time the session began, Mr. Green had them: a young couple with a three-week-old baby, a couple well into middle age, some fellow folk musicians, and approximately equal numbers of those who seemed just old enough to remember the hootenannies of the Fifties and those who looked to have been children in the Sixties, not of them.
>
> ...his most forceful and moving numbers were those about workers, such as "Millhand and Farmers," a driving celebration of honest labor, and "Down the Road and Over the Hill" and "The Murder of Ella May Wiggins," rich in history, imagery, and symbolism of the struggles in the textile mills of the South.
>
> Mr. Green closed the night of the recording of his live album with "The Hammer," an anthem to unionism, receiving sustained applause and responding with a simple "thank you" —and a clenched fist raised high in the air."[183]

The Bread & Roses phone line was inundated with calls from managers wanting to book their artists and from other venues wanting to book me. Around the same time, my *Still At Large* album was starting to garner attention. Combined with the reputation of Bread & Roses Two, and the success of the package show, I was suddenly in demand for radio shows and as a performer.

My parody song *Jesus Christ Was A Republican* got national attention when the CBS TV show, *The Tomorrow Show With Tom Snyder*, played it in a segment in which Snyder interviewed evangelist Jerry Falwell (who was mentioned in my song). That spurred album sales, radio play, and unsolicited requests for me to play in venues all over the country.

Taking full advantage of all the public attention and exploiting the title of the album, *Still At Large*, we booked me as *The Outlaw Folksinger* and called my music *Outlaw Folk*. It was a deliberate play on the huge country music "Outlaw" movement of my old friends Waylon and Tompall along with Willie Nelson and others; at the same time, it was a not-so-tongue-in-cheek reference to my legal situation.

I accepted them all and as I traveled from New York to California, I would augment the appearances by having my two Bread & Roses bookers pitch me to venues along the way or in the areas. I spent the next year off and on traveling the old "folk circuit" as well as union halls, music bars, folk festivals, small concert venues, and an awful lot of colleges and universities all over the country. Some nights I slept on the floor in the back of venues, snuggled against a steam radiator; other nights I crashed in band houses, on buses, in tents outdoors at festivals, at cheap hotels, or supporters' spare bedrooms or even couches. I spent many-many nights in college dorm rooms around the country, and just as many nights on various Native reservations around the country. On a few rare occasions

---

[183] The Baltimore Evening Sun, Section B Page 1, *Live With Folk From Baltimore*, by Eric Seigel, Monday, August 2, 1982

when I was booked at high-paying venues, I stayed in nice suites at a Ritz-Carlton or four-and-five-star hotels.

I used a standard performance contract, but in the spirit of the 1980's I had a complex rider that spelled out specific details of for my appearances. I didn't have a "no brown M&M's" clause[184], but my rider made it clear that I was a vegetarian, and that any meal would have to be completely vegetarian.

More interesting were my lighting and sound requirements, especially as they related to opening acts. The house lights were to remain on full brightness for any opening acts and the sound mix for those vocals were to be adjusted for loud treble brightness. When I was introduced, the house lights were to go to total darkness and remain that way throughout my performance. One follow-spot was to cover me from the eaves to center stage and be the only light, and with no gels. The sound system was to be readjusted to mid-ranges but highlighting bass notes. It was an effective behavior manipulation tool to control the expectations and reactions of the audience, regardless of the quality of my performance.

Occasionally I would sing a *Johnny Cash, Waylon Jennings, Woody Guthrie, Townes Van Zandt, Dylan, Peter-Paul-and-Mary*, or country-roots song; but mostly I sang originals from my three albums or new songs that I had not yet recorded. Depending on the venue, I would throw in traditional union and civil rights songs (*Solidarity Forever, We Shall Overcome, We Shall Not Be Moved, Union Maid, Which Side Are You On*, etc.)

To my complete surprise, the most enthusiastic audiences for me were at various northeastern universities. I had thought that my defiant Southernism combined with unmistakable radicalism would have repelled rather than attract that student population.

Totally absorbed in the outlaw persona, I openly identified with *Jesse James, Doc Holiday*, and the noble banditry of *Zorro, Robin Hood, Joaquin Murrieta, Salvatore Giuliano, Dick Turpin*, and other historical or mythological swashbuckling scoundrels. Every promotion for my gigs

---

[184] For years cited as typical of the self-indulgent 80's rockers, the actual reason for Eddie Van Halen's odd written requirement made total sense. To ensure a promoter had read every single word in the contract, the band created the "no brown M&M's" clause. It was a *canary in a coalmine* to indicate that the promoter may have not paid attention to other more important parts of the rider —especially safety requirements, and that there could be other bigger problems at hand. If brown M&M's showed up, it was the proverbial red-flag that other things may have been over-looked. Eddie was not the self-indulgent dummy as he has been portrayed.

THE LEGEND DIES ON — GARY GREEN

was wrapped in old-west outlaw imagery, even down to six-guns and cowboy hats.

My performances were delivered by the classic "angry young man" who had been persecuted for trying to right various wrongs (though I never went into the details of my actual fugitive status). I let it be known that I was anything but a pacifist when it came to righting wrongs. I certainly never expected all of my audacious posturing to appeal to college students and especially not in the northeast.

One of the most rousing calls for encores and additional bookings came from students at the University of Delaware in Newark.[185] It was one of the few gigs where they didn't want me to leave. In one year, I was re-booked there more than a dozen times; and each time to larger audiences.

The other welcoming location that surprised me was Greenwich Village. The very clubs that had barred me five years earlier now welcomed me as their latest discovery. Even *The New York Times* and *The Village Voice* promoted and then praised my performances there.

Renowned New York jazz critic *Nat Hentoff* wrote, *"Come hear why I call Gary Green The Outlaw Folksinger"*. People did and I was starting to appreciate John Kander & Fred Ebb's lyrics (if I can make it there, I'm gonna make it anywhere; It's up to you New York, New York[186]).

After one gig in New York, I was having lunch with Pete Seeger and talking about the momentum of a new "folk revival". Pete wondered aloud what I could do to help raise funds for *Sing Out! Magazine* (the folk music journal co-founded by Seeger in 1950). I, of course, offered to do a benefit concert in Baltimore. Pete loved the idea and then in the midst of making suggestions for it he asked me what I thought of him doing the concert and making it a joint benefit for *Sing Out!* and for *Bread & Roses Two*. Gee, let me think: who could draw more people to a benefit, me or Pete Seeger? Duh. Of course, I thought it was a great idea.[187]

Pete asked me to call Harold to set it up. I did, and the benefit was set for December 4th. That gave us plenty of time to advertise and sell tickets.

---

[185] Which I learned was pronounced *New Ark* rather than like the homographic New Jersey city with the same spelling.

[186] ©WB Music Corp., Emi Unart Catalog Inc., Jalni Publications Inc., Keystone Movietunes

[187] Though I always felt that Mark Moss (then Sing Out!'s editor) was not much of a Gary-fan. In fact, I felt that I was perhaps too wrapped up in my whole "outlaw" identity to ever fit into the Sing Out! genre of folkniks and perhaps I had done something to alienate them. No one ever said that to me, but I always felt like "an outsider" when it came to Sing Out! Nonetheless, I loved the publication and admired Mark and the staff. So, I was thrilled to do anything I could for the magazine even if they maybe hated me.

THE POET LAUREATE SOUL OF FOLKIE ROCK & ROLL

I was now an old-hand at four-walling and Notre Dame was once again my target. This time I didn't need Father Tom's help.

Even though the gig was 90 days away, tickets sold out during the first two weeks of making them available. The crowd was phenomenal, covering the broadest demographics. This time instead of Maryland's two sitting United States Senators being the only politicians in attendance, they were joined by the entire Maryland Congressional Delegation, members of the State Legislature, and most of Baltimore's City Council.

There was one hootenanny regular, and Irish singer, who a few years later would become the Governor of Maryland (and after that the head of the Social Security Administration). There were labor leaders, rank-and-file workers, civil rights activists, students, musicians, the arts community, and... of course... the media.

The coffeehouse (and I) got great plugs both from Seeger and in the reviews. *The Baltimore Sun* wrote:

"Mr. Seeger encouraged people to go and sing at Bread and Roses II Coffeehouse (426 E. 31st Street) reorganized by Mr. Seeger's old friend and fellow singer Gary Green."

Enthusiasm over Pete's performance amidst the much-publicized "folk music revival" also drew lots of attention from the large commercial concert venues. Apparently, my folk revival had become a bankable thing!

The City of Baltimore owned and operated a 4,000-seat venue called *Pier Six Pavilion*[188] at the famed *Baltimore Inner Harbor*. They contacted Harold and asked to book Pete for their upcoming summer concert series. Harold, always hustling his stable, pitched a concert of Pete with Arlo Guthrie.[189] The city happily accepted and booked a July 22nd date.

The outdoor Pier Six concert was a sellout and the two of them had the crowd in the palms of their hands. At the end of the show, for the last few

---

[188] Since its opening in 1981, the venue has booked Al Green; Aicci; B.B. King; Britney Spears; Chuck Berry; Coldplay; Diana Ross; The Doobie Brothers; Donna Summer; Erykah Badu; Etta James; Fats Domino; Goo Goo Dolls; Hall & Oates; Harry Connick Jr.; Jackson Browne; Jethro Tull; Jill Scott; Johnny Cash; Judas Priest; Pierce the Veil; Ray Charles; Steely Dan; Stevie Ray Vaughan; Umphrey's McGee; The Used; Tom Jones; Tracy Chapman; and many others.

[189] I had only met Arlo once, about seven or eight years earlier when I had a freelance assignment from *Circus* music magazine to interview him about an album that he had just released on Warner Brothers' Reprise Records. We had moved off topic to discuss Sis & Gordon's bitterness and the scope of topical music in general. It was a good conversation. Of course, I knew Arlo's mother, Marjorie, a lot better and had spent many hours with her during my time in New York and in D.C. (She had introduced me from the stage on the National Mall when I played at the Smithsonian's Folklife Festival.)

THE LEGEND DIES ON — GARY GREEN

songs (and the encore), Pete gave a plug to Bread & Roses Two and then called me onto the stage to join him and Arlo for the rest of the songs.

I didn't have a guitar with me, and Arlo looked surprised; though he knew Pete well enough to know he should never be surprised. At the microphone, I thanked Pete and added, "and it is good to see you again Arlo Davy". I am pretty sure Arlo didn't remember me, but if he did, he didn't really acknowledge it. Instead, he looked puzzled and put both hands up as if to question and wonder "who-the-hell?". The audience laughed and that was good. Pete started singing *This Land*, and to my delight, the audience recognized me and applauded when I stepped to the microphone.

Bread & Roses really had been the launching pad that I needed to step back into music —much more intensely than ever before. Moreover, though I was writing, my focus was on exactly what Reba Hancock, Kris Kristofferson, and Gil Veda and told me to do: me performing my songs.

The Outlaw Folksinger persona suited me perfectly, from the reality of my situation, from my personality, and from my personal interests. Even better, for me, things were happening fast, and I was completely absorbed in the matrix of it all.

With all the press, the new broad-based audience, and especially after the Seeger benefit, Bread and Roses Two was on a roll to become both a national driver of a folk revival and equally (or more) importantly, an influential and desirable local venue in Baltimore.

At the same time, albeit not in the direction I would have predicted back when I was walking Music Row back in Nashville, my own career was taking off. The whole *Outlaw Folk* thing was sticking and thanks to the Nat Hentoff review was becoming a genre —not just a description of what I was doing. I even booked other "outlaw folksingers" at the coffeehouse.

I suppose I should have been happy; should have been thrilled. I wasn't. I didn't feel "right" about either the positioning of the coffeehouse or my own role.

For Bread & Roses, I was bothered by how homogenized my creation had become. I mean, yes, we had large audiences, and the business was making money as well as providing a forum for struggling artists; but... there's always a "but", isn't there? In this case the "but" was that I was irritated by exactly *who* was in the audiences we were drawing: for the most part, white, upscale, well-educated, powerbrokers by day.

Even our "middle class" audiences (mostly coming to hear up-and-coming local performers) were lily-white, educated, "professionals". In any of the Bread & Roses audiences, I almost never saw non-white people, working people, poor people, or people not in one popular clique of another. Even on hoot-nights, the faces on stage were a sea of white and almost all males. It was a rare event whenever a woman was on stage; it

THE POET LAUREATE SOUL OF FOLKIE ROCK & ROLL

was almost unheard-of. For a citadel of liberal culture, there wasn't much diversity either on the stage or in the audiences.

I was not going to be happy with the coffeehouse until that situation changed. Though I tried to hide it, I began to view the followers of the coffeehouse with disdain; almost as much as I had disliked the whole *Mouse In A Blender* element. I am sure my contempt was more transparently visible than I wanted it to be, and I knew it was driven by my anger with what had happened to me from powerbrokers in Tennessee. Regardless of the source of my scorn, it was very real.

To expand our base of performers, I tried reaching out to *The Baltimore School for the Arts* (a public performing arts high school) and to the private *Maryland Institute College of Art*. Both schools had reputations for terrific diversification and outreach to minority artists; and both schools were known for their avant-garde breaching the boundaries of traditional artistic and especially business structures.

The high school was Baltimore's version of New York's *Fiorello LaGuardia High School of Music and Art and Performing Arts*, which had been immortalized in the 1980 MGM movie *Fame*. The Baltimore high school had a great admission policy that ignored academic performance, instead basing entrance on auditions and portfolios. They had successfully recruited talent from Baltimore's poorest neighborhoods and minority populations.

Both schools seemed like ideal matches for what I wanted to do with the coffeehouse. Disappointingly, both had fallen into a sort of artistic-academic elitism; and a southern-accented white man that self-identified as an "outlaw" did not fit that elitist model. The students, of course, were a different deal; but the administrations were much more interested in New York and Los Angles art and entertainment meccas than in an inner-city coffeehouse. Additionally, their paradigms just didn't congeal with my public image; so, attracting those students was a struggle.

That image of mine, self-inflicted for the most part, was certainly getting out of hand. My sardonic defiance of my legal situation and unrestrained anger over being in the situation in the first place... were a combination that made it much too easy for me to go deeper-and-deeper into a bottomless rabbit hole of bitterness.

At the same time, all of the traveling for gigs made it impossible for me to be at the every-weekend shows at Bread & Roses or even at many of my hootenannies. Fortunately, I found a surrogate host who, as it turned out, was ideally suited for that role and many others.

At my very first hoot, back on May 1st, one of the musicians who showed up had been a Baltimore singer-songwriter named *Gary Blanchard*. I was immediately taken by his voice, phrasing, and playing; he reminded me of the very best of *Peter-Paul-and-Mary, The Kingston*

THE LEGEND DIES ON — GARY GREEN

Trio, and that entire genre of 1960's commercial folkies. On top of the smooth and very-pleasing sound, he had written a peace song, aptly titled *The Peace Song*, that I felt then (and still feel today) is one of the finest genuine peace songs I have ever heard.

This cat was THE absolutely perfect host for my hootenannies. More than forty years later, he recalled:

> *"I remember playing some of my topical songs at a hootenanny; Gary Green came up to me afterward and commented on the music. He had recorded it, and it would be played on a local radio station.*
>
> *There was something about Gary's energy and outlook that drew me. It was just a matter of time until he felt like a brother to me; one more accepting of my unique look at things than anyone in my family.*
>
> *As time progressed, I began to feel more confident in my writing. Gary and I often did performances together. Gary's role as a Folkways recording artist helped to boost my profile. I somehow became the frequent host of the Hootenannies at Bread and Roses, allowing me to start to come out of my protective shell and to be better at social interaction.*
>
> *When I met Gary Green, I was in a period of trying to find my direction. I started writing music when I was 16 years old but had been out of the scene for a while. Where many of my musician friends were inspired by rock and roll, I came from the world of folk music, especially music with a social message. I wasn't sure if there was a place for my style of music in 1980. Once I walked into Baltimore's Bread and Roses Coffeehouse, I began to have a sense of hope.*
>
> *I remember when Gary brought me to New York for a meeting of the People's Music Network. It was my first time there and Gary was a great tour guide. He knew many people and always made sure that I was introduced as a friend and fellow musician. My songwriting grew stronger, and Gary often encouraged me to share the songs I was writing. His enthusiasm for one of my songs, The Peace Song, has continued to this day.*
>
> *My music has gone through changes over the past forty years, but it all builds from the folk roots that Gary Green appreciated and encouraged. I am proud to call Gary my mentor and my friend."*

As laudatory as his words were, what remained very true is that he really was the ideal person to take the lead at the coffeehouse while I was out playing "outlaw" at venues across the country. In fact, I loved his performances so much that even when I was in town, I would give him the stage and I would remain in the background.[190]

---

[190] An incredible talent! One of my regrets about that era of my career is that I could not do more for him. He should have had a widely-distributed commercial album with a lot of radio and television plays. I wish I could have facilitated that for him.

THE POET LAUREATE SOUL OF FOLKIE ROCK & ROLL

Gary Blanchard also was key in discovering, bringing in, screening, and scheduling many of the hoot-night performers —some of which became regular performers with shows of their own and in some cases launched national touring careers.

One night, when I was home from the road, I walked into Bread & Roses Two after a hoot had begun. The room was packed, and Gary Blanchard was in perfect form, alternating between playing guitar and folk-banjo between various performers. He had a real knack for keeping the show moving; a complex task given the set-up time that many performers took. Without his interludes, there would have been a lot of dead-time on stage between acts. "Dead air" (as they call it on the radio) is the quickest way to lose the attention of any audience. Gary Blanchard made sure we never suffered that death-knell.

I walked in just as he finished one of his interludes and was introducing the next act. I wasn't looking at the stage, but instead was checking the food and beverage inventory behind the bar. From the stage came the most incredible version of *House of The Rising Sun* I had ever heard. For years I had thought that Josh White had the best version; then I decided that Odetta held that honor; then I was certain that B.B. King had the best version; but that was before I heard *Steve Wilson* at Bread and Roses Two.

He used the well-known goofy chord progression and wacky arpeggio that Alan Price and Hilton Valentine had created for *The Animals* version; but he sang it with Odetta's passion and King's phrasing... all meshed into his own arrangement that was like nothing I'd heard. I was totally transfixed. It wasn't just me either; a hush fell through the entire audience as Steve sang and played guitar. This guy was major. Steve Wilson was an early-thirty-something African American corrections officer for the *Maryland State Prison System*; as anthesis to my world, he was *The Man*. He also had an angelic voice that was somewhere between a classic Irish tenor, a delta bluesman, and a New Orleans line jazz master.

Gary Blanchard had found for me the first step of the diversity that I was seeking; but much more importantly, he had found a major new talent. I was so taken by Steve that I began joining him on stage to play lead guitar behind him and on rare occasions attempted to provide vocal harmony. I also saw to it that he was frequently booked as a solo act at the coffeehouse, in addition to his regular hootenanny appearance. His day job limited his ability to travel to gigs, but whenever I had a local or regional booking, I would include him and Gary Blanchard on the billing.

Around the same time, through the Communist Party, I met an exceptionally talented Peruvian ethnomusicologist and performer. A fellow Johns Hopkins student and a researcher at *The Smithsonian Institution* in Washington, *Laura Larco* had an incredible repertoire of South American folk and revolutionary songs which she sang and accompanied herself on

THE LEGEND DIES ON — GARY GREEN

guitar. She also could tell great background stories for each song, making for terrific stage patter. I didn't find out until later that she was the daughter of the socialist (*American Popular Revolutionary Alliance*) Prime Minister of Peru, Guillermo Larco-Cox.

With Laura and Steve as part of Gary Blanchard's stable of performers, I felt comfortable turning the coffeehouse management over completely to an Armenian-American, classically-trained Goucher College dancer, and single mother who operationally had been running things since shortly after I took over.

She had solid roots in the Baltimore and suburban D.C. folk communities and was far more organized and detail-focused than I could possibly be. She made the ideal operator for Bread and Roses Two.

She also was a respected member of the famously-pacifist *Sandy Spring Quaker Meeting House* community, and as such, I am sure that she was a welcomed relief to my over-the-top gun-toting outlaw persona and dogmatic authoritarianism; just as I am certain that dealing with me during that era of my life was a ridiculous strain on such a kind-hearted person. Though some of my followers didn't seem to mind that since the FBI visited my mother, I had been carrying three guns on me at almost all times; that behavior had to be unacceptable to a Quaker; so, in hindsight, I apologize, but I needed to not be assassinated.

Though I still wasn't completely happy with the diversity level, I felt comfortable that it was on the right track and in good hands. There was little that I could add, other than the use of my name for publicity.

I refocused on my classes and on a new-found curiosity about something called "counting cards" at the recently-opened Atlantic City New Jersey casinos (only an hour-and-a-half from Baltimore). I thought that a pinko-fugitive beating the casinos out of their ill-gotten gains would be a delicious irony. Little did I know that I would come to rely on *that* in the not-to-distant future.

Meanwhile, as I continued to gig around the country, I was no longer identifying myself as a folksinger or a singer-songwriter; instead, I called myself as a "revolutionary cultural worker". Rather than exclusively a creative artist, I saw myself as a laborer in music and literature and not unlike a working-class laborer in any other industry; only the product of my praxis was "working for social change".

That decisively Marxist attitude also served to further alienate me from fellow musicians — especially those in the mainstream or those whose ideals revolved around *l'art pour l'art* (art for the sake of art). I condemned the latter as confused dilettantes and cited the *ars gratia artis* corporate slogan of Wall Street darling entertainment giant Metro-Goldwyn-Mayer.

THE POET LAUREATE SOUL OF FOLKIE ROCK & ROLL

Rather than be content to brush them off and ignore them, I was openly hostile to many musicians and performers, calling them out as feigning interest in the arts without real commitment or knowledge of how they were being manipulated and used by corporate American. I ranted that they were little more than mindless cogs for the corporate structure singing songs to fit the commercial requirements (even down to the three-minute-15-second song length).

As you might imagine, this attitude didn't win me any friends in the commercial music world and only intensified my alienation from the industry as a whole. Clearly, my bitterness over my own situation was driving me away from even the left-leaning liberals in the music industry (the more conservative performers had less-than-zero interest in me). And the curse of it was that I couldn't really tell anyone *why* I was so bitter; it was too much of a risk.

My attitude about my music peers was (like my attitude about most everything) tainted with my considerable psychological baggage. The vote-buying schemes in Tennessee had soured me on the electoral process; especially when I learned that the "walk-around money" voter fraud was rampant in almost every state, not just Tennessee. The jurisprudence system was meaningless to me since it had been perverted to manipulate a Grand Jury into indicting me on trumped up charges.

These very personal affronts convinced me that the only way to deal with oppression was with direct action. I often explained to people, *"If someone is hitting you in the head with a hammer, you don't take an aspirin for the headache and you don't politely ask him to please be gentle. No. You shoot that motherfucker and that makes sure he never hits anybody every again. The end."*

My anger, bitterness —and acute fear— made that new outlook even more volatile. Making matters even worse was my personal history of anger issues that I often, seemingly unprovoked, visited on family, friends, and complete strangers; all of which now, a half century later, I truly regret. But at that time in my life, I was genuinely out-of-control.

My father was known for his explosive, often violent, temper. Throughout my own life I had demonstrated many of those behaviors learned from him. But, when the weight of the trumped-up charges came down on me and actually threatened my life (to the point that I was ready to shoot a Federal agent) my bad temper moved from anger-management issues to near-psychotic explosions.

With cavalier abandonment I took to heart the John Wayne line from the 1977 film, The Shootist, expanding it paraphrasingly to, *"I nor those under my care will not be wronged. I won't tolerate insults to me or them. We won't be laid a-hand on. I don't do these things to other people, and I require the same from them."* I made it clear that violation of that mantra would be met with my full

THE LEGEND DIES ON — GARY GREEN

wrath, vengeance, and violence. *"Gods forgive; outlaws take revenge,"* I often warned.

Declaring myself "a revolutionary, not a reformer", I openly taunted power and dared authorities to come after me. In near-comical haughtiness, I stepped beyond advertising myself as an "outlaw" to actually printing (with a union label) business cards with my contact information and a new logo that transitioned my guitar into an M-16 5.56-mm assault rifle. Both brazen and absurdly defiant.

It was an unstable and bad time for me, and I did nothing to make it better; either for myself or for people around me. For the most part I ignored my own behavior and focused on that damned outlaw persona and the whole concept of being a revolutionary cultural worker.

𝄢𝄢𝄢𝄢

When legendary World War II flying ace Greg "Pappy" Boyington picked up his grandfatherly moniker he was an "ancient" 31 years old; but he was given that handle because he was a decade older than the Marine flyers answering to him. I turned 30 in 1984 and found myself in the bizarre "pappy" roles of elder statesman of the political music world.

It turned out that there was a young sub-culture that actually appreciated my "cultural workers" approach and my rudely defiant attitude. To my amazement, I became a mentor to a number of young, up-and-coming musicians, though not always because of the political bent of my music.

A young singer-songwriter-guitar-player named *Scott Henkel* did the most spot-on Neal Young one could imagine.[191] His solo performances brought more people to the coffeehouse than anyone (including my live album) had ever done. It was not uncommon for almost 500 Scott fans to crowd the coffeehouse, the street, the alley, and the sidewalk. Those

---

[191] He once entered a radio contest for Neal Young tribute artists and the judges disqualified for him because they refused to believe that he had not submitted a tape of Young himself. (It was all Scott.)

I was never sure if he understood what I was trying to do with the music, though he seemed more-than supportive of at least individual issues that arose. He gladly performed at various peace concerts; though I never really knew if it was fundamental support or part of his whole Neal Young mimicry. I guess it didn't matter, because he successfully drew people who otherwise would not have heard the message of the speakers at the events.

I would have liked to have helped Scott get to a national audience, but his drug usage was so extreme that even at our local venue he was often just "out of it." Despite my own personal opposition to illegal drugs (originally because it made users such an easy target for government harassment), I have always quietly tolerated people who chose that lifestyle (besides, there was no denying the medical benefits of THC). But Scott seemed to me to be high more frequently than being straight; and that was problematic as well as disappointing.

THE POET LAUREATE SOUL OF FOLKIE ROCK & ROLL

audiences were mostly high school students or recent high school graduates, and very rarely of legal drinking age.

If the goal had been profits, then his concerts would have been massive failures. But the goal was the work of generating change through cultural work; and on that front, Scott was a massive success for *Bread and Roses*.[192]

Another eager young musician that came to me (without a drug habit, incidentally) was 17-or-18-year-old *Jim Callahan*. Jim was an excellent musician (especially on electronic keyboard) and a terrific songwriter. He didn't pull the kind of crowd that Scott did; but no one did, Besides, the coffeehouse wasn't about crowd size as much as it was about quality.

Quality-wise, Jim was phenomenal. Even better for my goals, the crowds that came to see him were blue-collar working people — a population that I really wanted to reach. Jim was from the working-class suburb of Brooklyn Park and his father was a Baltimore City firefighter. His parents always came to his shows (I loved that level of support) and as word-of-mouth spread in his own community, he began drawing larger crowds who had not heard him before or only heard about him.

He was a phenomenal talent and one of the most creative artists that we showcased; he was exploring 1980's creative paths that were truly cutting-edge experimental art. But notably different from the established Avant Garde wave of the era, he was egalitarian and not the slightest bit aloof. He truly was a working-class artist; and that was exactly the kind of young talent I wanted to see come along.

I saw more potential in him than I had in most of the dozen or so young kids that had been hanging around up until then. Jim was decades ahead of his time creatively. In the mid-1980's he created a one-man show of highly-advanced (for the time) all electronic music. Beyond just synthesizer MIDI music, he was pioneering computer-controlled multi-track live music (using a *Commodore 64*).

At the time, what he was doing was both technically beyond my understanding and audibly outside of my personal tastes. Nonetheless, it clearly was cutting-edge and brilliantly creative. It took me another decade-and-a-half to grow into even a rudimentary understanding of the technology

---

[192] If there was a happy biproduct of my time with him, it was that I stayed in touch with his then-girlfriend and eventually hired her as my assistant. She embraced the political work and made several humanitarian trips to El Salvador as well as becoming part of the labor movement.

THE LEGEND DIES ON — GARY GREEN

involved, and another decade to develop a genuine appreciation of it. I wish I had "got it" back then[193].

Jim was one of many people that I genuinely wish I could have helped more; but I just didn't know what to do with him. He was too far ahead of his time; or at least ahead of me. He also was one of a handful of young musicians that came to me for mentoring who both understood what I was doing and didn't freak out over my outlaw image (and my guns). In fact, one night when he and his parents were mugged on the street coming into Bread and Roses, he ran into the coffeehouse calling for me to "go get them".

Sometime during that period when he played at Bread and Roses, he changed his stage name to *Solitaire* and launched an amazing career with a large international following. I lost track of him over the years, but he clearly did not need me. His technical prowess combined with genuine musical and lyrical creativity was powerful enough that I believed he could have a significant impact on the entire world of music; and clearly, I was correct, based on the worldwide following that he developed.[194]

While the hoot nights remained free-admission, we always "passed the hat" (often literally my hat, but sometimes a large coffee can). Those collected funds were divided equally among the hoot performers (with the coffeehouse keeping nothing).

For non-hoot performances, we usually charged a cover at the door; but, unlike my experiences in New York almost a decade earlier, 100% of our door usually went to the performers. With all those additional hours (and paid gigs) available, we became even more overwhelmed with people wanting to play at Bread and Roses. We switched the coffeehouse hours from weekends-only to seven-nights-a-week. On weekends, we opened at noon. That created a lot of time slots for live music.

---

[193] When he saw the letter from Pete Seeger that said there should be a *Ballad of Gary Green*, young Jim wrote that song and sent it to Pete. That embarrassing tribute to me did not, at all impact my admiration for his talent; if anything, it made me embarrassingly uncomfortable that he included that song in many of his sets.

[194] Forty years later, after *Googling* Jim Callahan, I reached out via email and telephone to reconnect with Jim. As brilliant then as he had been in his teens, I learned that he had both continued writing songs and had pursued careers in technology (where he pioneered modern 911 technologies in use by emergency services in some of America's largest cities). Along the way, he had become a Captain in the *Baltimore City Fire Department*. Even after a series of personal health challenges and tragedies in his family (including the untimely death of his wife), the voice I heard on the phone was filled with the same creative passion that I had heard on the stage at Bread and Roses Two in Baltimore. Even pushing sixty-years-old, he remained a creative force that people should hear!

THE POET LAUREATE SOUL OF FOLKIE ROCK & ROLL

My own criteria for bookings were multi-faceted. I felt like there were (at least) two schools of thought about music: one was that a musician's job was to entertain and take people's minds away from whatever was going on in the world. I respected and appreciated that goal. But I leaned toward Woody Guthrie's thought that a musician's job was *"to comfort disturbed people and disturb comfortable people"*.

Subscribing to the Guthrie description, I wanted to provide a place for artists that, as Moe Asch had said, "have something to say". People that needed to be heard and who might not otherwise have a place to find an audience for their work. I also wanted to provide a venue where more established artists could be comfortable, with no pressures, and could commune with like-minded people.

For everyone who played, established or newbie, I wanted to instill in them an understanding that work of supporting (and upholding) anti-racist, anti-sexist, peace, LBGTQ, and "progressive" culture required the proverbial pen as much as it required the proverbial sword. More specifically, I wanted the performers to understand that their words, their music, their voices, were positioned to educate, organize, and incite... while at the same time making people feel good.

Also, I wanted to provide a location where genuine community groups could hold meetings and events and everyone else would know that if an event was held at Bread and Roses Two, then it was cool. The challenge of that was policing against various sectarian and community groups with no community nor following. Fortunately, between Howard Ehrlich and myself, we knew enough of that alphabet soup that we could on-the-fly determine which groups were real and which were just full of shit.

I wanted the coffeehouse to be a safe haven for people outside the mainstream and without a community. Finally, I wanted everything that happened at Bread & Roses to be fun. Howard was fond of quoting early 20th century anarchist *Emma Goldman*, "If I can't dance, I don't want to be part of your revolution". Amidst all of the seemingly heavy-duty "cultural work", I wanted to rock and roll; I wanted people to come have a good time.

Those goals, especially the final one, made the coffeehouse a lot less dogmatic than one might think. More importantly, it seemed to work, and we drew a broad base of people who subscribed to part, or all, of our mission.

We repeatedly booked a local Irish folk group that included future Maryland Governor *Marty O'Malley*. We booked famous folkies, like my dear friend *Mike Seeger*. We booked labor troubadours like the amazing feminist singer *Bobby McGee*. We booked new folk stalwarts like the great *Charlie King* with a (then)-modern incarnation of the Almanac Singers called *Bright Morning Star*.

THE LEGEND DIES ON — GARY GREEN

Despite my then-well-known single-minded focus on acoustic folk, we booked rock bands, new wave bands, electronic bands, even a high school marching band. We booked three different rappers, though I was extremely sensitive to their poetry, rhymes, and delivery more than their beats (then again, I did have that rhythm issue). We booked comedians, theater troupes, tribute artists, classical pianists, and string/woodwind ensembles, even magicians.

We also continued to book performers who were geared toward raising social, political, and spiritual consciousness with their art. At the apex of those artists was *Ngoma Hill* (who decades later would be named *New York State National Beat Poet Laureate*). At the time he was performing with his then-wife, *Jaribu*, in a duo they called *Serious Bizness*. I had shared a gig in New York with them and I was so overcome by the precision performance and the crowd-inciting passion that I immediately asked the Bread & Roses booking team to arrange to get them to Baltimore.

Ngoma[195] sang with the intensity of labor organizing, civil rights struggles, the peace movement, and strengthening poor people. It was exactly what I wanted Bread & Roses to be known for. The more performers we could find with their passion, talent, and organizing skills, the closer we would be to those goals.

Altogether, we probably booked 200 performers a year; and every one of them adhered in some way to our missions. More than being a generic concert hall, we wanted to impact and influence the artists and their art; and there was strong evidence that we did so, for the most part.

More and more I stepped back from bookings and the day-to-day work, turning both over to a more-than-capable team of really good people.

My primary focus became mentoring, educating, and inciting; with my music and with the people we would bring to the coffeehouse (as well as to local churches, community centers, and larger concert venues that we began booking as well).

Major national talent brokers and booking agents frequently called me or visited me to pitch their stables. One big-name agent flew to Baltimore and offered me several well-known acts "at no cost"; other than my providing cocaine[196] —and that was *not* an unusual request for the 1980's.

---

[195] Nigerian: Ngoma Osayemi Ifatunmise

[196] In later years, decades later, I came to personally know those performers and I found it hard to believe, though not implausible, that the agent was truly representing what they wanted. I have never had the proclivity to ask them directly: but if you are reading this and know that I rejected you from Bread & Roses, please feel free to ask me if your booking agent wanted dope as pay; and please feel free to either fess up or tell me he was full of shit!

THE POET LAUREATE SOUL OF FOLKIE ROCK & ROLL

Of course those agents had no way of knowing about my fierce opposition to drug usage. Too many of my radical political friends had been framed on drug charges; so, for years I had made it a policy that I would not use nor tolerate around me any illegal drug. Further, the whole control-freak aspect of my behavior prevented me from drinking or getting high (with legal or illegal substances). So those agents that asked me to pay performers with coke had no idea why I shut them out and refused to take their calls. One was so persistent that when I politely told him no, he dropped the "price" to half of the amount of cocaine he had originally asked me to "pay". *(That one broke my heart, because the act is was pitching for drugs was one that I really liked.)*

Though the agents wanting me to pay in cocaine were plentiful, realistically, many of the people who approached me personally were looking for a stepping-stone into the music "business" and not a drug connection.

Little did they know that I was about as far from "business" as one could be. Most were not expecting me, at 30-years-old, to take that elder-statesman role where I found myself planted.

THE LEGEND DIES ON — GARY GREEN

Opus Twenty-One:
Túpac Meets Revolutionary Cultural Work & Communists

"From little G chords, mighty revolutions come"

— Rosanne Cash[197]

One of the women who did bookings for Bread & Roses Two, *Sally*, lived about eight blocks north of the coffeehouse on Greenmount Avenue. Some late nights, I would drop her off at her apartment rather than have her walk even that short distance in the cold; besides, it was on my way home. Her row-house (as Baltimore multi-story connected apartments were called), was not in a good area at the 3900 block of Greenmount Avenue; in fact, it was pure ghetto, and the entire block was infested with rats, roaches, and whatever other vermin haunted inner-city slums.

One night as I was driving her home, she told me that she had a new neighbor a couple of doors down that I should meet. She said that it was a single mom who at one time had been a "famous" Black Panter Party leader. Over the years, I had come across a lot of people who claimed to have been part of the Panthers, but really were never actually involved (except maybe accepting a free breakfast every now and then). I sort of shrugged off her recommendation and said, "Sure, bring her by the coffeehouse one night." I thought that was the end of it; but I am really glad it was not.

A few nights later at the coffeehouse, I was playing for a meeting of a subgroup of NECO (Baltimore's *Northeast Community Organization*). The group had called a meeting in response to white absentee landlords who had been purchasing ghetto row-houses, increasing rents, and failing to provide adequate maintenance. *(Shades of the South Bronx!)*

I ended my set with my powerfully bitter anti-racist call-to-action song, *Snakebite Poison*. Either the song or my performance drew a standing ovation and actual cheers. My stepping off stage disrupted the agenda of the meeting as most of the attendees surrounded me and began asking questions or requesting that I perform at various church groups or neighborhood organizations.

When the commotion died down, I spotted Sally with a woman who I'd never seen before. She introduced me to her new neighbor, a fellow North Carolinian and former Black Panther activist, *Afeni Shakur*.

---

[197] From a social media post in 2024; verified as original in a direct message to the author from Rosanne Cash's husband, John Leventhal.

THE POET LAUREATE SOUL OF FOLKIE ROCK & ROLL

I instantly knew the name; she had been one of the *Panther Twenty-one*[198]. Afeni Shakur was a legend. As soon as Sally introduced her, I recognized the name and the history; she truly was a revolutionary doyenne[199].

To my amazement and delight, she had heard of me too. She knew *Sherman*, who had told her about his crazy hillbilly-radical, folk-singing white friend. (It was from her that I learned that Sherman was in prison.)

We talked for about an hour. She told me that less than a month after she and all of her co-defendants were acquitted, she gave birth to her son. A year later she had renamed him *Túpac*, replacing his birth name of *Lesane* (which she viewed as a "slave name" like her own birth name, *Alice Williams*).

Afeni told me that she originally had created the name on her son's birth certificate to protect him from her FBI-targeted legacy.[200] *I knew THAT sentiment well;* and it was further confirmation of the kind of targeting that had plagued Phil Ochs and others ... alas, including me.

For the decade after her trial, she had tried to make a living in New York City and be an attentive mother. But after a divorce (from Baltimore-native and Black Liberation Army activist Mutulu Shakur) then

---

[198] *The Panther 21* were members of the Black Panther Party who had been arrested in New York City and accused of bombing four police stations, the Board of Education Building, five department stores, and the Bronx Botanical Gardens. Afeni, pregnant and facing a 300-year prison sentence, defended herself in what turned into the longest trial in New York history and one of the most publicized at the time.

New York Philharmonic Director (and composer) *Leonard Bernstein*, author *Tom Wolfe* (who I would meet two decades later), and even my old Miami compadre *Abbie Hoffman*, were among scores of celebrities who raised money for their bail and their defense. Two of the defendants jumped bail and fled to Algeria, where *Eldridge Cleaver, Huey P. Newton*, and other Panthers had been granted political asylum.

[199] Despite the District Attorney reading aloud from Chinese Communist Party Chairman Mao Zedong's Little Red Book of quotations and showing the court a two-hour Italian movie called The Battle of Algiers, Afeni famously shattered the prosecution's case and became somewhat of a folk hero in the process.

With no legal training, during her cross examination of one of the prosecution-witnesses she got him to admit that he was one of three of the 21 defendants who actually was an undercover police mole. Under oath, during her cross, he admitted the and the other two agent-provocateurs had organized all of the illegal activities for which the group was accused. Even further, she got him to admit that he had only seen her do "powerful, inspiring, and beautiful" community work.

[200] Her son was named either for *Túpac Amaru* the 16th-century Incan chief or for *Túpac Amaru II*, an 18th century Peruvian revolutionary; there were, apparently, a lot of people named *Túpac*. At various times she cited both stories to me. Her own name, Afeni, was a Nigerian Yoruba word meaning "lover of the people".

THE LEGEND DIES ON — GARY GREEN

losing her job (probably because of her notoriety), and apparently sinking into the drug world, she decided that New York was no longer healthy for her and her children. She packed up her nine-year-old daughter and 13-year-old son and moved to Baltimore. Shortly after that, she had met her neighbor, Sally, who had taken her to the coffeehouse that night.

Afeni told me that she was "retired" from political action, and she just wanted to be a "regular mom for my babies". I didn't believe her for a minute; despite how sincere she sounded and apparently believed it herself. If it had really been the case, I would never have seen her again; but in fact, I saw her many-many more times.

I saw her periodically at *Sam's Belly Food Co-op*, across the street from the coffeehouse. "The Belly" (as we called it) offered discounted and free food for poor people in the neighborhood.[201] Sally had taken Afeni there, introducing her to the many services in the Waverly-Charles-Village community (including the *Peoples' Health Clinic* and my coffeehouse).

Afeni had not been able to find work in Baltimore, despite ten-years' experience as a paralegal in New York (and that legendary job of defending herself). So, discounted or free food was a welcome addition to welfare and food stamps that kept her and her children alive.

The landlord of the dump-of-an-apartment (in the same row but a couple of doors down from Sally) had qualified for Federal Section 8 grants;[202] so, Afeni's rent was either reduced or granted.

I also saw her periodically at community gatherings where I would appear to do one or two songs or where I would just show up. The one unexpected place where I ran into her was at a holiday pot-luck lunch at the home of one of the leaders of the Baltimore chapter of the *Communist Party USA* (CPUSA).

I thought seeing her there was exceptionally interesting ... since she supposedly was "retired" from political activism. Actually, it was interesting seeing *any* Panther there, given the on-again-off-again relationship between the Panthers and CPUSA throughout the 1970's.

At that lunch she asked me a question that I thought was the most off-the-wall thing I'd ever been asked at a gathering of hard-core political people: *"What do you think of Rap?"*

---

[201] Another of the *Black Panther Party* and leftist founded neighborhood support services, *The Belly* was named from the ancient Greek myth of the Minotaur, "in the belly of the beast"; with "Sam" being *Uncle Sam*. The double entendre of it being that it was a food cooperative to feed hungry bellies in the community.

[202] Section 8 of the Housing Act of 1937 (42 U.S.C. § 1437f) authorized the payment of rental housing assistance to private landlords on behalf of low-income families.

THE POET LAUREATE SOUL OF FOLKIE ROCK & ROLL

Whew. That was complicated. We had booked some rappers at Bread and Roses, and I definitely had some strong opinions. But I assumed she was just making small-talk, and I responded with a polite small-talk answer that avoided giving an opinion.

She was much too astute to let me get away with a brush-off answer. "I'm asking for a reason," she sharply insisted and continued, "How is rap like or different from anything else? Do you think it's political?"

It was clear that she had an agenda for asking. Never known as a diplomat, I unleashed my thoughts; after all, she DID ask, so I began lecturing.

"To me, for any kind of music to be complete it needs to be dialectical; it needs to be about form *and* about content —the two intertwined together. One without the other makes the music empty to me," I began.

She held up her hand like a safety-patrol officer indicating she wanted me to pause. Then she motioned to her young-teen son to come closer. From the other side of the room, I had seen him straining to hear as soon as she asked the question and I had begun to wax philosophically. As he crossed the room and sat down beside me, she told me to "go on". I did.

"Well let me be clear that this is just my personal taste in music; it's not some political philosophy or anything that deep. It's just how I look at music," I pre-apologized for the rant of strung-together soapbox lectures I felt that I was about to give.

"Go on with what you were saying to me," she encouraged me as she waived her hands in circle, like a rolling wheel.

I continued, "For me, music is about the content *and* the form. If either one is not there, then I probably won't like it; but if they both are there, then it is great. There are exceptions, but to me it doesn't matter if it is rap or bluegrass or opera or headbangers or Nashville sound; it's all about the form with the content". I raved (flashing back to the Pancake House and Waylon Jennings lecturing me, *"Country, Hillbilly, Rock and Roll, Folk, Gospel. It's all the same thing"*).

Túpac asked me, "I don't see what you are saying

"Okay, you hear my accent; I'm a hillbilly, no two ways about that..."

Afeni didn't interrupt me, but she sort-of snortled a chuckle, as if I had just made the biggest understatement of the year.

I continued, "So, when I hear Northern or Midwestern or California people singing Appalachian music, a couple of things go through my head. I mean, it is cool that they are digging my culture and singing our songs. BUT... when those same people phony-up a Southern accent when they don't have one otherwise, THAT outrages me.

"It's like rich, white, academic anthropologists coming to study "the creatures" and mimicking what they find so they can communicate with "the primitives". I don't find a damned-thing about *that* to be flattering or

THE LEGEND DIES ON — GARY GREEN

charming. I call it "cultural misappropriation". I could see Afeni nod in agreement with the term, So I continued.

"I mean, if I was singing a Yip Harburg or Irving Berlin song, I wouldn't affect a New York or a Yiddish accent to make the song somehow more authentic. In fact, if I had been so crass as to do so, it would have been at best condescending and at worst out-and-out racist. For Christ's sake, if I had a gig in The Bronx, I wouldn't spice my phrasing with a bunch of *"not-for-nothing"* and *"get-outta-heah"*. It just would not be appropriate.

"It's the same with those fake Southern accents from Northerners singing hillbilly songs. And... from the get-go... I feel exactly the same way about *white* people rapping. White rappers are guilty of cultural misappropriation and disrespectful to an entire culture. In that regard, I find it racist. The same is basically true of Black rappers who were educated at Oxford and whose normal speech is formal English; they are just as bad when they fake street-speak and pretend to be all ghetto when in reality they roll up their windows and lock the doors when they have to drive by our neighborhoods."

I felt myself rising to a typical Gary-soapbox lecture, but surprisingly, I didn't lose her or Túpac. In fact, they both became more attentive and more engaged. So, I continued, repeating many things I'd said over the years but all strung-together for them.

"So, let's talk about rap, and remember this is for me personally. First is the form. Even if it has awesome beats and unthinkable rhymes...any of those things; then it is nice, but for me not interesting to me and certainly not complete; it feels like something is missing.

"If you have great music, amazing instruments, terrific rhythm —which I don't have— (they laughed with me on that) ... if you have all that but your lyrics are a jumble that no one can understand, then your music is nice but incomplete. It failed to communicate; not just with white hillbilly boys but with *anyone*.

"You may have great form; but without the content, I am not interested," I paused to breath and make sure they were still with me.

"I mean, it's not just rap; it's any musical form. I love me some rockabilly and some rock & roll and some country music and some high-brow shit. But if I listen to the lyrics, I am often like, *what-the-fuck*?

"The music can be pure escapism; forget about everything and just ride with the sound! It's like alcohol or drugs; pure escape from life. And some of it is absolutely brilliant at doing that," I said, thinking of my infatuation with Jerry Lee Lewis.

They were intently listening, so I continued, "So, I look at the content. What do those rhymes say? What are those words about? Are they from

THE POET LAUREATE SOUL OF FOLKIE ROCK & ROLL

the heart? Do they have something to say or are they just filler rhymes? What exactly IS the content that is being presented?

"That doesn't mean it has to preach, or lecture, or be political. It just needs to be real! Even Little Richard's *Long Tall Sally* or *Tutti Frutti* with its *"awop-bop-a-loo-mop, alop bom bom"* —those were written to be too fast or too hard to say for Pat-fucking-Boone to record them. *That* made them real when Little Richard sang them, regardless of the gibberish!

"Or listen to Jerry Lee Lewis sing *Whole Lotta Shakin*; he takes that Curlee Williams song (famously recorded by Big Mabel Smith) and makes it his own. You hear him do it and you believe they are his words; it becomes HIS song!

"That's why I dig people like Waylon Jennings; they have the ability to make a song theirs —as if THEY wrote it about themselves. It's *sincere*.

"Johnny Cash totally stole *Folsom Prison Blues* from Gordon Jenkins' *Crescent City Blues*; but almost everyone that hears the Cash song not only believes HE wrote it, but believes he spent time in the joint.

"Again, it is the authenticity; the ability to make it your own. A song really doesn't have to preach; it just has to FEEL. It doesn't have to be political; it is just the act of being *authentic* and that within itself is political.

"But just like one-sided form, content is the same deal. You can have the most moving and powerful lyrics ever written; you can make Shakespear look like a piker. But, if your music is so fucked up that no one wants to listen to what you are saying, then you have failed to communicate. You have nice poetry, but it is incomplete.

"Look, it's basic dialectics. The whole is always greater than the sum of its parts. Human beings are made up of a bunch of chemicals and water; but if you put all of those components in a bottle, you don't have a human. The whole is *always* greater than the sum of its parts," I emphasized as I sort-of concluded my rambling.

I saw Túpac's eyes widen and his mother paying close attention to what I was saying. They both looked like I was supposed to say something else, so I continued pontificating.

"Now, all of that is very general. But you asked me what *I, personally,* think of rap; what is MY opinion.

"Okay. First, I look at the dialectics of it, all those things I just described. I do that with *any* kind of music and most art of any kind.

"But for me, the most important thing is: does that combination of content and form —the whole— fulfill the job of a cultural revolutionary? Is the content revolutionary? Is the form revolutionary? Is the new whole made from them revolutionary?

"Rap, like the pure raw mountain hillbilly music of my culture, has the powerful potential to tell the story of the people; or it can teach, guide, and educate people; or it can do both. When it does both, then it is magic. Then it is truly great. If the form, the music, can move me and the lyrics can move me, guide me, teach me, or even just make me say *WOW*, then it is great.

"Sometimes just an instrumental or a rhythm pattern or a beat can be *SO* brilliantly composed that it evokes images, thoughts, memories; and THAT is true MUSICAL genius," I finally really did finish.

Afeni thanked me and said sharply, "That's a lot to think about; especially for a young man thinking about writing poetry."

Obviously, there was something going on with this young Túpac kid that I didn't know anything about. But, as soon as I finished, Túpac perked up as if a classroom bell had rung indicating time to go home. Without saying a word, he jumped up and went back to the other side of the room with the other kids. I figured I'd never see him again. And, once again, was I ever wrong!

The next Saturday afternoon, unexpected, Túpac walked into the coffeehouse. Somewhat sheepishly, he introduced himself as if I had somehow forgotten him; I had not. Besides, we didn't get a lot of 13-or-14-year-old kids at Bread & Roses and he definitely looked his young age.

Unlike the *Thug Life* and later bravado that came to be associated with him, the young Túpac was quiet, shy, and seemed a little insecure...at least at first. He had come by the coffeehouse on-his-own, not at his mother's prodding, and he was clearly unsure of what to say to me.[203]

I tried my best to put him at ease so that I could understand what had motivated him to walk nine blocks in the Baltimore cold. After a little bit of small talk about the holiday lunch where we'd met, he asked me if I would mind reading some of his poetry (not him reading it for me, mind you, but me reading it).

It didn't take a genius to see that this kid was internalizing a lot of very complex baggage; stress that would have been overwhelming for almost anyone, but especially intense for a 14-year-old to have to deal with daily.

I already knew that he lived in a horrible Section-8 apartment that was attached to a row that I knew (from Sally) was overrun with rats and roaches; so much so that they often invaded beds and shoes.

Eventually, he told me that though Section-8 covered the cost of rent, there often was not enough money to pay *Baltimore Gas & Electric*. I knew *The Belly* helped with food; but it wasn't enough for two growing children. He said that his mother got some *welfare* money monthly, but it wasn't much.

---

[203] Túpac said that the group THUG LIFE was an acronym for "The Hate U Give Little Infants Fucks Everybody".

THE POET LAUREATE SOUL OF FOLKIE ROCK & ROLL

While living in that squalor and dealing with the poverty, he attended Eighth Grade via a court-ordered desegregation busing plan that sent him to *Roland Park Middle School*[204] in the wealthiest neighborhood in Baltimore City *(and one that even in the 1980's continued to have deed restrictions prohibiting Black and Jewish residents)*.

This kid, with the odd-sounding name and from the ghetto, shared classes with the children of white millionaires who wanted for nothing. Then every afternoon he would come home to no-food-in-the-house, frequently turned-off electricity, only one pair of shoes, and not many more changes of clothing. I couldn't imagine the psychological trauma of being the single "have-not" in that sea of "haves".

Beyond the abject poverty that was thrown in his face daily, he watched his mother's disappointments as she struggled to be a "normal mom" and he tried to be a big-brother to his younger sister (a small child who I never met other than seeing from a distance, but clearly, he worshipped). Added to those struggles was the recurring specter of drug addiction that had haunted his mother in New York.

He was a complex kid. He knew a lot of television pop-culture, so it seemed clear to me that he was watching a lot of TV somewhere. He told me that he was surrounded by a community of drug users and dealers, but other than marijuana, he avoided drugs.

Besides the debilitating drug culture, the community was wrought with burglary, robbery, and the standard catalog of ghetto violent crime. He told me he didn't like it at all, but it was where he lived and other people were afraid to come into that community; and he didn't blame them.

He struggled in his classes at school, but outside of school he had long intellectual discussions that were beyond the capability of most college students that I knew.

He wrote adolescent poetry but had rhyming schemes that rivaled the best crossword dictionaries and poetic meter that surpassed most Lit majors and nearly all songwriters that I had known. Like I said, young Túpac was one complex kid.

At first, he was quiet, reflective, shy, and an introvert; but his mother was one of the most dynamic (and among the five most-famous) Black Panther Party figures in the country (along *with Bobby Seale, Huey Newton, Eldridge Cleaver*, and *Angela Davis*). Clearly not intimidated by powerful women (or anyone else), still he obviously was starving for

---

[204] I knew Túpac before his much-publicized tenure at T*he Baltimore High School For The Arts*, where he famously met *Jada Pinkett* and "came out of his shell". When I knew him, he was bused to school, first in hoity-toity *Roland Park* and then to the traditionally all-Black *Dunbar High School* in east Baltimore near the *Douglass Homes* housing project.

THE LEGEND DIES ON — GARY GREEN

adult-male role-model guidance (something that prima-facie was just impossibly non-sequitur to come from a white Southern country singer).

Nonetheless, during the course of the dozens of days that he came to spend hours-at-a-time with me, his speech patterns noticeably began to be peppered with some of the eccentricities that were part of my day-to-day lingo; mostly 1950's beat slang, 1960's hippie jargon, and scattered jazz-jive talk. He began calling people *squares* and *goofballs*, referring to males as *cats*; dropping a whole new lexicon into his vocabulary, some of which he carried for the rest of his short life.

On that first visit to Bread & Roses, he wanted me to read his poetry, and he wanted to talk to me about what I had meant at that lunch when I had said that content and form had to fulfill the job of a cultural revolutionary. After that coffeehouse visit, he was less shy and eventually became enthusiastic and genuinely over-the-top with excitement, ambition, and humor. During the next few weeks, he clearly became more comfortable with being himself around me. I saw him transformed from that introverted reflective kid to an animated, aggressive, passion-driven *performer*. It definitely was *performance* that he was honing.

My lecturing and mentoring became more of collaboratively bouncing ideas off of each other. It was different than a mere cultural exchange; it was a mutual respect without creative or intellectual boundaries... with a kid half my age.

Túpac had heard about revolution for his entire life. He was raised amongst revolutionaries. The Black Panther Party identified itself as the vanguard revolutionary party; multiple family members on the Shakur side had been or *were still* wanted fugitives for their revolutionary activities. Even the people at that CPUSA lunch (where we met) were talking about "the revolution". In *that regard* I was not much different from a lot of adults in his life.

But in all of that, he had never heard anyone talk about a *cultural revolutionary*; no one had said that music, poetry, art could be revolutionary. He wanted to know what that meant; he *needed* to know what I meant. But beyond that, he wanted to know ... HOW.

During that first visit we talked about all of those things going on in his life and we talked about his poetry; those would be subjects that we'd always talk about regardless of any other subjects that would creep into our conversations. Yet those were the two subjects that he was most reluctant to discuss.

He wasn't ashamed of nor embarrassed about the poverty and his life situation; he gave no indication of that at all. Instead, he seemed genuinely interested in shielding me (and everyone else) from what he was going through. At that young age he was setting himself as a barrier between the painful ugliness and his friends.

THE POET LAUREATE SOUL OF FOLKIE ROCK & ROLL

It was quite remarkable to see, and it was extremely difficult to crack through; though slowly I eventually was able to get him comfortable enough to do so. I did that by making him feel like my awareness of it all was no big deal, just another aspect of life.

For that first visit, the real subject was poetry and music in a revolutionary context. In the coffeehouse I had a cassette tape of songs from my *Folk Music and the American Left* class, so I played for him Lead Belly's *Bourgeois Blues*:

Them white folks in Washington they know how	*I tell all the colored folks to listen to me*
To call a man a nigger just to see him bow	*Don't try to find you no home in Washington, DC*
Lord, it's a bourgeois town	*'Cause it's a bourgeois town*
Uhm, the bourgeois town	*Uhm, the bourgeois town*
I got the bourgeois blues I'm	*I got the bourgeois blues and I'm*
Gonna spread the news all around	*Gonna spread the news.* [205]

That got his attention. I showed him the big blue letters written around the body of my guitar. We talked about how music could be considered dangerous. I shared the stories of Queen Mary and of Plato. I introduced him to Woody Guthrie's lyrics and one of my favorite Woody quotes, *"one good song is worth 10,000 of your best speeches and a couple of armies"*.

I could see that he was fascinated, but I wanted to caution him as well. I shared what Huey P. Newton had said about being a revolutionary, because I knew Túpac would be familiar with him: *"A revolutionary must realize that if he is sincere, death is imminent due to the fact that the things he is saying and doing are extremely dangerous."* To hammer the point in, I told him the story of Ella May Wiggins.

We talked for three, maybe four, hours; and probably would have gone longer, but that night's performers began arriving to set up just as the evening staff and early-bird customers began to drift in. I invited him to stay, but he was still much too shy and had a lot to think about. THAT would change by the next visit.

𝄞𝄢𝄞𝄢𝄞𝄢

My attendance at the pot-luck lunch with members of the *Communist Party USA* was no happenstance of hanging out with the alphabet soup of leftists. Beginning a couple of years earlier, I had become more-than merely close to The Party — just as Túpac Shakur was beginning to do.

Some of Túpac's later biographers tacitly apologized for his membership in the Party's youth organization by brushing it off as his somehow being under the beguiling influence of his white girlfriend. While it's true that Túpac was dating *Mary Jean Baldridge* whose parents were activists

---

[205] The Bourgeois Blues © Huddie Ledbetter, Arvee Music

in The Party[206]; but that was not even Túpac's motivation. In fact, he came to the Young Communist League through his mother and probably met Mary Jean that way (though Mary Jean was already deeply involved in the arts and they could have connected there[207]).

That *innocently being duped* nonsense was the same kind of bullshit that many Woody Guthrie biographers had written; that Woody was some kind of naïve hick that was never actually a member of the Communist Party. Woody (and apparently Túpac) supposedly were so simple-minded that those conniving commies were able to run circles around them, manipulating them into blindly following.

Make no mistake about it; neither man was tricked. Neither was simple-minded. Both knew exactly what they were doing and were quite committed.

As for Woody, Gordon Friesen told me, many times, that he and Woody had been members of the same Communist Party Club in New York[208]. Woody wrote a weekly column for the Communist Party's national newspaper[209]. Moreover, anyone who ever heard Woody's song *The Flood and The Storm* (from his *The Ballads of Sacco and Vanzetti* album) knows that song could not have been the product of anyone who was naïve to Communist philosophy.

Likewise, I was even more certain about Túpac's politics. When he began coming to hang out with me, no he wasn't a member of anything; he was barely 14-years-old. But unequivocally, three years later he joined the Party's *Young Communist League*; I have seen his membership application, and I saw him participate in Party campaigns.

The *Baltimore YCL*[210] was made up mostly of *Red Diaper Babies* (leftist lingo for children of political activists who were raised with their parents' ideals). Multiple times Túpac, Mary Jean, and other YCL kids

---

[206] Multiple people have incorrectly identified either Margaret or Jim Baldridge (Mary Jean's parents) as the Chairperson of the CPUSA in Baltimore. At the time, that simply was not true. The District Chair of The Party was an elderly African American man (who shared my last name); the Baldridge's where white. Margaret *did* eventually become Maryland party chair; but not until later.

[207] Though I am casually still in touch with her, via Facebook, I have never raised the subject with her.

[208] Communist Party "Clubs" were the basic organizational unit for members; often called "cells" by Federal agents and anti-communists.

[209] *Woody Sez* was an answer to Will Rogers' *Will Rogers Says* syndicated main-stream column.

[210] YCL is the Party's acronym for their Young Communist League

accompanied me as I would leaflet Baltimore neighborhoods promoting coffeehouse events or various community-organizing gatherings.

By the time he officially joined the Young Communist League, Túpac was committed and focused; and it had nothing to do with who he was dating. In fact, he probably was more focused and politically clear than most of the other YCL members[211].

From the first afternoon that Túpac Shakur showed up at my coffeehouse until 1988 when he joined the YCL, I was close enough to The Party that I was aware of his activities; so, my observations about his political activism in those days are absolutely empirical.

The CPUSA, both in Baltimore and nationwide, was extremely kind to me during my fugitive years; even more so than any of the alphabet soup of "New Left" and "Traditional Left" organizations of Maoist, Trotskyist, Social Democrats, Anarchists, Socialists, and whoever else clamored around my music. In fact, for much of the "new left" of the era I was a pariah; either because of my Southern heritage (which raised prejudicial suspicions) or because of my perceived "authoritarian" attitude *(which manifested as my blatant refusal to accept liberal principles of freedom of speech to all sides of any issue —I railed against free speech for racists, rapist, and fascists.)*

After my parents left Baltimore and before I found the coffeehouse, I was in dire need of a job. The Party hired me to revamp and then manage their *New Era Bookshop* at 408 Park Avenue. Besides the godsend of a much-needed paycheck, three-floors of philosophy, political, and religious books was heaven for my burgeoning academic life at Hopkins, Towson, and Morgan. Since academically I was delving into the aforementioned philosophical reconciliation of B.F. Skinner's *behavioral psychology* with Hegelian *dialectics,* you can see why the treasure-trove in the bookstore was great for me; that scholarly journey led me to *Pavlov* and then toward *Hegel's Logik*. From there, it was a short intellectual journey to Marx and then to Lenin.[212]

---

[211] In the 21st century, the Baltimore YCL Club was renamed *The Tupac Shakur Club.*

[212] Some of the most esoteric books in the store were important research works that simply were not available even in the best university libraries; like the complete works of *Lenin* published in the Soviet Union, the complete works of North Korea's *Kim il-sung*, books by East German's *Erich Honecker*, and even books by *Joseph Stalin*, along with the complete works of *Marx* and *Engels*. But there was also a treasure trove of non-political but equally rare Soviet-published works by physiologist *Ivan Petrovich Pavlov*, philosophers *Georg Wilhelm Friedrich Hegel, Ludwig Feuerbach, Immanuel Kant, Bruno Bauer, Pierre-Joseph Proudhon, Charles Fourier, Henri de Saint-Simon,* and even *Charles Darwin.* Eventually I was able to buy many of those rare books for my own library.

THE LEGEND DIES ON — GARY GREEN

Admittedly, I had initially approached CPUSA because I anticipated the potential of needing their help if my fugitive status came to an ugly head forcing me to actually flee the country. I never told any of their leadership about my situation, but I wanted to have them available if I needed to seek political asylum. It was the worst-kept secret among leftists (and the FBI) that CPUSA had close ties and received much funding directly from the Soviet Union. I mean come on: the party published two daily newspapers without advertising revenue, for God sakes! Duh! No one had to wonder how they could afford to do that[213]. *(And we won't even speculate how Party General Secretary Gus Hall paid for his home.)*

I was creating options for what to do if worse had come to worse and my only way to avoid assassination would have been political asylum in the Soviet Union. As I said earlier, such asylum was constitutionally guaranteed to people who were persecuted for defending the interests of the working people —for which I definitely qualified.[214] While my potential need to escape was my initial reason for making contact with The Party, my association with them grew to much more. My dire life-or-death situation should not be seen as an apologist explanation for my early 1980's association with The Communist Party... no more than Túpac's membership in the Party's YCL should be written off as his trying to appease his then-girlfriend (as those bad biographers have done).

Beyond political asylum and beyond university graduate-level studies, I became more and more impressed with CPUSA's involvement in labor unions, the civil rights movement, the anti-war and anti-nuclear-arms movement, and even anti-drugs in some of the inner-city's toughest neighborhoods. I felt more-and-more drawn to them, politically. And, of course, there was the historic connection to The Party through Sis & Gordon, Pete, and other old time New York City folkies.

Once I began the Bread & Roses adventures, Party members went out of their way to be supportive, help turn out crowds and recommend performers for us to book. So, the support between me and the Party was a two-way street.

The relationships developed to such a degree that (just like Túpac) I applied for Party membership and began attending Club meetings. Of

---

[213] Despite the "official" claims of donations from high-net-worth celebrities (of which there actually were some), reality was that the *Communist Party of the Soviet Union* purchased a large number of "subscriptions" at prices high enough to support the daily tabloid. In the USA, subscriptions (and postage) were free.

[214] Article 129 of the Soviet Constitution read, *"The U.S.S.R. affords the right of asylum to foreign citizens persecuted for defending the interests of the working people, or for their scientific activities, or for their struggle for national liberation".*

course, I didn't reveal my legal status; among the many reasons, I didn't want to subject anyone to the pressures of "harboring a fugitive". In fact, Túpac, his mother, and two Party board members were the only ones that knew my situation. Nonetheless, for a while I really became a "card-carrying" member; and yes, we really had cards and really called each other "comrade". *Far-out, huh?*

Even without knowing about the legal specter hanging over me, the leadership was more-than welcoming, encouraging, and supportive. They arranged for me to perform at the party's national convention at *Cobo Hall* in Detroit, and when I would play in New York (the Party headquarters) there would always be "comrades" in the audience.

When *Boris Yeltsin*, the *First Secretary of the Moscow City Committee of the Communist Party of the Soviet Union* visited Washington DC, he made a side trip to Baltimore. Five years before he became the Russian President, I was asked to be part of the official CPUSA delegation that hosted a reception for him and his aides. When his advance team learned that a "famous folksinger" was to be part of the welcoming group, they prepared a gift-package for me, including a miniature *balalaika*, the obligatory *matryoshka* (nesting dolls) souvenirs, and a handful of Soviet Communist Party pins and trinkets. (Most of which I still have.)

Apparently, as Kunstler had negotiated, no one was looking really hard for me; because God-knows the FBI and CIA certainly would have been monitoring anyone that met with Yeltsin. It's just hard to believe that there wouldn't be some cross-reference analyst who would say, "hey, that *famous folksinger* is a wanted fugitive". Their inaction further emboldened my cavalier behavior.

Yes, the Party was supportive of me; and I, in turn, participated in Party activities, educationals, newspaper distributions, leafleting, and a variety of social functions. The pot-luck lunch where I met Túpac was one of those social functions; it was all Party members and people close to the party near-joining. Afeni was among that latter group; young Túpac wasn't really on a recruitment radar at that time; he and his sister were just there with their mom.

Eventually I separated from the party (or it separated from me).[215]

---

[215] Eventually, some long-forgotten sectarian nonsense within the *Left* put me at odds with the leadership of The Party. Club meetings became intellectually taxing rather than stimulating as they originally had been. The retirement of the two (elderly) leaders who had hired me at the bookshop, the general Reagan-era chaos in the socialist world, and

THE LEGEND DIES ON — GARY GREEN

I frequently ranted against people compartmentalizing their lives, but ultimately, I was the most-guilty of that offense. Still a wanted fugitive (and given the unrestrained anger that added to my considerable baggage) I had to be very careful about who I associated with and what I said. Despite my outwardly cavalier attitude, I simultaneously was very guarded in what I would allow anyone to know about me; different parts of me for different purposes and different people. I completely compartmentalized.

It was a level of paranoia that would stay with me for the rest of my life; as the often-quoted *Joseph Heller* wrote in *Catch-22*, "Just because you're paranoid doesn't mean they aren't after you". Hence, my *omertà*[216] was something I would never shake, and wouldn't really want to discard.

Túpac Amaru Shakur, however, was a harmless 14-year-old kid with his own baggage. He had moved to Baltimore the year that I turned 30 when I was deep into a transition of my outlaw stage persona to a genuine lifestyle outside of laws, regulations and social mores born of payoffs, lust, bigotry, sexism, racism, bribes, lies, profiteering and usury.

The 14-year-old was the next generation of that same revolt against oppressive hypocrisies. I didn't feel particularly compelled to conceal anything specific from him, and that attitude apparently put him more at ease around me. With each successive visit, he would open up more and more.

On his second visit to the coffeehouse, again on a Saturday afternoon before the evening crowd arrived, he wanted to know more about Ella May Wiggins. Clearly, he'd been thinking about our last conversation.

"Was she a White lady or Black?" he wanted to know. I explained that she was White who lived in the Black community. "Well, that's what got her murked," he surmised, in wisdom beyond his years but very indicative of his background.

I talked more about her story and the Gastonia strike, but it was clear that he felt that he knew all he needed to know once he understood that she was a strong White woman living among Black people. When I next paused to breath, he interjected, "Yeah, but that's like ancient history or

---

my own demons combined to alienate me from most everything CPUSA was doing. The defections of *Angela Davis, Charlene Mitchell, Michael Meyerson,* and a lot of others, pushed me even further away from what struck me as absurd internal discussions.

I met with one of the National Board members who I had come to respect and shared my concerns with him. He confessed that he, too, was thinking about leaving. That was pretty-much the proverbial *straw-that-broke-the-camel's-back*. I wrote a somewhat bitter, and painful, resignation from my friends.

[216] *Omertà* is the Sicilian tradition of silence to authorities and outsiders.

THE POET LAUREATE SOUL OF FOLKIE ROCK & ROLL

something. That shit don't happen no more like that. Not for singing songs anyway. Just for political action."

I sat silently for a few seconds and then decided to tell him *MY* story. He listened intently, but I could see that he wasn't shocked or surprised. His entire life had been in the shadow of police violence against revolutionaries. The fact that cops had trumped up charges against me to execute me was absolutely nothing out of the norm of his life; and that was tragic. The only variation was that I am lily-white and Southern and the impetus to kill me had been my music and writing.

As he processed my story, he nodded empathetically and in a low-voice near-muttered, "So that's why you got blicky." It wasn't a question, just a sort-of acknowledgement. *("Blicky" was then-contemporary street-speak for a handgun; I silently noted how fucked-up it was that a 14-year-old was fluent in stone-cold hood lingo.)*

I didn't know that he had spotted any of my guns, but clearly, he had, And just like with my story, he wasn't fazed at all. I told him, "actually, I go heeled with at least three smokers". *(More street-slang: I carry at least three guns.)*

He looked at me, as if sizing me up for the first time, and just said, "Shit." It was a calm statement, not exclamation. From then on, he seemed to be more relaxed and at ease with me. If there was a seminal instance when our relationship changed from my lecturing to becoming our collaborating concepts, that was probably it.

On his next visit, he was eager for me to hear a recording that he had made. Despite his poverty and living conditions, somehow, he'd managed to make a cassette recording of himself rapping two of his poems.

I connected a high-end cassette deck through the coffeehouse's Sony tube-amplifier and piped it to the two huge speaker towers on opposite sides of the big room. So, when I dropped in his tape, the sound echoed through the room. I also had connected a graphic equalizer to channel each speaker tower, so I was able to adjust his sound so that it maximized the depth he had created.

As superb as the playback was, I could tell that he was more interested in what I thought of it than what I had done to the sound. The truth is, I was really surprised —*in a good way*— at what I heard; and I told him that. He had the beat, the melody, and a genuine vibe. His lyrics had perfect meter, spot-on rhymes, not contrived or forced, and very sophisticated syllable count.

What I heard was not the expected haphazard presentation of a junior-high-school poem. Rather, it was architecturally engineered with precision. This kid had carefully planned not just every line but every syllable and even every tonal emphasis of his voice. And I told him that.

THE LEGEND DIES ON — GARY GREEN

Above all of that complexity, he metaphorically used the language to trick the listener into thinking the poem was going one direction when actually it was headed somewhere else.

All of this came from a 14-year-old, who told me he'd been writing poetry since he was 10. I couldn't help but think of Kristofferson's lyric, *Billy Dee was seventeen when he turned twenty-one.*[217] Older than the years he held, I didn't question his depth at all; the quality indicated lots of experience and besides, I'd started young too.

He understood that everything I had said about his work was about the form. He wanted to know if I thought that his content and form made *the whole* that I had talked about. Clearly, he had been paying attention to my lectures. His lyrics were way outside of the mainstream and carried heavy-duty references to prisons, wrongful convictions, and very Panther-like themes of Black liberation, and self-defense against police brutality. Those were some very advanced themes to come from someone his age; but it was totally understandable given his back-ground. I didn't ask him about the source of that knowledgebase, but I assumed it came from his immediate or extended family and was as close to first-hand as it could be without suffering it himself.

It reminded me of my meeting Reba Hancock and Johnny Cash when I was exactly the same age, 14. The encouragement they gave me was one of the most important things that shaped my musical life. Even though they were never part of anything I did after the Folkways contract, I would never have gotten to Folkways without their encouragement and push. Even at 30-years-old in Baltimore, when I wrote songs I felt the Johnny-Cash-geist.

I wanted to give the same encouragement to my 14-year-old friend. I wanted him to carry-for-life the spirit that Reba and J.R. had instilled in me. I had submitted my *Jailbird* song to Cash, and he had said that he liked it and saw potential in me. Johnny Cash, of course, didn't record it. The song was sophomoric, unknowledgeable, and not very good; BUT... thematically it was there. Cash was accurate when he told me that I needed more experience to one day be a great writer. Most importantly, he and Reba told me that I was on the right track, and I should continue.

I wanted to give that same encouragement … and that same critique … to Túpac. But that is a dangerous line to walk; the wrong presentation could be discouraging and shut down or even completely destroy the creative process. But the right presentation could push him toward incredible adventures in music —*I knew that from experience*— as long as he didn't fall into the outlaw traps that had snared me. Without omniscient

---

[217] "Billy Dee" by Kris Kristofferson © Sony/ATV Music Publishing LLC

THE POET LAUREATE SOUL OF FOLKIE ROCK & ROLL

soothsaying abilities to see the dark roads ahead for him, I decided to go for it and give him the Reba-Hancock-Johnny-Cash encouragement.

(For those keeping score, you can officially note that, therefore, at least in this regard, Johnny Cash was an (indirect) influence on Túpac Shakur, arguably the most influential and successful rapper of all time.)

My encouragement-strategy must have worked, because for the next several months Túpac would come to the coffeehouse a couple of times a week and spend anywhere from three to five hours with me. About 75% of the time, we would talk about political topics, cultural misappropriations, bad lyrics versus good ones, and *audience manipulation* techniques. Occasionally we would discuss movies, television, acting, the socio-political role of actors, commercialism, and stage presence. The rest of the time he rapped poetry for me. We also discussed why I thought his ninth grade transfer to Dunbar would be a more well-rounded experience than being among the "children of the ruling class" in Roland Park.

Interestingly enough, in historical context, we did not talk about CPUSA or the YCL or any kind of organization. We also didn't talk about the *High School for the Arts*; it wasn't really on his radar at that time, despite it later playing such a pivotal role in his life.

On the afternoon before one of the hootenannies, Túpac came by a little later than his normal early-afternoon visits. After we talked for a few minutes, I realized that he was ready to appear on stage.

Forty-something years later the details are hazy; and at the time there was no reason to landmark the night, so I don't think my archives even have a tape of that hoot —though I do have several hoots preserved on high-end metal and chrome cassette tapes.

I don't think Gary Blanchard was present that night, but the circumstances of that are unclear too. I do recall that we later laughed at the mispronouncing of his name by whoever it was that introduced him from the stage. They made it sound like "Ta-PACK" (which struck the nerd-me as more of a Klingon greeting than a person's name).

I also recall that his performance was anything but low-key. It was totally a cappella; we didn't play any beats or music behind him. In that regard, it was more like Ginsberg reading *Howl* than like a song. But he delivered it with such rhythmic syncopation that the entire audience was into the beat and the mood that he created.

The poem itself was at first an indictment of supposed-friends who refused to visit him because they were "afraid of the neighborhood". Then, like with many of his pieces, he took the listener in an entirely unexpected direction by empathizing with that fear and then inditing the violence and the drug culture that surrounded children in the neighborhood. It was a pissed-off rap about protecting his little sister; and it was *very* good.

THE LEGEND DIES ON — GARY GREEN

I suppose he would have performed more at Bread & Roses and our regular multiple-times-a-week get-togethers would have continued into his Baltimore School for the Arts days and even the move his move to the Bay Area out in California...

... if it had not been for the MY demons of self-destruction.

After the coming explosion in my life, I never saw Túpac again; he moved on in life, became involved in the High School for the Arts, developed new friendships, created an entire life for himself, and to my knowledge never looked back.

He was from a world of people abandoning him and in that regard I lived up to his expectations. I don't even know if anyone told him what happened to me. I've never read (or heard) any reference that he ever made to those afternoons at Bread & Roses, so as far as I know we were *out-of-sight-out-of-mind*. It was probably for the best that he moved along and forgot about me.

The doorway that I was stepping through was pure self-destruction and not destined for a happy ending.

THE POET LAUREATE SOUL OF FOLKIE ROCK & ROLL

Opus Twenty-Two:
I Can Never Play Again, You Racist Bastards

> You, who are on the road
> Must have a code that you can live by
> And so become yourself
> Because the past is just a goodbye
> — Graham Nash, *Teach Your Children*, ©1970 Nash Notes; Spirit One Music

Poor people and transients were the usual residents of the *rent-by-the-week* rooms (acyrologically called "apartments") above the bar on the corner of 31st and Greenmount. Almost at the midpoint of the Greenmount Avenue corridor from North Avenue to Cold Springs Road, the bar was next door to Bread and Roses Two located at 426 East 31st Street. One of the flop-house "apartments" had been rented to two down-on-their-luck white guys; rare tenants in the almost-all-Black Waverly neighborhood.

Those two guys had somehow gotten their hands on two T-bone steaks and a charcoal grill. Downing several cans of beer that they had purchased at the bar but consumed on the street, they set up their grill on the sidewalk between the coffeehouse and Greenmount Avenue. Closer to the coffeehouse than the bar, they plopped their steaks onto the grill and waited for dinner to cook.

As the steaks sizzled over the coals, they ran out of beer. For some inexplicable reason, they *both* decided to go into the bar and order more beer, leaving their steak dinners and grill unattended on the sidewalk. To no one's surprise, except their own, when they returned the steaks were gone; someone had swiped them from the unattended grill.

The duo had set up the backyard-cookout along a street in the middle of not only one of the poorest areas of Baltimore City, but arguably one of the roughest ghettos in America. Had they not already been intoxicated they might have decided that one of them should have stayed with the steaks while the other went for the beer. But no! These cats both disappeared for about 10 to 15 minutes.

It was a Saturday afternoon, and I was onstage inside the coffeehouse. It was a chilly Baltimore afternoon, so the front door was closed to keep the heat inside. There was only a small crowd that had gathered, and we hadn't charged a cover. I was alone on stage with my guitar, two microphone stands, and two large stage monitors (so that I could hear what was going out into the room). It was loud, probably too loud for such a small crowd. Nonetheless, from on stage, with the door shut and the monitors blaring, I could hear those two guys on the street screaming about their

THE LEGEND DIES ON — GARY GREEN

missing steaks. Their ranting was punctuated by almost every known racial epithetical slur, as the generically blamed the Black population of America for the loss of their meals.

I felt the rage rising inside me. That damned burning acid rose from my stomach and seared my esophagus. I felt the muscles across my shoulders tense, and I knew my face was flushing bright red. It was always like that when my anger was about to be out of control.

Then it happened. In the middle of a song, I abruptly stopped and slammed my guitar down on the stage, oblivious to any damage that might have done to the Gibson instrument's sensitive wood. The stunned audience sat silently as I stormed toward the door and bolted down the steps to the sidewalk.

Screaming loud enough that I could be heard inside any of the buildings along the street, I bolted close enough to the two guys that I was spitting all over them. In their faces, I bellowed, *"I left the South to get away from that fuckin' racist bullshit; I will be god-damned if I am going to listen to it here in Baltimore Maryland. You need to shut the fuck up, NOW!"*

There is no way those two guys could have known the danger they were confronting; all they saw was a half-pint hippie yelling at them. In hindsight, I really wish they could have seen it.

That's the problem with violent confrontations; you never know what kind of lunatic you are dealing with. They could not know that I was a fugitive outlaw who carried my life in the palm of my hand. They had no idea that I felt like I had nothing to lose because there was already a death warrant out on me; killing them would have meant nothing to me, because I already was in the worst-possible legal position.

They sensed no danger at all, so the first one aggressively responded to me, shoving me and yelling, "another nigger-lover".

THAT did it. I exploded. I picked up the grill, full of hot coals, and smashed it against his face, burning him as he fell to the ground. His compadre charged at me, and I thrusted a hard roundhouse kick into his solar plexus — knocking his breath from him and causing him to vomit that beer he had been drinking for the past couple of hours.

With both of them down, I was satisfied ... and calmed. Now quite composed, I walked back up the steps into the coffeehouse and peacefully closed the door behind me.

I didn't see that the big guy, who I had burned, was charging up the steps behind me. It wasn't until he started screaming his racist tirade that I realized it wasn't over. But I was calm after my outburst; it always was like that. So, I wasn't nearly as dangerous as I had been (nor as angry).

I turned toward him in time to see him charging toward the door. Defensively, I crashed my right palm toward him with such force that it knocked him down the metal steps and onto the sidewalk. By then a crowd, mostly African American, had gathered around them and the two goofballs elected to gather their belongings and flee to their apartment.

It was only then that I realized the disaster that I had created. When I had thrust my palm toward his face, I had not stopped to open the door; I had crashed my hand through the heavy plate-glass window taking up half the doorway.

Crashing through the glass to knock him on his ass was fine; but when I pulled back, my hand went numb. I looked down at the blood covering my clothes. Rather than flowing, the blood was pumping in rhythm to my heartbeat. I realized I had sliced an artery, and I was starting to black out from the loss of blood.

I called out to the barmaid for a rag, which she tossed to me. I tried to tie a tourniquet but was unconscious before I could finish it.

On a stretcher I briefly regained consciousness, long enough to hear one of the paramedics say, "He's lost too much blood; there's no hurry. He won't make it."

I awoke again on an operating table with a surgeon looking over me. I tried to speak and was able to ask, "Doctor, I am a guitar player and..."

Before I could finish my sentence, he responded with the worst bedside manner in the history of Hippocratic medicine, *"Not anymore, you're not."*

I keep repeating it, but I can't emphasize enough what my legal situation had done to me psychologically. It had put me on a fast track that had no foreseeable happy ending.

A cultural Twilight Zone is how Brother Huey P. Newton (co-founder of the Black Panther Party) once described the plight of middle-class white youth who had become part of *The Movement*. He argued that we were estranged from our roots by our choices to oppose many of the fundamental tenets that defined those roots. At the same time, he argued, our education, experiences, understanding, and way we were raised, all fundamentally alienated us from the very people we were trying to serve. He added that the "New Left" hippies, through our hair and clothing, alienated ourselves from "the establishment". But at any time we could cut our hair, put on a suit, and take a seat at the table of the ruling class; something our black, brown, yellow, and red skinned comrades could not do.

If it only had been so simple for me! My situation was much more complicated. Yes, I was guilty of the self-alienating Twilight Zone that Newton had described; but beyond that, I was trapped in much more complex isolation. I was estranged from my deep roots in traditional hillbilly music and early rock and roll. *That* had practically got me thrown out of Nashville because I had audaciously combined our musical form with "radical" poetry.

THE LEGEND DIES ON — GARY GREEN

Because of that "product" I created and my attendant attitude for egalitarianism, I had become outcasted from many clubs and venues that otherwise would have welcomed roots music with a rock tinge.

All of that had come about not by any planned radical activity or intellectual journey. Rather, I had reacted to an entire school administration labeling our one black student "watermelon". I reacted to the campus church revealing what our government was perpetrating in Vietnam. I reacted to the legacy of murdering Ella May Wiggins for singing songs about unionism. I reacted to the genocidal campaigns against Native Americans.

Frankly, that alienation had come from my belief in (as the Superman television show used to say) *truth, justice, and the American way*. In my mind, I had become alienated because I believed in the ideals of America.

But there were tens of thousands, if not millions, in my generation that were part of those same isolating realities; that is why Huey P. Newton could generalize about it. None of those issues were a result of my legal problems, though my legal status contributed to having those problems in the first place. But there was much more.

I was further isolated because my reactions and activities were seen by many of the people who had shaped my life as betrayal; disloyal, infidelity, even treachery to my culture, my music, my history, even to my race.

I used to get SO angry at my father when he would chastise me for my choices and scream that I should *"everyday thank God that you were born white and male"*. At the time, I rejected his ranting as reactionary and racist; but, over the years I came to realize that it was his way of acknowledging the inequities that I was discovering. He was telling me that I had been *born into privilege* and he was disappointed at my failure to embrace that and exploit it.

Even when I was accepted as a comrade by members of the Panthers, The Black Liberation Army, and a handful of black-nationalist groups, we all knew that I would always be an outsider. Even as a fugitive who was terrified every time that I spotted a police car, I knew that being white and educated I could probably talk my way out of suspicion (as long as they didn't run wants and warrants on me).

That was a *privilege* that I would prove time and again in decades to come when I would do such things as take a seat with *Donald Trump* and others; a haircut, a shave, and a nice suit might disguise my past and my philosophy, but it could not conceal skin color and all the things that came with that. It was a license that Sherman and my Black, Brown, Asian, and Native friends could never exercise. Hence, I would always be an outsider in that regard and my father too was right in pointing out my privileged position; *privileged* even though I was born poor working class —it was *white* working class.

THE POET LAUREATE SOUL OF FOLKIE ROCK & ROLL

Many of my father's peers, though never my father, also condemned me for "betraying my race", with my open resistance to the brutality of my white "brethren" against any minority (physically, economically, socially, and even electorally).

My fourth classic alienation manifested as my loss of objectivity; what many people at the coffeehouse called my *dogmatism* —or what kinder people called my stubbornness. The truth is it was much more than obstinance; it was a loss of my ability to be neutral. In fact, it was almost losing myself to all of the disillusionment.

Still all of that psychological complication just laid the groundwork for what I was becoming and the wall-of-death spiral that I had been speeding around.

The stress of multiple arrests back in Tennessee should have been enough to break me; but instead, it just made me angry. My over-reaction to the FBI at my mother's door should have signaled to me that I was out-of-control; but instead, it just terrified me. Every day, it seemed to get more and more intense, and I seemed to get angrier and more afraid.

Magnifying those complexities, I began assembling an arsenal of weapons: various caliber revolver and automatic handguns; taser devices; switchblade knives; and most bizarrely, a Soviet-made combat knife that looked like Sly Stallone's Rambo knife but with a high-tension spring that could release the blade like a missile. I also had a small stash of incendiary bombs, heavy-duty fireworks (M-80's and cherry bombs), boxes of ammunition, and manuals provided to me by various underground organizations detailing how to convert various hunting rifles to fully automatic machine guns.[218]

Clearly, I was so terrified and so angry that I was out of control. All of that because I was writing songs that some people in power didn't want to hear?? Even saying it aloud sounded absurd, but obviously it was very real to me.

Finally, adding to that, was my volatile temper. The slightest afront would set me off, screaming, yelling, and potentially violent. My face would turn red, the veins in my neck would swell, and I would nearly-foam-at-the-mouth in unrestrained rage.

A racist comment, disrespect, bullying behavior, uncalled-for aggression would set me off beyond control. Repeatedly, I physically assaulted people a foot taller than me and 50 pounds heavier, I pistol-whipped

---

[218] All of this is shit that by the 2020's sounds like the arsenal of a far-right kook; but in the 1980's it was me, the far-left kook.

unsuspecting offenders, and at least once actually shot a guy who was brutally beating his girlfriend in an alley.

My unrestrained explosion at the two racist assholes on the street was not at all inconsistent with my intolerance nor with my temper outbursts. But that street-confrontation changed my life forever.

At the *Curtis Hand Center of Union Memorial Hospital* in Baltimore, surgeons elected to use a nerve block to anesthetize my arm rather than put me to sleep. They wanted me to be awake to react to what they were doing so that I could tell them when I had feeling in the hand.

The shards of glass had severed the carpal-tunnel nerve-bundle in my right wrist, effectively cutting off all nerve sensation to my hand. That severe damage is what had prompted the doctor's heartless pronouncement that I was no longer a guitar player.

Using a then-state-of-the-art micro-surgery technique, they attempted to reconnect the nerves. Unfortunately for me, nerves are not color-coded or otherwise individually identifiable. When multiple nerves had been severed there was no way to determine which sliced piece belonged to which other piece (at least at that time); and for some nerves, they just could not be stretched enough to fit.

While the doctors did a sci-fi-worthy job of reconnecting nearly-microscopic nerve endings so that I could have *some* level of feeling in my hand, it was far from perfect. I only had about 70% of the original feeling in my hand. My index finger was still practically numb; while it had a little hyper-sensitive feeling, I could immerse it into boiling water and feel almost nothing.

Further complicating my recovery, some of the nerves had been reconnected to the wrong endings. That meant that I could touch certain spots on my wrist but not feel it there; instead, I would feel it on my ring finger. Conversely, I could apply pressure to my middle finger but feel it in the palm of my hand. Quite simply, the nerves were "cross wired".

Following the crisscross surgery, I devotedly attended my several-times-a-week physical therapy sessions at the hospital, but it soon became clear to me that the goal was to reteach me range-of-motion, the ability to pick up objects, to close my fingers into a fist, and have the basics of a working hand. There was no pathway for me to ever be 100% again.

The first doctor had been correct, my guitar days were finished. My music was finished. *I was finished.*

If there was a silver-lining to that dark cloud, I could take some solace knowing that what the Federal government and the State of Tennessee had been trying to do —*silencing me and my guitar*— they ultimately had failed because I did it to myself.

THE POET LAUREATE SOUL OF FOLKIE ROCK & ROLL

I had come dangerously close to doing exactly what William Kunstler had repeatedly warned me against doing: getting arrested. I was damned lucky that the police had not run a check on me and transferred me to a hospital jail cell.

I can thank the quick-thinking of my coffeehouse coworkers for saving me from being arrested. I later learned that when the police came, they questioned my two victims and then the coffeehouse employees.

The two racists, still drunk and belligerent, wildly ranted and raved to the two uniformed Baltimore City cops that had come to investigate. They told him that a crazy hippie musician had attacked them because they were too close to the door of the coffeehouse.

The barmaid, who had tossed me the rag for a tourniquet, heard what the two told the cops. A middle-eastern minority, herself, she was no more amused at their racism than I had been. She looked at the two Black police officers and almost-whispered to them, "can I tell you exactly what happened?"

The cops escorted her inside, away from the crowd and my victims. She told them, "We had a performer on stage, and those two guys on the sidewalk started scream obscene racial slurs because somebody stole their steak, It was loud and racist and wouldn't stop. The guitar player went outside to ask them to quit, and they called him racist names and then assaulted him."

That was all the cops needed to hear. They stepped back outside and arrested the two guys, charging them with public intoxication and assault. The cops never asked my name and there was no follow-up with me at the hospital.

I dodged that bullet; but I was still a fugitive, though I couldn't pull the trigger of a gun to defend myself from an assassin's attack. It seemed that it was only a matter of time until a hired gun came for me; and I would be functionally helpless.

In the bigger picture, that didn't really matter to me. Without an assassin's intervention, I had robbed myself of my identity; of the very reason for being that had fueled me since that late night in July in 1957. My music life was over. I lost interest in the coffeehouse; after the hospitalization, I never went back. I wouldn't write songs anymore. I couldn't perform. I didn't even want to hear a record or a tape. It was over.

The coffeehouse itself operated barely solvent, mostly because of my policy of giving 100% of the door-charge to the performers. Of the hundreds of performers we booked, only two had contract riders that cost us extra money; the majority were willing to work with whatever we could provide. It was extremely generous and supportive of the venue.

Nonetheless, keeping the venue open month-to-month was always a struggle. Paying the landlord and the utility bills solely from food &

THE LEGEND DIES ON — GARY GREEN

beverage revenue was, at best, a delicate balancing act. The truth is it was more like "robbing Peter to pay Paul" (as the cliché goes). The business made money; but we spent more-than a lion's share to make certain the performers were treated fairly.

With me gone, and completely washing my hands of it, survival was impossible. I think it might have lasted two weeks, until rent was due. Briefly, staff tried relocating to a rent-free community center; but that location was so far away from the heart of Waverly and the Charles Village student ghetto that crowds were minute. I think they might have done three shows there before closing forever.

It was sad to see the legacy gone. But I just didn't have the energy, enthusiasm, nor inclination to do anything in the music world; especially run the venue where I had lost the use of my hand.

My biggest regret about it (and there were many), was losing contact with so many really good people. We had built a genuine community around Bread & Roses Two, and it wasn't fair or nice that I just abandoned them, even if it was necessary.

On top of all that abandonment, I had no savings, no money, and no way to generate income. I couldn't risk applying for government disability benefits, because I was concerned the Social Security Administration's database might be cross-referenced with the FBI's NCIC (National Crime Information Center) database. As a newspaper Police Reporter, I had seen cops rely on NCIC to find dirt on all sorts of "suspects".

Even that previous career, newspapering, was not a solution for me. It had been destroyed by the union battle. Even if it had not been, writing of any kind was out of the question. I couldn't use my right hand. I couldn't feel the touch of the typewriter keys. I couldn't hold a pen.

It was worse than needing a "change of direction" or a "reinvention"; I needed a new life, because as it was, I had no life. Hell, I couldn't even pay my upcoming apartment rent.

I decided that a clandestine trip to visit my parents might be in order. Maybe down there I could figure out what to do next.

I was confident that my expertise "living underground" was well-honed enough that I could slip in and out of North Carolina "under the radar" of law enforcement. Howard Ehrlich advised me against it, but I believed my skills (combined with my intimate knowledge of police tactics) would almost guarantee an uneventful trip. I was correct.

I am certain that my parents could read my gloomy dejection and lack of direction, even without me explaining it. Trying to be encouraging, Mother assured me that not being able to use my hand should not deter me from music.

THE POET LAUREATE SOUL OF FOLKIE ROCK & ROLL

"You know there's a lot of music that is like the *Concerto for the Left Hand*. She went to her music cabinet and pulled out an entire book of one-hand piano pieces.

"I don't want to be Wittgenstein[219]," I whined to her and walked away from the book she had found. I'm sure she saw how depressed I was over my loss of music in my life.

During the next few days, I could see that she and my father were watching how I used my hand (or rather, how I did *not* use it). They didn't patronize me or offer to assist when I struggled; they just watched.

I couldn't even use my right hand to hold a fork to eat meals. My index finger seemed always to be pointing, even when my fist was closed. My range of motion looked like it had returned to near-normal; but the fingers were more-or-less deadened when it came to feeling anything. I couldn't even detect pressure or grasp anything.

My mother rarely got angry, or at least didn't *show it*. Daddy had plenty of anger for the whole family (a trait I, unfortunately, learned from him). But after about a-week-and-a-half of watching me, she showed me anger.

"You need to stop feeling sorry for yourself. Get in there to the piano, sit down and start playing," she scolded; and she wasn't kidding.

"I can't", I protested; "even the doctors say I can't".

She wouldn't accept that whining from me, "you are smarter than any doctor. Since when are you going to listen to anybody? Sit down at that piano and start practicing until you can play."

My protests were impotent. Not only did she walk me to the piano, but she pulled out those damned red *John Thompson* music books that she taught to her students (and to me decades earlier). "Play," she demanded, opening the first page of the *First Grade Book*, but placing the *Thompson For Left Hand Alone* book with it.

What choice did I have? She wasn't budging until I started playing. At least my stubbornness against the left-hand only book prevailed; but I had to start with the songs in the first-grade piano primer. I knew each piece by heart from hearing them every day of my childhood as her students banged them out but also from my own memorizing them to fake sight reading. This time, however, I actually read the music and struggled to play; and used my right hand —or at least tried to use it. I knew exactly

---

[219] Paul Wittgenstein was a concert pianist whose right arm was amputated after a World War I accident. Rather that stop playing, he commissioned French composer Maurice Ravel to write a series of one-handed piano concert pieces. The most famous, *The Piano Concerto for the Left Hand in D Major*, was premiered by Wittgenstein performing with the Vienna Symphony Orchestra in the early 1930's.

THE LEGEND DIES ON — GARY GREEN

where the keys were, corresponding to the notes on the staff; but my fingers just couldn't feel the ivories when I touched the keyboard.

Runaway River, The Traffic Cop, the three-sharps *Air From Mozart, The Fairy Court* recital piece, the three-hand-positions of *Silent Night, Dublin Town, John Peel*, and all the drills in the John Thompson First Grade book; I spent about four hours a day on them for the next few weeks, struggling to follow the music and not the sound in my head for each one. Every time I would stumble on one of Thompson's rhythm exercises, my mother would appear from nowhere with her wind-up metronome and verbally count-off the beats, pointing at me when to play the notes.

After about a month, she dug out the *Southern Baptist Sunday School Board's Broadman Hymnal*; her go-to Sunday sheet music source. She began drilling me on those traditional hymns the same way she'd done with Thompson. Frankly, it was a great relief to practice in the realm of gospel music rather than Euro-classical drills.

I started at the front of the book and spent a few hours a day playing ten songs from the book. When I felt that I was "okay" with each group of ten, I would move on to the next ten. They were all very basic pieces; single or two simultaneous notes with the right hand and equally simple dyads with the left hand.

Then came Number 160, *What A Friend We Have In Jesus* in the key of F; and on the same page, Number 161, *Amazing Grace*, in the key of G. I played the first as it was written, but when I came to Number 161, something happened.

I was so board that I couldn't resist. Eleven bars into the song, it was written to have a tied quarter and eighth notes moving to two eighth notes for the lyrics "but now (I) am found". They were simple notes: d-e-g-e-d. But I couldn't take it; it was too... boring. Between the quarter notes and the eighth notes, I abruptly changed the key signature from G to a G-minor pentatonic scale and threw in a quick string of sixteenth notes punctuated with a quick blues run between the lyric phrase; so, the printed five notes became: d-e-g-B-B$^{\flat}$-A-G-e-d.

With the left hand, I decided to deviate from the uber-boring dyads, replacing them with inverted full chords, but corresponding with each treble clef note walking down half of a chromatic bass scale.

Along the way, with my rhythmic challenges, I changed the time-signature from 3/4 to 4/4, to accommodate the blues run.

In short, I changed Amazing Grace from a church-choir waltz to a soulful bluesy rock song. As soon as I threw in the extra four treble notes and the full-chord bass, my mother again magically appeared. "Keep going," she encouraged. As I stumbled a little with the rhythm (as was my way), she began tapping the count and telling me when to apply the left-hand

THE POET LAUREATE SOUL OF FOLKIE ROCK & ROLL

chords. When I finished the song, she immediately encouraged me with, "See. You're back. Do it again."

I whine-complained that I was not "back" because it didn't feel the same; I couldn't feel the touch of the keys. Rather than hit me with some patronizingly inane "it sounded fine", she bluntly told me, "It never will feel the same. Things change, but the world doesn't end."

That, actually, was the most encouraging thing that could have been said to me. It allowed me to come to grips, immediately, with the reality that there was no going backwards but there could be a going forward.

Just because I could play piano as well as a school kid, did not mean that I could go back to guitar, banjo, mandolin, fiddle, or any of the stringed instruments. Even though my left hand, my fretting-hand for individual notes and chords, was not affected at all, the irreversible damage to my right hand prohibited me from finger picking, holding a pick, strumming, and especially from the complexities of *The Carter Lick*.

My musical life was over; I came to terms with that. But what I learned from my mother was that it did not mean that my whole life was over. As she said, "it's not the end of the world"; it is just something different.

The problem was that I had already reinvented myself once; so, even though I had experience "starting over", I had already used-up the two skillsets that seemed most viable: journalism and music.

The task before me, then, was to determine what else might be viable. Just as a matter of survival, I had to take stock of exactly what it was that I was "good" enough at to be able to eat and pay the rent.

Daddy gave me enough money to pay the rent and buy groceries in Baltimore for two months. We all knew that as long as I was a fugitive, I would be much safer up there than in the South.

THE LEGEND DIES ON — GARY GREEN

Opus Twenty-Three:
My Dada Life As A Media Event Scoundrel

Patriotism is the last refuge of the scoundrel.
— Samuel Johnson, 1774 in The Patriot

Ned Buntline was, for me, the architype great American scoundrel. He did it all and along the way he created dozens of enduring American myths including *"Wild Bill" Hickock, "Buffalo" Bill*, and a fictionalized super-pistol called the *Buntline Special*. He wrote songs, books, and even Broadway plays. He lectured. He taught. He ran investments. He was the spokesman for social, moral, and political causes. He created touring shows. *And it was all hokum.* He was the best at what he did.

Oh, there have been other classic contenders for that (dis)honor of being top scoundrel —*Blackjack Bouvier, Aaron Burr, "Doc" John Holliday, Bernie Cornfeld, Robert Vesco*, and a myriad of colorfully nefarious characters— but Edward Zane Carroll Judson, aka Ned Buntline, was by far the grand master. Having said that, after the loss of use of my right hand I was right on his tail for inclusion into that school of smoke and mirrors.

I returned to Baltimore desperately looking for something that I was good enough at to pay the bills. With music and journalism gone and me already over 30 (traditionally over-the-hill for aging hippies), I had to decide what else I could do. The conclusion that I came to was not good.

The truth was, I was an outstanding *outlaw*, living outside the law. Not at breaking laws, mind you; I was really good at *evading* the law.

I was great at being on the outside and looking in. It was a genuine skill, and I had several years of experience at it. All I needed to do was to figure out a way to monetize those skills... legally.

Before I had left my parents' house, one of my brothers told me that a good friend of his, who I knew well, was preparing to see his uncle for the first time in a few years. The uncle had just been released after spending 25 years in prison, and no one was sure how the reunion would go. The friend asked me to come along for moral support. I agreed, just before my departure for Baltimore.

Fifteen to twenty years older than me, the uncle extended his hand to shake mine and introduced himself as *Casey L. Mane*; a surprisingly formal full-name intro that struck me as institutionally rehearsed.

Casey was one very scary-looking cat. He looked like a cross between Charles Manson and an outlaw biker. More concerning, I spotted two small round tattoos with a little "x" inside each, between his left thumb and his forefinger. They were adjacent to a tattoo of five dots: four corners with one dot in the center.

As a fugitive myself, deeply immersed in outlaw culture of the era, I recognized the meaning of his tattoos. The five dots were an announcement that he had "been in the joint"; that he was a convict. The circle-x tattoos where his "buttons"; each a "badge of honor" showing that he had killed someone. Like I said, *one scary cat*. Nonetheless, my brother and I agreed to go to a local restaurant for lunch with the two of them.

At lunch, Casey began telling some nonsensical tall tale full of gangster bravado; to me, it sounded like pure bullshit. I was a fugitive, living in one of the most crime-invested inner-cities in America; I carried my life in my hand every single day, and I had no patience for gangster macho nonsense. When his silly tale turned to a story of how he had killed rattlesnakes while mining for gold in Alaska, I'd had enough, and I called him out on it.

Casey abruptly stopped talking and stared at me with an obviously long-rehearsed attempt at an *evil-eye*. I laughed at him, and said, *"Man, you are so full of shit that it's not funny. I bet you were a standup comic in the joint."* "You got a problem with me?" he asked in his best confrontational voice.

"Nope, I just know bullshit when I see it," I snapped back with just as much swagger. "Why you say that?" he demanded.

I shook my head, "Well, first, rattlesnakes are cold blooded, you didn't find any in Alaska. As a matter of fact, there are no snakes of any kind in Alaska. So, I gotta wonder, since that is bullshit, what else about you is bullshit. Have you ever even been locked up?"

He glared at me and tilted his hand toward me so that I would see his inked dots and buttons. I guess I was supposed to be intimidated, but I didn't break my stare back at him. I knew *that* game of gangster machismo bullshit; and he wasn't going to back me down.

Continuing to play his little posturing bullshit game, I threw open the side of my jacket so that he could see the 9-mm automatic (pistol) in my shoulder holster and the snub-nose .38 in my belt. Two could play the intimidation game; and even though with my crippled right-hand I couldn't pull a trigger, I was still a fugitive, so I still went heeled most places. Besides, he didn't know about my infirmity and my left-hand worked just fine.

Casey took it all in and there were several long minutes of awkward silence before he finally spoke. "I have been telling that snake story for about five years, and you are the first son-of-a-bitch to ever call me out on it. You are all right, man," he smiled for the first time.

Then he turned to his nephew and said, "I like this guy. You done good bringing him to me."

THE LEGEND DIES ON — GARY GREEN

What should have been a half-hour lunch turned into about six hours as Casey and I talked about —as Arlo Guthrie had described of his "Group W" bench experience— *talking about crime, mother stabbing, father raping, and all kinds of mean, nasty, and groovy things that we was talking about on the bench; And everything was fine.*

Fine it was, indeed. On some perverse level of the outlaw brotherhood, Casey and I bonded as his nephew and my brother looked at us both like we were crazy (and in fact we WERE).

When it was time for me to go, I told Casey that I was heading back to Baltimore Maryland and if he was ever up that way, we should hook up and do some business[220]. I assumed I would never hear from that comical character again; oh, but I would!

₯♪₯♪₯♪

Back in Baltimore and still unsure of how to make a living, I plied my attention toward my formal education. Part of my studies focused on debunking the field of psychology as scientistic nonsense (*scientistic* as opposed to scientific).[221]

In conjunction with my philosophical studies in symbolic logic along with dialectical & historical materialism, I dove deeply into the world of psychology academia to try to show that the entire discipline was based on logical fallacies. Instead of the pseudo-science of Freudian, post-Freudian, and DSM[222] chicanery, I offered up the methodologies of behaviorism.

Doctor B.F. Skinner was still alive and my interest in his studies of behaviorism reached far beyond his pop-culture trade paper-backs (*Beyond Freedom and Dignity* and *Walden Two*). As noted earlier, I struck up a long series of correspondences with him, which I am sure was only possible because I could flash the credential of *Johns Hopkins University* in my academic *curriculum vitae*. As I began assembling a panel of interested academics, Skinner agreed to advise me on that one limited level.

---

[220] "Business" was outlaw slang for committing crimes.

[221] It was the old philosophical schism between idealism and materialism. That is what had led me to Hegel, Feuerbach, and Marx. Hegel's *Logik* also lead me, coincidentally, to the work of Austrian philosopher Ludwig *Wittgenstein* and the field of symbolic logic (coincidental, because Ludwig was the brother of the aforementioned Paul Wittgenstein who was the one-handed piano maestro). That led me to the Frankfurt School of critical theory philosophers, *Horkheimer, Marcuse, Adorno, Habermas,* and their contemporaries.

[222] DSM = the *Diagnostic and Statistical Manual of Mental Disorders*, from the *American Psychiatric Association*; a supposed "medical" manual that historically changes with the changing attitudes of society (most notably many changes like classifying homosexuality as a mental illness and later retracting that).

THE POET LAUREATE SOUL OF FOLKIE ROCK & ROLL

My piano exercises with my mother had developed enough motor control that I could type again. So, I became relatively prolific, turning out long academic tomes weekly along with one really long thesis paper. I also began presenting at academic conferences, graduate seminars, and public forums.

Comme d'habitude, it didn't take me long to reach my critical mass to trigger academic boredom. I was fortunate to have access to all four campuses; so, I was able to see that my impatience with academia was not ignited by only one institution but was systematic.

In hindsight, I suspect my issues were my own restlessness and lack of discipline. I felt stagnated, especially when I looked at the same-old-same-old careers of Walt, Howard, and the other PhD's in my orbit. Whatever the underlying causes, I soon lost all interest in university life. I began looking for something else to do.

At Towson State University's Student Union building I had smirked at a line of student-run booths promoting various mainstream political candidates for the upcoming U.S. Presidential elections. Just to amuse myself, I decided to stop at each stand and harass the supporters about their *Tweedledum and Tweedledee* candidates, Republican or Democrat.

I scolded them, saying that regardless of which flavor was elected that the ghettos wouldn't go away. I thought back to the *Song About What's Happening Now* that Moe had commissioned me to write for my Allegory album; the lyrics said basically the same thing. I briefly entertained myself haranguing the "Students For…" fill-in-the-blank for the name of the candidate.

Then I got to the little card table set up for *U.S. Senator Gary Hart*. I actually felt sorry for the young naïf working that booth. She was either incredibly unsophisticated or absolutely sincere, but either way rather than brush me off, she asked questions about what I meant in my near-canned condemnation of mainstream politicians. I stayed a little longer than I had at the other booths and continued to talk to her.

That is when it turned weird, and when my devious fugitive survival-scheming kicked in. It turned out that the young woman operating that booth was a neighbor of the candidate and had grown up as a close friend of his daughter. In effect, she was a member of the candidate's family; and she began telling me details of her experiences with the Senator and his family.

As she talked, it occurred to me that IF —*on a long shot*— her candidate actually became President of the United States…

… and IF —on a *longer* shot— I could use her family-connection to ingratiate myself to the Future President of the United States…

THE LEGEND DIES ON — GARY GREEN

... then there could be a *Presidential Pardon* for the Federal offense (*Interstate Flight To Avoid Prosecution*) and a Justice Department investigation into the Tennessee voter fraud that I had exposed ...

... and *THAT* would make the charges against me go away and the criminals behind the charges could be brought to justice.

Seriously, who was the naïf here? My desperation had reached such a height (or a low point) that a fantasy like that actually seemed viable. My directionless anxiety was so intense that I actually pursued that as a course of action. Naïve would be an understatement for ME.

At first, I offered my services to the Towson campus student group, as "a former newsman and aide to legendary Congressman Joe L. Evins". As I Machiavelli-connived, my young cohort told Senator Hart about her "discovery". He, in turn, sent word to his Maryland campaign office. And poof: just like that, I was recruited by the "adult" campaign and installed in the role of Maryland Press Secretary for the campaign — a full-time job and a *paid* position. *Rent issue solved!*

With income from the Presidential campaign, I embarked on a series of adventures that, with the benefit of decades of hindsight, were pure comedy but at the time seemed super-serious. The zenith of the absurdities was when the United States Secret Service, the protectors of the lives of Presidential candidates, assigned me —*an "armed and dangerous" Federal fugitive*— to be in charge of security clearances for a high-end suburban Washington DC fundraiser.

The invitation list included members of Congress, billionaire corporate figures, and a who's-who of Washington powerbrokers who lived in the DC burbs. That "bluebook A-list" was massive and millions of dollars were at stake; so naturally, rather than take the time to run background checks on such a highfalutin' gathering, our nation's executive protectors assigned a trusted campaign staffer to be in charge of approving access to the high-end party at a billionaire's home.

That trusted campaign staffer? *ME!* Seriously. And apparently, no one bothered to run a check on me. So, I became the gatekeeper, the approving authority, for the all-important access list.

I mean, seriously, forget that I was a wanted outlaw; just given my radical background going back to my Miami days, given my albums, given the rallies where I played for years: what kind of goofball would have ME approve access to a major Presidential candidate (who was also a United States Senator and Chairman of the *Senate Armed Services Committee*). If I was so goddamned dangerous, then ... *what-the-fuck?*

While that probably was the most absurd of the Gary Hart adventures, it certainly wasn't the most over-the-top. As the state press secretary, I decided to do something that at that time had never happened: I created the first modern era "media event". *Hard to believe, but true.*

THE POET LAUREATE SOUL OF FOLKIE ROCK & ROLL

The concept of a media event was so dada-out-there that it made the cover-story of *Time Magazine* —not the event itself, but the idea of having an event for no purpose other than to generate media coverage.

I know for sure that, historically, there had been many-many activities created for no purpose other than media coverage (God knows P.T. Barnum was all about that, as was Ned Buntline). Even in the political world it was not new; LBJ's helicopter landings throughout rural Texas were legendary attention-getters.

But I took it to such a level of absurdity that it actually garnered its very own label. I created a *non-event* and turned it into a media frenzy; and in those days the press was naive enough that they fell for lock-stock-and-barrel. In this case, I had the candidate's daughter come to the Baltimore campaign headquarters and make peanut butter and jelly sandwiches for campaign volunteers. That was it; nothing more.

But I pitched it nationwide with carefully worded allusions paralleling "what if Caroline Kennedy had made sandwiches for daddy's campaign". (Nevermind that Andrea Hart was 20 and Carolina Kennedy was 4 when their respective fathers first ran for the Presidency.)

It was just absurd enough that it worked. Worse than catching on, the creation of media events became a paradigm-changer in politics and marketing in general. *Jeeze!* Local media came, of course; but I also attracted all three national television networks and the major national newspapers. They actually covered making PB&J sandwiches as if it were news.

That cartoonish press coverage launched a whole new potential career for me. Apparently impressed with the peanut butter sandwich flash, Hart's campaign chief, Pat Caddell, called me to offer the job of Press Coordinator for several east coast states. For the rest of the campaign, I bounced between Harrisburg Pennsylvania, DC, Baltimore, Dover Delaware, and Richmond Virginia.

Nonetheless, my hopes for a Presidential pardon were dashed by Walter Mondale winning the nomination rather than Hart. That left me both without a pardon and once again unemployed.

Cadell, who had hired me, was one of the country's premier pollsters; his data analysis and targeting techniques were revolutionary in the political world. I studied the technique and the actions based on the data. It occurred to me that those same targeting techniques, using publicly available voter data combined with census data could be used for surgically targeting all sorts of marketing beyond specific political campaigns.

I decided to experiment with that possibility, beginning with non-candidate campaigns — more public relations or marketing than political campaigning. Combined with what I knew about manipulating the media (from my newspaper days and from having created the genre of "media events" for the Hart campaign), I set up a consulting company with the

THE LEGEND DIES ON — GARY GREEN

intentionally pompous name *The Columbia Policy Institute* (going for the association with District of Columbia).

I also embarked on a new reinvention for myself. I had been an award-winning journalist. I had been a recording artist and touring musician. I had been a venue operator. I had been a national political operative. This time, I reinvented myself as a *public relations guru*; and I launched a publicity campaign to prove it.

During the next few months, I was hired as the strategist and spokesman for a DC suburban county's civil rights commission to lead a ballot measure for an LGBQ housing equal rights law. I was hired by a Baltimore City School Board chairman who was amid a public relations disaster of some sort. I was hired by two different civic groups that wanted to lobby the State Legislature for their causes. I was hired by a mayoral campaign and one U.S. Senate campaign.

Among the dozen or so campaigns that called on my services, was an overly ambitious State Senator who *Forbes Magazine* had identified as one of the wealthiest people in America. It was with him that my new identity plans started to fall apart. Despite his seemingly progressive Democratic Party politics, his real interests were more aligned with maintaining the elitist privileges of his wealth and class; and that was in stark contrast to everything that I was all about. It wasn't that we didn't get along; it was just that our interests and motivations were vastly different. That led to an estrangement from the get-go and eventually to hostile clashes between us.

While my theory was sound for using the Cadell methodology for public relations marketing and non-candidate campaigns, my attention-span and my associated intolerance of nonsense just drained my interest in that reinvention, so I closed The Columbia Policy Institute and continued my search for what I wanted to do; or what I *could* do. For the next few months, with my crippled right hand, I dabbled in a dozen or more "grey area" (if not out-and-out criminal) activities and a few daredevilish mainstream activities (that probably should have got me arrested).

Around that same time, Casey, the recently-released-from-prison acquaintance, showed up in Baltimore. I had, after all, invited him. The first thing on his agenda was that he needed a State identification card or drivers' license so he could present identification other than his prison release card. I agreed to drive him to the drivers' license bureau where such cards were issued. I waited in the car while he made the quick run inside to get the card. The office was staffed by State Troopers, and I wasn't particularly interested in loitering inside a building full of cops, given my status.

Unbeknownst to either of us, once inside there was a two-hour waiting line. I waited in the car, as patiently as I could; but patience has never been a trait where I had strong affiliation. As the minutes ticked by, I became more and more irritated. Finally, after about an hour and forty-five minutes I decided to go inside and make certain everything was going smoothly. Once inside, I surmised the wait-in-line issue, and I turned to leave. Casey saw me and gave me an "OK" hand signal and a thumbs up; so, I returned to the car.

In another fifteen minutes or so he returned to the car with his ID card. Once inside the car, tears began rolling down the cheeks of the big scary man. I looked at him but before I could ask what was wrong, he spoke. "Nobody's ever done that for me before, man," he choked.

I had no idea what-the-hell he was talking about, so I let him continue.

"I saw what you were doing. It was taking so long; you thought the cops grabbed me. You came in there with all your hardware, and you were gonna throw-down on all of them and bust me out of there," he continued with unexpected passion. "Even my own family wouldn't do that for me. You were gonna off all those Johnny-Laws for me. You are a stand-up guy. I ain't never had a friend that tight. You're my brother," he sobbed. I decided it best to let him continue to think that, so I just nodded an acknowledgement and drove silently back into the city.

He needed a place to crash, and he needed some kind of job that would hire an ex-con. He could stay with me until we could find him a job to afford rent somewhere. The task at hand, then, was to find income for him. His first thought was to return to the trades that he knew best: burglary, armed-robbery, prescription forgery, pimping, and drug trafficking.

As a wanted fugitive, a self-described outlaw, and living the way I had to, none of that particular shocked or repelled me. However, my survival sense was well honed, and I realized that what he was proposing was a really bad plan that was destined for failure. I had a good deal of expertise in reinventing and evading the law. I decided *that* would be the best direction for Casey as well; and it would leave his criminal past behind him.

Living in Baltimore, I had continued to visit Atlantic City casinos frequently and agreed to a contract with a junket provider to fill his buses with gamblers for a *per-head* bounty. It wasn't really a career path for me (I didn't think), but it provided cash flow.

Casey had told me that when he was in the joint he operated inmate poker and blackjack games on behalf of the C.O.'s (correction officers / guards). When he told me that, I tossed him a deck of bicycles and asked him to wash and shuffle[223].

---

[223] I was deliberately using poker jargon that seasoned players and dealers would know. I was testing his knowledge base as well as his skill with cards. "Bicycles" meant cards (named for a brand); "Wash" meant to spread the cards face down and mix them up before shuffling.

THE LEGEND DIES ON — GARY GREEN

Back when I was getting the weekly special-event permits to serve alcohol at Bread & Roses, I learned that the city also issued special permits for "casino night" fundraisers for non-profits. Basically, the same bureaucracy of paperwork and no background checks as the special alcohol permits, the casino night permits allowed weekend operation of casino games to raise money.

I located a vacant room above a bar in the tourist-heavy *Fells Point* district of Baltimore. I contacted gaming equipment providers and fronted the money for Casey to rent the space and fill it with poker and blackjack tables. Casey asked me, "what happens if something goes wrong?" and I answered, "then we're up shit creek".

That stuck! We named the weekend casino, *SHT CREEK EMPORIUM* and it was "up" on the second floor. We printed signs and cards and listed Casey (as K.C.) as the proprietor. (It was illegal to call it a "casino", so we called it an "emporium".) I was strictly the silent partner and the financing behind the endeavor, which included the first month's rent, deposits, equipment, cards, cheques (chips), and the bankroll, as well as living expenses for Casey. I also bought a futon for him to use as a bed so that he could live there as well.

Things went fine for about three months. Sometime during that period, Casey decided that all of his dealers were going to be topless females. He reasoned that addition would bring in better players who would be watching the girls rather than notice the cheating that he was teaching his dealers. *What could possibly go wrong?*

That recipe for disaster turned out exactly as one might have predicted. In the early morning hours after the last customers and most of the staff had left, Casey and one of his dealers decided to get high and have fun on the futon. Sometime later, they both passed out from their intoxication, but left their cigarettes burning. As they slept, the cigarettes ignited a fire which ultimately burned the entire block of buildings. Miraculously, Casey and his guest escaped unharmed, more or less. But *Sht Creek* was permanently out of business, and Casey was homeless.

Around the same time that Casey was running the quasi-legal casino, I was contacted for help by one of the former Gary Hart staff volunteers. That staffer would eventually graduate from college, go to law school and one day be the Deputy Attorney General of her home state. But when she contacted me, she was an undergraduate at one of the Baltimore universities and was on the verge of losing her family home following the death of grandmother (her parents were already deceased). She wanted to know if I had any ideas about what she could do; her credit was horrible, and she could not get a loan to save the house.

I concocted an off-the-wall plan which began with me sitting for the *State Real Estate Licensing Exam*. The test was absurdly easy, and once licensed I was able to create a purchase to save the house from foreclosure. I just needed a strawman buyer who I could arrange cash-back financing for and who would then transfer ownership back to the student.

I set up a real estate investment firm and Casey became my strawman. All I charged the student was housing in the basement for Casey for a few months.

The scheme worked brilliantly and probably could have been cookie-cutter repeated dozens of times; strawman buying, pulling cash out at closing, renting the property, and then flipping it before the first payment was due. But the problem was the hatred that I had developed for landlords after I had seen the South Bronx situation a decade earlier.

More frequently than not, I used my scheme to buy a house or an apartment building, take the cash-at-closing to rehab the property, and then let the tenants skate on paying rent; after all, I wasn't going to own it long anyway.

It turned out that I was more-than proficient at structuring and then funding impossible-to-finance deals; but I lacked the insensitive ferocity to be a landlord. As the song on my second album had said, *There's no such thing as a good landlord; if he was good, he be bankrupt*[224].

Despite phenomenal success at *wheeling and dealing*, I discovered that the landlording racket just wasn't for me. Scratch another career option.

In conjunction with all of the real estate paperwork, bureaucracy, and legalese, it occurred to me that lawyers charged way-too much for what was basically clerical work. At the library I began reading various bar association magazines, where I discovered advertisements for software to help law firms speed up some of the most routine administrative functions: writing simple bankruptcies, wills, uncontested divorces, and so on.

I invested a couple of thousand dollars in the software and a basic office computer. I hired a full-time clerical and set up a paralegal business. I reasoned, incorrectly I might add, that as long as all we did was fill in the forms and show customers how to file *pro se* (representing themselves without a lawyer), then the business would be completely legal.

I learned, however, that the *Bar Association* (as the only professional association that regulates itself without government intervention) was less-than amused by my little business. It probably would have gone unnoticed had I not started buying display ads in *The Baltimore Sun* offering bankruptcies, divorces, etc. at about 10% of what even cut-rate law firms were charging for the same clerical work.

---

[224] *The Siege of Fort Apache*, by Gary Green, 1977, as recorded for Folkways Records album FH5353, *Allegory*

THE LEGEND DIES ON — GARY GREEN

When the Bar Association wrote the *cease-and-desist* they cited hundreds of thousands of dollars that I had cost their profession by "stealing" their business. It turned out there was actually a law called "*UPL*", unauthorized practice of law, and it was a *felony*. Obviously, I couldn't afford an arrest, so when that threat came, I immediately shut down that company. *Another career-dead end.*

That legal software had led me to the world of personal computers; first configuring them for various specialized software, then building them, repairing them, training people to use them. Before *Microsoft Windows*, I became a *DOS*-nerd memorizing all sorts of command strings to fine tune PC's. I was one of the first users of the *GEM* overlay to DOS that allowed a Windows-like experience before Windows existed. That, combined with my knowledge of printing and publishing led me to become one of the initial users of *Ventura Publisher* —the first PC-based desktop publishing program.

In my newspaper days, especially on the editing side, I had learned to typeset and maintain typesetting machines for both hot type and phototypesetting processes. Ventura was a universe beyond those technologies and cemented my attention. With it I was able to freelance typeset for a half-dozen publishers, as well as import lengthy documents from *WordPerfect*™ to format them in book or newspaper style. It didn't seem very practical in the mid-late 1980's, but it certainly was interesting.

As part of that hobby computer play, I began experimenting with dialing into H&R Block's *CompuServ*™ *Network* that allowed remote communication and file-sharing over phone lines. I added a second computer network service called *Prodigy*™, which was a joint-venture between CBS, AT&T, and Sears Roebuck. Unlike CompuServe, Prodigy had a graphic user interface, though it was less rich in content. Like desktop publishing, those online services and the little bit of programming that I toyed with were more hobbies than career paths.

I continued booking buses filled with gamblers bound for Atlantic City casinos, but I was still restless to find something to do. Music was still calling my name; but that remained impossible.

So, during the next eight or nine months, I went through a half dozen other hare-brained schemes to make a living. I didn't merely try out a few different careers; I became obsessed with each one and dove into the depths of each discipline.

In hindsight, I might call it a *psychotic mania* in each field, as I worked 18+ hours a day seven days a week with single focus. Yet, none of them held my attention for any longer than a few months; I just couldn't find the passion for any of those fields that had for my music, for my lyrics.

As I started measuring my available skill sets it occurred to me that one thing I actually had passion about was unions: *the labor movement*. I

THE POET LAUREATE SOUL OF FOLKIE ROCK & ROLL

decided to reach out to Ernie Crofoot. Timing, as Shakespear noted in Julius Caesar, is everything. Ernie's two public relations guys were leaving; one moving to another career and the other retiring.

Ernie appointed me, at first, his *Director of Public Relations* for his 28-union district council headquartered in Baltimore. In that role I wrote and published the union's newspaper, handled press, provided themes and design for leaflets for organizing drives, positioned the union with government bodies and other unions, was a public spokesperson for the district council (along with Crofoot himself), set up meetings and conventions, and even oversee internal elections.

Eventually, he expanded my role beyond union public affairs to serving as business agent and representative for a number of local unions across the state. In that latter role, I served as legal representative for disciplinary hearings, employee advocate before administrative law judges, and chief negotiator for contract enforcement matters. In short, I became a key player in the inner-workings of the district council.

Separate from that, Ernie Crofoot partnered with me to bankroll my continuing side-gig of sending buses to the casinos in Atlantic City; and he referred various locals and other unions to fill the buses. That, however, was a sideline that we kept secret from the staff and the board.

I was careful not to let anyone associated with the unions know about my legal situation. Looking back at it, I am certain that must have made the staff, the board, and some of the local leadership wonder how-the-hell this mysterious crippled eccentric character became so embedded in the organization. It was an enigma that would never be fully clarified for them, though I occasionally served up glimpses of my music life, my newspaper experiences, and my academic focus. Even those tiny glimpses must have been too improbably complex to be believable; especially taken out the twisted intricacies of my life story (even up to that point).

My survival paranoia made me keenly aware of the suspicious distrust my presence generated; but I decided not to act on it and just let their doubts simmer.

One of the duties of my union job was to organize and manage the annual convention for the district council. Crofoot had made a deal with a hotel-casino on Paradise Island in The Bahamas to host the gathering. My role was to charter the plane, book the rooms, arrange the meals, and set an agenda for the 200+ attendees.

The very first convention went off with only a few humorous hitches; barroom fable-worthy hilarity. But the chartered return flight, after landing back at BWI Airport, turned into a disaster.

Upon arrival, my fugitive years abruptly came to an end... with my arrest at the Baltimore airport.

THE LEGEND DIES ON — GARY GREEN

Opus Twenty-Four:
Arrested At Border Control; Now What?

All the Federales say
They could have had him any day
They only let him slip away
Out of kindness, I suppose
— *Pancho and Lefty*, by Townes Van Zandt, ©Wixen Music Publishing

*L*uck of the draw, or *unluck* of the draw; either way, once again a law enforcement service revolver was pointed at my head and cold handcuffs were clamped onto my wrists. Oh, and unlike bad-television shows, they don't handcuff you in front of your body; they handcuff you behind your back. (At least they weren't using plastic zip-ties back then, so nothing cut into my skin as the restrained me.)

The Immigration and Naturalization Service (an agency that ceased to exist after the Department of Homeland Security was created following 9-11) only randomly checked passports for returning charter flights of American citizens. On the union-chartered flight of 200+ passengers, I was one of a half-dozen randomly checked. Lucky me.

The agent routinely took my passport and typed my information into the NCIC terminal. I saw the expression on his face change as he hit a button under his countertop.

I searched for an escape route, but the only way out was to pass two armed uniformed officers. Seconds later, they were on top of me with guns drawn and then I was cuffed. They led me to a small, windowless office with only one door.

"Where are you taking me?" I asked (or maybe demanded) "You're going to prison. Write a song about that," one of the gunmen snorted. Visions of Victor Jara's hands being cut off before his assassination once again filled my head again. This was going to be ugly.

There they handcuffed me, again behind my back, to a wheeled office chair and pushed me down into the seat. "I want to make my phone call," I demanded. "You don't get a phone call," one of the surly agents gut-growled. "I have the right to talk to my attorney," I pushed.

The nastiest toned agent responded that I had not been admitted into the United States yet, so I had no constitutional rights. He added, "We're holding you pending disposition. We don't need any more communists in the country."

Fuck! They knew who they were holding. International political asylum was no longer an option. They had me; so now it was a matter of staying alive.

THE POET LAUREATE SOUL OF FOLKIE ROCK & ROLL

It was before-noon on a Sunday morning; so, getting ahold of anyone concerning my "disposition" was not going to be quick; I knew that. They left me sitting in the room for a little more than two hours before another agent, not in uniform, showed up.

The new guy apparently was some kind of supervisor who had been disturbed on a Sunday to come in and deal with this dangerous international fugitive that his team had caught. He was not a happy boy as he sat at the desk and began dialing numbers, evidently trying to get in touch with the FBI agent on call for Sunday situations.

I could hear his side of the conversation when he finally reached an agent after two or three attempts. He reported that they had nabbed a fugitive. They were debating what to do with me. Apparently, the FBI agent wanted me locked in the Baltimore City Jail until Monday when they could arrange extradition to Tennessee; but the INS supervisor needed paperwork in order to admit me to the United States. The FBI guy seemed to be objecting to the additional work that would require.

They finally resolved that since I was at the airport already, they could contact Tennessee officials immediately and resolve the whole thing within a couple of hours. Whether the legalities were right or not, they reasoned that since I had not been admitted to the United States yet, then no extradition hearing would be required. With authorization from Tennessee, the U.S. Marshall service could transport me to Nashville that very day. *(In hindsight, I question that armchair legal logic.)*

Though I knew that incarceration in Tennessee was a pre-trial death sentence, I actually held out a little hope for their plan. The Federal Marshall for the Nashville District was a relative of Congressman Evins and his appointment had been arranged by the Congressman. So, there was a chance I would not be killed if I could be in his custody.

On the other hand, if I was admitted to Maryland and sent to the City Jail, I was probably safe there too. I was the union representative for the correctional officers there; they would probably keep me safe and somewhat privileged. I might even be able to arrange an escape from there.

It's funny what absurd scenarios one's mind conjures when the fear of assassination is hanging above your head. Well, less than funny, it was testimony to my desperation.

When the call ended, the agent left me alone in the room for about five more hours. No water, no bathroom, handcuffed to a chair. I searched the desktop, trash can, and anything on the walls for something to use to pick the lock of the handcuffs and then a weapon to take out the agent when he returned to the room. There were not a lot of possibilities, and with my right hand crippled I was pretty sure that I couldn't hold a pick anyway.

Two or three hours later, the agent came back in; this time he was accompanied by another plain clothes guy who I assumed was either the

THE LEGEND DIES ON — GARY GREEN

FBI agent or a Federal Marshall, though he didn't offer his credentials or even acknowledge me. I silently wondered if he was the same FBI agent that I had almost shot at my mother's front door a couple of years earlier.

He sat at the desk, dialed a number, and instructed the person on the other end of the phone to call him back when they were able to connect with the district attorney in Tennessee. He must have been expecting an immediate connection because he sat at the desk staring at the phone.

Those expectations were spot on. In less than ten minutes, the phone rang. I could tell from his side of the conversation that his office had managed to reach the District Attorney General in Tennessee.

He apologized for calling on a Sunday and then announced the good news that he had captured a dangerous fugitive. I heard him say, "his name is Gary Green," and then he abruptly stopped.

After listening intently, he responded, "but the computer says he is still..." And he stopped again to listen. He spoke again, "that doesn't dismiss the Federal charges, flight to avoid...". Then silence again before he spoke more, "yes Sir, I would agree that if there is no prosecution then there could be flight to avoid it, but...". Silence once more. Then, "So, wait. *He was never served?*" More silence, then a few more apologetic sentences for bothering him on a Sunday afternoon. He hung up, walked out the door, and still didn't speak to me.

A few minutes later, the INS agent came into the room. He unlocked my handcuffs, and said, "you're free to go". He handed me my passport, stamped with my admission to the country, and told me where I could pick up my suitcase.

I asked, "that's it?" Very matter-of-factly he answered, "that's it." Rather than ask anything else, I got-the-hell out of there and went home.

First, I called my parents and told them what had happened. My mother conjected that the charges just "went away". Next, I called Kunstler to tell him what had happened. He said he would "get to the bottom of it" on Monday and meanwhile, I should get some sleep. I was not looking forward to Monday; I was going to have to explain to Crofoot what had happened in front of union members, and why.

The next morning, I chickened out; I called the receptionist and told her that I would be late and wouldn't be in until noon. Then I sat and waited to hear from Bill Kunstler. It seemed like forever, but middle Tennessee was in the Central time zone, so everything was off by an hour for me. I waited and waited. When he finally called, I felt like my heart was pounding so hard that it would explode; but it didn't.

Bill had talked with the Tennessee prosecutor. He said that when the FBI called on Sunday, the prosecutor had told them, "hell no; we don't want him back here." Kunstler told me that when the Federal agent objected, the prosecutor told him that the term of the Grand Jury had expired, the indictments expired without ever being unsealed *and served*.

My lawyer told me that it was all over. "It went away with a thud, not a bang. They don't want you back there, and you don't want to go back."

I called Howard, Walt, and many of the people who had supported me during the worst of my ordeal. Then I went in to see Crofoot.

Ernie listened intently and then finally spoke, "Holy shit. Well, that explains a lot." I offered to resign, but Ernie would hear nothing of it. He confessed that he was contemplating retirement and would like for me to remain with the union at least until then. *(Besides, he liked the residual income from our secret side business of running gambling buses to Atlantic City.)* I agreed to stay on.

He insisted that we should not let my full story be known to the staff nor the membership, though he acknowledged my suspicions that some staff members were aware that "something was up" with me as they had pieced together information from my day-to-day conversations.

They knew I had a music background but didn't know how I ended up at their union. They, obviously, knew that I had become crippled; but they didn't know how. They ascertained that I was some kind of lefty radical, but it wasn't clear what flavor. They were highly suspicious about my academic connections. Even my two Pulitzer nominations and the hundred or so state press awards raised questions about "why would he want to be at *our* newspaper?"

Then, they had seen the INS handcuff me; and that waved so many red flags, that there might not be any acceptable explanation short of full transparency (which Ernie wanted to avoid). Ernie suggested that I take a two-week paid vacation while he would "smooth things over". I agreed; but it turned out that my vacation choice just made matters worse.

The labor movement that I had joined as a member in the 1970's and as staff under the auspices of Ernie Crofoot in the mid-1980's was a lot different than the 21st century labor movement. At the time, neoconservative commentator Ben Wattenberg called AFL-CIO president, Lane Kirkland the "five-star general of the Cold War". [225] The columnist also noted that "during the decades of the Cold War it was the AFL-CIO that was the most stalwart institutional bastion of anti-communism in America."

It is no secret that near the end of that cold war era, the AFL-CIO worked closely with the CIA to topple left-leaning governments in South America and Europe. Republican U.S. Senator Orrin Hatch's office said

---

[225] Under Kirkland's leadership, union membership in American *decreased* by 51% according to *The Washington Post* and there were massive organizing losses with the air traffic controllers, Hormel meats, Federal Prison Industries, and others.

THE LEGEND DIES ON — GARY GREEN

Kirkland was "to the right of Reagan." Many on the left referred to the federation as the "AFL-*CIA*." My being entrenched in organized labor did me no favors with my lefty peers.

Domestically, the labor federation was just as vehemently anti-leftist as it was internationally; if not more so. Beginning in the McCarthy era, hundreds of "suspected communists" were expelled from unions; a practice that continued well into the 1990's. (Fortunately, as I write this —*almost a half-century later*— that seems to have changed; at least as I can see as a rank-and-file member these days, rather than as paid staff.)

Despite the presence of several progressive (or at least neutral) labor leaders across the country (including Ernie Crowfoot) rabid anti-leftist fervor dominated the top ranks of the Federation. Even the labor music and cultural programs of the George Meany Center for Labor Studies[226] was still screening and boycotting the more left-leaning labor musicians (though many, less-overt than me, passed muster).

It was in the context of *that* labor movement that I chose to take my Crofoot-ordered vacation to —*of all possible bad-decision places*— behind the "Iron Curtain". Specifically, I ended a London-Paris-Rome-Milan-Frankfurt European vacation with a week in *The German Democratic Republic*, aka "East Germany".

Though I was no longer a fugitive and relatively free to do whatever I chose, I was still in an outlaw state of mind and I was still philosophically aligned with the Communist Party on many issues. I wanted to see firsthand what it would have been like if I had been forced to seek political asylum; if I had no choice but to defect. And I wanted to keep my options open in the event I ever again became a fugitive.

Apparently my visiting the DDR (the *Deutsche Demokratische Republik*) was a lot more of a big deal than I had thought it would be.

Firstly, I wasn't going through the regular western-tourism channels; I had used the New York contacts of the Communist Party to arrange my visa. Besides calling attention to the trip, it also meant that I would be

---

[226] The center's *Great Labor Arts Exchange* was created and run by the self-pro-claimed "labors troubadour", Joe Glazer, who had recorded 25+ albums (and even several on Folkways in the 1950's before he turned on Seeger and others. Woody Guthrie called him "Joe Glassy-ear" because during the 1950's red-baiting he had written right-wing parodies of Pete Seeger songs and allegedly had testified before the House Un-American Activities Committee naming "known communist folk singers".

When I first became known in labor-song circles, Glazer invited me to meet with him; but when he found out that I was "a leftist", he made me persona-non-grata at the center; painting me not as a leftist but as an extreme ultra-leftist and disrupter of good unions. *I have been told in recent years that my perception of Glazer and the Meany Center was totally incorrect and that I was ostracized because I was so hostile toward him, rather than any other reason.*

THE POET LAUREATE SOUL OF FOLKIE ROCK & ROLL

entering the country through a German Party-approved checkpoint rather than the standard *Checkpoint Charlie* that American visitors normally used.

Secondly, it didn't occur to me until I arrived, but as the Public Affairs Director of a huge regional council of the largest union in the AFL-CIO, I was the highest-ranking labor union official ever to visit East Germany.

Finally, as a Folkways Records recording artists (with the political slant of some of my songs), I was somewhat of a "celebrity" to the *Socialist Unity Party* (Sozialistische Einheitspartei Deutschlands), the East German communist party that controlled the country.

What all this meant was that my vacation raised the attention of the *Stasi* (the East German version of the KGB, often referred to by Americans as the "secret police"). It also raised the attention of the CIA, which reported it to the headquarters of the AFL-CIO, who in turn reported it to the FBI. And, since I went directly through *New York* Communist Party members rather than on the recommendation and support of the Baltimore party, the CPUSA was suspiciously eyeing me as well.

All of that translated to every one of those groups, while adversarial to each other, were united in suspicions that I was some kind of spy for one of the others. Looking back on the whole thing, it is hilarious; but at the time it was some heavy-duty international spook stuff and pretty intense.

When I arrived in East Germany (through a bad-movie-style series of underground former subway tunnels), I was met by a Stasi agent who was my "tour guide" and escort for my visit. Apparently, Stasi determined that I wasn't a western agent or any other kind of threat, so after a few days my guide informed me that I would be own my own except for a few official state dinners and meetings at my various stops in the country.

I was scheduled to spend time in East Berlin, Dresden, Leipzig, and Weimar. In Berlin, he arranged meetings with top bankers, union officials, and academics, all ending with an official State dinner attended by big-shot Party officials (but disappointingly not *Party Chairman Erich Honecker*). The next couple of days were sight-seeing touristy stuff in Berlin.

In Dresden, I met with a Soviet military contingent that was assigned to a Russian "translator" to meet with me. Within seconds of meeting the supposed-translator, it was clear to me that he was probably KGB using that translator bullshit cover. About my age or maybe a couple of years older, his name was Vladimir Vladimirovich Putin. Yup, *that* Vladimir Putin; *who would have thunk?*

By the time that Dresden meeting ended, at Karl Marx University, the Stasi apparently had their determination confirmed by the KGB that I was not a planted spy (or at least no kind of threat to them). After Dresden they *completely* abandoned me and let me visit without escort the towns

THE LEGEND DIES ON — GARY GREEN

of Leipzig, Weimar, and the memorial at the *Buchenwald Nazi Concentration Camp*. Unlike the stories I'd heard of restricted travel behind the Iron Curtain, no one seemed to care where-the-hell I went in the country.

I was driven around in god-awful *Trabant* cars, flew on a very-iffy airline called *Interflug*, and rode on the DR (*Deutsche Reichsbahn*) passenger rail system; all with no apparent Stasi escort. I returned to East Berlin, spent a couple more nights there, mostly wandering around department stores, grocery stores, and shopping districts to see the often-reported shortages, bare shelves, and long lines for food —*none of which existed.* I visited schools, factories, prisons, libraries, and yes even churches.

Naïvely, it never occurred to me that my trip would be controversial; just as it never occurred to me that, since I was no longer a fugitive, the CIA would take notice or even care. So, when the CIA informed their partners at the AFL-CIO who informed my union's national office which in turn informed Crofoot, I was completely shocked.

Once again, I offered to resign. At a Sunday afternoon meeting at his home in Bowie Maryland, Ernie made fried corn-fritters as part of an early dinner for me and four of his key advisors. Cloaked as a casual social gathering, it was clear to me that the real purpose was to discuss damage control for the repercussions of my vacation. The strategy agreed on by the assembled brain trust proved to be disastrous; it was decided that I should write a first-person feature story about my experiences in East Germany, and we would print it as the front-page cover story for the next issue of the union newspaper.

I guess everyone had expected me to write a scathing review of harsh life behind the iron curtain; but instead, I reported that I didn't find the supposed shortages and long lines. It got worse: I reported on free health care, free college, and wage parity among blue collar workers with doctors and white-collar jobs. Then, as if deliberately sealing my own doom, I compared the living and working conditions to the average laborer or inner-city resident in the U.S.

That did it; calls came from the Meany Center for me to be fired. Joe Glazer ranted against me. Conservative union staffers, members, and officials of other unions all pressured Crofoot; but he defiantly refused to let me leave. When that failed, an organized campaign to find other ways to force me to resign.

Instead of getting rid of me, all of that drama contributed to Crofoot's already intense fatigue and thus his motivation to retire; and he did, announcing that it would be three-months later at the end of the election cycle. I hung on for almost another year or so.

During the 90 days before Ernie left and, in the following year before I resigned, I witnessed (or was asked to participate in) every imaginable corrupt practice that I had always thought could only be anti-union fiction.

THE POET LAUREATE SOUL OF FOLKIE ROCK & ROLL

From huge cash kickbacks to election rigging to sweetheart deals with exclusive vendors binding employers, even strong-arm death threats.

I saw it all... culminating in the police discovering a car-bomb waiting for me one evening after work. That, believe it or not, was not the last straw (as it should have been). I hung on for another 18 months; and probably should not have. *Yup, they found a bomb in my car!*

I mean, I certainly was accustomed to people wanting to murder me; but this shit was *not* what I had signed up for in a union; and it was a long way from picking and singing country-folk songs in Nashville or movement songs in New York and California. Since music was over for me, I had come to Crofoot a couple of years earlier in the hope of finding direction. It was, admittedly, a godsend; and I did a lot of good for a lot of union members. Clearly, though, it wasn't the right match for me.

During the years with the union, I had continued to run those buses to Atlantic City, which was a profitable little endeavor though not particularly interesting. Much more interestingly, very clandestinely I had been exercising my right hand to play piano and to try to play guitar.

My right thumb had recovered about 80% of its feeling; at least on the outside left part of it. That meant that I could do the bass and lead part of the Carter Family lick; but... alas... I could not use my index finger or middle finger at all. My ring finger was more like my thumb; it had about 75% to 80% feeling returned. My "pinky" finger seemed to be normal. The palm of my hand against my wrist, which I used to deaden strings at different times, was functional but hyper-sensitive. I could not, however, either hold a pick or wear finger picks or even a thumb pick. Since my left hand, used for fingering, was not damaged, I could play guitar; probably better than most amateur pickers, but nothing like I had been able to do before the fiasco. Still, I practiced.

I had heard repeatedly from friends that "Nashville has changed", and that I would be welcomed with open arms; especially with the "street cred" of being a "famous" Folkways recording artist. The Folkways connection carried a lot of weight nationwide.

Despite the crippled hand, I couldn't stop that incessant call of music that had awakened me that July night almost exactly 35 years earlier. I couldn't help myself. Moreover, I decided to go back into the state where they had vowed to murder me. I decided to go back to Tennessee. I decided to go to Nashville. Terrifying as that was, I also was still outlaw-arrogant and willing to dare anyone to come after me since I was "legal".

I put together a pretty elaborate pitch-package, including studio photos, a glossy four-page bio brochure, bumper stickers, buttons, balloons, recommendation letters, and a demo cassette tape. I carefully targeted the packages to Nashville, not looking for a record contract or a publishing deal this time; I was looking for venues to play.

THE LEGEND DIES ON — GARY GREEN

My old Grand Ole Opry friend Justin Tubb, the son of Hall of Fame legend "Texas Troubadour" Ernest Tubb, immediately booked me to play his father's *Midnight Jamboree* national radio show. It was a syndicated live broadcast that went out over clear-channel WSM right after the Opry.

Nervous as I was about going back into Tennessee, I swallowed hard and pulled up my "big-boy-pants". I flew directly into Nashville (avoiding small towns along the way), rented a car and... there I was... back in Tennessee. Scared shitless, but back.

Despite the fear, I was thrilled to be back with my "country music family" and Justin and his band welcomed me like a long-lost brother. His live audience was filled with people that I considered the royalty of Nashville music; including on the front row *Mae Axton* (who had written Elvis' first number-one song, *Heartbreak Hotel*).[227]

I opened with *The Wreck of the Old 97* —the arrangement that Moe Asch had ordered me never to perform. With Justin's band backing me up (with no rehearsal), I threw them for a loop when I switched to cut-time at the first break; but that band was made up of Nashville pros and they instantly made the adjustment. They were brilliant; much better than my performance (especially with my cracking voice and gimp hand).

The applause was robust, and after my performance Justin —to the live national radio audience— lavished accolades, praise, and thanks to me. He told the audience:

> "Gary Green has been gone too long. This is a man that has done just about everything somebody can do in this business, and we are so happy to welcome him home. We hope we will see him a regular now that he's back."

It could not have gone better. I could not have been happier. I was back in Nashville, and not just performing with my Opry family, but welcomed with loving arms and raucous applause. It was near-perfect.

On the same trip, I was also invited to play at *Exit/In*; the venue that I had heard so much about representing the "new" Nashville. On the heels of my Ernest Tubb Midnight Jamboree appearance, I could not have been more thrilled.

Finally, I was sure, Nashville and Gary were on the same page. I was welcomed in the Country Music Family and then I was about to be welcomed in the next generation; my people had finally arrived. *I thought.*

---

[227] She also was the mother of *Hoyt Axton*, himself a legendary songwriter who wrote *The Pusher* (recorded by Steppenwolf), *Joy to the World* (recorded by Three Dog Night), as well as dozens of other well-known songs including *Green-back Dollar, Della and the Dealer,* and *Never Been to Spain*. He also starred in a bunch of movies, including The Black Stallion and Gremlins.

THE POET LAUREATE SOUL OF FOLKIE ROCK & ROLL

Unfortunately, my arrival was a few years too-late for the venue to want the likes of me. Their much touted new-generation vegetarian cuisine had been long abandoned, which should have been a tell-tale sign of *something*. The club itself had become more of a rock venue than country, and not *even* folkie. In that regard, it was like a Nashville version of the transition of my old friends at CBGB in New York.

I miscalculated, at best; I didn't realize the changes and I Pollyanna-like expected a progressive, hippie-like, new Nashville within the walls of the little shopping center storefront club. I thought I was coming into Greenwich Village or Bread & Roses... with a Southern accent. I really believed that.

With my assumptions firmly in place, I decided to open with *Snake Bite Poison*, my tirade against the Ku Klux Klan, racism, and the old South. As I was singing, I could see shocked looks on the faces in the audience; clearly, they weren't expecting a topical song, especially one that pointed fingers so close to home. I saw no faces getting into the song.

When I finished, there was almost no applause. Again, from the audience's faces, I was surprised they didn't boo me off stage. In a flashback of that open mike during my freshman orientation back at UT, the proprietor (or at least somebody that seemed to be in charge) escorted me from the stage and lectured me about preaching versus "good-time" songs. I was politely invited to leave and never return.

That was devastating. If that represented the "new" Nashville, then it meant the problem was not about the lyrics, the anti-racism, or the politics. Pure and simple, it meant that I was just... bad. The new progressive outlaw-friendly Nashville was telling me that I sucked.

That splash of cold water completely extinguished the fire that Justin Tubb had ignited in me. Only worse: it wasn't a matter of Nashville not being "ready" for it; it was a matter that I simply was not good enough. Period. I cancelled the remaining two days that I had planned to spend in Music City. I didn't go see Reba. I didn't go to the Opry. I didn't go looking for any old friends or acquaintances. I didn't even go to Hillbilly Central (which is what Tompall's studio had been christened).

Nope. I packed up and got the first flight back to Baltimore. This time I really was finished. What's worse than a crippled wanna-be guitar picker? A BAD crippled wanna-be guitar picker!

♭♪♭♪♭♪

Back in Baltimore, once again I had to figure out what I wanted to be when I grew up; and I'd better hurry because I was creeping up on 40 years old! I had to job-hunt along the way.

With several years of union experience under my belt, even with the (quite accurate) red-baiting, I had a whole new resume track to list along

THE LEGEND DIES ON — GARY GREEN

with everything else. Being in commuting proximity to Washington DC, I could see multiple potential opportunities.

I began looking at the specialized DC jobs subculture of *associations*. DC was overrun with "*The American Association of __*" fill-in-the-blank outfits. Every affinity group in the country, from dentists to pipe fitters to bookbinders and everything in between, had an office in the District of Columbia. There were people whose entire careers were a string of association-hopping; for three years they represented butchers, for nine years they represented casino owners, and for six years they represented brake manufacturers. Seriously, there were hundreds of association operatives.

Associations, in structure, were similar to unions and by their nature were generally alienated from unions. So, I thought, I might have a shot. It worked; I spent the next couple of years association-hopping.

My first association gig was a huge consumer organization that published a 250,000-circulation monthly slick magazine. They were looking for an editor & publisher. Between my newspaper experience, my association (union) experience, and my magazine-publishing experience (Broadside), I was a shoe-in. Seriously, how many associations get a two-time Pulitzer nominated journalist editing their bullshit trade journal?

I could have stayed there a long time, I suspect; but I was aching for music and audiences… even after I had crashed and burned at Exit/Inn. So, after about a year I restlessly began looking for other things.

My daily commute from Baltimore to Washington and back became a real drag; sardine-packed with the *salaryman* commuter dilettantes for the hour-and-a-half train trip. After a few weeks of it, I discovered that for a few dollars more I could take the high-speed *Amtrak Metroliner* train that made the trip in one-third of the time (and not nearly as crowded); those trains also had the added benefits of a club car and meal service. Rather than rudely packed commuters, the people on the Amtrak train were generally on board for a longer trip and were more interested in comfort, socializing, and relaxation; none of the tenseness of commuter life.

A couple of times a week I would share a seat compartment with an up-and-coming United States Senator from Delaware —a liberal state where I had received my warmest welcomes as a topical folksinger. I wouldn't say we were close friends, but Senator *Joe Biden* and I certainly knew each other, acknowledged each other, and frequently shared idle chit-chat about nothing profound[228].

---

[228] In light of the disparaging image that ended his presidency in 2024, I probably should point out that even at age 48 he was somewhat of what I termed a "goofball". He was an off-the-cuff short-attention span happy-go-lucky guy. So, when the 21st century politicians questioned his lucidity, I scoffed because he was always like that (in a good way).

THE POET LAUREATE SOUL OF FOLKIE ROCK & ROLL

During the next couple of years, I bounced between associations and large labor unions (some, apparently, didn't know that I had been branded a commie). With Crofoot serving as a reference for me (and not mentioning the DDR), I landed several. I also did political consulting for several of his projects. Along the way I continued the Atlantic City bus junkets.

The most amazingly ambitious of those union gigs turned out to be a hard-won battle that technically was the largest union organizing drive in American history: 66-thousand people in one bargaining unit; unheard of!

The best, by far, was an untitled and ambiguous-duties but very hard-working position with Local 1923 of the *American Federation of Government Employees* (AFGE); representatives of the Social Security Administration, the Health Care Finance Administration, and a handful of smaller agencies. Working with some incredibly good —and unbelievable cool— people, it was the best union-insider experience that I ever had.

My boss, who eventually became the international president of the union, knew a lot about my background, the dropped charges, and even East Germany. He didn't care as long as I did my job, and it didn't enter into my work for the union. It wasn't that he agreed with me at all, or even sympathized; the fact was, he really didn't give a shit as long as I did what he needed me to do for his members. It was an awesome gig.

While I was working for AFGE, I received a call from a community organization in Waverly called *The Progressive Action Center*. They wanted me to help them put together a ten-year reunion tribute concert for Bread & Roses Two. They wanted to organize it almost like a Hoot; but not as an open mike; they wanted curated performers who fit their mission but also reflected the history of my coffeehouse.

Of course, I agreed to do it; with the proviso that I would not be performing; that I had permanently retired from music. I reached out to Gary Blanchard to see if he was willing to emcee the program and perform. He was. He had expanded from folk to some very 1980's / early-1990's electronica; and was making quite a splash in that world.

Gary Blanchard also booked *Geo Kendall*, a Bread & Roses Two alumnae who was a terrific jazz-folkie and always reminded me of Harry Chapin. He was an incredibly good guitarist, an excellent songwriter, and a damned fine performer. We booked him both as a solo and to play lead behind Blanchard's electronic keyboards.

We booked Steve Resnick, a young political folk singing guitar picker, who was a great representation of the kind of new talent that we were known for introducing. Dressed in American flag shirt *(à la Abbie Hoffman)*, he gave a great performance of contemporary topical music.

We also booked Laura Larco Gentile, the Peruvian ethnomusicologist who had been a regular at Bread & Roses Two. She gave a really nice performance of Latin American songs that were spiced with her history-

THE LEGEND DIES ON — GARY GREEN

lesson explanations of each song. That alone would have made the evening worth attending.

Gary Blanchard himself sang my favorite, *The Peace Song*, and another of his peace movement songs called *We Need Bread Not Bombs*. He masterfully added patter between an entire set of originals, mixing his Bread & Roses repertoire with his progressed electronica as well as some near-standup jokes from the stage.

His role as emcee was perfect. He gave the audience a nostalgic flashback to the heyday of Bread & Roses Two, and at the same time he showed that he, all of the performers, and the music itself had moved on to new levels. And each of the performers lived up to that theme.

He, and the Progressive Action Center, had prepared flip-chart pages of the history of the coffeehouse, from its original founding to the change into Bread & Roses Two and the highlights of concerts and events there until its closing. They walked the enthusiastic audience through that nostalgic journey, and I could see faces light up at different waypoints in the story.

It was 1993, ten years since I as a Federal fugitive had seized the coffeehouse from the *Mouse In A Blender* collective. The flip-chart history positioned me as a colorfully eccentric character who put Bread & Roses on the national radar. Kindly, their eventful history flow did not recount that along the way I had burned more bridges than General Sherman; and they graciously skipped over my then-well-known explosive temper outrages like the one that had crippled my hand and ended my music career.

About two weeks before the show, the community organizers and Gary Blanchard came back to me and insisted that an anniversary show would be vastly incomplete without a performance from me. They claimed that Bread & Roses Two really was *the Gary Green coffeehouse* and without me performing, it would not be an accurate reflection of the history.

After effectively being booed off stage at Exit/Inn, I had vowed that I really would never return to performing in front of people again. Ever. I preferred to just let it all die with fond memories rather than appear as a shadow-of-myself that was never all-that-good in the first place. Nonetheless, they insisted that I appear on stage; just being present and speaking would not be enough.

I still had no direction for what I wanted to do in life. At 39 years old, I was ready to walk from the labor movement permanently; I'd done all I could do there, and I was losing my enthusiasm for it. The association world was never interesting to me, only a layover. My work with Atlantic City casinos, successful as it had been, was winding down as the landscape there was changing; and that had only been a hobby anyway.

The truth is, I had no idea of what I wanted to do or could do; and I had pretty-much decided to leave Baltimore permanently. I had come there 14 years earlier to hide. I'd done so in plain sight until I had been caught. I had built a music career and ended it by failing to control my own demons.

With the mindset of closure on my Baltimore life, I reluctantly agreed to one last stage appearance. I asked to be sandwiched between performers rather than showcased; and they agreed. Gary Blanchard opened, he was followed by Steve, then Laura, then me followed by Geo, and then the show closed with Gary Blanchard's new material accompanied by Geo and then a house sing-along of *The Peace Song*.

I agreed to that lineup and put together a six-song set selected to reflect my thoughts about the last 14 years of my life. I opened with a medley of Billy Joe Shaver's *I've Been to Georgia On A Fast Train* and Cowboy Joe Babcock's *I Washed My Hands In Muddy Water*. I followed up by telling the story of being asked to leave Exit/Inn in Nashville and then performed my *Snake Bite Poison* for the room (they were considerably more enthusiastic than the Nashville crowd had been). I followed with my "hit", *Jesus Christ Was A Republican*.

When sustained applause for that recognizable song finally died down, I decided to tell the assembled crowd about the circumstances that had brought me to Baltimore. Without too-much yada-yada, I told them about being a fugitive and escaping to their city where I seized the coffee house, attended school, was arrested, saw the charges dropped, and I lost the use of my right hand.

Before their stunned expressions could turn to any reaction, I broke into my song *There Ain't No Easy Way*. I followed that with *I Wore His Gun*. I closed my set talking about my work in the labor movement for the past half-decade and then I performed Woody Guthrie's *Union Maid* as an audience sing-along. I ended my set as I ended many of my sets over the years, with a clinched power fist high in the air and the Black Panthers' slogan *All Power to the People!*

As I stepped off the stage, both Gary and Cliff (the organizer of the Progressive Action Center) rushed to the stage to thank me for coming out of retirement for one last performance. After a couple of lauding minutes, they led the room in an ovation as I made my farewell.

Unknown to anyone, it would be one of my last nights in Baltimore. I had already made complex arrangements to leave for good.

Through the labor grapevine I had heard that the recently-opened Euro-Disney, outside of Paris was embroiled in labor problems and their lawyers, professional negotiators, and even AFL-CIO consultants had reached a dead-end in negotiations. The giant corporation and Mike Eisner's team were looking for a peacemaker between the two sides; someone who the radicalized French workers would accept as a comrade but at the same time could convey the positions of the company. They didn't want a negotiator; they wanted a *peacemaker*.

THE LEGEND DIES ON — GARY GREEN

I had the labor relations cred and certainly the radical-left credentials; so, it was altogether possible that I could fit the bill. It also helped that I had been speaking French since second grade back in Kingsport.

The sole assignment for the short-term consulting gig was to get both sides back to the table; nothing more. I wouldn't have to negotiate, resolve the issues, or even be involved. It was pure-and-simple: get everyone to the table. Period. And it meant a few months all-expenses covered in France, along with a hefty payday.

Even though the Disney complex was only about 45 minutes east of Paris, I chose a base that was an hour-and-twenty-two-minute flight (or six-hour high-speed train trip) south on the French Rivera. I mean, if I was going to be a corporate stooge, I might as well spend corporate money improperly. Besides, I could have them buy me an open-ended ticket and once the assignment ended, I could hang out in Europe for a few months and return whenever (or IF ever) I felt like it.

I left Baltimore, still with no plan, but ready to move to the second part of my life. When the assignment ended, I spent the next weeks *and months* wandering around Paris, Rome, Florence, Munich, and other cities. Like the bohemians and beats before me, I was "looking for myself".

I went back to see what had become of East Berlin after the Reagan *"Mister Gorbachev, tear down this wall"* demand. I didn't like it. Probably most troubling was that the anti-Nazi memorial that the East German Government had built, with "an eternal flame never to be extinguished so the world will always remember" ... had been extinguished, plowed over, and was a parking lot for a casino.

Depressed and saddened, I boarded a train for Zurich to spend a couple of nights in a remote Swiss hotel, away from the world. I arrived during a blizzard, far worse than the average Swiss snowstorms. The hotel had closed down except for one group that had rented an entire wing of the hotel to ride out the blizzard. Taking pity on my having no place to go, the hotel graciously checked with the private party and obtained permission for me to stay until the storm let up.

It turned out that the private party that had rented the secluded hotel was *The Rolling Stones*. I spent the next two days dining with and generally hanging with Mick, Keith, and the gang in rural Switzerland.

My open-ended ticket was set to fly from Geneva, but I was not ready to go back to the States. I still hadn't answered any of my own questions about what to do with the rest of my life now that music was gone.

I needed to find some musical inspiration, or some live music, or something, I decided to travel back to Paris where I ended up spending my 40th birthday. I needed clarity. Damnit, I *needed* to rock and roll.

THE POET LAUREATE SOUL OF FOLKIE ROCK & ROLL

Opus Twenty-Six:
God forgives; Outlaws Take Revenge *(and own a circus)*

I planned each charted course
Each careful step along the byway
And more, much, much more
I did it, I did it my way[229].

It was a time. Moe Asch died in October of 1986, just before my arrest. Brother Kirk had died almost exactly two months earlier. Congressman Evins died the same year. My biggest California supporter, Malvina Reynold had died about the same time that I was preparing to flee Tennessee for Baltimore. Marjorie Guthrie died the week I gained control of Bread & Roses. Ewan MacColl died about the time the plate glass sliced open my right wrist. Bill Kunstler would die in the next year or so, while I would be cavorting in the Philippines. Then, Gordon Friesen would die less than a year after that.

It indeed was a time; a time to evaluate what I wanted to do … and COULD do… with my music and with my life; a time to address my bitterness head-on and extract restitution if that's what I wanted.

It was a time for either restoration or metamorphosis. It was a time to revisit my musical direction. In the fourteen tumultuous Baltimore years, my musical landscape turned inside out. I had gone from country folkie poet recording artist to outlaw radical folk-"slinger" to concert promoter and venue operator.

My walkabout through Europe *did* provide me with a calming perspective on my life; what was and what was *not* actually important. I resolved nothing; but I did come to understand that so much was out-of-whack with my life that I needed to seriously evaluate "what now".

With Moe's death, my in-the-works *Live At Bread & Roses* album disappeared and my *come in and record any time* arrangement with Folkways evaporated. It briefly looked like my remaining records from Moe's warehouse would be sold off as cutouts by *Rounder Records* (who told me that they had no interest in me as an artist for their label).

My friend Mike Seeger assured me that his nephew, Tony, and a very cool cat named Jeff Place would be "taking care of" Folkways in a special

---

[229] Claude Francois, Gilles Thibaut, Jacques Revaux, Paul Anka, "My Way" (comme d'habitud", © CONSALAD CO., Ltd., BMG Rights Management, SUISA, CONCORD MUSIC PUBLISHING LLC, WARN-ER CHAPPELL MUSIC FRANCE, JEUNE MUSIQUE EDITIONS

THE LEGEND DIES ON — GARY GREEN

arrangement with the renowned *Smithsonian Institution*. I had never met either, but Marilyn Averett Conklin told me that the Smithsonian would keep the recordings alive forever; just as Moe had willed. Still, just to be safe, I bought the entire stock of my vinyl records that Rounder had threatening to destroy.

Music had driven my life since that night in 1957 when I first met Rock & Roll; what could possibly go wrong with *that* as a life plan? At 40-years-old I arguably was old enough to know better (as the Oscar Wilde cliché reminded).

By that age, most people knew what they wanted to be when they grew up and were well into professions. More-likely-than-not, by that age, they were nearing or already at their career apex... or (with less aggrandizing) at least accepting their lot in life, whether self-defining careers or simply what they do in life.

Not me. Murderous thieves had stolen 14 years of my life by driving me underground; so, perhaps, my growth had been stunted at 26-years-old. Though it is arguable that I didn't exactly remain hidden, it is not debatable that I was muted by the stress and by the very real dangers hanging over my head.

Additionally inhibiting, my earlier vacillations between music and journalism may have independently retarded any trajectory toward Southern white middle-class normalcy (probably knocking another five or six years off of my development).

Whether victimized or self-destructive (or both), my psychological maturity was about 20-years-old while physically I was 40. I amused myself with a potential "outlaw" alias of *The Tennessee Kid*. Despite such fanciful silliness, what those transformative years actually provided was relief from my out-of-control *John-Osborne-esque* angry young man behavior.

Punching through the plate glass in Baltimore took me a long way toward letting that go; but actual closure came in my sojourning hajj through Europe. *That* closure allowed me to move from hopeless disillusionment to focused resolve.

I was neither abandoning my music nor finding some sort *eight-fold path to enlightenment*; in fact, it was much more Hegelian than Buddhist. I looked back at the previous 20 years not as aimlessly developing a random collection of events and skillsets, but rather as a logical and rational progression towards something.

That "something" was an intense focus on how to use the diverse skillset that necessity had created for me. *That* was not necessarily a good thing, either; because the "clarity" that I found had a name and it was REVENGE. Not a pretty picture; but a very focused one.

That intensity manifested as a quiet, systematic, carefully played chess board rather than the out-of-control panicked rage of my fugitive years;

and in that regard, it was much more dangerous to my targets (and ultimately to myself) because instead of random breakdowns, I recalcitrantly connived complex pathways for revenge: not against the handful of haughty idiots in Tennessee (time would take care of them); but rather, aimed at the elements that allowed all of it to happen in the first place.

For the first time, it put my music goals in a focused direction rather than a hope-it-sticks vision. So, from Europe I flew back to Baltimore-Washington to pack up and drive to South Carolina. Yup, *South Carolina*.

In the past few years, while I had been bouncing between DC associations, organizing unions, and traipsing around Europe, my parents permanently retired and moved to Myrtle Beach South Carolina. It was not an unexpected retirement location for them. Since the early 1960's, that Grand Strand resort town had been my family's go-to vacation spot for at least two weeks every year (and often four to six weeks).

Myrtle Beach is the focal point of a 60-mile stretch of the South Carolina coast called the "Grand Strand". With 85+ golf courses, almost 2,000 restaurants (that's not a typo), it is the number three driving destination in the country for vacationers[230]; attracting (at that time) 12-million mostly blue-collar tourists annually (and double that many by the 21st century). It also was a major retirement destination; with many of the benefits of Florida, but without the costs.

My mother was a "sun worshiper" who spent endless hours "tanning"; and Daddy loved the laid-back carefree atmosphere. Both were die-hard Southerners, so, Myrtle Beach made perfect sense to them.

What was unexpected was the timing of the retirement. On the cusp of his sixties, my father had suffered a massive heart-attack and had a triple-bypass as well as having a pig's aortic valve installed in is heart. After the operation his energy level observationally dropped, and his once lightning-fast brain slowed to… normal or less.

In my youth, my father could out-think me; he was faster. I often likened it to either Davy Crockett's first speech to Congress[231] or to Walter Brennan as Will Sonnett[232]. After the heart surgery, my father's speed and drive had noticeably slowed down. Retirement for him was more of a necessity than a luxury; and he was only in his not-elderly sixties.

---

[230] Behind only Orlando (Disney World) Florida and Washington DC.

[231] In 1827 Crockett, a Tennessean staunchly opposed to Jackson's Indian Removal Act, purportedly introduced himself to the floor of Congress with a speech that, among other colorful things said, *My father can whup any man in Kentucky, and I can whup my father*.

[232] The Will Sonnett character frequently said *My son is the fastest gun in the west and I am faster than him.*

THE LEGEND DIES ON — GARY GREEN

Social Security payments (that they should have been able to live off of) had been reduced by his participation in the *Railroad Retirement Board* (a Federal agency that predated the Social Security Act) and by his retirement income from his last job in sales. To supplement his retirement income, he began publishing and selling advertising for a small neighborhood newsletter, *The Upshot*, distributed to the few hundred homes in the retirement community where they had moved.

It was a modest income; not enough to live from, but a healthy unreported supplement to retirement benefits. Expanding it would help; but as it was, the little extra money was adequate.

Even while living in Europe, I had called them almost daily or at least every few days (as I had done for the previous 22 years). During one of the calls from the south of France, my father asked me to move to Myrtle Beach and help him with his little neighborhood newsletter.

In my new focused resolve, I was heading to South Carolina. Convoluted as it might have appeared, my next steps were deliberately calculated to reinvent my music direction. I was making moves to transform myself from outlaw hippie-poet-folksinger recording artist to mainstream music impresario-producer. Amidst that transformation was my hidden agenda of extracting revenge on the system that came after me.

THAT would not be an overnight "career change" if it was going to work. It was going to have to be a total caterpillar-to-butterfly metamorphosis where an observer would never know that the dark side existed.

Rather than it being a random next-stop, I had a plan that would put to use my last two decades of acquired skills. Slow, conniving, step-by-step, the intention was to create an entirely new person who could seemingly glide into major production and promotion projects. Psychotic, huh?

The first move would be with my father as a co-conspirator, beginning with his *The Upshot* newsletter. I was experienced publishing large-circulation magazines (from the associations and the unions). I had writing and production experience (from newspapers). For that era, I had much more-than-average computer experience and genuinely pioneering desktop publishing experience. My father was a seasoned salesman and a damned genius at selling advertising. We both knew more about the Myrtle Beach Grand Strand than most of the current population.

My first goal was to expand The Upshot from a black-and-white offset newsletter to a glossy four-color magazine. That would require vastly increasing circulation and a corresponding substantial increase in the price of advertising. In order to reach those goals, a radical revamping of the business would be necessary.

My parents had retired to the *south-strand* part of the greater Myrtle Beach: the area of *Murrells Inlet* and *Garden City*. The area was known for its dozens of seafood restaurants (and being the home of pulp-mystery writer Mickey Spillane). I rebranded the magazine from Daddy's neighborhood-centric *The Upshot* to a broader-based *Murrells Inlet & The South Strand Magazine.*

Next, I needed the local businesses, especially the Murrells Inlet seafood restaurants, to accept the magazine as *THE* official organ of the inlet. To accomplish that, my father and I joined the local merchants' association; after all, we were merchants as publishers of the little magazine.

Though certainly no one ground up a mouse in a blender, the organization — or, rather, lack thereof— was an instant flashback to my first meetings with the Bread and Roses Collective in Baltimore. Directionless, mission-less, and short-term visioned, the group seemed to just exist but accomplishing nothing.

I immediately concocted a similar "take-over" plan, to gain control of the association and hence control endorsement for the magazine. In the process, I would provide the merchants with desperately-needed promotion and marketing; they were in a battle-to-the-death with a North Myrtle Beach area that promoted itself as "Restaurant Row". And, if my promotion was successful, it would almost guarantee regular advertisers for our magazine.

I was a *Johnny-come-lately* as a local resident; but my father was established. So, my strategy was to place him as the front man. After dealing with the multi-agenda sharks in academia, in lefty collectives, and Northeastern labor unions, the board of the merchants' association was a walk in the park. The board "hired" him as their President and passed a unanimous resolution to advertise. From my Baltimore-acquired public relations skills, I immediately made a press announcement of the major changes. Then my next steps were even more Machiavellian.

Before the fiasco back in Tennessee, I had become press-friendly with the Congressman who had replaced Joe Evins: *Albert Gore, Jr.* By the time I arrived in Myrtle Beach, Al was the sitting Vice President of the United States. Name-dropping *that* connection along with my significant Baltimore-gained experience as a powerhouse political consultant, I jumped into the local Democratic Party.

Just as our work with the restaurants was conceived (sincerely) to draw more business to them, likewise my local Democratic Party involvement was genuinely to offer my considerable skills and expertise to the party. That I had additional personal agendas for both adventures did not detract from the sincerity of publicly-known plans. Working with the Democratic party, I became involved in the gubernatorial campaign of the sitting lieutenant governor. That was business-useful because the lieutenant governor introduced me to the state's tourism board.

With his endorsement and armed with the endorsement of the merchants' association and the advertising pitch-package, I was able to convince the state's official tourism board to allow distribution of the new magazine in all of the state's official welcome centers along the interstate highways, as well as at state welcome desks at airports and anywhere else the state promoted tourism.

As a final step, I convinced members of the approximately four-hundred-member Myrtle Beach hotel association to offer the magazine in their lobby racks of tourist attractions. Some of those hotels also agreed to put a copy of the magazine in each guest room.

Between the hotels, the order from the state, and distribution in the restaurants, we had a demand for about a *quarter-of-a-million* copies of each issue of the magazine. *That* justified a significant advertising rate.

I put together an advertising rate card justifying the new pricing and also teaching local merchants how to get *co-op advertising money* from national brands. That allowed our advertisers to afford larger and more expensive ads by offsetting the cost.[233]

I also imported two of my union co-workers from Baltimore to handle the physical distribution and some additional advertising sales for our new magazine. They both moved in and began new careers.

I settled into an inlet-front home with a detached office building, just three doors down from Mickey Spillane (who I got to know fairly well at the local barber shop). The magazine gave me a solid base from which to re-address music; and as I began that phase of my planning, the *fickle-finger-of-fate* scratched on my door.

One of our advertisers was a tourist attraction called "*EuroCircus*"; which was a *Cirque du Soleil* style nouveau circus (with lots of acrobats and no animals). Made up of elements of the former *Moscow Circus* and with all Russian performers, the owners had purchased several full-page ads from us on a standard "net 30" contract.[234] Unfortunately, they were unable to pay after the first thirty days and asked for an extension to a net-60 and continuation of full-page ads.

South Carolina, at that time, was one of the states that still had a "printer's lien" statute. [235] Under that kind of law, if the debt were not

---

[233] Also called MDF (Market Development Funds), these were advertising dollars given to local merchants by national brands to prominently feature the brand in the merchants' print advertising.

[234] A standard 30-day length of time for payment, beginning the day they received the invoice.

[235] Also known as "naked liens", these were laws that allowed printers (or other businesses) who rendered services before they were paid to be granted an immediate lien against the debiting business. Such an action was not considered unusual nor radical; and it required only a court filing, not even a hearing.

satisfied, I could foreclose on the circus and, if I wanted to, sell off the assets to satisfy the debt.

As we know, I was a jailhouse lawyer (having litigated illegally in Baltimore and having argued legally in front of those Federal administrative law judges on behalf of various unions). When I lived there, South Carolina had one of the last laws in the country that allowed people to "read the law". [236] I had been apprenticing under a local lawyer and had planned to take the bar, but four months before my statutory apprenticeship would have ended, the loophole closed, and I was shutout of the practice of law.

Nonetheless, operating *pro se* I exercised our magazine's options under the printers' lien statute. After the circus owners received service for my filing, I sat down to discuss the situation with them. Daddy and I had no desire to own their circus or sell off their assets; we just wanted to be paid for the ads.

The primary owner, speaking for his Russian partner, offered an interesting solution. Rather than pay the back bills, they would form a three-way partnership between themselves and me; I would become one-third owner of the circus and be responsible for the advertising and public relations. It helped too that (as a result of my Soviet-interest years) I could speak Russian and knew a great deal about the country's history (and still had the gifts from Yeltsin).

Suddenly our little publishing company was also a circus owner. That also meant that I had a venue; so, we had become an *entertainment* company as well. I made plans to move the circus out of its leased space, using a fiberglass tent that had been purchased from Cirque du Soleil, and into a building that we would own —a space for a multi-purpose entertainment venue and where I could take advantage of South Carolina's casino gaming law that allowed video poker machines in certain businesses[237].

Suddenly, we owned a publishing company, a marketing company, a circus, an entertainment venue, and a small casino. That opened an absurd flurry of opportunities knocking at our door.

---

[236] *Reading The Law* was a way for people to take become lawyers without going to law school (or, for that matter, with no formal education required at all). It basically was an extended apprenticeship under a licensed lawyer and then taking the Bar exam. Though the South Carolina Supreme Court had prohibited the practice and required lawyers to graduate from an accredited law school, there were several loopholes that still allowed non-law-school apprentices to sit for the Bar Exam and become attorneys without law school.

[237] The law allowed only five video machines per *business*; so, I established sixty Limited Liability Companies and connected the "independent businesses" by renting each one space from the circus company; mimicking the Deadwood South Dakota configuration of casinos.

THE LEGEND DIES ON — GARY GREEN

Also through the Democratic Party I had met and then become a close friendship with former U.S. Congressman *John Jenrette*. Johnny and I became almost inseparable for months; having lunch together every day and spending six to eight hours a day working together on any of dozens of projects that he brought to me[238].

We partnered on a massive Interstate Highway median strip landscaping project with former *President Jimmy Carter*, using peanut shells in the fertilizer mix. We worked on a dredging project for the Intercoastal Waterway to allow an expansion of shipping. The was a never-ending flow of "deals" that Johnny brought to me.

Using the advertising sales network that my father had put together, Johnny brought me into a startup *airline* that he helped establish to bring tourists to Myrtle Beach. My role was to provide advertising-rich ticket jackets (it was in the days before electronic ticketing) as well as the seat-back-pocket inflight magazine. It also allowed me to fly for free to our gateway cities (including *Baltimore, Boston, Chicago, Cleveland, Detroit, New York, Newark, Philadelphia,* and *Savannah*). The ticket jackets and magazines soon expanded to more general marketing functions to fill the seats. Add to my eclectic resume: *Airline Executive*.

Also, through Congressman Jenrette and his network, I met *Salvador "Doy" Laurel*, the Vice President of the *Republic of the Philippines*. The Philippines government engaged me for three unrelated projects; each of which matched some piece of my background.

In Washington DC, I met with the *Philippines Ambassador Raul Ch. Rabè* who engaged my lobbying and political services to help obtain U.S. military benefits for Philippines citizens who fought as members of the U.S. armed forces during the second world war.

On a trip to Manila, Doy wanted me to help plan the Philippines centennial celebration scheduled for 1998 put together by the organizers of the often-maligned New Orleans World's Fair. Specifically, the Vice President and the Fair organizers wanted me to be part of the planning committee; with me bringing in entertainment, casino gambling, and American corporate *financing* for the celebration (I was able to bring in *AT&T* and *FedEx*, as well as a handful of others who were looking to take advantage of the land at the former Subic Naval Base.)

Finally, and related to the casino portion of the project, Doy asked me to meet with the *Philippine Amusement and Gaming Corporation* (PAGCOR) to help craft regulatory language for the burgeoning casino industry likely to be spurred by the centennial project.

---

[238] Johnny is usually remembered for his conviction and prison sentence in the *Abscam* corruption scandal or for being the husband of playboy model Rita Jenrette.

THE POET LAUREATE SOUL OF FOLKIE ROCK & ROLL

Adding diplomat-lobbyist and developer to that virtual resume, I was fired-up about the ability to book entertainment worldwide —controlling venues in the Philippines as well as on the east coast of the United States; and that was about to expand further.

Back in Myrtle Beach, through another Democratic Party contact, I was introduced to another... *character*: a convicted bank robber, sometimes gangster, accused murder, former Federal inmate, and once-upon a time construction executive who allegedly had the contract to build part of the CIA complex in Langley Virginia. Whatever was true or not true with him, he did bring to the table (and I met with) financiers from the Saudi *Khashoggi* family, from several large commercial real estate trusts, and from a futures-trading group. Okay, now add *"financier"* to that C.V.

That interesting collection of characters brought me a proposed entertainment project with a bar, restaurant, concert theater, and casino. As part of that development, they brought in *ABC-Dunhill* recording artist and San Diego nightclub owner *Fred "Mickey" Finn*; a brilliant ragtime performer and band leader who I knew of from his 1966-1967 NBC television variety show. The plan was for Fred to headline a showroom in the new project.

Effectively, that would put four separate music venues under my control, with plans for a fifth in the Los Angeles area. I began booking acts that once-upon-a-time were big; incredibly talented musicians who had been big a decade or two earlier but who had become marginal in the music "business" world.

I viewed it as a resurrection project for them; but within the industry I was viewed as an artist-friendly venue and promotional megalith. My music life was systematically being transformed into the next-logical-step from Bread & Roses and four-walling; I was becoming a sort of music promotional impresario *à la Bill Graham* of secondary or tertiary venues.

All of those projects initially revolved around the magazine and then refocused around the circus and around Congressman Jenrette. Meanwhile, to further complicate my life, the Washington DC based DCCC (*Democratic Congressional Campaign Committee*) contacted me and asked me to run for Congress from South Carolina's First District. Republican Congressman Arthur Ravenel had decided not to run for reelection, opting instead to run for Governor (he lost). That opened up the seat and some wag in the party thought that I would have a good chance of capturing the seat. (They of course didn't bother to do their homework to learn about my communist-fugitive life; but they *did* know that Congressman Evins had touted me 15 years earlier).

The Republican Primary was crowded and ended in a runoff election between a George Bush operative and a real estate developer / restaurant entrepreneur named *Mark Sanford*. At the request of the DCCC, I

THE LEGEND DIES ON — GARY GREEN

attended several public debates between the Republicans and determined, at least from my perspective, that Sanford was an idiot. He won the runoff.

The DCCC wanted me to run against him. They offered to fund my campaign and promised that I would be unopposed in the state's Democratic Primary. *No way!* The Tennessee ordeal still weighed heavily on my mind. In my place, the Democrats recruited a very capable State Legislator named Robert Barber Jr.; but Sanford defeated him with twice-as-many votes.[239] I would have done much worse, given that the Republicans undoubtedly would have uncovered my background.

૭੭੭੭

Shortly after I had moved to Myrtle Beach in 1993, the *National Center for Supercomputing Application*s (NCSA) launched the first public web browser and thus began public access to the internet via the *World Wide Web*. By the end of 1993, there were 623 websites, according to a study by *Massachusetts Institute of Technology*; by the end of 1994, the total number was 2,278, and by 1995 that number had mushroomed to 23,500 sites. Today *Internet Live Stats* projects that there are more than two-billion sites. It really was a new world in 1993!

In those early days, there was no online shopping, no way to process credit cards, and with so few websites not a lot of content. At best the world wide web was a bunch of interactive billboards for large corporations that had the budgets to launch online ads. Public access to the web was only available through a dial up connection through *America On Line* or before that a handful of small local Internet Service Providers.

As a veteran of *CompuServe, Prodigy*, and *AOL*, I was intrigued by the median. I thought that once enough content could migrate out of the paid services and to the web, there could be millions of eyeballs looking at those ads. With that in mind, and little more than a hobby, I became two of those very first web sites; *GaryGreen.com* for my personal site and a billboard site for our circus.[240]

For my personal site, I used it to play with the new *hyper-text-markup-language* to create fun graphics and sounds. For the circus site, I made a one-page billboard that advertised circus seats, prices, and gave a fax

---

[239] Sanford went on to become governor of the state and then stunned the nation when, as governor, he disappeared for four days telling his staff he was hiking the Appalachian trail but in fact had clandestinely flown to Argentina for an extra-marital affair.

[240] My internet service provider told me at the time that I launched GaryGreen.com, my personal site was one of the first 625 in the world; but the *Internet Archive Wayback Machine* (which as of this writing has cataloged 869-billion individual web pages) began saving my personal site on December 23, 1996 —when there were approximately 257,600 websites. Whatever the count, it is clear that my site was pioneering in the big picture of online presence.

number where tickets could be ordered (but only by fax machine). Surprisingly, our fax machine received a few hundred ticket orders. I was amused; but nothing beyond that.

By the time I started developing multiple entertainment venues, I was approached by a book publisher who produced regional travel guides. They were launching an *Insiders' Guide To Myrtle Beach* as part of their series of a few dozen travel titles. They had a primary writer for the book, but they wanted some local color writing thrown in and asked me if I would be interested. Though I never met my "co-writer", I accepted the assignment and did a lot of promotion of my projects and businesses, as well as of my Murrells Inlet supporter businesses.

Around that same time, Daddy told me that he was concerned that the scope of our magazine and all of the peripheral projects had left behind his original concept for a neighborhood newsletter that would list birthdays and anniversaries, be peppered with articles reflecting on the post-World War II era and offering retirement tips. He had become very personal-computer-proficient with the *CorelDraw* vector graphics program and the *Lotus 1-2-3* spreadsheet software.

We decided to relaunch *The Upshot*, his initial neighborhood newsletter. The timing could not have been better; the centerpiece of our little empire, the circus, was about to take a big hit.

One afternoon, sitting in my lawyer's office musing over the Philippines project, my after-lunch pontification was interrupted by the arrival of a Russian thug-looking character showed up demanding (not asking, but demanding) to buy the circus. What followed in the next few days was an intriguing book-worthy complexity of offers, threats, and deadlines filled with FBI agents, the U.S. Attorney's office, Vladimir Putin ally and oligarch Vagit Alekperov, Russia's Lukoil company, and an exceptionally shady international currency trader and owner of a chain of topless bars. No, really; just when my life was supposedly staid.

In the midst of the drama and intrigue, both of our partners in the circus died mysteriously. One from a supposed mugging when he returned to Russia *(the U.S. Attorney told us that evidence indicated that he was actually murdered by Russian mobsters over the circus situation)*. The second had a heart attack and died after he heard of the drama going on in Myrtle Beach.

Technically, because of a "surviving partner key man" agreement that the three of us had signed, I was the sole owner of the circus. That was certainly how the big Russian suitor was viewing it when he told me that if I sold the circus to him then I might avoid a "tragic accident like your two partners had".

The various heirs of the partners didn't agree with that surviving partner assessment, but "on the advice of legal counsel" (as well as the

THE LEGEND DIES ON — GARY GREEN

recommendation of the Federal Bureau of Investigation, despite my historical distrust of them) I accepted the purchase offer. The Russians immediately closed the circus and liquidated all associated projects under my entertainment umbrella.

My father and I agreed that it was safer for the family if we became less high-profile. My over-the-top life had already cost him that lucrative court trustee position about 20 years earlier and between that memory and what I'd gone through after Tennessee, he insisted that we *lay low*. The once-bitten twice shy cliché certainly fit his thinking over the whole circus situation; and the nightmarish fugitive years that I had suffered added to the cliché to cement his opinion.

Hence, once again it was time for me to assess my plan. Music, with its roots deep into my childhood, had been at first an obsession for me and then a psychotic reaction to my own *Paradise Lost*. In Europe, though, I had come to terms with my (as Buddhists warn) delusions and ignorance obscuring the basics of who I was.

The sale/loss of my venues did not change the *outlaw-to-impresario* plan; but it did redirect it. For one thing, it made me realize I needed a *lot* of money to pull it off effectively. Practically, that only meant that it was time to revisit the retribution that I had been orchestrating since my perception-clarity on the Parisian streets.

♭♪♭♪♭♪

I knew the supposed mafia adage that revenge doesn't have a statute of limitations; but I also knew that Hamlet's hesitation to take revenge against Claudius ended up with a poisoned sword stabbing the Danish prince himself. So, generally, I was more inclined to lean toward Sinatra's saying that *the best revenge is massive success*.

That definitely was where I was headed with my post-Baltimore maneuvering; but I couldn't deny that my outlaw years had caused a moral death in me that insisted on exacting cruel retribution and then laughing about it and moving on. Even in my newfound external tranquility, I still rode with my dark Machiavellian demons; and they fully had taken the reigns after the sale of the circus.

In my labyrinthine planning I decided to begin by going online to see what venue or other music opportunities I might dig up as a steppingstone toward closure reprisals.

Most newspapers were not online yet, but many papers had taken their display advertising online; the internet was still pretty much just a series of billboards. Some few newspapers also posted their classified ads online; among those were the classified sections of several national newspaper chains, including the *Chicago Tribune* group of 20 or so papers.

While scanning that group for venue possibilities, I came across an interesting, but non-music, posting in the Tribune's *Fort Lauderdale Sun-*

THE POET LAUREATE SOUL OF FOLKIE ROCK & ROLL

Sentinel newspaper. In one of their ads, a company was looking for an "internet guru". The ad didn't give much more information than that along with the name and address of the company and instructions to mail or fax a resume to an H.R. office.

I had not had a resume in almost 20 years; and even if I had one, I was certain it would get lost among the flood of mail that their human resources department would receive. Besides, who-the-hell would believe the shit on MY resume?

So, instead, I made the assumption that the company already had a website or at least a domain service. It turned out that there was no website, but they did have a dot-com registration.

Next, I went to the library (there were no well-known search engines yet) to research the organizational structure of the company; I found the name of the CEO. Finally, I speculated on possible name conventions for email addresses (first and last name, first initial last name, inverted order, first name dot last name). I tried about 20 different possibilities and sent them each the same email.

The emails said that I had seen their ad "online" and that I was the "guru" that were seeking. I said that I don't "do resumes", but if they wanted to know my qualifications they could go to my website or the circus website (and I provided the URL's).

Within minutes I had a return email from the CEO asking me if I was serious. I assured him I was, and we exchanged a series of emails over the next few minutes.[241] At the end of the exchange, he invited me to South Florida to interview for the job.

The company was the largest software and hardware provider for an *ERP* system for the mail order catalog industry.[242] Most major catalog companies and major mail order operations used their multi-million-dollar software solution on a mini-mainframe computer. Those companies were eyeing the new medium of "the internet" and suspected that one day soon consumers would want to place orders via the world wide web. Most turned to their ERP software provider for a solution.

A little more than 19% of all retail sales in the country were mail order sales. By the time I arrived in Florida, 34% of the US homes had internet access (though much of it was through other services like AOL). There was, indeed, real opportunity on the horizon.

---

[241] Outside of the services like AOL and Prodigy, there was not much instant messaging, and few corporate types understood IRC.

[242] ERP was "enterprise resource planning" (ERP) software that managed orders, inventory, customer data, day-to-day business activities, accounting, procurement, project management, risk management and compliance, and supply chain operations.

THE LEGEND DIES ON — GARY GREEN

On-line ordering, through static storefront websites, emails, faxes, or phone numbers on those billboard-like pages became known as "e-commerce"; and that made up a little less than 1% of all retail sales. Credit card processing, real-time inventory, secure web pages, and the other elements of the e-commerce boom *did not exist*.

I was hired, initially, to work within the company's software programming department to help facilitate making the *ERP* features available for companies that wanted to create or expand their businesses into the new vertical. In less than a month, it became clear that the market was going to be much larger than the company had anticipated.

In relatively short order, demand from the customer base was so great that the company created an entirely new business unit to develop and sale the product.

I became the *Director* of the new business unit, and the company assigned dozens of hardcore programmers to me to translate my marketing vision for "e-commerce" to reality.

Specifically, I focused on *Customer Personalization & Merchandising; An Order Taking & Shopping Cart system; Methodologies for Automated Payment & Security; Order Management; Warehousing* (pick-pack-ship); *Customer Service; Inventory Accounting* real time with each transaction; *System Interoperability;* and Business processes & marketing the sites.

While today those are routine (if not mundane) features of any good website, in the 1990's they were unheard of innovations. Our timing could not have been better; it was the beginning of the dot-com bubble and the consumer explosion into the internet.[243]

Two years in a row, our innovations became a finalist for the era's leading technology award, *Best of Comdex*; and by 1998 our software was handling more than 5% of all transactions on the planet. With the growth of the new internet vertical, my new business unit was soon out-performing the rest of the company. Like so many dot-com companies of the era, we opportunistically popped an IPO and made a lot of people very wealthy.

Among the Fortune 1000 companies that began using my innovations were *Microsoft* (their Developers Network), *AOL* (their product

---

[243] This was right around the same time that Jeff Bezos and MacKenzie Scott quit their jobs at New York's D.E. Shaw Hedge Fund to start an online bookstore in a Seattle garage. The complexities that we were creating were not even on the Amazon radar for them at that time. (And when we pitched it to giant bookseller *Barnes and Noble*, we were dismissed outright with the admonition that no one would ever purchase anything on the new internet; especially not books!)

THE POET LAUREATE SOUL OF FOLKIE ROCK & ROLL

fulfillment), *Compaq* (HP), *Nordstrom, Hickory Farms, Star-Trek.com* and more than 200 other companies.[244]

My industry notoriety had me moving in the oddest circles; at least odd *for me*, given my background. I became friendly with *"Chainsaw" Al Dunlap*, the corporate "turn-around" monster who ruined thousands of lives as he orchestrated mass-layoffs in the companies he helmed.[245] I spent most Sunday afternoons with him and his bodyguard,[246] sharing our mutual hatred for corporate America. Al often repeated to me, "corporate America, especially the CEOs, have their heads so far up their asses, they will never see the light of day." I couldn't disagree with that assessment, albeit for vastly different reasons.

---

[244] Among the companies using my software were: Microsoft (MSDN), American On Line (AOL) via AB&C Fulfillment, WWF.com (Suresource), StarTrek.com, i-legions.com, StarWars.com, LogicConcepts, Sony Music, Time Life Customer Service, 4-Dshopping.com, A.M. Leonard, Adam's Headwear, Affinity Express, Alpha Memory, Alpine Trading, America's Hobby Center, American Supply, Antenna 3 Directo, Aquascape Design, Asset Marketing, Bailey's, Ballard Design, Beren Shoes, Best Uniforms, Baseball Express, Big Toe Sports, Bluewater Books & Charts, Bravanta.com, Brookstone, Burden Sales, Bu-reau for at Risk Youth, CRT Associates, Carlton Industries, Carnell, Case Logic, Casual Male, Catalog Ventures, Century 21 Promotions, Chaparral Motorsports, Childcraft Education, ClassroomDirect.com, ClubMac, Coach, Coldwater Creek, Compactappliace.com, Cornerstone Brands, Corral West Ranchwear, Cosmetique, Country Home Products, Country Supply, Crestline, Cyberguys, Out-post.com, Daniel Smith, Delia's, Desantis Collection, Design Within Reach, Dexter Shoe Company, DiamondDepot.com, Direct Source, Direct To Home, ERB Industries, Ear-lychildhood.com, MACWarehouse, Educational Experience, Ethel M. Chocolates, Fahrney's Pens, Fantastic Media, Fire Mountain Gems, Flag-house, Footsmart, Fruitful Yield, Gaim, Galls, Geiger, Gemplers, Genesis Direct, Girlfriends, LA, Beauty and the Best, Global Video, Golf Warehouse, Golfven-turesonline.com, Guideposts, HCI Direct, Hallmark, Hallmark Flowers, Hamakor Judaica, Hammacher Schlemmer, Heritage Collections, Hickory Farms, Home Trends, Home-Showcase, Homeclick.com, Hot Topic, Humbolt Industries, I/D/E/A, IMT Harrowbrook, Idea Art, Indiana Botanic Gardens, Informal Educa-tion, Insect Lore, JC Penney Logistics, Jenson USA, Johnson Smith, Journal Edu-cation, Junonia, KBkids, King Schools, Knight/Williams Corp., LFP, Inc., Lab Safety Supply, Lego Systems, Leisure Time Entertainment, Levenger, Library Video, Lit-tlewoods, Logistix, Mailcome PCL, Make Up Art Cosmetics, Malaco, Marketing Concepts, Marriot Desert Springs, MasterGrip, McFeely's Square Drive, MvGlen Micro, Melitta, Meyer Distributing, Miami Dolphins, Mile Post Four, Miles Kim-ball, MilesTex, Misco Canada, Mitchell's Newspaper, Model Expo, Monterey Bay, Musician's Friend, Mustangs Unlimited, My Twinn, NVE Pharmaceuticals, New Braunfels Smokehouse, New England Serum Co., Nine West, Nordstrom, Norm Thomson, Northern Saftey Co., Old Glory, On Campus Marketing, One Ste-pAhead, Open Enterprises, Overtons, PC Nation, PCMall, Peachtree Business Products, Personal Creations, Pet Doors USA, Pinch A Penny, Precision Response Corp., Price Point, Pro Sound & Stage Lighting, Professional Uniforms, Program-mers Paradise, Promotional Resources, Pure Encapsulations, QVC Television, Quadratec, Quartermaster, Readers Digest, Reading Etc., Red Envelope, Right Stuff, Rimmer Brothers, Rocky Mountain Motorworks, Rodale Press, Ross-Si-mons, Rue de France, Satisfusion, Savory Foods , Schneider Saddlery, Scully & Schully, Seeds of Change, Sensational Beginnings, Shar Products, The Shopping Channel, Sid Savage Auto Dealer, Siegel Display Products, Softmart, 3rd Wave Marketing, Sound City, Southern Tier Athletics, Specialty Pool Products, Stand-ard Tools, Staples, UK, Star Struck, Steeda Auto Sports, Steuben Glass, Story House, Stumps, Sun Precautions, Sunbelt Sportswear, MACMall, Swell.com, Tlavideo, Tafford Manufacturing, Taylor Gifts, Teacher's Discovery, That Fish Place, That Pet Place, Kingshill Collection, Lakeside Collection, Pfaltzgraff Co., Republic of Tea, Thor Tek, Tiger Direct, Time Customer Service, A-3 Services, Ti-tle Nine Sports, Tom Snyder Productions, Topix Innov. Gallery, USCO Distribu-tion, United Methodist Publish, Ultimate Office, USI, Urban Outfitters, Valen-tineOne, Valu-Bilt Parts, Victorian Paper Co., Vitacoast.com, Western Athletic Supply, Wetmore & Company, What On Earth, Wine Country Gift Baskets, Wine Enthusiast, Wine Watch, Winterthur, World Almanac, Zale Corporation, Zomax, PCZone, MACZone, PCWarehouse, ClickMail ...*and many others*

[245] *Fast Company Magazine* labeled him one of the worst CEOs of all time. Al was eventually forced to retire after accusations of his cooking the books to make his turnarounds look better came to light.

[246] He went everywhere with an armed bodyguard because of the dozens of death threats he received weekly as reaction to his vicious layoffs. With my outlaw background and demeanor, I wasn't fazed by mere threats.

THE LEGEND DIES ON — GARY GREEN

After the SEC-mandated waiting period for people with founders' shares and friends-and-family shares, I sold my stock and resigned. I bought cars, houses, and investments in technology companies. I wrote a short book telling businesses how e-commerce should work; *Pay No Attention To The Man Behind The Curtain; Navigating the Information Yellow Brick Superhighway*. That booklet beget a string of invitations to be a keynote speaker at internet conventions and trade shows all over the country; I spoke at a dozen or more of them in the course of the next twelve months.

My parents had always wanted to visit Hawaii, so I had them flown to Honolulu for two weeks after which they moved near me to South Florida.

Meanwhile, I was booked two and three times a month for speaking engagements or seminars. I had become extremely high-profile in the internet-company frenzy era. So, after many of my public appearance bookings I would be approached by companies with internet start-up ideas and wanting to hire me to consult on or invest in their projects.

Even "big blue", IBM, courted me; flying me to their west-coast internet services center in San Francisco and pitching me an executive role heading that corporate division. Can you even imagine *ME* as an operative within the bowels of corporate America? I couldn't. I took their hospitality in San Francisco, truthfully because it was one of my favorite cities in America and I loved being there as their guest. I held up at the Four Seasons Hotel[247] for a few weeks and emersed myself into the city's life; especially the old South Beach beat district.

The offers that came in were diversely from startups with no money to the *next-great-things* funded by billionaires. I listened to all of them and even accepted several. After one keynote at the Javits Center in New York, I agreed to meet one of those company-founders for dinner at a restaurant that he owned. In his private dining room at the upper-eastside high-end eatery, I was seated at a table to discuss his project. He sat at the head of the table with his corporate legal counsel at his left and around the table an eclectic collection of New York characters that included author *Tom Wolfe* (dressed in his "costume" of a white suit, purple shirt, and white wide-brim fedora), real estate developer (and future President of the United States) *Donald J. Trump*, and several non-celebrity New York movers-and-shakers.

I accepted that consulting gig; and ended up living in New York City again —moving out on September 10, 2001, the day before the notorious 9-11 attacks. My condo on John Street, downtown, was two blocks from

---

[247] Now called *The Clift Hotel* at the intersection of Geary Street and Taylor Street.

THE POET LAUREATE SOUL OF FOLKIE ROCK & ROLL

the *World Trade Towers* where I had breakfast every morning the entire time I lived there. Once more in my life, I "dodged a bullet".

I accepted another gig from a genuine marketing genius who dropped (mailed) 20-million paper catalogs every quarter and collected unimaginable cash payments from his customers. There were probably a half-dozen or so of these high-paying gigs where all I did was pontificate; *good work if you could get it.*

After another keynote at the recently-opened Staples Center in Los Angeles, I was approached by the CEO of an old "blue chip" Fortune 100 company. He pitched a startup technology company for which his corporation would provide *partial* funding. He wanted to use my reputation in the industry as "bait" for investors; in exchange, he offered me the CEO role in the startup as well as investment opportunity at the *founders-share* level. I accepted that one as well.

The latter was packed with multiple "red flags" that should have kept me far away, but I was feeling bulletproof. More importantly, I was well down the road toward the reckoning that I was orchestrating.

If anything did go wrong, I was connected enough that bouncing back would not be unsurmountable. I was too-well-connected in the legitimate world to ever be outcasted again; and I wasn't a 20-something-year-old kid with no experience dealing with sharks.

Still, shit happens on all levels. That CEO was indicted for a Dunlap-style cooking-the-books. Facing 25-years in prison, he cut a deal with prosecutors and the SEC. Meanwhile valuation of my founders' shares fell from $42-per-share to $14-per-share and then around $3.

That would have been or should have been devastating to a normal corporate kind of person; but this was *me*. I'd been rock-bottom down before and, more importantly, the accumulation of wealth wasn't my goal. My goal was the retribution.

Meanwhile, during the entire internet development stage of my life, four or five years, I had switched my casino focus from Atlantic City to Las Vegas. Early in my original dot-com role, I had worked with Steve Wynn's technology team to solve a problem they had sharing data between the two casinos that Wynn owned. I had sketched, on a cocktail napkin, the solution that I had used to take the mainframe ERP system to the internet. It never occurred to me that my solution could be monetized —until it created a buzz in the casino industry. I learned from that experience and vowed to monetize any of my "free advice" from then forward.

After that, I began researching how casinos used customer data and the relationship of that data to technology. I postulated that if the collected data was combined with publicly available data sources (like census, NCOA, voter records, and other public information) and if it was parsed

THE LEGEND DIES ON — GARY GREEN

using the three-dimensional methodology of the mail-order industry, then a tremendously powerful casino marketing tool could be created.

To develop that, I needed to understand the state of casino data usage. I launched a nationwide tour of casinos, testing their player tracking systems and their marketing responses.

I wrote my findings in the form of another booklet, similar to what I had done for e-commerce a few years earlier. It was that booklet, and my speaking appearance on a panel at a major casino industry conference in Las Vegas that got the attention of iconic casino owner *Bill Bennett*.

Known for creating the family-friendly Las Vegas, William G. Bennett owned *Circus-Circus* casino, and created the Camelot-themed *Excalibur* casino, *Luxor casino, Mandalay Bay* casino, and later owned the legendary *Sahara* casino. We developed a genuine friendship and began to plot ways to use my proposed system to revolutionize casino marketing.

There were a handful of ahead-of-their-time casino marketers (most notably at Harrah's and at one of the Trump-owned properties in New Jersey) that were using advanced data techniques; and what they were doing was both impressive and advanced. But none were using the direct-marketing (catalog industry) methodology that I was suggesting; so, in my mind, "advanced" (as well as the data-usage awards they were winning) were decades behind the state-of-the-art in other industries.

I wasn't impressed, though the casino industry was. In fact, I was openly hostile to an entire cadre of self-proclaimed marketing and data experts who truly were at the top of the *casino marketing* game but were cavemen (and women) compared to the best direct marketers in the world —those world-class companies that had been my e-commerce customers.

In order to develop that first e-commerce solution, I had spent hundreds of hours under the personal tutelage of the best-of-the-best cataloguers, direct mailers, and super-marketers in the world. To make their software solution ideal for their needs, they had to teach me the intricacies of their businesses. I learned targeting, segmentation, offer creation, tracking, evaluation, list testing, and all the tenets of direct customer contact from, quite literally, the best in the world.

Hence, not just arguably, but empirically, the very best casino marketing gurus were bush league hobbyists compared to the sophistication and intricacies of the direct marketing world. My hostility toward those casino operatives, then, was aimed at their arrogant attitudes. If they had owned up to their incompetence rather than touted it as genius, I would have been fine with them. But the state of skill levels and knowledge base was sometimes irritating, sometimes comical, and most times both. So, this time, rather than sketch my system on a cocktail napkin, I filed a patent application on the process and created a massive public relations campaign.

THE POET LAUREATE SOUL OF FOLKIE ROCK & ROLL

The press coverage and the booklet put me in front of a lot of casino-industry big-wigs. It was how I first connected with my new friend Bill Bennett. In turn, Mister Bennett taught me the casino operations business. He loved to talk about his past glories and the history of developing Las Vegas; and I was an eager listener and learner.

He also got a kick out of introducing me to his old friends who also owned casinos; people like *Jackie Gaughan* (who allegedly had taken over *Bugsy Siegel, Meyer Lansky, Gus Greenbaum, Moe Sedway*, properties), as well as *Ralph Engelstad* (who owned the Imperial Palace Casino and with Bill had built the Las Vegas Motor Speedway).

Besides the colorful introductions to dozens of old-Vegas characters, Mister Bennett spent hours-on-end for a couple of years hammering into me his vision of the intricacies of casino operations and customer service. It was a "masterclass" in the industry. He insisted that I learn everything from the executive suite to the casino floor and every role in between.

Mister Bennett always said that the "magic" of casino profits was on the casino floor; understanding the customer: the player.[248]

The casino games —*especially the slot machines that generated 80% of the property's revenue*— were purely mathematical. There was no element of luck or "gambling" on the side of the house. Pure and simple, the casino kept *eight-and-a half cents of every dollar wagered*. The math was universal from casino to casino; so, the differentiator for competition was all about the customer's perception; customer service: the player.

Other than that, for the games, Mr. Bennett used to joke that people could stay home and just mail him a check every month for eight-and-a half percent of their wages. His laser-like focus was always on the blue-collar customers, not the *high rollers*. Middle class was his target.

So, as we focused on his players, we scoured over the customer data that I was able to match through multiple databases and then sort using my patented methodology. What I found was that the majority of casino customers, at least at his casinos, were: white, older than 50, lower-middle-class-ish, cigarette smokers, from the "middle-America" states, poorly educated, anti-intellectual, politically conservative.

In short, they were the people that had supported segregation, the Vietnam war, the oppression of Native Americans, and ... *the very kind of folks that had driven me underground and out of Tennessee.*

My search for revenge imagined no better way to extract that reprisal than to collect about nine percent of their paychecks every week. All I

---

[248] That was part of why he insisted that I know everything about every job; things even he had not done, like working the drop team or slot maintenance or housekeeping or any of other dozen "worker-bee" jobs in the casinos.

THE LEGEND DIES ON — GARY GREEN

needed to do was position myself as the legal beneficiary of that extraction. Even more importantly in my conniving, was harnessing that restitution for Native America.

Over the years one thing had led to another and my sovereignty work focused on the right to operate gaming on Tribal lands. Once I understood William Bennett's operational and financial model for casinos, it put the sovereignty fight around casinos in an entirely new light for me. Retribution where it would hurt the oppressors the most: in their pocketbooks.

Both retribution thoughts made for delightful fantasy but were unreachable for me; without some heavy-duty reinvention, I just didn't have the chops to either own a casino or offer little more to Native casinos than my patent segmentation and targeting system.

What I *could* focus on, though, were the music resources in the casino world. Mr. Bennett also agreed to open up for me his casino showrooms and entertainment facilities. His outrageous temper tantrums (as bad or worse than some of *mine* during my fugitive years), his extreme alcoholism, and his far-right-wing neo-fascist politics were all things that should have made me stay as far away from him as possible. But I saw him as a great teaching resource for my nefarious needs. So, we never talked politics and his infamous temper never aimed at me. Alcoholism was another matter; I saw it retard his plans, memories, and ability to get things done.

Nonetheless, my thoughts were that if I could learn as much about Vegas entertainment as I had learned the about Greenwich Village folk scene and about The Grand Ole Opry, or even the circus, then I would be well on the way to a role as a major impresario in arguably the most high-profile venue in the world: *Las Vegas!*

Sometime in early 2002, the alcohol-related disease combined with the remnants of a heart attack he had suffered five or six years earlier, all began to catch up with him. I had been living in Vegas hotels for about 11 months and we were making plans for a less transient move there. During one of my return trips back to Florida, I received a message from him that we needed to either postpone or cancel our plans. Never admitting his obvious alcohol problems to me, he simply said that his legs had been amputated and he was losing his will to enter into new fights (presumably involving the revolution we were creating on the casino marketing front, though he didn't elaborate). We talked several more times and I continued to focus on talking with his entertainment people as well as show producers at multiple properties on the Las Vegas strip.

Then in December of 2002 William G. Bennett died. But rather than kill my transformation, it fired me up with even more determination to go after that Vegas music scene with an eye toward Los Angeles.

THE POET LAUREATE SOUL OF FOLKIE ROCK & ROLL

The 4ᵗʰ Movement
coda/nascence: *one last shot, just for old times*

THE LEGEND DIES ON — GARY GREEN

Opus Twenty-Seven:
My Most Absurd Musical Reinvention

I already got a guilty conscience; Might as well have the money too.
— Kevin Jarre, *Tombstone* original screenplay, fourth draft, March 15, 1993

It's hard to decide which turned out to be the biggest absurdity: the Gary Green *bobbleheads* that were distributed of me as a "casino boss" or winning an advertising award for the TV commercial with me wearing one of Elvis' original jumpsuits along with a wig and fake sideburns. I think it was a tossup of farces; but they were among the easiest-to-explain of the absurdities that were part of my newest reinvention.

Probably the *MOST* non-sequitur, given my crazy history, was when I became a *Vice President of Trump Hotels & Casinos* — yup, THAT Trump. It was reinvention at its finest. It was deception at its zenith. And it was all tied to America's love for scoundrels and the mystique of Las Vegas gambling.

Vegas has long been known as the home of reinvention. *Moe Dalitz*, the notorious bootlegger for Detroit's Purple Gang and Cleveland's Mayfield Road Mob, famously became one of Vegas' leading citizens and founded Sunrise Hospital, the Las Vegas Country Club, and the LV Convention & Tourism Bureau. Accused Texas murderer *Benny Binion* became such a pillar of the Las Vegas community that the only civic statue ever erected there was of him, horseback.

And there are many others whose images were totally *reformed*. Vegas history is filled with converted gangsters, failed businessmen, has-been celebrities, and pie-in-the-sky dreamers who completely metamorphosed into successful business and community leaders. In short, Las Vegas Nevada was ripe for what I had in mind; a total reinvention... or at least the illusion of that.

Leveraging my connection with the late Bill Bennett, my booklet on casino data, and my substantial chops from a decade of running busses to Atlantic City casinos, I convinced the organizers of the preeminent casino-industry conference, the *World Gaming Congress & Expo* to book me for two of the panels at their upcoming convention.

First, I shared the stage with the marketing vice-presidents of four major Las Vegas casinos to discuss the effective use of marketing data. My second panel was sharing the dais with the CEOs of the three largest casino corporations in the country; the topic was a discussion of various ways of projecting revenue for individual business units at casinos.

In the kindest terms, I treated those executives of publicly-traded corporations as if they were my apprentices (rather than as the lords of Las

THE POET LAUREATE SOUL OF FOLKIE ROCK & ROLL

Vegas as they perceived themselves). More accurately, in my usual caustically over-the-top outlaw manner, I argued, debated, and called my panel mates blockheads (among other things).

My performance on those two stages immediately established "street cred" for me within the casino industry. I mean, who-the-hell shares a stage with that level of industry titans except for their peers?[249] I supposed that my high-level technology CEO experiences also contributed to allowing me a seat at that elitist table. Who knows what actually got me there; but there I was.

Suddenly I was in demand; or at least was my officiously lecturing on the failings of casino marketing. Consulting proposals and job offers began filling my email box from casinos, from slot machine companies, and from various trade shows and conventions.

I took every consulting gig that came my way; mostly either revamping or in some cases developing new casinos. Despite the new public image that I had cultivated as a casino marketing guru, my actual criteria for the assignments I accepted were dependent on the *entertainment potential* of the project. Along the way, I was working at a wide range of casinos sizes and types, gathering information at every stop.

With a few dozen consulting gigs under my belt, I decided that it was time to move toward another of my goals for the reinvention: *helping (in some minor way) restitution in Native America.* I had absolutely no silly racist fantasies of being the *great white hope* coming to Indian Country nor even some kind of *Lone Ranger Kemosabe* bullshit.

Instead, I had amassed, and frankly, mastered some seriously in-depth knowledge of the universe of casino players. I knew that if I made these techniques available to Tribal casinos it would give them a set of power tools for generating revenue and (more personally satisfying to me) adding a distinct advantage over the white-owned and corporate-owned commercial casinos. Moreover, the methodologies were totally teachable, so I could pass them along to Tribal members and then get my white ass out of their business.

My patented-system of three-dimensional targeting was unprecedented. In every casino where I had introduced it, the system had never failed to

---

[249] It is probably footnote-worthy to point all of the executives that were on that dais with me succeeded in bankrupting their respective companies. One orchestrated one of the ten largest corporate frauds in American history; another resigned in disgrace after it came to light that his entire resume was bogus; and a third was forced to resign for allegedly cooking the books. Nonetheless, all left their positions with incredibly large "golden parachutes"; one was $11.7 million.

THE LEGEND DIES ON — GARY GREEN

increase revenue by at least 40%. Even the skeptical casino operators couldn't argue with the hard numbers.

The more casino marketing programs I stepped into, the more I realized that the problems were not so much marketing failures as they were failures of general casino management philosophy. I decided I needed to further fine-tune my reinvention expanding to operational management and to finance.

Adding to the unheard-of performance of my marketing methodology, I plugged in a financial performance structure based on the Texas Instruments Company's *zero-based budgeting* system. That addition allowed me to put together an entire customer-focused (thank you Bill Bennett) casino operational management strategy.

Applying those strategies led to even more renown in the casino business. Industry magazines interviewed me; trade shows offered me keynote-speaker roles; television, radio, and major newspapers called me for quotes. In relatively short order, I was the most written about figure in then-modern casino business circles. During the next few years, I operated or developed dozens of casinos in Indian Country and commercially.

Early in that process I was hired as *Marketing Director* by a New Jersey born casino General Manager who was operating a Tribal casino on the west coast on behalf of a management contract between the Tribe and Donald Trump's New Jersey casino empire. In a relatively short time, that manager was dismissed and operation of the casino was turned over to a triumvirate of the Chief Financial Officer, the Atlantic City based Vice President of Table Games, and... me.

Besides marketing duties, my role expanded first to being the "hatchet man" for the other two; assigned to fire employees that they disliked *(to this day, decades later, some of those former employees are still mad at me, thinking I terminated them)*. That role soon expanded when the three of us divvied up the management of the operating units between us.

At the same time, my marketing methodology began to make waves in the Trump corporate ranks; our property was the only "successful" one amidst the bankruptcy of his properties. The company flew me to Atlantic City and then to New York, and I was installed as *Vice President of Marketing and Player Development* for *Trump Hotels & Casinos*.

The first season of *The Apprentice* debuted on NBC (yes, I have a cameo in it) and we created a branding behemoth —almost all smoke-and-mirrors, but an incredible learning and experimentation process in manipulating people en mass. It was all façade, showmanship, and misrepresentations —*lies*— having very little to do with reality; but, again, it was a tremendous educational experience.

It is indisputable that we created one of the most powerful brands in the history of the world; one that with absolutely zero substance manipulated

THE POET LAUREATE SOUL OF FOLKIE ROCK & ROLL

enough people that he was able to become President of the United States, riding on that brand.

Privately, Trump mocked, ridiculed, belittled, and laughed at his legions of devoted followers and fans. He said they were stupid, would buy anything he told them to buy, and would mindlessly do anything he demanded. He marveled at how much "smarter" he was than the "stupid fuck" masses that near-worshipped him and handed him their money.

We had a player who lost about $500,000 at our tables in one week. He would not accept any comps, not even free meals; but he had one request: he wanted a dinner at *Mar-a-Lago* in Palm Beach (about 20 minutes from my home). We asked Trump and he respond with great delight, "tell the fuck that when he loses a million dollars, I will *think* about it".

Trump's arrogance and disdain for almost everyone would have been either comical or (more likely) intolerantly unacceptable to me had it not been for my blood-lust for revenge against the entire behavior-strata that had driven me underground; against them and their racist, xenophobic, hatred-spewing intolerance of anyone different.

So, the whole Trump experience for me was about a marketing lollapalooza, a manipulative apocalypse, and the greatest mass revenge I could have hoped to create against an entire social strata!

Unfortunately for the rest of the country, it had far-reaching side-effects that I could not have predicted. And though I left the Trump organization (on good terms) long before his foray into politics, my adventures in Trump-land and interactions with Donald J. Trump are themselves booklength stories and escapades, but not in *this* context.

Using those Trump years as a practicum laboratory, I went on to star in an award-winning series of television commercials (playing a created "casino boss" character), and then played off of that character creating bobbleheads, billboards, and public appearances. At one casino we even issued poker chips with my picture on them.

The recognition was not merely hollow role-playing like Trump's; I actually *did* become one of the country's leading authorities on casino development, operations, and marketing. I generated tens of millions of dollars for client companies. I put together a team of top casino-industry professionals from every discipline within the business; and they became part of my plug-and-play turnaround or development package for casinos.

We developed software, management systems, marketing techniques, and most-importantly a training-mentoring program to teach people to replace us and far surpass us —especially in Indian Country *(which has been done many times over)*. I even opened my own small casino, with only 300 slot machines; and I co-founded a slot machine company.

At the height of my casino successes, I was approached by a big-name Hollywood agent who wanted to represent me. He had absolutely no

THE LEGEND DIES ON — GARY GREEN

interest in my music career but wanted to represent me because of my fame (or notoriety) from the casino world. In relatively short order, he presented me with a book contract (to write a book about the history of modern Indian casinos) and he began negotiating with two television networks to create a TV "reality" series based on my casino turnaround work.

Maybe I couldn't be a folk-singing songwriter anymore, but I had spent the majority of my life on stage, on radio, in print, and in front of television cameras. The television series seemed like the next-best-thing to my lost music career; so, I was all in for it. Besides, it really was legitimate; I was pretty well-known as the casino turnaround dude. At least I would be in front of an audience again; and the agent was much more than the-real-deal —he was genuine Hollywood royalty with tentacles deep into the entertainment world.

I had orchestrated an amazing, and somewhat complete, reinvention, not just of image but in content as well as form. It certainly was not an overnight process, nor did it spin haphazardly out of control. It was a carefully executed strategic application of an amalgamation of the skills I had developed before, after, and during my exile. It took more than a decade to pull it off; but in the big picture, that was a short time compared to the fourteen years I had spent in Baltimore.

The odd thing was that my intense decade of building the new persona combined with the previous decade-and-a-half marketing Atlantic City and then combined with more-than a quarter-century fighting for sovereignty in Indian Country... all added up to making me legitimately a senior "executive" with an unmatched track record. *The reinvention was bizarrely successful; and I really got into it.*

I had constantly reinvented myself throughout life. I went from science-nerd-boy to music hippie. Then I became newspaperman and then outlaw folk-slinger. Then union official. Then publishing magnate and circus owner. Then dot-com tech guru. And then, casino authority.

At best it was eclectic; at worse it was insanity. Nonetheless, at each twist, turn, and reinvention I threw myself manically into the role and equaled or surpassed people who'd spent their lives in each discipline. Each was very real and legitimate.

So, while I went through multiple reinventions over the years, none of them were disingenuous. As the vice-president of a technology company told a reporter for a national newspaper chain when interviewed about me in the early 2000's, *"Gary Green is the real thing. It sounds crazy. But if he says he's going to do something, it is the real deal."* Though at the time I didn't really appreciate (nor sanction) that interview, in hindsight I am both grateful and humbled by it.

Using the skills from all of those "past lives" that I had lived, I had successfully become a major casino figure. Still, music would not let go

THE POET LAUREATE SOUL OF FOLKIE ROCK & ROLL

of me and the real benefit of the amazing casino reinvention was gaining control of showrooms and other entertainment venues. In that regard, it was like Bread & Roses on steroids.

From the very beginning of my casino-world notoriety —*long before I had an agent or a television show*— I began focusing on entertainment and the life-long hold it had on me. This time, though, it was quantitatively different; I had huge budgets to play with; state-of-the-art huge showroom/auditoriums; and broad audiences beyond just one genre.

While all those resources were incredible to control, I still needed immersive lessons on what-the-hell to do with those resources. Operating a 2,500-seat casino showroom was a lot different from a seat-of-your-pants folk venue. I needed an adviser and guide to the world of Vegas shows.

I found that mentor in the person of Frank Sinatra's favorite lounge lizard; a savvy Philadelphia piano playing singer who'd spent three-quarters of his life on the Las Vegas strip. If you had called *Central Casting* and asked them to send you the archetypal Las Vegas lounge act, *Howie Gold* would have knocked on your door. When I met Howie in early 2000, he'd already been playing Vegas for more than 40 years.

Sinatra loved his work so much that when Old Blue Eyes moved to Palm Springs, he demanded that Howie move there to play at the local country club for Frank's entertainment.[250] Howie and I became good

---

[250] When Howie refused, he found himself fired and blackballed from every casino in Vegas. He finally accepted Sinatra's offer and moved to Palm Springs for a few years, until Frank finally allowed him to go back to Vegas.

I witnessed Tom Jones, after finishing a show at a major Strip casino, showing up at the lounge where Howie was gigging. It was already almost midnight and for the next six-fucking-hours, Tom Jones jammed with Howie in the little bar; until just after six-o'clock-the-next-morning.

When Arnold Palmer opened his steakhouse in the California desert, he insisted that Howie was the grand opening entertainer. And, when a well-known Mafia boss heard that a comedian with the same name was booked into casino across town from where the boss was throwing an anniversary gala for made guys, he sent two "button men" to make sure Howie showed up at the anniversary. He refused to believe that there were two Vegas entertainers with the same name.

In 1969 when the San Diego Padres were founded, Howie leveraged his Vegas "friends" to directly contact owner C. Arnholt Smith and convince him that the new San Diego Stadium should have a live organist rather than the canned music that had taken over Major League Baseball. With the blessings of his Vegas sponsors, Howie took two years off and played for seventh inning stretches in San Diego.

THE LEGEND DIES ON — GARY GREEN

friends and besides showing up at his various gigs, I booked him regularly for lounges, parties, conventions, and other special events. In turn, he fully indoctrinated me into the world of Vegas shows.

He introduced me to showroom managers, booking agents, working musicians, and *Local 369 of the American Federation of Musicians*. I had marched on a picket line with local members when Strip casinos first began replacing live music with canned recordings.

Beyond the introductions, Howie took me to after-hours parties that would be full of backup musicians from strip shows, understudies, and even headliners. Usually at a bar or room way off the Strip and away from tourists, the music community relaxed with each other and lamented about the tribulations of trying to make a living in Las Vegas.

During daytime hours, Howie arranged tours for me of stage lighting, sound systems, dressing rooms, costumers, set designers, and the gamut of elements that made the back-of-the-house for Vegas shows of that era and previous eras. Some of the room operators he took me to meet were

---

When he returned to Vegas two years later, he moved right back into his role of premier lounge act. The headliners continued to flock to see him; I saw Tony Bennett walk into a lounge where Howie was playing, interrupt the gig and start singing with him.

The funny thing was, Howie never wanted to be a headliner; that just wasn't his thing. He just wanted to work and entertain. Unlike anything I had ever set out to do in music, Howie Gold was the happiest when he could entertain people; and nothing more.

From his tuxedo to the brandy-snifter-tip-jar on the edge of the grand piano, Howie exuded Las Vegas. The patter, the one-liners, the impossible-to-stump repertoire, even the cheap cologne —they were all Howie and they all screamed Las Vegas. He played casino lounges, restaurants, as part of bands in major shows on the strip, at VIP events, and just about anywhere one could hear live music in Las Vegas.

In the early part of the century, when I was living in Vegas parttime and working with Bill Bennett, I had dinner almost every night at a well-known local's favorite Italian restaurant a couple of miles off the Strip. I was such a regular there that I didn't even order; the owner knew what I always ate and when I would walk in, he would put my order to the kitchen (house-made gnocchi pomodoro). To this day and as of this writing, every time I return to Vegas I still dine with the legendary restauranteur to the stars, Gino Ferraro.

In those days, Gino had hired Howie to play six nights a week during happy hours. That is where I met him. Howie had a routine in which he did a knock-off of the Johnny Carson and Doc Severinsen "stump the band" act. If a patron could name any song in any genre that was a legitimate song, and if Howie didn't know it then he would buy the patron a drink.

I was the outlaw folksinger of Nashville Tennessee, or at least I had been in a past life. There wasn't an obscure country song in existence that I didn't know something about; remember Don't Blow Smoke In A Kangaroo's Face To Get Your Kicks from Cecil Null? For weeks I stumped ... or tried to stump... Howie nightly. He was good. But I think I won more than lost. And it cost him nothing since I don't drink.

Even during the Covid pandemic of the early 2020's, I was still booking Howie.

THE POET LAUREATE SOUL OF FOLKIE ROCK & ROLL

genuine organized-crime-era legends or at least Vegas show-producer legends.

Howie's world wasn't my world; but I could not have asked for a better tutor to guide me through all aspects of Vegas shows entertainment. Talent aside (though he had oodles of it), what he really provided for me was the behind-the-scenes inner workings of his industry. He showed me the proverbial good, bad, and ugly of casino showrooms and lounges.

That intense tutelage combined with my substantial show-operational experience from Bread & Roses allowed me to create or operate venues that were differentiated from anything else available. I brought a performer's perspective, an owner's sensibilities, and a marketer's intensity. Though, that intensity wasn't always as well-received as I had hoped.

For a Don Rickles appearance that I booked, I began an advertising campaign that ran a single hockey puck on a black background with the only words on the ad "Comedy Coming Soon..." (and the name of the casino. Rickles was known for referring to people as "hockey pucks". Dozens of phone calls (including from members of the Tribal Counsel that owned the property) came in asking when we were getting ice hockey. Okay! Note to self: don't be too "insider" with promotional jargon.

During those casino operations years, I produced dozens —probably hundreds— of shows with almost no limit of genres. I booked *Charlie Daniels, Patti LaBelle, Earth Wind & Fire, Howie Mandell, George Lopez, Don Ho (*and his daughter *Hoku) Peter Frampton, The Mills Brothers, The Righteous Brothers, Tony Orlando, Paul Anka*, the aforementioned *Don Rickles, The Doobie Brothers, The Pointer Sisters, The Village People, Travis Tritt, Chubby Checker, The Coasters, The Chippendales, Donna Summer, Brian Setzer, Teresa Teng, Brad Paisley, Christina Aguilera,* my childhood hero *Jerry Lee Lewis, Art Garfunkel, Styx, The Moody Blues, Paul Rodriguez,* and many, many, many others. In addition to the headliners, I booked even more second tier acts, local and regional performers, tribute artists, lounge lizards, Mariachi bands, folk singers, and almost any touring group that would be driving by one of the casino properties.

A decade later, by the time I was filming the pilot for my television show, I was a recognized casino operations, marketing, finance, and development guru. More importantly personally to me, I had a pretty good handle on producing major casino shows.

I turned my focus to financing the purchase of my own casino and putting a management team in place to operate it and assigning an entertainment operator. Even with my industry reputation, that was no simple task; nonetheless, I began chasing capital stacks for investments.

THE LEGEND DIES ON — GARY GREEN

I constantly was scheduled to fly from somewhere to somewhere else for a speaking engagement or to be interviewed or to chase investors or something. The truth is, I was averaging about 150 trips a year (keep in mind that there are only 52 weeks in a year), so even at the time it was hard to remember where I was supposed to be and when. Thank God for administrative assistants and later electronic calendars.

There was one of those trips early on in my casino-world adventures, just when I was starting to let go of my music aspirations, that I found myself looking for the *Delta Airlines Crown Room* lounge at the San Jose airport; I didn't even know if they had one.

As I approached a gate agent to ask for directions, I noticed several genuinely derelict-looking guys standing in front of me at the counter. They were about twenty years older than me and their shaggy unkemptness, their faded and filthy jeans, and their generally spacey demeanor indicated to me that either a litter of old homeless men had wandered in off the street, or they were musicians heading to a gig. There were no guitar cases, but before I went with the homeless theory, I decided to ask one of the guys. "Are you guys in a band?" I questioned.

A tall skinny guy, with a Southern accent heavier even than mine, answered with a friendly grin, *you wouldn't believe it, but you are looking at the world's greatest rock and roll band.*

I almost bit my tongue to refrain from saying, *damn, you don't look like The Rolling Stones*; but I successfully restrained myself (and ultimately I was damned glad that I did —*because it turned out that those cats really WERE the world's greatest rock-and-roll band!*)

Equally amused by his teasing response, I struck up a music conversation with him. After a few minutes of conversation as we waited in the line, I realized that his claim might not have been nearly as grandiose as it had sounded. I was talking to *Kenny Lovelace*, longtime guitar and fiddle sideman to *Jerry Lee Lewis*; exactly where my whole music journey had begun.

When he introduced himself, I immediately acknowledged that I knew who he was and that indeed they might just be the world's greatest rock and roll band. Delighted, and surprised, that I recognized his name he immediately stepped out of the spotlight and pointed to the man standing in front of him and said, *then I guess you know who this guy is. This is James Burton.* Damn. I was almost tongue-tied. I told James that I had spent months trying to sound like him after I heard the *Buddy Cagle* song.

Planes were grounded for a weather delay, so we all retired to the executive lounge. There they told me they were headed to Vegas for a gig with Jerry Lee Lewis. A few seconds later they introduced me to him.

And that was where it had all started for me a half-century earlier. Talk about full circle!

THE POET LAUREATE SOUL OF FOLKIE ROCK & ROLL

We all talked for another hour, mostly about music and our experiences. Okay, I talked like a fanboy, and they talked like old rockers. Both descriptions were accurate. When the ground-stop was finally lifted and it was time to go, Kenny said, *"It's a shame you're going to Florida instead of Vegas. We could hang out after the show..."*

Before he could finish his sentence, I was on my feet announcing that I would be changing my ticket for Vegas. He told me that he'd arrange a backstage pass and an auditorium seat for me at the *Will Call* window at the gig. They boarded their flight, I changed my ticket to the next flight to Las Vegas, and I called my mother to tell her what had just happened. She, of course, was as thrilled as I was.

In Vegas, late at night after the show, we all talked for hours more. At some point I lamented about my lost career and the strange direction I had taken. I did not, however, mention the fugitive years though I certainly mentioned my hand.

For the first time in the few hours that I had known them, Kenny addressed me in a very serious tone, though still with his ever-present grin.

He pointed at Jerry Lee Lewis and then demanded to me, "Do you think this guy gave up when things didn't go the way they were supposed to?"

Jerry Lee, who was listening, answered the question, in third person, *No sir-eeeee, The Killer never stopped. Never did. Never will.*

Kenny continued, Look at this bunch of old men here. *Do you think we stopped because we are too old and decrepit?*

He was on a roll and went on as he pointed to James and asked, Do you think he quit because the Rock and Roll Hall of Fame rejected him? The greatest Rock and Roll guitar man of all time!"

Whoa. Wait. What? Why did they reject you? I asked James Burton. He explained that the bylaws of the Hall of Fame excluded "sidemen" from induction.[251]

---

[251] I already was no fan of the Rock & Roll Hall of Fame because I felt that its Cleveland location was stolen from Memphis through payoffs and bribery. I felt that its very existence was an afront to Sam Phillips, who I considered a founding father of Rock & Roll. Their board justified their locating in Cleveland by citing it as being the base of rock impresario – the DJ *Alan Freed*. The fact that Freed is most often remembered for the payola scandal seemed, to me, totally appropriate for the decision to locate the Hall of Fame in Cleveland.

Nonetheless, I took it on myself to correct the injustice perpetrated on James Burton (and other incredible non-frontman performers). I started a telephone and letter-writing campaign; but I didn't go the "grassroots" route. Instead of rallying fans, I organized

THE LEGEND DIES ON — GARY GREEN

Kenny convinced me that I should not stop. I should not abandon my music; such an essential part of my very being. That night was what kept me focused on entertainment during the casino years, rather than just hanging it all up. Once again, Jerry Lee Lewis had pulled me to music.

Still ... heading into my sixties, I at long last resolved, albeit very sadly, that my music days were long gone. My reinvention as a casino guru actually had been entirely *too* good.

Worse than believing my own press, I had *become* my own creation. I'd moved from being *Doctor Frankenstein* to become *Frankenstein's Monster*.

As the cliché goes, *It Is What It Is*. Good, bad, or indifferent, it had been one hell of a ride. I had made a ton of money and lost a ton of money, but that didn't matter at all. I had lived dreams that most could never get near. While many of my generation were content to vicariously live melodrama, I had jumped in headfirst —often to my detriment. I had made lots of friends but had lots of detractors too.

At speaking engagements when I would be introduced with a list of supposed accomplishments (especially in the casino realm) I always responded that I just wanted to be a little hillbilly guitar picker.

But I finally resolved to accept the reality of whatever it was that I unwittingly had become... so I thought.

---

corporate executives, billionaires, major entertainment figures, and people that I knew would sway the Hall of Fame's board. (I even convinced one of the board members to join my movement.)

It didn't take long at all; the next induction, the bylaws were changed, and James Burton was inducted, by Keith Richards.

Still, I refer to the organization as *The Pop Music Hall of Fame*, rather than credit it with Rock & Roll.

THE POET LAUREATE SOUL OF FOLKIE ROCK & ROLL

Opus Twenty-Eight:
The Worst Year Of My Life & My Coda

And she cried, 'Singer of sad songs
I need your services today
Doctor of broken hearts
I've got some early hybrid corn for your pay'
— Alex Zanetis, *Singer of Sad Songs*, Diamond Garden Music & Universal Music

Tombstone Arizona 1881 and Doc Holliday. The Northfield Minnesota bank robbery of 1876 and Jesse James. Waterloo 1815. October 1917. Awakening the sleeping giant in 1941. September 11, 2001. In various big picture scenarios, those were dates that changed everything. For me in all of my pictures, it was October of 2011. That month everything changed for me... forever.

An eight-year roller-coaster-ride of events actually began in 2003 with the death of Johnny Cash. It didn't hit me like the 1977 death of Elvis had; it didn't put me to bed coming to terms with mortality. Nonetheless, it started a series of episodes that changed a lot of things in my life.

Even before the teenaged me was invited to that guitar pull at his house in Hendersonville Tennessee, I was fancying myself as a Johnny-Cash-wannabe; *I've been pretty clear about that in this book.* As his status in country music sank and mine rose in the folk world, my imagined bond to him strengthened; helped along in no small part by the mentoring friendship of his sister and the guitar lesson from his mother-in-law. So, I really did feel some kind of personal loss when he died; though it was not clear, even to me, what that was all about.

After the Rick Ruben albums, Cash had phoenixed out of the *Mercury Records* ashes (where he'd landed after *Columbia* dumped him) and graduated from aging country music star to become a genuine American icon. *June Carter Cash* had died in May of 2003 after heart-valve replacement surgery. Then J.R. died in September, technically from diabetes complications; but I believed it was from a broken heart after losing June.

Death elevated him further to become almost some sort of minor deity. (Then the 2005 biopic film, *Walk The Line*, totally consecrated his legend.) For me, there was some silly minor satisfaction in being able to say, *"I knew him back when..."*

I suspected that the funeral and memorial services would be media events garnished with the special obnoxious Nashville social-climbing that I had learned to hate decades before; so, I avoided it like a plague. I decided to wait until the dust settled before reaching out to Reba Hancock.

THE LEGEND DIES ON — GARY GREEN

Though we had not talked in two decades, she remembered me and, as always, was very welcoming when we talked. But I could hear fatigue and age in her voice, though she was only in her late sixties or early seventies. We talked briefly, and I told her that I was thinking of coming back through Nashville in a few months. She asked me to give her a call when I did. Of course, I said I would.

It actually was about a year or so later when I finally decided to go to Nashville; and my sole purpose was for a one-last-time drive by Johnny Cash's house and his four-and-a-half lakefront acres in Hendersonville. It was my own private "goodbye" to him. After that I called Reba.

She sounded even more weary, but just as welcoming. I told her that I had just driven by the lake house, and she sounded surprised as she asked me, "Oh? Are you thinking about buying it? It would be great if it stayed with family and friends and people we know."

Okay, trying to put aside for a minute that Johnny Cash's sister just referred to me as "family and friends" (wow); I was stunned that the house was on the market.

"Is it for sale?" I asked, trying not to sound star-struck. She told me that it was on the market and her brother Tommy was handling the sale for the family through Crye Leike Realtors where he was licensed as an agent.

First, who-the-hell knew that *Tommy Cash* was a real estate agent? I knew *of* Tommy from a couple of hit records he had on his own, including one of my favorite country songs, 1969's crossover hit *Six White Horses* written by Larry Murray.

Tommy also had charted with *I Recall A Gypsy Woman*, (which Waylon later covered) and with a Carl Perkins song, *Rise and Shine*. I was actually a Tommy Cash *fan*, having nothing to do with his iconic brother.

I told Reba that I wasn't aware that it was for sale, but yes, I would be interested. She gave me Tommy's home number and I promised to call him.

The other thing she said to me, unrelated to the house, was that my name came up after one of the memorial services for J.R. *How is THAT even possible*, I wondered. She asked me if I knew *Jack Clement*. Only by reputation and fame, but I simply replied, "I know *who* he is, but I don't *know*-KNOW him".

"Well, he certainly "know-knows" you", she told me. She said that he had approached her after one of the services and asked if she knew how to get in touch with me.

Apparently, he told her that he had read a liner note on one of my albums where I had thanked her, and he was wondering about the connection. She responded that she hadn't heard from me in years and didn't have current contact information, but that if I contact her again, she would pass it along to me.

THE POET LAUREATE SOUL OF FOLKIE ROCK & ROLL

Once again, WOW! *Cowboy Jack Clement*. Double-wow!! She gave me his home address but didn't have a phone number. She thought it might be listed.

We talked for a few more minutes and I promised to call Tommy and to write to Jack. She wished me luck; but her voice trailed as if she was sick and thought her end was near too. I don't know; it was just weird. She died about a year later, so it really was the last time I would speak with her. It just seemed like she knew that it would be our *goodbye*.

When Tommy Cash ran my bona-fides and then found out that I knew his music and was a fan, we hit it off really well. He was interested in selling the house, but he was equally (or more) interested in me booking him to play at casinos. We talked probably two dozen times during the next few weeks and at one point, at his request, I visited his booking agent on Music Square (the former Music Row).[252]

For the purchase of the Johnny Cash home, I was one of about a half-dozen suitors seriously considering buying it. I had no idea how many "looky-loos" were lined up to star-chase; but that's why Tommy and Crye Leike did due diligence on potential buyers. Apparently, I passed.

Tommy told me that house would be sold "as is", which also meant that some of John and June's furniture would be included (as well as the really-creepy mural of June's face that J.R. had someone paint on the elevator doors after she died).

The 14,000-square-foot house was listed for $2.9-million, and I had managed to raise just under $2-million. Tommy encouraged me to formally offer that or a little bit more *in writing*. He thought the trustees of the estate would accept that lowball offer.

Up until that point I had assumed that the house was being sold by J.R. and June's son, *John Carter Cash* (who I had only met when he was *very* young and in the hospital after being in a jeep wreck with Reba). I had no idea that there was a trustee handling the estate; but I was not aware of all the family drama going on between John Carter and June's kids and J.R.'s kids with Vivian. *(I later heard there were lawsuits and all sorts of hard feelings. To this day, I don't know where all of that ended or if it did. I don't even know if the lawsuit rumors were true. Actually, I don't know anything at all about the relationships in the family(ies).)*

---

[252] I can't say Tommy Cash became a close friend, but we did come to know each other and stay in contact over the years; almost as close as I had been to Reba in those early years. As some kind of closure, in September of 2024 I was asked to attend his funeral in Hendersonville (and I did). It was a small gathering of friends and family and no press or any sort of Nashville hoopla. In departing, Rosanne Cash (JR's daughter) melancholily said to me, "there are too many of these lately".

THE LEGEND DIES ON — GARY GREEN

Whatever the drama, the property was being sold by *the trustees* of a revokable trust and it looked like the pool of potential buyers got narrowed down to just two or three of us.

One of the other serious contenders for the property was *(Sir) Barry Gibb*, of the Bee Gees. He offered $2.3-million along with a "business plan" to renovate it and turn it into a songwriters' retreat in the spirit of the guitar pulls that had been held there in the 60's and 70's *(and where I had first met J.R.)*.

Truthfully, I had no plans for the house whatsoever. I certainly wasn't going to move back to Nashville (or Hendersonville); and I thought turning it into some sort of museum or the like was just too crass —even for Nashville *(and that is saying a lot: to be too tactless for Nashville!)*. I simply wanted to buy it for the nostalgia of having been there decades before and to have an occasional getaway near Music City.

Needless to say, the disco king's offer beat me out before I could raise money to up my offer sufficiently to submit a second offer in writing. He apparently *actually had* the money and didn't have to raise it like I did.

Disappointed, I flew back to Florida. I was conspiracy-theory puzzled, at least, when about a year-and-a-half later the house mysteriously burned to the ground and the Gibb project was abandoned. That feeling did not subside when I later read that the City did not approve zoning for the property for any purpose other than single family residential; the songwriting retreat would not be approved without a major zoning amendment which likely would be opposed by the other Caudill residents. It was all just one of those things that makes one wonder, *hmmmm*.

Shortly after returning to Florida, I decided to write to the legendary producer, Jack Clement. I wasn't sure what to say to him, but nevertheless, I wrote him a letter, a seemingly out-of-the-blue cold-call letter; more or less an introduction to me and my musical past with an explanation that Reba Cash Hancock had asked me to contact him. I included my return address, email address, and phone number.

I had a less-than-zero expectation that the celebrated Jack Clement would even read the letter, much less respond to it. Whew, as was repeatedly the case with my suppositions; I was quite wrong. He called me.

𝄢?𝄢?𝄢?

Beginning with that very first conversation, Cowboy Jack (who by then had dumped the "cowboy" label and was calling himself *Pineapple Jack*) pulled no punches with me... ever. He told me that he didn't agree with almost anything I was "preaching" in my political songs, but he absolutely loved some of my other songs.

Specifically, he praised *There Ain't No Easy Way, That Burnt Out Rock and Roll, I Can Never Go Back Home Again, The Last Minstrel, I Wore*

THE POET LAUREATE SOUL OF FOLKIE ROCK & ROLL

His Gun, The Cowboy, and *Ashes of a Fire.* I could tell, he actually had listened to my albums.

Then he lectured me, kindly but still lecturing, "You are not a folk singer. Stop calling yourself that. *Peter, Paul, and Mary. The Kingston Trio, Simon and Garfunkel.* They are folk singers. It has a sweet sound. I am okay with the 'outlaw' thing; but you aren't New-York-City-folk. You are a country rock and roll poet."

I have to admit, he found the right buttons to push to get my attention. He said all the key words; and there was that "poet" thing again.

He asked me if I wanted to record, because, he said, he would like to produce me. Before I could answer, he added, "but I have one more question for you".

After a long pause, he asked, "Do you want to do this for the satisfaction of knowing that you can make a real country album, or do you want to do it to sell records for people to hear you?"

Without hesitation I answered, "I don't need to record me singing in the shower; I know what I am and am not. I have things to say, and I want people to hear me."

I could almost hear his smile as he responded, "That is exactly what I hoped you were going to say. Let's make a record."

Still hesitant, I asked, "You've heard my albums. You had to hear my rhythm issues. What do we do about that?"

He brushed my objection aside, "That's a production issue. You aren't the worst I have ever heard. I could tell you some stories about some of the most famous singers you know; they were much worse than you at keeping time. That rhythm thing is MY problem, not yours. Let me take care of that."

Then he added, "Besides they couldn't play guitar half as good as you do. You are a real picker; it just needs to be highlighted a little better. We can do a lot with that."

Like a true technician, he wanted to know what kind of guitar and what kind of strings I used on the albums.

I told him that on the first album, recorded in Charlotte, I used my *Western Auto Truetone Jumbo* which was manufactured by *Kay Guitars*, the last year Kay was in business. I used *Black Diamond* medium gauge strings then.

On the second album, recorded at the Broadside office in New York, I used that same Kay but with *Gibson mono-steel* medium gauge with a wound third string. I also played a Brazilian *Giannini* spruce and mahogany nylon *AWN-25A* with *Augustine Classical Black Silver* strings.

On the third record, I played the same Giannini, a borrowed pre-CBS *Fender Stratocaster,* and my own vintage *Gibson J-100* (the same model

THE LEGEND DIES ON — GARY GREEN

that Little Jimmy Dickens used). I used the same Gibson mono-steel medium strings.

Jack was also a fan of the big Gibson J-100, often called "the poor man's J-200". He had a Gibson J-200, which he told me was his favorite guitar; he called it his baby. He said that he thought the subtle difference in tone between the J-100 and J-200 was really interesting. He said that the J-100 was usually a rhythm-only instrument while the 200 was more for flatpicking. He told me that he wanted to experiment with that difference sounds when we got together.

When we got together? Okay! So, this thing with one of America's most legendary —and notoriously eccentric— record producers was for real. I mean, my God, this was the cat that added the trumpets to *Ring of Fire* with Johnny Cash, the producer of Waylon's *Dreaming My Dreams* album, not to mention dozens of other credits beginning back at Sun Records in Memphis!

For the next couple of months, we talked on the phone once or twice a week. Finally, he suggested that we needed to get together in person and "do some picking together".

During one email exchange, I finally asked him when he wanted me to come to Nashville, and he told me that he was planning a trip to Florida, and he would get back to me.

Sometime right after that, his email apparently went down, and I didn't hear from him for a week or two. Eventually, about a week after my birthday, I received a letter from him asking if I wanted to meet in Florida.

I called him immediately to set a meeting. He sounded really pleased and added that he'd bring his *J-200* with him so we could trade some guitar licks.

It could not have possibly gone better. He had started making a list of studio musicians that he wanted on my new record. The list included some of the best session players in Nashville, many who had played on records he produced of *Johnny Cash, Charlie Pride, Waylon Jennings*, and even *Doc Watson*.

He also put together a list of my songs that he wanted me to record with that group. He said that he wanted me to redo some of my Folkways stuff, but he also listed a few new songs that I had sent to him (or at least they were "new" since my last Folkways recordings).

Though we were then talking on the phone at least weekly, it still wasn't clear to me what he had in mind, sound wise, for me. One afternoon, he asked me if I was familiar with *Don Williams*. Jack had produced most of Don's fifty-plus charted country hits.

I was already a fan and thought that Don Williams' interpretation of songs by one of my favorite writers, *Bob McDill* (*Amanda, Gypsy Woman, Good Ole Boys Like Me*) were outstanding. I also liked Williams'

THE POET LAUREATE SOUL OF FOLKIE ROCK & ROLL

work on *Rake and Ramblin' Man*, and (of course) his mega-hit *Tulsa Time* (which later was covered by Eric Clapton). So yes, I was very familiar with Don Williams.

Jack told me that I reminded him of Don Williams, and he wanted me to get Don's albums and practice playing along with them.

He especially wanted me to focus on the Townes Van Zandt song *If I Needed You*[253] (Which Jack constantly mistakenly called *If You Needed Me*) that Don did as a duet with Emmylou Harris.

Jack wanted me to be able to flawlessly play along and sing along so that Don's timing (read "rhythm") would become second nature to me.

I didn't want to "sound like" Don Williams; or for that matter anyone else. I wanted to sound like *Gary Green*. But I took the homework assignment seriously and every week, on the phone, Jack would quiz me on my Don-Williams-progress. I practiced and practiced.

For the next year and few months, Jack drilled me on Don Williams songs; all the while praising my guitar playing and my writing. He kept encouraging me enough to keep me from becoming disillusioned. He told me that he didn't want me to cover the songs; he just wanted me to listen to the phrasing, as he put it.

I got *that*. There was, for example, a vast difference in the phrasing of Don Williams' version of *Amanda* and Waylon Jennings version of the same song. I favored Waylon's version; but Jack was adamant that I needed to understand Don's version. He kept telling me that the Williams' version was much more like *ME*.

Frankly, the whole Don-Williams-thing became sort of monotonous to me and I was on the verge of abandoning the whole "Gary is back" project. I was starting to feel that there was no real appreciation for MY work per se, within itself.

Then out-of-the-blue, in June, alternative rocker *Frank Black* released *93–03*; a compilation album highlighting the 10 years of his solo career after ending things for his influential band *The Pixies*.[254] Side Two, Track Five of that album was a song he had been including for a while in his live performances: my *Burnt Out Rock and Roll*.

In his initial stage-patter about my song, he told WOXY internet radio in Dayton Ohio and WVXU public radio in Cincinnati:

---

[253] As noted in a previous chapter, that was the song that my friend Rhinestone (David Allan Coe) unceremoniously coopted into his *Would You Lay With Me In A Field of Stone*.

[254] With the stage name of Frank Black, Charles Michael Kittridge Thompson IV, also went by the name Black Francis. His record label described him as: "*Best known as the frontman of iconic alternative rock band Pixies, Black Francis' music has inspired generations of musicians from Nirvana to Radiohead*".

THE LEGEND DIES ON — GARY GREEN

> "I've been downloading some music recently off of a site called *The Smithsonian Archive*. I got some old rock and roll stuff. There's this poet guy, I think he might be a DJ now, his name is Gary Green, I think he's from Georgia originally. Don't know much about him. I've Googled him. I've learned a little bit about him on the internet of course, and he's got this great song called *That Burnt Out Rock and Roll* which I've been obsessed with ever since I heard it a couple weeks ago."

Later, in many of his live-concerts he gave variations of it as:

"There's a guy called Gary Green who is a very obscure folksinger. I think he does a lot of lawyering now for Native Americans. I found this great wonderful song on the Smithsonian website, which is sort of like iTunes but smarter."

Whatever the between-songs dialog, his live performances and the album brought new attention to my song and to me (as did his 2022 release of a nine-disc boxset which closed with my song). I will always be grateful to him for finding the song and making it his own.[255]

Besides calling attention to the song, Frank Black's recording did several much-more important things for me personally: First, without ever meeting me, he inspired me to keep going; once again, it appeared that *somebody* liked my songs. But, also, by recording my song, he instantly took away the self-doubt and uncertainty that I was feeling from months of playing Don Williams songs over-and-over-and-over-and... thinking my producer wanted me to be a Don Williams clone. Secondly, in his patter *(albeit not exactly accurate)*, he referred to me as a "poet-guy"; just as Alan Ginsberg had done thirty years earlier and just as Kristofferson had said to me in Nashville. THAT was a huge reinforcement to me.

Finally, who he was —*an icon of alternate rock*— showed me (and the world) that my music, my poetry, reached out to more than a just a niche genre. In that sense, Frank Black legitimized to me that what I was doing was ... actually a thing.

Meanwhile, Pineapple Jack and I continued working toward creating an album. We finalized a list of eleven songs that we wanted to put on the record —all originals with no covers. We jointly chose some of my old ones and some of my new ones.

Jack suggested a first session at his studio, in late fall of 2011. He lined up the sessions players that he wanted, and we agreed on a date just after the Fourth of July. I booked a first-class flight to Music City and a suite at the Marriott in Donelson, near where I used to live.

Then It Was 2011, the worst year of my life.

---

[255] On YouTube: https://youtu.be/YRVYGxvxiVo

THE POET LAUREATE SOUL OF FOLKIE ROCK & ROLL

There would be nothing but misery that year. As a harbinger of the dark year ahead, in January, my Oklahoma assistant and topical musical Phil-Ochs-super-fan died. In March, my companion for 19 years, my Baltimore rescue cat died.

Storm clouds were gathering.

In late June, about a month before my recording session, Jack's Belmont Avenue home and studio burned to the ground. It was a devastating loss of not just his home and his studio, but more importantly, of a lifetime of papers, tapes, and memories. He was shattered. Needless to say, and quite appropriately, the recording sessions would postpone until... at the earliest... sometime the next year.

Then came the 12th day of October in 2011.

I received a call that once again my mother was in a coma and death was at her door. By the time my delayed plane arrived, both of my brothers had been at her bedside constantly for almost 20 hours. They went home to get some sleep as I sat down beside the bed and spoke aloud, "I am here now." She made a slight whimpering sound, as if in pain, and then she gasped for a last breath.

It was, of course, medically expected; but for me it was unexpected and that is how it hit me. Two-and-a-half years earlier, she had been hospitalized and comatose for more than 36 hours. By the time I arrived on another delayed flight, the rest of the family had gathered around her in the hospital room that time too. It was the day before Thanksgiving. The doctors told us that the end was imminent. I leaned over the hospital bed and whispered to her, "Nope. We're not ready for you to die." A minute later she opened her eyes and spoke for the first time in days, "I've got to get home and cook Thanksgiving dinner; let's get out of here." By God, the cavalry DID arrive; she actually did go home the next day and for the next couple of years, things were near-normal.

But in 2011, there was no cavalry; she died. Did she hold on to life until the return of her wastefully extravagant, oldest, prodigal son? My brothers thought so.

For more than a half-century I had talked with my parents either on the phone or in person almost every day. Even when my own self-inflicted social-alienating demons repeatedly haunted me as an adult, my parents always welcomed me home. *"Family first, no matter what"*; that was my mother's true belief. Regardless of what madness I visited on the world or on myself (and God knows there was much madness), the family was all that mattered. Maybe that was why she could not die until the family was reunited; maybe that was how she was able to wait until my return.

The next night we reported her death to our father, who was tucked away in a nursing home and guessing the puzzle solutions to *Wheel of Fortune* on television when we arrived. He was never a religious or even

THE LEGEND DIES ON — GARY GREEN

spiritual man; in fact, I often quote his snarky observation, *"the only thing wrong with Christianity is that they cut back on the lions about 2,000 years too early".*

But on that night, he looked upward at the ceiling and loudly yelled, "Goodbye Dot." Seventy-two hours later, he too was dead. It was the all-too-cliché long-time ending of a 60-year marriage (15 days before that anniversary).

Their deaths changed *everything*. The family had always been closer than most. Being orphaned at 57 years old was just... just... not possible in my mind. There was no "home" to "go home" to anymore. Only emptiness.

There hadn't been enough time. The stolen years had slowed me down; and my own squandering of time had me acting like Shel Silverstein's Unicorn —missing Noah's Ark because I was out frivolously playing.[256] I just didn't have enough time to do everything I wanted to do for them and with them. I fucking ran out of time.

Even if Jack's studio had not burned, I lost all will to do anything; especially anything musical. The heart of my music had always been my mother, and the heart of my poetry was my father.

With their deaths, I shut down. I was worthless for the remaining few months of the year, all of 2012, and into 2013. I mean absolutely nothing motivated me; I didn't return calls and I answered very few emails. I wrote nothing.

Jack, too, was shut down for a while; it was near the end of 2012 before he next called me. I had called his cell phone right after I heard about the fire, but he didn't know about my parents' deaths, and we had not talked since I called him. When we finally did talk again, in 2013, I sensed something else was wrong, but I couldn't put my finger on it.

During that bottoming-out period of my life, the only thing that I did that was even remotely music-related was to push getting Jack into the *Country Music Hall of Fame*. It was more of a "closure" project for me than anything else. I was just closing the books on everything outstanding in my life. Since the early 1990's I had been an on-again-off-again voting member of the *Country Music Association*, the gatekeepers of the Hall of Fame.[257] Much like my ferocity of getting James Burton into the Rock & Roll Hall of Fame, I was a champion of Jack's induction to the CMA's

---

[256] *The Unicorn*, by Shel Silverstein, Copyright 1962 Hollis Music Inc.

[257] I should have joined earlier but the whole political-folk thing and my bad experiences with the Nashville music "industry" had kept me from applying for membership. I finally overcame my reluctance during my circus years and was welcomed by the CMA with open arms.

THE POET LAUREATE SOUL OF FOLKIE ROCK & ROLL

Hall of Fame. Only with Jack didn't run into any resistance at all, and to my delight, the move to induct him was well underway by the time I was onboard for it. In April of 2013 it happened![258]

Then in late July or early August Jack died. What I had heard in his voice was the unshared information that I only found out later: he was battling liver cancer. It was a battle that he lost; and consequently, we all lost.

That was it. Not like my previous maniacal on-again-off-again in-and-out of music breaks, this time it really felt like the coda. My parents were dead. My producer was dead.

The spiral that ensued could have no happy ending. I dropped out of doing *anything*. No music. No working. No interests. No anything. I lost everything, not just willingness and inspiration but tangible things as well. Eventually, my stagnation drained all saving. I lost my home. I lost friends. I became a hermit, for all practical purposes.

Just to afford to keep eating, I jumped back into the casino world focusing mostly on developing new casinos and bringing new slot machine companies into the market. After all, through my last reinvention I had genuinely become a somewhat authoritative, if not iconic, elder statesman of the casino business world.

It was easy for me to step back into *that*; and I really didn't want to even think about music or anything else. It made for an excellent escape from my painful realities and of course, I told no one of my woes.

It was a world full of deserving victims begging to be parted from their money. I just didn't care *(and especially if their losses went to a good cause, like Tribal restitution)*. Revenge… or reckoning?

One of the great things about personal reinvention is that when it is real, it is VERY real. My reinvention into a casino marketing and operations guru was the real deal. For Christ's sake, I had been a vice-president of *Trump Hotels & Casinos*, had developed patent-rights to a proprietary operations management system, developed and operated a score of casinos, created a financial structure that always increased bottom-line revenue, … and had stood at the forefront of Native sovereignty *(as much as any white guy could)*. I had shot the pilot of a fucking television series about how I save casinos. No one knew better than me the financial dynamics and potential of a properly-run casino-hotel-resort; no one. I had written two highly-praised books about the casino business.

---

[258] …and in 2019 that *Gibson J-200* that he loved so much, was permanently placed in the *Hall of Fame Museum*. I choke up every time I see it; just as I do when I see Mother Maybelle's guitar that I had played.

THE LEGEND DIES ON — GARY GREEN

There were more magazine and radio interviews than I could even remember; I stopped saving clips decades ago because there were just too many. When one reviewer wrote that I was *"the most written about figure in modern casino business circles"*, it wasn't just good P.R.; it was empirical fact. In my not-so-secret-identity, I in fact was the *Casino Cat*.

THE POET LAUREATE SOUL OF FOLKIE ROCK & ROLL

Opus Twenty-Nine:
One More Shot, Just For Old Times

> One more shot, just for old times
> One Last Stand
> One more hit ought to do it
> Then I quit while I can
> — Paul Kennerley, *One More Shot*, ©1980 Randor Music, London

What's the line from *The Godfather Part III*? *"Just when I thought I was out, they pull me back in!"* That is exactly what happened to me. But it wasn't music that brought me out of my self-imposed exiled retirement. Nor was it some kind of sappy *moving on with my life* dynamic. It wasn't even a Zen-soaked fanciful bright-colors-and-flowers romantic *embracing of life's joys*. Nope, none of that bullshit.

Instead, it was the bony fingers of a cold dark specter resurrected from the pits of hell; a demon who returned to earth with the most-vile abominations that many of my generation thought were forever behind us. Darkness from the abomination was something to which I could relate and react; I had lived through the best they could throw. (Ozzy's *Prince of Darkness* moniker had nothing on reality; it was pure showbiz puffery compared to anguish unleased on earth).

On the 17th day of June in 2015 a 21-year-old white supremacist cacodemon incarnate shot ten people during a *bible study* at the oldest Black church in America. In fellowship and brotherhood, the young man had been welcomed into the group and repaid the kindness with hollow-point rounds from a Glock 41.

It wasn't just the unthinkable action; *it was the very atmosphere in the country that allowed such horrendous behavior to resurface*; to resurface *repeatedly* from mass shootings to twisted manifesto-driven individual assaults and assassinations. It was a national pattern of social changes that empowered such atrocities and during the next few years would become *almost* officially-endorsed: i.e. *"you also had people that were very fine people, on both sides"*[259] —NO there fucking are NOT!

Even four years before that kind of tacet endorsement of racist violence, the details of that Charleston attack hit me like an epiphanical gut punch.

---

[259] (My former employer) President Donald J. Trump, remarks to the press – Friday, April 26, 2019. (To be clear, those remarks were *not* about the Charleston murderer but rather were about the Charlottesville Virginia racist attacks four years later and are attributed to WhiteHouse.gov, Remarks by President Trump Before Marine One Departure.)

THE LEGEND DIES ON — GARY GREEN

It reeked with the putrid stench of a rolling rancidity that was trying to become a smothering blanket to freeze the warm progress of the past few decades. It was handwriting-on-the-wall, at least for me.

I smelled the uncontrolled rhetoric from demagogic anti-politicians moving from eccentric nonsense fringe to sanctioned emboldening (if not tacitly endorsing) the reemergence of subcultures that had been driven underground by civility, education, and struggle. *The bastards were back,* and they were edging toward being the "mainstream".

From their Charleston graves, I heard the crying for the Outlaw's return ... with vengeance. And I trembled with a long-suppressed rage. The horror called out to me like a long-stored-away and cobweb-covered *Bat-Signal* that had been rolled out and desperately aimed into the night sky. Even more metaphorically, I could hear Victor Laszlo saying to Rick Blaine, *"Welcome back to the fight. This time I know our side will win"*. Melodramatically, I could see myself going to the locked-away gun cabinet, opening the hand-carved box with my custom *Peacemaker*, and strapping it to my side. Realistically and *actually* though, I opened a long-locked wooden Stickley armoire cabinet, removed an Anvil flight case, and from inside that case I took out the *long-stored-away-to-be-forgotten* guitar with those big blue words painted around the body: These Six Strings Neutralize The Tools Of Oppression. *I am back, you motherfuckers!*

It would be another full year before the new furor of hatred could become sufficiently obfuscated within a cloud of economic nationalism, border hysteria, regulatory deregulation, and opposition to globalist perspectives. Though a whipped-up mass furor would become the dernier cri by then, at the moment there was sufficient outcry to force at least a token policy response to the Charleston church killings.

With political posturing reminiscent of Ronald Reagan's "tear down this wall," much of America called out to South Carolina Governor *Nikki Haley* to *"take down that flag"* even though she openly had been opposed to doing so before the shootings. South Carolina was the last state to fly the *Confederate Battle Flag* over the State Capitol Building. She finally ordered it retired on the 10th of July: a little less than a month after the murderous rampage at the church in her state.[260]

---

[260] Twenty years earlier, when I had raised the flag issue to official circles, South Carolina Democratic Lieutenant Governor Nick Theodore arranged to have it taken down and given to me in a presentation box (which I still have) on his last day in office. But literally the next fucking day, the new governor, banking dynasty scion David Beasley, sanctioned a replacement to be raised in its place. It took another two decades and those mass murders in church to force that century-over-due action.

THE POET LAUREATE SOUL OF FOLKIE ROCK & ROLL

Once again, the official moral compass was set by political convenience rather than genuine integrity. I wasn't shocked at Haley because she is a renowned political opportunist, but damn I was pissed.

Nine days later, I flew with my brother Ron (who had become a much better guitar picker than I) to *Tony Cohen's* mountaintop recording studio above Santa Rosa California. I updated the lyrics to *Snake Bite Poison* to address the church massacre and Tony engineered the recording.[261]

For *Snakebite Poison,* Tony did a brilliant job mixing and producing the session. Ron was superb on lead guitar (he always was —as was evidenced by the awesome rock cover band he fronted decades earlier in Myrtle Beach[262]). But even with their expertise guiding me, I wasn't happy with what I had created. *Something was missing.*

The sound was digital. It was updated. It was more polished than the original. All of that was great; in fact, I wanted those things. But basically, all we had was ...nothing more than a 21st century version of what I had been doing in the mid-20th century.

To me, it showed none of the progress that should have reflected the changes in my life. The lyrics weren't the issue; the issue was *the sound itself.* I wanted it to be a sound that would drive behavior. I wondered if it needed a band; a band that could steer reaction from the sound itself.

Secondly (and even more importantly) after Tony sent me the final mix a few weeks later, it occurred to me what my real issue was: *what-to-do-with-it.* Distribution!

Decades earlier, Walt Fuchs had said to me, "it doesn't do any good to philosophize in your closet; if people don't read or hear what you are

---

[261] Tony was a 70-something-year-old hippie lawyer who I'd become close to when we worked together on several Native American projects. A fine guitarist himself (with a couple of very-cool vintage guitars), he had become a certified digital recording engineer and built a studio at his home. He and I had formed a personal bond over music and reminiscences of the Sixties counterculture; all from his west coast perspective and my east coast. From almost the first time we met, he began encouraging me -pushing me- to "come back" to music. He had no agenda, no subterfuge, no reason for pushing except to dig what I was doing. To me, he was the living embodiment of The Movement culture. His opening up his studio, his time, and his heart was the push (or pull) that I need-ed to come back to music. It was the public resurfacing of hatred that pulled my head out of the sands of grief; but it was Tony's laid-back California-eze that brought me back to music. Damn, gotta love California hippie musicians. (Unfortunately, both the studio and Tony's home were completely destroyed in the 2017 Tubbs Fire that burned 5,000 homes and killed 22 people.)

[262] That band was locally known as "FOX PASS"; but that was because most visitors didn't understand the band's name or how to pronounce it when they read it: *Faux Pas*. I always said that was reflective of the demographic that visited Myrtle Beach.

THE LEGEND DIES ON — GARY GREEN

saying, then why bother?" Clearly, the same wisdom applied to my music in the 21st century.

I didn't have a Moe Asch to call up and put out a record. Hell, vinyl records almost didn't exist anymore; even CDs were going the way of eight-track-tapes. Most music was downloaded or more-likely streamed. *(As a technology-guru in one of my reinventions, I certainly was cool with that change.)* But the music "business" itself had changed a lot since the 1970's and 1980's; and not in a way that was friendly to either artists or distribution of songs.

It was a problem that required more thought than merely going into the studio had required. It was a monumental issue. Other than an un-promoted *YouTube* posting, I let the recording stagnate. It was a topical song anyway; like a daily newspaper it was time-fixed, so I didn't mind doing nothing with it.

The overall music issue, however, needed more attention. I needed to learn about the "new" business of music. Since the end of my Bread & Roses days, I had been focusing on venues and live shows for various artists; not on the recording world and certainly not on MY music (other than the incessant Don Williams mimicking).

On top of those shortcomings, I needed to make some decisions about what I wanted to do in light of my newfound drive toward California music that Tony's encouragement had sparked for me. I had stubbornly refused to move to California throughout the 70's, 80's, and 90's, despite family urging to do so and friends there constantly inviting me. *I probably should have listened.* But instead I needed to figure out the paradigm for the "new" world of music for an artist rather than for a promoter.

Meanwhile, back in Vegas, I reconnected with my old friend *Monica Maciel*.[263] In the past quarter-century, Monica had become a dynamo at the center of entertainment management. She opened her own entertainment company, *Talent Concepts Inc.*, booking headliners and lounge acts while managing acts, events, and benefits nationwide.

When I first met Monica in Oklahoma, I didn't know about her music background; I only knew her as a slot machine technical whiz. Shortly after I hired her, she left Oklahoma for a better job in Vegas and to be with her fiancé (who she married). For whatever reasons, Monica took me under her proverbial wing to tutor me in what I had missed in the

---

[263] I had met her a decade earlier when she came to work for me as a slot machine manager at an Oklahoma casino. A native of the West Tennessee / Eastern Missouri border area, she had grown up in country music, literally. Her early industry "chops" came under personal guidance from country legend Razzy Bailey and from her neighbor and dear friend Loretta Lynn.

THE POET LAUREATE SOUL OF FOLKIE ROCK & ROLL

music "business" in the past thirty years. *Wow:* there was a lot; and it was almost more than I was willing to absorb that late in my life.[264]

Around that same time, the Harrahs casino in Las Vegas signed a residency deal for a production of the Broadway show, *Million Dollar Quartet*. The show was what the industry called a "jukebox show"; and this one was a *sort-of-based-on-fact* musical dramatization of the historic impromptu jam session of Elvis Presley, Jerry Lee Lewis, Carl Perkins, and Johnny Cash and clandestinely recorded by Sun Records' engineer-at-the-time *Jack Clement*.

How could I resist THAT show? *Cash! Jerry Lee!* My producer *Pineapple Jack!* Add to that *Elvis* and *Carl Perkins!*[265] It was impossible for me *not* to go see it. It was like a concert of all of the early influences on my music. Despite the less-than-stellar adherence to the actual history of the Million Dollar Quartet session, I fell in love with the musical show at Harrahs. I saw it, then saw it again the next night. Then another night.

---

[264] Working with headlining 1980's rockers Kevin Chalfant (*707, The Storm, Journey Experience*) and Jimi Jamison (*Target, Cobra, Survivor*), she created "Music to The Rescue" which was instrumental in getting FEMA help for the area of The Great Flood in Tennessee and Mississippi. Her organizational skills were already legendary in the music industry. She produced (and helped build a brand with the cofounder) highly-successful *Voices of Rock Radio* stage show and served as either producer, co-creator, or agent for a handful of other popular live (and syndicated) Vegas-based and touring shows. (I frequently made fun of her booking of so many 1980's rock bands, calling her the "queen of the hair bands".) A talented singer herself, I had heard a cassette tape of her singing with a very drunk (or high or both) Jerry Lee Lewis; that association within itself cemented me to her.

Her fiancé who became her husband, *Patrick Maciel*, it turned out was a high-tech brainiac that made my own substantial technology knowledge look like merit-badge stuff. He was also a superb photographer and stepped into the role of documenting Monica's various music productions. And he became a really go friend.

[265] I adored Carl Perkins as much as any of the quartet, and for more than just his Blue Suede Shoes that most people knew from him. He had many other hits as well as some fine songs that he wrote and were covered by other people: Daddy Sang Bass (Johnny Cash), Silver and Gold (Dolly Parton), Rise and Shine (my friend Tommy Cash), Let Me Tell You About Love (The Judds), So Wrong (Patsy Cline), and others.

After the death of Cash's original Tennessee Two guitar picker, Luther Perkins (unrelated to Carl), Carl Perkins filled in for about ten years (until Bob Wooten was hired). I loved that crazy constant hammer-on thing he did on chords that turned even rhythm accompaniment into lead guitar; it was a pre-Jerry-Reed version of that same style playing. Carl Perkins also played with George Harrison, and dozens of other pickers. Paul McCartney purportedly once said "if there were no Carl Perkins, there would be no Beatles".

So, I definitely was a Carl Perkins fan. When I visited his display at the Rockabilly Hall of Fame, I was thrilled when the director of the museum invited me to play one of Carl's last guitars. Yes, I was a fan.

THE LEGEND DIES ON — GARY GREEN

Then on my next Vegas trip I booked a front row seat for every night that I was in town. Altogether I saw the show more than *65 times*. I got to know the cast, the understudies, and the alternates. I became such a regular that occasionally some of the actors would break the fourth wall and address me directly.

When Harrah's made the decision to end the show's run, I reached out to the owners of the show to investigate buying it from them; not merely licensing it like Harrahs had done; rather, buying outright the unlimited and perpetual Las Vegas license for the show.

In anticipation of the purchase, I arranged a high-end dinner for much of the cast at the Italian restaurant where I had met Howie Gold, *Ferraro's*. At the dinner, I outlined my plans and announced the creation of a new company that Monica and I had decided to form.

Gary Green Productions was to be the launch pad for my maybe-soon-to-be-reborn music career; but at the dinner, I was inviting attendees to come along for the ride! The new company would be a mainstream version of Bread & Roses; combining the application of all I had learned about big-box show productions in the casino world along with my personal music goals and a handful of related projects.

We immediately began putting together a team to operate the new company. Monica would serve as the Chief Executive Officer. Tony Cohen agreed to serve as the company's head of A&R, responsible for finding promising new artists and developing them. Patrick Maciel (Monica's husband) agreed to be our chief technology officer (a key position in the digital music universe and one well-suited to his technology background).

Since we were focusing on stage shows as well as music, My old friend Emmy-award winning actor (and horror film superstar) *Bill Oberst Jr.* signed on as a third co-founder. Bill's film and live stage show background was exactly what we needed for that role; and when married to his celebrity-status in Hollywood, it brought an additional level of credibility to the project.

Still reaching back to my hippie days, I decided to reach back into my teen years and ask my closest high school friend from Gastonia, *Tom Boshamer*, to join the team for the hands-on implementation of company policies and philosophies and to be our direct liaison with artists and productions. His background as a renowned festivals actor was ideal for that role. Monica and I rounded out the team with well-known Memphis record producer and studio owner *Niko Lyras* serving as music producer and recording executive for the company; and I began negotiating with Niko to buy his famous Memphis studio.

As negotiations with the rights holders of Million Dollar Quartet continued, Monica and I began looking at Las Vegas venues to four-wall a theatre, visiting several and actually entering into early negotiations with

THE POET LAUREATE SOUL OF FOLKIE ROCK & ROLL

two of them. As scheduled, Harrahs closed the show, and I threw that big wrap party. The audience for the final performance was filled with luminaries and my associates; many of whom attended my party at Gino Ferraro's restaurant in Vegas.

Troubled by the lack of enthusiasm from the owners of the play, we began looking at other possibilities including other rockabilly history shows with "tribute" artists, more dramatic shows with ac-tors rather than imitators, and promotion of individual artists from the MDQ cast.

Several of the show's former cast members had projects they wanted to pitch to us; and none of them really had any gigs lined up and ready to go when the show closed. One of Million Dollar Quartet actors brought us our first project; a *Rat-Pack-style* Christmas charity. He was pretty far along in planning the show and production; but he wanted us to provide funding to four-wall a small venue and promote the show.

Monica and I thought it would be a good market-entry project for us. Marc had no idea about my background, and we decided to keep it that way; my interest was presented strictly as a casino operator and fan. For budgeting purposes, he was looking at small, somewhat out-of-the-way venues. My grandiose fantasies *(not to mention my over-the-top approach to everything)* leaned more toward a high-profile major strip casino's main showroom.

The pushback from my target venues, however, was the one-two punch of what they wanted to charge to rent their space *and* the casinos' general reluctance to host charitable shows that were not aimed at drawing a *gambling* crowd. Leveraging my casino-industry reputation, I made some CEO-level calls (rather than showroom-manager-level) and after a little "string-pulling" (or perhaps perceived strong-arming) I finagled the *rent-free* usage of one of Vegas' historic main showrooms.

The show was a tremendous success and more importantly for our fledgling little company, it established us as the producers of a major Las Vegas casino production show. Overnight, we were major movers-and-shakers in the entertainment space. Even more impactful, we could now add to our corporate C.V. that *Gary Green Productions* produced a major Las Vegas casino showroom extravaganza show. That was a whole different world from the informal hootenannies at folkie coffeehouses. It *was*, however, the next logical step after owning a circus. *We had become major show producers in the entertainment capital of the world!*

Shortly after that success, one of the understudies for Million Dollar Quartet pitched us a Jerry Lee Lewis *tribute show* for himself. Because he had developed a personal friendship with the *real* Jerry Lee (and had visited him multiple times in his home), the young actor was certain that he could get the legend's official sanction to do the show. His concept

THE LEGEND DIES ON — GARY GREEN

(and I suspected added inducement to get Jerry Lee's approval), was to include Lewis's real-life younger sister in the cast *playing herself.*

The pitch from a twenty-something year old understudy to star as Jerry Lee Lewis with a "little sister" on stage that was 50 years older than him… was not a terribly plausible show concept. Though the understudy himself was extremely talented, tribute shows were second or third tier shows; not headliner shows; and this concept came dangerously close to being easily a target of ridicule.[266]

Nonetheless, I more-than-welcomed meeting the sister, *Linda Gail Lewis,* during an upcoming trip I had scheduled to Austin Texas, where she lived. Once we met, my mind started racing with ideas for booking her as well as a Million Dollar Quartet style "jukebox" play about her wild-ass life. I had read her autobiography, *The Devil, Me, and Jerry Lee,* and I was certain that her story plus the powerful boogie-beat of her piano playing could be nightly sell-out material at the box office. *If I put Bill Oberst to work on a stage-play script, I would have a sure-fire winner!*

Linda and her husband arrived for the meeting at the restaurant of Austin's historic *Driskill Hotel.* Given Linda's very *rock-and-roll* history,[267] I had no idea what to expect of the hubby. But the first clue that *this* marriage might be different from her well-known reputation was that it already had lasted about 20 years; *a record, by far, for Linda Gail Lewis.*

---

[266] I was looking for a headliner show that would fill a major casino's main showroom six nights every week along with at least three matinees every week. I was looking for a show that could expect a very long run. A tribute artist show would be a hard-sell to casino entertainment directors and even to top management (despite what juice my reputation might carry with them). Even my beloved Million Dollar Quartet had not been in a large main showroom; instead, tucked away upstairs on the second floor of Harrahs with another mid-size room. Tribute shows on-their-own just didn't have the pizazz needed for people to plan their trips to Vegas around the show.

[267] Even though she was only six or seven years older than me, I had been watching Linda Gail Lewis's career since I was in high school in Nashville when she appeared with her brother on those locally syndicated television shows. In those days I knew of her as a country singer in the shadow of her brother; but over the years I had come to know her as a true rock and roller. All of the hell-raising and bad behavior that Jerry Lee Lewis was known for was matched (and believe it or not, in some cases surpassed) by his sister. The remarkable thing with such out-of-control behavior was that she actually had talent; and a lot of it. The more we talked, the clearer it became to me that Linda Gail Lewis had been vastly under-marketed throughout her career. I mean, it made perfect sense that the initial "hook" to draw attention to her was her big brother. There definitely was a certain panache to being the hell-raising little sister of "The Killer" (as Jerry Lee was known); but the woman I was talking with had a much different potential on her own. By the way, it turned out that Kenny Lovelace, who I'd met in San Jose and who introduced me to Jerry Lee, was one of Linda's ex-husbands.

THE POET LAUREATE SOUL OF FOLKIE ROCK & ROLL

Watching the two of them interact, it was equally clear that this one was going to last and be *THE* one for them.

Beyond that, from the get-go it was obvious that this cat, *Eddie Braddock*, had a story of his own and wasn't merely riding on the skirt-ruffles of his famous wife. It only took about ten minutes into the conversation for me to realize that I was talking to a genuine living legend in the *business* side of music. Eddie Braddock was the almost-mythically legendary *Super Whitey* —the white former Memphis Tennessee redneck DJ who almost single-handedly had integrated Southern rock and roll radio station airways![268]

My supposedly-maximum 90-minute meeting with Linda turned into about four-and-a-half hours, which in hindsight I feel sort of bad about because most of that time was dominated by me and Eddie talking about the record business. It wasn't an intentional slighting of Linda, at all; in fact, I had determined in very short order that she was "a keeper" and had huge potential that we needed to act on.[269] Eddie, though, was a treasure-trove of information, stories, ideas, and raw brain-storming. An absolute inspiration.

It was the beginning of a maniacally intense adventure with Eddie. From that first meeting, I followed up by bringing Eddie and Linda both

---

[268] Eddie Braddock was the almost-mythically legendary *Super Whitey* —the white former Memphis Tennessee redneck DJ who almost single-handedly had integrated Southern rock and roll radio station airways!

His storied career had taken him from celebrated DJ to regional promoter for Leonard and Phil Chess' eponymic rhythm & blues record label (Chess Records) then to Ahmet Ertegun's Atlantic Records before becoming THE promotions guy for the fabled Al Bell's Stax Records and Volt Records.

I had heard the legends, but Eddie confirmed for me that he would show up at a radio station with 45's: the latest Stax 45-rpm record and a Colt .45 automatic. He would ask the DJ which they'd like to deal with. Inevitably, the DJ would choose to play the record. Make no mistake about it, whatever technique he actually used, without Eddie Braddock, white girls and boys (like me) may have never heard many artists that were only getting play on Black stations. It was a horrible time in American cultural history when even over-the-airways segregation kept white America from hearing Otis Redding, Sam & Dave, Rufus & Carla Thomas, Booker T, & the MG's, and others.

Eddie Braddock, without a doubt, was instrumental in the success of crossing America's 1960's racial barriers by using music (even if it was under a perceived threat). He was a most unlikely civil rights crusader whose day-to-day work changed the world. I loved that kind of story!

[269] I had come to Austin with the plan to have an hour-or-so meeting with Linda Gail Lewis and to determine if there could be some synergies for us to work together through my new Gary Green Productions company. I absolutely found those synergies in Linda; she was awesome —and not nearly as spacey as I had found Jerry Lee when I met him a decade or so earlier.

THE LEGEND DIES ON — GARY GREEN

to Vegas to meet with the whole Gary Green Productions team to plan the next steps. A few weeks after that, I flew Eddie, Tom, and Tony to Nashville for the *Americana Music Association's Americanafest* workshops. And from that we decided to launch a record label!

With no Moe Asch in the world and the Smithsonian keepers of the Folkways legacy being a historical curatorial role, I felt there was either a void to be filled or an opportunity to be realized. Besides, even if Moe had been around, the kind of music styling that I was targeting went in a different direction from the "something to say" mantra and added a "something to hear" flavor to it. It was to be a first-of-its-kind consensus of content and form; the precious dialectic.

Based on what Eddie taught me about the independent commercial record companies and what Monica had told me about artist relations, I envisioned a different kind of label in an era when record labels were dying. I pulled our team together in Vegas to work out the vision for the new label. I wanted to reintroduce the record companies' long-lost *Artist Development* departments. Because I came up through Moe Asch and the Folkways philosophy, the idea of focus on *the talent* seemed the most natural way of doing business. But the new paradigm of the record business was about *product* not *people*.

I was beginning to formulate a new model for a record company; and that would mean a new direction for me. I began writing a manifesto to codify my thoughts, research, and conversations (that long industry-detailed document is available online still). I envisioned a fusion of the old models and the new for a different kind of record company vertical.

Our new label was certainly not going to be a "major" (especially by the AIM definition); but we also were not an "indie" in the vanity sense or in the near-obscure under-marketed sense. I wanted a synthesis of the best of all worlds with a new flavoring to them.

I was building on the old artist development intensity of the 1950's and 1960's independents, combining that with the marketing intensity of the majors, and added the new-business take on the digital age and creating a marketing-centric business model. *That* was what my new label would be about.

Focusing on "bottom up" distribution to create channel-demand and taking control of the entire "big picture" artist development scenario *(including recording, publishing, licensing, presentation, touring, positioning, social media, and scores of other disciplines)* —we planned to be neither indie nor major (in modern parlance). We were, in fact, a *new oldstyle* label. Our vision was that we wanted to be the 21st century version of Sun, Stax, Chess, and even Atlantic. Hence, we created TENARE RECORDS; named from a Latin idiom that means *Touches the Soul*.

THE POET LAUREATE SOUL OF FOLKIE ROCK & ROLL

As I pushed forward, the thing that I did not tell any of the Gary Green Production team was the source of funding for all of my over-the-top grandiosity. Up to this point, I had paid for *everything* out-of-pocket. The several-thousands-dollars dinner for the MDQ cast, the Vegas-Nashville-Austin-Memphis travel for the team, the hotel rooms, meals around the country, show tickets, conference fees; everything out of *my* pocket. And my pockets weren't nearly as deep as they once had been in my software magnate days. The source of the money that I was spending came from my mercenary casino consulting practice. An accounting review of my *one-last-shot* period indicates that I spent about $1.3-million on music-related projects up through the plans to launch the record label. As long as I could keep up my very lucrative consulting practice and high-profile role in the casino business world, we were good.

Formally launching Gary Green Productions, buying Niko's studio, launching the label, creating a venue, and starting a viable music business-entity was going to take a considerable amount of money beyond the basics that I could provide from casino *consulting* income; especially since I had let so much go after my parents' deaths.

To further complicate things, the more time I spent focusing on the new music project, the less time (and energy and focus) I had for the *casino* business. That was problematic on multiple levels. Of course, it meant that there was less income; but more complexly, it also meant that I was in front of the casino industry less-and-less and therefore less relevant, at least not actively on the minds (and agendas) of casino operators. The less I was on their minds, the fewer opportunities for income came my way. The fewer opportunities then the less money to pour into the music project. Before it even began, I recognized the treadmill cycle of that dynamic and began working on a more viable financial model.

To make the music projects work, I needed to leverage my casino industry notoriety to attract investors for the cash dynamo of casino ownership —*my own casino*. Buying an existing casino or developing a new one, operating it properly, and flipping it —all using my proven methodologies— could be an investor's dream-come-true.

The method to that madness? My personal profits could more-than-cover the costs of all the music projects. Moreover, I could use the casino showrooms, lounges, and attractions to launch the music projects. *Perfect.*

I decided to pursue that very viable model to push forward with funding the music projects. I called on my network of top casino professionals to join with me under a single banner and share in the equity; and I was able to put together a blue-chip team. With that team in place, I then decided to push forward with the pilot episode for my television show and I lined up an industry sponsor to cover costs. I reasoned that it would garner some

THE LEGEND DIES ON — GARY GREEN

much-needed industry attention as well as provide validation for potential investors.

The show's Canadian producer flew to California and together we drove up to Lake Tahoe Nevada for the videoing. Our last day of filming turned out to also be the last day that airports were open for a while! After a frantic drive through a blizzard, over the storied *Donner Pass*, I got him on the very last flight to Toronto before the shut down for the Covid-19 pandemic.

That, as might be expected, put everything in a phantom zone of frozen time. When time finally began to thaw out, a year and a half later, the dynamics of television-show demand had changed for the new reality. A mid-pandemic meeting at the television network's New York headquarters turned into a major change in direction for my show.

The network was now wanting a show that was not be a travelogue of casino rescues across America, but instead, a *Casino Insider* look behind the scenes of me buying and rehabbing a Las Vegas casino. They wanted a six-to-twelve-episode series showing the drama, the secret Vegas stories, the folklore and mythology, the stress, and everything involved in turning a failing also-ran Las Vegas casino into an over-the-top *Garyesque* casino. As an alternative to that network concept, they would accept a show about the trials and tribulations of buying raw land on the Las Vegas strip and building a cutting-edge casino resort from scratch.

Great! All I had to do was raise about a half-billion dollars to develop a Las Vegas Strip casino, to launch the television show that I would use to raise the money to buy the casino. Holy *Circulus In Probando*! That sounded a whole lot like a circular argument.

Then, once more, as I spent the necessary time putting together capital stacks and investment packages to pitch that project (even with the added benefit of a national television series to draw customers), I had no time for my consulting practice. My full-time job became putting together the casino development project.

I supplemented that with a few speaking engagements to talk about casino marketing, and occasional consulting gigs for a handful of international slot machine companies wanting to enter the U.S. market.

For all practical purposes, the music production projects were, once again, on hold until I could finagle a casino purchase and the development cash flow channel.

Relief to that situation surfaced with a most unexpected throwback to my Folkways days and to Moe Asch's right-hand, *Marilyn Averett Conklin*. When Moe would play the grumpy old curmudgeon, Marilyn would be the maternally friendly face that also watched out for me. I am

THE POET LAUREATE SOUL OF FOLKIE ROCK & ROLL

sure that in her quarter-century at Folkways she filled that role for many that were intimidated by Moe (including me).

Marilyn had a son, *Charles*, who was my same age; born the same year. He was part of Folkways, one way or another, as long as his mother was. As he puts it, his early life was all about *growing up Folkways*.

A good part of that growing up took place at the Folkways Records offices, where young Charles would accompany his mother to work, and the office would serve as his daycare playground. Moe Asch took on the role of a sort of surrogate father to him; even coming to Marilyn's home for birthdays, holidays, and family occasions.

When he reached his teens, Charles accepted Moe's offer to come to work for him full-time in the warehouse, and later filling a variety of jobs as well as becoming Moe's daily lunch companion. *(Charles was working in the warehouse when the FBI showed up with the warrant for the Bob Dylan interview album that I produced.)*

As the last living member of the original core of Folkways Records, he truly was the antipodal torchbearer of the small inner-circle of what grew to be one of the largest and most influential record companies in the world. By the time Charles was in his late sixties, he decided to create a syndicated radio series called *Growing Up Folkways*, an interview and musical recollection of life at Folkways Records.

The series was more than Averett's front-row seat to the chronicling, documenting, disseminating, and shaping those cultural events. In each episode, his audience would experience the power of Folkways' capturing the spirit of a nation, reflecting its triumphs, struggles, and the diverse voices that shaped the American identity.

While the stories were framed with Averett's Growing Up Folkways, it was really about *America* Growing Up Folkways. Focused around never-before-assembled interviews with key players of that legacy and spiced with the recordings themselves, the series went deep into the heart and soul of Folkways' impact on American culture and rebounding into the contemporary world.

For episode number one, he wanted to interview *me* about the infamous *Bob Dylan – A.J. Weberman* album and adventure. We talked on the phone several times and seemed to really "click". We marveled at the many times that we crossed paths but never actually met other than a brief "hello" at the record company's office.

A few weeks later he flew to Florida, and we met in person for the first time. As we talked, we discovered that we played off of each other really well and especially extemporaneously we could keep the Folkways story engaging by talking to each other and taking the audience into our confidences. He invited me to change from interview subject to *co-hosting* the series with him. It sounded like a really exciting project, so I flew to

THE LEGEND DIES ON — GARY GREEN

Dayton Ohio where we recorded the pilot episode at the flagship NPR (National Public Radio) station at Antioch College: *WYSO Radio*.

Things went so well that we pitched the concept to Moe's son Michael, who agreed to serve in an advisory role and appear on the show.[270] We also pitched it to The Smithsonian, the stewards of Moe's legacy; we wanted their endorsement and sponsorship.

It also occurred to me that the story was good, under-told, and held potential beyond syndicated radio; it could be a multimedia stage presentation. Spiced with guests, rare pictures and tapes, and some great stories, the stage show could be our personal remembrances of Folkways, Moe, Broadside, and the artists who were part of those worlds. The idea was to make it like a *Ken Burns* PBS documentary on musical steroids; maybe even a television series *(though my initial TV inquiries about it brought more interest in exploiting the Bob Dylan lawsuit story than the Folkways story; and THAT did not interest me at all).*

I called Monica to see what she thought of the stage show idea; the core of her business was booking nostalgic-type shows at Indian casinos across the country as well as on college campuses. I placed a lot of value on her experience and instincts about book-ability of shows.

Somewhat surprisingly, at least to me, she loved the idea; but with a different take on it than I had. In *my* mind the show was all about Folkways Records and the hook to the show was the fact that the show's star, Charles, had an intimate inside seat for 27 years.

I saw *MY* role only as a facilitator to keep the patter going, since I had significant extemporaneous stage experience. Monica, however, saw the show as about two icons: Folkways Records and... *me*. I just didn't see it. She saw Charles' role as the voice of Folkways, of Moe and of his Mom; and my role as being an artist that Moe chose against the grain and proved to be an influence across the industry.

I, literally, laughed out loud. I was sure that she was making a joke. When she innocently and matter-of-factly asked, "what?"

Certain that it was a joke, I pleaded with her, "Come on, I am serious about this show; what do you think? Don't joke around."

She insisted that she was serious, and I was just as insistent that I was *not* the story and had not influenced ANY one in the music world. *(In part it was my old journalism sensibility of being an invisible observer and never part of the story—despite the "Gonzo" trend from Doctor Hunter S. Thompson)*

---

[270] Moe's son became a well-respected anthropologist and professor in Canada and was not in the day-to-day office world at Folkways, but certainly was a survivor of the Folkways legacy.

THE POET LAUREATE SOUL OF FOLKIE ROCK & ROLL

Not letting it go; she scoffed at my reaction and began reciting a litany of my music-adventures and individuals I had touched —*mostly the escapades that I have detailed in this book*. She added to those the names of other musicians who I had never met but who had told her that either I or something I did had a direct impact on their musical lives.

I told her that I understood what she was saying and could even see why she *might* think that; but I just wasn't buying into it. Her response was completely perplexing to me. She simply said that she'd show me. I let it go and we moved on to other topics.

The other subject that I wanted to discuss with her was bringing back to life my jukebox show idea; a *replacement* for *Million Dollar Quartet* since continuing that show was impossible for us. Though several of the cast members had gone off on their own and created tribute-shows for the characters they played in MDQ, I was not interested in a knock-off of the original show. They just were not over-the-top enough for my tastes and it wasn't universal; it was genre-trapped.

The roots of my concept for a new show reached back to my teen years in Nashville, when I was spending time backstage at the Grand Ole Opry at the old pre-Opryland Ryman auditorium in the 1960's. I never let go of that and continued to be infatuated with the *structure* of the Opry as much as with the content. It was the format that I wanted to reinvent for the 21st century. There was a good solid historical base for these show.

The Grand Ole Opry, The Louisiana Hayride, The Renfro Valley Barn Dance, The National Barn Dance, and more than 140 others were examples of an early-to-mid twentieth century genre of live radio broadcasts called "Jamboree" shows. Those shows played a significant role in introducing audiences to a wide range of styles from both established and emerging artists to showcase their talents and connect with listeners across the country.

THAT was what intrigued me about the Opry: the format. With The three-and-a-half-hour shows were divided into 15-minute or 30-minute segments. Each segment opened with a tier-one major-name star as the segment's host. After an opening song, the headliner would introduce a tier-two minor-name star who would sing one song (or tell jokes, in the case of a comedy act). The host then would return for a second song, after which the headliner would introduce a lesser-known or even unknown performer who would do one song. The segment would end with the headliner performing one of their hits.

It occurred to me that the *Opry* format possibly could defy the jukebox show inability to hold a major showroom; especially if those "tier-one" acts were actual headliners and rotated frequently. It just might work! Each segment had a sponsoring company (i.e. *The Acme Boot Show*, or *Martha White Self-rising Flour Presents The Grand Ole Opry*, or any of

THE LEGEND DIES ON — GARY GREEN

dozens of companies). Between each song, either an announcer or the headlining host would read a commercial for the host company. (Bluegrass stars *Flatt and Scruggs* even wrote a song for *Martha White Flour* that was released as a single and actually charted on Billboard.)

Content aside *(though it is noteworthy that the Louisiana Hayride was the first show to introduce newcomer Elvis Presley)*, the *format* was fascinating to me. It was basically a radio-version of what I had grown up knowing as television *variety shows*. I was sorely disappointed that a genuine piece of Americana had disappeared; but I was also inspired by the apparent market for it that the *MDQ*-style jukebox shows indicated still existed.

Monica loved the idea and thought it would be ideal both on the Vegas Strip but out in "the real world" as well. She lined up a show production staff and a cowriter to move the project forward; and she began looking for cast members. From her encouragement, I made some calls and secured a commitment from a major Las Vegas casino showroom to partner with us for the production. That would keep my upfront costs to a minimum; and the format of the show itself—*with 15-minute sponsorship segments*— reduced out-of-pocket expenses even more.

As we further explored the expected budget for the show, Monica and I both hit on an idea that pulled from our mutual expertise in the casino world as well as in the music world: branded slot machines.

Casinos pay a premium price for slot machines that have a celebrity brand attached to them. Among the better-known have been slot machines with images and sounds of *Elvis, Sinatra, The Rolling Stones, Brittney Spears, Michael Jackson, Johnny Cash, Willie Nelson*, and dozens of others. Between us we had a network of top name music personalities and decision-making management at hundreds of casinos (not to mention executives at multiple slot machine manufacturers). We quickly put together a slot machine company that signed exclusive intellectual property deals with the stars and revenue-share lease deals with the casinos. That venture would provide additional funding for the proposed show.

We moved forward with show research and recruiting, we set out on a road trip from Tulsa Oklahoma to Nashville via Memphis. Along Interstate 40 about halfway between Memphis and Nashville, Monica pointed to a piece of land she owned at the highway exit near Loretta Lynn's attraction in Hurricane Mills.

As we drove, it occurred to both of us that the location could possibly make a good spot for a new music venue: a destination-resort themed around a country music show. That train of thought got us brainstorming about using the concept for our Vegas show to create a contemporary version of what those Jubilee shows had been a century earlier.

THE POET LAUREATE SOUL OF FOLKIE ROCK & ROLL

Calling on my technology reinvention days, it occurred to me that if we created such a show and could secure a "home base" traditional radio station ... using a series of AI-generated delivery personalizations we could deliver our weekly live show not just nationwide in the clear-channel style, of 1925, but worldwide in streaming style of 100 years later. We continued to explore venue needs, staging models, and technology models that would reach the largest audience. I couldn't find a hole in the plan anywhere.

My only hesitation was that I did not want to become a parody of The Grand Ole Opry; I wanted to become an entirely new thing, but with solid roots. I didn't want to mimic other broad-audience knock-offs (most of which made me cringe).

With our planning, the Vegas venue signed on, and with the groundwork for financing that Monica and I had lined up, suddenly we were in the production business, with three major projects in the works: *Growing Up Folkways* series with Charles T. Averett; my jukebox Broadway-style show at a major Las Vegas casino resort; and our own Tennessee venue for live music and an Artificial Intelligence plan to deliver it worldwide and become a major destination resort.

During that whole *One Last Shot* era, beginning with the *Eddie-Braddock-Tom-Boshamer-Tony-Cohen-Monica-Maciel-Patrick-Maciel* trip to that Americana Music Fest in Nashville, I had begun further exploring that "new" musical genre called *Americana*. Though I had been sniffing around the genre long before that trip, I still was really surprised at the existence of it as a separate genre from Country or Folk (though God-knows country music had long ago morphed into pop-music-with-a-southern-accent). Americana was more like the original concept of CBGB in New York.

Apparently, I wasn't alone in my raised-eyebrows. September 13, 2017, issue of *Rolling Stone Magazine* defined the genre:

> "Americana" first came to fashion as a descriptive musical phrase in the mid-Nineties, when a group of radio promoters and industry outsiders dispersed throughout Nashville, California, and Texas sought to carve ou a distinct market-place for a wave of traditionally minded songwriters like Guy Clark, Darrell Scott and Jim Lauderdale, artists whose work was no longer being served by a country music industry riding high on Garth Brooks and Shania Twain."

Just as I was coming to terms with Americana and trying to understand how a hillbilly-folkie-poet might fit into that world, Monica hit me with another totally unexpected proposal. She wanted me back in the studio to record a new album; she wanted to pick up from where Pineapple Jack had left off. I tried to balk; but she would not take "no" as an answer.

THE LEGEND DIES ON — GARY GREEN

To pressure me into acquiescence, she took the extraordinary step of lining up singers and musicians to join me on the album. Unlike sessions players that Jack had brought in, Monica brought in some of the legendary hall-of-fame rock and country musicians that she represented. These legends actually wanted to be on an album with *ME*, doing Gary Green songs! As if that was not enough, she arranged for the album to be recorded at one of the most famous studios in the industry and engineered by multiple Grammy winners.

Baffled by the whole thing, I asked her "why?". She answered by telling me that my music, my productions, my life had served as inspiration to generations of musicians. She again sited many of the episodes that I now have written about for this book. It was a wasted argument from me; she set about making arrangements for me to record the album, lining up the roster for luminaries to appear on it with me, and making a list of Gary Green songs to include on it.

Even *THAT* was not all she had lined up. Near the end of 2023 she informed me that I would be inducted into the *California Music Hall of Fame* during their April 2024 ceremony.

WOW. It had begun with a pre-kindergarten kid in Atlanta mesmerized by a televised wild man's piano antics. With a healthy ingestion of Southern Baptist hymns and Appalachian culture, I had survived the angst of growing up in Nashville and awakened to learning that some songs could get people killed.

Radicalized, rejected, and dejected, I had drifted to New York's folk scene where I recorded, learned, grew, and emerged a fugitive militant. Through unlikely reinventions, over-the-top controversies, I weathered impossible successes and predictable failures.

Amongst the ridiculousness along the way were completely non-sequitur voyages from the Governor of Kentucky ordaining me as a *Colonel* to a Native American Tribe in South Carolina issuing credentials announcing that I was an *"honorary"* Tribal member[271] to my approving security clearances for the United States Secret Service. Oh, and I owned a circus. *Crazy shit!*

I was fortunate to have personal encounters and interactions with the likes of *Pete Seeger, Moe Asch, Sis Cunningham & Gordon Friesen, Johnny Cash & Reba Hancock, Floyd Westerman, Don Rickles, Frank Sinatra Jr.,* and dozens of others.

---

[271] THAT always reminds me of the old Native joke about giving a white man "an Indian name" of *Walking Eagle* —meaning that the white guy is so full of shit that he is too heavy to fly if he was a bird.

THE POET LAUREATE SOUL OF FOLKIE ROCK & ROLL

Seriously, who-the-hell regularly has midnight pancakes with *Waylon Jennings*, swaps poetry with *Túpac Sakur*, gets *Bob Dylan* to sue them for millions, becomes a Federal fugitive, gets guitar lessons from *Maybelle Carter*, produces Las Vegas shows, ends up in the Smithsonian, and... well, just who-the-hell?

Kris Kristofferson, Alan Ginsberg, Cowboy Jack Clement, and *Frank Black*, all had called me a poet (rather than a folksinger or a hillbilly picker).

Through it all, I saw myself as *the influenced* and never as *the influencer*. Then, officially "elderly", it seemed I really was getting *one last shot, just for old times*.

THE LEGEND DIES ON — GARY GREEN

Librettist's Cadenza:
These Six Strings Neutralize The Tools of Oppression

He's a walking contradiction partly truth and partly fiction
Taking every wrong direction on his lonely way back home
— Kris Kristofferson, *The Pilgrim: Chapter 33,* ©Iron Madon Music

At the cusp of my eighth decade on earth, I stood over the bronze plaque marking where my parents' ashes had been dropped, in plastic bags, 12 years earlier at *Rutherford County Memorial Cemetery* near Forest City North Carolina. There was a chilled misty rain blowing across my face as I looked at the grave marker and spoke aloud to Mother and Daddy … or to nobody.

"Ho-ho-ho", I began because it was Christmas. "Merry Christmas. It won't be long now. We'll be back where we started; the three of us in North Carolina", I choked. "I'll be home soon", I said as I turned to walk away, fully aware of my mortality and that there were fewer days ahead than there were behind me.

I pulled my fedora lower toward my brow to keep the rain off my glasses, zipped my leather jacket, and took a deep breath of the pollution-free mountain air. I hated cold weather *(and compared to my home of the last 28 years in Florida, ANY-where was cold)*; but there was no denying the serenity of rural Appalachia.

Really, if it wasn't for the damned cold, it would be a great part of the country for a final retreat. But I just knew that if I lived there, I would be living out one of Daddy's favorite poems that he had often recited: Robert Service's *The Cremation of Sam McGee* (if you don't know the poem, I encourage you to read it).

My life had been one long dactyl of intense adventures; so, it was altogether fitting and proper, then, that I would be concerned about such poetical fancies.

Often when I would visit their graves in the winter I would wonder if at Daddy's cremation he had been "looking cool and calm, in the heart of the furnace roar; And he wore a smile you could see a mile, and he said: Please close that door".[272]

As I shivered away from the cemetery, I mused at whether it was the climate or my icy miscreants that brought the chill. I mean, James

---

[272] *The Cremation of Sam McGee*, by Robert W. Service, the Bard of the Yukon, ©1907 in *Songs of a Sourdough*.

THE POET LAUREATE SOUL OF FOLKIE ROCK & ROLL

Baldwin had said, "artists are here to disturb the peace"; I certainly have lived up to *that* depiction for my entire life.

There had been something stirring in me since that 1957 night in Atlanta; and maybe before, but that night was when I first became aware of it. On one Euclidean plane it was as if I was born to ramble with a fever in my soul; but far beyond that one-dimensional universe I have always walked with a perilous treachery rebelling against all probity.

Clearly, I have lived a life full of rich adventures, episodes, encounters, and escapades. While the stories in this book are just the reports of my day-to-day existence, the reality of my life is that I just wanted to make music and tell stories.

After the April 2024 induction ceremony at the California Music Hall of Fame, the official magazine of my union *(the American Federation of Musicians, AFL-CIO)* ran a very kind news report of the event[273] that summarized my musical life in a handful of paragraphs with a photo.

Even as I stood on stage at the induction ceremony, it was surreal to me; made even more unreal as I performed my *"That Burnt Out Rock & Roll"* for that audience. The ceremony featured my friend Chalé (Charles Averett) introducing me; not with the traditional list of accolades that such events typically garner, but instead with an explanation of Moe Asch's contribution to American culture and why Moe was attached to *ME*. It was as if Folkways was still alive and Moe was able to say: *see, I was right about Gary*. That was the message that Chalé said he wanted to convey; and he did ... even down to his own costuming.

Then, a couple of weeks after the induction, I received an official proclamation from the sitting Governor of Maryland, Wes Moore, citing my *"demonstration of high integrity and ability, meriting our great trust and respect"* ... *"in appreciation of your outstanding services to the citizens of this state."* Again, *WOW*. All those years in Baltimore were finally *officially* appreciated. All of the community organizing, mentoring young writers and singers, the union work, teaching, concerts; officially recognized! Such an honor!

Just as I was trying to digest all of the kind acknowledgements, even more over-the-top citations came in, commending the apparent influence I had wielded. It all really was quite overwhelming. The Hall of Fame induction was something I could never have imagined. It just wasn't on my radar or for that matter even a realistic thought. Then there was the seemingly impossibility of the State of Maryland officially recognizing

---

[273] Page 20, International Musician, May 2024

THE LEGEND DIES ON — GARY GREEN

my work during the Bread & Roses years ... and my being welcomed to Baltimore when I was a political fugitive in the South.

On the heels of all that, in another unbelievable tribute, United States Congresswoman Lois J. Frankel, representing Palm Beach County Florida (which has been my primary residence for three decades) added her kind regards, by praising me in *The Congressional Record*—the official record of the proceedings of the United States Congress. Like the inclusion of my albums in the Smithsonian Folkways collection, being read into The Congressional Record *(which began publication in 1873 and is kept as the official history of The United States)* was a proclamation of immortality. That record will be there as long as there are archives of the United States of America.

Suddenly I Had a Genuine Musical/Poetic Legacy

What greater legacy could one even fantasize than to be part of both the official records of the nation *(even as a minor footnote)* and to have my poetry/songs preserved for ever in the official museum system (the Smithsonian)!

With the benefit of decades of social growth behind me, it finally appeared that *maybe* I was no longer the pariah that had been a fugitive hiding in plain sight in Baltimore. Perhaps *Moe, Kris, Túpac, Cash, Alan,* and others really did see something enduring in my work.

The reality is that I never set out to be extreme, over-the-top, or even weird. I didn't set out to be a radical; in fact, I really tried to *avoid* politics but was labeled "political" because I was raised believing in *"truth, justice, and the American way"* and that meant standing up and objecting when I saw something wrong —*even when it was unpopular to do so.*

Write it off to those aforementioned great 1950's American passion plays of black & white television that had me truly believing in the arrival of *"a fiery horse with the speed of light, a cloud of dust, and a hearty Hi-yo Silver"*; the last-minute arrival of the calvary when otherwise all seemed lost; or Superman suddenly appearing from nowhere to catch that helicopter with one hand and Lois with the other as they fall from the roof of the building.

Believing in that mythology guided my life into a lot of good stories; and I love to tell those stories and have made a life of doing just that.

But make no mistake about: there was no exceptionalism, no secret code, no specialized knowledge. The reality is that I was fortunate to be in the right places at the right times *(and sometimes the wrong places at the wrong times)*. I was privileged to cross paths with some truly exceptional people; and at times I blindly stumbled into some very special historical circumstances.

While I have hungered to mimic Shelley's lyrical intellect in *Queen Mab*, honestly, I am thinking that nothing matches the genius of *"I shot a*

THE POET LAUREATE SOUL OF FOLKIE ROCK & ROLL

man in Reno just to watch him die." Know what I mean? That's all I wanted: that simplicity in communication.

In fact, it was in that sought-after straightforwardness that I rediscovered the basics that had brought me to music in the first place —before the ghost of Ella May and my 1950's delusions of justice-warrior.

Spending time at the Hall of Fame Induction Ceremony with true rockers; becoming friends with people like Linda Gail Lewis; returning to the backstages of pure rock & roll shows; reexperiencing the front-porch joy of hillbilly Americana…

…all of those things (and more) helped frame for me that the music itself could be the *message* that I had hungered to write. Sometimes, in fact, *it's only rock & roll.*

In the innocence of "just living", there were no *actual* dark demons driving me; just counter-social survivalist reinventions —which for decades I flippantly cloaked as "*I only do fun things in life, and when they cease to be fun, I cease to do them*".

As people have asked me, over the years, "why do you do so many things?", I have to answer that I think THE saddest thing is to be in the last few minutes of life and on your death bed your very last thoughts are "*I wonder what it would have been like if only I had…*" I was determined that would not be my fate.

Ultimately, at the end of this tome, this book is only a digest of my musical life. I have other books and other stories; but if you are looking for more, for some perceived greater truth, then listen to my songs. I never really thought about my "legacy" until I crossed the 70-years threshold. I never really thought about actual *immortality* until a doctor told me that testing indicates that I likely was suffering the same cancer that had killed my father. If you are looking for my legacy and living immortality, then listen to my recordings; I am always there. But if you are looking for the underlying story, then … as I began this journey… **Let's Rock & Roll!**

Made in the USA
Middletown, DE
06 February 2025